LOEB CLASSICAL LIBRARY
FOUNDED BY JAMES LOEB 1911

EDITED BY
JEFFREY HENDERSON

ARISTOTLE
XVI

LCL 317

ARISTOTLE

PROBLEMS

BOOKS 20–38

EDITED AND TRANSLATED BY

ROBERT MAYHEW

RHETORIC TO ALEXANDER

EDITED AND TRANSLATED BY

DAVID C. MIRHADY

HARVARD UNIVERSITY PRESS
CAMBRIDGE, MASSACHUSETTS
LONDON, ENGLAND
2011

First published 2011

Library of Congress Control Number 2011925635
CIP data available from the Library of Congress

ISBN 978-0-674-99656-4

*Composed in ZephGreek and ZephText by
Technologies 'N Typography, Merrimac, Massachusetts.
Printed on acid-free paper and bound by
The Maple-Vail Book Manufacturing Group*

CONTENTS

CONTENTS

RHETORIC TO ALEXANDER

PREFACE

For information on the nature and authorship of the Aristotelian *Problems*, see the introduction in LCL 316. This volume contains books 20–38, the titles of which are:

20. Problems Connected with Shrubs and Vegetables
21. Problems Connected with Barley Meal, Barley Cake, and the Like
22. Problems Connected with Fruit
23. Problems Connected with Salt Water and the Sea
24. Problems Connected with Hot Water
25. Problems Connected with Air
26. Problems Connected with Winds
27. Problems Connected with Fear and Courage
28. Problems Connected with Moderation and Licentiousness, Continence and Incontinence
29. Problems Connected with Justice and Injustice
30. Problems Connected with Intelligence, Understanding, and Wisdom
31. Problems Connected with Eyes
32. Problems Connected with Ears
33. Problems Connected with the Nostril
34. Problems Connected with the Mouth and the Things in It
35. Problems Connected with What Depends on Touch

ARISTOTLE'S PHYSICAL PROBLEMS ARRANGED ACCORDING TO KIND

BOOK XX

INTRODUCTION

Diogenes Laertius (5.25) and the *Vita Hesychii* (no. 96) both attribute to Aristotle a work, in two books, with the title Περὶ φυτῶν (*On Plants*). Aristotle on at least nine occasions refers to (the need for) such a work.[1] If he himself did write one, it was likely lost by the second century AD, for Alexander of Aphrodisias (*in Sens*. 87.7–12 = fr. 341 Gigon) reports that unlike Theophrastus' *On Plants*, Aristotle's is not extant (οὐ φέρεται).[2] Whatever Aristotle may have written on the subject, the serious study of botany in the Lyceum was left to Theophrastus.

Pr. 20–22 were likely grouped together because they all deal in some sense with plants. Though all three discuss plants as sources of nutrition, Book 20 is the most botani-

[1] *Mete*. 339a5–9, *Sens*. 442b23–26, *Long*. 467a30–b6, *Juv*. 468a13–b9, *HA* 539a16–25, *PA* 655b28–56a7, *GA* 715b25–16a2, 731a14–33, 783b8–26. For the other ancient references to this work, see frs. 326–49 Gigon.

[2] The Περὶ φυτῶν in the *corpus Aristotelicum* is not the same work. It is in fact a Byzantine Greek translation of a Latin translation of an Arabic translation (likely of a Syriac translation) of an otherwise lost Περὶ φυτῶν by Nicolaus of Damascus (which may have included material from Aristotle's Περὶ φυτῶν). See H. J. Drossaart Lulofs, "Aristotle's ΠΕΡΙ ΦΥΤΩΝ," *Journal of Hellenic Studies* 77, no. 1 (1957): 75–80.

cal. In general, its topic is the nature of plants, especially with a view to their cultivation. We can further divide its thirty-six chapters as follows: plant physiology (1, 2, 3, 7, 17, 19, 21, 24, 26, 31, 36); taste and odor of plants (10, 11, 20, 22, 23, 25, 30, 33, 35); gardening (8, 9, 12–15, 18, 27–29, 32); cooking (4–6); medicine (16, 34).

We can merely speculate that Aristotle's *On Plants* may have been one of its sources, though the major source was certainly Theophrastus' *De Causis Plantarum* (and especially Book 5).

ΟΣΑ ΠΕΡΙ ΘΑΜΝΟΥΣ ΚΑΙ ΛΑΧΑΝΩΔΗ

923a 1. Διὰ τί τὸ ἁλυκὸν ὕδωρ τὰ μὲν σέλινα δέχεται, τὸ δὲ πράσον οὔ; ἢ ὅτι τοῦ μὲν ἀσθενεῖς αἱ ῥίζαι, τοῦ δὲ ἰσχυραί; τὸ δὲ ἰσχυρότερον ἀπαθέστερον.

2. Διὰ τί λέγεται "μίνθην ἐν πολέμῳ μήτ' ἔσθιε 10 μήτε | φύτευε"; ἢ ὅτι καταψύχει τὰ σώματα; δηλοῖ δὲ ἡ τοῦ σπέρματος φθορά. τοῦτο δὲ ὑπεναντίον πρὸς ἀνδρείαν καὶ θυμὸν ταὐτὸν ὂν τῷ γένει.

3. Διὰ τί ἔνια ἄνθος ἔχοντα ἄκαρπά ἐστιν, οἷον σίκυος καὶ κολόκυνθα καὶ ῥόα; ἢ οὐκ ἄκαρπα, ἀλλὰ 15 ταῦτα καρπός | ἐστιν; περικάρπιον γοῦν ἐστὶ τὸ ἀνθοῦν, ὁ δὲ σίκυος περικάρπιον.

4. Διὰ τί τῶν φυομένων τὰ μὲν ἑψανά, τὰ δὲ ὠμὰ βρωτά; ἢ ὅσων οἱ χυμοὶ μὴ εὐθὺς ἐδώδιμοι, τούτων πυρωθέντων γλυκύτεροι γίνονται ὑπὸ τοῦ θερμοῦ, 20 ὅσων δὲ εὐθύς, | καὶ ὠμὰ ἐδώδιμα;

---

[1] This saying is not otherwise known. It is included in the Byzantine *Collectio paroemiarum* (11.6) by M. Apostolius.

[2] That is, its corruption of sperm proves that mint cools bodies. See Hp. *Vict*. 2.54: "If one eats mint often, it melts the semen

PROBLEMS CONNECTED WITH SHRUBS AND VEGETABLES

1. Why does celery tolerate salt water, whereas leeks do not? Is it because the roots of the latter are weak, whereas those of the former are strong? And what is stronger is less affected.

2. Why is it said: "Neither eat nor plant mint in wartime"?[1] Is it because mint cools bodies? Now its corruption of seed proves this.[2] And this is contrary to courage and spirit, being the same in kind.

3. Why are some (*plants*) that have flowers fruitless, such as cucumber, gourd, or pomegranate? Or are they not fruitless, but these (*flowers*) are fruit? In any case, the flowering part is a fruit case, and the cucumber is a fruit case.

4. Why are some plants edible when boiled, and others raw? Is it that the juices of any that cannot be eaten straightaway when put on the fire are made sweeter by the heat, but any that can be eaten straightaway are edible raw as well?

(τὴν γονὴν) such that it runs, and prevents erections and makes the body weak."

5. Διὰ τί τὰ μὲν ἑψανά, τὰ δὲ ὀπτανά; ἢ ὅτι τὰ μὲν ὑγρότερα οὐ τοσοῦτον,[1] τὰ δὲ ξηρότερα οὐ μᾶλλον ξηρανθῆναι δεῖ; ἑψόμενα δὲ πάντα ὑγρότερα καὶ μαλακώτερα. τὰ δὲ ἧττον ὑγρὰ ἂν πυρωθῇ, γίνεται ξηρά. |

25 6. Διὰ τί δὲ τὰ μὲν ἄβρωτά ἐστι τὰ δὲ βρωτά; ἢ διὰ τοὺς χυμούς; ὅσα γὰρ καὶ ὠμὰ ἀπέπτους ἔχει καὶ πυρούμενα μὴ μεταβάλλει, ἄβρωτα. ὅσων δὲ βρωτὸς μὲν ὁ χυμὸς ἰσχυρότερος δέ, ταῦτα ἡδύσματά ἐστιν· τὰ γὰρ ἐν μικρῷ ἔχοντα πολλὴν δύναμιν τῶν βρωτῶν ἡδυντικὰ τῶν ἐν πολλῷ. |

30 7. Διὰ τίνα αἰτίαν τὰ μὲν μέχρι σπέρματος τῶν φυτῶν ζῇ, εἶτα ἐνεγκόντα αὐαίνεται, οἷον ἡ πόα καὶ τὰ καλούμενα λάχανα, τὰ δὲ οὔ, ἀλλὰ πολλάκις φέρει; καὶ τῶν μέχρι σπέρματος ζώντων τὰ μὲν πολλὰ ἐπέτεια,[2] τὸ δὲ ἱπποσέλινον τῷ ὑστέρῳ ἔτει φέρει καρπόν, 35 καὶ ἐνέγκαν ἐξαυαίνεται; | ἢ ἅπαντα μὲν μέχρι τούτου ἀκμάζει, ἕως ἂν καὶ[3] τὸ σπέρμα ἀκμάζῃ; ἐπεὶ καὶ οἱ ἄνθρωποι μέχρι τριάκοντα ἐτῶν ἐπιδιδόασιν, ὁτὲ μὲν τῷ μήκει,[4] ὁτὲ δὲ τῇ παχύτητι. ὅταν δὲ μηκέτι δύνηται 923b φέρειν, ὥσπερ ἐκεῖ, || αὐαίνεται καὶ καταγηράσκει· τὰ

[1] post τοσοῦτον add. <ὑγρανθῆναι> Forster ex Gaza
[2] ἐπέτεια Sylburg : ἐφέτια C^a Y^{a1} : ἐπέτια Ap. X^a Y^{a2}
[3] καὶ Platt : καὶ κατὰ Y^a : κατὰ cett. codd.
[4] μήκει Bonitz : πλήθει codd.

5. Why are some boiled, whereas others are roasted? Is it because the moister ones are not (*dry*) enough, whereas the drier ones should not be dried any further? Now anything that is boiled becomes moister and softer. But if the less moist ones are put on the fire, they become dry.

6. But why are some inedible, whereas others are edible? Is it because of their juices? For those that when raw have unconcocted[3] juices and when heated do not change, are inedible. And those the juice of which is edible but too strong—these are seasonings; for the (*plants*) that have a lot of power in a small (*quantity*) are seasonings for the foods (*that have a lot of power*) in a large (*quantity*).

7. For what reason do some plants live until (*the production of*) seed, then having borne it they wither, such as grass and the so-called vegetables, whereas some do not, but bear many times? And of those that live until (*the production of*) seed, (*for what reason*) are the majority annuals, whereas horse parsley[4] bears fruit in its second year, and withers away after bearing it? Or do they all flourish until this point: till the seed too has flourished? For humans too grow until their thirtieth year, sometimes in length, and sometimes in bulk. But when they are no longer able to bear (*seed*), just as in this case,[5] they wither

[3] See *Pr.* 1.6, trans. n. 10, on the process of concoction in Aristotle's biology, and note that πέττειν and cognate terms are used in *Pr.* 20 not only in the technical sense to describe concoction, but also in its standard sense of ripening. Cf. *Mete*. 4.3.

[4] *Smyrnium olusatrum*; also known in English as alexanders. The Greek (ἱπποσέλινον) is literally "horse celery."

[5] I.e., when plants are no longer able to bear seed, just as in the case of humans, etc.

δὲ βραδέως καὶ κατὰ λόγον. δι' ἣν μὲν οὖν αἰτίαν τὰ μὲν βραχύβια τὰ δὲ μακρόβιά ἐστιν, ἄλλος ἔστω λόγος· ἐπεὶ δ' ἔστι πᾶσιν ὅρος ἡ τοῦ σπέρματος
5 τελείωσις, ἀνάγκη τοῖς μὲν βραχυβίοις ἅπαξ | ἢ ὀλιγάκις [τὸ][5] ἐνεγκεῖν καρπόν, τοῖς δὲ μακροβίοις πολλάκις, ὥστε τὰ μὲν ἀσθενέστατα ἅπαξ ἐνεγκεῖν[6] (διὸ ἀνάγκη αὐαίνεσθαι)· καὶ τούτων τὰ μὲν δυνάμενα ἐνιαυτῷ ἐπέτεια εἶναι, τὰ δέ, ὥσπερ τὸ ἱπποσέλινον, τῷ ὑστέρῳ ἔτει †ὥσπερ τὰ δένδρα καὶ τὰ φυτά†.[7] |

10 8. Διὰ τί σελίνου, ἐάν τις περιορύξας μέχρι κάτω πρὸς τὰς ῥίζας περιβάλλῃ τῶν καχρυδίων, εἶτα ἄνωθεν τὴν γῆν, καὶ οὕτως ἄρδῃ, παμμεγέθεις γίνονται αἱ ῥίζαι; ἢ διότι τὸ καχρύδιον θερμὸν ὂν καὶ σομφὸν κατέχει μὲν σύνολκον τὴν τροφὴν καὶ οὐ προΐεται[8]
15 ἄνω, πέττει δὲ θερμὸν ὄν, ὥστε | πολλὴν τὴν αὔξησιν γίνεσθαι;

9. Διὰ τί, ἐάν τις τὰς κολοκύνθας εὐθὺς μικρὰς οὔσας κρύψῃ τῇ γῇ ἢ τοὺς σικύους, μείζους γίνονται; ἢ διότι τὰ πνεύματα καὶ ὁ ἥλιος ξηραίνοντα ἀφαιροῦνται τὴν αὔξησιν, καὶ τοὺς ὄγκους ἐλάττους μὲν
20 ποιοῦσιν πάντων, στιφροτέρους | δέ, ὥσπερ καὶ τῶν δένδρων τά τε <ἐν>[9] προσηνέμοις καὶ εὐείλοις[10] καὶ τὰ

[5] [τὸ] Sylburg [6] ἐνεγκεῖν Bonitz : ἐνέγκοι codd.

[7] †ὥσπερ τὰ δένδρα καὶ τὰ φυτά† codd. (obel. incl. Flashar) : καὶ τὰ φυτά secl. Louis : ante ὥσπερ lac. indic. Forster || cf. Gaza, *quae vero praevalida surgunt, haec annis plusculis post fructificare incipiunt, diuque vitam agere possunt, fructiferareque saepius ut abores* [8] προΐεται Sylburg : προσίεται codd.

and grow old—some slowly and in proportion?[6] Now the reason why some are short-lived and some long-lived, let that be (*the topic of*) another account;[7] but since the full development of the seed is the limit in all cases, the short-lived ones necessarily bear fruit once or a few times, whereas the long-lived do so many times, so that the weakest bear fruit only once (this is why they necessarily wither); and those able to bear in a year are annuals, and others, like horse parsley, are able to bear in the second year †just like trees and plants†.[8]

8.[9] Why, if one digs down to and around the roots of celery and surrounds them with barley husks, and then puts earth over and waters them, do the roots become extremely large? Is it because the barley husks, being hot and spongy, retain the nourishment in a mass and so it does not rise up, but, being hot, concocts it, so that a great deal of growth occurs?

9.[10] Why, if one buries gourds or cucumbers in the ground when they are still small, do they become larger?[11] Is it because the winds and the sun, through drying, prevent growth, and make the bulk of all (*plants*) less but more compact, just like trees in windy and sunny places,

[6] I.e., not immediately, but in proportion to their longevity.
[7] See Arist. *Long*. 6.
[8] The text of the end of this chapter is certainly corrupt, and something is probably missing.
[9] Source: Thphr. *CP* 5.6.3. [10] Source: Thphr. *CP* 5.6.4.
[11] I.e., they grow to be larger than they would otherwise.

---

[9] ‹ἐν› Sylburg [10] εὐείλοις scripsi ex Thph. *CP* 5.6.4 : ἑλώδεσιν codd. : εἱλώδεσιν Bussemaker

ἐν κοίλοις καὶ ἐφύδροις (τὰ μὲν γὰρ μεγάλα γίνονται καὶ σομφά, τὰ δὲ μικρὰ καὶ πυκνά)· ἐν δὲ τῇ γῇ κρυφθέντα ἐναντία πάσχοντα ἐναντίως ἀποβαίνει. ὁμοίως δὲ καὶ τὰ εἰς ἀγγεῖα τιθέμενα, σίκυοι εἰς |
25 νάρθηκας κοίλους ἢ καλυπτῆρας καὶ ῥοιαὶ καὶ μῆλα εἰς χύτρας, τὰ μὲν μεγάλα σομφὰ δέ, †οἱ δὲ μικροὶ στερροὶ αὐξανόμενοι μὴ εἰς ἀντίτυπον†.[11] αἰτία δὲ ἡ τροφὴ πλείων γινομένη διὰ τὸ μήτε ἀποπνεῖσθαι μήτε ξηραίνεσθαι· τὸ γὰρ ἀποστέγον κωλύει ταῦτα πάσχειν. |

30 10. Διὰ τί τὰ σπέρματα τῶν δριμέων φυτῶν δριμύτερά ἐστιν ἢ αἱ ῥίζαι καὶ τὰ φύλλα; ἢ διότι ἐκ τοῦ σπέρματος γίνεται ἅπαντα, καὶ εἰς τὰ ἄλλα δίδοται μέρη ἐκ τούτου, οἱονεὶ ἐνυπάρχοντα, ὥς φασί τινες, καὶ οἱ χυμοὶ καὶ αἱ ὀσμαί, ἐπεὶ καὶ αἱ ὀσμαὶ ἴδιοι
35 γίνονται ἅμα τοῖς σπέρμασιν | ἅπασιν; εἰ οὖν ἐκ τούτου καὶ τοῖς ἄλλοις ἡ δριμύτης ὑπάρχει, εὔλογον καὶ αὐτῷ[12] ὑπάρχειν μάλιστα.

11. Διὰ τί αἱ ῥαφανῖδες αἱ λεπταὶ δριμύτεραι; ἢ ὅτι αἱ μείζους διὰ τὸν χρόνον πεπεμμέναι μᾶλλον; ||

924a 12. Διὰ τί ἡ κάππαρις οὐκ ἐθέλει ῥᾳδίως ἐν τοῖς ἐργασίμοις γίνεσθαι χωρίοις; πολλοὶ γὰρ πεπείραν-

[11] οἱ δὲ μικροὶ στερροὶ αὐξανόμενοι μὴ εἰς ἀντίτυπον codd. (obeli inclusi) : οἱ δὲ μικροὶ στερροὶ <δὲ>, αὐξανόμενοι [μὴ] εἰς ἀντίτυπον Forster : †οἱ δὲ μικροὶ στερροὶ <δὲ> αὐξανόμενοι, μὴ εἰς ἀντίτυπον† Flashar

[12] αὐτῷ B x D : αὐτὸ cett. codd.

and trees in hollow and wet places (for the latter become large and spongy, the former small and dense)? Now being buried in the earth, which is the contrary condition,[12] produces contrary results. And similarly too are things put into receptacles (cucumbers into hollow fennel stalks or boxes, pomegranates and apples into jars) the latter (*becoming*) large and spongy, †the former small and solid, growing into a resisting surface†.[13] The reason is that the amount of nourishment becomes greater, because it is neither blown away nor dried up; for the covering prevents these from happening.

10. Why are the seeds of the acrid plants more acrid than the roots and the leaves? Is it because everything comes from the seed, and is distributed to the other parts from this, as if preexisting therein, as some claim,[14] both the flavors[15] and the odors, since the odors become distinctive at the same time in all the seeds? Therefore, if the acridness exists from this and so in the other parts, it is reasonable that it should exist in the seed especially.

11. Why are thin radishes more acrid? Is it because the larger ones are more concocted owing to the amount of time?

12.[16] Why does the caper plant tend not to grow easily in cultivated ground? For many have made the attempt,

[12] I.e., contrary to a windy and sunny condition.

[13] Hett's note *ad loc*: "The text here is quite uncertain, but there seems to be an allusion to the practice of enclosing cucumbers in narrow receptacles so as to shape them for water-vessels." I have followed Forster's suggestion in translating this line.

[14] This reference is unclear. Cf. Anaxagoras 59B4 D–K.

[15] *οἱ χυμοὶ* could also be translated "the juices."

[16] See Thphr. *CP* 3.1.4–6 and *HP* 1.3.6.

ται καὶ ῥίζας μεταφέροντες καὶ σπέρματα καταβάλλοντες (ἐνιαχοῦ γὰρ λυσιτελεῖ μᾶλλον τῶν ῥόδων),
5 ἀλλὰ φύεται μάλιστα ἐπὶ | τῶν τάφων, ὅτι ἀβατώτατος ὁ τόπος ἐστίν. περὶ δὲ δὴ τούτου καὶ ὅσα ἄλλα τοιαῦτα, δεῖ λαβεῖν ὅτι οὐχ ἅπαντα ἐκ τῆς αὐτῆς ὕλης γίνεται οὐδ' αὔξεται, ἀλλ' ἔνια ἐξ ἄλλων φθορᾶς καὶ ἐξ ἀρχῆς γίνεται καὶ αὐξάνεται, οἷον οἱ φθεῖρες καὶ αἱ
10 τρίχες ἐν τῷ σώματι διαφθειρομένης τῆς τροφῆς, | καὶ αὐτοῦ[13] χεῖρον ἔχοντος. ὥσπερ οὖν καὶ τῶν ἐν σώματι ἔνια γίνεται ἐκ περιττώματος τροφῆς, τοῦτο δ' ἐστὶν ἀπεψία, καὶ οὗ μὴ ἐδύνατο κρατῆσαι ἡ φύσις, τὰ μὲν προχειρότατα εἰς κύστιν καὶ κοιλίαν ἀποκρίνεται, ἐξ ἐνίων δὲ ζῷα γίνεται (διὸ καὶ αὐξάνονται ταῦτα ἐν
15 γήρᾳ καὶ νόσοις), οὕτως ἐν τῇ | γῇ τὰ μὲν ἐκ πεπεμμένης τῆς τροφῆς γίνεται καὶ αὐξάνεται, τὰ δὲ ἐκ περιττωμάτων καὶ ἐναντίως ἐχόντων. ἡ δὲ γεωργία πέττει καὶ ἐνεργὸν ποιεῖ τὴν τροφήν· ἐξ ἧς συνίστανται οἱ ἥμεροι καρποί. ἃ μὲν οὖν ἐκ τοιαύτης γίνεται ἡμερότητος, ἥμερα καλεῖται διὰ τὸ ἀπὸ τέχνης ὠφε-
20 λεῖσθαι | ὥσπερ παιδευόμενα· ὅσα δὲ μὴ δύναται ἢ καὶ ἐξ ἐναντίως ἔχοντος συνίσταται, ταῦτα ἄγριά ἐστιν καὶ οὐκ ἐθέλει γίνεσθαι ἐν γεωργησίμῳ. ἡ γὰρ γεωργία φθείρει[14] αὐτὰ παιδεύουσα· ἐκ γὰρ φθορᾶς γίνεται. ὧν καὶ ἡ κάππαρίς ἐστιν.

[13] αὐτοῦ Forster : ἀεὶ τὸ codd. : ἀεὶ τοῦ Richards
[14] φθείρει Bussemaker ex Gaza : φέρει codd.

transplanting roots and sowing seeds (for in some places they are more profitable than roses), but they grow best on graves, because the ground is untrodden? Now regarding this and all other such issues, it must be accepted that not everything is born or grows out of the same matter, but some things are born from the beginning and grow out of the decay of others—such as lice, and the hair on the body when its nourishment is corrupted, i.e., when *(the body)* itself is in a worse condition. Therefore, just as in the body as well some things grow out of the residue of nourishment (and this is unconcocted), and what nature is unable to master, the most common are secreted into the bladder and stomach, while animals come to be from others (and this is why these grow during old age and diseases),[17] so in the earth some *(animals)* come to be and grow out of concocted nourishment, others out of residues and what is in an opposite condition.[18] Now farming[19] concocts and makes productive the nourishment; from this, cultivated fruits are formed. What grows from such cultivation, then, are called "cultivated" because they are benefited by expertise, as if being trained; but those that are unable to be *(cultivated)* or even are formed out of an opposite condition, these are wild and tend not to grow in farmed land. For farming ruins these by training them, since they come to be out of corruption. The caper plant is one of these.

[17] For nature is then least able to master "the residue of nourishment" (i.e., the urine and excrement).

[18] In *Mete.* 381b9–13, Aristotle seems to refer to this passage or at least to these ideas, and writes that animals coming to be in excrement has been discussed in other works (ἐν ἑτέροις), which Alexander of Aphrodesius takes to mean ἐν τοῖς προβλήμασι (*in Mete.* 107.16–17).

[19] And specifically tilling the ground.

13. Διὰ τί, ἐάν τις ῥαφανίδων, ὅταν μάλιστα ἀκμά-
25 ζωσι | τοῦ χειμῶνος, ἀποτεμὼν τὰ φύλλα περισάξῃ τὴν γῆν καὶ καταπατήσῃ ὥστε ἀποστέγειν τὸ ὕδωρ, αὗται ἐν τῷ θέρει γίνονται ἄπλετοι τὸ πάχος; ἢ ὅτι τοῦ μὲν μὴ φθείρεσθαι τὸ περισεσάχθαι αἴτιον, κωλῦον τὸ ὕδωρ σήπειν; ἡ δὲ τροφή, ἣν ἄνω ἀφίει εἰς τὸν βλα-
30 στόν, εἰσέρχεται εἰς αὐτήν, ὥστε | ἀνάγκη αὐτὴν μείζω γίνεσθαι ἢ ἀφιέναι παραβλαστάνουσαν ἄλλας ῥίζας, ὥσπερ τὰ κρόμμυα; καὶ γὰρ ταῦτα, ἐὰν μή τις ἐκτίλῃ ἐπέτεια ἀλλ᾽ ἐάσῃ τὸν χειμῶνα, πολλαπλάσια γίνεται. τὰ μὲν οὖν κρόμμυα τῶν παραβλαστανόντων ἐστίν, ἡ δὲ ῥάφανος οὔ, ὥστε ἀνάγκη αὐτὴν γίνεσθαι
35 παχεῖαν | διὰ τὸ πᾶσαν λαμβάνειν τὴν τροφήν.

14. Διὰ τί, ἐάν τις σικύους ἢ κολοκύνθας περὶ φρέαρ φυτεύσας, ὅταν ὡραῖοι ὦσι, καθεὶς εἰς τὸ φρέαρ ἀποστεγάσῃ, γίνονται δι᾽ ἔτους χλωροί; ἢ διότι ἥ τε ἀπὸ τοῦ ὕδατος ἀτμὶς ψύχουσα κωλύει ξηραίνεσθαι
924b καὶ παρέχει θάλλοντα, καὶ || τὸ ἀποστέγειν τούτους καὶ τὰ πνεύματα τρέφει τὰ ηὐξημένα; τοῦ δὲ διαμένειν αἴτιον τὸ ἔχειν τροφὴν ἐωμένων τῶν ῥιζῶν. καὶ γὰρ ἐάν τις ἀφελὼν τὴν βλάστην, ὅταν καρποφορήσωσι, καὶ ἀποτεμὼν περισάξῃ καὶ καταπατήσῃ τὴν γῆν περὶ
5 τὰς | ῥίζας, πρωΐμους οἴσει σικύους, ὡς δυναμένων σώζεσθαι τῶν ῥιζῶν· οὐ γάρ ἐστι[15] σίκυος τῶν προετείων. θᾶττον δὲ αὐτοὶ τῶν σπειρομένων οἴσουσι καρπὸν διὰ τὸ πολὺ προϋπάρχειν τοῦ ἔργου τῇ φύσει

[15] ἐστι Cᵃ : ἔσται cett. codd.

13.[20] Why, if one cuts the leaves off radishes (when they flourish most of all, during the winter) and then packs earth around them and treads it down, so as to provide a covering against moisture, do these become immense with respect to thickness in the summer? Is it because the packing around is a cause of their not decaying, by preventing the water from rotting them? And the nourishment, which ⟨*the plant*⟩ was sending up into the shoot, enters into ⟨*the radish*⟩, so that it must either itself become bigger or, sprouting lateral shoots, send forth other roots, as onions do? Indeed these latter, if one does not pull them out annually but lets them be during the winter, become multiplied. Thus onions are among the ⟨*plants*⟩ that sprout lateral shoots, whereas the radish is not, so that it must become thick because it receives all the nourishment.

14.[21] Why, if one plants cucumbers or gourds near a well, and when they are in season puts them into the well and covers them up, are they green throughout the year? Is it because the water vapor, by cooling them, prevents them from drying and allows them to thrive, and covering them up also maintains the breath that has grown in them? Now the reason for their preservation is that they have nourishment as long as their roots are left alone. For even if one removes the shoot when they have borne fruit, and cutting away packs earth around the roots and treads it down, it will bear cucumbers early, because the roots can be preserved; for the cucumber is not a biennial. They themselves will bear fruit more quickly than what is sown, because the roots—the mightiest part of the thing—is al-

[20] Source: Thphr. *CP* 5.6.2–3.
[21] Source: Thphr. *CP* 5.6.5.

τὰς ῥίζας, τοῖς δὲ σπειρομένοις δεῖν γίνεσθαι τοῦτο πρῶτον. ἔτι δ' ἡ περίσαξις[16] ἀλέαν ποιεῖ,[17] ὥστε
10 σώζεσθαι | καὶ θᾶττον ἐνιέναι βλαστόν. διὸ καὶ ἐάν τις χειμῶνος φυτεύσῃ σπέρμα σικύου ἐν ταλαρίσκοις καὶ ἄρδηται θερμῷ καὶ εἰς τὸν ἥλιον ἐκφέρῃ καὶ παρὰ πυρὶ τιθῇ, πρώϊμοι σφόδρα ἔσονται, ἐὰν ὡς ἔχει ἐν τοῖς ταλάροις εἰς τὴν ἱκνουμένην ὥραν εἰς τὴν γῆν φυτεύσῃ. |

15 15. Διὰ τί ἀρδεύουσιν ἕωθεν ἢ νυκτὸς ἢ δείλης; πότερον ἵνα μὴ ὁ ἥλιος ἀναλώσῃ; ἢ ὅτι, ἐὰν ᾖ θερμὸν τὸ ὕδωρ, διαφθείρει τὰ ἀρδόμενα;

16. Διὰ τί τὰ εὐώδη οὐρητικὰ καὶ σπέρματα καὶ φυτά; ἢ ὅτι θερμὰ καὶ εὔπεπτα, τὰ δὲ τοιαῦτα οὐρη-
20 τικά; ταχὺ | γὰρ λεπτύνει ἡ ἐνοῦσα θερμότης, καὶ ἡ ὀσμὴ οὐ σωματώδης, ἐπεὶ καὶ τὰ μὴ εὐώδη, οἷον σκόροδα, διὰ τὴν θερμότητα οὐρητικά, μᾶλλον μέντοι συντηκτικά. θερμὰ δὲ τὰ εὐώδη σπέρματα, διότι ὅλως ἡ ὀδμὴ διὰ θερμότητά τινα γίνεται· ἀλλὰ τὰ δυσώδη
25 ἄπεπτά ἐστιν. δεῖ δὲ μὴ μόνον εἶναι | θερμὰ ἀλλὰ καὶ εὔπεπτα, εἰ ἔσται οὐρητικά, ὅπως συγκατιόντα λεπτύνῃ τὰ ὑγρά.

17. Διὰ τί θᾶττον ἐκκαυλεῖ τῶν λαχάνων τὰ ἐκ παλαιοτέρου σπέρματος, οἷον τριετοῦς ἢ διετοῦς, ἢ τὰ ἐκ τῶν προσφάτων; ἢ ὅτι ὡς ἐπὶ τῶν ζῴων θᾶττον

[16] ἔτι δ' ἡ περίσαξις Forster ex Thph. *CP* 5.6.4 : ἐν ᾗ περισάξεις codd.

[17] ποιεῖ u : ποιεῖν cett. codd. : δεῖ εἶναι Vat.1904^mg

ready present in their growth, whereas in what is sown this part must grow first. Further, the packing around produces warmth, so that it is preserved and sends out a shoot more quickly. And this is why if one plants cucumber seeds in baskets in winter, and gives them hot water and carries them out into the sun and places them by a fire, they will appear very early if one plants them into the earth just as they are, in their baskets, when the season arrives.

15.[22] Why do people water either in the morning, or at night or late afternoon? Is it so that the sun may not consume (*the water*)? Or is it because, if the water is hot, it ruins what is watered?

16.[23] Why are fragrant seeds and plants diuretic? Is it because they are hot and easily concocted, and such things are diuretic? For the internal heat liquefies quickly and the smell is not corporeal, since even the ones that are not fragrant, like garlic, are diuretic owing to their heat, though they are more productive of colliquation. Fragrant seeds are hot, because the smell generally comes to be owing to a certain heat; but malodorous things are unconcocted. Now if something is to be diuretic, it must not only be hot but also well-concocted, in order that it may liquefy the moist elements as they move downward with them.

17.[24] Why do vegetables that come from old seed—e.g., two or three years old—send up a stem more quickly than those that come from fresh seed? Is it because, as in

[22] See Thphr. *HP* 7.5.2.

[23] This chapter is virtually identical to *Pr.* 12.12. See also 1.48.

[24] Source: Thphr. *CP* 4.3.5–6. See also *HP* 7.3.4.

30 σπέρμα φέρει τὸ ἀκμάζον, | οὕτω καὶ τῶν σπερμάτων τὰ μὲν λίαν παλαιὰ ἐξίκμασται τὴν δύναμιν, τὰ δὲ ἀσθενέστερα διὰ τὸ ἔτι ἔχειν περίττωμα μὴ οἰκεῖον, τὰ δὲ μέσα τῷ χρόνῳ ἰσχυρότατα ἀπεληλυθότος τοῦ ὑγροῦ; θᾶττον οὖν σπέρμα φέρει. τὸ δὲ ἐκκαυλεῖν τοῦτό ἐστιν· ἐκ γὰρ τοῦ καυλοῦ τὸ σπέρμα. |

35 18. Διὰ τί πήγανον κάλλιστον καὶ πλεῖστον γίνεται ἐάν τις ἐκφυτεύσῃ εἰς συκῆν; ἐκφυτεύεται δὲ περὶ τὸν φλοιὸν καὶ περιπλάττεται πηλῷ. ἢ ὅτι θερμότητος δέονται αἱ ῥίζαι τοῦ πηγάνου καὶ ἀλέας (διὸ καὶ τὴν τέφραν ἐάν τις περιβάλλῃ, ὀνίνανται), ἡ δὲ συκῆ 925a θερμή ἐστιν; δηλοῖ δὲ καὶ ὁ || ὀπὸς πάντων δριμύτατος ὤν, καὶ ὁ πολὺς καπνός. ἔχει οὖν τοιαύτην θερμότητα καὶ ἰκμάδα οἵαν καὶ ἡ τέφρα, ὥστε εἰ ἐκείνη[18] ὀνίνησιν, ἀναγκαῖον καὶ ἐν τῇ συκῇ μάλιστα εὐσθενεῖν, ὅσῳ ἡ μὲν τέφρα οὐκ ἐπιρρεῖ, τὸ δ' ἀπὸ τῆς συκῆς ἀεὶ | 5 ἐπιρρεῖ, οὐκ ἀναλισκομένου τοῦ ὑγροῦ τῇ συκῇ.

19. Διὰ τί ἔνια τῶν φυτῶν ἀεὶ κενὸν φέρει τὸν καυλόν;[19] ἢ ὧν ἀνάγκη ἄλλο φύειν;[20]

20. Διὰ τί ἐν τῇ Ἀττικῇ οἱ μὲν ἄλλοι καρποὶ

[18] ἐκείνη Bussemaker ex Gaza : ἐκείνην codd.

[19] καυλόν : αὐλόν Ap^a

[20] ἢ ὧν ἀνάγκη ἄλλο φύειν : post φύειν lac. indic. Sylburg : (sc. ἢ ὧν) ἡ φύσις ἀσθενεστέρα D^{mg} (cf. Gaza, *an illis quarum natura imbecillior est, has rarum inanemque emittere caulem necesse est*)

---

[25] I.e., vegetables that come from old seed.

the case of animals what is in its prime bears seed more quickly, so too (*in the case of vegetables*) the very old seeds have their power evaporate, while the (*fresh ones*) are weaker because they still contain residue that does not belong to them, but those intermediate in age are strongest because the moisture has left them? They[25] therefore bear seed more quickly. And this is sending up a stem; for the seed comes from the stem.

18.[26] Why does rue[27] grow finest and best if one grafts it onto a fig tree? It is grafted into the bark and plastered with clay. Is it because the roots of rue require heat and warmth (and this is why they are benefited if one surrounds them with ashes), and the fig tree is hot? Both its sap, which is the most acrid of all, and the quantity of smoke (*it produces when burned*) show this. It therefore contains the same sort of heat and fluid as ash does, so that if ash benefits (*the rue*), it would necessarily thrive most of all on the fig tree, as the ash does not produce any flow of liquid, whereas what comes from the fig tree flows continually, since the moisture in the fig tree is not consumed.

19. Why do some plants always bear an empty stem? Are they among those that must produce something else?[28]

20. Why are the other fruits in Attica very sweet, while

[26] Source: Thphr. *CP* 5.6.10.

[27] Rue is a genus (*Ruta*) of shrub, many species of which have medicinal and culinary uses.

[28] Judging by a marginal comment in ms. D and by the translation of Gaza, there may have been an alternative text for the second question, which made reference to the greater weakness of such plants.

γλυκύτατοι γίνονται, τὸ δὲ θύμον δριμύτατον; καίτοι
10 καὶ τοῦτο καρπός | τίς ἐστιν.[21] . . . ὥστε οὐ πολὺ ὑγρὸν
τὰ φυόμενα ἔχει; ὅσα μὲν οὖν φύσει γλυκέα ἐστί διὰ
μετριότητα τοῦ ἐνυπάρχοντος ὑγροῦ, ὅταν ἀπάγῃ ὁ
ἥλιος τὸ πλεῖστον, τὸ ὑπολειπόμενον ῥᾳδίως πέττεται·
τὸ γὰρ πολὺ ἔργον πεπάνθαι, τὸ δὲ μέτριον ῥᾷον.
15 ὥστε γίνονται οἱ φύσει γλυκεῖς γλυκύτεροι. | ἐν δὲ
τοῖς φύσει ξηροῖς τε καὶ μὴ γλυκέσι καρποῖς λείπεται
δι' ὀλιγότητα τὸ οἰκεῖον, τοῦτο δ' ἐστὶν ἥκιστα γλυκύ·
ἀφαιρεῖται γὰρ ὁ ἥλιος τὸ γλυκύτατον καὶ κουφό-
τατον· οὗτοι δὲ οὐκ ἔχουσι περιττὸν ὑγρόν, ὥσπερ οἱ
ἄλλοι καρποί.

21. Διὰ τί γλήχων καὶ τὰ λείρια καὶ τὰ κρόμμυα τὰ |
20 κρεμάμενα ὑπὸ τὰς τροπὰς ἀνθεῖ; ἢ ἐνυπάρχει αὐτοῖς
τροφὴ ἄπεπτος, ἣ τοῦ μὲν χειμῶνος οὐ πέττεται διὰ τὸ
ψῦχος, ὑπὸ δὲ τὰς τροπὰς πεττομένης διὰ τὴν ὥραν ἡ
αὔξησις γίνεται; αὕτη δὲ διὰ τὸ μὴ ἔχειν ἐπίρρυσιν
ταχὺ μαραίνεται. οὐ γάρ τινα ἔχουσα ἀρχὴν οὐδέ τινα
25 ἐπίρρυσιν | ἀποξηραίνεται, ὥσπερ Σκύθαις διὰ τὸ
πολλὴν τὴν χιόνα γίνεσθαι συμβαίνει τὸν σῖτον μέ-
νειν καὶ ταχὺ ἀνατρέχειν.

22. Διὰ τί τὸ κρόμμυον μόνον οὕτως περιττῶς
δάκνει τὼ ὀφθαλμώ (διὸ καὶ τοὔνομά φασι τοῦτ' ἔχειν
αὐτό, ὡς τὴν κόρην ποιεῖν συμμύειν), ἡ δὲ ὀρίγανος

[21] post ἐστιν lac. indic. Casaubon· ἴσως λείπει : ἢ ὅτι ἀγρὸς ἐκεῖνος λεπτός τε καὶ ξηρός ἐστι Xa mg (cf. Gaza, *an quod ager ille tenuis dulcisque est*)

thyme is very acrid? Yet thyme too is a kind of fruit. (*Is it because this ground is thin and dry*),[29] so that the plants do not have much moisture? Therefore, in those that are sweet by nature owing to the moderate amount of moisture existing in them, when the sun draws off most of it, what is left over is easily concocted; for it is hard work for a large quantity to be ripened, but easier for a moderate amount. So (*fruits*) that are sweet by nature become sweeter. But in those fruits that are by nature dry and not sweet, the (*moisture*) proper to them falls short because there is so little, and this is least of all sweet; for the sun removes the sweetest and lightest part; and these do not have excessive moisture, like the other fruits.

21.[30] Why do pennyroyal, lilies, and onions bloom when hung up at the summer solstice? Is unconcocted nourishment present in them, which is not concocted in winter because of the cold, but when it is concocted at the summer solstice owing to the season, growth occurs? But this growth is quickly exhausted because there is no flow of moisture. For if they do not have some source or some flow of moisture, it is dried up, just as among the Scythians, because of the quantity of snow that falls, the result is that the grain remains (*in the ground*) and then suddenly shoots up.

22. Why does the onion alone sting the eyes so excessively (and they say this is why it has its name, because it makes one cover the pupil),[31] but marjoram does not, nor

[29] This insertion is based on the marginal comment in ms. X[a] and the translation of Gaza.

[30] Cf. *Pr.* 20.26 and 28. See Thphr. *CP* 1.7.4.

[31] The author is claiming (incorrectly) that *κρόμμυον* ("onion") is derived from *κόρη* ("pupil") and *μύειν* ("to close"). Cf. Ath. 367A.

30 οὔ, οὐδ' ἄλλα δριμέα | ὄντα; καὶ γὰρ τὸ ἀνάρρινον μᾶλλον δάκνον οὐ ποιεῖ ὁμοίως δακρύειν προσφερόμενον, τὸ δὲ <κρόμμυνον>[22] προσφερόμενον καὶ κατατρωγόμενον. ἢ ὅτι διαφοραὶ πολλαὶ ἀκολουθοῦσιν ἑκάστοις τῶν δριμέων, ἃ ποιεῖ τὴν ἰδίαν ἑκάστου δύναμιν; τὸ μὲν οὖν ἀνάρρινον διὰ τὸ θερμότερον εἶναι
35 ξηραντικώτερόν ἐστι τῆς | γινομένης ὑπ' αὐτοῦ συντήξεως, ἐπεὶ ποιεῖ γε δάκρυον ἐσθίοντι, προσφερόμενον δὲ οὔ, ὅτι οὐκ ἀπατμίζει ἀπ' αὐτοῦ λεπτόν τι· ξηρότερον γάρ ἐστι καὶ θερμότερον. ἡ δὲ ὀρίγανος ||
925b καὶ τὰ τοιαῦτα θερμὰ ξηρά ἐστιν ἠρέμα.[23] δεῖ δὲ τὸ μέλλον δάκρυον ποιήσειν δηκτικὸν καὶ ὑγρὸν εἶναι καὶ γλίσχρον. διὸ καὶ τὸ ἔλαιον ποιεῖ δακρύειν, ἀσθενῆ ἔχον δῆξιν· διὰ γλισχρότητα γὰρ καὶ λεπτότητα
5 παραδῦνον ποιεῖ | τὸν πόνον, καὶ τὴν σύντηξιν διὰ τὸν πόνον. τὸ δὲ κρόμμυον τοιαύτην ἔχει τὴν δύναμιν ὥστε καὶ τὸ ὑγρὸν καὶ τὴν ἀτμίδα αὐτοῦ θερμὴν καὶ λεπτὴν καὶ γλίσχραν εἶναι. ὥστε προσφερόμενον μέν, διὰ τὸ τὴν ἀτμίδα τοιαύτην εἶναι καὶ συναφιέναι
10 ὑγρότητα λεπτήν, ποιεῖ δακρύειν, ἐσθιομένου δὲ | ἡ ἀναθυμίασις διιοῦσα . . .[24] τὸ δὲ σκόροδον θερμὸν μὲν καὶ δριμύ ἐστι καὶ ὑγρότητα ἔχει, ἀλλ' οὐ γλίσχρον· διὸ οὐ ποιεῖ δακρύειν.

23. Διὰ τί τὰ μύρτα ἐν τῇ χειρὶ θλιβέντα γλυκύ-

[22] <κρόμμυον> Ruelle

[23] θερμὰ ξηρά ἐστιν ἠρέμα : fort. *θερμά ἐστιν ἠρέμα καὶ ξηρά* ex Barth. et Gaza (*calida et sicca*)

[24] post διιοῦσα lac. hab. codd. : add. *ταὐτὸ ποιεῖν δύναται* Sylburg ex Gaza

do the other acrid (*plants*)? Indeed, though the nasturtium stings more, it does not produce tears to the same extent when brought near (*the eyes*), but the onion does when brought near or eaten. Is it because many differences accompany each of the acrid (*plants*), which produce the special capacity of each? So the nasturtium, because it is very hot, has an ability to produce dryness that is greater than the colliquation that it generates, and so it produces tears when eaten, but not when brought near (*the eyes*), because it does not produce a thin vapor, since it is very dry and very hot. But marjoram and similar hot (*plants*) are slightly dry.[32] But to produce tears (*a plant*) must be acrid and moist and sticky. And this is why olive oil produces tears, although its sting is weak; for it gets through because of its stickiness and thinness and so causes pain, and there is colliquation because of the pain. Now the onion has this capacity, such that both its moisture and vapor are hot and thin and sticky. So that when it is brought near (*the eyes*), because its vapor is of such a character and it gives off thin moisture, it produces tears, and when it is eaten the evaporation passes through . . .[33] Garlic, however, is hot and acrid and contains moisture, but is not sticky, which is why it does not produce tears.

23. Why do myrtle berries crushed in the hand seem to

[32] We should perhaps follow Bartholmew and Gaza and translate "and similar (*plants*) are slightly hot, and dry."

[33] The mss. indicate a lacuna here. If we follow Gaza and Sylburg, we should supply "and can produce the same effect."

τερα ἡμῖν δοκεῖ εἶναι τῶν μὴ τεθλιμμένων; ἢ καθάπερ
15 καὶ αἱ | ῥᾶγες τετρυγημέναι τῶν βοτρύων γλυκύτεραί
εἰσιν τῶν ἀτρυγήτων; ὑπὸ γὰρ τοῦ γλεύκους ὄντος
φύσει ἡδέος αἱ μὲν τετρυγημέναι ῥᾶγες ὥσπερ ἐοίκασιν
ἡδυσμέναι (ἀνάπλεῳ γάρ εἰσι καὶ ἔξωθεν), αἱ δ'
ἐπὶ τῶν βοτρύων ἀνήδυντοι. ὁμοίως οὖν καὶ ἐπὶ τῶν
20 μύρτων φύσει γλυκέων καὶ τὴν γλυκύτητα | ἐχόντων
ἐντός. ὥσπερ αἱ ῥᾶγες οὖν, ὅταν θλιφθῇ, ἀναπίμπλαται
ἀπὸ τῆς ἐντὸς γλυκύτητος καὶ ἔξωθεν διαφαίνεται
γλυκύτερα ὄντα.

24. Διὰ τί τῶν τε μύρτων τὰ ἐλάττω ἀπυρηνότερά
ἐστι, καὶ ἐν τοῖς φοίνιξι καὶ ἐπὶ τῶν βοτρύων, ἔνθα
25 δ'[25] αἱ μικραὶ | ῥᾶγες οὐκ ἔχουσιν ἢ ἐλάττους πυρῆνας;
ἢ διὰ τὸ ἀτελέστερα εἶναι οὐκ ἔχει ἀποκεκριμένον;
τέλος γὰρ ὁ πυρὴν ἔχει τὸ σπέρμα. διὰ τοῦτο
δὲ καὶ ἐλάττους εἰσίν, ὡς ὄντα παραφυάδες καὶ ἀτελῆ.
καὶ ἧττον δὲ γλυκέα τῶν ἐχόντων πυρῆνας· ἀπεπτότερα
γάρ ἐστιν, ἡ δὲ πέψις τελείωσίς ἐστιν. |

30 25. Διὰ τί τῶν περικαρπίων τὰ μὲν[26] πικρότερα τὰ
πρὸς τὴν ῥίζαν ἔχει, οἷον σίκυοι, τὰ δὲ πρὸς τὸ ἄκρον
τὸ ἄνω, οἷον αἱ βάλανοι; ἢ ὅτι τῶν μὲν ταύτῃ ἄπεπτος
ἡ τροφὴ διὰ τὸ ἐπιρρεῖν κατὰ τὴν ῥίζαν ἀεί, τὰ δὲ
ξηρὰ φύσει ἐστίν, ὥστε ἀπαγομένου τοῦ γλυκέος ἐκ
35 τοῦ ἄκρου καὶ πεπεμμένου | ἤδη ξηραίνεται, καὶ λείπεται
τὸ πικρὸν ὥσπερ οἱ ἅλες; ξηραινόμενον δὲ

[25] δ' secl. Forster
[26] μὲν om. Louis

be sweeter than those that have not been crushed? Is it for the same reason that grapes that have been gathered are sweeter than bunches of grapes that have not been gathered? For grapes that have been gathered, so it seems, are flavored by their sweet juice, which is naturally pleasant (for they are saturated with it even externally), whereas grapes that are still in bunches are not so flavored. It is the same, too, in the case of myrtle berries, as they are naturally sweet and have sweetness within them. Therefore, just like grapes when they are crushed, ⟨*myrtle berries*⟩ are saturated with the sweetness within and are clearly sweeter externally.

24. Why do the smaller myrtle berries tend to be stoneless, as in dates and bunches of grapes (and here the small grapes have no stones or small ones)? Is it because, being more imperfect,[34] they do not have differentiated ones? For the stone's goal is to hold the seed. Now the reason why they are smaller is that they are offshoots and imperfect. And they are less sweet than those that have stones, since they are more unconcocted, and concoction is their perfection.

25.[35] Why are some fruit cases more bitter toward the root (for example, cucumbers), others toward the upper part (for example, acorns)? Is it because in the former the nourishment of those parts is unconcocted, because it is always flowing down along the root, while the latter are dry by nature, so that when the sweetness is drawn off from the upper part and concocted, it is already dry, and what is bitter is left behind, like salt? And becoming dry it grows

[34] "More imperfect" (ἀτελέστερα), i.e., less complete or finished.

[35] Source: Thphr. *CP* 6.10.7.

μᾶλλον πικρὸν γίνεται, καθάπερ ἐλαῖαι καὶ βάλανοι παλαιούμεναι πικραὶ γίνονται. ||

926a 26. Διὰ τί ἔνια βλαστάνει οὐκ ἐν τῇ γῇ ὄντα ἀλλ' ἐκτετμημένα, τὰ δὲ κείμενα, οἷον οἱ τῶν κρίνων καυλοὶ καὶ σκόροδα καὶ κρόμμυα; ἢ ὅτι ἔχουσι τροφὴν ἅπαντα ἐν αὑτοῖς, ἀλλ' οὐκ ἐν ἀφωρισμένῳ τόπῳ [οὐθὲν
5 φυτόν];[27] [ἡ περιουσία οὖν | ἐστὶ τῆς τροφῆς ἡ ποιοῦσα βλαστάνειν. δῆλον δέ· καὶ γὰρ καὶ αἱ σκίλλαι καὶ οἱ βολβοὶ ταὐτὸ ποιοῦσιν.][28] αὔξεται δ' ἕκαστον οὐ τῷ ἔχειν, ἀλλ' ὅταν πεφθῇ καὶ διανεμηθῇ. ἔχει μὲν οὖν καὶ ἔμπροσθεν, αὔξεται δέ, ὅταν ἡ ὥρα ἔλθῃ ἐν ᾗ τοῦτο γίνεται πεττούσης <τῆς>[29] ὥρας, οἷον καὶ τὰ τῶν
10 κροκοδείλων | ᾠά. συνεχὲς δὲ οὐκέτι, ὅτι οὐκ ἐπιρρεῖ ἄλλη τροφή.

27. Διὰ τί ποτε τὰ σκόροδα καὶ τὰ κρόμμυα ὅσῳ ἂν ξηρότερα φυτεύηται, τοσούτῳ βελτίω γίνεται, τὰ δὲ ἄλλα χείρω; ἢ ὅτι πάντα τὰ τοιαῦτα μάλιστα ὑγρασίας ἐστὶ πλήρη; εὔκρατα οὖν γίνεται τοῦτον τὸν
15 τρόπον φυτευθέντα. | καὶ ὅτι ἧττον σήπεται, ὅταν ξηρανθέντα φυτευθῇ.

28. Διὰ τί ποτε τὰ σκόροδα καὶ τὰ κρόμμυα μόνα τῶν φυτῶν κείμενα βλαστάνει; ἢ διότι ὑγρασίας ἐστὶ πλήρη καὶ τροφῆς; ἡ περιουσία οὖν ἐστὶ τῆς τροφῆς ἡ ποιοῦσα βλαστάνειν. δῆλον δέ· καὶ γὰρ αἱ σκίλλαι

27 [οὐθὲν φυτόν] Hett : ἔξωθεν φυτοῦ Forster
28 ἡ περιουσία—ταὐτὸ ποιοῦσιν seclusi, om. Ya Ca, cf. *Pr.* 20.28, 926a18–20 29 <τῆς> Forster

more bitter, just as olives and acorns become bitter as they grow old.

26.[36] Why do some (*plants*) sprout when they are not in the ground but are cut off, and others do so in storage, like lily stems, garlic, and onions? Is it because they all contain nourishment within themselves, and not in some separate place? [Therefore, their surplus nourishment is what makes them sprout. And this is clear, for squills and bulbs do the same thing.][37] Now each of them grows not simply by containing nourishment, but when this is concocted and distributed. It therefore contains (*the nourishment*) beforehand, but it grows when the season arrives during which this occurs (the season producing concoction), like crocodile's eggs. But this is not continuous, because further nourishment does not flow in.

27.[38] Why do garlic and onions grow that much better, the drier they are when planted, whereas the other (*plants*) grow worse? Is it because all such (*plants*) are especially full of moisture? So they are in a mild condition when planted in this way. It is also because they are less likely to rot when they are planted after having been dried.

28.[39] Why are garlic and onions the only plants that sprout when placed in storage? Is it because they are full of moisture and nourishment? Therefore, their surplus nourishment is what makes them sprout. And this is clear, for

[36] Cf. *Pr.* 20.21 and esp. 28.

[37] This line is not found in the two oldest mss., and is repeated verbatim in *Pr.* 20.28, where it is a better fit.

[38] Cf. Thphr. *HP* 7.4.10–12.

[39] Cf. *Pr.* 20.21 and esp. 26.

20 καὶ οἱ βολβοὶ ταὐτὸ ποιοῦσιν. | αὔξεται δέ, ὅταν ἡ ὥρα ἔλθῃ ἑκάστῳ.

29. Διὰ τί τὰ τῷ ψυχρῷ ὕδατι ἀρδόμενα γλυκύτερα ἢ τὰ τῷ θερμῷ; πότερον ὅτι ἐγκατακλειόμενον τὸ θερμὸν ἁλμυρώτερον, ὥσπερ καὶ τὸ ἁλμυρώτερον θερμότερον, τὸ δὲ γλυκὺ ἐναντίον, ὥσπερ ψυχρόν; τροφὴ
25 δὲ τοῖς λαχάνοις | τὸ ὑγρόν, καὶ οἱ χυμοὶ ἐντεῦθεν.

30. Διὰ τί τὰ σκόροδα ὄζει μᾶλλον ἐγκαυλοῦντα ἢ νέα ὄντα; ἢ ὅτι νέων μὲν ὄντων ἔτι πολὺ ὑγρὸν ἀλλότριον ἐνὸν ἀφαιρεῖται τὴν δύναμιν αὐτῶν, ὅταν δὲ πεπανθῇ, ἐκκεκριμένου ἤδη τούτου, τότε τὴν οἰκείαν
30 ἔχει ὀδμήν; αὕτη δέ ἐστι | φύσει δριμεῖα.[30] ὁμοίως δὲ καὶ οἱ ἄλλοι καρποὶ οἱ πρόσφατοι ὄντες ὑδαρέστεροι. διὸ καὶ τὰ κρόμμυα ἧττον δριμέα τὰ νεώτερα.

31. Διὰ τί τῶν μυρρινῶν μὲν μὴ τεταριχευμένων τὰ μύρτα ἀπορρεῖ μᾶλλον τῶν φύλλων, ταριχευομένων
35 δὲ τῷ φύκει | τὰ μὲν φύλλα ἀπορρεῖ, τὰ δὲ μύρτα οὐκ ἀπορρεῖ; ἢ ἀταριχεύτων μὲν ὄντων οὕτως ἔχει διὰ τὴν φύσιν; ὅταν γὰρ πεπανθῇ, ἀπορρεῖν πέφυκε τὰ μύρτα. τοῦτο δὲ οὐ συμβαίνει κειμένων, ἀλλὰ μόνον κωλύει ἡ ἰκμὰς τοῦ φύκους μεταβάλλειν τὸ ἐν τῷ μύρτῳ ὑγρόν.
926a τὰ δὲ φύλλα ἀποπίπτει || τοὐναντίον αὐτῶν ξηραινο-

[30] δριμεῖα Ap : om. cett. codd.

---

[40] Squills or *Scilla*, a genus of bulb-forming plants in the family *Hyacinthaceae*. "Bulbs" (οἱ βολβοί) here likely refers specifically to grape hyacinth (*Muscari comosum*).

squills and bulbs[40] do the same thing. But they grow when the season for each arrives.[41]

29. Why are (*plants*) that are watered with cold water sweeter than those watered with hot? Is it because the hot water enclosed (*in the plant*) is saltier, just as what is saltier is hotter, but what is sweet is the opposite, that is to say, cold? Now nourishment in vegetables is the moisture, and hence their juices.

30. Why does garlic have more of an odor when it has sent out a stem than when it is young? Is it because, when it is young, there is still a lot of foreign moisture in it that diminishes its power, but when it is concocted,[42] this moisture having already been excreted, it then has its proper odor? And this is naturally acrid. Similarly, the other fruits too when they are fresh are more watery. And this is why young onions are less acrid.

31. Why, when myrtle branches are not preserved, do the myrtle berries fall off rather than[43] the leaves, but when they are preserved in seaweed, the leaves fall off, but the myrtle berries do not fall off? Is this the condition they're in, owing to their nature, when they are unpreserved? For when it is concocted,[44] it is natural for the myrtle berries to fall off. But this does not happen when they are in storage, rather the fluid in the seaweed only prevents the moisture of the myrtle berries from changing. The leaves, by contrast, fall off when they[45] get dry, and the

[41] I.e., squills and bulbs, unlike garlic and onions.
[42] Or "has ripened."
[43] Or "more than."
[44] Or "has ripened."
[45] The leaves themselves or, more likely, the branches.

μένων, τὸ δὲ φῦκος ξηραίνει ἁλμυρὸν ὄν. οὐ ταὐτὸ οὖν συμβαίνει ἐπί τε τῆς μυρρίνης οὖσι καὶ κειμένοις τοῖς φύλλοις.

32. Διὰ τί οἱ σίκυοι πέπονες[31] ἄριστοι γίνονται ἐν
5 τοῖς ἑλώδεσι | πεδίοις, οὖσιν ἐνύγροις, οἷον περὶ Ὀρχομενὸν καὶ ἐν Αἰγύπτῳ; δοκεῖ δ' ἔνυδρος αὕτη ἡ χώρα εἶναι. ἔστι δὲ τὰ ἑλώδη ἔνυδρα· οἱ δὲ σίκυοι[32] αὐτοὶ ὑγρότεροι· διὸ καὶ οἱ κηπαῖοι φαῦλοι εἰσίν. πότερον ὅτι εἰς βάθος διὰ σκληρότητα τῆς γῆς ἀναγκάζονται φυτεύεσθαι; ἡ γὰρ πηλώδης καὶ πεδιὰς |
10 μάλιστα γίνεται σκληρά, οἱ δὲ εἰς βάθος φυτευθέντες βελτίους. ἢ διότι ξηρὰν δεῖ εἶναι τὴν γῆν διὰ τὸ αὐτὸ εἶναι ὑγρὸν φύσει; οὕτω γὰρ ἀντισπώμενον ἐπὶ τὸ μέσον ἥξει. ἡ δὲ ἑλωδεστέρα μὲν βαθεῖα δὲ τροφὴν ἴσχει καὶ διὰ τὸ βάθος τῆς γῆς καὶ διὰ τὸν τόπον, καὶ
15 οὐχ ὑπερβάλλουσαν διὰ | τὸ ξηραίνεσθαι τὴν γῆν πάλιν.

33. Διὰ τί τὸ πήγανον δυσώδεις τοὺς ἱδρῶτας ποιεῖ, καὶ ἔνια τῶν μύρων; ἢ ὅτι ὅσων ἐν τῇ ὀσμῇ βαρύτης ἔνι καὶ δριμύτης, ταῦτα κεραννύμενα ταῖς περιττωματικαῖς ὑγρότησι κακωδεστέραν ποιεῖ τὴν ὀσμήν; |

[31] ante πέπονες add. ‹οἱ› Richards
[32] σίκυοι Bekker : σίκυες codd.

---

[46] The meaning seems to be "when they are still on the tree."

[47] Hp. *Vict.* 2.55 reports that "unripe cucumbers" (σίκυοι ὠμοὶ) are difficult to concoct (or undigestible, δύσπεπτον), whereas ripe (πέπονες) ones are not. Jones (LCL nn. 4–5 *ad loc.*)

seaweed being salty dries them. So the same thing does not happen to the leaves when they are on the myrtle branch[46] and when they are in storage.

32. Why do ripe cucumbers[47] grow best in marshy plains, which are wet, for instance around Orchomenos and in Egypt? This country seems to be wet. Now marshy areas are wet, and cucumbers are themselves very moist; and this is why those grown in a garden are poor. Is it because they must be planted deep owing to the hardness of the ground? For clayey and flat ground becomes very hard, and what is planted deep does better. Or is it because the ground should be dry because the ⟨*plant*⟩ itself is naturally moist? For being drawn in contrary directions in this way it will arrive at the mean. Now ground that is very marshy but deep contains nourishment both because of the depth of ground and because of the locality, but not in excess, because the ground becomes dry again.

33.[48] Why do rue and certain perfumes[49] make the sweat malodorous? Is it because those things that have a heavy and acrid scent, when mixed with residual moisture, make the scent have a more evil odor?

suggests that the unripe *σίκυοι* are cucumbers, while the ripe ones are melons. Similarly, Forster and Hett translate *σίκυοι πέπονες* (in *Pr.* 20.32) "melons." Nevertheless, the distinction could be referring to two stages in the growth of the same species of plant. [48] This chapter is virtually identical to *Pr.* 2.13; see also 8.9. Source: Thphr. *Sud.* 10. Cf. Thphr. *Od.* 10.

[49] The word translated "perfumes" (*μύρων*) might also be rendered "ointments" or "unguents" or "myrrh oil." If the author has in mind specifically this last, then he is referring to the oil derived from the dried sap of trees in the genus *Commiphora*, which is used primarily in perfume.

20 34. Διὰ τί τὸ πήγανον βασκανίας φασὶ φάρμακον εἶναι; ἢ διότι βασκαίνεσθαι δοκοῦσι λάβρως ἐσθίοντες, ἢ ὑφορώμενοί τινας δυσχερείας καὶ περὶ τὰ προσφερόμενα ὑπόπτως ἔχοντες; ἐπιλέγουσι γοῦν, ὅταν τῆς αὐτῆς τραπέζης ἰδίᾳ τι προσφέρωνται, μεταδιδόν-
25 τες, "ἵνα μὴ βασκάνῃς με." ἅπαντες | οὖν μετὰ ταραχῆς τῶν βρωμάτων προσοίσονται τὸ διδόμενον ὑγρὸν ἢ σιτίον, ὑφ' ὧν ἢ καταλαμβανομένων ἢ ἀπεμουμένων μετεωρισθέντα τὰ σιτία συνεξέπεσεν καὶ τὰ πνεύματα ὑπὸ τῶν ὑγρῶν καὶ[33] πόνους καὶ στρόφους παρέχει. τὸ πήγανον οὖν προεδεσθέν, θερμαντικὸν ὂν τῇ φύσει,
30 ἠραίωσε τὸ | δεχόμενον ἀγγεῖον τὰ σιτία καὶ τὸ ἄλλο σῶμα. διὸ ἐξίεσθαι[34] τὸ ἐγκαταλαμβανόμενον πνεῦμα συμβαίνει.

35. Διὰ τί ἡ ὀρίγανος ἐμβαλλομένη τῷ γλεύκει γλυκὺν ποιεῖ τὸν οἶνον; ἐμβάλλονται δὲ δύο κοτύλαι εἰς τὸν ἀμφορέα. ἢ ὅτι ἐξαίρει δι' ὧν ἡ αὐστηρότης
35 γίνεται, τὸ ὑδατῶδες | καὶ τὸ τρυγῶδες ἀναδεχομένη τῇ ξηρότητι εἰς αὑτήν; σημεῖον δὲ ὅτι ἐκ τούτων τὸ αὐστηρόν· οἱ γὰρ οἶνοι ἧττον μαλακοί, ἐὰν ὕδωρ παραχεθῇ, καὶ ἐὰν ἐν τῇ τρυγὶ πλείω χρόνον ἐάσῃ τις.

[33] καὶ om. Bekker [34] ἐξίεσθαι Bussemaker ex [Arist./Alex.] *Sup.Pr.* 3.6, 4 : ἔξωθεν codd. : ἐξωθεῖν Forster

---

[50] Cf. [Arist./Alex.] *Sup.Pr.* 3.6.

[51] βασκανία ("bewitchment") is often translated "evil eye" (a rendering supported by Plu. *QC* 5.7 [*Mor.* 680C–83B]). According to Orion (fifth century AD), *Etymologicum* 159.8–9, βάσκα-

34.[50] Why do they say that rue is a remedy against bewitchment?[51] Is it because they seem to be bewitched when eating greedily,[52] or when suspecting some unpleasantness and being suspicious about what is offered them? At least, when they are offered something from the same table particularly for them, they share it and add: "lest you bewitch me." So all will take with trouble[53] what is offered, whether liquid or solid, of those foods the constriction or vomiting forth of which causes the solid food to rise and be ejected and the winds from the liquids to produce pain and writhing. Rue eaten beforehand, therefore, being by nature capable of heating, makes porous the receptacle receiving food and the rest of the body. This is why the result is that the wind enclosed within is released.

35. Why does marjoram, thrown into the grape juice, make the wine sweet? Two cups are thrown into an amphora. Is it because it removes the cause of harshness, receiving into itself by means of its dryness the watery part and the dregs? A sign of this is that the harshness comes from these; for wines are less soft if water is poured into them or if one leaves them for a long time in the dregs. And

νος comes from *φάσκανος* (otherwise unattested), which in turn comes from *φάεσι καίνειν* ("kill with the eyes," as *φάος* ["light"] can also mean "the light of the eyes" and, by extension, simply "the eyes").

52 The evidence for this, according to the version in [Arist./Alex.] *Sup.Pr.* 3.6 (as emended by Bussemaker), is the flatulence that often accompanies eating greedily.

53 Here, "with trouble" (*μετὰ ταραχῆς*) could refer to mental trouble ("with misgivings" [Hett]) or physical trouble ("with [gastrointestinal] discomfort").

καὶ ὅταν ποιῶσι γλυκύν,[35] ἡλιῶσι τὰς σταφυλὰς πο-
927a λὺν χρόνον, καὶ ὁ ἥλιος ἀφαιρεῖ τὸ ὑδατῶδες καὶ ‖ τὸ λοιπὸν συμπέττει. ταὐτὸ δὲ τοῦτο ποιεῖ καὶ ἡ ὀρίγανος· ξηρὰ γὰρ καὶ θερμή, ὥστε εἰκότως διαμένει.

36. Διὰ τί αἱ μέλαιναι μυρρίναι πυκνοφυλλότεραί[36] εἰσι τῶν λευκῶν μυρρινῶν; ἢ ὅτι ἀγριώτεραι τὸ γένος;
5 σημεῖον | δὲ ὅτι γίνονται ἐν τοῖς ἀγροῖς[37] καὶ ἥκιστα μεταβάλλουσιν ὑπὸ τῆς ἐπιμελείας. τὰ δὲ ἄγρια πάντα πυκνοφυλλότερα· διὰ γὰρ τὸ ἧττον πέττειν τὸν καρπὸν εἰς τὰ φύλλα ἡ τροφὴ τρέπεται.

[35] γλυκύν (sc. οἶνον) Forster : γλυκύ codd.
[36] πυκνοφυλλότεραί Y^a : πυκνοφυλλότεροί cett. codd.
[37] ἀγροῖς : fort. ἀργοῖς Bussemaker (cf. Gaza *locis rusticis*)

when they make sweet wine, they expose the bunches of grapes to the sun for a long time, and the sun removes the watery part and concocts the remainder. Now marjoram too produces this same effect; for it is dry and hot, so that it naturally produces a permanent result.

36. Why do dark myrtle trees have thicker foliage than light myrtle trees? Is it because they are a wilder kind? A sign of this is that they grow in the fields[54] and change very little under cultivation. But all wild *(plants)* have thicker foliage; for because the fruit is less concocted, the nourishment is diverted into the leaves.

[54] Or perhaps, following the suggestion of Bussemaker, "in untilled ground."

BOOK XXI

INTRODUCTION

The twenty-six chapters of *Pr.* 21 raise and attempt to deal with (to borrow a phrase from Louis) *problèmes de la boulangerie*.[1] To be more specific, with few exceptions the chapters of Book 21 discuss the nature and appearance of different kinds of grains (barley and wheat most of all) and especially the products made from them, and changes to their nature and appearance from processes like kneading and heating. Chs. 2, 8, and 15, however, discuss the medical or nutritional value of various kinds of bread. In the case of these three chapters alone are possible sources identifiable (Hp. *Vict.* 2.40–44 and *VM* 13–14).

Pr. 21.14 seems to be off topic, as it asks: "Why do the same things appear pleasant when we are getting accustomed to them and not very pleasant when we take them continuously?" More appropriate to a discussion of moderation and weakness of will, I suspect it was placed where it is in Book 21 as a follow-up to ch. 13, which asks: "Why can we enjoy some forms of nourishment . . . for a long

[1] Louis, vol. 2, p. 136.

time, for instance nourishment that comes from barley meal and wheat flour, and unadorned wine and water, but others we cannot so enjoy, even though these are more pleasant?" *Pr.* 21.13 and 14 are the two longest chapters, and arguably the most interesting.

ΟΣΑ ΠΕΡΙ ΑΛΦΙΤΑ ΚΑΙ ΜΑΖΑΝ ΚΑΙ ΤΑ ΟΜΟΙΑ

927a10 1. Διὰ τί ἡ πτισάνη καὶ τὸ ἄλευρον ἐλαίου ἐπιχεομένου λευκότερα γίνεται; καίτοι τὸ ἔλαιον πυρρόν. ἢ ὅτι πέφυκεν μιγνύύμενον τῷ ὑγρῷ ἀφρίζειν; τοῦτο δὲ ἡ λευκότης. ἡ δὲ μῖξις τρίψει καὶ κινήσει. μίγνυται δὲ
15 μᾶλλον τοῖς σωματικοῖς· | ἐν δὲ τοῖς ἑψήμασι τοῦτο συμβαίνει, διὸ καὶ λευκότερα ποιεῖ.

2. Διὰ τί ἡ ἐκ τοῦ πυροῦ τροφὴ μάλιστα ἁρμόττει τοῖς σώμασιν καὶ μᾶλλον τρόφιμος ἢ ἡ ἐκ τῶν κριθῶν; ἢ διότι μετρίαν ἔχει γλισχρότητα; δεῖ δὲ τὴν
20 τροφὴν ἔχειν τοῦτο· | προσφῦναι γὰρ δεῖ καὶ προσκολληθῆναι τῷ σώματι· οὗ αἴτιον τὸ γλίσχρον. ἀλλὰ <ἡ κριθὴ>[1] ψαθυρώτερον· διὸ αἱ τετριμμέναι σφόδρα μᾶζαι τροφιμώτεραι τῶν ἀτρίπτων.

3. Διὰ τί τῶν μὲν ἀλεύρων τὰ πρῶτα, τῶν δὲ ἀλφίτων τὰ τελευταῖα λαμπρότερα; ἢ διότι τὸ μὲν

[1] <ἡ κριθὴ> Bussemaker ex Gaza

---

[1] I.e., the color of flame (πυρρόν).
[2] The oil, or the wheat or barley.
[3] I.e., foam.

PROBLEMS CONNECTED WITH BARLEY MEAL, BARLEY CAKES, AND THE LIKE

1. Why do barley gruel and wheat flour become paler when oil is poured on them? Yet oil is yellowish red.[1] Is it because when mixed with what is moist, it[2] naturally foams? And this[3] is pale. Now mixture occurs through rubbing and moving. But it is mixed more by what has body; and this effect occurs in boiled liquids, and this is what makes it paler.

2.[4] Why is nourishment that comes from wheat best suited to the body and more nourishing than what comes from barley? Is it because wheat has a moderate amount of stickiness? And nourishment should have this, since it must grow into and adhere to the body—the cause of which is stickiness. But <barley> is very friable;[5] this is why cakes made of well-kneaded barley are more nourishing than those of unkneaded barley.

3.[6] Why is the first of the wheat flour to be ground the brightest, but the last of the barley meal? Is it because the

[4] Source: Hp. *Vict.* 2.40.

[5] The friable (ψαθυρός)—or crumbly or loose-textured—is the contrary of the sticky or viscous (γλίσχρος) (see *Mete.* 385a17).

[6] Cf. *Pr.* 21.4, 7, 15.

25 καπυρὸν ὂν περιθραύεται, | τὸ δὲ μαλακὸν ἐνθλίβεται; λαμπρότερον δὲ ἐν ἀμφοτέροις τὸ ἐντός.

4. Διὰ τί οἱ ἄρτοι λευκότεροι φαίνονται ψυχροὶ ὄντες ἢ θερμοί; ἢ διὰ τὴν αὐτὴν αἰτίαν τρόπον τινὰ καὶ τὸ ἔλαιον λευκότερον τοῦ προσφάτου τὸ παλαιόν; 30 αἴτιον γὰρ τῆς μελανίας | τὸ ὕδωρ, τοῦτο δὲ ἐν ἀμφοτέροις πλεῖον προσφάτοις οὖσιν· χρονιζομένοις δὲ διὰ τὸ ἐξατμίζειν λείπεται ἔλαττον τὸ ἐπιπολῆς. ἐξατμίζει δὲ τοῦ μὲν ἐλαίου ἢ ὁ χρόνος ἢ ὁ ἥλιος· ἐκ δὲ τῶν ἄρτων ψυχομένων τὸ θερμὸν ἐξιὸν, ψυχρῶν μὲν ὄντων ἐξελήλυθεν, ἐν δὲ θερμοῖς οὖσιν ἔτι ἔνεστιν. |

35 5. Διὰ τί οἱ ἄναλοι ἄρτοι πλείονα σταθμὸν ἔχουσι τῶν ἡλισμένων, τῶν ἄλλων[2] αὐτοῖς ἴσων ὑπαρχόντων; εἰκὸς δὲ ἦν τοὐναντίον· οἱ γὰρ ἅλες πρόσκειταί τε καὶ βαρύτεροι τοῦ ὕδατός εἰσιν. ἢ ὅτι ξηραίνουσιν οἱ ἅλες; διὸ καὶ σώζεται ἄσηπτα τὰ ταριχευμένα· ἀνα- 927b λίσκεται γὰρ καὶ ξηραίνεται || τὸ ὑγρὸν ὑπ᾽ αὐτῶν, ὃ σήπεται ὑπὸ τοῦ θερμοῦ. καὶ ἐν τῷ ἄρτῳ οὖν ἀναλίσκεται τὸ ὑγρὸν ὑπὸ τοῦ ἁλός, καὶ ἀποπνεῖ ἔξω. διὸ καὶ οἱ ἕωλοι ἄρτοι κουφότεροί εἰσι τῶν θερμῶν, ψυ- 5 χρότεροι ὄντες. ἐν δὲ τοῖς μὴ ἡλισμένοις τοῦτο | τὸ ὑγρὸν πλεῖον ἐνυπάρχον ποιεῖ βαρυτέρους αὐτούς.

6. Διὰ τί οἱ μὲν ψυχροὶ ἄρτοι ἂν βρεχθέντες ἅψωνται ἀλλήλων, οὐ συνέχονται, οἱ δὲ θερμοί; ἢ ὅτι οἱ μὲν ψυχροὶ μετὰ τῆς ἀτμίδος ἀφιᾶσι[3] τὸ ἐν αὐτοῖς γλί-

[2] ἄλλων β a^m D Y^a pc E^mg : ἁλῶν cett. codd.
[3] ἀφιᾶσι : ἀφῆκαν [Arist./Alex.] *Sup.Pr.* 3.8, 2.

latter, being dried out, breaks up, while the former, being soft, is crushed? And in both the interior is brightest.

4.[7] Why do loaves of wheat bread appear paler when they are cold than when they are hot? Is it in some way for the same reason that old oil is paler than fresh? For water is the cause of its being dark, and more of this is present in both[8] when they are fresh; but after a time less remains on the surface owing to evaporation. Now either the time or the sun causes evaporation from the oil; but the heat exits out of the loaves as they cool, and when they are cold it has gone, but while they are hot it is still present.

5.[9] Why do unsalted loaves[10] have more weight than salted, assuming the other things in them are the same? The opposite would seem to be the case; for salt is added and is heavier than water. Is it because salt causes drying? And this is why things preserved in salt do not putrefy. For the moisture, which is putrefied by the heat, is consumed and dried by the salt. So in the loaf as well the moisture is consumed by the salt, and evaporates to the outside. And this is why stale loaves—which are colder—are lighter than hot ones. But in unsalted loaves, this moisture being present in greater quantities makes them heavier.

6.[11] Why, if cold loaves that have been wetted touch each other, do they not cohere, whereas hot ones do? Is it because the cold ones give off the sticky moisture in them

[7] Cf. *Pr.* 21.3, 7, 15.

[8] Oil and loaves of bread.

[9] Cf. [Arist./Alex.] *Sup.Pr.* 3.7.

[10] Unless otherwise specified, "loaves" refers to loaves of wheat bread.

[11] Cf. [Arist./Alex.] *Sup.Pr.* 3.8.

σχρον ὑγρόν, οὗ ἐξελθόντος οὐ κολλῶνται (τὸ γὰρ
10 ὕδωρ ᾧ ἐβρέχθησαν, | ψαθυρώτερόν ἐστιν), οἱ δὲ
θερμοὶ ἔχουσί τινα γλισχρότητα; ὅταν μὲν οὖν βε-
βρεγμένων αὐτῶν ἡ ἀτμὶς ἐξίῃ, τὸ μὲν θερμὸν διαπνεῖ
διὰ λεπτότητα, τὸ δὲ κολλῶδες συνεξιὸν αὐτῷ καὶ
μιγνύμενον τῷ ὑγρῷ προσέχεσθαι ποιεῖ ἑαυτοῖς.[4] |

15 7. Διὰ τί τῶν ἀλεύρων τὰ πρῶτα[5] λαμπρότερά ἐστι,
τῶν δὲ ἀλφίτων τὰ τελευταῖα; ἢ ὅτι τὸ μὲν ἄλφιτον
καπυρὸν ὂν περιθραύεται, οἷον μάλιστα πάσχει πλεῖστον χρόνον κοπτόμενον, τὸ δὲ μαλακὸν καὶ λεπτὸν
ἄλευρον, ὅ ἐστιν ἐντὸς τοῦ πυροῦ, ἐκθλίβεται πρῶτον;
20 λαμπρότατον δέ | ἐστιν ἐν ἀμφοτέροις τὸ ἐντός.

8. Διὰ τί ἡ μὲν μᾶζα ὅσῳ ἂν μᾶλλον τριφθῇ,
δυσδιαχωρητοτέρα γίνεται, ὁ δὲ ἄρτος εὐδιαχωρητό-
τερος; ἢ διὰ τὸ τριφθῆναι σφόδρα τὸ σταῖς μικρότε-
ρον γίνεται; τὸ δὲ[6] γλίσχρον τοιοῦτόν ἐστιν, ὑπὸ δὲ
25 τοῦ πυρὸς πάντοθεν ἐξῄρηται | τὸ ὑγρὸν τοῦ ἄρτου,
ὥστε ψαθυρώτερον γίνεται τοῦ ὑγροῦ ἐξαιρεθέντος
ὅλως, ὅσῳ ἂν μᾶλλον τριφθῇ, διὰ τὸ ἐν τῇ τρίψει
μικρομερέστερον γεγονέναι· τὸ δὲ ψαθυρὸν εὐπεπτό-
τερόν ἐστιν. ἡ δὲ μᾶζα ὅσῳ ἂν μᾶλλον τριφθῇ,
γλισχροτέρα γίνεται τοῦ ὑγροῦ μεμιγμένου· τὸ δὲ
30 γλίσχρον οὐκ | εὐδιαίρετον. τὰ δὲ τοιαῦτα δύσπεπτά
ἐστιν· δεῖ γὰρ τὸ πεφθησόμενον διαιρεθῆναι εἰς
μικρά.

[4] προσέχεσθαι ποιεῖ ἑαυτοῖς Bussemaker ex Gaza : προσ-
έρχεσθαι ποιεῖ ἐν αὐτοῖς codd.

together with the vapor, and when this is gone they do not adhere (for the water with which they were wetted is more friable), but the hot ones have a certain stickiness? So when they are wetted and the vapor exits, the heat is blown off owing to its lightness, and the adhesive part comes off with it, and being mixed with the moisture causes them to hold together.

7.[12] Why is the first of the wheat flour to be ground the brightest, but the last of the barley meal? Is it because the barley meal, being dried out, breaks up, which happens especially when it is ground for a very long time, while the flour that is inside the wheat, being soft and thin, is crushed out first? And in both the interior is brightest.

8.[13] Why is it that the more barley cake is kneaded, the more indigestible it becomes, whereas a loaf of wheat bread becomes easier to digest? Does the dough become smaller through being kneaded a great deal? Now such is the sticky part, and the moisture is removed from the entire loaf by the fire, so that when the moisture is removed completely it becomes more friable, the more it is kneaded, because in the kneading it has become divided into smaller parts; and what is friable is more easily concocted. But the more the barley cake is kneaded, the stickier it becomes when mixed with water; and what is sticky is not easily divisible. Such things are difficult to concoct; for what is to be concocted must be divided into small parts.

[12] Cf. *Pr.* 21.3, 4, 15.
[13] Source: Hp. *Vict.* 2.40.

---

5 *πρῶτα* Vat.1904mg, cf. *Pr.* 21.3, 927a23 : *ἄλφιτα* cett. codd.
6 *δὲ* : *γὰρ* Ya Ca

9. Διὰ τί ἡ μὲν μᾶζα τριβομένη ἐλάττων γίνεται, τὸ δὲ σταῖς μεῖζον; ἢ ὅτι τὸ μὲν ἄλφιτον βρεχθὲν καὶ τριβόμενον συνίζει τῇ τοῦ ὑγροῦ κολλήσει διὰ τὸ
35 ἀραιὸν εἶναι | καὶ χονδρόν, τὸ δὲ ἄλευρον μετεωρίζεται διὰ τὸ πυκνὸν σφόδρα εἶναι; τὰ γὰρ πυκνὰ τριβόμενα θερμαίνεται, θερμαινόμενα δὲ καὶ πνευματούμενα μετεωρίζεται, καθάπερ καὶ ἡ σάρξ.

10. Διὰ τί δὲ πυρούμενον τὸ σταῖς μεῖζον γίνεται ἢ
928a ἡ || μᾶζα; ἢ ὅτι ἔχει ὑγρὸν οὐ κεχωρισμένον, ὥστε ἐξιέναι θερμαινόμενον διὰ τὴν τρῖψιν; ἐξ οὗ θερμαινομένου πνεῦμα γίνεται, ἐκ δὲ τοῦ πλείονος ὑγροῦ ἀνάγκη γίνεσθαι πλεῖον πνεῦμα. |

5 11. Διὰ τί τοῦ μέλιτος κολλητικωτέρου ὄντος ἢ τοῦ ὕδατος, τὸ τῷ μελικράτῳ φυραθὲν ἄλευρον ψαθυρώτερον γίνεται, ὅταν ἑψηθῇ ἢ ὀπτηθῇ, ἢ τὸ τῷ ὕδατι; ἢ διότι τὸ μὲν ὑπὸ τοῦ πυρὸς πήγνυται καὶ συνίσταται, [τὸ ὕδωρ][7] τὸ δὲ μέλι συνιστᾷ μὲν ἀλλ' ἐπιξηραίνει;
10 διὸ μᾶλλον ψαθυρὸν ποιεῖ· | ἡ γὰρ ψαθυρότης ὑπὸ ξηρασίας γίνεται.

12. Διὰ τί οἱ δίπυροι ἄρτοι ψυχθέντες οὐ γίνονται σκληροί; ἢ ὅτι ἔχει τινὰ ἐν αὑτῷ ὁ πυρὸς γλυκὺν καὶ γλίσχρον χυμόν, ὅς ἐστιν αὐτοῦ καθάπερ ψυχή; σημεῖον δέ· ξηραινόμενος μὲν γὰρ ὅλως κενοῦται, νοτιῶν
15 δὲ ἐκφύεται.[8] | τοῦ οὖν χυμοῦ τούτου ἐνυπάρχοντος καὶ ἐν τῷ ἀλεύρῳ καὶ μάλιστα τῷ καθαρωτάτῳ, σταιτὸς

[7] [τὸ ὕδωρ] Bussemaker
[8] ἐκφύεται : ἐκφυσᾶται Forster

9.[14] Why does barley cake when kneaded become less bulky, whereas dough becomes larger? Is it because barley meal when wetted and kneaded unites owing to the adhesiveness of the moisture, because it is porous and gritty, whereas wheat flour rises because it is very dense? For what is dense, when kneaded, becomes hot, and when they become hot and inflated they rise, just as the flesh does.

10.[15] But why does heated dough become larger than barley cake does? Is it because dough contains moisture that is not separated, such that it escapes when heated owing to kneading? Breath arises from it when it is heated, and a greater amount of air necessarily arises from a greater amount of moisture.

11.[16] Why, although honey is more adhesive than water, does wheat flour mixed with honey-water become more friable, when boiled or baked, than mixed with water? Is it because the one[17] is solidified and set by the fire, whereas the honey[18] sets but also dries? This is why it makes it more friable; for friability comes to be owing to dryness.

12.[19] Why do twice-baked loaves, when they cool, not become hard? Is it because wheat has in it some sweet and sticky juice, which is as it were its soul? There is a sign of this: for when it is dried it is completely empty, but when it is wet it grows out. Therefore, as this juice also exists in wheat flour, especially in the purest, when the flour be-

[14] Cf. *Pr.* 21.22. [15] Cf. *Pr.* 21.23.

[16] Source: Hp. *Vict.* 2.41.

[17] I.e., the flour mixed with water.

[18] In the flour and honey-water mixture.

[19] Cf. *Pr.* 21.25.

γενομένου τοῦ ἀλεύρου καὶ τριβομένου συμβαίνει
ταὐτό.[9] σημεῖον δέ· ἑψόμενον γὰρ διαχωρητικώτερον
γίνεται. ὀπτωμένου μὲν οὖν τὸ πρῶτον τοῦ ἄρτου, τὸ
ψαθυρὸν καὶ ἐλαφρὸν τοῦ [δὲ][10] ὑγροῦ τοῦ ἐκ τοῦ
20 ἄρτου | ἀπατμίζει, καὶ τοῦ ἀλεύρου τὸ ἀχυρωδέστατον
ἀποκαίεται. ἐξαιρεθέντος δὲ καὶ τριβομένου πάλιν τοῦ
σταιτός, τό τε τοῦ ἀλεύρου λειότατον καὶ ⟨τὸ⟩[11] τοῦ
ὑγροῦ γλισχρότατον λειπόμενα μίγνυται μᾶλλον ἑαυτοῖς, διά τε τὸ τοιαῦτα καὶ μᾶλλον γεγονέναι, καὶ διὰ
25 τὴν πύρωσιν· βαφῇ γὰρ | ἡ μῖξις αὐτῶν ὁμοία γίνε-
ται, ὥστε γίνεσθαι τὸ ὕστερον τριφθὲν σταῖς ὅμοιον
τῷ ἑψομένῳ ἀλεύρῳ. καὶ γὰρ ἐκείνου[12] τριφθέντος τοῦ
σταιτὸς καὶ λειφθέντος τοῦ λεπτοτάτου ἀλεύρου καὶ
τοῦ γλισχροτάτου ὑγροῦ, πυρωθὲν κολλῶδες γίνεται
καὶ ἀνεξίκμαστον· τό τε γὰρ γλίσχρον δυσδιαίρετον,
30 καὶ τὸ | πυκνὸν οὐθὲν δι' αὑτοῦ προΐεται ὑγρόν. ταὐτὸ
οὖν τοῦτο καὶ δίπυρος[13] πάσχει ἄρτος διὰ τὰ εἰρη-
μένα· ἔχων δὲ ἀεὶ ὑγρότητα οὐ γίνεται σκληρός.

13. Διὰ τί τῆς τροφῆς καὶ τῆς ξηρᾶς καὶ τῆς ὑγρᾶς
ἐνίοις δυνάμεθα πολὺν χρόνον χρῆσθαι, οἷον τῇ γινο-
35 μένῃ | τροφῇ ἐξ ἀλφίτων καὶ ἀλεύρων καὶ τοῖς οἴνοις
τοῖς αὐστηροῖς καὶ ὕδατι, τοῖς δὲ οὐ δυνάμεθα, καὶ
ταῦτα ἡδίοσιν οὖσιν; ἢ ὅτι τὰ μέν ἐστι τῶν προσφερο-
μένων ἐπιπολαστικὰ καὶ τρόφιμα, ὥστε καὶ ὅταν κε-
νωθῶσι, τῆς πρώτης τροφῆς ἀναλωθείσης ἔτι ἔνεστιν

[9] ταὐτό Forster : αὐτό codd. [10] [δὲ] Bussemaker
[11] ⟨τὸ⟩ Forster [12] ἐκείνου Forster : ἐκεῖνο codd.

comes dough and is kneaded the same thing happens. And there is an indication of this: for when it is boiled it is more digestible. When the loaf is baked for the first time, therefore, the friable and light part of the moisture evaporates from the loaf, and the most chafflike part of the flour is burned out. But when the dough is removed (*from the oven*) and kneaded again, the smoothest part of the flour and the stickiest part of the moisture that are left mix more with one another, both because they have become smoother and stickier and because of the heat; for their mixing is similar to dyeing, so that the dough being kneaded a second time becomes similar to boiled flour. For when this dough is kneaded and the lightest part of the flour and the stickiest part of the moisture are left, when put on the fire it becomes adhesive and damp; for what is sticky is difficult to divide, and what is dense does not release any moisture. The twice-baked loaf, therefore, also undergoes this same process, for the reasons given; and as it always contains moisture it does not become hard.

13. Why can we enjoy some forms of nourishment, both dry and liquid, for a long time, for instance nourishment that comes from barley meal and wheat flour, and unadorned wine and water, but others we cannot so enjoy, even though these are more pleasant? Is it because some of the things we take lie on the surface (*of the stomach*) and are very nourishing, so that when they are voided, although their first nourishment is consumed they still have

---

[13] *ὑγρόν. ταὐτὸ οὖν τοῦτο καὶ δίπυρος* Forster (*δίπυρος* pro *διὰ πυρὸς* Bussemaker ex Gaza) : *ὑγρότατον οὖν τοῦτο καὶ διὰ πυρὸς* codd.

928b ἐν τῷ σώματι πολλὴ δύναμις, ὡς || μὲν πρὸς τὴν πρώτην ἐργασίαν τοῦ σώματος πεφθεῖσα, ὡς δὲ πρὸς τὸ τέλος καὶ τὴν ἐκ διαδοχῆς γινομένην ἄπεπτος; τοιαῦτα δέ ἐστι καὶ τῶν ἡδέων τὰ πλεῖστα; τὰ μὲν γὰρ λιπαρὰ καὶ γλυκέα καὶ πίονα ἥδιστα δοκεῖ εἶναι | 5 γευομένοις ἡμῖν, ταῦτα δέ ἐστι πάντα τρόφιμα[14] καὶ οὐκ ἄπεπτα καὶ ἐπιπολαστικά, ἐν ᾗ ἂν ᾖ διαφορᾷ· ὥστε ἔναυλον εἶναι τὴν δύναμιν, ἐάν τις αὐτῶν πληρωθῇ, καὶ μὴ ταχὺ ἐκλίπῃ[15] τὴν αἴσθησιν. οὐ γὰρ μόνον ἐν τῇ κοιλίᾳ ἐνόντων γίνεται ἡ πλήρωσις, ἀλλὰ 10 καὶ διαδοθείσης | τῆς τροφῆς ἐν ἄλλοις μέρεσιν. ἢ οὐ μόνον τοῦτο αἴτιον, ἀλλὰ καὶ τὸ τῇ φύσει ἔνια σύμμετρα εἶναι καὶ οἰκεῖα ἡμῖν; πάντα γὰρ τὰ τοιαῦτα διὰ τὸ κατὰ φύσιν εἶναι μᾶλλον προσίεται τὰ σώματα, τὰ δὲ παρὰ φύσιν ἧττον. ἄλλα τε ἄλλῃ κράσει ἁρμόττει, 15 οἷον τὸ μέλι ταῖς μελίτταις | κατὰ φύσιν ἐστὶν ὥστε προσφέρεσθαι μόνον· καίτοι ἀσθενεῖς γέ εἰσι τὴν δύναμιν. ὥστε δεῖ λείπειν τὸ ἀναλισκόμενον, ἀλλ' εἶναι ἀνάλογον τὸ πλῆθος πρὸς τὴν ἰσχὺν τὴν ἀπὸ τῶν ἀνθρώπων· ὥστε ὅσα τῶν ἡδέων τοιαῦτά ἐστι, διὰ μὲν τὸ ἐν τῇ φύσει ἧττον ὑπάρχειν ἡδέα φαίνεται, | 20 ὀλίγον δὲ χρόνον· εἶτα πληροῖ ταχύ. τῶν δὲ κατὰ φύσιν ἀεὶ δέονται, ὥστε καὶ προσφερομένων συνεχῶς δι' αὐτὰ οὐ τῶν ἡδίστων, ἀλλ' ἑτέρων ἧττον πληροῦνται.

14. Διὰ τί τὰ αὐτὰ συνεθιζομένοις τε ἡδέα φαίνεται

a great deal of power in the body, being concocted for their first bodily function, but unconcocted for the final function and what succeeds it? Now such are most of the pleasant (*forms of nourishment*). For those that are oily and sweet and fat seem to us to be the most pleasant when we taste them, but these are all nourishing and not difficult to concoct and inclined to lie on the surface, though they may differ (*in other ways*); so their power is enduring, if one is full of them, and the sensation does not cease quickly. For this feeling of fullness is not only while the nourishment is in the stomach, but also when it is distributed to other parts of the body. Or is this not the only reason, but it is also that some nourishment is naturally in harmony with and proper to us? For our bodies are more likely to accept all such (*nourishment*) because it is natural, but less likely to accept what is contrary to nature. And different (*nourishment*) is suitable to different temperaments, for instance, honey is for bees according to nature, such that they take it in alone; and yet they are weak with respect to their power. So what they consume must lacking, but the quantity must be proportionate to their strength, as (*the quantity of what we consume*) is for humans; hence all of the pleasant (*nourishment*) is of this sort, because what is present in small amounts in us by nature appears pleasant, but for a short time, and then they fill us quickly. But people *always* want what is natural, so that when they take in nourishment continually—not what is most pleasant in itself, but the other kind—they feel less full.

14. Why do the same things appear pleasant when we

---

[14] *πάντα τρόφιμα* B x D A[m] R w : *πάντα τὰ τρόφιμα* cett. codd. [15] *ἐκλίπῃ* : *ἐκλιπεῖν* Forster

καὶ λίαν συνεχῶς προσφερομένοις οὐχ ἡδέα; τὸ δὲ
25 ἔθος ἐστὶ τὸ | πολλάκις καὶ συνεχῶς τι ποιεῖν. ἢ ὅτι τὸ
μὲν ἔθος ἕξιν δεκτικήν τινος ἐν ἡμῖν ποιεῖ, οὐ πλήρωσιν, τὸ δὲ συνεχῶς προσφέρεσθαί τι πληροῖ τὴν
ἐπιθυμίαν, καὶ καθάπερ ἀγγεῖον;[16] ἔστι γάρ τι κενὸν[17]
ἡ ἐπιθυμία. αἱ μὲν οὖν ἕξεις[18] γυμναζόμεναι αὔξονται
30 καὶ ἐπιδιδόασιν· τὰ δὲ ἀγγεῖα σαττόμενα | οὐδὲν
μείζω γίνεται. διόπερ τὸ μὲν ἔθος ὂν γυμνάσιον αὔξει
τὴν δεκτικὴν ἕξιν· τὸ δὲ συνεχῶς προσφερόμενον
σάττει μὲν καὶ πληροῖ τὴν ἐπιθυμίαν, ἧς πληρωθείσης οὐκέτι προσιέμεθα, αὔξει δὲ οὐθὲν αὐτὴν διὰ
τὰ προειρημένα ἐπὶ τῆς σάξεως. ἔτι τὸ ἔθος οὐ τῷ ἀεὶ
35 ἡδύνειν ἡδύ ἐστι | (λυπεῖ γὰρ καὶ τὰ τοιαῦτα, ἐάν τις
συνεχῶς ποιῇ) ἀλλὰ τῷ τὴν ἀρχὴν τοῦ ἔργου ἡδέως
ἡμᾶς προσίεσθαι, καὶ πλείω χρόνον δύνασθαι ταὐτὸν
ποιεῖν ἢ ἀσυνήθεις ὄντας. ἐν ᾧ οὖν καὶ τοῦτο λυπεῖ
ἡδὺ ὄν, ἐν ταὐτῷ καὶ τὰ ἄλλα ἡδέα. συνεχῶς γὰρ
929a γινόμενα ἢ προσφερόμενα ἀμφότερα λυπεῖ. || αἴτιον
δὲ τὸ μὴ ἀπείρους ἡμᾶς ἐν αὑτοῖς δυνάμεις ἔχειν τὰς
δεκτικὰς καὶ ποιητικάς, ἀλλὰ πεπερασμένας, αἳ τυγχάνουσαι τοῦ συμμέτρου αὐταῖς (τοῦτο γὰρ συνεχῶς
ἐστὶν αἰσθητὸν εἰς ἐπίδοσιν) αἱ μὲν πληροῦνται, αἱ δὲ
5 ἀδυνατοῦσιν | ἐνεργεῖν.

15. Διὰ τί τὸ μὲν σταῖς γίνεται τριβόμενον λευκόν,

[16] ἀγγεῖον Bonitz : αἴτιον codd.
[17] κενὸν Bonitz : καὶ codd.
[18] αἱ . . . ἕξεις : fort. τὰ . . . ἔθη

are getting accustomed to them and not very pleasant when we take them continuously? Yet habit is doing something often and continuously. Is it because habit produces in us a state receptive of certain things, not fullness, whereas taking something continuously fills[20] the appetite, just like a filled vessel? For the appetite is a kind of void. States[21] when exercised, therefore, grow and increase; but vessels do not grow any larger by being stuffed full. This is why habit, being an exercise, causes the receptive state to grow; but what is taken continually stuffs and fills the appetite, and when filled we no longer accept (*what was taken continually*), and nothing can cause this to grow, for the reasons already stated in the case of the stuffing full (*of the vessel*). Furthermore, habit is pleasant not by always giving pleasure (for such things even cause pain, if one does them continuously), but by our approaching the beginning of the process with pleasure, and we are able to do the same thing for a longer time than when we are unaccustomed to it. Thus, in the same way that habit, which is pleasant, also causes pain, so too do all other pleasant things. For both occurring and being taken continuously cause pain. Now the reason is that the powers of reception and action that we have in ourselves are not unlimited, but limited, and when they reach their point of due measure (and this is continually perceptible with each addition), the former are filled, while the latter cannot function.

15.[22] Why does dough become pale when kneaded,

[20] πληροῖ, i.e., satisfies.

[21] "Habits" (τὰ ἔθη) seems a better fit than "states" (αἱ ἕξεις), but has no mss. support.

[22] Cf. *Pr.* 21.3, 4, 15.

ἡ δὲ μᾶζα μελαντέρα; πότερον ὅτι ξηραίνεται μᾶλλον τὸ ἐπιπολῆς ἐν τῷ ἀλφίτῳ, τὸ δὲ[19] ἐν ὑγρῷ θερμόν ποιεῖ[20] τὴν λευκότητα; ἢ διὰ τὸ πεπυρῶσθαι ἕλκει τὸ
10 ὑγρὸν εἰς αὑτό, | μεγαλομερέστερον ὄν;

16. Διὰ τί τὰ ἄλφιτα μᾶλλον τῷ ὕδατι συμμένει φυρόμενα ἢ τῷ ἐλαίῳ, ὄντι γλισχροτέρῳ; καίτοι κολλητικώτερον τὸ γλίσχρον, τὸ δὲ ἔλαιον τοῦ ὕδατος γλισχρότερον. ἢ ὅτι λεπτότερον τὸ ὕδωρ, ὥστε εἰσέρ-
15 χεται εἰς ἅπαν καὶ | μαλακὰ ποιεῖ, συμφύεταί τε μᾶλλον καὶ συνθλίβεται πρὸς ἄλληλα, καίτοι θλιβόμενα χωρὶς[21] τῆς τρίψεως;

17. Διὰ τί οἱ ἄτριπτοι ἄρτοι καὶ οἱ σφόδρα τετριμμένοι ῥήγνυνται; ἢ[22] οἱ μὲν ἄτριπτοι διὰ τὸ ἀσύνδετοι εἶναι; ἡ γὰρ τρῖψις συνδεῖ· προωδοποίηνται οὖν τὸ
20 ῥήγνυσθαι. ἔτι | ἀμιγὲς καὶ πολὺ ἔχουσι τὸ ὑγρόν. οἱ δὲ τετριμμένοι σφόδρα λίαν εἰσὶ ξηροὶ διὰ τὸ ὀλίγον ἔχειν ὑγρόν· θερμαινομένων γὰρ πᾶν ἐξέρχεται. ὥστε ἄμφω διὰ τὸ πολὺ ὑγρὸν ἐξιέναι ῥήγνυνται· πολὺ γὰρ ἐν μὲν τοῖς ἀτρίπτοις ἁπλῶς ἔνεστιν, ἐν δὲ τοῖς τετριμμένοις πρὸς τὸ ὑπόλοιπον <ἔξεισι>.[23] |

25 18. Διὰ τί κουφότερον τὸ φύραμα γίνεται ἢ ἄμφω, τό τε ὑγρὸν καὶ τὸ ἄλφιτον; πότερον ὅτι μιγνυμένων πνεῦμα συγκατακλείεται; ἢ ὅτι ὑπὸ τοῦ θερμοῦ τοῦ ἐν τοῖς ἀλφίτοις ἐξατμίζεται τοῦ ὕδατος, ὥστε ἔλαττον

[19] τὸ δὲ Forster ex Gaza : οἷον codd.
[20] ποιεῖ Yᵃ : ὄν ποιεῖ Cᵃ : ὃ ποιεῖ cett. codd.
[21] χωρὶς Cᵃ et Barth. : καὶ χωρὶς cett. codd.
[22] ἢ Yᵃ Ap. Xᵃ : ἢ ὅτι cett. codd.
[23] <ἔξεισι> Forster

while barley cake becomes darker? Is it because in barley meal the surface becomes drier, and the heat in the moisture produces the paleness? Or does it, by being put on the fire, draw the moisture into itself, because it consists of larger particles?

16. Why does barley meal hold together better mixed with water than with oil, which is stickier? And yet what is sticky is more adhesive, and oil is stickier than water. Is it because water is thinner, so that it penetrates to all (*of the grains*) and makes them soft, and they grow together more and are crushed into each other, even if they are crushed apart from the kneading?

17. Why do both unkneaded loaves and those excessively kneaded break up? Do the unkneaded loaves do this because each is not bound together? For kneading binds, so they are predisposed to break up. Further, they contain a lot of moisture not mixed in. The excessively kneaded loaves, however, are dry because they contain very little moisture, since it all escapes when they are heated.[23] So that both types break up because a lot of moisture goes out: in unkneaded loaves a lot of moisture is present on its own,[24] and in kneaded ones a lot escapes in comparison to what is left behind.

18. Why is the mixture of liquid and barley meal lighter than both (*together but unmixed*)? Is it because when they are mixed air is enclosed within? Or is it because the water is evaporated by the heat in the barley meal, so that

[23] Owing to the excessive kneading.

[24] Literally, "simply" (ἁπλῶς), as opposed to being an integrated part of a composite of flour and water. In this (somewhat dubious) sense, the water can be said to escape.

γίνεται τὸ μεμιγμένον; ὁ δὲ ἀήρ, εἰ καὶ μίγνυται, οὐθὲν
30 ἂν κουφότερον ποιοῖ· | ἔχει γὰρ βάρος καὶ ὁ ἀὴρ ἐν τῷ
ἀέρι.

19. Διὰ τί μετὰ τοῦ ἀλφίτου πινόμενον τὸ γάλα καὶ ὁ γλυκὺς φαίνεται γλυκύτερα; πότερον[24] παρὰ τὸ μὴ γλυκὺ μᾶλλον φαίνεται; τὸ γὰρ ἄλφιτον οὐ γλυκύ. ἢ ὅτι ἐνδιατρίβει τὸ ἄλφιτον ἔχον γλυκύτητα, ὥστε
35 πλείονι χρόνῳ ἡ | αἴσθησις;

20. Διὰ τί ἧττον ἄκρατον φαίνεται τὸ αὐτὸ πόμα μετὰ τοῦ ἀλφίτου πινόμενον; πότερον ἢ ὅτι κεράννυσιν ἄλλο ἔχον μετ᾽ ἄλλου; ἢ ὅτι ἀντιφράττει τῷ πόματι καὶ ἀφανίζει, ἀντισπῶν εἰς αὑτό; ||

929b 21. Διὰ τί ὁ χόνδρος πλεῖον ὕδωρ δέχεται ἢ οἱ πυροὶ ἐξ ὧν ὁ τοιοῦτος ἐγένετο χόνδρος; ἢ ὅτι ἀλευρά πώς ἐστιν ὁ χόνδρος, τὰ δὲ ἄλευρα πλεῖον δέχεται; καὶ γὰρ γίνεται ὁ ὄγκος πλείων ἢ ὁ τῶν πυρῶν· σέσακται
5 γὰρ καὶ τὰ ἐν τοῖς | πυροῖς. τὰ δὲ πλείω χωρεῖ πλεῖον, καὶ <διὰ>[25] τοῦτο καὶ ὅτι ἔχει θερμότητα καὶ τὰ ἄλευρα καὶ ὁ χόνδρος. τὸ δὲ θερμὸν καὶ ἕλκει μᾶλλον τὸ ὑγρόν, καὶ ἐξαναλίσκει ἐξατμίζον.

22. Διὰ τί τὸ ἄλευρον τριβόμενον μεῖζον πολὺ γίνεται ἢ τὸ ἄλφιτον κατὰ λόγον; ἢ ὅτι τὸ μὲν πολὺ
10 ὕδωρ δέχεται, | τὸ δὲ ὀλίγον; διὰ τί δὲ δέχεται πλεῖον; μᾶλλον γὰρ εἰκὸς τὸ ἄλφιτον· πεπύρωται γάρ, τὸ δὲ ἄπυρον· μᾶλλον δὲ ξηρὸν τὸ πεπυρωμένον. ἢ διότι

[24] πότερον Sylburg : πότερα Xa : πότερα οὖν cett. codd. (πότερον οὖν Ya teste Bekker) [25] <διὰ> Bonitz

the mixture becomes smaller? But the air, even if it were mixed in, would not make it lighter; for even air (*enclosed*) in air has weight.

19. Why do milk and sweet wine appear sweeter when drunk with barley meal? Do they appear sweeter in contrast to what is not sweet? For barley meal is not sweet. Or is it because the barley meal continues holding the sweetness, so that the perception of it lasts longer?

20. Why does the same drink appear less diluted when drunk with barley meal? Is it because (*the barley meal*), having one (*quality*), mixes with what has another? Or is it because it counteracts the drink and conceals it, drawing it into itself?

21. Why does gruel take up more water than the wheat from which such gruel comes? Is it because the gruel is in a way wheat flour, and wheat flour takes up more moisture? Indeed, its bulk is greater than that of wheat; for even what is in the wheat[25] is compact. Now that which is more makes room for more, both for this reason[26] and because both the wheat flour and the gruel contain heat. And the heat draws the moisture more and expends it by evaporation.

22.[27] Why does wheat flour when kneaded become much larger in proportion than barley meal? Is it because the former takes up a lot of water, but the latter a little? But why does wheat flour take up more? For one would expect barley meal to take up more, since it has been put on the fire while the other has not; and what has been put on the

[25] I assume this refers to the composition of the grains of wheat themselves.

[26] That the grains of wheat are all packed tight.

[27] Cf. *Pr.* 21.9.

τρῖψιν μᾶλλον δέχεται τὸ ἄλευρον; τούτου δὲ αἴτιον τὸ μικρομερέστερον εἶναι. ὥσπερ οὖν ὁσαπλάσιόν ἐστι
15 δυνάμει τῇ μικρότητι, τοσαυταπλάσιον δέχεται | τὸ ὕδωρ. κόλλῃ γὰρ χρῆται τῷ ὕδατι, ὥσπερ καὶ Ἐμπεδοκλῆς μετήνεγκεν ἐν τοῖς Φυσικοῖς[26] εἰπὼν "ἄλφιτον ὕδατι κολλήσας." καὶ ἀναλίσκει πολὺ διὰ τοῦτο.

23. Διὰ τί δὲ καὶ πεπυρωμένον τὸ σταῖς μεῖζον γίνεται ἢ ἡ μᾶζα; ἢ ὅτι ἔχει ὑγρὸν οὐ κεχωρισμένον,
20 ὥστε ἐξιέναι | θερμαινόμενον,[27] ὃ πνεῦμα[28] γινόμενον καὶ οὐ δυνάμενον ἐξιέναι ὁμοίως καὶ ἐν τῇ μάζῃ διὰ τὴν πυκνότητα τοῦ σταιτός (πυκνὸν γὰρ τὸ ἐκ μικρομερεστέρων), αἴρει[29] καὶ ποιεῖ τὸν ὄγκον; ἔτι δὲ καὶ πλεῖον ἔχει τὸ ὑγρόν, ἐξ οὗ θερμαινομένου πνεῦμα
25 γίνεται, ἐκ δὲ τοῦ πλείονος ἀνάγκη γίνεσθαι | πλεῖον.

24. Διὰ τί οἱ περὶ τὴν τῶν σιτίων ἐργασίαν, οἱ μὲν περὶ τὰς κριθὰς ἄχροοι γίνονται καὶ καταρροϊκοί, οἱ δὲ περὶ τοὺς πυροὺς εὐεκτικοί; ἢ διότι εὐπεπτότερος ὁ πυρὸς τῆς κριθῆς, διόπερ καὶ αἱ ἀπόρροιαι; |

30 25. Διὰ τί ὁ ἄρτος, ἐὰν μέν τις αὐτὸν ὀπτᾷ, σκληρότερος γίνεται, ἐὰν δέ τις αὐτὸν χλιαίνῃ, ὑγρότερος

26 Φυσικοῖς Meursius (ex *Mete.* 382a1) apud Ruelle : Περσικοῖς codd. 27 θερμαινόμενον : θερμαινομένου β
28 ὃ πνεῦμα w R^pc : πνεῦμα β : οὐ πνεῦμα cett. codd.
29 αἴρει Y^a Ap C^a : αἴρει οὖν cett. codd.

---

28 Cf. *Mete.* 381b31–82a1 = 31B34 D–K. The words translated "glue" (κόλλῃ) and "gluing" (κολλήσας) are elsewhere in *Pr.* 21 rendered "adhesive" and "adhere," etc.

fire is drier. Is it because the wheat flour admits of more kneading? And the reason for this is its having smaller parts. Therefore, as manifold as it is through the capacity of the smallness (*of its parts*), to such an extent it takes up water. For it uses the water as a glue—like Empedocles employed as a metaphor in his *Physics*, saying "gluing wheat flour with water."[28] It consumes a lot of water in this way.

23.[29] But why does dough that has been heated become larger than barley cake does? Is it because (*dough*) contains moisture that is not separated, such that it escapes when heated, and this (*moisture*), becoming breath and not being able to escape to the same extent as in barley cake owing to the density of the dough (for what consists of smaller parts is dense), makes it rise and produces its bulk? And further, it also contains more moisture, from which breath arises when it is heated, and a greater amount (*of breath*) necessarily arises from a greater amount (*of moisture*).

24.[30] Why, of those whose work is connected to grain, do those who deal with barley become pale in complexion and subject to discharges, while those who deal with wheat are healthy? Is it because wheat is more easily concocted than barley, and thus so are the emanations from it?

25.[31] Why does a loaf, if one bakes it, become harder, whereas if one warms it, it becomes moister (up to a cer-

[29] Cf. *Pr.* 21.10.

[30] *Pr.* 21.24 and 38.10 are virtually identical. See also 1.37. Apollonius (*Mir.* 7) paraphrases this material and attributes it to Aristotle's *Problems*.

[31] Cf. *Pr.* 21.12.

ἄχρι τινός; ἢ ὅτι ὀπτωμένου αὐτοῦ τὸ ὑγρὸν ἐκπορεύεται; σκληρότερος οὖν γίνεται· ἐπιθερμαινομένου δὲ τὸ ὑγρὸν συσταθὲν διαχεῖται ὑπὸ τοῦ πυρός, διὸ ὑγρότεροι γίνονται. |

35 26. Διὰ τί τὰ μὲν ἄλευρα ψυχόμενα ἧττον σάττεται, τὰ δὲ ἄλφιτα μᾶλλον; ἢ ὅτι τὰ μὲν μικρομερῆ οὐ διαλείπει χώραν, καὶ τὰ βαρέα τῇ θλίψει τὰ πλείω <ἢ>[30] ἐλάττω κατέχει τὸ ἴσον; τὰ μὲν οὖν ἄλφιτα ἁδρά ἐστιν. ψυχόμενα οὖν ἐλάττω γίνεται, ὥστε τὸ ἔλαττον 930a συμπιέζεται[31] πλέον. τὰ || δὲ ἄλευρα ὑπάρχει μὲν μικρομερῆ ὄντα, ὥστε οὐ διὰ τοῦτο ψύχεται, ἀλλ' ἵνα ᾖ κουφότερα καὶ μὴ σάττηται διὰ τὴν θλῖψιν· βαρύτερον γὰρ φύσει τὸ ἄλευρον τοῦ ἀλφίτου ἐστίν.

[30] <ἢ> Forster

[31] συμπιέζεται Forster ex Gaza : συμπιέζει τὸ codd.

tain point)? Is it because the moisture leaves when it is baked? It therefore becomes harder; but when it is reheated, the congealed moisture is liquefied by the fire, so it becomes moister.

26. Why does wheat flour become less compact as it cools, whereas barley meal becomes more so? Is it because what has small parts has no spaces in between, and heavy things, owing to pressure, occupy equal space, whether there are more or fewer? Barley meal then is coarse. So as it cools it grows less (*bulky*), such that the less is squeezed together more. But wheat flour has small parts to begin with, so that it does not cool because of this, but so as to become lighter and not to become more compact owing to pressure; for wheat flour is by nature heavier than barley-meal.

BOOK XXII

INTRODUCTION

According to its title, the topic of Book 22 is fruit (ὀπώρα). More specifically, its fourteen chapters deal with the different effects of fruit on our system—in most cases with an eye on their nutritional value. The sources for, or background to, this material seem to be the Hippocratic writings on the nutritional and medicinal value of fruit (see especially *Vict*. 2.55, the topic of which is fruit, and also, for example, *Vict*. 3.68 and *Aff*. 61).

It is worth noting that there are three Greek words that can be translated "fruit": The title's ὀπώρα—which can refer specifically to the individual piece of fruit, as a whole—is used by the author four times in *Pr*. 22; περικάρπιον—which can refer specifically to the fleshy part surrounding the seeds or pit—is used twice; and καρπός—which can refer specifically to fruit as an agricultural product—does not appear in this book, though it is used eleven times in Book 20. In 22, the author often refers to a species of fruit (e.g., figs) or to a basic sort of fruit (e.g., sweet or acrid), in the latter case leaving the subject ("fruit") implied.

ΟΣΑ ΠΕΡΙ ΟΠΩΡΑΝ

930a5 1. Διὰ τί τὴν ὀπώραν ὕστερον ἢ πρότερον φαγοῦσιν οὐκ ἀνάλογος[1] τοῖς αὐτοῖς ὁ ὄγκος τῆς πληρώσεως γίνεται; ἢ ὅτι βαρυτέρα ἐστὶν ἡ ὀπώρα πολὺ τῶν σιτίων; δηλοῖ δὲ καὶ[2] τὰ σῦκα, ἐὰν ὕστατα βρωθῇ· 10 τελευταῖα γὰρ ἐμεῖται. ἐὰν | μὲν οὖν πρῶτα, διὰ βάρος κάτω πορευόμενα εὐρυχωρίαν ἄνω ποιεῖ, ὥστε ῥᾳδίως δέχεσθαι τὸν ὄγκον τῶν σιτίων. ἀνάπαλιν δὲ εἰσελθόντα τὰ σιτία, διὰ τὸ μὴ κάτω φέρεσθαι, ταχὺ τοῦ ἄνω κενοῦ προσλαμβάνει.

2. Διὰ τί τῶν γλυκέων ὄντων ὁμοιοτέρων ἡμῖν ἢ 15 τῶν δριμέων, | θᾶττον πληρούμεθα ὑπὸ τῶν γλυκέων; εἰκὸς δὲ ἦν ἧττον· ὑπὸ γὰρ τῶν ὁμοίων ἧττον ἦν εἰκὸς πληροῦσθαι. ἢ ὅτι οὐχ ὁμοίως τό τε ἀγγεῖον πληροῦται ταχύ, ἐξ οὗ πληρούμεθα,[3] καὶ τὸ τρεφόμενον, ἀλλ' ἐνίοτε ἡ μὲν κοιλία πλήρης ἐστίν, οἷον τῶν διψώντων, 20 τὸ δὲ δίψος οὐδὲν ἧττόν ἐστιν; οὐ | γὰρ τῷ ταύτην εἶναι πλήρη παυόμεθα διψῶντες, ἀλλὰ τῷ ἕκαστον τῶν τοῦ σώματος τὸ αὐτῷ οἰκεῖον ἐσπακέναι, καὶ ὅταν

[1] ἀνάλογος Cᵃ Ap. : ἀνάλογον cett. codd.
[2] καὶ om. Yᵃ Cᵃ [3] πληρούμεθα : τρεφόμεθα Bonitz

PROBLEMS CONNECTED WITH FRUIT

1. Why is the volume (*of food needed*) for fullness not proportionate in the same people, if they eat fruit after or before a meal? Is it because fruit is much heavier than solid foods? Indeed figs prove this, if they are eaten at the end, since they are vomited last. So if they are eaten first, owing to their weight they move down and create plenty of space above, so as to receive easily the volume of solid food. Conversely, when the solid food enters, because it does not travel downward, it quickly takes up the upper empty space.

2.[1] Why, although what is sweet is more akin to us than what is acrid, are we filled more quickly by what is sweet? It seems natural that we should be less so, since it seems natural to be filled less by what is akin to us. Is it because the vessel from which we are filled and the body that is nourished are not filled equally quickly, but sometimes the stomach is full, for example in those who are thirsty, but the thirst is no less? For we do not cease being thirsty through the stomach being full, but through each part of the body having drawn in its own proper liquid, and when

[1] Cf. *Pr.* 22.3, and see also 21.13.

ἐκεῖνα ἀπολάβῃ ἱκανῶς, τότε παυόμεθα διψῶντες. καὶ πεινῶντες δὲ ὡσαύτως.

3. Διὰ τί θᾶττον πληρούμεθα ἀπὸ τῶν γλυκέων ἢ
25 ἀπὸ | τῶν δριμέων; ἢ ὅτι θᾶττον παυόμεθα ἐπιθυμοῦντες τῶν γλυκέων; ἢ ὡς μὲν ἡ κοιλία πληροῦται, οὕτω καὶ ἡμεῖς ὑπὸ τῶν γλυκέων, οὐχ ὁμολογεῖται, ὅτι δὲ ἡ ἐπιθυμία θᾶττον ὑπ' αὐτῶν πληροῦται, τοῦτ' ἂν εἴη λεκτέον; ἢ ὅτι ἡ μὲν ἐπιθυμία, ὡς ἁπλῶς εἰπεῖν, ἔστι
30 μὲν ἔνδεια, καὶ ὅταν μηκέτι ἔχωμεν | τροφὴν ἢ ὀλίγην; τὰ μὲν οὖν δριμέα οὐκ ἔστι τρόφιμα, ἀλλὰ τροφὴν μὲν ὀλίγην ἔχει, τὸ δὲ περίττωμα πολύ. εἰκότως οὖν πολλὰ ταῦτα ζητοῦμεν ἐσθίειν, καὶ οὐκ ἐμπιπλάμεθα αὐτῶν τὴν ἐπιθυμίαν, διὰ τὸ ἔτι προσδεῖσθαι τροφῆς, ταῦτα δὲ μὴ ἔχειν τροφήν. τὰ δὲ γλυκέα ἅπαντά ἐστι τροφή, |
35 καὶ ἀπὸ μικρῶν τοιούτων πολλὴν λαμβάνει τὸ σῶμα. ὅταν οὖν ἀπολάβῃ πολλὴν τροφήν, οὐκέτι δύναται ἐσθίειν διὰ τὸ μὴ ὑποφέρειν. εἰκότως οὖν θᾶττον ὑπὸ τῶν γλυκέων πληρούμεθα.

4. Διὰ τί τὰ περικάρπια καὶ τὰ κρέα καὶ ὅσα
930b τοιαῦτα, || ἐν τοῖς ἀσκοῖς ἄσηπτα γίνεται, ὅταν σφόδρα φυσηθῶσι, καὶ τὰ ἐν τοῖς ἀκριβῶς περιπωματιζομένοις ὡσαύτως; ἢ διότι σήπεται μὲν κινούμενα πάντα, τὰ δὲ πλήρη ἀκίνητα; ἀδύνατον γὰρ ἄνευ κενοῦ κινηθῆναι, ταῦτα δὲ πλήρη. |

5 5. Διὰ τί μετὰ τὰ σαπρὰ τῶν περικαρπίων ὁ οἶνος πικρὸς φαίνεται πινόμενος; ἢ ὅτι τὴν πικρότητα ἔχει ἡ σαπρότης ἡ τοιαύτη; τὸ οὖν ἐπιμένον ἐπὶ[4] τῇ γλώττῃ, μιγνύμενον τῷ πόματι καὶ διαχεόμενον, πικρὸν ποιεῖ

they have received this sufficiently, then we cease being thirsty. And it's the same way with being hungry.

3.[2] Why are we full more quickly from what is sweet than from what is acrid? Is it because we cease desiring what is sweet more quickly? Or, though it is not admitted that as the stomach is filled by what is sweet, so also are we, it might be said that our desire is more quickly filled by them? Or is it because desire, to speak simply, is a need, and exists when we no longer have nourishment or have a little? Now what is acrid is not nourishing, but contains a little nourishment and much residue. Naturally, therefore, we seek to eat a lot of them, and do not satisfy our desire with them, because nourishment is still required and these do not contain nourishment. But all sweet things are nourishment, and the body receives a lot of it from a few of them. When it has taken in a lot of nourishment, therefore, it is no longer able to eat because it cannot bear it. Naturally, therefore, we are filled more quickly by what is sweet.

4.[3] Why do fruits and meats and all such things not putrefy in leather skins, when they are blown up, and similarly things in vessels with their lids closed? Is it because all things set in motion putrefy, and things that are full are unmoving (*within*)? For it is impossible for something to be set in motion without empty space, and these are full.

5. Why does wine drunk after eating rotten fruit appear bitter? Is it because such rottenness contains bitterness? What remains on the tongue, therefore, mixing with the drink and running through it, makes the drink bitter. But

[2] Cf. *Pr.* 22.2, and see also 21.13. [3] Cf. *Pr.* 25.17.

---

[4] ἐπιμένον ἐπὶ : ἐπὶ μὲν Ca : ἐπὶ Louis

τὸ πόμα. αὐτὸ δὲ καθ' αὑτὸ ἧττον φαίνεται ἐσθιόμενον
10 διὰ τὸ πολλῶν | ἅπτεσθαι καὶ εἰς μικρὰ διανενεμῆσθαι τὸν τοιοῦτον χυμόν.

6. Διὰ τί τὰ τραγήματα ἐδεστέον; ἢ ἕνεκα τοῦ πιεῖν ἱκανόν; οὐ γὰρ μόνον ποτέον τῆς δίψης χάριν τῆς ἐπὶ τοῖς σιτίοις, ἀλλὰ καὶ μετὰ τὸ σιτίον. |

15 7. Διὰ τί τὰ ὀπτὰ κάρυα ψυχθέντα χείρω γίνεται, καὶ ὁ ἄρτος δὲ καὶ ὁ βάλανος καὶ πολλὰ τῶν τοιούτων, θερμανθέντα δὲ πάλιν βελτίω; ἢ διότι ψυχθέντος μὲν πέπηγεν ὁ χυμός, ἀναχλιανθέντος δὲ πάλιν χεῖται; ἡ δὲ ἡδονὴ γίνεται διὰ τὸν χυμόν. |

20 8. Διὰ τί ἐπὶ τῇ ἀπολαύσει τῆς ὀπώρας, οἷον σύκων καὶ τῶν τοιούτων, ἢ οἶνον ἄκρατον δεῖ ἐπιπίνειν ἢ ὕδωρ; ταῦτα δὲ ἐναντία. ἢ ὅτι ἡ ὀπώρα καὶ θερμή ἐστι καὶ ὑγρὰ διὰ τὴν γένεσιν; ἔχει γὰρ πολὺ πῦρ καὶ ὑγρότητα, ὥστε διὰ μὲν τὸ πῦρ οἷον ζέσιν ποιεῖ ὁ
25 χυμὸς εἴσω, ὅπερ ἔξω τὸ | γλεῦκος ποιεῖ. ἧττον δὲ ἔχει δύναμιν καὶ τὰ ἄλλα τὰ ἀκρόδρυα. τὸ δὲ τῆς ὑγρότητος πλῆθος ἀπεψίαν ποιεῖ. τὸ μὲν οὖν ὕδωρ διὰ τὴν ψυχρότητα σβεννύει τὴν ζέσιν, ὁ δὲ οἶνος διὰ τὴν θερμότητα ὡς ἐπὶ τὸ πολύ· ὥσπερ γὰρ πῦρ ἐνίοτε πυρός, ἐὰν ᾖ ἔλαττον, ἀφαιρεῖται τὴν ἰσχύν. μᾶλλον |
30 δὲ τῇ θερμότητι πεπτικός ἐστι τῆς ὑγρότητος, καὶ διὰ βάρος κατακρατεῖ τὸν τῆς ζέσεως ἐπιπολασμόν.[5]

[5] τὸν . . . ἐπιπολασμόν : τῶν . . . ἐπιπολασμῶν Y[a] X[a]

---

[4] One possible translation of *τὰ τραγήματα* is "dried fruits" (suggested by the topic of *Pr.* 22); another is "dessert" (suggested

the fruit when eaten by itself appears less bitter, because such juice touches many places and so is divided into small parts.

6. Why should one eat dried fruits?[4] Is it for the sake of drinking enough? For one should drink not only because of the thirst that comes while eating solid food, but also after solid food.

7. Why do roasted nuts become worse when they are cooled, and also wheat bread and acorns and many such things, but better when they are heated again? Is it because when they cool the juice is solidified, but when they are warmed up it flows again? And the pleasure is due to the juice.

8.[5] Why, for the enjoyment of fruits such as figs and the like, should one drink unmixed wine or water with them? For these are opposites. Is it because fruit is both hot and moist owing to its origin? For it contains much fire and moisture, so that owing to the fire, the juice produces something like boiling within, just as the sweet juice produces outside. (The other, hard-shelled fruits, have less of this power.) But the large quantity of moisture prevents concoction. Thus the water owing to its coldness extinguishes the boiling, whereas the wine does so in most cases owing to its heat, just as one fire sometimes takes away the strength of another fire, if it is smaller. So wine, with its heat, is more conducive to concoction than moisture, and owing to its weight it gains mastery over the surface of the boiling.

by "after solid food"). In any case, dried fruit was likely a common dessert.

[5] Cf. Heracleides of Tarentum fr. 68 (Guardasole) = Ath. 79E–80A.

9. Διὰ τί τῶν ἰσχάδων γλυκύταται αἱ δίχα ἐσχισμέναι, οὔτε δὲ αἱ πολυσχιδεῖς οὔτε αἱ ἀσχιδεῖς; ἢ διότι ἐκ μὲν τῶν πολυσχιδῶν διαπέπνευκε καὶ ἐξίκμα-
35 κε μετὰ τοῦ | ὑγροῦ τὸ πλεῖστον τοῦ γλυκέος, ἐν δὲ ταῖς μεμυκυίαις πολὺ[6] τὸ ὑδατῶδές ἐστι διὰ τὸ μὴ ἠτμικέναι; αἱ δ' ἐσχισμέναι μέν, μὴ εἰς πολλὰ δέ, ἀμφοτέρων τούτων ἐκτός εἰσι τῶν παθημάτων.

10. Διὰ τί ταῖς καμίνοις ξηραινόμενα[7] τὰ σῦκα
931a σκληρότερα ‖ γίνεται, ἐὰν ψυχθῇ ἐν τῇ καμίνῳ, ἢ ἂν ἐξαιρεθέντα ψυχθῇ; ἢ ὅτι ἐν μὲν τῇ καμίνῳ ἐξατμίζει πᾶν τὸ ὑγρὸν ὑπὸ τοῦ θερμοῦ, ἔξω δὲ περιεστηκὼς ὁ ἀὴρ ψύχων κωλύει τὸ ὑγρὸν ἐξιέναι καὶ συνίστασθαι;
5 †μᾶλλον γὰρ ἐξατμίζει.†[8] | ἔστι δὲ τὰ μὲν ξηρὰ σκληρά, τὰ δὲ ὑγρὰ μαλακά.

11. Διὰ τί παρὰ τὰ στρυφνὰ ὁ οἶνος καὶ τὸ ὕδωρ φαίνεται γλυκύτερα, οἷον ἐάν τις βαλάνους ἢ μύρτα ἤ τι τῶν τοιούτων διατράγῃ; ἢ εἰκότως, καθάπερ καὶ ἐπὶ τῶν ἄλλων; πᾶν γὰρ τὸ αὐτὸ παρὰ τὸ ἐναντίον μᾶλλον
10 φαίνεται, οἱ | δὲ τῶν ἐναντίων χυμοὶ ἀντικείμενοί πώς εἰσιν. ἢ ὅτι, καθάπερ ἐπὶ τῶν βαπτομένων, ὑπὸ τῶν στρυφνῶν ἡ γλῶττα προδιεργάζεται καὶ τοὺς πόρους ἀνοίγεται, ὥστε μᾶλλον διιέναι τὸ γλυκύ; καὶ γὰρ τὰ βαπτόμενα τούτου ἕνεκεν προβρέχουσιν ἐν τοῖς στρυ-
15 φνοῖς, τῷ <τὸ>[9] διεργασθὲν μᾶλλον δέχεσθαι | τὴν βαφήν.

[6] πολὺ : πλεῖον Y[a] C[a] [7] ξηραινόμενα Sylburg ex Gaza : ψυχόμενα codd. [8] συνίστασθαι; μᾶλλον γὰρ ἐξατμίζει codd. (obelis inclusi) : συνίστασθαι μᾶλλον ἢ ἐξατμίζει Forster [9] <τὸ> Forster

9. Why are the sweetest dried figs those that have been cut in half, and not those cut many times nor the uncut? Is it because most of the sweetness from those cut many times has blown off and evaporated with the moisture, whereas in those that are closed up the watery part is larger because it has not evaporated? Now figs that are cut, but not into many parts, are outside of both of these results.

10. Why do figs that are being dried in ovens become harder if they are cooled in the oven, than if they are taken out and cooled? Is it because in the oven all the moisture is evaporated by the heat, whereas outside, the surrounding air cools (*the figs*) and prevents the moisture from escaping and condensing? †For there is more evaporation.†[6] Now dry things are hard, whereas moist ones are soft.

11. Why do wine and water appear sweeter when taken along with what is sour, for instance, if one munches acorns or myrtle berries or some such food? Or is this natural, as in other cases as well? For anything appears to be what it is itself more alongside its opposite, and the flavors of opposites are in a way antithetical. Or is it because, as in the case of things being dyed, the tongue is worked through beforehand by what is sour and opens its pores, so that the sweet goes throughout it more? And indeed, it is for this reason that they presoak what is being dyed in sour[7] liquid, because what is worked through takes the dye more readily.

[6] If this is to make any sense, it must refer to the former case (dried figs left to cool in the oven). The line may have been a marginal gloss.

[7] In the context of dyeing cloth, one of the other meanings of *στρυφνός* ("harsh" or "astringent") would be more apt than "sour."

12. Διὰ τί τὰ γλυκέα ἧττον δοκεῖ γλυκέα εἶναι θερμὰ ὄντα ἢ ὅταν ψυχθῇ; πότερον ὅτι ἅμα δύο αἰσθήσεις γίνονται ἀμφοῖν, ὥστε ἡ τοῦ θερμοῦ ἐκκρούει τὴν ἑτέραν; ἢ ὅτι καὶ τὸ γλυκύ[10] θερμόν; ὥσπερ
20 οὖν πῦρ γίνεται ἐπὶ πῦρ. | κωλύει οὖν ἡ θερμότης. ἢ ὅτι τὸ πῦρ ἀφαιρεῖται τὰς δυνάμεις ἁπάντων διὰ τὸ κινητικὸν εἶναι; ἐγγυτέρω οὖν τοῦ μεταβάλλειν ἐστὶ θερμὰ ὄντα, ἀποψυχθέντα δὲ ἕστηκεν.

13. Διὰ τί ποτε τὰ ἄχυρα τὰ μὲν σκληρὰ πέττει, τὰ δὲ πεπεμμένα οὐ σήπει; ἢ ὅτι τὰ ἄχυρα θερμόν τε καὶ |
25 ὁλκόν ἐστιν; τῇ μὲν οὖν θερμότητι πέττει, τῷ δὲ ὁλκὸν εἶναι τὸν ἰχῶρα τὸν σηπόμενον δέχεται· διὸ οὐ σήπει.

14. Διὰ τί τὰ σῦκα μαλακὰ καὶ γλυκέα ὄντα λυμαίνεται τοὺς ὀδόντας; ἢ διὰ τὴν γλισχρότητα προσέρχεται τοῖς οὔλοις, καὶ παρεμπίπτει διὰ τῶν ὀδόντων εἰς
30 τὰ διὰ μέσου | διὰ τὸ μαλακὰ εἶναι, καὶ σῆψιν ποιεῖ ταχέως ἅτε θερμὰ ὄντα; τάχα δὲ ἴσως καὶ διὰ τὴν σκληρότητα τῶν κεγχραμίδων ἐν τῇ τούτων κατεργασίᾳ πονοῦσι ταχέως οἱ ὀδόντες.

[10] γλυκύ Forster : γλεῦκος codd.

12. Why do sweet things seem to be less sweet when they are hot than when they have cooled? Is it because two sensations of both qualities occur simultaneously, so that the sensation of the hot knocks out the other? Or is it because what is sweet is hot as well? So it is like fire added to fire. Therefore, the heat prevents it.[8] Or is it because fire takes away the power of everything, owing to its being a cause of motion? Being hot, therefore, is nearer to changing, but when cooled they stand still.

13.[9] Why does chaff concoct the hard *(fruits)*, but does not putrefy what has been concocted?[10] Is it because chaff is both hot and absorbent? Therefore, it concocts by means of its heat, whereas by being absorbent it receives the liquid that is putrefying; hence *(chaff)* does not putrefy *(what has been concocted)*.

14. Why do figs that are soft and sweet harm the teeth? Do they go onto the gums because of their stickiness, and slip into the spaces between the teeth because they are soft, and quickly cause putrefaction because they are hot? And perhaps the teeth also quickly suffer in chewing them because of the hardness of the little seeds.

[8] I.e., it prevents the full sensation of the sweetness.

[9] Cf. *Pr.* 20.9.

[10] The contrast here is between unripe (i.e., hard) fruit and ripe (i.e., concocted) fruit.

BOOK XXIII

INTRODUCTION

Books 23–26 deal with topics that fall under meteorology (as understood in the Lyceum): the sea and salt water (23), hot water (24), air (25), and winds (26).[1]

Aristotle's *Meteorology* 2 opens: "Let us speak about the sea (*περὶ δὲ θαλάττης*): what its nature is, and for what reason such a mass of water is salty (*διὰ τίν' αἰτίαν ἁλμυρὸν τοσοῦτόν ἐστιν ὕδατος πλῆθος*), and further, about its origin from the beginning" (353b32–34). *Mete.* 2.1–3 are devoted to these topics, and this discussion probably serves as the background for *Pr.* 23, though there is little direct connection between them. The most prominent subject of Book 23 is salt water (including the sea and

[1] Johannes Camotius, in his edition of the Aldine *Problems* (Venice, 1552), appends the following intriguing note to the end of *Pr.* 25 (so between the discussions of air and wind):

> Some of the wisest say that Aristotle's "(*Problems*) Connected with Fire" and "(*Problems*) Connected with Light" are missing here, and that these two are finest of the *Problems*.
>
> *ἐνταῦθα φασί τινες τῶν σοφωτάτων ἐλλείπειν Ἀριστοτέλους ὅσα περὶ τὸ πῦρ καὶ ὅσα περὶ τὸ φῶς καὶ ταῦτα δύο κάλλιστα εἶναι τῶν προβλημάτων.*

I know of no other evidence for these books.

other saltwater bodies), especially as compared to (bodies of) fresh water (see chs. 7, 8, 10, 13–16, 18–22, 25–27, 30–32, 35, 37–39). Other topics are waves (1, 2, 4, 11, 12, 17, 23, 24, 28, 29, 33, 36), the colors of bodies of water (6, 8, 9, 23, 38, 41), lakes (6, 33, 34, 40), and the behavior of ships (3, 5).

Aside from *Mete*. 2.1–3, other possible sources are the relevant works of Theophrastus: *On Water(s)* (DL 5.45, frs. 210–21 FHSG), *On Salts, Soda, and Alum* (DL 5.42, frs. 222–23 FHSG), and *On Winds*.[2]

Plutarch, *QC* 1.9 (*Mor.* 626E–27E), which discusses "why clothes are washed better in fresh water than in sea water," seems to refer to passages in *Pr.* 23, which he does not name, though he does attribute the passages to Aristotle.

[2] Theophrastus' *Meteorology*, or what survives of it (existing solely in Syriac and Arabic translations), does not discuss the seas and salt water. For introduction, texts, commentary, and an English translation of the Arabic version of Ibn Al-Khammar, see Hans Daiber, "The *Meteorology* of Theophrastus in Syriac and Arabic Translation," in William W. Fortenbaugh and Dimitri Gutas, eds., *Theophrastus: His Psychological, Doxographical, and Scientific Writings* (New Brunswick, N.J.: Transactions, 1992), pp. 166–293.

ΟΣΑ ΠΕΡΙ ΤΟ ΑΛΜΥΡΟΝ ΥΔΩΡ ΚΑΙ ΘΑΛΑΤΤΑΝ

931a35 1. Διὰ τί τὸ κῦμα οὐκ ἐπιγελᾷ ἐν τοῖς βαθέσι πελάγεσιν, ἀλλ' ἐν τοῖς μικροῖς καὶ βραχέσιν; ἢ ὅτι τὸ μικρὸν ὑγρὸν φερόμενον μᾶλλον διαιρεῖται ὑπὸ τοῦ πνεύματος ἢ τὸ πολύ;

2. Διὰ τί τὰ κύματα πρότερον φοιτᾷ ἐνίοτε τῶν ἀνέμων; ἢ ὅτι πρὸς τῇ ἀρχῇ τοῦ πνεύματος ἡ θάλαττα 931b ὠσθεῖσα ‖ ⟨ἡ⟩[1] πρώτη τὴν ἐχομένην ἀεὶ ταὐτὸν ποιεῖ; διόπερ οὔσης αὐτῆς συνεχοῦς καθάπερ μιᾷ πληγῇ συνεχεῖ πάσαις ⟨κίνησις⟩[2] γίνεται. τὸ δὲ ἐν ἑνὶ χρόνῳ γίνεται, ὥστε συμβαίνει τήν τε πρώτην καὶ τὴν ἐσχά- 5 την ἅμα κινεῖσθαι. ὁ δὲ ἀὴρ οὐ πάσχει τοῦτο, ὅτι | οὔτ' ἐστὶν ἓν σῶμα συνεχές, τῷ πολλὰς πάντοθεν ἀντικρούσεις λαμβάνειν, αἳ πολλάκις κωλύουσι τὴν πρώτην καὶ νεανικωτάτην κίνησιν, τήν τε θάλασσαν οὐ ποιοῦσι τοῦτο διὰ τὸ βαρυτέραν καὶ δυσκινητοτέραν αὐτοῦ εἶναι.

3. Διὰ τί τὰ πλοῖα γέμειν δοκεῖ μᾶλλον ἐν τῷ

[1] ⟨ἡ⟩ Richards [2] ⟨κίνησις⟩ Richards

PROBLEMS CONNECTED WITH SALT WATER AND THE SEA

1.[1] Why doesn't a wave ripple in the deep open seas, but it does in the small and shallow ones? Is it because a small amount of liquid as it travels is more divided by the wind than a large amount?

2.[2] Why do the waves sometimes begin to move before the winds do? Is it because the first part of the sea, near the origin of the wind, being pushed, always produces the same effect on the adjoining part? So, since the sea is continuous, motion comes to every part of it as if by one continuous blow. Now this occurs in one time, with the result that the first and the last parts are moved simultaneously. But the air does not experience this, because it is not one continuous body, through receiving from every direction many checks, which often hinder the first and most vigorous motion; but (*these checks*) do not do this to the sea, because it is heavier and harder to move than the air.

3.[3] Why do ships seem to be fuller in the harbor than

[1] Cf. *Pr.* 23.17 and 24.

[2] Cf. *Pr.* 23.11, 12, 28. Source: Thphr. *Vent.* 35.

[3] Source: *Mete.* 359a7–15.

10 λιμένι | ἢ ἐν τῷ πελάγει, καὶ θεῖ δὲ θᾶττον ἐκ τοῦ πελάγους πρὸς τὴν γῆν ἢ ἀπὸ τῆς γῆς εἰς τὸ πέλαγος; ἢ ὅτι τὸ πλέον ὕδωρ ἀντερείδει μᾶλλον [ἐκ][3] τοῦ ὀλίγου, ἐν δὲ τῷ ὀλίγῳ δέδυκε διὰ τὸ κρατεῖν αὐτοῦ μᾶλλον; ὠθεῖ γὰρ κάτωθεν[4] τὸ ὕδωρ ἄνω.[5] ἐν μὲν οὖν
15 τῷ λιμένι ὀλίγη ἐστὶν ἡ θάλαττα, | ἐν δὲ τῷ πελάγει βαθεῖα. ὥστε καὶ ἄγειν πλέον δόξει ἐν τῷ λιμένι καὶ κινήσεται χαλεπώτερον διὰ τὸ δεδυκέναι μᾶλλον καὶ ἧττον ἀντερείδειν τὸ ὕδωρ. ἐν τῷ πελάγει δὲ τἀναντία τούτων ἐστίν.

4. Διὰ τί, ὅταν τι ῥιφθῇ εἰς τὴν θάλατταν κυμαί-
20 νουσαν, | οἷον ἡ ἄγκυρα, γαλήνη γίνεται; ἢ διότι ἵσταται ἡ θάλαττα τῷ φερομένῳ, μεθ' οὗ ἀὴρ συγκαταφέρεται, ὃς ἐπ' εὐθείας κάτω φερόμενος καὶ ἐνταῦθα ἐπισπασθεὶς συνεπισπᾶται τὸ ἐκ πλαγίου κινοῦν τὴν θάλατταν; ὁ δὲ κλύδων τῆς θαλάττης οὐκ ἄνωθεν κάτω γίνεται ἀλλ' ἐπιπολῆς· οὗ λήξαντος |
25 γαλήνη γίνεται. ἔτι συνιοῦσα ἡ θάλασσα εἰς τὰ διαστάντα τῷ φερομένῳ δίνην ποιεῖ. ἡ δὲ δίνη κύκλῳ φέρεται. ἐπεὶ δὲ ἡ εὐθεῖα τοῦ κύκλου κατὰ σημεῖον ἅπτεται, τὰ δὲ κύματα ἐπ' εὐθείας λοξῆς φέρεται, συμβαίνοι ἂν αὐτὰ τοῦ ἐξωτάτου τῆς δίνης κατὰ
30 σημεῖον ἅπτεσθαι, διά τε τὰ | εἰρημένα καὶ διὰ τὴν τῆς δίνης φοράν, ἣ προσιοῦσα[6] ἀπωθεῖται αὐτά. ἀκύ-

[3] [ἐκ] Sylburg [4] κάτωθεν Ya Ap : κάτω cett. codd.
[5] ἄνω Ya Ca : ἄνωθεν plur. codd. : κάτωθεν Xa
[6] προσιοῦσα : fort. περιοῦσα

they do in the open sea, and run more quickly from the open sea toward the land than from the land toward the open sea? Is it because the greater quantity of water offers more resistance than the small, and a ship sinks in the small quantity because it masters it more? For it pushes the water up from below.[4] Now in the harbor there is a small quantity of sea,[5] whereas in the open sea it is deep. And so a ship will seem to carry more in the harbor and will move with more difficulty, because it is sunk more and the water offers less resistance. But in the open sea the opposite of these is true.

4. Why, when something (such as an anchor) is thrown into a wave-tossed sea, is calm established? Is it because the sea is brought to a standstill by the traveling object, with which air is carried down, which is traveling in a straight line downward and, drawn thither, draws with it that which moves the sea in a lateral direction? Now the sea wave does not come down from above but along the surface; and when it abates, calm is established. Further, the sea, as it reaches the area separated by the traveling object, produces an eddy. And an eddy travels in a circle. But since the straight line touches the circle at a point, and waves travel in an oblique straight line, the result would be that these touch the outermost part of the eddy at a point, owing to what has been said and owing to the movement of the eddy, which, as it comes into contact with them,[6]

[4] Or, if we accept the reading of other mss., "down from above."

[5] Literally, "the sea is small."

[6] Or perhaps "as it goes around."

μου δὲ ὄντος τοῦ κατ᾽ αὐτὴν τόπου, γαλήνην ἐν τῇ ῥήξει αὐτῆς συμβαίνει γίνεσθαι, ὅτι συγκαταβὰς ὁ ἀὴρ τῷ ἐνεχθέντι κάτω, ἀναφερόμενος καὶ ὠθῶν ἄνω τὴν θάλατταν ὥσπερ πομφολυγοῖ αὐτήν· ἡ γὰρ πομ-
35 φόλυξ | ὑγροῦ ὑπ᾽ ἀέρος κάτωθεν ἀνωθουμένου ἐστίν. πομφόλυξ δὲ πᾶσα λεία καὶ γαληνός ἐστιν. σημεῖα δὲ τῶν εἰρημένων ἐστίν· μετέωρος γὰρ ἡ κατὰ τὸ ἐνεχθὲν κάτω θάλαττα τῆς πέριξ γίνεται μικρὸν ὕστερον.

5. Διὰ τί ἐνίοτε πλοῖα θέοντα ἐν τῇ θαλάττῃ εὐδίας
932a καταπίνεται || καὶ ἀφανῆ γίνεται, ὥστε μηδὲ ναυάγιον ἀναπλεῖν; ἢ ὅταν ἀντρώδης τόπος ἐν τῇ ὑπὸ τὴν θάλατταν γῇ ῥαγῇ, ἅμα εἰς τὴν θάλατταν καὶ ἔσω ἀκολουθεῖ τῇ τοῦ πνεύματος[7] φορᾷ; ὁμοίως δὲ καὶ
5 πάντῃ φερομένῃ κύκλῳ | φέρεται κάτω. τοῦτο δ᾽ ἔστι δῖνος. τὰ δὲ περὶ Μεσήνην ἐν τῷ πορθμῷ πάσχει μὲν τοῦτο διὰ τὸν ῥοῦν (γίνονται γὰρ αἱ δῖναι ὑπὸ τούτου) καὶ καταπίνεται εἰς βυθὸν διὰ ταῦτά τε καὶ ὅτι ἡ θάλαττά βαθεῖα τε[8] καὶ <ἡ>[9] γῆ ὕπαντρος μέχρι πόρρω. φέρουσιν οὖν εἰς ταῦτα ἀποβιαζόμεναι αἱ
10 δῖναι· διὸ οὐκ | ἀναπλεῖ αὐτόθι τὰ ναυάγια. ὁ δὲ ῥοῦς γίνεται, ὅταν παυσαμένου τοῦ προτέρου ἀντιπνεύσῃ ἐπὶ τῆς θαλάττης ῥεούσης τῷ προτέρῳ πνεύματι, μά-

[7] πνεύματος : ῥεύματος Bonitz

[8] ἡ θάλαττά βαθεῖα τε Y^a Ap C^a : θάλαττά τε βαθεῖα cett. codd.

[9] <ἡ> Ruelle

pushes back the waves. As the place where the eddy is lacks waves, the result is that calm is established in its cleft,[7] because the air that went down with the object that traveled downward travels back up and thrusting the sea upward, as it were causes it to bubble; for a bubble comes from moisture pushed up by air from below. And every bubble is smooth and calm. There is a sign of what has been said: the sea where the object traveled downward[8] rises higher a little later than the surrounding area.

5. Why is it that sometimes ships running on the sea in good weather are swallowed up and disappear, such that *no* wreckage floats up? Is it that when a cavernous place in the earth beneath the sea breaks open, at the same time a ship follows the movement of the wind[9] into the sea and inside (*the cavern*)? And similarly, the sea, traveling in a circle in every direction, is carried downward. This is a whirlpool. Now ships in the Straits of Messina experience this because of the current (since the whirlpools are produced by this), and they are swallowed up into the abyss both owing to this and also because the sea is deep and the earth is cavernous beneath it to a great distance. Therefore the whirlpools, forcing the ships away (*from the surface*), carry them into these caverns; this is why wreckage does not float up at the spot (*where the ship disappeared*). Now a current occurs when, the previous wind having stopped, wind blows in the opposite direction over a sea that is flowing under the influence of the previous wind, and espe-

[7] I take "in its cleft" to refer to the center of the eddy, where the surface was broken by the object thrown into the sea (cf. Hett's "where the surface is broken"). [8] I.e., the object "thrown into a wave-tossed sea." [9] Or, with Bonitz, "the current."

λιστα δὲ ὅταν νότος ἀντιπνεύσῃ. ἀντιπνέοντα γὰρ ἀλλήλοις τὰ ῥεύματα[10] παρεκθλίβεται ὥσπερ ἐν τοῖς
15 ποταμοῖς, καὶ γίνονται αἱ δῖναι. φέρεται δὲ | ἑλιττομένη ἡ ἀρχὴ τῆς κινήσεως ἄνωθεν ἰσχυρὰ οὖσα. ἐπεὶ οὖν εἰς πλάγιον οὐκ ἔστιν ὁρμᾶν (ἀντωθεῖται γὰρ ὑπ' ἀλλήλων), ἀνάγκη εἰς βάθος ὠθεῖσθαι, ὥστε καὶ ὃ ἂν ληφθῇ ὑπὸ τῆς δίνης, ἀνάγκη συγκαταφέρεσθαι. διὸ ἀνάσιμα τὰ πλοῖα ποιοῦνται· ἤδη γὰρ ὀρθόν ποτε
20 μνημονεύεται | καταποθέν.

6. Διὰ τί ἡ θάλαττα λευκοτέρα ἡ ἐν τῷ Πόντῳ ἢ ἡ ἐν τῷ Αἰγαίῳ; πότερον διὰ τὴν ἀνάκλασιν τῆς ὄψεως τὴν γινομένην ἀπὸ τῆς θαλάττης εἰς τὸν ἀέρα; ὁ μὲν γὰρ περὶ τὸν Πόντον ἀὴρ παχὺς καὶ λευκός, ὥστε καὶ
25 τῆς θαλάττης | ἡ ἐπιφάνεια τοιαύτη φαίνεται, ὁ δὲ ἐν τῷ Αἰγαίῳ κυανοῦς διὰ τὸ μέχρι πόρρω εἶναι καθαρός, ὥστε καὶ ἡ θάλαττα ἀνταυγοῦσα τοιαύτη φαίνεται. ἢ ὅτι πᾶσαι αἱ λίμναι λευκότεραι τῆς θαλάττης, ὁ δὲ Πόντος ἐστὶ λιμνώδης διὰ τὸ πολλοὺς ποταμοὺς
30 εἰς αὐτὸν ῥεῖν; αἱ δὲ λίμναι διαλευκότεραι | τῆς θαλάττης καὶ τῶν ποταμῶν· γράφουσι γοῦν οἱ γραφεῖς τοὺς μὲν ποταμοὺς ὠχρούς, τὴν δὲ θάλατταν κυανέαν. ἢ ὅτι διὰ μὲν τοῦ ποτίμου οὐ[11] διέρχεται ταχὺ ἡ ὄψις ἀλλὰ[12] ἀνακλᾶται πρὸς τὸν ἀέρα, ἀπὸ δὲ τῆς θαλάσσης οὔ,[13] οὔτ' ἄνω ἀνακλᾶται διὰ τὸ μὴ λεῖον εἶναι τὸ ὕδωρ, |

[10] ῥεύματος : πνεύματος Bonitz
[11] οὐ Xa Bs x Am D : om. cett. codd.
[12] ἀλλὰ Xa Bpc x Am D : καὶ οὐκ cett. codd. : καὶ [οὐκ] Forster
[13] οὔ om. Bussemaker ex Gaza

cially when it is a south wind blowing in the opposite direction. For the currents[10] blowing at each other in opposite directions thrust each other aside, just as they do in rivers, and whirlpools are formed. And the original motion,[11] being strong, is carried turning round and round from above. Therefore, since it is not possible for the currents to rush sideways (for they push against each other), they must be pushed down into the depths, and so whatever is caught by the whirlpool must be carried down with it. This is why ships are made turned up at the ends: it is recollected that sometime before a straight one had been swallowed up.

6.[12] Why is the sea whiter in the Pontus[13] than in the Aegean? Is it through the refraction of the visual ray coming from the sea into the air? For the air around the Pontus is dense and white, so that the surface appearance of the sea appears this way, whereas the air in the Aegean appears blue because it is clear to a great distance, so that the sea reflecting it also appears this way. Or is it because all lakes are whiter than the sea, and the Pontus is lakelike because of the many rivers flowing into it? Lakes are more bright-white than the sea and than rivers—at any rate, painters paint rivers as pale, and the sea as blue.[14] Or is it because the visual ray does not go quickly through fresh water but is refracted to the air, but not from the sea, and it is not refracted upward *(from the sea)* because the water is not

[10] Or, with Bonitz, "the winds."

[11] Literally, "the origin of the motion."

[12] Cf. *Pr.* 23.23 and 41, 26.37.

[13] The Pontus is the Black Sea; "whiter" could also be rendered "paler."

[14] And, the implication is, in painting lakes they make them (bright) white.

35 κάτω δὲ ἀποκάμνει βαδίζουσα; διὸ μέλαινα φαίνεται. ἐν δὲ τοῖς λιμνώδεσιν ἐπιπολῆς ὄντος τοῦ ποτίμου, κάτω δὲ τοῦ ἁλμυροῦ, οὐ διέρχεται, ἀλλ᾽ ἀνακλᾶται πρὸς τὴν αὐγήν· διὸ φαίνεται λευκὴ ἡ ἐπιφάνεια αὐτῆς.

7. Διὰ τί ἡ θάλαττα τοῦ ποτίμου ὕδατος ἧττον
932b ψυχρά, ‖ καὶ τὰ ἁλυκὰ τῶν γλυκέων; πότερον ὅτι πυκνότερον ἡ θάλαττα καὶ μᾶλλον σῶμα; τὰ δὲ τοιαῦτα ἧττον ψύχεται, ὥσπερ καὶ θερμαίνεται μᾶλλον· σωστικωτέρα γὰρ τοῦ θερμοῦ διὰ τὴν πυκνότητα. ἢ
5 ὅτι λιπαρωτέρα ἡ θάλαττα; | διὸ καὶ οὐ σβέννυσι τὴν φλόγα (ὁμοίως καὶ[14] ἐπὶ τῶν ἄλλων). τὸ δὲ λιπαρώτερον θερμότερον. ἢ ὅτι γῆς πολὺ ἔχει, ὥστε ξηρότερον; τὸ δὲ ξηρότερον θερμότερον.

8. Διὰ τί ἡ[15] θάλαττα εὐδιοπτοτέρα τοῦ ποτίμου, παχυτέρα οὖσα; λεπτότερον γὰρ τὸ πότιμον τοῦ ἁλμυ-
10 ροῦ. ἢ οὐ | τὸ λεπτὸν αἴτιον, ἀλλ᾽ εὐθυωρίαι τῶν πόρων πλεῖσται καὶ μέγισταί εἰσιν; τὸ μὲν οὖν πότιμον πυκνὸν διὰ λεπτομέρειάν ἐστιν, τὸ δὲ ἁλμυρὸν μεγάλα ἔχει τὰ διάκενα. ἢ ὅτι καθαρώτερον ἡ θάλαττα; γῆ μὲν γὰρ οὐκ ἔστιν, ἡ δὲ ἄμμος βαρεῖα οὖσα
15 ὑφίσταται. τὰ δὲ πότιμα γεώδη. αὕτη[16] δὲ ἐν | τῷ μεταξὺ φερομένη ἀναθολοῦται ταχύ.

[14] καὶ Yª Cª : δὲ καὶ cett. codd. [15] ἡ om. Ruelle
[16] αὕτη (sc. ἡ γῆ) Forster : αὐτὴ codd.

---

[15] There is a problem with the text, and the attempts at emendation have not made the sense of this question clear.

smooth, but proceeding below it fails?[15] This is why the sea appears black. But in lakelike bodies, since the fresh water is on the surface and the salt water is below, the visual ray does not go through, but is refracted toward the daylight; this is why the surface appearance (*of a lakelike sea*) appears white.

7. Why is the sea less cold than fresh water, and brackish waters less cold than sweet?[16] Is it because the sea is denser and has more body? Now such things are cooled less readily, just as they also are heated more readily; for owing to their density they are more able to retain heat. Or is it because the sea is oilier? And this is why it does not extinguish the flame (and similarly in other cases).[17] And what is oilier is hotter. Or is it because it contains a lot of earth, such that it is drier? And what is drier is hotter.

8.[18] Why is the sea more transparent than fresh water, although it is denser? For fresh water is thinner than salt water. Or is thinness not the cause, but the fact that the direct passages (*in the sea*) are many and large? Fresh water, therefore, is dense because it consists of small parts, whereas salt water has large empty spaces. Or is it because the sea is purer? For there is no earth there, but the sand, being heavy, has sunk to the bottom. But fresh water is earthy. And this (*earthy material*) traveling in the middle of it is quickly stirred up.

[16] I take the first half of the question to refer to bodies of water, and the second more generally to salt water and potable water per se.

[17] I.e., other oily substances too "do not extinguish the flame" (which is another way of saying they retain heat).

[18] Cf. *Pr.* 23.9 and 38.

9. Διὰ τί ἐν τοῖς βορείοις εὐδιοπτοτέρα ἡ θάλαττα ἢ ἐν τοῖς νοτίοις; ἢ ὅτι ἐν τῇ γαλήνῃ χρῶμα ἔχει ἡ θάλαττα; λιπαρὸν γὰρ ἔνεστιν ἐν τῷ ἁλμυρῷ χυμῷ. σημεῖον δέ· ἐκκρίνεται γὰρ ἔλαιον ἐν ταῖς ἀλέαις.
20 εὐδίας | οὖν οὔσης καὶ ἀλεεινοτέρας τῆς θαλάττης, διὰ κουφότητα ἐπανθεῖ ἄνω ὁ τοιοῦτος χυμός. τοῖς δὲ βορείοις ἧττον διὰ τὸ ψῦχος. ἔστι δὲ τὸ ὕδωρ εὐδιοπτότερον τοῦ ἐλαίου· τὸ γὰρ ἔλαιον χρῶμα ἔχει, τὸ δὲ ὕδωρ ἄχροον παρεμφαινόμενον σαφεστέραν ποιεῖ τὴν ἔμφασιν. |

25 10. Διὰ τί λουσάμενοι τῇ θαλάττῃ θᾶττον ξηραίνονται, βαρυτέρᾳ οὔσῃ τῶν ποτίμων; ἢ ὅτι παχυτέρα καὶ γεώδης ἡ θάλαττα; ὀλίγον οὖν ἔχουσα τὸ ὑγρὸν ξηραίνεται θᾶττον.

11. Διὰ τί τὰ κύματα ἀνεμώδη; ἢ ὅτι σημεῖά ἐστι
30 πνεύματος | ἐσομένου; ἔστι γὰρ τὸ πνεῦμα σύνωσις ἀέρος, ᾗ[17] διὰ τὸ ἀεὶ προωθεῖσθαι γίνεται; προωθεῖ δὲ οὐ συνεχές πω ὂν τὸ πνεῦμα, ἀλλὰ ἀρχόμενον. τὸ μὲν δὴ πρῶτον ὥσπερ προεμαράνθη, ἄλλο δὲ τοῦτο προέωσε καὶ ἄλλην πυκνότητα ἤγαγεν καὶ ἀπεμαράνθη.
35 ὥστε δῆλον, ὅταν ἤδη | τὸ προωθούμενον παρῇ, ὅτι ἥξει καὶ τὸ κινοῦν· ἀρχόμενον γὰρ τοῦτο ποιεῖ.

12. Διὰ τί τὸ κῦμα προεκπίπτει τοῦ πνεύματος; ἢ

[17] ᾗ Bonitz : ἢ codd.

---

[19] Cf. *Pr.* 23.8 and 38.

[20] Or "when the wind is from the north than when it is from the south."

9.[19] Why is the sea more transparent in the north than in the south?[20] Is it because the sea has color in calm weather? For there is something oily in salty juice. And there is a sign of this: oil is excreted in warm weather. When the sea is tranquil and warmer, therefore, such juice forms up on the surface owing to its lightness. But this is less so in the north[21] because of the cold. Now water is more transparent than oil; for oil has color, but water, outwardly appearing colorless, produces a clearer appearance.

10. Why do those who wash in the sea become dry more quickly, although it is heavier than fresh water? Is it because the sea is denser and earthy? Therefore, as it contains little moisture, one becomes dry more quickly.

11.[22] Why are waves windy?[23] Is it because they are a sign of a coming wind? For wind is a pushing together of air, which occurs because it is continually being pushed forward. But the wind pushes forward when it is not yet continuous, but is beginning (*to blow*). So the first (*breath of wind*) as it were dies away, but it pushes forward another and leads on another mass (*of air*) and then dies away. So it is clear, when that which is pushed forward is already present, that which sets it in motion will also come; for it causes this when it begins (*to blow*).

12.[24] Why does the wave break before the wind?[25] Is it

[21] Or "when the wind is from the north."

[22] Cf. *Pr.* 23.2, 12, 28. Source: Thphr. *Vent.* 35.

[23] Hett's less literal "Why do waves imply wind?" may better convey the meaning.

[24] Cf. *Pr.* 23.2, 11, 28. Source: Thphr. *Vent.* 35.

[25] I.e., before the wind arrives or is perceived.

ὅτι οὐχ ἅμα παύεται τὸ πνεῦμα [τὸ][18] πνέον καὶ ἡ θάλαττα κυμαίνουσα, ἀλλ' ὕστερον ἡ θάλαττα; ἐν-
933a δέχεται[19] τὸ κινῆσαν ‖ πνεῦμα φθαρῆναι πρὸ τοῦ γενέσθαι αἰσθητόν. ὥστε οὐ πρότερον τὸ κῦμα πνεύματος, ἀλλὰ τὸ μὲν λανθάνει τὸ δὲ οὔ. ἢ οὐχὶ τὰ πνεύματα ἅμα πανταχοῦ πνεῖ, ἀλλ' ὅθεν ἡ ἀρχὴ πρότερον; ἅμα δὲ πνεῖ καὶ τὴν πλησίον θάλατταν |
5 κινεῖ, αὕτη δὲ τὴν ἐχομένην· καὶ οὕτως ἂν ἐνδέχοιτο πρότερον τὸ κῦμα ἐκπίπτειν. ὑπὸ γὰρ τῆς θαλάσσης καὶ οὐχ ὑπὸ τοῦ πνεύματος ἡ κίνησις, ἡ θάττων τοῦ ἀέρος, ἡ[20] τῆς θαλάττης.

13. Διὰ τί ἐν τῇ θαλάττῃ μᾶλλον νεῖν δύνανται ἢ ἐν
10 τοῖς | ποταμοῖς; ἢ ὅτι ὁ νέων ἀεὶ ἐπιστηριζόμενος ἐν τῷ ὕδατι νεῖ; ἐν δὲ τῷ σωματωδεστέρῳ μᾶλλον ἀποστηρίζεσθαι δυνάμεθα, σωματωδέστερον δέ ἐστι τὸ θαλάττιον ὕδωρ τοῦ ποταμίου· παχύτερον γάρ ἐστι καὶ μᾶλλον ἀντερείδειν δυνάμενον.

14. Διὰ τί ποτε ἐν τῇ θαλάττῃ πλείω χρόνον δια-
15 τελεῖν | δύνανται ἢ ἐν τῷ ποταμῷ; ἢ διότι τὸ ποτάμιον ὕδωρ λεπτόν ἐστιν; μᾶλλον οὖν παρεισδυόμενον πνίγει.

15. Διὰ τί ἡ μὲν θάλαττα καίεται, τὸ δὲ ὕδωρ οὔ; ἢ καίεται μὲν κἀκεῖνο, ἡ δὲ θάλαττα ἧττον σβέννυσι τὸ πῦρ διὰ τὸ λιπαρωτέρα εἶναι; σημεῖον δὲ ὅτι λιπαρω-
20 τέρα· ἀπὸ | γὰρ τῶν ἁλῶν ἔλαιον ἀφαιρεῖται. ἢ καὶ

[18] [τὸ] Bekker [19] post ἐνδέχεται add. <γὰρ> Forster
[20] ἡ Bonitz : ἢ codd.

because the wind blowing and the sea being wave-tossed do not stop at the same time, but the sea stops later? It is possible that the wind that set (*the wave*) in motion dies before becoming perceptible. So the wave is not prior to the wind, but the latter goes unnoticed whereas the former does not. Or do the winds not blow everywhere at the same time, but they blow from the origin first? Now the wind blows and moves the sea nearby at the same time, and this (*moves the sea*) connected to it; and in this way it would be possible for the wave to break before the wind. For the motion of the sea, which is quicker than that of the air, is due to the sea and not to the wind.

13.[26] Why is one better able to swim in the sea than in rivers? Is it because the swimmer swims while continually being supported in the water? And we are better able to be supported in water that has more body,[27] and sea water has more body than river water; for it is denser and better able to offer resistance.

14.[28] Why is one able to spend more time in the sea than in the river? Is it because river water is thin? It therefore penetrates more (*into the body*) and causes choking.

15.[29] Why does the sea burn,[30] whereas water does not? Or does the latter too burn, whereas the sea is less able to extinguish fire because it is oilier? And there is a sign that it is oilier: for oil is extracted from salt. Or are the passages

[26] Cf. *Pr.* 23.14.

[27] I.e., contains more solid particles.

[28] Cf. *Pr.* 23.13.

[29] Cf. *Pr.* 23.32.

[30] Hett's note *ad loc.*: "Presumably Aristotle only means that sea-water burns in the sense that it does not easily extinguish fire."

ἧττον δύνανται οἱ πόροι ἁρμόττειν τῷ πυρὶ διὰ τὸ παχύτεροι εἶναι, καὶ μᾶλλόν γε δή, ἅτε καὶ τῶν ἁλῶν ἐνυπαρχόντων; ὥσπερ οὖν τὸ ξηρὸν τοῦ ὑγροῦ ἧττον σβεστικόν, καὶ τὸ ξηρὸν μᾶλλον κατὰ λόγον καυστι-
25 κόν ἐστι, καὶ ἕτερον ἑτέρου μᾶλλον, | τῷ ἐγγυτέρω τοῦ θερμοῦ εἶναι[21] τὸ ξηρότερον· τῇ δὲ[22] θαλάττῃ ἄμφω [δὲ][23] ταῦτα μᾶλλον ὑπάρχει.

16. Διὰ τί ἀπὸ μὲν τῆς θαλάττης οὐκ ἀποπνεῖ ἕωθεν ψυχρόν, ἀπὸ δὲ τῶν ποταμῶν; ἢ ὅτι ἡ μὲν θάλαττά ἐστιν ἐν ἀναπεπταμένοις τόποις, οἱ δὲ ποτα-
30 μοὶ ἐν στενοῖς; | ἡ μὲν οὖν ἀπὸ τῆς θαλάττης αὔρα εἰς πολὺν τόπον σκίδναται, ὥστε εἶναι ἀσθενής, ἡ δὲ ἀπὸ τῶν ποταμῶν ἀθρόως φέρεται καὶ μᾶλλον ἰσχύει, διὸ μᾶλλον εἰκότως φαίνεται ψυχρά. ἢ οὐ τοῦτό ἐστιν αἴτιον, ἀλλ᾽ οἱ μὲν ποταμοὶ ψυχροί εἰσιν, ἡ δὲ θάλατ-
35 τα οὔτε θερμὴ οὔτε ψυχρά; γίνεται | δὲ ἡ αὔρα καὶ ἡ ἀναπνοὴ[24] θερμαινομένων ἢ ψυχομένων τῶν ὑγρῶν· ὁπότερον γὰρ ἂν τούτων πάσχῃ, ἐξαεροῦται, ἐξαερουμένου δὲ τοῦ ὕδατος ὁ ἀὴρ ὁ γινόμενος φέρεται, ὅ ἐστιν αὔρα. τὸ μὲν οὖν ἀπὸ τῶν ψυχρῶν ψυχρὸν εἰκότως ἀποπνεῖ, τὸ δὲ ἀπὸ τῶν σφόδρα θερμῶν ἀπο-
40 πνέον ψύχεται | καὶ γίνεται ψυχρόν. τοὺς μὲν οὖν
933b ποταμοὺς ψυχροὺς || ἅπαντας εὕροι τις ἄν, ἡ δὲ θάλαττα οὔτε ψυχρὰ οὔτε θερμὴ σφόδρα ἐστίν. οὔτε

[21] post εἶναι lac. indic. Louis
[22] τῇ δὲ Bonitz ex Gaza : δὲ τῇ codd. [23] [δὲ] Bonitz
[24] ἡ ἀναπνοὴ : ἀποπνοὴ *Pr.* 26.30, 943b12

(*in the sea*) less able to adjust to the fire, because they are too thick—indeed even more so, because salt is present as well? Therefore, just as what is dry is less able to extinguish than what is moist, and what is dry is proportionally more able to burn, the one is also more than the other,[31] what is drier being more akin to the hot. And both of these[32] are more present in the sea.[33]

16.[34] Why doesn't the wind blow cold from the sea in the morning, but it does from the river? Is it because the sea is in spread-out areas, whereas rivers are in narrow ones? Thus the breeze from the sea is dispersed over a large area, so that it is weak, whereas the breeze from rivers travels in a mass and is stronger, which is why it naturally seems cold. Or is this not the reason, but it's that rivers are cold, whereas the sea is neither hot nor cold? Now a breeze or an exhalation comes from the heating or cooling of what is moist: for whichever of these is experienced, there is evaporation, and when water evaporates the air that comes to be travels, which is a breeze. So what comes from cold (*bodies of water*) naturally blows cold, whereas what comes from very hot ones, when it blows, cools and becomes cold. Now one would find that all rivers are cold, but that the sea is neither cold nor very hot. Therefore,

[31] This may mean "what is dry is also proportionally more able to burn than what is moist," or, more likely, "the sea is also proportionally more able to burn than water."

[32] I.e., heat and dryness.

[33] There are textual problems with the last sentence of this chapter.

[34] This chapter is virtually identical to 26.30.

οὖν τὸ ἀποπνέον ψυχρὸν ἀπ' αὐτῆς ἐστί, διὰ τὸ μὴ ψυχρὰν εἶναι, οὔτε ψύχεται ταχύ, διὰ τὸ μὴ θερμὴν εἶναι σφόδρα. |

5 17. Διὰ τί ἐν τοῖς μείζοσι πελάγεσι βραδύτερον καθίσταται κύματα ἢ ἐν τοῖς βραχέσιν; ἢ ὅτι ἐκ τῆς πολλῆς κινήσεως βραδύτερον καθίσταται πᾶν ἢ ἐκ τῆς ὀλίγης; ἐν δὲ τοῖς μεγάλοις πελάγεσι πλείων ἡ ἄμπωτις γίνεται ἢ ἐν τοῖς βραχέσιν. οὐθὲν οὖν ἄλο-
10 γον τὸ πλεῖον βραδύτερον | καθίστασθαι.

18. Διὰ τί τὸ ἁλμυρὸν ὕδωρ ψυχρὸν μὲν οὐ πότιμον, θερμαινόμενον δὲ μᾶλλον γίνεται πότιμον, καὶ θερμὸν δὲ ὂν καὶ ἀποψυχόμενον; ἢ διότι εἰς τὸ ἐναντίον ἀπὸ τοῦ ἐναντίου πέφυκε μεταβάλλειν; ἔστι δὲ τὸ πότιμον
15 τῷ ἁλμυρῷ | ἀντικείμενον· καὶ θερμαινομένου μὲν ἀφέψεται τὸ ἁλμυρόν, ψυχομένου δὲ ὑφίσταται.

19. Διὰ τί τὰ πρὸς τῇ θαλάττῃ ὡς ἐπὶ τὸ πολὺ γλυκέα ὕδατα[25] ἀλλ' οὐχ ἁλμυρά; ἢ διὰ τὸ ποτιμώτερα διηθούμενα γίνεσθαι; διηθεῖται δὲ τὸ ἐγγύτερον τῆς
20 θαλάττης | μᾶλλον.

20. Διὰ τί τὸ ἁλμυρὸν ὕδωρ οὐκ ἀπόρρυτόν ἐστιν; ἢ διότι τὸ μὲν βαρὺ στάσιμον, τὸ δὲ ἁλμυρὸν βαρύ; διὸ καὶ τὰ θερμὰ μόνα τῶν ἁλμυρῶν ὑδάτων ἀπόρρυτά ἐστιν. ἔχει γὰρ κουφότητα ἐν αὐτοῖς, ἢ κρατεῖ τῆς
25 κατὰ τὴν ἁλμυρίδα | βαρύτητος· τὸ γὰρ θερμὸν κουφότερόν ἐστιν. ἔτι τὰ μὲν ἀπόρρυτα διηθεῖται διὰ τῆς γῆς· ἠθουμένων δὲ ἀεὶ μάλιστα ὑφίσταται τὸ παχύτατον καὶ βαρύτατον, ἐκκρίνεται δὲ τὸ κοῦφον καὶ καθα-

what blows from it is not cold, because *it* is not cold, nor does it cool quickly, because it is not very hot.

17.[35] Why do waves subside more slowly in larger open seas than in shallow ones? Is it because everything subsides more slowly coming out of a lot of motion than out of little? And the tide is greater in larger open seas than in shallow ones. There is nothing absurd, therefore, in what is greater subsiding more slowly.

18. Why is salt water not drinkable[36] cold, though it becomes more drinkable when heated, and when it is hot and then cooled off? Is it because it is natural to change from one opposite to the other? Now the drinkable is the opposite of the salty; and the salty part is boiled out when (*salt water*) is heated, and settles below when it cools.

19. Why are waters close to the sea in most cases sweet and not salty? Is it because water becomes more drinkable when it is filtered? And what is nearer the sea is filtered more.

20. Why is salt water not free-flowing? Is it because what is heavy is stationary, and salt water is heavy? And this is why the hot among salt waters alone are free-flowing. For they have lightness in themselves, which masters the heaviness from the salt; for what is hot is lighter. Furthermore, free-flowing waters are filtered through the earth; and as they are filtered, most of the densest and heaviest parts always settle below, while the light and pure part is

[35] Cf. *Pr.* 23.1 and 24.

[36] In other contexts, *πότιμος* is translated "fresh."

---

[25] *γλυκέα ὕδατα* B x Am D A E Lamb.1204 : *ὕδατα γλυκέα ὕδατα* plur. codd. : *ὕδατα γλυκέα* (et alt. *ὕδατα* in marg.) s

ρόν· ἔστι γὰρ τὸ μὲν ἁλμυρὸν βαρύ, τὸ δὲ γλυκὺ
30 κοῦφον. διόπερ ἐστὶ γλυκέα τὰ ἀπόρρυτα. τὸ | δ' αὐτὸ
αἴτιόν ἐστι καὶ διὰ τί τὸ ἁλμυρὸν ὕδωρ κινούμενον καὶ
μεταβάλλον γλυκύτερον γίνεται· κουφότερον γὰρ καὶ
ἀσθενέστερον διὰ τὴν κίνησιν γίνεται.

21. Διὰ τί ἐν τῇ Λιβύῃ ἐὰν ὀρύξῃ τις παρὰ τὴν
θάλατταν, τὸ πρῶτον πότιμον, εἶθ' ἁλμυρὸν γίνεται
35 ταχύ, ἐν δὲ | τοῖς ἄλλοις τόποις ἧττον ποιεῖ τοῦτο;
πότερον ὅτι τὸ μὲν πρῶτον τὸ ὑπάρχον ὕδωρ ἐν τῷ
τόπῳ καὶ τὸ πεπεμμένον ὑπὸ τῆς γῆς ἐστίν, ὅταν δὲ
χρονισθῇ, ἡ θάλαττα προσδιηθουμένη[26] διὰ τὸ πρόσ-
φατον εἶναι ποιεῖ ἁλμυρώτερον; ἐν δὲ τοῖς ἄλλοις ἢ
40 οὐκ ἔστι[27] ἢ πολὺ ὕδωρ διὰ τὸ μὴ ξηραίνεσθαι | τὸν
τόπον. ||

934a 22. Διὰ τί τοὺς ἅλας θᾶττον τήκει τὸ ἁλμυρὸν ὕδωρ
ἢ τὸ πότιμον; ἢ διότι τὸ μὲν τήκεσθαί ἐστι τὸ ὑπὸ τοῦ
ὑγροῦ ἢ[28] θερμοῦ εἰσιόντος διαιρεῖσθαι, ὥστε ὑγρὸν
εἶναι; οὐ τήκει δὲ ἢ τὰ ὅλως μὴ δυνάμενα εἰσιέναι, ἢ
5 τὰ οὕτως ὥστε μὴ θιγγάνειν. | μόλις δὲ τήκει τὰ
ῥᾳδίως διεξιόντα· τὰ δ' ἐπιόντα βιαζόμενα, ταῦτα
τάχιστα διαιρεῖ. οὐκ εἰσέρχεται δὲ τὰ λίαν μεγαλο-
μερῆ· ὑπερέχει γὰρ τῶν πόρων. τὰ δὲ μικρομερέστερα
διέρχεται οὐ ψαυόμενα. ἔστι δὲ τὸ μὲν πότιμον λεπτόν,

[26] προσδιηθουμένη : προσιερχομένη Grumach apud Flashar [27] ἔστι Forster : ἔχει codd. [28] ἢ om. Xa

---

[37] Cf. *Pr.* 23.37. See also [Arist.] *Mir.* 134 and [Arist./Alex.] *Sup.Pr.* 2.34.

separated; for salt water is heavy, and sweet water light. This is why free-flowing waters are sweet. Now it is for the same reason as well that salt water becomes sweeter by being moved and by changing (*its location*): for it becomes lighter and weaker because of the motion.

21.[37] Why, in Libya, if one digs near the sea, is the first (*water one encounters*) fresh, then it quickly becomes salty, whereas in other places this happens less?[38] Is it because the first is water that was in this place to begin with and has been concocted by the earth, but as time passes, the sea is filtered through and, because it is new, makes (*the water*) saltier? But in other places either there is no (*fresh*) water or a lot, because the place is not dried.[39]

22. Why does salt water melt salt more quickly than fresh water? Is it because being melted *is* being broken apart by the entering of either moisture or heat, such that it[40] is moist? Now things that are completely unable to enter do not cause melting, nor do things that are such that they enter but do not come into contact with it. Things that pass through easily scarcely cause melting; but things entering forcefully, these break it apart most quickly. Things having very large parts do not enter; for they exceed (*the size*) of the passages. But things having very small parts pass through without touching. Now fresh water is thin,

[38] It is unclear, here and in the last line, what is supposed to happen in other places. Perhaps in other places one finds either no fresh water at all or much more of it.

[39] Something is wrong with this line, which Forster brackets. I follow Flashar and Louis and take it to be referring to fresh water.

[40] I.e., the substance being melted (which is left to implication throughout the text).

10 τὸ δὲ ἁλμυρὸν παχύτερον. ὥστε τὸ μὲν ῥᾳδίως | διὰ τὴν λεπτότητα διαδῦνον μόλις τήκει, τὸ δὲ εἰσέρχεται μὲν, ἧττον δὲ διὰ τὸ μεγαλομερέστερον εἶναι διαιρεῖ,[29] καὶ βιάζεται θᾶττον.

23. Διὰ τί τὸ ὕδωρ ἧττον φαίνεται λευκόν, ἐὰν κινῆται, οἷον καὶ ἡ φρίκη; διὸ καὶ Ὅμηρος ἀρχομένου
15 φησὶ τοῦ | πνεύματος "μελάνει δέ τε πόντος ὑπ' αὐτοῦ." ἢ διὰ δύο αἰτίας; ἐγγύθεν μὲν τῆς ὄψεως οὔσης, διὰ τὸ διιέναι τὴν ὄψιν μᾶλλον ἠρεμοῦντος, κινουμένου δὲ μὴ εὐθυπορεῖν· τὸ δὲ διαφανὲς λευκὸν φαίνεται. δι' οὗ γὰρ μὴ διέρχεται ἡ ὄψις, μέλαν φησὶν
20 εἶναι. διὸ καὶ ὁ ἀὴρ πόρρωθεν μέλας φαίνεται, | ὁ δὲ ἐγγὺς λευκός, καὶ θαλάττης τὸ μὲν ἐγγὺς λευκόν, τὸ δὲ πόρρωθεν κυανοῦν καὶ μέλαν. πόρρωθεν δέ, κινουμένης πως τῆς ὄψεως, διὰ τὸ[30] διανακλᾶσθαι ἀθρόον τὴν ὄψιν, ἐὰν ἠρεμῇ, πρὸς τὸ φῶς, κινουμένου δὲ μὴ δύνασθαι. |

25 24. Διὰ τί ἐν τοῖς βαθέσι πελάγεσι τὸ κῦμα οὐκ ἐπιγελᾷ, ἀλλ' ἐν τοῖς μικροῖς; πότερον ὅτι τὸ μικρὸν φερόμενον ὕδωρ διαιρεῖται ὑπὸ τοῦ ἀέρος μᾶλλον ἢ τὸ πολύ; διὸ θραύεται πατάξαν μᾶλλον. ἐν μὲν οὖν τῷ βαθεῖ πολὺ τὸ κινούμενον, ἐν δὲ τῷ βραχεῖ ὀλίγον. |

30 25. Διὰ τί οἱ πρὸς νότον τόποι ἁλυκώτερα τὰ ὕδατα

[29] διαιρεῖ : διαρρεῖ Forster
[30] διὰ Forster (cf. 934a16) : καὶ codd. || τὸ Y^a Ap C^a : τῷ X^a

while salt water is thicker. So the former, slipping through easily because of its thinness, scarcely causes melting, whereas the latter enters, but flows through to a lesser extent because it has very large parts, and forces its way more quickly.

23.[41] Why does water appear less white, if it is set in motion, for instance even a ripple? This is why Homer says that when the wind begins "the sea becomes black under it."[42] Is it for two reasons? (1) Because, when the sight is near, the sight passes through more ⟨*directly*⟩ when the water is at rest, but when the water is in motion the sight does not travel in a straight path, and what is transparent appears white. For that through which the sight does not pass Homer says is black. And this is why the air from a distance appears black, but the air nearby appears white, and the part of the sea nearby appears white, whereas the distant part appears blue or black. (2) Because, when the sight is at a distance and moving in some way, the sight is refracted in a mass toward the light, if the water is at rest, but this is not possible when the water is in motion.[43]

24.[44] Why doesn't a wave ripple in deep open seas, but it does in the small ones? Is it because a small amount of water as it travels is more divided by the air than a large amount? This is why as it strikes more it is broken up. Therefore, in deep water what is set in motion is large, whereas in shallow water it is small.

25. Why do places facing the south wind[45] have more

[41] Cf. *Pr.* 23.6 and 41, 26.37.

[42] Hom. *Il.* 7.64.

[43] There seems to be a problem with the text of this last line. I adopt Forster's emendation, but without much confidence.

[44] Cf. *Pr.* 23.1 and 17.

[45] Or simply "facing south."

ἔχουσιν; ἢ διὰ τὸ τὴν θάλατταν ὑπὸ νότου ὠθεῖσθαι ὑπὸ τὴν γῆν κεράννυται;

26. Διὰ τί τῶν ὑδάτων τὸ ἁλμυρὸν ἐπὶ τῷ γλυκεῖ οἴνῳ μᾶλλον ἐπιπολάζει ἢ ἐπὶ τῷ αὐστηρῷ; πότερον
35 ὅτι μᾶλλον | ἔχει γῆν ὁ γλυκύς, ὥσπερ ἡ ἀσταφίς; ἢ ὅτι βαρύτερος καὶ γλισχρότερος ὁ γλυκύς, ὥσθ' ἧττον μίγνυται, μὴ μιγνύμενον[31] δὲ ἐφίσταται;

27. Διὰ τί ὅλως ἐφίσταται γεῶδες ὄν; ἡ γὰρ οἰκεία φορὰ κάτω. [πότερον ὅτι μᾶλλον ἔχει γῆν ὁ γλυκύς;
934b ἢ][32] διὰ τὴν || θερμότητα, καθάπερ οἱ ἅλες; ὅμοιον γὰρ ἐξανθήματι. ἢ δι' ἄλλην αἰτίαν; εἰ γὰρ οὐ, διὰ τοῦτο καὶ ἐπὶ τῷ γλυκεῖ μᾶλλον οὐκ ἄλογον· θερμότατος γάρ.

28. Διὰ τί τὰ κύματα πρότερον φοιτᾷ ἐνίοτε τῶν
5 ἀνέμων; | ἢ διότι καὶ τελευτᾷ ὕστερον; τὸ γὰρ πρῶτον πνεῦμα ὡσανεὶ προδιαλύεται τοῦ ὠσθέντος κύματος· ἀφικνεῖται δὲ οὐκ αὐτὸ τὸ πρῶτον ὠσθέν, ἀλλ' ἀεὶ ἡ ὦσις γίνεται τοῦ ἐχομένου.

29. Διὰ τί αἱ κυματωδέστεραι γαῖ στερραὶ γίνονται
10 πολλάκις | οὕτω σφόδρα ὥσπερ ἠδαφισμέναι; καὶ ἡ μὲν κυματώδης γῆ στερρά, ἡ δὲ ἄποθεν χαῦνος; ἢ διότι ἡ μικρὰ ἄμμος οὐ πόρρω[33] ἐκβάλλεται ὑπὸ τοῦ κύματος, ἀλλὰ ἡ μείζων μᾶλλον, ὥσπερ καὶ τῇ χειρὶ βάλλειν πόρρω οὐ τὸ ἐλάχιστον μάλιστα δυνατόν;

[31] μιγνύμενον : μιγνύμενος Cᵃ : μιγνυμένου Ross apud Forster

[32] πότερον—ἢ seclusi, om. Yᵃ : ὅτι—ἢ om. Cᵃ

[33] πόρρω Cᵃ : πόρρωθεν cett. codd.

brackish waters? Is it because the sea, pushed by the south wind under the earth, becomes mixed?

26. Why does the salty part of waters come to the surface of sweet wine more than of dry? Is it because sweet wine, like raisin wine, contains more earth? Or is it because sweet wine is heavier and stickier, so that it mixes less, and (*the salty part*) stays on the surface without mixing?

27. Why does it,[46] being earthy, stay on the surface at all? For its proper motion is downward. [Is it because sweet wine contains more earth?][47] Is it because of its heat, just like salt? For it is similar to an efflorescence. Or is it for another reason? For if not, it is not more unreasonable for this to be why it stays on the surface of sweet wine; for this is the hottest wine.

28.[48] Why do the waves sometimes begin to move before the winds do? Is it because they also die down later? For the first breath (*of wind*), so to speak, dissipates before the wave that it pushed; and the first wave pushed does not itself come, but the push continually comes from (*the water*) connected to it.

29. Why does the more wave-beaten ground often become so very solid, as if it were (*purposely*) leveled? And why is wave-beaten ground solid, whereas the ground farther (*from the sea*) is loose? Is it because a small grain of sand is not thrown out far by the waves, but rather the larger is, just as it is not possible to throw far with the hand

[46] I.e., the salty part. This chapter is a continuation of the previous one. [47] This line is repeated from the previous chapter (see 934a39); it is not found in the oldest ms.

[48] Cf. *Pr.* 23.2, 11, 12. Source: Thphr. *Vent.* 35.

15 ἔπειτα πολλῶν κυκωμένων | τὰ ἐλάχιστα ἐμπίπτοντα πυκνοῖ. ἡ δὲ τοῦ κύματος λωφῶντος κίνησις ἐδαφίζει, κινεῖ δὲ οὐκέτι. διὰ μὲν οὖν τὸ τὰ μικρότατα μὴ πόρρω δύνασθαι πηδᾶν, ἐκ μικρῶν σφόδρα συντέθειται· διὰ δὲ τὸ πολλάκις κινεῖσθαι συνεχὲς γίνεται πιπτούσης
20 ἄμμου, ἕως ἂν συναρμόσῃ· διὰ δὲ τὸ | κῦμα τὸ τελευταῖον ἐδαφίζεται, καὶ τὸ ἠρέμα ὑγρὸν συγκολλᾷ. ἡ δὲ πόρρω ξηρά τε οὖσα διίσταται, καὶ ἐκ μειζόνων ἐστὶ λιθιδίων καὶ ἀνεδάφιστος.

30. Διὰ τί τῆς θαλάσσης τὰ ἄνω τῶν ἐν τῷ βάθει ἁλμυρώτερα καὶ θερμότερα; ὁμοίως δὲ καὶ ἐν τοῖς |
25 φρέασι τοῖς ποτίμοις τὸ ἐπιπολῆς ἁλμυρώτερον τοῦ εἰς βάθος· καίτοι ἔδει τὸ κατωτέρω· βαρύτερον γὰρ τὸ ἁλμυρόν. ἢ διότι ὁ ἥλιος καὶ ὁ ἀὴρ ἀνάγει ἀεὶ τὸ ἐλαφρότατον ἀπὸ τῶν ὑγρῶν; τὸ δὲ ποτιμώτερον ἀεὶ κουφότερον, μᾶλλον δὲ ἀπάγει ἀπὸ τῶν ἐγγυτέρων[34]
30 τόπων. ὥστε καὶ τῆς θαλάττης | ἀπὸ τῶν ἐπιπολῆς καὶ τῶν ποτίμων ἀνάγκη τὸ λειπόμενον ἁλμυρώτερον εἶναι, ἀφ᾽ ὧν ἀνῆκται, ἢ ἀφ᾽ ὧν μηθὲν ἢ ἔλαττον τὸ γλυκύ.[35] διὰ τοῦτο δὲ καὶ θερμότερα τὰ ἄνω· τὸ γὰρ ἁλμυρὸν θερμότερον τοῦ ποτίμου. διὸ καὶ φασί τινες τῶν ἡρακλειτιζόντων ἐκ μὲν τοῦ ποτίμου ξηραινο-
35 μένου | καὶ πηγνυμένου λίθους γίνεσθαι καὶ γῆν, ἐκ δὲ τῆς θαλάττης τὸν ἥλιον ἀναθυμιᾶσθαι.

[34] *ἐγγυτέρων* codd. (teste Louis) || *ἐγγυτέρω* codd. (teste Bekker) || *ἐγγυτέρων* Y^a : *ἐγγυτέρω* cett. codd. (teste Ruelle)
[35] *τὸ γλυκύ* secl. Hett

what is very small? Then, when many (*grains of sand*) are stirred up, the smallest fall upon (*the ground*) and become compact. And the motion of the receding wave levels them, but no longer moves them. Thus, because the smallest ones cannot leap very far, (*the solid ground*) is formed out of very small ones; and because it is moved often, it becomes continuous as the sand falls, until they fit together; and it is leveled by the final wave, and the slight moisture[49] glues it together. But the ground farther away being dry disintegrates, and consists of larger pebbles and is not leveled.

30.[50] Why are the upper parts of the sea saltier and hotter than the parts in the depths? Similarly, even in freshwater wells the surface is saltier than the depths. Yet the lower ought to be, since what is salty is heavier. Is it because the sun and the air always bring up the lightest part of the liquid? Now the fresher is always lighter, and the sun and the air bring up more from the parts that are nearer. And so what remains on the surface both of the sea and of fresh waters, from which (*the lightest part*) has been brought up, must be saltier than that from which little or no sweet water has been brought up. For this reason too the upper parts must be hotter; for what is salty is hotter than what is fresh. And this is why some of those who are Heraclitean claim that whereas stones and earth come to be from fresh water drying and solidifying, the sun produces evaporation from the sea.

[49] Literally, "what is slightly moist."
[50] Source: Hp. *Aër* 8.

31. Διὰ τί τῆς θαλάττης τὰ πρὸς τῇ γῇ γλυκύτερά ἐστιν; ἢ διότι ἐν τῇ κινήσει μᾶλλόν ἐστιν; κινούμενον δὲ τὸ ἁλμυρὸν γλυκύτερον γίνεται. ἢ ὅτι καὶ ἐν τῷ
935a βάθει ἁλμυρώτερόν ‖ ἐστι τὸ ὕδωρ, τὰ δὲ πρὸς τῇ γῇ ἧττόν ἐστι βαθέα; διὸ καὶ τἀγχιβαθῆ ἁλμυρά ἐστι καὶ οὐχ ὁμοίως γλυκέα. τούτου δ' αἴτιον ὅτι βαρὺ ὂν τὸ ἁλμυρὸν φέρεται μᾶλλον εἰς βάθος. |

5 32. Διὰ τί ἡ θάλαττα μόνον τῶν ὑδάτων κάεται, τὰ δὲ πότιμα καὶ ποτάμια οὔ; πότερον ὅτι γῆν πολλὴν ἔχει; δηλοῦσι δὲ οἱ ἅλες. ἢ διότι λιπαρά; δηλοῖ δὲ τὸ ἐν τοῖς ἅλασιν ἐφιστάμενον[36] ἔλαιον.

33. Διὰ τί ἐν ταῖς λίμναις ἄμμος οὐ γίνεται ἢ ἧττον
10 ἢ | ἐν τῇ θαλάττῃ καὶ τοῖς ποταμοῖς; ἢ ὅτι ἐν τῇ θαλάττῃ πέτραι γίνονται, καὶ ἡ γῆ ἐκκέκαυται μάλιστα; ἡ δὲ ἄμμος ἐστὶ πέτρα ἐψηγμένη εἰς μικρὰ καὶ ἐλάχιστα μόρια. ψήχεται δὲ διὰ τὴν πληγὴν τῶν κυμάτων. ἐν δὲ ταῖς λίμναις οὐ γίνονται ὁμοίως πέ-
15 τραι καθαραί, οὐδὲ θραύονται | ὁμοίως διὰ τὸ μὴ γίνεσθαι κύματα ὁμοίως. ἐν δὲ τοῖς ποταμοῖς μᾶλλον, ὅτι τὴν μὲν γῆν καταφέρουσι, τὰς δὲ πέτρας τῇ πληγῇ θραύουσιν.

34. Διὰ τί, ὅταν ἡ λίμνη ἢ κοπάσῃ ἢ ξηρὰ γένηται, ἀποκάεται ὁ σῖτος ἐν τῷ πεδίῳ μᾶλλον; πότερον ὅτι τὸ |
20 ὑγρὸν τὸ ἐν τῇ λίμνῃ ἀπατμίζον τῇ ἀτμίδι θερμαίνει τὸν ἀέρα, ὥστε ἐλάττους καὶ ἀσθενεστέρους ποιεῖ τοὺς πάγους ἢ ἐν τοῖς κοίλοις καὶ προσελώδεσι τόποις; ἢ ἐκ τῆς γῆς, ὥσπερ λέγεται, τὰ ψύχη ἄρχεται καὶ λανθάνει εἰσδυόμενα; ξηρᾶς οὖν οὔσης τῆς λί-
25 μνης, διὰ πλείονος τόπου ἡ ψυχρότης | πλείων προσ-

31. Why are the parts of the sea by the land sweeter? Is it because they are in motion more? And salt water becomes sweeter when it moves. Or is it also because the water is saltier in the depths, and the parts by the land are less deep? And this is why deep waters near the shore are salty and not so sweet. Now the reason for this is that, being heavy, the salty part is carried more into the depths.

32.[51] Why does the sea alone of waters burn, whereas fresh water and river water do not? Is it because it contains a lot of earth? The salt proves this. Or is it because it is oily? The oil forming on salt proves this.

33. Why does sand not form in lakes, or less than in the sea or in rivers? Is it because rocks form in the sea, and the earth has mostly been burned out of them? Now sand is rock worn down into small and tiny parts. It is worn down by the pounding of the waves. But in lakes pure rocks are not formed to the same extent, nor are they broken up to the same extent because there are not waves to the same extent. But in rivers there is more sand, because they carry down the earth, and break up the rocks by pounding them.

34. Why, when a lake is exhausted or becomes dry, is the grain in the (*adjoining*) plain more likely to be burned off (*by frost*)? Is it because the moisture evaporating in the lake heats the air with its vapor, so that it makes less and weaker frost than in hollows and marshy places? Or does the cold originate from the earth, as they say, and enter without being noticed? When the lake is dry, therefore, the greater cold falling upon a greater space solidifies and

[51] Cf. *Pr.* 23.15.

36 ἐφιστάμενον Y[a] Ap : ὑφιστάμενον cett. codd.

πίπτουσα πήγνυσι καὶ ἀποκάει μᾶλλον. ἐν δὲ ταῖς τοιαύταις χώραις τὰ ψύχη κάτωθεν γίνεται, ὥσπερ καὶ δοκεῖ. καίτοι ἡ γῆ θερμὴ τοῦ χειμῶνος· ἀλλὰ διὰ τὸ ἔφυγρον εἶναι κατέψυκται τὸ ἐπιπολῆς θερμὸν τὸ ἐν τῇ γῇ. τὸ γὰρ ὑγρὸν οὔτε οὕτω πόρρω ἐστὶν ὥστε
30 μὴ ψύχεσθαι, | διὰ τὴν ἐνοῦσαν θερμότητα ἐν τοῖς ὑγροῖς, οὔτε οὕτως ὀλίγον ὥστε μηθὲν ἰσχύειν, διὰ τὸ διάβροχον εἶναι τὴν γῆν. οἷον οὖν διὰ τὴν ψύξιν αὐτοῦ συμβαίνει ἐπὶ κρυστάλλου περιπατεῖν καὶ οἰκεῖν.

35. Διὰ τί ἡ θάλαττα ἁλμυρὰ καὶ πικρά ἐστιν; ἢ ὅτι |
35 ἐν τῇ θαλάττῃ πλείους εἰσὶν οἱ χυμοί; καὶ γὰρ τὸ ἁλμυρὸν καὶ τὸ πικρὸν ἅμα φαίνεται.

36. Διὰ τί τὰ ἐν τῇ θαλάττῃ ὄστρακα καὶ λίθοι στρογγύλα γίνεται; ἢ ὅτι ὁμοίως περιθραυόμενα τὰ
935b ἔσχατα εἰς || τὸ στρογγύλον σχῆμα ἔρχεται; τούτου γὰρ τὸ ἔσχατον ὅμοιον, ἡ δὲ θάλαττα πάντῃ κινοῦσα ὁμοίως περιθραύει.

37. Διὰ τί ἐνιαχοῦ, ἐάν τις ὀρύξῃ παρὰ τὴν θάλατταν, τὸ μὲν πρῶτον πότιμόν ἐστιν ὕδωρ, εἶθ' ἁλμυρὸν
5 γίνεται; ἢ | ὅτι αὐτῆς ἐστὶ τῆς θαλάττης τῆς διηθούσης ὑπὸ τὴν γῆν τὸ ὕδωρ; εἰκότως οὖν τὸ πρῶτόν ἐστι γλυκύ· ἐλαφρότερον γάρ ἐστι τὸ γλυκὺ τοῦ ἁλμυροῦ, καὶ ἡ θάλαττα ἔχει τι τοῦ γλυκέος, ὃ μιχθὲν τῇ γῇ μᾶλλον ἐπιπολάζει. τὸ δὲ ἁλμυρὸν διὰ τὸ βάρος καὶ
10 διὰ τὸ τμητικὸν εἶναι κάτω φέρεται. | εἴτε οὖν οὕτως εἴτε κατὰ τὰς φλέβας ἐκ τῆς ἠπείρου ῥεῖ ἐπὶ τὴν θάλατταν τὸ γλυκὺ ὕδωρ, εἰκότως ἂν ἐπιπολῆς εἴη τῆς

burns off more. And in such areas the cold comes from below, as indeed seems to be the case.[52] Yet the ground is (*still*) hot in winter; but because there is moisture, the surface heat on the ground is cooled. For the moisture is neither so far away that it does not become cold, owing to the heat existing in liquids, nor so little in amount that it does not prevail, owing to the ground being wet. So, for instance, owing to its cooling one is able to walk and dwell upon ice.

35. Why is the sea salty and bitter? Is it because the juices in the sea are numerous? And indeed, saltiness and bitterness appear at the same time.

36. Why do shells and stones that are in the sea become round? Is it because their extremities, being broken equally all around, tend toward a round shape? For the extremity of this shape is equal, and the sea, moving things in every direction, breaks (*their extremities*) equally all around.

37.[53] Why, in some places,[54] if one digs near the sea, is the first water (*one encounters*) fresh, then it becomes salty? Is it because the water comes from the sea itself which is filtered under the earth? So naturally the first water is sweet; for sweet water is lighter than salt water, and the sea contains some sweet water, which when mixed with the earth[55] tends to come to the surface. But the salty part, owing to its weight and its ability to pierce,[56] travels downward. Therefore, whether in this way or through the veins (*of the earth*) the sweet water flows from the mainland into

[52] Or perhaps, "as is even believed to be the case."

[53] Cf. *Pr.* 23.21.

[54] Or "sometimes," though ch. 21 specifies "in Libya."

[55] I assume this refers to the filtering mentioned earlier.

[56] I.e., to penetrate into the earth.

θαλάττης, ᾗ μίγνυται αὐτῇ. ἀνοιχθέντων δὲ τῶν πόρων, ὕστερον διὰ πλῆθος τὸ ἁλυκὸν κρατοῦν τοιοῦτο πᾶν ποιεῖ. συμβαίνει γὰρ πεφραγμένων τῶν πόρων |
15 *ἄνω*[37] *ἄλλην ὁδὸν ζητεῖν τὸ ἐπιρρέον· ἀνοιχθέντων δὲ ἐνταῦθα πᾶν φέρεται, καθάπερ ἐπὶ τῶν τοῦ σώματος φλεβῶν.*

38. *Διὰ τί ἡ θάλαττα οὖσα βαρυτέρα τοῦ ποτίμου ὕδατος μᾶλλόν ἐστιν εὐδίοπτος; πότερον ὅτι λιπαρωτέρα; τὸ δὲ ἔλαιον ἐπιχυθὲν ποιεῖ μᾶλλον εὐδίοπτον.*
20 *ἔχουσα δὲ ἐν* | *αὐτῇ λίπος εἰκότως μᾶλλον εὐδίοπτός ἐστιν. ἢ οὐχ ἅπαν τὸ ἐλαφρότερον καὶ εὐδιοπτότερον; αὐτὸ γὰρ τὸ ἔλαιον ἐλαφρότερον τοῦ ὕδατος, εὐδιοπτότερον δὲ οὔ. ἢ οὐκ εὐδιοπτότερόν ἐστιν, ἀλλὰ φαίνεται; τὸ γὰρ πότιμον ὕδωρ ἀπὸ τῆς γῆς ἢ ἀπὸ*
25 *ῥευμάτων ἐστίν, ἡ δὲ πηγὴ συναφίησι μετὰ* | *τοῦ ὕδατος καὶ γῆν, ὥστε τῷ μὴ καθαρὰ εἶναι τὰ ῥεύματα συγκατάγει τὴν γῆν καὶ ἰλύν. αὕτη οὖν ἐστὶν ἡ αἰτία τοῦ ἧττον εἶναι εὐδίοπτον.*

39. *Διὰ τί οἱ νέοντες ἐν τῇ θαλάττῃ λαπαροὶ*[38] *γίνονται; εἰ γὰρ ὅτι πονοῦσι, καὶ οἱ τροχιζόμενοι*
30 *ἰσχυρὸν πονοῦσι πόνον* | *καὶ οὐ λαπάττονται. ἢ ὅτι οὐ πᾶς πόνος ποιεῖ λάπαξιν, ἀλλ᾿ ὁ μὴ ποιῶν σύντηξιν; ἡ δὲ ἐν τῇ θαλάττῃ διατριβὴ καὶ ὅλως δοκεῖ βρωτικωτέρους ποιεῖν καὶ λαπαρούς·*[39] *θερμή τε γάρ ἐστι καὶ ξηρὰ ἡ ἀπ᾿ αὐτῆς ἀτμίς.*

[37] *πόρων ἄνω* Ap Xa : *ἄνω πόρων* cett. codd.
[38] *λαπαροὶ* Sylburg ex Gaza : *λιπαροὶ* codd.
[39] *λαπαρούς* Sylburg ex Gaza : *λιπαρούς* codd.

the sea, it would naturally be on the surface of the sea, which is mingled with it. But later, when the passages are opened, the brackish part, owing to its quantity, prevails and makes it all salty. For when the passages are blocked, it happens that what is flowing finds another way upward,[57] but when they are opened it all travels there, as in the case of the veins of the body.

38.[58] Why is the sea, which is heavier than fresh water, more transparent? Is it because it is oilier? Now oil poured on to water makes it more transparent. And having oil in it, ⟨*the sea*⟩ is naturally more transparent. Or is not everything that is lighter also more transparent? For oil itself is lighter than water, but is not more transparent. Or is the sea *not* more transparent, but only appears to be so? For fresh water comes from the earth or from streams, and the source sends forth earth as well with the water, so that not being pure, the streams carry down with them earth and mud. Therefore, this is the reason ⟨*fresh water*⟩ is less transparent.

39. Why do those who swim in the sea have loose stools? For if it is because they exert themselves, then those who run intensely also exert themselves with strong exertions, but they do not have loose stools. Is it because not every exertion produces loose stools, but only that which does not produce colliquation? Now spending time in the sea seems generally to produce both much greater hunger and loose stools; for the vapor from it is both hot and dry.

[57] Or, with the other mss., "when the upper passages are blocked, it happens that what is flowing finds another way."

[58] Cf. *Pr.* 23.8 and 9.

40. Διὰ τί Παῖσα λίμνη[40] πότιμος οὖσα πλύνει καὶ
35 ῥύπτει | τὰ ἱμάτια; πλύνει μὲν γὰρ τὸ γλυκύ, ῥύπτει δὲ τὸ πικρόν, ἅμα δὲ οὐχ οἷόν τε ἔχειν ταῦτα. ἢ οὐ τῷ πικρὸν εἶναι οὐθὲν ῥύπτει, ἀλλ' ἡ γλισχρότης ῥυπτικόν; διὸ καὶ τὰ ἀκροκώλια καὶ ὅσα μυξώδη τοιαῦτα,
936a ὥστε καὶ τῶν πικρῶν || ὅσα τούτου μετέχει. ἐν δὲ τῇ λίμνῃ ταύτῃ συμβέβηκε τοῦτο, ὥστε τῆς νιτρώδους δυνάμεως τὸ μὲν πικρὸν ἐκκεκαῦσθαι, ἐμμένειν δὲ τὸ λιπαρὸν καὶ γλίσχρον. τούτῳ μὲν οὖν ῥύπτει, πλύνει δὲ τῷ ποτίμῳ αὐτῆς. |

5 41. Διὰ τί τὸ γαληνίζον τῆς θαλάττης λευκὸν φαίνεται, τὸ δὲ καταφέρον[41] μέλαν; ἢ ὅτι τὸ ἧττον ὁρώμενον μελάντερον μᾶλλον φαίνεται, ἧττον δὲ φαίνεται τὸ κινούμενον τοῦ ἠρεμοῦντος; ἢ διότι τὸ μὲν διαφαινόμενον λευκόν, τὸ δὲ μὴ διαφαινόμενον μέλαν;
10 ἧττον δὲ διαφαίνεται τὸ | κινούμενον.

[40] Παῖσα λίμνη Sylburg ex Gaza (*Lacus Paesa*) : πᾶσα λίμνη codd. : ἡ Ὑρκανία λίμνη [Arist./Alex.] *Sup.Pr.* 3.45, 1 : cf. ἐν Παλαιστίνῃ . . . λίμνη *Mete.* 359a17

[41] καταφέρον : καταφερόμενον C[a] : κατάφορον Sylburg

---

[59] Cf. [Arist./Alex.] *Sup.Pr.* 3.45. Source: *Mete.* 359a17–22. See also [Arist.] *Mir.* 53 and Phaenias fr. 34 Wehrli.

[60] Unknown. Herodotus mentions a city Paesa, near Lampsacus, on the Hellespont (5.117). One might speculate that "Paesa" is a corruption of "Palestine," as Aristotle mentions "a lake in Palestine" (no doubt the Dead Sea) fabled to have similar characteristics. But that lake is said to be so salty and bitter that no fish can

40.[59] Why does Lake Paesa,[60] which is fresh water, wash *and* scrub[61] clothes? For what is sweet washes and what is bitter scrubs, but (*water*) cannot have both qualities at the same time. Or does nothing scrub by being bitter, but stickiness is suitable for scrubbing? And this is why the extremities and all mucus-containing parts are such, so that anything bitter also partakes of this characteristic.[62] Now in this lake it happens to be the case that the bitter part of the nitrous power[63] has been burned out, and the oily and sticky part remains. So by virtue of this it scrubs, whereas by virtue of its fresh water it washes.

41. Why does the part of the sea that is calm appear white, whereas the part that is traveling[64] appears black? Is it because what is less visible appears blacker, and what is moving appears less[65] than what is still? Or is it because what is transparent is white, whereas what is not transparent is black? And what is moving is less transparent.

live in it (*Mete*. 359a16–22), which contradicts the freshwater nature of Lake Paesa.

[61] πλύνω and ῥύπτω both mean "wash" or "cleanse," but in the present context, the former seems to refer specifically to rinsing, the latter to scrubbing or scouring.

[62] The precise meaning of this line is unclear. "Extremities" refers to animal parts like pigs' feet. The author seems to be saying that certain things are both bitter and sticky, but it is the stickiness that makes them suitable for scrubbing.

[63] The nitrous power likely refers to sodium carbonate.

[64] *καταφέρον* actually means "traveling downward" or "carrying down," and as a contrast to being calm probably refers to the choppy, up-and-down motion of the sea. Most editors accept Sylburg's emendation (*κατάφορον*), but it is not much of an improvement.

[65] I.e., is less visible.

BOOK XXIV

INTRODUCTION

The subject of Book 24 is hot water. Most of the chapters (3–11) deal with various effects or powers of hot (and especially boiling) water. The last four chapters (16–19) raise questions about hot waters or springs (some of which, at least, are bathing places); and the two preceding them (14–15) seem connected, in that they discuss the supposedly unhealthy nature of bathing in water heated by the sun. The remainder (1, 2, 12, 13) cover miscellaneous topics.

The sources that can be identified with a reasonable degree of probability come from Theophrastus—*On Fire*, *On Stones*, and (the lost) *On Waters*. Although not often a clear source, the author of *Pr.* 24 is certainly drawing on principles presented in Aristotle's *Meteorology*.

ΟΣΑ ΠΕΡΙ ΤΑ ΘΕΡΜΑ ΥΔΑΤΑ

1. Διὰ τί τὸ θερμὸν ὕδωρ, ἐὰν ἐπικεχρισμένοι ὦσιν ἐλαίῳ, ἧττον θερμόν ἐστι καταχεόμενον, τοῦ ἐλαίου 936a15 θερμοῦ ὄντος; ἢ | διὰ τὸ λεαίνειν ὀλισθαίνει καὶ ἧττον ἐνδύνει;

2. Διὰ τί τὰ ὕδατα ἐν τοῖς φρέασι μετὰ μεσημβρίαν γίνεται τοῦ θέρους θερμά; ἢ διότι τηνικαῦτα ἤδη κεκράτηκε τὸ θερμὸν τὸν ἀέρα; πρὸ μεσημβρίας δὲ τὸ θερμὸν λύει τὸ ψυχρὸν καὶ παύει· οὐχ ἅμα δὲ 20 πέπαυται καὶ κρατεῖ, | ἀλλ' ὅταν ἐπιχρονίσῃ.

3. Διὰ τί τὸ ὕδωρ θερμότερον ἐνίοτε τῆς φλογὸς γινόμενον οὐ κατακάει τὰ ξύλα, ἡ δὲ φλὸξ κατακάει; ἢ ὅτι ἡ μὲν φλὸξ λεπτομερές, καὶ τὸ ἀπ' αὐτῆς πνεῦμα, τὸ δὲ ὕδωρ μεγαλομερές, ὥστε οὐκ εἰσδύεται; ἡ δὲ 25 φλὸξ καὶ τὸ | ἀπὸ τῶν ἀνθράκων διὰ λεπτότητα εἰσιὸν διαλύει.

4. Διὰ τί τὸ μὲν ὕδωρ τὸ ζέον οὐ τήκει, ἡ δὲ κοιλία τήκει; πότερον ὅτι τὸ μὲν θερμὸν τὸ ἐν τῇ κοιλίᾳ εἰσέρχεται διὰ λεπτότητα, τὸ δὲ ὕδωρ οὐκ εἰσέρχεται

---

[1] I.e., owing to the oil smoothing down the body.

[2] Source: Thphr. *Ign*. 40.

PROBLEMS CONNECTED WITH HOT WATER

1. Why, if people are covered with oil, is the hot water poured over them less hot, although oil is hot? Is it because owing to the smoothing[1] the water slides off and so penetrates less?

2. Why does the water in wells in summer become hot after midday? Is it because by that time the heat has mastered the air? Now before midday the heat is dissolving and stopping the cold; but the one is not stopped at the same time the other gains mastery, but after some time has passed.

3.[2] Why does water, which sometimes becomes hotter than flame, not burn wood, whereas flame does burn it? Is it because flame consists of thin parts, as does the breath that comes from it, whereas water consists of large parts, and so does not penetrate? But flame, and the (*breath*) from the coals, entering owing to its thinness, destroys (*the wood*).

4.[3] Why does boiling water not cause melting, whereas the stomach does cause melting? Is it because the heat that is in the stomach enters because of its thinness, but water does not penetrate because of its density? Or is it be-

[3] Sources: Thphr. *Ign*. 40 and 45.

διὰ παχύτητα; ἢ διότι καὶ τὰ ἄλλα κωλύει τήκεσθαι τὸ
30 ὑγρόν; | οὐθὲν γὰρ ἐν ὑγρῷ τήκεται. ἐν δὲ τῇ κοιλίᾳ τὸ ὑγρὸν εἰς τὴν κύστιν ὑπονοστοῦν οὐ κωλύει.[1]

5. Διὰ τί τῶν ἀγγείων ὁ πυθμὴν οὐ κάει ἐνόντος τοῦ ὕδατος καὶ ζέοντος, ἀλλὰ καὶ φέρουσι τοῦ πυθμένος ἐχόμενοι, ἐξαιρεθέντος δὲ κάει; ἢ ὅτι σβέννυται τὸ
35 ἐγγινόμενον | θερμὸν ἐν τῷ πυθμένι ὑπὸ τοῦ ὕδατος; διὸ καὶ οὐ τήκεται τὰ τηκτά, ἂν ὑγρόν τι[2] ἐμπέσῃ.

6. Διὰ τί οὐχ ὑπερζεῖ τοῦ χειμῶνος ὁμοίως καὶ τοῦ θέρους τὸ ὕδωρ, οὐ μόνον ὁμοίως θερμαινόμενον ἀλλὰ καὶ μᾶλλον, καὶ ὁμοίως θερμὸν ὂν καὶ ἔτι μᾶλλον; ἢ
936b διότι ἡ || ὑπέρζεσίς ἐστιν ἡ ἀναβολὴ τῶν πομφολύγων; τὸ μὲν οὖν ὕδωρ αὐτὸ θερμαίνεται τότε οὐθὲν ἧττον ἢ τοῦ θέρους,[3] αἱ δὲ πομφόλυγες αἴρεσθαι οὐ δύνανται ὁμοίως διὰ τὸ τὸν περιέχοντα ἀέρα εἶναι
5 ψυχρόν, ἀλλ' ἐλάττους τε τὰ μεγέθη | αἴρονται ὑπὸ τοῦ ψύχους θλιβόμεναι, καὶ διακόπτοντος τοῦ ἀέρος ταχὺ διαπίπτουσιν. ὥστε ἐλάττους τε τῷ ὄγκῳ καὶ τῷ πλήθει γίνονται τοῦ χειμῶνος, τοῦ δὲ θέρους τοὐναντίον. ἡ δὲ ὑπέρζεσις γίνεται διὰ τὸ πλῆθος καὶ τὸ μέγεθος τοῦ ἀφροῦ. |

10 7. Διὰ τί τὸ μὲν θερμὸν ὕδωρ ῥυτιδοῖ, τὸ δὲ πῦρ θερμὸν ὂν οὔ; ἢ ὅτι τὸ μὲν πῦρ ποιεῖ πνεῦμα, ὥστε

[1] οὐ κωλύει Forster : οὕτω λύει codd.
[2] ὑγρόν τι Barnes ex Gaza : μὴ ψόφος codd.
[3] θέρους Bonitz : ψύχους codd.

---

[4] Cf. *Pr.* 24.8, Thphr. *Ign.* 68, and [Arist./Alex.] *Sup.Pr.* 3.42.

cause liquid in fact prevents other things from melting? For nothing melts in liquid. But in the stomach the liquid sinks into the bladder and does not prevent (*melting*).

5.[4] Why does the bottom of vessels not burn when water is present and boiling, but people even carry them holding them by the bottom, whereas when the water is removed it burns? Is it because the heat developing in the bottom is extinguished by the water? And this is why things that can be melted do not melt, if some liquid is thrown in.[5]

6.[6] Why does water not boil over to the same extent in winter and in summer, not only when it is heated to the same extent but even more, and both when it is hot to the same extent and still more? Is it because boiling over is the tossing up of bubbles? Now the water itself is heated no less at this time than in summer, but the bubbles are not able to rise to the same extent because the surrounding air is cold, but they rise smaller in size being compressed by the cold, and they soon burst when the air breaks through them. So they become less both in bulk and in number in winter, but in summer it is the opposite. Now boiling over occurs because of the number and the size of the foam.[7]

7.[8] Why does hot water cause wrinkling, but fire, which is hot, does not? Is it because fire produces breath, and so

[5] I translate Barnes's emendation, which is based on Gaza. The mss. reading would be rendered "unless a noise occurs," which seems to make no sense (but cf. the opening of Thphr. *Ign*. 68, which refers to the noise made when a fire is extinguished by water). If the mss. reading is correct, then *Pr.* 24.5 was probably longer originally.

[6] Source: Thphr. *Ign*. 16.

[7] I.e., the number and size of the bubbles that make up the foam.

[8] Cf. *Pr.* 24.10.

ὀγκοῖ; περιτείνεται γὰρ τὸ δέρμα. ἡ δὲ κάμψις ῥυτίς ἐστιν.

8. Διὰ τί τῶν ἀγγείων οἱ πυθμένες θερμαινομένου τοῦ ὕδατος, ἕως ἂν ᾖ ψυχρὸν τὸ ὕδωρ, θερμότεροί
15 εἰσιν; ἢ | διότι ψυχροῦ μὲν ἔτι ὄντος τοῦ ὕδατος ἐγκατακλείεται τὸ θερμὸν καὶ ἀντιπεριίσταται εἴσω, κωλυόμενον ἐξιέναι, ὅταν δὲ διαθερμανθῇ τὸ ἐνὸν ὕδωρ, οὐκέτι ἀποστέγοντος ἀλλὰ διαπνέοντος καὶ ἐλάττονος γινομένου τοῦ πυρὸς[4] ψυχρότερος γίνεται ὁ
20 πυθμήν, ὁμοίως ὥσπερ καὶ τὰ βαλανεῖα; καὶ | γὰρ ταῦτα τοῦ χειμῶνος θερμότερα ἢ τοῦ θέρους διὰ τὸ ἐγκατακλείεσθαι τὸ θερμὸν ἐν τῷ χειμῶνι μᾶλλον ἢ ἐν τῷ θέρει ὑπὸ τοῦ περιέχοντος ἀέρος ὄντος ψυχροῦ.

9. Διὰ τί τὸ μὲν ὕδωρ ζέον οὐκ ἐκπαφλάζει, τὸ δὲ ἔτνος καὶ ἡ φακῆ; καίτοι κουφότερον τὸ ὕδωρ τούτων,
25 τὰ | δὲ κοῦφα ῥᾷον ῥῖψαι πόρρω. ποιεῖ δὲ καὶ τὸ ἀργύριον ταὐτό, καὶ τοῦτο καθαιρόμενον· διὸ οἱ ἐν τῷ ἀργυροκοπείῳ καλλύνοντες κερδαίνουσιν· τὸ γὰρ διαρριπτούμενον συγκαλλύνοντες λαμβάνουσι τὰ λείψανα. ἢ διότι ποιεῖ μὲν τὸν ἐκπαφλασμὸν τὸ θερμὸν
30 ἐξατμίζον καὶ βιαζόμενον τὰ | ἀντικρούοντα τῇ κατὰ φύσιν αὐτοῦ φορᾷ; τὸ μὲν οὖν ὕδωρ διὰ κουφότητα καὶ λεπτότητα οὐκ ἀποβιάζεται, ὥστε οὐκ ἀθροίζεται πολὺ θερμόν, ἀλλὰ πρὶν ἁλισθῆναι φθάνει διακόψαν τὸ ἀεὶ προσελθόν. τὰ δὲ ἔχοντα ἐν αὑτοῖς σῶμα, οἷον

[4] πυρὸς : fort. ὕδατος

causes swelling? For it stretches the skin all around.[9] But a wrinkle is the creasing (*of skin*).

8.[10] Why, when water is being heated, are the bottoms of vessels hotter while the water is cold? Is it because when the water is still cold the heat is enclosed and contained within (*the bottom of the vessel*),[11] being prevented from going out, but when the water inside becomes thoroughly hot, as the fire[12] no longer retains (*the heat*) but evaporates and becomes less, the bottom becomes colder, in the same way baths do as well? And in fact these are hotter in winter than in summer because the heat is enclosed more in winter than in summer by the surrounding air, which is cold.

9. Why does boiling water not burst out in bubbles, whereas pea soup and lentil soup do? And yet water is lighter than these, and it is easier to throw light things a distance. Silver too does the same thing, i.e., when it is being refined; this is why the cleaners in a silversmith's gain by it; for those who clean up what is scattered about take the remains. Or is it because the heat—vaporizing or forcing what counteracts its own natural movement—produces the bursting out in bubbles? Water, therefore, owing to its lightness and thinness, is not forced out, such that not much heat is collected, but before it gathers together, the heat continually coming in first cuts its way through. But with respect to the (*liquids*) that have body in them, like

[9] Or "the skin is stretched all around."

[10] Cf. *Pr.* 24.5 and [Arist./Alex.] *Sup.Pr.* 3.42.

[11] Following Kapetanaki and Sharples, [Arist./Alex.] *Sup.Pr.* p. 275.

[12] One might instead expect "the water," but such a reading has no mss. support.

35 τὰ ῥοφήματα ἢ ὁ ἄργυρος, διὰ βάρος τὸ | σωματοειδὲς ἔχοντα πολύ, καὶ ἀνταπωθοῦντα διὰ τὸ ἀποβιάζεσθαι, βίᾳ ἐξιόντος ἀποσφαιρίζεται ᾗ ἂν κρατήσῃ τὸ θερμόν· οὐ γὰρ δίεισι διὰ πυκνότητα, ἀλλὰ κρατεῖ, ἕως ἂν ὑπὸ τοῦ ἐπιρρέοντος θερμοῦ ἀπορριφθῇ. γίνεται δὲ πληγή, οὐκ ὦσις, διὰ τὸ ταχὺ φέρεσθαι τὸ θερμὸν κάτωθεν ἄνω. ||

937a 10. Διὰ τί τὰ μὲν ὀλίγον χρόνον ἐν τῷ θερμῷ βρεχόμενα ἀνοιδεῖ, τὰ δὲ πολὺν συμπίπτει καὶ γίνεται ῥυσά; ἢ διότι τὸ θερμὸν ἐκ τοῦ[5] πεπηγότος ὑγρὸν ποιεῖ, ἐκ δὲ ὑγροῦ πνεῦμα, τὰ δὲ πυκνὰ ἀραιοῖ; τὸ μὲν 5 οὖν πρῶτον θερμαῖνον | τὰ πεπηγότα ὑγρότερα ποιεῖ, καὶ ἐξ ὑγρῶν πνευματοποιοῦν ὀγκηρὰ ποιεῖ διαχέον· ὅταν δὲ μᾶλλον θερμαίνῃ, τὸ πέριξ ἀραιὸν ποιεῖ, ὥστε ἀποπνεῖται ἡ ἀτμίς, καὶ τὸ ὑγρὸν ξηραινόμενον συμπίπτειν ποιεῖ τοὺς ὄγκους. συμπιπτόντων δὲ ῥυσοῦται 10 τὸ πέριξ δέρμα πάντων. ᾗ δὲ ἀνωμάλως, | ταύτῃ ῥυσὸν γίνεται.

11. Διὰ τί ὑπὸ τῶν θερμῶν ὑδάτων μᾶλλον ἢ ὑπὸ τῶν ψυχρῶν πήγνυνται λίθοι; πότερον ὅτι τῇ τοῦ ὑγροῦ ἐκλείψει γίνεται λίθος, μᾶλλον δὲ ὑπὸ τοῦ θερμοῦ ἢ τοῦ ψυχροῦ ἐκλείπει τὸ ὑγρόν, καὶ ἀπολι15 θοῦται δὴ διὰ τὸ θερμόν, καθάπερ | καὶ Ἐμπεδοκλῆς φησὶ τάς τε πέτρας καὶ τοὺς λίθους διὰ[6] τὰ θερμὰ τῶν

[5] τοῦ Xᵃ : om. cett. codd.
[6] διὰ Forster : καὶ codd.

gruel[13] or silver, having a lot of bodily material owing to their weight, and counterthrusting by applying force, the heat—exiting with force—forms bubbles (*in such liquids*) wherever it achieves mastery; for owing to their density it cannot pass through them, but (*the density*) achieves mastery, until it is thrown off by the inrush of heat; and a blow occurs, not a thrust,[14] owing to the heat quickly traveling upward.

10.[15] Why do things steeped in hot water for a short time swell, whereas things steeped for a long time collapse and become wrinkled? Is it because the heat produces moisture from what is solidified, and breath from moisture, and makes porous what is dense? Therefore, what produces heat at first makes the solidified things moister, and producing breath from moisture it spreads and makes them bulky; but when it heats them more, it makes the outside porous, so that the vapor blows off, and the moist becoming dry causes their bulk to collapse. Now when anything collapses, the outside skin wrinkles. And where it is uneven, there wrinkles form.

11.[16] Why are stones solidified by hot water more[17] than by cold? Is it because a stone is formed by the departure of moisture, and moisture departs more under the influence of heat than of cold, and in fact there is petrifaction through heat, just as Empedocles says[18] that both rocks and stones are formed through hot waters? Or does heat

[13] Likely any thick liquid food, such as pea soup or porridge.
[14] I.e., not a gradual application of pressure, but a sudden strike. [15] Cf. *Pr.* 24.7.
[16] Cf. Thphr. *Lap.* 3 and *Ign.* 46.
[17] Or "rather." [18] 31A69 D–K.

ὑδάτων γίνεσθαι; ἢ τὸ θερμὸν ἀπολιθοῖ, καὶ ὑπὸ τοῦ ψυχροῦ δὲ λιθοῦται διὰ τὸ τὴν ὑπερβολὴν τοῦ πάγου τὸ ὑγρὸν ἀναλίσκουσαν σκληρύνειν; δῆλον οὖν ἐκ τῆς ὑπερβολῆς καὶ τὸ ἁπλῶς. |

20 12. Διὰ τί ἐν τῷ θερμῷ ὕδατι ἐὰν τὸν πόδα ἔχῃ τις, ἠρεμοῦντος μὲν ἧσσον δοκεῖ εἶναι θερμόν, ἐὰν δὲ κινηθῇ, θερμότερον; ἢ ὥσπερ καὶ ἐπὶ τοῦ σώματος, ἐὰν ἐν τῷ πνεύματι τροχάζῃ τις; ἀεὶ ὁ προϊστάμενος ἀὴρ ψυχρότερος, εἰς δὲ τὸ πορρώτερον εἰσιὼν[7] μᾶλλον αἰσθάνεται. |

25 13. Διὰ τί ἐν τῷ ἡλίῳ μᾶλλον ἢ τῇ σκιᾷ τὰ θερμὰ ψύχεται; πότερον ὅτι τὸ θερμὸν τὸ ἔλαττον ὑπὸ τοῦ πλείονος φθείρεται; ἢ ὅτι ἐν μὲν τῇ σκιᾷ τὸ ψυχρὸν περιεστηκὸς θλίβει τὸ ἐνὸν θερμὸν καὶ οὐκ ἐᾷ ἐπεξιέναι, ὅπερ[8] καὶ τοῖς ἐκθνήσκουσι[9] ποιεῖ τὸ ψυχρὸν 30 προσχεόμενον; ἐγκατακλείει | γὰρ τὸ θερμὸν καὶ κωλύει ἐξιέναι· καὶ ὅλως τοῦ χειμῶνος ἅπασι συμβαίνει τὰ ἔσωθεν θερμότερα· ἐν δὲ τῷ ἡλίῳ οὐδενὸς ἀντιφράττοντος φέρεται καὶ θᾶττον ἀπολείπει.

14. Διὰ τί τὸ ἐν τῷ ἡλίῳ θερμαινόμενον ὕδωρ ὥστε 35 λούεσθαι | οὐκ ἔστιν ὑγιεινότερον; πότερον ὅτι διὰ τὸ ψύχεσθαι καὶ ἔτι ἐπὶ τῷ σώματι ὂν[10] φρίττειν ποιεῖ; ἢ ποιεῖ μὲν καὶ τοῦτο, ἀλλὰ κἂν πολλάκις λούηταί τις, νοσερόν ἐστιν; τὸ μὲν γὰρ θερμὸν ὅλως πεπτικόν ἐστι καὶ ξηραντικόν, τὸ δὲ ψυχρὸν σταλτικόν, ὥστε ἄμφω

[7] εἰσιὼν : ἀεὶ ἰὼν Bonitz [8] ὅπερ Y^a : ὥσπερ cett. codd.
[9] ἐκθνήσκουσι Bussemaker (cf. Thphr. *Ign.* 15,1 λειποψυχήσασι) : θνήσκουσι codd.

petrify, but there is also petrifaction under the influence of cold because the excess of frost uses up the moisture and hardens it? So it is clear from the excess that (*cold*) without qualification also (*petrifies*).

12.[19] Why, if one holds a foot in hot water, does it seems to be less hot when it stays still, but hotter if it is moved? Is it just like in the case of the body, if one runs in the wind? The air being encountered is always colder, and the farther one goes into it[20] the more one perceives (*the cold*).

13.[21] Why are hot things cooled more in the sun than in the shade? Is it because the lesser heat is destroyed by the greater? Or is it because in the shade the surrounding cold presses the inner heat and does not allow it to escape, the very thing the pouring of cold water produces in those who are fainting?[22] For it encloses the heat and prevents it going out; and generally, in all things it happens that in winter the inner parts are hotter; but in the sun, as there is no obstacle against it, it travels and quickly departs.

14.[23] Why is water being heated in the sun for washing not healthier? Is it because, owing to its cooling and also being on the body, it produces shivering? Or does it produce this too, but also if one washes in it often, it causes disease? For in general what is hot promotes concoction and drying, whereas what is cold promotes constriction,

[19] Cf. *Pr.* 5.36 and 38.6.
[20] I.e., the longer one runs against the wind.
[21] Source: Thprh. *Ign.* 15. [22] Or "dying" if we follow the mss. reading. [23] Cf. *Pr.* 24.15.

---

[10] ἐπὶ τῷ σώματι ὄν Forster ex Gaza : ἐπεὶ τὸ σωμάτιον codd.

937b ποιεῖ τι ἀγαθόν. διὸ καὶ ‖ τὸ ὕδωρ καὶ τὸ ψυχρὸν λουομένοις καὶ τὸ θερμὸν τὸ ὑπὸ τοῦ πυρὸς χρήσιμον· τὸ δὲ ὑπὸ τοῦ ἡλίου διὰ τὴν ἀσθένειαν τῆς θερμότητος οὐδέτερον τούτων ποιεῖ, ἀλλὰ ὑγραίνει ὥσπερ τὸ τῆς σελήνης φῶς. |

5 15. Διὰ τί τὸ ἐν τῷ ἡλίῳ θερμανθὲν ὕδωρ οὐκ ἀγαθόν; ἢ ὅτι τὰ ψυχόμενα ῥιγοῦν ποιεῖ;

16. Διὰ τί τὰ ἐν Μαγνησίᾳ καὶ τὰ ἐν Ἀταρνεῖ θερμὰ πότιμά ἐστιν; ἢ διότι ἐμβάλλει ὕδωρ πλεῖον ἀπορρέοντι τῷ θερμῷ, οὗ ἡ μὲν ἁλμυρότης ἀφανί-
10 ζεται, ἡ δὲ θερμότης | διαμένει;

17. Διὰ τί ἐν Μαγνησίᾳ τὰ θερμὰ τοῦ μὲν θερμὰ εἶναι ἐπαύσατο, ἁλμυρὸν δὲ ἦν τὸ ὕδωρ; ἢ πλεῖον ἐπεχύθη ἅμα ψυχρὸν ἐπὶ τὰς πηγὰς ἀλλότριον, καὶ ἐναπέσβεσε τὴν θερμότητα; ἡ δὲ γῆ ἁλμυρὰ μὲν ἦν,
15 θερμὴ δὲ οὔ, διὰ τὸ | πλῆθος τοῦ ὕδατος τοῦ ἐμβάλλοντος. ὅμοιον οὖν συνέβη τῷ διὰ τῆς τέφρας ὕδατι ἠθουμένῳ· καὶ γὰρ τοῦτο διὰ θέρμης ἠθούμενον ἐκείνην μὲν καταψύχει, καὶ αὐτὸ ψυχρὸν γίνεται, ἁλμυρόν τε[11] καὶ πικρὸν διὰ τὴν τέφραν ἐστίν. ἐπεὶ δὲ τὸ προσιὸν ἠλλοτριωμένον ἐστί, δι' ἄλλην αἰτίαν ἐκρά-
20 τησεν | ἡ θερμότης ἐνοῦσα ἐν τῇ γῇ τῆς ψυχρότητος τοῦ ὕδατος δι' ὀλιγότητα, καὶ ἐγένετο πάλιν θερμά.

[11] τε : δὲ Cᵃ

---

[24] Plu. *QC* 3.10 (*Mor.* 657F–59D), which asks why flesh rots more quickly in moonlight than in sunlight, discusses the pur-

such that both produce something good. And this is why water—both cold, and hot from the fire—are useful to those who are washing; but water heated by the sun, owing to the weakness of the heat, produces neither of these goods, but moistens as does the light of the moon.[24]

15.[25] Why is water heated in the sun not good? Is it because what is cooling produces chills?

16.[26] Why are the hot waters in Magnesia and Atarneus fresh?[27] Is it because more water comes into the hot water flowing off, of which the saltiness disappears, while the heat remains?

17. Why did the hot waters in Magnesia cease to be hot, whereas the water continued to be salty?[28] Did more cold water from elsewhere pour into the springs at the same time, and extinguish the heat? Now the earth was salty, but not hot, owing to the amount of incoming water. A similar thing happens to water filtered through ashes; for this water filtering through hot ashes cools them down and itself becomes cold, and also salty and bitter owing to the ashes. But when the added water had become altered, for a different reason the heat present in the earth mastered the coldness of the water owing to its small amount, and the waters again became hot.

ported moistening effect of moonlight and refers to a number of ancient sources.

[25] Cf. *Pr.* 24.14.

[26] Possible sources for *Pr.* 24.16–18 are Arist. *Mete.* 359b4–26 and Thphr. *On Waters* frs. 212–14C FHSG.

[27] Or "drinkable."

[28] This contradicts *Pr.* 24.16. As Hett notes *ad loc.*, "This is an unsatisfactory Problem."

18. Διὰ τί τὰ ὅλα τῶν θερμῶν ὑδάτων ἁλμυρά; ἢ διότι τὰ πολλὰ διὰ γῆς ἠθεῖται στυπτηριώδους (δηλοῖ δὲ ἡ ὀσμὴ αὐτῶν) κεκαυμένης δέ; ἡ δὲ τέφρα πάντων
25 ἁλμυρὰ καὶ | θείου ὄζει. διὸ καὶ συγκάει οὕτως ὥσπερ ὁ κεραυνός. πολλὰ οὖν θερμά ἐστιν ἀπὸ ἐπισημάνσεως κεραυνῶν.

19. Διὰ τί τὰ θερμὰ λουτρὰ ἱερά; ἢ ὅτι ἀπὸ τῶν ἱερωτάτων γίνονται, θείου καὶ κεραυνοῦ;

18. Why are the totality of hot waters salty? Is it because the majority are filtered through alum-rich earth (their smell proves this) and have been burned? Now the ashes of anything are salty and smell of sulfur. And this is why the way it burns[29] is just like a lightning bolt. In fact, many of these waters are hot from the stroke of lightning bolts.

19. Why are hot bathing places sacred? Is it because they come from two very sacred things, sulfur and lightning bolt?

[29] I.e., the way the earth burns the water.

BOOK XXV

INTRODUCTION

The background to Book 25 is Peripatetic meteorology, and possible sources for some of its chapters are Aristotle's *Meteorology*, Theophrastus' *Meteorology* and *On Wind*, and Strato's *On the Void*.

The main topic is air as it is connected to the weather, including (though not primarily) wind: see chs. 2, 4–7, 14–16, 18–19, 21–22. Other topics are air and water—either their interactions or the contrast between them (3, 10–12, 20), the properties of inflated and deflated wineskins (1, 8, 13, 17), and air and putrefaction (17 and 20). *Pr.* 25.9 raises and attempts to answer the question "Why does air, which is thicker than light, pass through solid things?"

ΟΣΑ ΠΕΡΙ ΤΟΝ ΑΕΡΑ

937b30 1. Διὰ τί ἐν τοῖς ἀσκοῖς τοῖς πεφυσημένοις ἐναπολαμβανόμενα τὰ μέλη πόνον παρέχει; πότερον διὰ τὴν πίεσιν τοῦ ἀέρος; ὥσπερ γὰρ οὐδὲ τοῖς ἔξωθεν πιέζουσι τὸν ἀσκὸν ἐνδίδωσιν ὁ ἀήρ, ἀλλ' ἀπωθεῖ,
35 οὕτω καὶ τὰ ἐντὸς ἐναπολαμβανόμενα | θλίβει ὁ ἀήρ. ἢ διότι βίᾳ κατέχεται καὶ πεπίληται; ἔξω οὖν πάντῃ ὁρμῶν κατὰ φύσιν προσαπερείδεται πρὸς τὸ ἐντὸς ἀπειλημμένον σῶμα.

2. Διὰ τί ἐν τοῖς ἕλεσι τοῖς παρὰ τοὺς ποταμοὺς γίνονται οἱ καλούμενοι βούμυκοι, οὓς μυθολογοῦσι
938a ταύρους ἱεροὺς || εἶναι[1] τοῦ θεοῦ; ἔστι δὲ τὸ γινόμενον ψόφος ὅμοιος φωνῇ ταύρου, ὥστε αἱ βόες οὕτω διατίθενται ἀκούουσαι ὥσπερ ταύρου μυκωμένου. ἢ ὅτι ὅσοι ποταμοὶ λιμνάζουσιν εἰς ἕλη, [ἢ ὅσα ἕλη λιμνά-
5 ζονται][2] ἢ ὑπὸ θαλάττης ἀντικρούονται, ἢ τὸ | πνεῦμα ἀφιᾶσιν ἀθροώτερον, ἐν τοῖς τοιούτοις γίνεται τοῦτο; αἴτιον δὲ ὅτι αἱ κοιλίαι τῆς γῆς γίνονται. οὕτως οὖν

[1] εἶναι : ἀφεῖναι vel ἀφιέναι Bonitz (cf. *Mete*. 368a24 ἀφίησι) : ἱέναι Ross apud Forster

[2] [ἢ ὅσα ἕλη λιμνάζονται] Forster

PROBLEMS CONNECTED WITH AIR

1.[1] Why do limbs enclosed in inflated wineskins produce pain? Is it due to the pressure of the air? For just as the air does not give in to outside pressure on the wineskin, but pushes back, so too the air exerts pressure on what is enclosed in it. Or is it because the air is held fast by force and compressed? Therefore, naturally moving outward in every direction it presses against the enclosed body.

2.[2] Why in marshes near rivers do the so-called "ox bellowings" occur, which they say in myth are the sacred bulls of the god? Now what occurs is a noise similar to the sound from a bull, so that cows are affected in the way they are when they hear a bull bellowing.[3] Or is it that those rivers stagnating into marshes [or those marshes becoming stagnant], or those resisted by the sea, or those discharging a very large quantity of wind—this occurs in such places? The reason is that hollows in the earth are formed. There-

[1] See Hp. *Art.* 77 and *Mochl.* 25.

[2] See *Mete.* 2.8, and the opening of Thphr. *Mete.* (Daiber p. 261).

[3] See [Arist.] *Mu.* 396a11–16.

κλυζόμενον τὸ ὕδωρ, διὰ τὸ ἐνεῖναι ῥεῦμα ἐν τῇ τοιαύτῃ λιμνασίᾳ, ἀπωθεῖται τὸν ἀέρα διὰ στενοῦ εἰς εὐρυτέραν κοιλίαν, οἷον εἴ τις εἰς ἀμφορέα κενὸν κατὰ
10 τὸ στόμιον ποιοῖ | ψόφον, μυκήματι ὅμοιον γίνεται· καὶ γὰρ ἡ μύκησις διὰ τοῦτο γίνεται τὸ σχῆμα τοῖς βουσίν. πολλὰς δὲ καὶ ἀτόπους φωνὰς ποιοῦσι τὰ σχήματα τῶν κοιλιῶν ἀνώμαλα ὄντα, ἐπεὶ καὶ ἀμφορέως τὸν πύνδακα ἐάν τις ἀφελὼν διὰ τοῦ πυθμένος τρίβῃ ἕλκων ἔσω καὶ ἔξω, [εἰ τρίψει διὰ τοῦ κατα-
15 δήματος][3] | ψόφον ποιεῖ, ὥστε φεύγειν τὰ θηρία, ὅταν οἱ ὀπωροφύλακες κατασκευάσωσιν αὐτό.

3. Διὰ τί ὁ ἀὴρ οὐχ ὑγρός, ἁπτόμενος τοῦ ὕδατος; τῶν γὰρ ἄλλων οὐθὲν ὅ τι οὐχ ὑγρόν, ἂν ἅψηται. ἢ διότι τὸ ἔσχατον αὐτῶν ἅμα, τὸ δὲ ἐπίπεδον ἑκατέρου
20 [οὐχ][4] ἕτερον; | τὰ μὲν οὖν ἄλλα βαρύτερα, ὁ δὲ ἀὴρ οὐ ῥέπει κατωτέρω τοῦ ἐσχάτου. ἅπτεται μὲν οὖν, ὅτι οὐθὲν μεταξύ, οὐ βρέχεται δέ, ὅτι ἀεὶ ἄνωθεν τοῦ ὕδατος.

4. Διὰ τί μέσων νυκτῶν καὶ μεσημβρίας μάλιστα εὐδία γίνεται; ἢ διότι ἡ νηνεμία ἐστὶν ἀέρος στάσις,
25 ἕστηκε | δὲ μάλιστα, ὅταν κρατῇ ἢ κρατῆται, μαχόμενος δὲ κινεῖται; κρατεῖ μὲν οὖν μάλιστα μέσων νυκτῶν, κρατεῖται δὲ μεσημβρίας· τότε μὲν γὰρ ὁ

[3] [εἰ τρίψει διὰ τοῦ καταδήματος] Forster : *fonum per intercapedinem* Gaza : fort. ἐν τρίψει διὰ τοῦ κατάγματος Flashar (cf. Forster n. ad loc)

[4] [οὐχ] Richards

fore, as the water washes in, because of the flow going into stagnant waters of this kind, it pushes back the air through a narrow passage into a wider hollow, just as if one produced a noise through the opening into an empty vessel, generating something like bellowing; and indeed bellowing in oxen occurs through this shape. Now the shapes of hollows that are irregular produce many strange sounds, since if one takes off the base[4] of a vessel and rubs it through the bottom drawing it in and out, [if one will rub intermittently] one produces a noise, such as to make beasts flee, when orchard guards do this.

3.[5] Why is the air not moist, when it comes into contact with water? For none of the other things do not become moist, if it comes into contact with water. Is it because the limit of these[6] are at the same place, but the surface of each is distinct? So while the other things are heavier, the air does not sink below the limit of the water. It therefore comes into contact with it, because nothing is between them, but the air does not become wet, because it is always above the water.

4.[7] Why does fair weather occur most often at midnight and midday? Is it because calm is a stillness of air, and air is at a standstill most when it achieves mastery or is mastered, but when struggling it is in motion? Now it achieves mastery most at midnight, and is mastered most at midday;

[4] Translators often render *πύνδακα* here "lid," though its standard meaning is certainly "base." The latter makes sense, however, if the author is referring to a vessel with a narrow opening and with the base removed. Some object (likely the base itself) is then rubbed up and down the interior of the vessel to produce a sound.

[5] Cf. *Pr.* 25.10.

[6] I.e., the air and the water.

[7] Source: Thphr. *Vent.*18.

ἥλιος πορρωτάτω, τότε δὲ ἐγγυτάτω γίνεται. ἔτι ἄρχεται τὰ πνεύματα ἢ περὶ ἕω ἢ περὶ δυσμάς, λήγει δὲ
30 τὸ μὲν ἕωθεν, ὅταν κρατηθῇ, τὸ | δὲ ἀπὸ δυσμῶν, ὅταν παύσηται κρατῶν. συμβαίνει οὖν τὰ μὲν μεσημβρίας παύεσθαι, τὰ δὲ μέσων νυκτῶν.

5. Διὰ τί ὑποφωσκούσης ἕω καὶ ἤδη πρωῒ μᾶλλόν ἐστι ψῦχος ἢ τῆς νυκτός, ἐγγυτέρω ὄντος τοῦ ἡλίου ἡμῶν; ἢ ὅτι πρὸς ἡμέραν δρόσος καὶ πάχνη πίπτει,
35 ταῦτα δ' ἐστι | ψυχρά; ὥσπερ οὖν ῥανθέντος τοῦ παντὸς τόπου ὑγρῷ ψυχρῷ γίνεται κατάψυξις.

6. Διὰ τί ἐν τῷ Πόντῳ καὶ ψύχη μάλιστα καὶ πνίγη; ἢ διὰ τὴν παχύτητα τοῦ ἀέρος; τοῦ μὲν γὰρ χειμῶνος οὐ δύναται διαθερμαίνεσθαι, τοῦ δὲ θέρους,[5] ὅταν
938b θερμανθῇ, || κάει διὰ τὴν παχύτητα. ἡ δὲ αὐτὴ αἰτία καὶ διότι τὰ ἑλώδη τοῦ μὲν χειμῶνος ψυχρά, τοῦ δὲ θέρους θερμά. ἢ διὰ τὴν τοῦ ἡλίου φοράν; τοῦ μὲν γὰρ χειμῶνος πόρρω γίνεται, τοῦ δὲ θέρους ἐγγύς. |

5 7. Διὰ τί τῆς νυκτὸς αἰθρία μᾶλλον ἢ μεθ' ἡμέραν; ἢ καὶ τοῦ πνεύματος καὶ τῆς ταραχῆς ὁ ἥλιος αἴτιος; ταῦτα γὰρ κινήσεώς τινος γενομένης συμβαίνει γίνεσθαι. αἴτιον τοίνυν τὸ θερμόν. ὅταν οὖν τοῦτο μὴ παρῇ, ἠρεμεῖ τὸ πᾶν, καὶ αἰρομένου τοῦ ἡλίου μᾶλλον
10 ἢ τοὐναντίον· καὶ | τὸ "μή ποτ' ἀπ' ἠπείρου"[6] τοῦτ'

[5] δὲ θέρους : θέρους δὲ Y^a C^a

[6] "μή ποτ' ἀπ' ἠπείρου", cf. *Pr.* 26.57, 947a7–8 ("μή ποτ' ἀπ' ἠπείρου δείσῃς νέφος ἀλλ' ἀπὸ πόντου χειμῶνος, θέρεος δὲ ἀπ' ἠπείροιο μελαίνης").

for at the one time the sun is farthest away, while at the other it is nearest. Further, the winds begin either about dawn or about dusk, and the dawn wind abates when it is mastered, and the wind that begins at dusk abates when it stops achieving mastery. So as a result, the former winds stop at midday, and the latter at midnight.

5.[8] Why, when dawn is breaking and it is still early morning, is it colder than at night, although the sun is nearer to us? Is it because dew and frost fall toward daybreak, and these are cold? So when as it were the whole place is sprinkled with cold moisture, cooling occurs.

6.[9] Why do both extreme cold and stifling heat occur in the Pontus? Is it owing to the density of the air? For in the winter it cannot be thoroughly heated,[10] and in summer, when it is heated, it burns because of its density. And this same reason too is why marshy places are cold in winter, but hot in summer. Or is it because of the movement of the sun? For in the winter it is far away, whereas in the summer it is near.

7.[11] Why is there clear sky more at night than during the day? Is the sun also the cause of wind and turbulence? For these things occur when some movement occurs. The heat, therefore, is the cause. So when heat is not present, everything is still, and this is more the case when the sun is rising than when it's doing the opposite; and the saying "Do not (*fear a cloud*) from the mainland . . ."[12] means that

[8] Cf. *Pr.* 25.15 and 8.17. [9] Cf. *Pr.* 14.13.

[10] I.e., the air cannot be thoroughly heated because of its density. [11] Cf. *Pr.* 26.57 and Thphr. *Vent.* 60.

[12] The full proverb is given in *Pr.* 26.57: "Do not fear a cloud from the mainland in winter but from the open sea, and in summer from the dark mainland" (947a7–8; cf. Thphr. *Vent.* 60).

ἐστίν, ὅτι οὗ πλείστη κίνησις, ἐκεῖ ἥκιστα ἄν τι μένοι καὶ συσταίη, μὴ ὁμαλοῦ ὄντος καὶ κρατοῦντος τοῦ συνισταμένου. τοῦ μὲν δὴ χειμῶνος ἡ θάλαττα τοιοῦτον, τοῦ δὲ θέρους ἡ γῆ.

8. Διὰ τί, ὅταν διαχυθῇ τὸ ὑγρὸν εἰς ἀσκούς, οὐ
15 μόνον | τὸ ὑγρὸν δέχεται ὁ πίθος μετὰ τῶν ἀσκῶν, ἀλλὰ καὶ ἄλλο προσλαμβάνει; ἢ ὅτι ἐν τῷ ὑγρῷ ἐνυπάρχει ὁ ἀήρ; οὗτος οὖν ὅταν μὲν[7] ἐν τῷ πίθῳ ἐνῇ, οὐ δύναται ἐκκρίνεσθαι διὰ τὸ μέγεθος τοῦ πίθου· ἐκ γὰρ τοῦ μείζονος χαλεπώτερον ἐκθλῖψαι ὁτιοῦν καὶ
20 ὑγρὸν καὶ πνεῦμα, ὥσπερ καὶ ἐκ τῶν | σπόγγων. ὅταν δὲ μερίζηται εἰς μικρά, ἐκθλίβεται ἐκ τοῦ ἀσκοῦ μετὰ τοῦ ἐνόντος, ὥσθ' ἡ τοῦ ἀέρος χώρα κενὴ γίνεται· διὸ καὶ τοὺς ἀσκοὺς καὶ ἔτι ἄλλο ὑγρὸν δέχεται ὁ πίθος. καὶ μᾶλλον ἐπὶ τοῦ οἴνου τοῦτο γίνεται, ὅτι πλείων ἀὴρ ἐν τῷ οἴνῳ ἔνεστιν ἢ ἐν τῷ ὕδατι. ὅμοιον δὲ τούτῳ
25 καὶ τὸ | ταὐτὸ ἀγγεῖον τήν τε κονίαν καὶ τὸ ὕδωρ χωρεῖν ἅμα, ὅσον ἑκάτερον χωρὶς ἐγχεόμενον. ἔοικε γὰρ πολλὰ εἶναι τὰ διάκενα τῆς τέφρας. ἅτε οὖν λεπτότερον τὸ ὕδωρ διαδύνει μᾶλλον καὶ συσσάττει ἤδη ὥστε πυκνοῦσθαι, καὶ[8] διὰ τὸ παρ' ἕκαστον τῶν
30 μερῶν εἶναι τὴν σάξιν (μᾶλλον γὰρ | σάττεται κατὰ μικρὸν σαττόμενον ἅπαν ἢ ἀθρόον), τούτου δὲ γινομένου ὑποκαταβαίνειν τὴν κονίαν· ἅμα δὲ καὶ ἡ τέφρα εἰς αὑτὴν δέχεται τὸ ὑγρὸν διὰ τὸ ἔχειν κοιλίας. ἡ δὲ

[7] μὲν Bussemaker ex Gaza : μὴ plur. codd. : om. B x A^m D
[8] καὶ secl. Forster

where motion is greatest, there least of all would something remain the same and be stable—that which causes stability not being uniform nor gaining mastery. Indeed, the sea is in such a state in the winter, whereas the land is in summer.

8.[13] Why, when liquid is poured into wineskins, does the jar receive not only the liquid with the wineskins, but it also takes in something else besides? Is it because air is present in the liquid? So when this[14] is in the jar, it cannot be given off owing to the size of the jar; for it is more difficult to press out anything, liquid or air, from what is large, just as it is from sponges as well. But when it is distributed into smaller parts, it is pressed out of the wineskin with what is inside, so that the space containing the air becomes empty; and this is why the jar holds the (*content of the*) wineskins and other liquid as well. This occurs even more in the case of wine, because there is more air in wine than in water. And similar to this too, the same vessel can contain as much ash and water together as it can of each poured in separately. For there seem to be many empty spaces in ash. Therefore, as the water is lighter, it slips into the ash more and then packs it together, so that it becomes dense, indeed because the packing is by each of the parts individually (for anything being packed little by little becomes more packed than if it happens all at once), and when this happens the ash settles down; and at the same time the ash also receives the liquid into itself because it

[13] For the opening, cf. [Arist./Alex.] *Sup.Pr.* 3.11. The entire chapter is extremely obscure. A possible source is *Phys.* 4.6.

[14] Either air or liquid, but which is unclear.

βαλλομένη τέφρα εἰς τὸ ὕδωρ θερμὴ οὖσα τέμνει αὐτὸ καὶ ἐξαεροῖ. καὶ πρότερον δὲ ὕδατος ἐγχυθέντος καὶ
35 ὕστερον | κονίας ἐμπιπτούσης τὸ αὐτὸ γίνεται, ὥστε καὶ τὸ ὕδωρ ἔχοι ἂν κοιλίας καὶ διάκενα αὐτὸ ἐν αὑτῷ. ἢ οὐ τὸ ὕδωρ τὸ δεχόμενον τὴν κονίαν, ἀλλ' ἡ κονία τὸ ὕδωρ; τὸ γὰρ λεπτομερέστερον εἰκὸς εἶναι τὸ εἰσιόν. ἔτι καὶ ἐκ τῆς πείρας δῆλον. ὅταν γὰρ ἐπιπάττηται ἡ
939a τέφρα, καθ' ὃν ἂν || τόπον ἐπιπάττηται, εἰς τοῦτον συρρεῖ τὸ ἄλλο[9] ὕδωρ· ἔδει δὲ τὸ ἐναντίον, εἴπερ ἦν τὸ ὕδωρ τὸ δεχόμενον. ἢ οὐ συμβαίνει τοῦτο, ἐὰν πρότερον ἐγχυθῇ τὸ ὕδωρ καὶ σφόδρα διαμεστώσῃ; ἀλλ'
5 ἐὰν ὁτιοῦν ἐπιβληθῇ, ὑπερχεῖται. ἐὰν δ' | ἅπαξ ὑπερχυθῇ καὶ ἐπιπέσῃ ἡ τέφρα, ἤδη συμβαίνει· ἡ γὰρ τέφρα ἦν δεχομένη. ταὐτὸ δὲ τοῦτο καὶ ὅτι οἱ βόθυνοι τὴν ἐκβληθεῖσαν ἐξ αὐτῶν γῆν οὐ δέχονται· ἔοικε γὰρ δὴ ἀήρ τις προκαταλαμβάνων τὸν τόπον καὶ διὰ τοῦτο μὴ δέχεσθαι. |

10 9. Διὰ τί ὁ ἀὴρ παχύτερος ὢν τοῦ φωτὸς διέρχεται διὰ τῶν στερεῶν; ἢ διότι τὸ μὲν φῶς κατ' εὐθεῖαν φέρεται μόνον, διὸ καὶ διὰ τῶν ἀραιῶν οὐ διορᾷ ἡ ὄψις, οἷον κισήριδος; ἐπαλλάττουσι γὰρ οἱ πόροι· ἀλλ' οὐκ ἐν τῇ ὑάλῳ. ὁ δὲ ἀὴρ οὐ κωλύεται διὰ τὸ μὴ
15 εὐθυπορεῖν οὗ | διέρχεται.

[9] ἄλλο secl. Forster

---

[15] Hett's note *ad loc.*: "This Problem is not very clear, but it seems to mean that if a substance containing air spaces (e.g. ashes)

contains cavities. (But ash thrown into water that is hot cuts it and then dissipates.) Now when water is poured in first and ash falls in after, the same thing happens, so that the water too would have cavities and empty spaces in it. Or is the water not receiving the ash, but the ash the water? For it is likely that what has lighter parts is what does the entering. Further, this is also clear from the experiment. For when the ash is sprinkled, on whatever place it is sprinkled, to this the other water flows; but the opposite should happen, if the water were receiving the ash. Or does this not occur, if the water is poured in first and fills up (*the vessel*) completely? But if anything else is thrown in, it overflows. But if once it overflows and the ash falls in, then it happens; for the ash is receiving. Now this same thing also (*explains*) the fact that the trenches do not receive the earth thrown out of them; for some air seems to occupy the space and because of this it is not received.[15]

9.[16] Why does air, which is thicker than light, pass through solid things? Is it because light travels only in a straight line, and this is why sight cannot see through porous things, like a pumice stone? For the passages overlap; but they do not in the case of glass. But air is not hindered, because it does not go straight through that which it passes.

is put into a vessel and water poured in afterwards, the water will replace the air and thus ashes + water will take up no more room than ashes alone. If the water is put in first, and then ashes, the water will overflow because the ashes will carry air down with them, but afterwards the air will escape and the whole subside."

[16] Cf. *Pr.* 11.49 and 58, and Strato frs. 28A–30 Sharples.

10. Διὰ τί ὁ ἀὴρ ψυχρὸς μὲν γίνεται διὰ τὸ ἅπτεσθαι τοῦ ὕδατος, δίυγρος δὲ οὔ, κἂν σφόδρα τις φυσᾷ εἰς τὸ ὕδωρ ὥστε κυμαίνειν; ὅτι δὲ ψυχρός, δηλοῖ μεθιστάμενος· ψύχει γὰρ <ὁ>[10] ἀπὸ τῶν ὑδάτων. ἢ ὅτι
20 ψυχρὸς μὲν πέφυκεν εἶναι | καὶ θερμός, ὥστε μεταβάλλει τῇ ἁφῇ οὗ ἄν τινος ἅπτηται, ὑγρὸς δὲ οὐκέτι διὰ τὸ κουφότερος εἶναι; καὶ οὐδέποτε εἰς τὸ βάθος τοῦ ὕδατος ἔρχεται, ἀλλ' ἀεὶ τοῦ ἐπιπέδου ἅπτεται, κἂν βιάζηται κάτω· καὶ τὸ ὕδωρ ἔτι κατωτέρω φέρεται, ὥστε μήποτε εἰς βάθος ἰέναι. |

25 11. Διὰ τί ὁ ἐκ τῶν πομφολύγων καὶ κάτωθεν ἀνιὼν οὐ διερὸς ἐξέρχεται; ἢ διότι οὐκ ἐπιμένει τὸ ὑγρόν, ἀλλ' ὀλισθαίνει τὸ ὕδωρ; τὸ δ' ἐπὶ τῇ πομφόλυγι καὶ ἔλαττόν ἐστιν ἢ ὥστε διερεῖν.[11]

12. Διὰ τί ὁ ἀὴρ οὐκ ἀναπίμπλησι, τὸ δὲ ὕδωρ; καὶ
30 εἰς | τὸν ἀέρα γὰρ μετατιθέμενον διερόν. ἢ ὅτι ὥσπερ οὐδὲ ὁ λίθος; οὐ γὰρ πᾶν ἐστὶν ἀναπληστικόν, ἀλλὰ τὸ γλίσχρον ἢ ὑγρόν.

13. . . . ἢ[12] ὅτι ὁ ἀὴρ ἄνω φέρεται; ὁ γὰρ ἀσκὸς ὅταν μὲν κενὸς ᾖ κάτω φέρεται, ὅταν δὲ φυσηθῇ, ἄνω
35 ἐπιμένει διὰ | τὸ τοῦτον ἀναφέρειν. εἰ δὲ ὁ ἀὴρ ἀνακουφίζει καὶ κωλύει κάτω φέρεσθαι, διὰ τί βαρύτεροι γίνονται φυσηθέντες; καὶ πῶς, ὅτε μὲν βαρύτερός ἐστιν, ἐπιμένει, κουφότερος δὲ γενόμενος καταφέρεται;

[10] <ὁ> Bonitz [11] διερεῖν Y^a Ap^b (*humectare* Barth., *humefacere* Gaza) : διαιρεῖν cett. codd.

[12] ante ἢ lac. indic. Ruelle, add. *Cur utres inflati valeant fluitare* Gaza : cap. 13 non vertit Barth.

10.[17] Why does air become cold by touching water, but not thoroughly moist, even if one blows hard into the water such that it makes waves? Now that it becomes cold is clear from the change it undergoes; for the air from water produces cold. Is it because air is by nature cold and hot, so that it changes through touch whatever it touches, but it is not moist because it is very light? And it never goes into the depth of water, but always touches its surface, even if forced downward; and the water travels lower still, so that the air never reaches its depth.

11. Why does the (*air*) from bubbles even rising from below not come out wet? Is it because the moisture does not remain on it, but the water slips off? And the water on a bubble is also not enough to make it wet.

12. Why doesn't air saturate, whereas water does? For even when transformed into air it is wet. Is it for the same reason as that for which a stone does not? For not everything is capable of saturating, but only what is viscous[18] or liquid.

13. . . .[19] Is it because air travels upward? For the skin, when it is empty, travels downward, but when it is inflated, it stays up because (*the air*) carries it upward. But if the air makes them lighter and prevents them from traveling downward, why are they heavier when they are inflated? And how does it stay up, when it is heavier, but when it is lighter it travels downward?

[17] Cf. *Pr.* 25.3.

[18] Elsewhere, γλίσχρον is translated "sticky."

[19] The opening question is missing from the text. Gaza supplies "Why are inflated skins able to float?"

14. Διὰ τί ὁ ἀὴρ οὐκ[13] ἄνω φέρεται; εἰ γὰρ τὰ
939b πνεύματα ‖ τούτου κινουμένου ὑπὸ τοῦ θερμοῦ γίνεται, πέφυκε δὲ τὸ πῦρ ἄνω φέρεσθαι, καὶ τὸ πνεῦμα εἰς τὸ ἄνω ἐβάδιζεν, εἴπερ τό τε κινοῦν εἰς τὸ ἄνω θεῖ καὶ τὸ κινούμενον οὕτω πέφυκε φέρεσθαι. νῦν δὲ φαίνεται λοξὴν τὴν φορὰν ποιούμενος. |

5 15. Διὰ τί τὸ ἀφ' ἕω ψυχρότερον ἢ τὸ ἀφ' ἑσπέρας; ἢ ὅτι τὸ μὲν ἐγγύτερον μέσων νυκτῶν, τὸ δὲ μεσημβρίας; ἔστι δὲ ἡ μεσημβρία θερμότατον διὰ τὸ εἶναι ἐγγύτατον ἡλίου, αἱ δὲ μέσαι νύκτες ψυχρότεραι[14] διὰ τὸ ἐναντίον.

16. Διὰ τί αἱ νύκτες τῶν ἡμερῶν ἐν ταῖς ἀλέαις
10 πνιγηρότεραι; | ἢ διὰ τὴν ἄπνοιαν; οἱ γὰρ ἐτησίαι καὶ πρόδρομοι τὰς νύκτας ἧττον πνέουσιν.

17. Διὰ τί τὰ ἐν τοῖς ἀσκοῖς ἄσηπτα φυσηθεῖσι, καὶ ἐν τοῖς περιπωματιζομένοις; ἢ διότι σήπεται μὲν κινούμενα, ἅπαντα δὲ τὰ πλήρη ἀκίνητα, ταῦτα δὲ πλήρη; |

15 18. Διὰ τί τῆς αἰθρίας μᾶλλον ψῦχος γίνεται ἢ ἐπινεφέλων ὄντων; τὰ δὲ ἄστρα καὶ ὁ οὐρανὸς θερμός. ἢ ὅτι οὐθὲν ἀποστέγει ἐν τῇ αἰθρίᾳ τὴν ἀτμίδα, ἀλλὰ διαχεῖται· ἐν δὲ τοῖς ἐπινεφέλοις ἀποστέγεται; καὶ βορείων γε ἢ νοτίων διὰ τὸ αὐτό· ὁ μὲν γὰρ νότος ἄγει

[13] ante *οὐκ* lac. indic. (et suppl. *ὑπὸ θερμοῦ κινουμένος* fort.) Ruelle [14] *ψυχρότεραι* : *ψυχρόταται* Forster

[20] Source: Thphr. *Vent*.22.

[21] This line contradicts the opening of the previous chapter.

14.[20] Why does air not travel upward?[21] For if the winds occur when the air is moved by heat, and fire by its nature travels upward, the wind too should go upward, since that which sets in motion runs upward and that which is moved travels by its nature in the same direction. But as it is, the air obviously produces a sideways movement.

15.[22] Why is it colder at dawn than at nightfall? Is it because the former is nearer to midnight, and the latter to midday? Now midday is warmest because it is nearer to the sun, whereas midnight is colder for the opposite reason.

16. Why are the nights more stifling than the days in hot weather? Is it because of the lack of wind? For the Etesian winds and the Forerunners[23] blow less at night.

17.[24] Why are things in inflated wineskins, and in vessels with their lids closed, not subject to putrefaction? Is it because things putrefy when they are in motion, but anything that is full is lacking in motion, and these are full?

18.[25] Why is it colder in clear weather than when it is cloudy? Yet the stars and the heavens are hot. Is it because in clear weather nothing contains the vapor, but it is diffused, whereas in cloudy weather it is contained? And for the same reason, it is colder when there are Boreas winds than when there are Notos winds: for the Notos wind attracts such things,[26] but the Boreas wind pushes them

Some editors suspect part of it is missing—something qualifying air, so that it originally read, for example, "Why does air *moved by heat* not travel upward?" [22] Cf. *Pr.* 25.5 and 8.17.

[23] The Forerunners precede the Etesian (literally, "annual") winds (see Thphr. *Vent.* 11).

[24] Cf. *Pr.* 22.4. [25] Cf. *Pr.* 25.21.

[26] I.e., clouds.

20 τὸ τοιοῦτον, ὁ δὲ | ἀπωθεῖ. καὶ ἀτμίζειν δὲ φαίνεται βορείοις μᾶλλον ἢ νοτίοις, καὶ χειμῶνος ἢ θέρους. ἢ παρὰ τὸ ἀνόμοιον; ἢ ὅτι θερμοῦ ψυχομένου ἐστὶν ἡ ἀτμίς;

19. Διὰ τί ἀὴρ ὁ ἐλάττων θερμότερος τοῦ πλείονος; αἱ γὰρ στενοχωρίαι ἀλεεινότεραι. ἢ διότι κινεῖται 25 μᾶλλον ὁ | πολύς, ἡ δὲ κίνησις ποιεῖ ψυχρόν; σημεῖον δὲ τούτου, ὅτι κινούμενα ψύχεται τὰ θερμά.

20. Διὰ τί ὕδωρ μὲν καὶ γῆ σήπεται, ἀὴρ δὲ καὶ πῦρ οὐ σήπεται; ἢ ὅτι θερμότερον[15] γίνεται τὸ σηπόμενον ἅπαν, πυρὸς δὲ οὐθὲν θερμότερον; ἢ ὅτι ψυχθῆναι δεῖ 30 πρότερον, | τὸ δὲ πῦρ ἀεὶ θερμόν, ὁ δὲ ἀὴρ πυρὸς πλήρης; σήπεται δὲ οὐθὲν θερμόν, ἀλλὰ ψυχθέν· γῆ δὲ καὶ ὕδωρ[16] καὶ θερμὰ καὶ ψυχρὰ γίνεται.

21. Διὰ τί τὰ ἐπινέφελα ἀλεεινότερα τῶν αἰθρίων; πότερον ὡς οἱ ἀρχαῖοι ἔλεγον, ὅτι τὰ ἄστρα ψυχρά; ἢ 35 λίαν | τοῦτό γε ἄτοπον, ἀλλὰ διότι ἀτμίζει; ἐπισημαντέον δὲ ὅτι ἐν νηνεμίᾳ ἡ δρόσος καὶ ἡ πάχνη γίνεται. ὅταν μὲν οὖν αἰθρία ᾖ, διαπνεῖ τὸ θερμόν, ὑφ' οὗ ἀνάγεται τὸ ὑγρόν, ὥστε ψυχρὸς ὁ ἀήρ· διὸ καὶ δροσίζει ἀφιέμενον τὸ ὑγρὸν ἀπὸ τοῦ θερμοῦ. ὅταν δὲ 940a ἐπινέφελον ᾖ, ἀποστέγεται, διὸ οὐ || γίνεται δρόσος οὐδὲ πάχνη ὄντων ἐπινεφέλων. περὶ οὖν τὴν γῆν ὑπομένον τὸ θερμὸν ποιεῖ τὴν ἀλέαν.

[15] θερμότερον Ap : θερμότατον cett. codd.
[16] καὶ ὕδωρ Ap : καὶ ὕδωρ καὶ ἀὴρ cett. codd.

back. And it also appears to evaporate more with Boreas winds than with Notos winds, and in winter than in summer. Or is it due to dissimilarity? Or is it because there is vapor when heat cools?

19.[27] Why is the smaller amount of air hotter than the larger? For confined spaces are warmer. Is it because the large amount is subject to more motion, and movement produces cold? Now a sign of this is the fact that hot things are cooled when they are moved.

20.[28] Why do water and earth become putrefied, whereas air and fire do not become putrefied? Is it because anything undergoing putrefaction becomes very hot, and nothing is hotter than fire? Or is it because ⟨*what becomes putrefied*⟩ must be cooled beforehand, and fire is always hot, and air is full of fire? Now nothing hot becomes putrefied, unless it has been cooled; and earth and water can become both hot and cold.

21.[29] Why is cloudy weather warmer than clear weather? Is it as the ancients said, because the stars are cold? Or is this very absurd, but it is in fact because ⟨*in clear weather*⟩ vapor is given off? And one must admit to the significance of the fact that in calm weather dew and frost form. So, when the weather is clear, the heat, by which the moisture is drawn up, is blown about, such that the air becomes cold; and this is why the moisture discharged from the heat forms dew. But when it is cloudy, ⟨*the moisture*⟩ is contained, which is why neither dew nor frost forms when it is cloudy. Therefore, the heat remaining near the earth produces warmth.

[27] Source: Thphr. *Vent*. 19. [28] Source: *Mete*. 4.1.
[29] Cf. *Pr*. 25.18.

22. Διὰ τί ἐν τοῖς ὑψηλοῖς τῶν οἴκων ὁ ἀὴρ διευριπίζει, καὶ μάλιστα ταῖς εὐδίαις; ἢ διότι ὁ ἀὴρ πολύ-
5 κενός τίς | ἐστι τὴν σύγκρισιν; ὅταν οὖν ἄρξηται εἴσω ῥεῖν, συγχωρεῖ ὁ ἐν τῷ οἰκήματι ἀὴρ καὶ συστέλλεται. τούτου δὲ συμπίπτοντος τῷ χρόνῳ πολυκενώτερος γίνεται ὁ ἔξωθεν, καὶ χώραν πολλὴν ἴσχει. εἰς ταύτην οὖν τὴν χώραν πίπτει ὁ ἐκ τοῦ οἰκήματος ἀήρ, ὢν
10 πλησίον, καὶ φέρεται εἰς ταύτην | τὴν χώραν διὰ τὸ κρέμασθαι καὶ τὴν τοῦ κενοῦ φύσιν μὴ δύνασθαι ἀντιστηρίζειν. κατὰ πολλὰ δὲ αὐτοῦ μέρη τούτου συμβαίνοντος, ἕπεται αὐτῷ ὁ πλησίον διὰ τὴν πρόωσιν·[17] εἶτα πολλοῦ ἔξωθεν φερομένου ὁ μὲν ἔσω τόπος πολύκενος γίνεται, ὁ δὲ ἔξω πυκνότερος, καὶ
15 πάλιν ἔξωθεν εἴσω φέρεται. | καὶ ταῦτα ἀλλάσσονται.

[17] *πρόωσιν* Sylburg ex Gaza (*propulsione*) : *πρόσοψιν* codd. : *πρόκοψιν* Ross apud Forster : fort. *πρόσπτωσιν* Ruelle

22.[30] Why in lofty rooms does the air ebb and flow throughout,[31] and especially in fair weather? Is it because the air, with respect to its composition, is something with a lot of empty space? So when (*the air outside*) begins to flow in, the air in the room gives way and is compressed. Now when the air collects together, in time the outside air becomes emptier, and so contains much space. Into this space, therefore, the air from the room falls, and it travels into this space because it is suspended and the nature of the void is not able to resist it. And when this happens in many parts of it, the nearby air follows it because of the forward thrust; then, when much air travels outside, the place inside comes to have a lot of empty space, whereas the outside air becomes denser, and so it travels back inside from the outside. And these[32] continue to interchange.

[30] Source: Strato, *On the Void,* frs. 28A–30B Sharples.

[31] The rare *διευριπίζει* comes from *εὔριπος*, which refers to a strait or narrow where the ebb and flow is especially strong. See Thphr. *Vent*. 26.

[32] I.e., the inward and outward motions.

BOOK XXVI

INTRODUCTION

Book 26 is the fourth longest in the *Problems*. Its topic —winds (*ἄνεμοι, πνεύματα*)—was a subject of great interest in the Lyceum, judging not only by the length of this book, but also by the number of extant Peripatetic treatments of it. See Aristotle, *Meteorology* 1.13 and 2.4–6; [Aristotle], *On the Cosmos* 4 (394b7–95a14); [Aristotle], *On the Locations and Names of the Winds*; Theophrastus, *On Winds*; Theophrastus, *Meteorology* 13;[1] and, Theophrastus (?), *On Weather Signs* (esp. §§ 26–37). Although these works are all part of the background for *Pr.* 26,[2] the primary source is clearly Theophrastus, *On Winds*.

At the opening of *Meteorology* 2.6, Aristotle writes: "Let us now speak about the position of the winds, and which ones are opposite to which, and which can blow simultaneously and which cannot, and what sort and how many there happen to be, and in addition to these about any other conditions that have not been discussed in the

[1] See Hans Daiber, "The *Meteorology* of Theophrastus in Syriac and Arabic Translation," in William W. Fortenbaugh and Dimitri Gutas, eds., *Theophrastus: His Psychological, Doxographical, and Scientific Writings* (New Brunswick, N.J.: Transactions, 1992), pp. 166–293 (see esp. pp. 268–69 for the translation of ch. 13, on winds).

[2] See also Hp. *Vict.* 2.38.

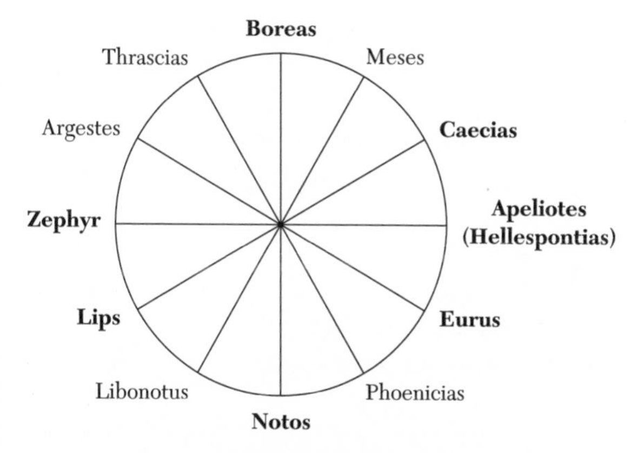

An Aristotelian Wind Rose[3]

Problems" (363a21–25). This seems to refer to *Pr.* 26, and suggests that Aristotle himself was the author of at least some of this book.

Virtually without exception, the sixty-two chapters in Book 26 raise and answer questions about the nature of the various winds (on which, see the wind rose above): in what season they blow, under what conditions or owing to what causes, whence and to where, and to what effect. There is a special interest in exploring connections between winds and other meteorological phenomena.

[3] I have relied heavily on D'Arcy Wentworth Thompson, "The Greek Winds," *Classical Review* 32, no. 3/4 (1918): 49–56. Names in bold are winds discussed or mentioned in *Pr.* 26. Many thanks to my daughter, Tessa, for creating an electronic version of the wind rose.

ΟΣΑ ΠΕΡΙ ΤΟΥΣ ΑΝΕΜΟΥΣ

1. Διὰ τί ὁ καικίας μόνος τῶν ἀνέμων ἐφ᾽ ἑαυτὸν ἄγει τὰ νέφη; ἢ ὅτι ἀφ᾽ ὑψηλοτέρων τόπων πνεῖ; ἔστι
940a20 γὰρ τὰ | πρὸς ἕω ὑψηλότερα τῶν πρὸς ἑσπέραν. σημεῖον δὲ τὸ τῆς πρὸς ἑσπέραν θαλάττης μέγεθος καὶ βάθος. πνέων δὲ ἄνωθεν εἰς τοὐναντίον γραμμὴν ποιεῖ τῇ φορᾷ τὰ κοῖλα[1] πρὸς <τὸν οὐρανὸν καὶ οὐκ ἐπὶ>[2] τὴν γῆν ἔχουσαν. προσπίπτων δέ, ὡς εἴρηται, τοῖς πρὸς ἑσπέραν τῆς γῆς τόποις, καὶ συστέλλων τὰ
25 νέφη διὰ τὸ | τῆς γραμμῆς σχῆμα, τῇ ἐκεῖθεν ἀνακλάσει ἐφ᾽ αὑτὸν[3] ὠθεῖ αὐτά. ποιεῖ δὲ μόνος τοῦτο τῶν ἀνέμων[4] τῷ τοὺς μὲν ὑψηλοτέρους, τοὺς δ᾽ ἐναντίους εἶναι τόπους, πρὸς οὓς ἐκ τοῦ κάτωθεν ἢ ἐπ᾽ εὐθείας τὴν φορὰν γίνεσθαι συμβαίνει, τὰ κυρτὰ[5] πρὸς τὴν γῆν ἐχούσης, ὥστε ἀνάκλασιν μὴ γίνεσθαι τοῦ |

[1] κοῖλα : κυρτὰ Forster ex Gaza
[2] <τὸν οὐρανὸν καὶ οὐκ ἐπὶ> Grumach apud Flashar (ex *Pr.* 26.26, 943b1–2 and Thphr. *Vent.* 39)
[3] ἐφ᾽ αὑτὸν Louis : ἐπ᾽ αὐτὸν codd. : ἐφ᾽ ἑαυτὸν Forster
[4] ἀνέμων conieci : λοιπῶν codd. : fort. πάντων
[5] κυρτὰ : κοῖλα Forster ex Gaza

PROBLEMS CONNECTED WITH THE WINDS

1.[1] Why does the Caecias[2] alone of the winds bring the clouds to itself? Is it because it blows from higher regions? For the parts toward the east are higher than the parts toward the west.[3] A sign of this is the size and depth of the sea toward the west. Now blowing from above to the opposite direction, it describes by its movement a line having curves toward <the sky and not to> the earth. And falling, as has been said, on regions of the earth toward the west, and gathering together the clouds because of the form of the line, by bending back from there it pushes the clouds toward itself. It alone of the winds does this, because some places are higher and some the opposite, toward which the movement (*of the Caecias*) comes either from below or in a straight line, having arches toward the earth,[4] so that a bending back of the wind does not occur because air does

[1] Cf. *Pr.* 26.29. Much of this chapter is obscure, and there are problems with the state of the text. Sources: Thphr. *Vent.* 37 and 39, Arist. *Mete.* 364b2–14.

[2] On the direction of Caecias (and all other winds discussed in Book 26), see the Aristotelian wind rose provided in the introduction. "Caecias" is derived from the river Caecus in Asia Minor.

[3] "West" (ἑσπέρα), literally, "the setting (*sun*)."

[4] I.e., its curve is downward, toward the earth.

30 πνεύματος τῷ μὴ πρὸς τὴν γῆν [ἐχούσης] ἀέρα[6] ἔχειν τὴν τελευτὴν τῆς φορᾶς, ἐν ᾧ οὐδὲ νέφη ἐστὶ περὶ τὴν γῆν· τοῖς δὲ ἧττον κοίλοις καὶ τῷ ἀπηλιώτῃ τῷ μὴ εἶναι ὑγρόν. ὥστε οὐ συνιστὰς ἧττον καταφανής ἐστιν αὐτοῦ ποιῶν τοῦτο ὃ ποιεῖ. |

35 2. Διὰ τί βορέαι μὲν ἐτήσιοι γίνονται, νότοι δὲ οὔ; ἢ γίνονται μὲν καὶ νότοι, ἀλλ' οὐ συνεχεῖς, ὅτι πόρρω ἡμῶν ἡ ἀρχὴ τοῦ νότου ἐστίν, ὑπὸ δὲ τῷ βορέᾳ οἰκοῦμεν; ἔτι οἱ μὲν ἐτησίαι βορέαι καθεστηκότος τοῦ 940b ἀέρος πνέουσι (θέρους || γὰρ πνέουσιν), οἱ δὲ νότοι ἦρος, ὅθ' ἧττον ἕστηκε τὰ περὶ τὸν ἀέρα. πρὸς δὲ τούτοις ὁ μὲν νότος ὑγρός, τῷ δ' ὑγρῷ ὁ ἄνω τόπος ἀλλότριός ἐστιν· διὸ ταχὺ διαλύεται τὰ ἐν αὐτῷ συν-5 ιστάμενα ὑγρά. καὶ τὰ ὑγρὰ πλανητικά ἐστιν, | ὥστε οὐ μένων[7] ἐν ταὐτῷ τόπῳ συμμεθίστησι καὶ τὴν τοῦ ἀέρος κίνησιν. κινουμένου δὲ μὴ ἐν ταὐτῷ πνεύματα ἄλλα συμβαίνει γίνεσθαι· ἔστι γὰρ πνεῦμα ἀέρος κίνησις.

3. Διὰ τί νότος πνεῖ μετὰ πάχνην; ἢ διότι ἡ μὲν πάχνη γίνεται πέψεως γινομένης, μετὰ δὲ τὴν πέψιν 10 καὶ | τὴν ἀποκάθαρσιν ἡ μεταβολὴ εἰς τοὐναντίον

[6] τῷ μὴ πρὸς τὴν γῆν ἐχούσης ἀέρα codd. (secl. ἐχούσης Hett) : τῷ περὶ τὴν γῆν [ἐχούσης ἀέρα] Ross apud Forster

[7] μένων : μένοντα Flashar

[5] The east wind, literallly, "from the (*rising*) sun." See *Pr.* 26.33.

not have the end of its course in relation to the earth, in which place there are no clouds around the earth; but in winds with less of a curve, and so in the Apeliotes,[5] there is no moisture. So that as it does not form (*clouds*), (*the Apeliotes*) is less obvious than (*the Caecias*) in doing what it does.

2.[6] Why are the Boreas winds Etesian,[7] whereas the Notos winds are not? Or are the Notos winds as well Etesian, but not continuous, because the source of the Notos is far from us, whereas we live under the Boreas? Furthermore, the Etesian Boreas winds blow when the air is still (for they blow in summer), whereas the Notos blow in the spring, when the regions around the air are less still. And in addition to these factors, the Notos is moist, whereas the upper region is unfavorable to what is moist; this is why the moisture forming in it is rapidly dissolved. And moisture has a tendency to wander, so (*the Notos*) not remaining in the same place[8] helps to change the movement of the air. And since (*air*) is not in the same place when it moves, the result is that other winds arise; for wind is a movement of air.

3.[9] Why does the Notos blow after a frost? Is it because frost occurs when concoction occurs, and after concoction and purification the change into the opposite occurs? Now

[6] Cf. *Pr.* 26.51. Sources: Thphr. *Vent.* 10–11, *Mete.* 362a11–22.

[7] I.e. annual: they come at the same time every year.

[8] It is unclear what the author is claiming does not stay in the same place. The Notos is most likely, especially as ὁ νότος agrees with μένων. If we follow Flashar's suggested emendation, the moisture stays in the same place.

[9] Source: Thphr. *Vent.* 50.

γίνεται; ἐναντίον δὲ τῷ βορρᾷ νότος ἐστίν. διὰ ταὐτὸ δὲ καὶ μετὰ τὴν χιόνα πνεῖ νότος. ὅλως δὲ καὶ ἡ χιὼν καὶ ἡ χάλαζα καὶ τὸ ὕδωρ καὶ πᾶσα ἡ τοιαύτη ἀποκάθαρσις πέψεως σημεῖόν ἐστιν. διὸ καὶ μετὰ τὸν

15 ὑετὸν καὶ τὰς τοιαύτας | χειμασίας πίπτει τὰ πνεύματα.

4.[8] Διὰ τί αἱ τροπαὶ πνέουσιν; ἢ διὰ τὸ αὐτὸ ὃ καὶ οἱ εὔριποι ῥέουσιν; μέχρι γὰρ τοῦ ῥεῖν καὶ ἡ θάλαττα φέρεται καὶ ὁ ἀήρ· εἶθ' ὅταν ἀντιπέσῃ καὶ μηκέτι δύνηται τὰ ἀπόγεια προάγειν διὰ τὸ μὴ ἰσχυρὰν ἔχειν

20 τὴν ἀρχὴν τῆς | κινήσεως καὶ φορᾶς, πάλιν ἀνταποδίδωσιν.

5. Διὰ τί αἱ τροπαὶ ἐκ τῆς θαλάττης εἰσίν; ἢ ὅτι ἡ θάλαττα πλησίον; ἢ ὅτι ἐναντίον ἐστὶ τῇ ἀπογείᾳ ἡ τροπαία, καὶ ἔστιν ἡ τροπαία οἷον ἀναστροφὴ ἀπογείας; ἡ δὲ ἀπογεία τὸ ἐκ τῆς γῆς πρὸς τὴν θάλατταν

25 πνεῦμα γινόμενον, | ἡ δὲ τροπαία ἡ τούτου παλίρροια. ὥστε ἀνάγκη ἐκ θαλάττης εἶναι. ἢ ἡ θάλαττά ἐστι . . .[9] διὰ τὸ εἰς τὴν θάλατταν ἀθροισθῆναι τὸν ῥυέντα ἀέρα; τοῦ δὲ μὴ εἰς τὴν γῆν τοῦτο συνίστασθαι καὶ τοῦ ἀνακάμπτειν ἀπιὸν[10] αἴτιον ὅτι ἡ θάλαττα ἐν κοίλῳ ἐστίν· ὁ δὲ ἀήρ, ὥσπερ τὸ ὕδωρ, ῥεῖ ἀεὶ εἰς τὸ κοιλότατον. |

30 6. Διὰ τί οἱ ἐκνεφίαι ὕδατος γενομένου θᾶττον

[8] cap. 4 et 5 post cap. 8 ponuntur in Yª Ap Barth. Gaza

[9] post ἢ ἡ θάλαττά ἐστι lac. indic. Flashar : ἢ ἡ θάλαττά ἐστι om. Cª (secl. Bekker) : ἢ [ἡ θάλαττά ἐστι] Forster

[10] ἀπιὸν secl. Richards

the Notos is opposite to the Boreas. For the same reason as well a Notos blows after snow. In general, snow and hail and rain and every such purification is a sign of concoction. And this is why after showers and such storms the winds fall.

4.[10] Why do alternating winds[11] blow? Is it for the same reason as that which makes the straits (*ebb and*) flow? For both sea and air are carried along until they flow; then, when offshore[12] winds encounter resistance and are no longer able to carry them forward because the source of their motion and course is not strong, they go back in the opposite direction.

5.[13] Why are alternating winds from the sea? Is it because the sea is nearby? Or is it because the alternating wind is the opposite of the offshore wind, and the alternating wind is, so to speak, a reversal of the offshore wind? Now the offshore wind is a wind coming from the land toward the sea, and the alternating wind is the flowing back of this. So it must be from the sea. Or the sea is . . . because the flowing air is collected on the sea? Now the cause of its not collecting on the land and of its bending back as it departs is that the sea is in a hollow; and air, like water, always flows into what is most hollow.

6.[14] Why do cloud winds[15] stop more quickly when rain

[10] Cf. *Pr.* 26.5, 40. Source: Thphr. *Vent.* 26.

[11] I.e., winds that change and blow in the opposite direction.

[12] Literally, "from the land."

[13] Cf. *Pr.* 26.4, 40. Sources: Thphr. *Vent.* 26 and 53.

[14] Source: Thphr. *Vent.* 50; see also Arist. *Mete.* 370b4–17.

[15] *οἱ ἐκνεφίαι* (sc. *ἄνεμοι*) can also be translated "hurricanes."

παύονται; ἢ ὅτι αἱ κοιλίαι συμπίπτουσι τοῦ νέφους, ὕδατος γενομένου, ἐν αἷς ἡ ἀρχὴ τοῦ πνεύματος συνίσταται;

7. Διὰ τί οὐχ οἱ αὐτοὶ ἄνεμοι πανταχοῦ ὑέτιοί εἰσιν; ἢ ὅτι οὐχ οἱ αὐτοὶ πανταχοῦ πρὸς <τὰ αὐτὰ>[11] ὄρη
35 ἀντιπνέουσιν, ἀλλ' ἕτεροι | κεῖνται πρὸς ἕτερα ὄρη; οἷον γὰρ πρὸς ἀνάντη μόλις ῥεόντων, ἐνταῦθα ὑφίσταται μᾶλλον τὰ νέφη, οὗ ἀδυνατεῖ ἔτι προωθεῖν αὐτὰ ἄνεμος. ὑφιστάμενα δὲ καὶ πιεζόμενα ῥήγνυται. ||

941a 8. Διὰ τί αἱ μὲν καθαραὶ δύσεις εὐδιεινὸν σημεῖον, αἱ δὲ τεταραγμέναι χειμερινόν; ἢ ὅτι χειμὼν γίνεται συνισταμένου καὶ πυκνουμένου τοῦ ἀέρος; ὅταν μὲν οὖν κρατῇ ὁ ἥλιος, διακρίνει καὶ αἰθριάζει αὐτόν, ὅταν
5 δὲ κρατῆται, | ἐπινεφῆ ποιεῖ. ἐὰν μὲν οὖν ἰσχυρὰ ᾖ ἡ σύστασις, εὐθὺς ἡμέρας γίνεται χειμών· ἐὰν δὲ ἀσθενεστέρα, μὴ παντάπασι δὲ κρατουμένη, τὸ συνιστάμενον ἐξωθεῖται πρὸς τὰς δύσεις. ἐνταῦθα δὲ μένει διὰ τὸ παχύτερον[12] εἶναι τὸν περὶ τὴν γῆν ἀέρα τοῦ
10 χειμῶνος. ταχὺ δὲ συνίσταται καὶ | ὁ ἄλλος διὰ τὸ ἔχειν ἀρχὴν καὶ ἔρεισμα, ὃ δέξεται καὶ ἀθροίσει τὸ προσιὸν †καθάπερ ὄρθρος†·[13] ὥσπερ γὰρ ἐν τροπῇ ἑνὸς ἀντιστάντος καὶ οἱ ἄλλοι μένουσιν, οὕτω καὶ ἐπὶ τοῦ ἀέρος. διὸ ταχὺ καὶ ἐξαίφνης ἐνίοτε γίνεται καὶ ἐπινέφελα. ὅταν οὖν αἱ δύσεις τεταραγμέναι ὦσι,

[11] <τὰ αὐτὰ> Flashar [12] παχύτερον Forster : παχύτατον codd. [13] καθάπερ ὄρθρος codd. (obelis inclusi) : secl. Forster ex Gaza : κατ' ὄρθρον Grumach apud Flashar

comes? Is it because, when rain comes, the hollows of the cloud, in which the source of the wind is formed, collapse?

7.[16] Why aren't the same winds rainy everywhere? Is it because the same winds do not everywhere blow against ‹the same› mountains, but different ones lie against different mountains? For instance, when winds flow with difficulty against steep mountains, the clouds are more likely to form there, where wind is unable to push them still further. And when they are formed and subject to pressure, they break.

8.[17] Why are clear sunsets a sign of fine weather, whereas disturbed sunsets are a sign of stormy weather?[18] Is it because a storm comes when the air condenses and thickens? Now when the sun achieves mastery, it separates and airs out the air, but when it is mastered, it makes the air cloudy. Therefore, if the density is strong, a storm comes as soon as it is day; whereas if it is weaker, but not completely mastered,[19] the condensed part is pushed out toward the sunset. And it remains there because the air about the earth is denser than the storm. And the rest quickly condenses because it has a source and support, which will receive and collect what comes to it †just like dawn†; for just as in a rout when one man resists the others also remain, so also in the case of air. This is why it sometimes quickly and suddenly becomes overcast. Therefore, when the sunsets

[16] Cf. Pr. 26.56. Source: Thphr. *Vent*. 5.

[17] Source: Thphr. (?) *Sign*. 38.

[18] The sunsets are "disturbed" by cloud cover. The word translated "stormy" (*χειμερινόν*) also means "wintry."

[19] I.e., if the air (the density of which is weak) is not completely mastered by the sun.

15 σημεῖόν ἐστιν | ἰσχυρὸν ὅτι οὐ κεκράτηκεν ὁ ἥλιος τῆς συστάσεως, πολὺν χρόνον ἐναντιούμενος αὐτῇ, ὥστε εἰκότως ἔστι συστῆναι πλέον. καὶ ἧττον δέ ἐστι φοβερόν, ὅταν προχειμάσαντος ἢ ὅταν ἐξ εὐδίας τοῦτο συμβῇ. ἐκείνως μὲν γὰρ ἔοικεν ὥσπερ ὑπόλειμμά τι εἶναι, οὕτω δὲ ἀρχὴ συστάσεως. |

20 9. Διὰ τί λέγεται "οὔ ποτε νυκτερινὸς βορέας τρίτον ἵκετο φέγγος"; ἢ διότι ἀσθενῆ τὰ πνεύματα τὰ ἀπὸ τῆς ἄρκτου, ὅταν ᾖ νυκτερινά; σημεῖον γὰρ ὅτι οὐ πολὺς ὁ κινηθεὶς ἀήρ, τὸ τηνικαῦτα πνεῦσαι, ὅτε ὀλίγη θερμότης ὑπῆρχεν· ἡ δὲ ὀλίγη ὀλίγον ἐκίνει 25 ἀέρα. τελευτᾷ δὲ ἐν τρισὶ πάντα, | καὶ τὰ ἐλάχιστα ἐν τῇ πρώτῃ τριάδι, ὥστε καὶ τοῦτο τὸ πνεῦμα.

10. Διὰ τί ὁ βορέας πυκνότερον πνεῖ ἢ ὁ νότος; ἢ ὅτι ὁ μὲν βορέας γειτνιῶν τῇ οἰκουμένῃ οὐ λανθάνει ὀλιγοχρόνιος ὤν (ἅμα γὰρ πνεῖ καὶ πάρεστιν), ὁ δὲ 30 νότος οὐκ ἀφικνεῖται | διὰ τὸ πόρρωθεν πνεῖν;

11. Διὰ τί ὁ νότος ‹οὐχ›[14] ἧττον μετὰ χειμερινὰς νύκτας πνεῖ ἢ μεθ' ἡμέρας; ἢ ὅτι καὶ τῆς νυκτὸς ὁ ἥλιος ἐγγύς ἐστι τῇ πρὸς νότον χώρᾳ, καὶ ἀλεεινότεραι αἱ νύκτες ἐκεῖ ἢ πρὸς ἄρκτον αἱ ἡμέραι, ὥστε 35 πολὺς κινεῖται ὁ ἀήρ, καὶ οὐθὲν | ἐλάττων ἢ μεθ' ἡμέραν; ἀλλ' αἱ θερμότεραι ἡμέραι κωλύουσι μᾶλλον πνεῖν, ξηραίνουσαι τὰς ὑγρότητας.

[14] ‹οὐχ› Septalius

---

[20] Cf. *Pr.* 26.14. The likely source is Thphr. *Vent.* 49.

[21] "Arctic" (ἄρκτος) is more transliteration than translation,

are disturbed, it is a strong sign that the sun has not mastered the density, though opposing it for a long time, so that (*the air*) has likely condensed much more. Now it is less alarming when this happens as a storm is brewing than out of calm weather. For in the former case it would seem to be some remnant of the storm, but in the latter it is the beginning of the condensing.

9.[20] Why is it said: "The Boreas (*blows*) not at night once the third daylight has come"? Is it because the winds from the arctic[21] are weak, when they come at night? Indeed, a sign that the amount of air that was moved is not great is the fact that it blew at a time when there was little heat; and little heat was moving little air. Now all things end in threes, and the smallest in the first triad, and that is what this wind does.

10.[22] Why does the Boreas blow more frequently than the Notos? Is it because the Boreas, being close to the inhabited world, does not escape our notice, though it is of short duration (for it blows and makes its presence known at the same time), but the Notos does not reach us because it blows from far off?

11.[23] Why does the Notos blow <no> less after stormy nights than after stormy days?[24] Is it because even at night the sun is close to the region of the south, and the nights there are warmer than days in the arctic, so that much air is moved, and no less than by day? But the hotter days prevent more blowing, by drying the moisture.

and here is simply another word for north, though it can refer specifically to the regions around the pole.

[22] Cf. *Pr.* 26.15. Sources: Thphr. *Vent.* 6 and 9 and Arist. *Mete.* 363a3–8.

[23] Source: Thphr. *Vent.* 49.

[24] Or "after wintery nights than after wintery days."

12. Διὰ τί ἐπὶ κυνὶ ὁ νότος πνεῖ, καὶ τοῦτο ὥσπερ τι ἄλλο γίνεται τεταγμένως; ἢ διότι θερμὰ τὰ κάτω, τοῦ ἡλίου ⟨οὐ⟩ πόρρω ὄντος,[15] ὥστε πολλὴ ἡ ἀτμὶς γίνε-
941b ται; καὶ πολλοὶ δὴ ἔπνεον, || εἰ μὴ διὰ τοὺς ἐτησίας. νῦν δὲ οὗτοι κωλύουσιν. ἢ ὅτι ἐπὶ πᾶσι μὲν σημαίνει τοῖς ἄστροις δυομένοις ἢ ἐπιτέλλουσιν, οὐχ ἥκιστα δὲ ἐπὶ τούτῳ; δῆλον οὖν ὅτι πνεύματα μάλιστα ἐπὶ τούτῳ
5 καὶ μετ' αὐτόν. ἐπεὶ δὲ πνίγει, καὶ πνεύματα | εἰκότως ἐπ' αὐτῷ τὰ θερμότατα κινεῖται· ὁ δὲ νότος θερμός ἐστιν. ἐπεὶ δὲ εἴθισται μάλιστα ἐκ τῶν ἐναντίων εἰς τὰ ἐναντία μεταβάλλειν, πρὸ κυνὸς δὲ οἱ πρόδρομοι πνέουσιν ὄντες βορέαι, εἰκότως μετὰ κύνα νότος πνεῖ, ἐπειδὴ ἐπισημαίνει μέν, ἐπιτέλλουσι δὲ τοῖς ἄστροις.
10 τὸ δὲ ἐπισημαίνειν[16] | ἐστὶ μεταβολὴν τοῦ ἀέρος ποιεῖν. μεταβάλλει δὲ πάντα εἰς τοὺς ἐναντίους ἢ τοὺς ἐπὶ δεξιὰ ἀνέμους τὰ πνεύματα. ἐπεὶ δὲ βορέας εἰς τοὺς ἐπιδεξίους ⟨οὐ⟩[17] μεταβάλλει, εἴη ἂν αὐτῷ λοιπὸν εἰς νότον μεταβάλλειν. ἔστι δὲ καὶ ἡ μετὰ τὰς χειμερινὰς τροπὰς πεντεκαιδεκάτη νότιος, διὰ τὸ τὰς |
15 μὲν τροπὰς ἀρχήν τινα εἶναι, κινεῖν δὲ τὸν κατ' αὐτὴν μάλιστα ἀέρα τὸν ἥλιον, εἶναι δὲ ἐν ταύταις ταῖς τροπαῖς πρὸς νότον. καθάπερ οὖν καὶ τὰ ἀπ' ἀνατολῆς

[15] ⟨οὐ⟩ πόρρω ὄντος Forster : πόρρω ὄντος codd. : παρόντος Röhr apud Flashar

[16] ἄστροις. τὸ δὲ κτλ. : ἄστροις τὸ [δὲ] κτλ. Forster

[17] ⟨οὐ⟩ Bonitz

12.[25] Why does the Notos blow at the time of the Dog Star,[26] and (*why does*) this occur just like any other orderly winds? Is it because the lower regions are hot, as the sun is not far away, so that a lot of vapor is produced? And many (*Notos winds*) would be blowing, if not for the Etesian winds. But as it is, these prevent them. Or is it because there are signs at the setting or rising of all stars, and not least at this one?[27] Now it is clear that there are winds at this time[28] and after it. But since it stifles,[29] naturally the hottest winds too are set in motion at this time; and the Notos is hot. And since things are most accustomed to change from opposites into opposites, and as the Forerunners, which are Notos winds, blow before the time of the Dog Star, naturally the Notos blows after the Dog Star, since there is a sign, and it occurs at the rising of the stars. And what is signified consists in a change in the air.[30] Now all winds change either into their opposites or to winds on their right.[31] But since the Boreas does <not> change into winds on the right, what would remain for it is to change into a Notos. And on the fifteenth day after the winter solstice it is in the south, because the solstice is a certain beginning, and the sun moves the air that is most of all near it, and during this solstice the sun is toward the south. Therefore, just as it rouses the Apeliotes winds when it moves the

[25] Cf. *Pr.* 26.32. Source: Thphr. *Vent*. 48.

[26] I.e., when the Dog Star (Sirius) rises.

[27] I.e., at the setting or rising of the Dog Star.

[28] Presumably, when the Dog Star rises.

[29] I.e., since the Dog Star gives rise to stifling weather—the dog days of summer.

[30] There are likely textual problems with this and the previous line.

[31] I.e., eastward.

κινῶν ἀπηλιώτας ἀνέμους ἤγειρεν, οὕτω καὶ τὰ ἀπὸ μεσημβρίας κινῶν νότους ἐγείρει. οὐκ εὐθὺ δὲ ἀπὸ
20 τροπῶν ποιεῖ τοῦτο διὰ τὸ | βραχυτάτας ποιεῖσθαι τὰς μεταστάσεις τότε, ἀλλ' ἐν τῇ πεντεκαιδεκάτῃ διὰ τὸ τὸν χρόνον τοῦτον συμμέτρως ἔχειν τῇ κατὰ τὴν μετάστασιν πρώτῃ φαντασίᾳ· ὅλου γάρ ἐστι μέρος εὐσημότατον ὁ εἰρημένος χρόνος.

13. Διὰ τί ἐπὶ Ὠρίωνι γίνονται αἰόλοι μάλιστα αἱ
25 ἡμέραι | καὶ ἀκαιρίαι τῶν πνευμάτων; ἢ ὅτι ἐν μεταβολῇ ἀεὶ πάντα ἀοριστεῖ μάλιστα; ὁ δ' Ὠρίων ἀνατέλλει μὲν ἐν ἀρχῇ ὀπώρας, δύνει δὲ χειμῶνος, ὥστε διὰ τὸ μήπω καθεστάναι μίαν ὥραν, ἀλλὰ τὴν μὲν γίνεσθαι τὴν δὲ παύεσθαι, διὰ ταῦτα ἀνάγκη καὶ τὰ
30 πνεύματα ἀκατάστατα | εἶναι διὰ τὸ ἐπαμφοτερίζειν τὰ ἐξ ἑκατέρας. καὶ χαλεπὸς δὴ λέγεται καὶ δύνων καὶ ἀνατέλλων ὁ Ὠρίων διὰ τὴν ἀοριστίαν τῆς ὥρας· ἀνάγκη γὰρ ταραχώδη εἶναι καὶ ἀνώμαλον.

14. Διὰ τί ὁ νυκτερινὸς βορέας τριταῖος λήγει;
35 πότερον | ὅτι ἀπὸ μικρᾶς καὶ ἀσθενοῦς ἀρχῆς, ἡ τρίτη δὲ κρίσιμος; ἢ ὅτι ἀθρόος ἡ ἔκχυσις,[18] ὥσπερ τῶν ἐκνεφιῶν; ταχεῖα οὖν ἡ παῦλα.

15. Διὰ τί βορέαι πλεῖστοι πνέουσι τῶν ἀνέμων; ἢ

[18] ἔκχυσις : ἔκρυσις Ruelle

---

[32] Literally, "of the rising (*sun*)." Presumably, the sun moves *the air* in the eastern regions.

[33] μεσημβρία can refer to both midday or noon and to the south.

eastern regions,[32] so too does it rouse the Notos winds when it moves the southern regions.[33] Now it does not do this immediately after the solstice, because the slightest changes are produced then, but it does so on the fifteenth day, because this time coincides with the first impression corresponding to the change; for the time mentioned is the most significant[34] part of the whole process.

13.[35] Why do the days and variability[36] of the winds become especially changeable at the time of Orion? Is it because during a time of change everything is always especially indeterminate? Now Orion rises at the beginning of autumn and sets in winter, so that because one season has not yet settled—but one is coming to be while the other is ending—for this reason the winds too must be unsettled, because they share the properties of those from each season. And indeed, Orion is called difficult, both rising and setting, because of the indeterminateness of the season, since it is necessarily turbulent and inconsistent.

14.[37] Why does the nighttime Boreas cease on the third day? Is it because it comes from a small and weak source, and the third day is critical? Or is it because its outpouring is all at once, like the cloud winds? Therefore, its cessation is quick.

15.[38] Why, of the winds, do Boreas winds blow the

[34] I.e., the activity on the fifteenth day is the most conspicuous or easily known by signs.

[35] Source: Thphr. *Vent*. 55. See also Arist. *Mete*. 361b30–35.

[36] Or unseasonable nature.

[37] Cf. *Pr*. 26.9. Source: Thphr. *Vent*. 49.

[38] Cf. *Pr*. 26.10. Sources: Thphr. *Vent*. 6 and 9 and Arist. *Mete*. 363a3–8.

διὰ τὸ πρὸς τούτῳ τὴν οἰκουμένην τῷ τόπῳ ὑποκεῖ-
942a σθαι ὄντι ὑψηλῷ ‖ καὶ ἔξω τροπῶν καὶ πλήρει χιόνος,
ἣ οὐδέποτε ἔνια ὄρη λείπει; τὸ πολὺ οὖν ὑγραινομένων
τῶν πεπηγότων πολλάκις πνεῦμα γίνεται. τοῦτο δ'
ἐστι βορέας, τὸ ἐκ τῶν ἀπὸ τῆς ἄρκτου τόπων πνεῦμα. |
5 16. Διὰ τί οἱ νότοι πνέουσι μὲν χειμῶνος καὶ ἔαρος
ἀρχομένου καὶ μετοπώρου λήγοντος, εἰσὶ δὲ κυματοει-
δεῖς καὶ συνεστραμμένοι, καὶ τοῖς ἐν Λιβύῃ ὁμοίως
ψυχροὶ ὡς οἱ βορέαι ἐνταῦθα; ἢ διότι πλησίον τοῦ
ἡλίου ὄντος ἀνάγκη κινεῖσθαι τὰ πνεύματα; ὁ δὲ ἥλιος
10 τοῦ χειμῶνος πρὸς νότον | φέρεται, καὶ τοῦ μὲν ἔαρος
ἀρχομένου τοῦ δὲ μετοπώρου τελευτῶντος ἤδη θερμαίνει, τὸ δὲ θέρος πρὸς βορέαν φέρεται, ἐκείνους δὲ
ἀπολείπει τοὺς τόπους. θερμὸς δέ ἐστι διὰ τὸ μίγνυ-
σθαι τὸ πνεῦμα τῷ κατὰ Λιβύην ἀέρι θερμῷ ὄντι· καὶ
διὰ τοῦτο †μεγαλοκύμων† νοτίζειν[19] ποιεῖ τὸ θέρος,
15 ἐμπίπτων | εἰς τὴν θάλατταν.

17. Διὰ τί ὁ νότος δυσώδης; ἢ ὅτι ὑγρὰ καὶ θερμὰ
ποιεῖ τὰ σώματα, ταῦτα δὲ σήπεται μάλιστα; οἱ δὲ ἐκ
τῆς θαλάττης νότοι ἀγαθοὶ φυτοῖς· ἐκ θαλάττης γὰρ
αὐτοῖς προσπίπτει. καὶ τῆς Ἀττικῆς τῷ Θριασίῳ πε-
20 δίῳ αἴτιον, | διότι ἀπεψυγμένος ἀφικνεῖται. αἱ δ' ἐρυ-
σίβαι γίνονται ὑπὸ ὑγρότητος θερμῆς μὲν ἀλλοτρίας
δέ.

[19] μεγαλοκύμων νοτίζειν plur. codd. (obelis inclusi) : post μεγαλοκύμων add. ‹ὤν› Platt : μεγάλως κυματίζειν Ap : fort. μεγάλως νοτίζειν

most? Is it because the inhabited world lies near this place, which is high and outside the solstice and full of snow, which never leaves some mountains? So, as most of the solidified material liquefies, wind often arises. And this is the Boreas, the wind from the regions of the arctic.

16.[39] Why do the Notos winds blow in winter and when spring begins and when autumn ends, and why are they wavelike and twisting, and why are they as cold to those in Libya as the Boreas winds are here? Is it because, the sun being nearby, the winds must be set in motion? Now the sun in winter travels toward the south, and when spring begins and when autumn ends it is already producing heat, whereas with respect to the summer it travels toward the north, and leaves those other places. Now it is hot because the wind mingles with the Libyan air, which is hot; and because of this . . . it causes the summer to be wet, falling to the sea.[40]

17.[41] Why is the Notos malodorous? Is it because it makes bodies moist and hot, and these most of all cause putrefaction? But Notos winds from the sea are good for plants; for they fall upon them from the sea. And this is the cause (*of the fertility*)[42] of the Thriasian Plain in Attica, because the Notos arrives having been cooled off. But mildew[43] comes from moisture hot but extraneous.

[39] Cf. *Pr.* 26.49. Source: Thphr. *Vent.* 10.

[40] I take this sentence to mean (1) that the south wind is hot (by the time it reaches the Greeks) because it mingles with the hot Libyan air, and (2) that it causes the summer to be rainy and/or humid, because it is hot and because it sweeps down on the sea. There is, however, a problem with the text.

[41] Cf. *Pr.* 1.23 and 26.50. Source: Thphr. *Vent.* 57–58.

[42] Following a suggestion of Louis.

[43] Or blight.

18. Διὰ τί ἄνεμος γίνεται πρὸ τῶν ἐκλείψεων ὡς τὰ πολλά, ἀκρόνυχον μὲν πρὸ τῶν μεσονυκτίων ἐκλείψεων, μεσονύκτιον δὲ πρὸ τῶν ἑώων; ἢ διότι ἀμαυροῦ-
25 ται τὸ θερμὸν | τὸ ἀπὸ τῆς σελήνης διὰ τὸ πλησίον ἤδη φορὰν εἶναι, ἐν ᾧ γενομένῳ ἔσται ἡ ἔκλειψις; ἀνιεμένου οὖν ᾧ κατείχετο ὁ ἀὴρ καὶ ἠρέμει, πάλιν κινεῖται καὶ γίνεται πνεῦμα τῆς ὀψιαίτερον ἐκλείψεως ὀψιαίτερον.[20]

19. Διὰ τί ὁ νότος οὐκ ἀρχόμενος ἀλλὰ λήγων
30 ὑέτιος; | πότερον ὅτι πόρρωθεν συνάγει τὸν ἀέρα; γίνεται δὲ συνιστάντος τὸ ὕδωρ, συνίσταται δὲ ὕστερον ἢ ἄρχεται. ἢ ὅτι ἀρχομένου θερμός ἐστιν ὁ ἀὴρ ἔτι διὰ τὸ ἐκ τοιούτου ἐληλυθέναι, ἐπιχρονιζόμενος δὲ ψυχθεὶς συνίσταται μᾶλλον εἰς ὕδωρ;

20. Διὰ τί ὁ νότος, ὅταν μὲν ἐλάττων ᾖ, αἴθριός
35 ἐστιν, | ὅταν δὲ μέγας, νεφώδης καὶ χρονιώτερος; πότερον, ὥσπερ τινὲς λέγουσι, διὰ τὴν ἀρχήν; ἐὰν μὲν γὰρ ἀπ' ἐλάττονος, αἴθριος, ἐὰν δὲ ἀπὸ πλείονος ὁρμήσῃ, νεφελώδης. ἢ ὅτι ἐλάττων ἀρχόμενός ἐστιν,
942b ὥστε οὐ πολὺν ἀέρα ὠθεῖ, ἐπὶ || τέλει δὲ εἴωθε γίνεσθαι μέγας; διὸ καὶ παροιμιάζονται "ἀρχομένου γε νότου καὶ λήγοντος βορέαο".

[20] τῆς ὀψιαίτερον (ὀψιαιτέρας Ap[a] mg) ἐκλείψεως ὀψιαίτερον : fort. ὀψιαίτερον, τῆς ἐκλείψεως ὀψιαίτερον <οὔσης> Forster

---

[44] Source: Arist. *Mete.* 367b25–32.

[45] The question concerns lunar eclipses.

18.[44] Why does wind occur before an eclipse in most cases, at nightfall before midnight eclipses, and at midnight before dawn eclipses?[45] Is it because the heat from the moon diminishes owing to its course already being near (*the earth*), during which occurrence there will be an eclipse? So when that[46] by which the air is held back and kept still is relaxed, it moves again and a wind occurs later as the eclipse is later.

19.[47] Why is the Notos rainy, not when it's beginning but when it's ending? Is it because it gathers together the air from far off? Now the water comes when the air is collected, and it is collected later rather than at the beginning. Or is it because when the Notos begins, the air is still hot, having come from such a region, but as time passes it cools and collects more (*air*) into water?

20.[48] Why is the Notos clear when it is smaller,[49] but cloudy and longer-lasting when it is great? Is it, as some say, because of its source? For if it is from a smaller source it is clear, but if it starts from a larger one it is cloudy. Or is it smaller when it begins, so that it does not push much air, but in the end it usually becomes great? And this is why they have the proverb "When the Notos begins and when the Boreas comes to an end."[50]

46 Presumably the heat.

47 Sources: Thphr. *Vent*. 7 and Thphr. (?) *Sign*. 35.

48 Cf. *Pr*. 26.38. Source: Thphr. *Vent*. 6–7.

49 Smaller in the quantity of air, or weaker or of shorter duration.

50 A fuller version is cited at *Pr*. 26.45, 945 a 29: "It is good to sail when the Notos begins and when the Boreas comes to an end." Cf. *Pr*. 26.27, 943a25.

21. Διὰ τί προΐεται τοῦ χειμῶνος ἀπὸ τῆς ἕω τὰ πνεύματα, τοῦ θέρους δὲ καὶ ἀφ' ἑσπέρας; ἢ ὅτι ὅταν
5 μηκέτι | κρατῇ ὁ ἥλιος, ἀφιέμενος ὁ ἀὴρ ῥεῖ; δύνων τε οὖν καταλείπει νέφη, ἀφ' ὧν οἱ ζέφυροι· καὶ ὅσον ἂν ἐπαγάγῃ ἐκείνοις τοῖς ἐν τῷ κάτω ἡμισφαιρίῳ οἰκοῦσιν, ἑωθινὸν πνεῦμα γίνεται. τἀναντία δέ, ὅταν δύνῃ ἐν τῷ κάτω μέρει, ἐκείνοις τε ζεφύρους ποιήσει καὶ
10 ἐνταῦθα ἑωθινὸν | πνεῦμα ἀπὸ τοῦ ἑπομένου ἀέρος αὐτῷ. διὰ τοῦτο κἂν καταλάβῃ ἄλλον ἄνεμον, μείζων γίνεται αἱρομένου, ὅτι προσέθηκεν.

22. Διὰ τί οἱ κύνες τὰ ἴχνη ἥκιστα εὑρίσκουσι ζεφύρου πνέοντος; ἢ διότι μάλιστα συγχεῖ διὰ τὸ
15 συνεχέστατος | εἶναι τῶν ἀνέμων καὶ μάλιστα ὑπὸ τὴν γῆν πνεῖν;

23. Διὰ τί, ὅταν ἀστέρες διάττωσιν, ἀνέμου σημεῖον; ἢ ὅτι ὑπὸ τοῦ πνεύματος φέρονται, καὶ πρότερον ἐκεῖ γίνεται πνεῦμα ἢ παρ' ἡμῖν; διὸ καὶ ἀφ' οὗ ἂν τόπου φέρωνται οἱ ἀστέρες, ἐν τούτῳ καὶ τὸ πνεῦμα γίνεται. |

20 24. Διὰ τί μεγίστας νεφέλας τῶν ἀνέμων ὁ ζέφυρος ἄγει; ἢ διότι ἐκ πελάγους πνεῖ καὶ κατὰ τὴν θάλατταν; ἐκ πολλοῦ οὖν καὶ συνάγει.

---

[51] Cf. *Pr.* 26.54. Source: Thphr. *Vent.* 47.

[52] This sentence is highly ambiguous: If the wind that becomes a Zephyr in the Southern Hemisphere and an Apeliotes in the Northern overtakes another wind, it (the original wind or the

21.[51] Why do the winds come from the east in winter, but also from the west in the summer? Is it because, when the sun no longer has mastery, the air flows moving freely? When the sun sets, therefore, it leaves behind clouds, from which the Zephyr winds come; and all that it takes with it to those residing in the lower hemisphere becomes an Apeliotes. Now in the contrary case, when the sun sets in the lower part, it will produce Zephyr winds for those (*living there*) and an Apeliotes here from the air following it. For this reason too, if it overtakes another wind, it becomes greater as the sun rises, because it adds something.[52]

22. Why do dogs find the scent least when a Zephyr is blowing? Is it that the Zephyr is most confusing because, of all the winds, it is the most continuous and blows most on the land?

23.[53] Why, when there are shooting stars, is it a sign of wind? Is it because they are carried by the wind, and the wind occurs there before it comes to us? And this is why the wind occurs as well in that place from which the stars travel.

24.[54] Why, of the winds, does the Zephyr carry the largest clouds? Is it because it blows from the open sea and so over the (*entire*) sea? Therefore, it collects clouds from a large area.

overtaken one?) becomes greater as the sun rises, because it (the rising sun or one of the winds?) adds something.

[53] Sources: Thphr. (?) *Sign.* 13 and 37; see also Thphr. *Vent.* 36.

[54] Source: Thphr. *Vent.* 42.

25. Διὰ τί οἱ ἐπὶ τέλει ἄνεμοι μέγιστοι; ἢ ὅτι ὅταν ἀθρόοι ἐκπνεύσωσιν, ὀλίγον τὸ λοιπόν;[21] |

25 26. Διὰ τί, ἐὰν περὶ ἰσημερίαν λὶψ πνεύσῃ, ὕδωρ γίνεται; ἢ ὅτι καθ' ὃν ἂν ᾖ ὁ ἥλιος τόπον τοῦ κόσμου, τὰ ἐντεῦθεν πνεύματα κινεῖ; διὸ καὶ ἡ τῶν πνευμάτων περίστασις κατὰ τὴν τοῦ ἡλίου φορὰν γίνεται. ἐπεὶ δ' ἡ ἰσημερία μεθόριόν ἐστι χειμῶνος καὶ θέρους, ὅταν 30 συμβῇ τὸν ἥλιον | κατὰ τὴν ἡμῖν φαινομένην ἰσημερίαν ὑπερβεβληκέναι ἢ ἐκλείπειν τοῦ ἀκριβοῦς ὅρου καὶ εἶναι μᾶλλον ἐν τοῖς χειμερίοις, συμβαίνει τοὺς ἐκ τούτου τοῦ μέρους ἀνέμους πνεῖν, ὧν ἐστὶ πρῶτος λίψ, ὢν ὑγρὸς φύσει. ὄντος δὲ τοῦ ἡλίου μᾶλλον ἐν τῷ 35 χειμερίῳ μέρει τοῦ κόσμου, καὶ κινοῦντος τὰ ἐν | αὐτῷ πνεύματα, τὰ χειμῶνος ἔργα συμβαίνει γίνεσθαι· τούτων δέ ἐστιν ὁ ὄμβρος. ἔτι δὲ ἐπειδὴ ἡ ἰσημερία ἐστὶ καθάπερ χειμὼν καὶ θέρος ἰσοκρατές,[22] ἐὰν ὁποτερῳοῦν αὐτῶν τι προστεθῇ, εὔσημον τὴν ῥόπην ποιεῖ, 943a καθάπερ ἐπὶ τῶν || ἰσαζόντων ζυγῶν. ἐπεὶ δὲ ὁ λὶψ ἔκ τε τῆς χειμερίου τάξεώς ἐστι καὶ ὑγρὸς φύσει, προστεθεὶς ἐν τῇ ἰσημερίᾳ ῥοπὴν χειμῶνος ἐποίησε καὶ ὄμβρον· ὁ γὰρ ὄμβρος χειμών ἐστιν οἰκειότατος τῷ πνεύσαντι πνεύματι. |

5 27. Διὰ τί ὁ νότος καὶ ὁ εὖρος θερμότεροι ὄντες τῶν

[21] λοιπόν Forster ex Thphr. *Vent.* 36. : θερμόν codd.
[22] ἰσοκρατές Y[a] : ἰσοκρατής cett. codd.

[55] Source: Thphr. *Vent.* 36.

25.[55] Why are the winds greatest at the end? Is it because when they blow out all at once, what remains[56] is little?

26.[57] Why, if the Lips[58] blows during the equinox, does rain come? Is it because in whatever region of the world the sun is, it sets in motion the winds from there? And this is why the veering of the winds corresponds to the course of the sun. Now since the equinox is the boundary between winter and summer, when it happens that the sun—according to what appears to us to be the equinox—has gone beyond or fallen short of the precise boundary and is rather in the wintry region, the result is that the winds from this part blow, of which the Lips is the first, being moist by nature. But when the sun is rather in the wintry part of the world, and sets the winds in motion in that region, the result is that wintry conditions occur; and rain is one of these. Furthermore, since the equinox is just as if winter and summer were equally powerful, if anything is added to either of them, it makes the tilt conspicuous, as in the case of balancing scales. But since the Lips is from the wintry order and is moist by nature, being added during the equinox it produces a tilt of the scales toward winter and rain; for rain is the condition of winter most closely related to the wind that is blowing.

27. Why are the Notos and the Eurus, which are hotter

[56] Following Forster and Thphr. *Vent.* 36; the mss. reading ("the heat") does not make sense.

[57] Source: Thphr. (?) *Sign.* 20.

[58] On the direction of Lips, see the Aristotelian wind rose provided in the introduction. The name is possibly derived from λείβω ("pour") or from Λιβύη ("Libya").

ἐναντίων, ὁ μὲν τοῦ βορέου, ὁ δὲ τοῦ ζεφύρου, ὑδατω-
δέστεροί εἰσιν; καίτοι διὰ ψυχρότητα ὕδωρ ἐξ ἀέρος
γίνεται. οὐ γὰρ διὰ τὸ ἀπωθεῖν τὸν βορέαν ἐντεῦθεν
γίνεται τὰ νέφη· ὁ γὰρ ζέφυρος καὶ ὁ εὖρος ἀπάγου-
10 σιν ἄμφω (ὁμοίως γὰρ πλάγιοι), | καὶ οἱ ἄλλοι δὲ
πάντες, ὅθεν πνέουσιν. πότερον ὅτι ἀντιπεριίσταται τὸ
ψυχρὸν εἴσω μᾶλλον, ὅταν ᾖ ἔξω τὸ θερμὸν μᾶλλον; ἢ
ἔστι μέν τι καὶ διὰ τὸ ὅθεν πνέουσιν, αἰθρίους εἶναι;
καὶ γὰρ εὖρος ἀπ' ἠοῦς ἐστίν, πρὸς <δὲ> ἑσπέραν
κεῖται [καὶ] ζέφυρος.[23] ἀλλὰ καὶ διότι πρότερον |
15 θερμαινόμενος ὁ ἀήρ, ὥσπερ καὶ τὰ ὕδατα, τάχιστα
καὶ μάλιστα ψύχεται. φέρεται οὖν ὁ μὲν ἀπὸ τοῦ εὔρου
ἀπ' ἀνατολῆς ἀὴρ θερμός, ὁ δὲ ἀπὸ τοῦ νότου ἀπὸ
μεσημβρίας. ὅταν οὖν ἔλθωσιν εἰς τὸν ψυχρότερον
τόπον, ταχὺ πήγνυνται καὶ συνίστανται εἰς ὕδωρ. καὶ
20 μᾶλλον ὁ εὖρος ποιεῖ | ὕδωρ, ὅτι ἀπὸ τοῦ ἡλίου
μᾶλλον φέρει τὸν ἀέρα, καὶ ὁμοίως θερμόν. ὁ δὲ νότος
λήγων ὑδατώδης, ὅτι ψυχρὸς ὁ πρῶτος φερόμενος ἀὴρ
ἀπὸ τῆς θαλάττης, ὁ δὲ τελευταῖος διάθερμος ὢν ἀπὸ
τῆς γῆς κομίζει. ἢ οὐ μόνον τοῦτ' αἴτιον, ἀλλ' ὅτι καὶ
25 μείζων λήγων ὁ νότος γίνεται; διὸ καὶ ἡ | παροιμία εἰς
αὐτὸν "ἀρχομένου τε νότου." οἱ δὲ μείζους ψυχρότεροι,
ὥστε πηγνύει ὕστερον τὰ νέφη. ἢ διὰ τοῦτο ὑδατω-
δέστερος ἢ ἀρχόμενος;

[23] *πρὸς ἑσπέραν κεῖται καὶ ζέφυρος* B x A^m D *Lamb.*1204 A E : *ἥδε δὲ ἡ χώρα πρὸς ἑσπέραν κεῖται καὶ ζέφυρος* cett. codd. (*κινεῖται* pro *κεῖται* β) : *ἥδε δὲ ἡ χώρα* <*θερμή*> *πρὸς* <*δὲ*> *ἑσπέραν κεῖται καὶ ζέφυρος* Forster || om. *καὶ* u et Berol.148

than their opposites (the Boreas and the Zephyr),[59] wetter? And yet water comes from the air through coldness. For clouds do not form owing to the Boreas pushing them away from here; for the Zephyr and the Eurus both drive away clouds from the direction whence they blow (for they are similarly at the sides), and so do all the other winds. Is it because the cold is contained within more, when there is more heat outside? Or is it also due somewhat to the direction whence they blow, that ⟨*the skies*⟩ are clear? And indeed, the Eurus is from the east, and the Zephyr lies toward the west. But it is also because air that has been heated previously cools most quickly and thoroughly, just as water does. Therefore, the air carried by the Eurus from the east is hot, as is the air carried by the Notos from the south. So when ⟨*the winds*⟩ go into the colder region, they quickly condense and are combined into rain. And the Euros produces more rain, because it brings the air more from ⟨*the direction of*⟩ the sun and this is similarly hot. But the Notos as it comes to an end is rainy, because the first air that it brings, from the sea, is cold, whereas the last air, being warmed through, arrives from the land. Or is this not the sole reason, but it is also because the Notos becomes stronger as it comes to an end? And this is why the proverb refers to it: "when the Notos begins."[60] But the stronger winds are colder, so that the Notos forms the clouds later on. Is this why it is rainier than when it begins?

[59] On the direction of Eurus, see the Aristotelian wind rose provided in the introduction (which makes clear that Eurus is not directly opposite the Zephyr).

[60] A fuller version is cited at *Pr.* 26.45, 945 a 29: "It is good to sail when the Notos begins and when the Boreas comes to an end."

28. Διὰ τί οἱ ἄνεμοι ξηραίνουσι ψυχροὶ ὄντες; ἢ διότι ἀτμίζειν ποιοῦσιν οἱ ψυχρότεροι; διὰ τί δὲ μᾶλ-
30 λον ἢ ὁ | ἥλιος; ἢ διότι ἀπάγουσι τὴν ἀτμίδα, ὁ δὲ ἥλιος καταλείπει; ὑγραίνει μὲν οὖν μᾶλλον, ξηραίνει δὲ ἧττον.

29. Διὰ τί ὁ καικίας μόνος τῶν ἀνέμων ἐφ' ἑαυτὸν ἄγει τὰ νέφη, ὥσπερ καὶ ἡ παροιμία λέγει "ἕλκων ἐφ' αὑτὸν ὥσπερ καικίας νέφος"; οἱ γὰρ ἄλλοι, ὅθεν ἂν
35 πνέωσιν, | ἐνταῦθα ἀναστέλλουσιν. πότερον αἴτιον ὅτι ἅμα ὁ ἐναντίος πνεῖ; ἢ οὐκ ἂν ἐλάνθανεν, ἀλλὰ πέφυκε τὸ πνεῦμα κύκλου γραμμὴν φέρεσθαι; οἱ μὲν οὖν
943b ἄλλοι περὶ τὴν γῆν πνέουσιν· || τούτου[24] δὲ τὸ κοῖλον τῆς γραμμῆς πρὸς τὸν οὐρανὸν καὶ οὐκ ἐπὶ τὴν γῆν ἐστίν, ὥστε ἐπὶ τὴν ἀρχὴν πνέων ἐφ' ἑαυτὸν τὰ νέφη ἄγει.

30. Διὰ τί ἀπὸ μὲν τῆς θαλάττης οὐκ ἀποπνεῖ
5 ἕωθεν | ψυχρόν, ἀπὸ δὲ τῶν ποταμῶν; ἢ ὅτι ἡ μὲν θάλαττά ἐστιν ἐν ἀναπεπταμένοις τόποις, οἱ δὲ ποταμοὶ ἐν στενοῖς; ἡ ‹μὲν›[25] οὖν ἀπὸ τῆς θαλάττης αὔρα εἰς πολὺν τόπον σκίδναται, ὥστε εἶναι ἀσθενής, ἡ δὲ ἀπὸ τῶν ποταμῶν ἀθρόως φέρεται καὶ μᾶλλον ἰσχύει,
10 διὸ μᾶλλον εἰκότως φαίνεται ψυχρά. | ἢ οὐ τοῦτό ἐστὶν αἴτιον, ἀλλ' οἱ μὲν ποταμοὶ ψυχροί εἰσιν, ἡ δὲ θάλαττα οὔτε θερμὴ οὔτε ψυχρά; γίνεται δὲ ἡ αὔρα καὶ ἀποπνοὴ[26] θερμαινομένων ἢ ψυχομένων ‹τῶν

[24] τούτου Bekker (vid. app. crit. ad loc.) : τοῦτο codd.
[25] ‹μὲν› addidi ex *Pr.* 23.16, 933a28

28.[61] Why do winds, which are cold, produce dryness? Is it because the colder winds cause evaporation? But why do they do so more than the sun? Is it because they carry off the vapor, whereas the sun leaves it behind? Therefore it produces more moisture but less drying.

29.[62] Why does the Caecias alone of the winds bring the clouds to itself, as the proverb says, "drawing to himself like Caecias does a cloud"? For the other winds raise up (*the clouds*) from the place where they blow. Is the reason that the opposite wind blows at the same time? Or would this not have escaped notice, but the wind naturally travels in a circular line? The other winds therefore blow round the earth; but the curve of the line of this wind is toward the sky and not to the earth, so that blowing toward its source it brings the clouds to itself.

30.[63] Why doesn't the wind blow cold from the sea in the morning, but it does from the river? Is it because the sea is in spread-out areas, whereas rivers are in narrow ones? Thus the breeze from the sea is dispersed over a large area, so that it is weak, whereas the breeze from rivers travels in a mass and is stronger, which is why it naturally seems cold. Or is this not the reason, but it's that rivers are cold, whereas the sea is neither hot nor cold? Now a breeze or an exhalation comes from the heating or cooling

[61] Source: Thphr. *Vent*. 60.

[62] Cf. *Pr.* 26.1. Sources: Thphr. *Vent*. 37 and 39 and Arist. *Mete*. 364b2–14.

[63] This chapter is virtually identical to *Pr.* 23.16.

---

[26] ἀποπνοὴ : ἡ ἀναπνοὴ *Pr.* 23.16, 933a35

ὑγρῶν⟩·[27] ὁπότερον γὰρ ἂν τούτων πάσχῃ, ἐξαεροῦται, ἐξαερουμένου δὲ τοῦ ὕδατος ὁ ἀὴρ γινόμενος
15 φέρεται, ὅ ἐστιν αὔρα. τὸ μὲν οὖν ἀπὸ τῶν | ψυχρῶν ψυχρὸν εἰκότως ἀποπνεῖ, τὰ δὲ ἀπὸ τῶν σφόδρα θερμῶν ἀποπνέοντα ψύχεται καὶ γίνεται ψυχρά. τοὺς μὲν οὖν ποταμοὺς ψυχροὺς ἅπαντας εὕροι τις ἄν, ἡ δὲ θάλαττα οὔτε ψυχρὰ οὔτε θερμὴ σφόδρα ἐστίν. οὔτε οὖν τὸ ἀποπνέον ψυχρὸν ἀπ' αὐτῆς ἐστί, διὰ τὸ μὴ
20 ψυχρὰν εἶναι σφόδρα, | οὔτε ψύχεται ταχύ, διὰ τὸ μὴ θερμὴν εἶναι σφόδρα.

31. Διὰ τί ὁ ζέφυρος εὐδιεινὸς καὶ ἥδιστος δοκεῖ εἶναι τῶν ἀνέμων, καὶ οἷον καὶ Ὅμηρος ἐν τῷ Ἠλυσίῳ πεδίῳ, "ἀλλ' αἰεὶ ζεφύροιο διαπνείουσιν ἀῆται";[28] ἢ πρῶτον μὲν ὅτι ἔχει τὴν τοῦ ἀέρος κρᾶσιν; οὔτε γὰρ
25 θερμὸς ὥσπερ οἱ ἀπὸ μεσημβρίας | καὶ ἕω, οὔτε ψυχρὸς ὥσπερ οἱ ἀπὸ τῆς ἄρκτου, ἀλλ' ἐν μεθορίῳ ἐστὶ[29] τῶν ψυχρῶν καὶ θερμῶν πνευμάτων· γειτνιῶν δὲ ἀμφοῖν τῆς δυνάμεως αὐτῶν κοινωνεῖ, διὸ καὶ εὔκρατός ἐστι καὶ πνεῖ ἔαρος μάλιστα. ἔτι τὰ πνεύματα περιίσταται ἢ εἰς τἀναντία ἢ εἰς τὰ δεξιά. μετὰ οὖν
30 τὸν | βορέαν πνέων (ἐπὶ δεξιὰ γὰρ ὁ τόπος) εὐδοκιμεῖ, ὥσπερ παρὰ χαλεπὸν πρᾶος. καὶ ἅμα ὅταν ἀποχειμάσῃ, εὐδία εἴωθε γίνεσθαι ὡς ἐπὶ τὸ πολύ. ὁ δὲ βορέας χειμέριος ἄνεμος. †καὶ ὁ ἀπηλιώτης δὲ ἐν τῷ μέσῳ ὢν τῶν θερμῶν καὶ τῶν ψυχρῶν πνευμάτων
35 ἧττον αὐτοῖς κοινωνεῖ. ἀπηλιώτης | μὲν γὰρ πνέων τὰ

[27] ⟨τῶν ὑγρῶν⟩ Forster ex *Pr.* 23.16, 933a36

<of what is moist>: for whichever of these is experienced, there is evaporation, and when water evaporates the air that comes to be travels, which is a breeze. So what comes from cold (*bodies of water*) naturally blows cold, whereas what comes from very hot ones, when it blows, cools and becomes cold. Now one would find that all rivers are cold, but that the sea is neither cold nor very hot. Therefore, what blows from it is not cold, because *it* is not very cold, nor does it cool quickly, because it is not very hot.

31.[64] Why is the Zephyr thought to be gentle and the most pleasant of the winds, and for instance even Homer says that in the Elysian Field "always the breezes of the Zephyr are blowing"?[65] Is it foremost because it contains a mixture of air? For it is neither hot like the winds from the south and the east, nor cold like those from the arctic, but it is on the border between the cold and the hot winds: being near both it shares in their capacities, and this is why it is well mixed and blows most in spring. Further, the winds turn either into their opposites or into those going to the right. Therefore, blowing after the Boreas (for it is on the right), the Zephyr is well thought of, as being mild in contrast with a difficult wind. And at the time when (*this difficult wind*) blows over, the weather usually, in most cases, becomes calm. But the Boreas is a wintry wind. †And the Apeliotes, though it is between the hot and the cold winds, shares in them less. For when the Apeliotes blows, it sets in

[64] Cf. *Pr.* 26.55. Source: Thphr. *Vent.* 38.
[65] *Od.* 4.567.

---

[28] Cf. ἀλλ᾽ αἰεὶ ζεφύροιο λιγὺ πνείοντος ἀήτας *Od.* 4.567
[29] ἐστὶ B x D Am A E *Lamb.*1204 : ἐπὶ cett. codd.

πρὸς νότου πνεύματα κινεῖ (ἐνταῦθα γὰρ ἡ μετάστασις αὐτοῦ ἐστίν), κινῶν δὲ οὐ μίγνυται αὐτοῖς. ὁ δὲ
944a ζέφυρος καὶ κινεῖται ὑπὸ τῶν νοτίων, καὶ ‖ πνέων κινεῖ τὰ βόρεια· τελευτᾷ γὰρ ἐνταῦθα ἡ περίοδος τῶν πνευμάτων. διὸ τῶν μὲν τὴν τελευτὴν τῶν δὲ τὴν ἀρχὴν ἔχων ἐν αὑτῷ δικαίως ἡδύς ἐστι καὶ δοκεῖ εἶναι.†[30]

32.[31] Διὰ τί ἐπὶ κυνὶ ‹ὁ›[32] νότος πνεῖ; ἢ ὅτι ἐπὶ πᾶσι
5 μὲν σημαίνει | τοῖς ἄστροις δυομένοις ἢ ἐπιτέλλουσιν, οὐχ ἥκιστα δὲ ἐπὶ τούτῳ; δῆλον οὖν ὅτι πνεύματα μάλιστα ἐπὶ τούτῳ καὶ μετ' αὐτόν. ἐπεὶ δὲ πνίγει, καὶ πνεύματα εἰκότως ἐπ' αὐτῷ τὰ θερμότατα κινεῖται· ὁ δὲ νότος θερμός ἐστιν.[33] | ἐπεὶ δὲ εἴθισται μάλιστα ἐκ τῶν ἐναντίων εἰς τὰ ἐναντία μεταβάλλειν, πρὸ κυνὸς δὲ οἱ πρόδρομοι πνέουσιν ὄντες βορέαι, εἰκότως μετὰ κύνα νότος πνεῖ, ἐπειδὴ ἐπισημαίνει μέν, ἐπιτέλλουσι δὲ τοῖς ἄστροις. τὸ δὲ ἐπισημαίνειν ἐστὶ μεταβολὴν τοῦ ἀέρος ποιεῖν. μεταβάλλει δὲ πάντα εἰς τοὺς ἐναντίους ἢ τοὺς ἐπὶ δεξιὰ ἀνέμους τὰ πνεύματα. ἐπεὶ δὲ βορέας εἰς τοὺς ἐπιδεξίους ‹οὐ›[34] μεταβάλλει, εἴη ἂν αὐτῷ λοιπὸν εἰς νότον μεταβάλλειν. ἔστι δὲ καὶ ἡ μετὰ τὰς χειμερινὰς τροπὰς πεντεκαιδεκάτη νότιος,

[30] καὶ ὁ ἀπηλιώτης—δοκεῖ εἶναι B x D A^m A E *Lamb*.1204 (obelis inclusi), cf. *Pr.* 26.55, 946b24–31 : om. cett. codd. et Barth. (secl. Sylburg) [31] cap. 32 non vertit Gaza

[32] ‹ὁ› addidi ex *Pr.* 26.12, 941a37

[33] post θερμός ἐστιν, add. ἐπεὶ δὲ—χρόνος (= *Pr.* 26.12, 941b6–23) Y^a Ap Barth., om. Bekker

[34] ‹οὐ› Bonitz

motion the winds toward the south (since its change is in that direction), but though it sets them in motion it does not mix with them. Now the Zephyr is moved by the Notos winds, and when it blows it sets in motion the Boreas winds; for the cycle of the winds ends there. This is why, having in itself the end of some winds and the beginning of others, the Zephyr justly is and is thought to be pleasant.†[66]

32.[67] Why does the Notos blow at the time of the Dog Star?[68] Is it because there are signs at the setting or rising of all stars, and not least at this one?[69] Now it is clear that there are winds at this time[70] and after it. But since it stifles,[71] naturally the hottest winds too are set in motion at this time; and the Notos is hot. And since things are most accustomed to change from opposites into opposites, and as the Forerunners, which are Notos winds, blow before the time of the Dog Star, naturally the Notos blows after the Dog Star, since there is a sign, and it occurs at the rising of the stars. And what is signified consists in a change in the air.[72] Now all winds change either into their opposites or to winds on their right.[73] But since the Boreas does <not> change into winds on the right, what would remain for it is to change into a Notos. And on the fifteenth day after the

66 The obelized passage is omitted from the major mss. It recurs, virtually identically, in *Pr.* 26.55, where it is a better fit.

67 This chapter is virtually identical to *Pr.* 26.12. Source: Thphr. *Vent.* 48.

68 I.e., when the Dog Star (Sirius) rises.

69 I.e., at the setting or rising of the Dog Star.

70 Presumably, when the Dog Star rises.

71 I.e., since the Dog Star gives rise to stifling weather—the dog days of summer.

72 There are likely textual problems with this and the previous line.

73 I.e., east.

διὰ τὸ τὰς μὲν τροπὰς ἀρχήν τινα εἶναι, κινεῖν δὲ τὸν κατ᾿ αὐτὴν μάλιστα ἀέρα τὸν ἥλιον, εἶναι δὲ ἐν ταύταις ταῖς τροπαῖς πρὸς νότον. καθάπερ οὖν καὶ τὰ ἀπ᾿ ἀνατολῆς κινῶν ἀπηλιώτας ἀνέμους ἤγειρεν, οὕτω καὶ τὰ ἀπὸ μεσημβρίας κινῶν νότους ἐγείρει. οὐκ εὐθὺ δὲ ἀπὸ τροπῶν ποιεῖ τοῦτο διὰ τὸ βραχυτάτας ποιεῖσθαι τὰς μεταστάσεις τότε, ἀλλ᾿ ἐν τῇ πεντεκαιδεκάτῃ διὰ τὸ τὸν χρόνον τοῦτον συμμέτρως ἔχειν τῇ κατὰ τὴν μετάστασιν πρώτῃ φαντασίᾳ· ὅλου γάρ ἐστι μέρος εὐσημότατον ὁ εἰρημένος χρόνος. |

10 33. Διὰ τί ὁ ζέφυρος πρὸς τὴν δείλην πνεῖ, πρωῒ δὲ οὔ; ἢ αἴτιος μέν ἐστιν ὡς ἐπὶ τὸ πολὺ τῶν πνευμάτων ὁ ἥλιος ἀνατέλλων καὶ δύνων; ὅταν γὰρ ὑγρὸν ὄντα τὸν ἀέρα διαθερμαίνων πέττῃ καὶ διακρίνῃ, εἰς πνεῦμα διακρίνει· ἐὰν δὲ ᾖ πνευματώδης ὁ ἀήρ, ἔτι μᾶλλον
15 ἐκπνευματοῦται ὑπὸ | τοῦ ἡλίου. ὅταν μὲν οὖν ἐπ᾿ ἀνατολῇ ᾖ ὁ ἥλιος, πόρρω ἐστὶ τοῦ ζεφύρου· ἀπὸ γὰρ δυσμῶν πνεῖ. ὅταν δὲ περὶ τὸ δύνειν ἤδη, τότε διακεκριμένον ἐστὶ τὸ πνεῦμα τελέως. ἀπὸ δὲ μέσου ἡμέρας καὶ πρὸς τὴν δείλην συμμετρότατα ἔχει πρὸς τὸ
20 διαθερμᾶναι καὶ διακρῖναι. διὰ ταῦτα δὲ καὶ ὁ | ἀπηλιώτης πρωῒ ἄρχεται πνεῖν· τοῦ γὰρ ὑπὲρ γῆς ἀέρος τῆς νυκτὸς ἐξυγραινομένου καὶ τῇ γῇ πλησιάσαντος διὰ βάρος, ἕωθεν διακρίνων αὐτὸν ὁ ἥλιος τὸν καθ᾿ αὑτὸν

[74] Literally, "of the rising (*sun*)." Presumably, the sun moves *the air* in the eastern regions. [75] μεσημβρία can refer to both midday or noon and to the south.

winter solstice it is in the south, because the solstice is a certain beginning, and the sun moves the air that is most of all near it, and during this solstice the sun is toward the south. Therefore, just as it rouses the Apeliotes winds when it moves the eastern[74] regions, so too does it rouse the Notos winds when it moves the southern regions.[75] Now it does not do this immediately after the solstice, because the slightest changes are produced then, but it does so on the fifteenth day, because this time coincides with the first impression corresponding to the change; for the time mentioned is the most significant[76] part of the whole process.

33.[77] Why does the Zephyr blow toward the late afternoon, but not in the early morning? Is the sun rising and setting the cause of the winds in most cases? For when the sun, by thorough heating, concocts and dissolves the air, which is moist, it dissolves it into wind; and if the air is full of wind, it is still further made windy by the sun. So when the sun is in the east, it is far away from the Zephyr; for this blows from the setting sun. And when the sun is already close to setting, the wind is then thoroughly dissolved. But from midday and to late afternoon (*the sun*) is in the most suitable position with respect to heating and dissolving the air. This is also the reason the Apeliotes begins to blow in the early morning: for as the air over the earth becomes moist during the night and owing to its weight comes close to the earth, at dawn the sun, dissolving it, sets in motion

[76] I.e., the activity on the fifteenth day is the most conspicuous or easily known by signs.

[77] Cf. *Pr.* 26.35.

κινεῖ πρῶτον. τὸ δὲ ἀπὸ τοῦ ἡλίου πνεῦμα ἀνατέλλοντος ἐντεῦθεν ἀπηλιώτης καλεῖται. |

25 34. Διὰ τί αἰρομένου τοῦ ἡλίου καὶ αὐξάνεται καὶ πίπτει τὰ πνεύματα; ἢ ὅτι τὸ πνεῦμά ἐστιν ἤτοι τοῦ ἀέρος ἢ τοῦ ἀναχθέντος[35] ὑγροῦ κίνησις; αὕτη δὲ ὅταν μὲν ἐλάττων ᾖ, ταχὺ καταναλίσκεται ὑπὸ τοῦ ἡλίου, ὥστε οὐ γίνεται πνεῦμα· ὅταν δὲ πλείων, κινεῖται
30 μᾶλλον τοῦ ἡλίου ἀνατείλαντος· ὁ | γὰρ ἥλιος ἀρχὴ τῶν κινήσεών ἐστιν.

35a. Διὰ τί ὁ ζέφυρος τῆς δείλης πνεῖ; ἢ ἅπαντα τὰ πνεύματα τοῦ ἡλίου διαχέοντος τὸ ὑγρὸν γίνεται; πρότερον[36] γὰρ συνεστηκός, ὅταν ἡ τοῦ θερμοῦ δύναμις πλησιάζῃ, ἐξάπτει.[37] ὁ δὲ ζέφυρος ἀφ᾽ ἑσπέρας
35 πνεῖ. εἰκότως οὖν τῆς δείλης | γίνεται· τότε γὰρ ὁ ἥλιος εἰς τὸν τόπον αὐτοῦ ἀφικνεῖται.

35b.[38] . . . καὶ ὁ βορέας καὶ ὁ νότος διὰ τοῦτο πλειστάκις πνέουσιν, ὅτι τὸ ἐναντίον ὑπὸ τοῦ ἐναντίου κρατούμενον κατ᾽ εὐθυωρίαν ἥκιστα δύναται διαμέ-
944b νειν, ἀλλὰ μᾶλλον ἐκ τοῦ πλαγίου. || ὁ μὲν οὖν νότος καὶ βορέας ἐκ τῶν ἐφ᾽ ἑκάτερα τόπων τῆς τοῦ ἡλίου φορᾶς πνέουσιν, οἱ δὲ ἄλλοι μᾶλλον ἐκ τοῦ κατ᾽ ἀντικρύ.

[35] ἀναχθέντος Y^{a} Ap : ἀναχυθέντος cett. codd.
[36] πρότερον Y^{a2} : πότερον Y^{a1} Ap C^{a} X^{a} Barth. : τότε Sylburg
[37] ἐξάπτει : ἐξάπτεται Louis : ἐκπέττει Forster
[38] nov. cap. Gaza : cap. 35a continuatur in codd. || lac. ante καὶ ὁ βορέας indicavi, add. *Cur aquilo et auster saepissime spirant? An quia . . .* Gaza

first the air that is near it. And the wind from the rising sun is called Apeliotes.[78]

34.[79] Why, when the sun rises, do the winds grow and fall? Is it because wind is movement either of the air or of the moisture carried up? Now when this movement is little, it is quickly expended by the sun, so that wind does not arise; but when it is greater, it is set in motion more when the sun rises; for the sun is a source of the movements.

35a.[80] Why does the Zephyr blow toward the late afternoon? Or do all the winds occur when the sun disperses the moisture? For when the power of the heat is near, it consumes[81] the moisture that previously collected. Now the Zephyr blows from the west. So it naturally occurs in the late afternoon; for then the sun reaches that place.[82]

35b.[83] . . . the Boreas and the Notos blow most often for this reason: when one contrary is mastered by the other, it is least able to remain on a straight course, but it is better able ⟨*to resist a wind coming*⟩ from the side. Now the Notos and Boreas blow from regions on either side of the path of the sun, whereas the others blow more from regions going against it.

[78] See n. 5 above.

[79] Source: Thphr. *Vent*. 48.

[80] Cf. *Pr.* 26.33.

[81] Literally, "enflames"—or "concocts" (if we follow Forster).

[82] I.e., the west—the place from which the Zephyr blows.

[83] I follow Gaza in dividing *Pr.* 26.35 in two; I mark a lacuna at the beginning of 35b. It is, however, possible that the two are part of what was once one longer chapter—see Arist. *Mete*. 361a4–21, which seems connected to both. The opening of 35b provided by Gaza can be translated "Why do the Boreas and Notos blow most often? Is it because . . ."

36. Πότερον τὸ πνεῦμα ἀπὸ πηγῆς τινὸς φέρεται
5 ὥσπερ | τὸ ὕδωρ, καὶ ταύτης οὐκ ἔστιν ἀνωτέρω αὐτὸ
ἐνεχθῆναι, ἢ οὔ; καὶ πότερον ἀπὸ ἑνὸς σημείου ἢ ἀπὸ
πλείονος τόπου; ἔνια μὲν οὖν ἐστὶν ὅμοια ἃ καὶ ἐπὶ
τῶν ὑδάτων συμβαίνει γίνεσθαι.[39] τό τε γὰρ ὕδωρ,
ὅταν εἰς τὸ κάταντες φέρηται, θᾶττον ῥεῖ ἢ ὅταν ἐν τῷ
10 ἐπιπέδῳ καὶ ὁμαλῷ[40] λιμνάζῃ. ὁμοίως δὲ καὶ | τὰ
πνεύματα· ἐπὶ μὲν γὰρ τοῖς ἄκροις καὶ τοῖς ὑψηλοῖς
ἀεὶ ἐν κινήσει ὁ ἀήρ, ἐν δὲ τοῖς κοίλοις ἠρεμεῖ πολλάκις καὶ ἄπνοια γίνεται. ἔτι ἐπὶ τοῖς σφόδρα ὑψηλοῖς
ὄρεσιν οὐ γίνεται τὰ πνεύματα, οἷον ἐπὶ τῷ Ἄθῳ καὶ
τοῖς ἄλλοις τοῖς τοιούτοις. σημεῖον δέ· ἃ γὰρ ἂν
15 καταλείπωσιν οἱ | τῷ προτέρῳ ἔτει θύοντες, εὑρίσκε-
σθαί φασι διαμένοντα τῷ ὑστέρῳ. δῆλον οὖν ὅτι
ὥσπερ ἀπὸ πηγῆς τινὸς καὶ ἡ τοῦ πνεύματος φορὰ
γίνεται. εἰς τὸ ἄνω οὖν οὐκέτι δύναται δικνεῖσθαι. διὰ
τοῦτο οὖν ἐπὶ τοῖς ὑψηλοῖς τοῦτο συμβαίνει. ὁμοίως δ'
ἂν καὶ ἐπὶ τοῦ ὕδατος εἴη· οὔτε γὰρ ὕδωρ λάβρον οὔτε |
20 πνεῦμα ἐξαίσιον ἐν τοῖς ὑψηλοῖς φαίνεται γίνεσθαι.

37. Διὰ τί ποτε τοῦ μὲν νότου πνέοντος ἡ θάλαττα
κυανέα γίνεται, τοῦ δὲ βορέου ζοφώδης; ἢ ὅτι ὁ
βορέας ἧττον τὴν θάλατταν ταράττει, τὸ δὲ ἀταρακτό-
τερον[41] ἅπαν μέλαν φαίνεται. |
25 38. Διὰ τί οἱ νότοι μικρὰ μὲν πνέοντες οὐ ποιοῦσιν

[39] συμβαίνει γίνεσθαι : φαίνεται συμβαίνει Y[a]
[40] ὁμαλῷ : ὁμαλεῖ Y[a] : ὁμαλοῦ Ruelle

36. Does the wind travel from some source, just like water does, and is it unable to travel higher than its source, or is this not so? And does it travel from one point or from a larger area? Now in fact there are some similarities with what also happens to occur in the case of water. For water, when it travels downhill, flows more quickly than when it stagnates on flat and level ground. And similarly the winds: for the air is always in motion on the peaks and the high places, whereas in the hollows the air is often still and it is windless. Further, on very high mountains there are no winds, for instance on Mount Athos and other such places. A sign of this: for what those who sacrifice in a previous year leave behind, they say is found to be still there in the next year. Therefore, it is clear that the course of the wind too is as it were from some source. So it is never able to penetrate upward. This then is why this happens on high ground. And it would be similar in the case of water; for neither turbulent water nor violent wind appear to occur in the high places.

37.[84] Why does the sea become blue when the Notos blows, but dark when the Boreas blows? Is it because the Boreas disturbs the sea less, and anything that is more undisturbed appears black?

38.[85] Why do the Notos winds, when they blow slightly,

[84] Gell. (2.30, 11) refers to this chapter and attributes it to Aristotle's *Problems*. Cf. *Pr.* 23.23.

[85] Cf. *Pr.* 26.20. Source: Thphr. *Vent*. 7.

---

41 *ἀταρακτότερον* Bussemaker (ex Gell. 2.30, 11 [sic]) : *ἀτακτότερον* codd.

ἐπίνεψιν,[42] μεγάλοι δὲ γενόμενοι ἐπινεφοῦσιν; ἢ διότι μικροὶ μὲν πνέοντες οὐ δύνανται πολλὰ νέφη ποιεῖν;[43] ὀλίγον οὖν τόπον κατίσχουσιν. ὅταν δὲ μεγάλοι γίνωνται, πολλὰ ἀπωθοῦσι, διὸ καὶ δοκοῦσι μᾶλλον ἐπινεφεῖν. |

30 39. Διὰ τί ὁ μὲν βορέας ἀρχόμενος μέγας, λήγων δὲ μικρός, ὁ δὲ νότος ἀρχόμενος μὲν μικρός, λήγων δὲ μέγας; ἢ ὅτι ὁ μὲν βορέας ἐγγὺς ἡμῶν, ὁ δὲ νότος πόρρω; ὁ μὲν οὖν ὅταν ἄρξηται, εὐθὺς παρ' ἡμῖν, τοῦ δὲ ἅτε διὰ πολλοῦ χρόνου ἡ ἀρχὴ διασκεδάννυται, καὶ 35 πρὸς ἡμᾶς μικρὸν ἐξικνεῖται | αὐτῆς τὸ πρῶτον· τῆς δὲ τελευτῆς τοῦ μὲν αἰσθανόμεθα, τοῦ δὲ ὅλως οὐκ αἰσθανόμεθα. ὥστε εἰκότως ὁ μὲν ἀσθενὴς παυόμενος (ἀσθενὴς γὰρ ἡ τελευτὴ πάντων), ὁ δὲ οὔ· τῆς γὰρ τελευτῆς οὐκέτι αἰσθανόμεθα αὐτοῦ. ||

945a 40. Διὰ τί οὗ μὲν κόλποι εἰσί, τροπαῖαι γίνονται, οὗ δὲ ἀναπεπταμένα πελάγη, οὐ γίνονται; ἢ διότι εἰς μὲν τοὺς κόλπους ῥέον οὐ διασπᾶται τὸ πνεῦμα μᾶλλον, ἀλλ' ἀθρόον ἐπὶ πολὺ φέρεται, ἐν δὲ τοῖς ἀναπεπτα-5 μένοις ἐξ ἀρχῆς τε αἱ ἀπογέαι | εὐθὺς διασπῶνται μᾶλλον, καὶ ὅταν ῥέωσι, ταὐτὸ πάσχουσι διὰ τὸ πολλαχῇ ἐξεῖναι ὁρμῆσαι; ἔστι γὰρ ἡ τροπαία ἀπογέας[44] ἀνάκλασις.

[42] post ἐπίνεψιν add. ἤτοι συννέφειαν Xa : ἐπίνεψιν· ἀντὶ τοῦ συννέφειαν Ya mg

[43] ποιεῖν : κινεῖν vel ὠθεῖν Bonitz

[44] ἀπογέας Ross apud Forster : ἀπόγεος codd.

not produce clouding over, but when they are strong they cause clouding over? Is it because when they blow slightly they are not able to produce many clouds? Thus they cover a small area. But when they become strong, they push along many clouds, and this is why they seem to cause more clouding over.

39.[86] Why is the Boreas strong when it begins, but slight when it comes to an end, whereas the Notos is slight when it begins, but strong when it comes to an end? Is it because the Boreas is near us, whereas the Notos is far away? Therefore, the former, when it begins, is upon us straightaway, whereas the beginning of the latter is spread out owing to the length of time, and little of it reaches us at first: so we perceive the end of the Boreas, but we do not wholly[87] perceive the end of the Notos. So it is natural that the Boreas is weak when it is stopping (for the end of everything is weak), but the Notos is not; for we never perceive its end.

40.[88] Why do alternating winds occur where there are bays, but they do not occur where there is wide-open sea? Is it because the wind flowing into bays is not more spread out, but for the most part travels in a mass, whereas in the wide-open seas the offshore winds are more spread out straightaway from the beginning,[89] and when they flow, they experience the same thing because it is possible to move in many directions? For the alternating wind is a bending back of an offshore wind.

[86] Cf. *Pr.* 26.19, 41, 45. Source: Thphr. *Vent.* 5–7.
[87] Or perhaps "do not at all."
[88] Cf. *Pr.* 26.4 and 5. Source: Thphr. *Vent.* 26.
[89] Or "from the source."

41. Διὰ τί λέγεται "ἀρχομένου τε νότου καὶ λήγοντος βορέαο"; ἢ διότι ὁ μὲν βορέας, διὰ τὸ ὑπείκειν[45]
10 ἡμᾶς αὐτῷ | καὶ εἶναι τὴν οἴκησιν πρὸς ἄρκτον, εὐθὺς μέγα πνεῖ; ἅμα γὰρ ἄρχεται καὶ πάρεστιν. διὸ παυόμενος ἡδὺ πνεῖ· τότε γὰρ ἀσθενὴς πνεῖ. ὁ δὲ νότος διὰ τὸ πόρρωθεν ὕστερον μείζων ἀφικνεῖται.

42. Διὰ τί ἐν τοῖς νοτίοις βαρύτερον ἔχουσι καὶ
15 ἀδυνατώτερον | οἱ ἄνθρωποι; ἢ διότι ἐξ ὀλίγου πολὺ ὑγρὸν γίνεται διατηκόμενον διὰ τὴν ἀλέαν, καὶ ἐκ πνεύματος κούφου ὑγρὸν βαρύ; εἶτα ἡ δύναμις ἀτονεῖ.

43. Διὰ τί ἐν τοῖς βορείοις βρωτικώτεροι ἢ ἐν τοῖς νοτίοις; ἢ διότι ψυχρότερα τὰ βόρεια; |

20 44. Διὰ τί ὁ νότος οὐ πνεῖ κατ' αὐτὴν τὴν Αἴγυπτον τὰ πρὸς θάλατταν, οὐδ' ὅσον ἡμέρας δρόμον καὶ νυκτός, τὰ δὲ ὑπὲρ Μέμφεως καὶ ἀποσχόντι δρόμον ἡμέρας καὶ νυκτὸς λαμπρός; καὶ πρὸς ἑσπέραν οὐ πνεῖ, ὅσον δύο ἡμερῶν καὶ νυκτῶν δρόμον, τὰ δὲ πρὸς
25 ἕω λίβες πνέουσιν; ἢ διότι κοίλη | τὰ κάτω ἡ Αἴγυπτός ἐστι, διὸ ὑπερπίπτει αὐτῆς, ἄνω δὲ καὶ πόρρω ὑψηλότεροι οἱ τόποι;

45. Διὰ τί ὁ νότος ἀρχόμενος μὲν μικρός ἐστι, λήγων δὲ μείζων γίνεται, ὁ δὲ βορέας ἀνάπαλιν, διὸ καὶ ἡ παροιμία λέγει "εὖ πλεῖν ἀρχομένου τε νότου

[45] ὑπείκειν : ὑποικεῖν Sylburg

---

[90] Cf. *Pr.* 26.39 and 45.

[91] A fuller version is cited at *Pr.* 26.45, 945 a 29: "It is good to sail when the Notos begins and when the Boreas comes to an end."

41.[90] Why do people say: "when the Notos begins and when the Boreas comes to an end"?[91] Is it because the Boreas—owing to our submitting to it and our habitation being toward the arctic—blows with strength straightaway? For it is with us as soon as it begins. This is why it blows pleasantly when it is stopping; for then it blows weakly. But the Notos reaches us later with more strength, because it is far away.

42.[92] Why do people feel heavier and more powerless in the Notos winds? Is it because moisture melted by the warmth becomes abundant instead of slight, and light breath is replaced by heavy moisture? So power is relaxed.

43. Why (*are people*) more inclined to eat in the Boreas winds than in the Notos? Is it because the Boreas winds are colder?

44.[93] Why does the Notos not blow in Egypt itself in the regions by the sea nor for the distance of a night and day run (*inland*), whereas in the regions beyond Memphis and extending for the distance of a night and day run, it is vigorous? And (*why*) does it not blow toward the west for the distance of a run of two days and two nights, whereas toward the east the Lips blows? Is it because Egypt in its lower regions is hollow, which is why (*the Notos*) passes over it, but up and farther away the regions are higher?

45.[94] Why is the Notos slight when it begins, but becomes stronger when it comes to an end, whereas the Boreas is the opposite, and this is why the proverb says "It is good to sail when the Notos begins and when the Boreas

[92] Cf. *Pr.* 1.24. Source: Thphr. *Vent.* 56.
[93] Source: Thphr. *Vent.* 8.
[94] Cf. *Pr.* 26.39 and 41.

30 καὶ λήγοντος βορέαο"; ἢ | διότι πρὸς ἄρκτον μᾶλλον ἢ πρὸς μεσημβρίαν οἰκοῦμεν, πνεῖ δὲ ὁ μὲν βορέας ἀπὸ τῆς ἄρκτου, ὁ δὲ νότος ἀπὸ τῆς μεσημβρίας; εἰκότως οὖν ὁ μὲν ἀρχόμενος εὐθὺς σφοδρὸς πρόσκειται τοῖς πλησίον τόποις μᾶλλον, καὶ μετὰ ταῦτα μεταλλάττει τὸ σφοδρὸν πρὸς ἐκείνους. ὁ δὲ νότος τοὐναντίον |
35 ἀρχόμενος μὲν τοῖς πρὸς μεσημβρίαν οἰκοῦσιν ἔγκειται, ἐπειδὰν δὲ παραλλάξῃ, τοῖς πρὸς ἄρκτον λαμπρὸς καταπνεῖ.

46. Διὰ τί λέγεται "εἰ δ' ὁ νότος βορέαν προκαλέσσεται, αὐτίκα χειμών"; ἢ διότι ὁ νότος τοιοῦτός ἐστιν οἷος νεφέλας καὶ ὕδωρ πολὺ συναίρειν;[46] ὅταν οὖν
945b τοιαύτης τῆς καταστάσεως || οὔσης ἐπιπνεύσῃ ὁ βορέας, πολλῆς αὐτῷ ὕλης ὑπαρχούσης πήγνυσι καὶ χειμῶνα ποιεῖ. διὸ λέγεται "εἰ βορρᾶς πηλὸν καταλήψεται, αὐτίκα χειμών". ὁ δὲ πηλὸς καὶ ὅλως τὰ ὕδατα ὑπὸ τοῦ νότου ἢ μάλιστα ἢ πλειστάκις γίνεται. |
5 47. Διὰ τί ἐπὶ μὲν τῷ νότῳ ταχὺς ὁ βορέας, ἐπὶ δὲ τούτῳ ὁ νότος οὐ ταχὺς ἐπιπίπτει; ἢ ὅτι τῷ μὲν ἐγγύθεν τῷ δὲ πόρρωθεν ἡ ἄφιξις; ἡ γὰρ οἴκησις πρὸς βορέαν ἡμῶν.

48. Διὰ τί τὰ πνεύματα ψυχρά ἐστιν, ὄντα ἀπὸ τῆς τοῦ θερμοῦ συγκινήσεως; ἢ οὐ πάντως ἡ ὑπὸ τοῦ
10 θερμοῦ κίνησις | θερμὴ γίνεται, ἐὰν μὴ τρόπον τινὰ γίνηται; ἀλλ' ἐὰν μὲν ἀθρόως ἐμπίπτῃ, καίει αὐτὸ τὸ

[46] συναίρειν : fort. συναιρεῖν Bussemaker

comes to an end"? Is it because we live toward the arctic rather than toward the south, and the Boreas blows from the arctic, whereas the Notos blows from the south? It is reasonable, therefore, that the Boreas, when it begins, straightaway attacks with violence those in regions nearer to it, and afterward transfers its violence to the others. But the Notos, on the contrary, when it begins, attacks[95] those living in the south, and when it has passed beyond them, blows vigorously on those who live toward the arctic.

46.[96] Why do people say: "if the Notos summons a Boreas, winter[97] comes forthwith"? Is it because the Notos is such as to gather clouds and much rain? Therefore, when the Boreas blows under such conditions, there being a lot of material with it, it freezes (*this material*) and produces winter. This is why people say: "If a Boreas lays hold of mud, winter comes forthwith." And mud and in general water come especially or most often due to the Notos.

47.[98] Why does the Boreas follow quickly on the Notos, but the Notos does not follow quickly on the Boreas? Is it because the arrival in one case is from nearby, whereas in the other it is from far away? For our dwelling is toward the Boreas.

48.[99] Why are the winds cold, though they come from the movement of heat? Or is the movement from heat not in every case hot, but only if it arises in a certain way? If it bursts forth in a mass, the heat burns the very thing which

[95] Presumably "straightaway attacks with violence."
[96] Cf. Thphr. *Vent*. 46.
[97] Or "stormy weather."
[98] Source: Thphr. *Vent*. 9.
[99] Source: Thphr. *Vent*. 19–20.

ἀφιὲν θερμή·[47] ἐὰν δὲ διὰ στενοῦ καὶ κατὰ μικρόν, αὐτὴ μὲν θερμή, ὁ δὲ ὑπὸ τούτου κινούμενος ἀήρ, οἷος ἄν ποτε τυγχάνῃ προϋπάρχων, τοιαύτην καὶ τὴν κίνη-
15 σιν ἀπετέλεσεν, ὥσπερ καὶ ἐπὶ τοῦ στόματος.[48] | φασὶ γὰρ ἐκ τοῦ αὐτοῦ θερμὸν καὶ ψυχρὸν ἡμᾶς πνεῖν, τοῦτο δὲ οὐκ ἀληθές, ἀλλὰ τὸ μὲν ἐξιὸν θερμὸν ἀεί. σημεῖον δὲ τὸ ἐγγὺς προσαγαγόντι τοιοῦτον φαίνεσθαι. διαφέρει δὲ ἡ ἔκπτωσις αὐτοῦ. ἐὰν μὲν γὰρ διὰ πολλοῦ ἀφίωμεν χανόντες, θερμὸν φαίνεται διὰ τὸ
20 αὐτοῦ αἰσθάνεσθαι, ἐὰν δὲ διὰ | στενοῦ, σφοδρότερον γινόμενον ὠθεῖ τὸν πλησίον ἀέρα, κἀκεῖνος τὸν ἐχόμενον. ψυχροῦ δὲ ὄντος τοῦ ἀέρος καὶ ἡ κίνησις αὐτοῦ ψυχρὰ γίνεται. μήποτε δὲ καὶ ἐπὶ τῶν πνευμάτων τὸ αὐτὸ συμβαίνει, καὶ διὰ στενοῦ ἡ πρώτη κίνησις· εἶτ' ἐκεῖνον μὲν διήνεγκεν, ἕτερος δὲ ἀὴρ ἐπιρρεῖ. διὸ καὶ
25 τοῦ μὲν | θέρους θερμά, τοῦ δὲ χειμῶνος ψυχρὰ τὰ πνεύματα, ὅτι ἐν ἑκατέρῳ τοιοῦτος ὁ ἀὴρ ὁ προϋπάρχων· ἐπεὶ ὅτι γε οὔτε αὐτὸς ὑφ' ἑαυτοῦ κινούμενος ὁ ἀὴρ οὔτε ὑπὸ τοῦ θερμοῦ κρατούμενος φέρεται ταύτην τὴν φοράν, δῆλον οὐ μόνον τούτῳ ὅτι θερμαίνει τὰ
30 πνεύματα πλείονος τοῦ θερμοῦ ἐνόντος, | ἀλλὰ καὶ ἄνω ἐφέρετο. τὸ γὰρ πῦρ τοιοῦτον, τὸ δὲ ψυχρὸν κάτω πέφυκε φέρεσθαι. τὰ δὲ πνεύματα πλάγια εἰκότως· ἐπεὶ γὰρ τὸ μὲν ἄνω τὸ δὲ κάτω βιάζεται, καὶ οὐδέτερον κρατεῖ, μένειν δὲ οὐχ οἷόν τε, λοξὴν τὴν φορὰν εἰκότως γίνεσθαι. |

[47] θερμή : θέρμη Y^a
[48] στόματος Forster ex Thphr. *Vent.* 20 : σώματος codd.

emits it. But if it comes gradually through a narrow passage, it is itself hot, whereas the air that is set in motion by this, completes the movement and in such a condition as it was before, just as in the case of the mouth. For people say we breathe both hot and cold from the same place, but this is not true, since what exits (*the mouth*) is always hot. A sign of this is that (*the breath*) appears (*hot*) to what is brought near (*the mouth*). Now its emission is what makes the difference. For if as we yawn we emit breath through a large opening, it appears to be hot because we perceive it; but if we emit it through a narrow opening, occurring more violently it pushes the nearby air, and this pushes the adjoining air. And when the air is cold its movement is cold as well. Perhaps the same thing happens in the case of the winds, and their first movement is through a narrow passage; then it carries this through, and other air flows in.[100] And this is why the winds are hot in summer, but cold in winter, because in each case the air that was there before was of this character. Now that the air travels this course, neither being set in motion by itself nor being mastered by the heat, is clear not merely from this—that it heats the winds when there is more heat in it—but also because it was traveling upward. For fire has such a character, whereas what is cold naturally travels downward. So it is reasonable that the winds travel from side to side: for since the heat forces itself upward and the cold downward, and neither achieves mastery, and yet they cannot remain still, it is reasonable that their course is sideways.

[100] I.e., the wind moves the neighboring air with it, making room for other (colder) air.

35 49. Διὰ τί οἱ νότοι ἐν τῇ Λιβύῃ ψυχροί, ὥσπερ παρ' ἡμῖν οἱ βορέαι; ἢ πρῶτον μὲν διὰ τὸ ἐγγυτέρω εἶναι ἡμῖν τε κἀκείνοις τὰς ἀρχὰς τῶν πνευμάτων; εἰ γάρ, ὥσπερ εἴπομεν, διὰ στενοῦ γίνεται τὰ πνεύματα, τοῖς ἐγγυτέρω ψυχρότερα ἔσται διὰ τὴν σφοδρότητα τῆς 946a κινήσεως· εἰς || γὰρ τὸ πόρρω προϊούσης διαχεῖται. διὸ καὶ παρ' ἡμῖν οἱ βορέαι ψυχροί, ὅτι ἐγγυτέρω καὶ παντελῶς πρὸς τῇ ἄρκτῳ οἰκοῦμεν.

50. Διὰ τί οἱ νότοι οἱ ξηροὶ καὶ μὴ ὑδατώδεις 5 πυρετώδεις; | ἢ ὅτι ὑγρότητα καὶ θέρμην[49] ἀλλοτρίαν ἐμποιοῦσι τοῖς σώμασιν; εἰσὶ γὰρ ὑγροὶ καὶ θερμοὶ φύσει, τοῦτο δ' ἐστὶ πυρετῶδες· ὁ γὰρ πυρετὸς ὑπ' ἀμφοτέρων τούτων ἐστὶν ὑπερβολῆς. ὅταν μὲν οὖν ὑπὸ τοῦ ἡλίου ἄνευ ὕδατος πνέωσι, ταύτην τὴν τάξιν,[50] ὅταν δὲ ἅμα τῷ ὕδατι, τὸ ὕδωρ καταψύχει. |

10 51. Διὰ τί οἱ ἐτησίαι ταύτην δὴ τὴν ὥραν ἀεὶ καὶ τοσοῦτοι πνέουσιν; καὶ διὰ τί ληγούσης τῆς ἡμέρας λήγουσι καὶ τῆς νυκτὸς οὐ πνέουσιν; ἢ τοῦτο μὲν διὰ τὸ τὴν χιόνα τηκομένην παύεσθαι ὑπὸ τοῦ ἡλίου πρὸς ἑσπέραν καὶ τὴν νύκτα; ὅλως δὲ πνέουσιν, ὅταν ὁ 15 ἥλιος κρατεῖν καὶ λύειν ἄρξηται τὸν | πρὸς βορέαν πάγον. ἀρχομένου μὲν οὖν οἱ πρόδρομοι, ἤδη δὲ λυομένου οἱ ἐτησίαι.

[49] *ὑγρότητα καὶ θέρμην* scripsi ex *Pr.* 1.23, 862a18 : *ὑγρότητα θερμὴν* codd.

[50] *ταύτην τὴν τάξιν* : *ταύτην ἐν ἡμῖν ποιοῦσι τὴν διάθεσιν* Forster ex *Pr.* 1.23, 862a21–22

49.[101] Why are the Notos winds cold in Libya, just as the Boreas winds are with us? Is it primarily because the sources of these winds are in the one case nearer to us, in the other to them? For if, as we have said,[102] the winds come through a narrow passage, they will be colder to those who are nearer, owing to the violence of their movement; for when the movement advances into the distance, they are dispersed. And this is why the Boreas winds are cold with us, because we live nearer and altogether toward the arctic.

50.[103] Why are the Notos winds that are dry and not watery fever-producing? Is it because they produce extraneous moisture and heat in the body? For they are moist and hot by nature, and this is fever-producing; for fever is due to an excess of both of these. Therefore, when these winds blow due to the sun and without water, this is the result,[104] but when they come with water, the water cools us.

51.[105] Why do the Etesian winds always blow in their season and with such strength? And why, when the day comes to an end, do they come to an end and not blow at night? Is this because the melting of the snow by the sun stops toward evening and at night? Now in general they blow when the sun begins to master and dissolve the ice in the north. When this begins, the Forerunners blow, but when it is already dissolving the Etesian winds do.

[101] Cf. *Pr.* 26.16. [102] In the previous chapter.

[103] Cf. *Pr.* 1.23 and 26.17. Source: Thphr. *Vent.* 57.

[104] Literally, "this is the order" or "position." The corresponding line in *Pr.* 1.23 has "they produce this condition in us," which makes more sense.

[105] Source: Thphr. *Vent.* 11.

52. Διὰ τί ὁ ζέφυρος λειότατός τε τῶν ἀνέμων καὶ ψυχρός, καὶ δύο ὥρας πνεῖ μάλιστα, ἔαρ τε καὶ μετόπωρον, καὶ πρὸς ἑσπέραν τῆς ἡμέρας, καὶ ἐπὶ τὴν
20 γῆν μάλιστα; | ἢ ψυχρὸς μὲν διὰ τὸ πνεῖν ἀπὸ τῆς θαλάττης καὶ πεδίων ἀναπεπταμένων; ἧττον μὲν οὖν ψυχρὸς τοῦ βορέου διὰ τὸ ἀφ' ὕδατος πνευματουμένου καὶ μὴ χιόνος πνεῖν, ψυχρὸς δὲ διὰ τὸ μετὰ χειμῶνα, ἄρτι τοῦ ἡλίου κρατοῦντος, πνεῖν, καὶ μετοπώρου, ὅτ'[51]
25 οὐκέτι κρατεῖ ὁ ἥλιος. οὐ γὰρ ὥσπερ ἐν | γῇ ὑπομένει τὴν εἵλην,[52] ἀλλὰ πλανᾶται διὰ τὸ ἐφ' ὑγροῦ βεβηκέναι. καὶ ὁμαλὸς διὰ τὸ αὐτό· οὐ γὰρ ἀπὸ ὀρέων πνεῖ, οὐδὲ βίᾳ τηκομένου, ἀλλὰ ῥᾳδίως ὥσπερ δι' αὐλῶνος ῥέων. τὰ μὲν γὰρ πρὸς βορέαν καὶ νότον ὀρεινά· πρὸς ἑσπέραν δὲ οὔτε ὄρος οὔτε γῆ ἐστίν, ἀλλὰ τὸ Ἀτλαν-
30 τικὸν πέλαγος, ὥστε | ἐπὶ τῆς γῆς φέρεται. καὶ πρὸς ἑσπέραν δὲ τῆς ἡμέρας πνεῖ διὰ τὸν τόπον· τότε γὰρ ὁ ἥλιος πλησιάζει τῷ τόπῳ. καὶ τῆς νυκτὸς παύεται διὰ τὸ ἐκλείπειν τὴν τοῦ ἡλίου κίνησιν.

53. Διὰ τί, ὅταν ὁ εὗρος πνεῖ, μείζω φαίνεται τὰ πάντα; ἢ ὅτι ζοφωδέστατον τὸν ἀέρα ποιεῖ; |

35 54. Διὰ τί τὸν μὲν χειμῶνα πρωῒ ἀπὸ τῆς ἕω τὰ πνεύματα πνεῖ, τὸ δὲ θέρος δείλης καὶ ἀπὸ δυσμῶν ἡλίου; ἢ ὅτι ἃ ἡμῖν συμβαίνει τοῦ θέρους, ταῦτα τοῦ χειμῶνος τοῖς τὸ ἐναντίον τῆς γῆς ἡμισφαίριον οἰκοῦσιν; ἡμῖν δὲ τοῦ χειμῶνος πρωῒ καὶ ἀφ' ἕω τὰ πνεύ-

[51] ὅτ' scripsi ex Thph. *Vent.* 40 (ὅτε iam Sylburg ex Gaza) : ὅτι codd. [52] εἵλην Y^a1 : ἴλην Ap Y^a2 : ὕλην cett. codd.

52.[106] Why is the Zephyr both the mildest of the winds *and* cold, and why does it blow mostly in two seasons—spring and autumn—and toward evening, and mostly on land? Is it cold because it blows from the sea and wide-open plains? Now it is less cold than the Boreas because it blows from evaporated water and not from snow, but it *is* cold because it blows after winter, when the sun is just achieving mastery, and in autumn, when the sun no longer has mastery. For it does not await the sun's heat, as if it were on land, but it wanders because it has gone over water. And it is steady for the same reason: for it does not blow from the mountains nor from what is melted by force, but flows easily as if through a channel. For the regions toward the north and south are mountainous; but toward the west there is neither mountain nor land, but the Atlantic Ocean, so that it travels in the direction of the land. And it blows toward evening because of the location (*from which it comes*): for at that time the sun comes close to that location. And it stops at night because the movement from the sun ceases.

53.[107] Why, when the Eurus blows, do all things appear larger? Is it because it causes the air to be very dark?

54.[108] Why, in winter, do winds blow in the early morning and from the east, whereas in summer they blow in the late afternoon and from the setting sun? Is it because what happens to us in the summer happens in winter to those living in the opposite hemisphere of the earth? Now for us, in winter the winds blow in the early morning and from the

[106] Cf. *Pr.* 26.31, 33, 55. Sources: Thphr. *Vent.* 38, 40, 41.

[107] Source: Arist. *Mete.* 373b10–13.

[108] Cf. *Pr.* 26.21. Source: Thphr. *Vent.* 47.

946b μ̣ατα πνεῖ διὰ τὸ τὸν ἀέρα κάθυγρον || <ὄντα>[53] ἐν τῇ
νυκτὶ διακρίνεσθαι καὶ κινεῖσθαι τὸ πρωῒ ὑπὸ τοῦ
ἡλίου, καὶ πρῶτον τὸν ἔγγιστα τοῦ ἡλίου. ποιεῖ δὲ
τοῦτο ὁ ἥλιος καὶ πρὸ ἀνατολῆς· διὸ αὖραι οὐχ ἧττον
πρὸ ἀνατολῆς πνέουσιν. ἐπειδὴ οὖν καὶ ἐφ' ἑαυτὸν
5 ἕλκει ὁ ἥλιος τὰ | ὑγρὰ καὶ κινεῖ πρὸ ἀνατολῆς τοῦ
χειμῶνος ὑγρὸν ὄντα τὸν παρ' ἡμῖν ἀέρα, δῆλον ὡς
καὶ ἐφ' ἑαυτὸν ἂν ἕλκοι, ὧν ἐν τῷ κάτω ἡμισφαιρίῳ,
καὶ δείλη ἐκείνοις ὃ ἡμῖν ἐστὶν ὄρθρος. ὥστε συμβαίνοι ἂν τὸν ὑπὸ τοῦ ἡλίου πρὸ ἀνατολῆς παρ' ἡμῶν
10 ἐφ' ἑαυτὸν ἑλκόμενον ἀέρα, τοῦτον τοῖς κάτω | γενέ-
σθαι ζέφυρον καὶ δείλης πνεῖν. ὃ δὲ ἐν τῷ παρ' ἡμῖν
χειμῶνι, τῆς ἕω ἐκείνοις συμβαίνει, ὃ δὲ ἐν τῷ θέρει,
τῆς δείλης ἡμῖν. ὅτε γὰρ παρ' ἡμῖν θέρος, ἐκεῖ χειμών
ἐστι, καὶ ἡ ἡμετέρα δείλη ἐκείνοις ὄρθρος, καθ' ἣν
ἐκείνοις μὲν αὔρας ἐξ ἑώας συμβαίνει πνεῖν, ἡμῖν δὲ
15 ζεφύρους διὰ ταὐτὰ | τοῖς προειρημένοις. τοῦ δὲ θέ-
ρους καὶ ἑῷαι μὲν οὐ πνέουσιν, ὅτι εἰς ξηρότερον ἔτι
τὸν παρ' ἡμῖν ἀέρα ὁ ἥλιος ἀνατέλλει διὰ τὸ ὀλίγον
χρόνον αὐτοῦ ἀπογεγονέναι· ζέφυροι δὲ οὐ πνέουσι
δείλης τοῦ χειμῶνος, ὅτι οὐδ' ἐν τῷ κάτω ἡμισφαιρίῳ
ἑῷοι ταύτην τὴν ὥραν διὰ τὰ προειρημένα, ὅθεν ὁ
20 ἥλιος | ἐφ' ἑαυτὸν ἕλκων τὰ ὑγρὰ τὸν παρ' ἡμῖν
ζέφυρον ποιεῖ.

55. Διὰ τί ὁ ζέφυρος εὐδιεινὸς καὶ ἥδιστος δοκεῖ
εἶναι τῶν ἀνέμων; ἢ ὅτι ἐν μεθορίῳ ἐστὶ τῶν θερμῶν

[53] <ὄντα> Richards

east, because the air, which is very moist at night, is dissolved and set in motion by the early morning sun, and first of all the air nearest to the sun. And the sun does this even before rising, which is why the breezes blow no less before sunrise. Therefore, since the sun draws the moisture to itself, and before rising, in winter, sets in motion the air around us, which is moist, it is clear that it would also draw the moisture to itself when it is in the lower hemisphere, and that their late afternoon is our morning. So it would happen that the air, which is drawn by the sun to itself before rising near us, would in the lower hemisphere become a Zephyr and blow in the late afternoon. And what happens in our winter happens at dawn for them, and what happens in our summer happens to them in the late afternoon. For when it is summer with us, it is winter there, and our late afternoon is their morning, at which time for them the breezes happen to blow from the east, whereas for us there are Zephyr winds for the reasons stated earlier. But in summer eastern winds do not blow, because the sun rises into the air around us, which is still very dry owing to the sun having been away for a short time; but Zephyr winds do not blow in the late afternoon in summer, because eastern winds do not blow in the lower hemisphere in this season, because of what was stated earlier, for which reasons the sun, drawing the moisture to itself, produces a Zephyr with us.

55.[109] Why is the Zephyr thought to be gentle and the most pleasant of the winds? Is it because it is on the bor-

[109] Cf. *Pr.* 26.31. Source: Thphr. *Vent.* 38.

καὶ ψυχρῶν πνευμάτων, γειτνιῶν δὲ ἀμφοῖν τῆς δυνάμεως αὐτῶν κοινωνεῖ· διὸ εὔκρατός ἐστιν. ὁ δὲ
25 ἀπηλιώτης ἧττον κοινωνεῖ, | ὢν ἐν τῷ μέσῳ τῶν αὐτῶν. ἀπηλιώτης μὲν γὰρ πνέων τὰ πρὸς νότον πνεύματα κινεῖ (ἐνταῦθα γὰρ ἡ μετάστασις αὐτοῦ ἐστίν), κινῶν δὲ οὐ μίγνυται αὐτοῖς. ὁ δὲ ζέφυρος καὶ κινεῖται ὑπὸ τῶν νότων καὶ πνέων κινεῖ τὰ βόρεια· τελευτᾷ γὰρ ἐνταῦθα ἡ περίοδος τῶν πνευμάτων. διὸ
30 τῶν μὲν τὴν | τελευτὴν τῶν δὲ τὴν ἀρχὴν ἔχων ἐν ἑαυτῷ δικαίως ἡδύς ἐστι καὶ δοκεῖ εἶναι.

56. Διὰ τί ἄλλοις ἄλλοι τῶν ἀνέμων ὑέτιοι, οἷον ἐν μὲν τῇ Ἀττικῇ καὶ ταῖς νήσοις ὁ Ἑλλησποντίας, ἐν Ἑλλησπόντῳ δὲ ὁ βορέας καὶ ἐν Κυρήνῃ, περὶ
35 Λέσβον δὲ νότος; | ἢ ὅπου ἂν ἄθροισις νεφῶν, ἐνταῦθα ὕδωρ; ἐνταῦθα γὰρ ἡ πύκνωσις ἀθροίζεται, ὅπου ἂν προκαθίζεσθαι ἔχῃ. διὸ καὶ ἐν τοῖς ὄρεσι μᾶλλον ὕει ἢ ὅπου ἂν τὸ πλῆθος ὑπεξάγειν δύνηται· περικαταλαμβανόμενον γὰρ πυκνοῦται. δεῖ δὲ τοῦτο γενέσθαι· καὶ ἐν ταῖς εὐδίαις μᾶλλον ὕει. ἐν Ἑλ-
947a λησπόντῳ ‖ μὲν οὖν ἄνωθεν ὁ βορέας πολλὰ συνωθεῖ νέφη, πρὸς δὲ τὴν Ἀττικὴν καὶ τὰς νήσους ὁ Ἑλλησποντίας, ὥσπερ ὕλην ἔχων· καὶ γὰρ περιίσταται τὰ πολλὰ ἐκ τοῦ βορέου. περὶ δὲ Λέσβον ὁ εὖρος καὶ ὁ
5 νότος ἐκ τοῦ πελάγους | φέροντες πολλὰ νέφη προσβάλλει τῇ χώρᾳ. τὸν αὐτὸν τρόπον καὶ ἐπὶ τῶν ἄλλων.

der between the hot and the cold winds, and being near both it shares in their capacities, which is why it is a well-mixed?[110] But the Apeliotes shares in them less, though it is between the hot and the cold winds. For when the Apeliotes blows, it sets in motion the winds toward the south (since its change is in that direction), but though it sets them in motion it does not mix with them. Now the Zephyr is moved by the Notos winds, and when it blows it sets in motion the Boreas winds; for the cycle of the winds ends there. This is why, having in itself the end of some winds and the beginning of others, the Zephyr justly is and is thought to be pleasant.

56.[111] Why are different winds rainy in different places? For example, in Attica and in the islands the Hellespontias[112] is rainy, in the Hellespont and in Cyrene the Boreas, and around Lesbos the Notos. Is it that wherever there is a gathering of clouds, there is rain? For wherever a density gathers, there it can settle. And this is why it rains more in the mountains than where the mass ⟨*of clouds*⟩ is able to escape; for being confined it condenses. Now this must occur; even in fine weather it rains more. So in the Hellespont, the Boreas coming from above pushes together many clouds, while the Hellespontias ⟨*pushes them*⟩ toward Attica and the islands, as they have the material; and indeed, most of the clouds come round from the north. But around Lesbos, the Eurus and Notos carry many clouds from the open sea and strike them against the land. It is the same way as well in the case of the other winds.

110 εὔκρατός also means "temperate."

111 Cf. *Pr.* 26.7. Source: Thphr. *Vent.* 5.

112 An alternative name for the Apeliotes.

57. Διὰ τί λέγεται "μή ποτ' ἀπ' ἠπείρου δείσῃς νέφος ἀλλ' ἀπὸ πόντου χειμῶνος, θέρεος δὲ ἀπ' ἠπείροιο μελαίνης"; ἢ διότι τοῦ μὲν χειμῶνος ἡ θάλαττα
10 θερμοτέρα, ὥστε | εἴ τι συνέστη, δῆλον ὅτι ἀπ' ἀρχῆς ἰσχυρᾶς συνέστηκεν; ἐλύθη γὰρ ἂν διὰ τὸ ἀλεεινὸν εἶναι τὸν τόπον. τοῦ δὲ θέρους ἡ μὲν θάλαττα ψυχρά, καὶ τὰ πόντια πνεύματα, ἡ δὲ γῆ θερμή, ὥστε εἴ τι ἀπὸ τῆς γῆς φέρεται, διὰ μείζονος ἀρχῆς συνέστη· διελύθη γὰρ ἄν, εἰ ἀσθενὲς ἦν. |

15 58. Διὰ τί ἐν τῇ Ἀρκαδίᾳ ὑψηλῇ οὔσῃ τὰ μὲν πνεύματα οὐθὲν ψυχρότερα τῶν παρὰ τοῖς ἄλλοις, ὅταν δὲ νηνεμία ᾖ καὶ ἐπινέφελα, ψυχρά, ὥσπερ ἐν τοῖς ὁμαλέσι τοῖς ἑλώδεσιν; ἢ ὅτι καὶ ἡ Ἀρκαδία ὁμοία γίνεται τοῖς ἑλώδεσιν; οὐ γὰρ ἔχει ἐξόδους τοῖς
20 ὕδασιν εἰς θάλατταν, διὸ καὶ βάραθρα | πολλὰ αὐτόθι ἐστίν. ὅταν μὲν οὖν ᾖ ἄνεμος, ἀπορριπίζει τὴν ἐκ τῆς γῆς ἀναθυμίασιν, οὖσαν ψυχράν· αὐτὰ δὲ τὰ πνεύματα οὐ ψυχρὰ διὰ τὸ ἀπὸ τῆς θαλάττης προσβάλλειν· ἐν δὲ ταῖς νηνεμίαις ἀνιοῦσα ἡ ἀτμὶς ἀπὸ τοῦ ἐμμένοντος ὕδατος ποιεῖ τὸ ψῦχος. |

25 59. Διὰ τί, ἂν ἕωθεν πνεῖν ἄρξηται, διημερεύει μᾶλλον; ἢ διότι ἀρχομένου τοῦ ἡλίου σφοδροτάτη ἡ φορά, διὸ ἐκτείνεται τοιαύτη οὖσα; σημεῖον δὲ ὅτι ἰσχυρὰ ἡ σύστασις.

60. Διὰ τί βορέας τὴν ἡμέραν μὲν λαμπρός, τὴν δὲ

---

113 Cf. *Pr.* 25.7. Source: Thphr. *Vent.* 60.

114 It sounds contradictory to say the winds are cold when the

57.[113] Why do people say "Do not fear a cloud from the mainland in winter but from the open sea, and in summer from the dark mainland"? Is it because in winter the sea is hotter, so that if any cloud forms, it is clear that it has formed from a strong source? For otherwise it would have been dissolved because the region is warm. But in summer the sea is cold, and so are the sea winds, whereas the land is hot, so that if any cloud travels from the land, it has formed from a greater source; for it would have been dissolved, if it were weak.

58. Why in Arcadia, which is high, are the winds not colder than around other regions, but when it is calm and cloudy, they are cold,[114] just as they are in flat marshlands? Is it because Arcadia is also similar to marshlands? For there are no exits for its waters to the sea, and this is why there are many gulfs there. Therefore, when there is wind, it winnows away the evaporation[115] from the earth, which is cold; but the winds themselves are not cold because they strike from the sea; but in calm weather the vapor rising from the still water produces the cold.

59. Why, if wind begins to blow at dawn, is it more likely to last throughout the day? Is it because, when the sun begins, the motion[116] is very violent, which is why it continues as it does? A sign of this is the fact that its composition is strong.

60.[117] Why is the Boreas vigorous during the day, but

weather is calm (i.e., windless). Perhaps the author is saying that if it is calm and cloudy, *when* the winds come they are cold.

[115] Or "exhalation."

[116] I.e., the motion or impetus the sun imparts to the wind.

[117] Source: Thphr. *Vent.* 49.

νύκτα πίπτει; ἢ διότι γίνεται ἀπὸ πεπηγότος ὑετοῦ,
30 ὅταν | ἀναθυμιᾶται διὰ τὸν ἥλιον; πίπτει δὲ νυκτός, ὅτι
οὐχ ἡ αὐτὴ γένεσις, ἀλλὰ τοὐναντίον ποιεῖ· τὰς γὰρ
νύκτας ἐκπνεῖ, τὰς δὲ ἡμέρας ἧττον.

61. Διὰ τί τὰ ἀράχνια τὰ πολλὰ ὅταν φέρηται,
πνεύματός ἐστι σημεῖα; πότερον ὅτι ἐργάζεται ὁ
35 ἀράχνης ἐν | ταῖς εὐδίαις, φέρεται δὲ διὰ τὸ ψυχό-
μενον τὸν ἀέρα συνιέναι πρὸς τὴν γῆν, τὸ δὲ ψύχεσθαι ἀρχὴ χειμῶνος; σημεῖον οὖν ἡ φορὰ τῶν
ἀραχνίων. ἢ ὅτι μετὰ τὰ ὕδατα καὶ τοὺς χειμῶνας
γίνεται τῶν ἀραχνῶν[54] ἀθρόα ἡ φορά, ἐν ταῖς εὐδίαις
ἐργαζομένων, διὰ τὸ ἐν τῷ χειμῶνι μὴ φαίνεσθαι; ||
947b δύσριγον γὰρ τόδε.[55] καὶ φερόμενοι ὑπὸ τοῦ πνεύματος πολὺ ἐκπηνίζονται. μετὰ δὲ τὰ ὕδατα εἴωθε
πνεύματα γίνεσθαι ὡς τὰ πολλά.

62. Διὰ τί οἱ βορέαι μεγάλοι τοῦ χειμῶνος ἐν τοῖς
5 ψυχροῖς | τόποις ἐπινέφελοι, ἔξω δὲ αἴθριοι; ἢ ὅτι ἅμα
ψυχροί εἰσι καὶ μεγάλοι, ἐγγὺς δὲ μᾶλλον ψυχροί,
ὥστε φθάνουσι πηγνύντες πρὶν ἀπῶσαι τὰ νέφη; ὅταν
δὲ παγῇ, μένουσι διὰ βάρος. ἔξω δὲ τῷ μεγέθει
ἐργάζονται μᾶλλον ἢ τῷ ψυχρῷ.

[54] ἀραχνῶν Forster : ἀραχνίων codd.
[55] τόδε (sc. τὸ θηρίον) Bonitz

falls at night? Is it because it comes from frozen rain, when it is evaporated by the sun? But it falls at night, because its origin is not the same, but does the opposite: for at night (*the Boreas*) blows itself out, but less during the day.

61.[118] Why, when many spiders' webs are in motion, is it a sign of wind? Is it because the spider works in fine weather, but (*their webs*) move because the cooling air collects on the ground, and this cooling is the beginning of winter? Therefore, the movement of the spiders' webs is a sign. Or is it because after rains and storms, the movement of spiders is incessant,[119] working in fine weather, because they do not appear in winter? For this (*animal*) cannot take the cold. And as they are carried by the wind, they let out a lot of thread. Now after rain winds usually come in most cases.

62.[120] Why are the strong Boreas winds in winter cloud-bearing in the cold regions, but clear elsewhere? Is it because they are at the same time cold and strong, and colder when they are near (*their origin*), so that they freeze[121] the clouds before pushing them away? And when they are congealed, the clouds stay where they are because of their weight. But outside of these regions, the effect they have is due more to their size than to their coldness.

118 Source: Thphr. (?) *Sign*. 29.
119 Or "concentrated."
120 Source: Thphr. *Vent*. 6–7.
121 Or "congeal."

BOOK XXVII

INTRODUCTION

On the face of it, Books 27–30 of the *Problems* deal with ethical philosophy: courage (27), moderation (28), justice (29), and the intellectual virtues (30). This might seem like a significant break from the natural philosophy predominant in the previous books; but in fact the focus of *Pr.* 27 is on the physiological side of ethical states.

According to Aristotle, courage is the state of character by which one is able rationally to choose the mean in those areas of life involving fear and confidence. This virtue receives substantial treatment in the *corpus Aristotelicum* (see *EN* 3.6–9, *EE* 3.1, *Rh.* 2.5, and *MM* 1.20). These works may provide the background or framework for the discussion in *Pr.* 27, but no sources for its eleven chapters can be identified.

The primary concern of Book 27 is discovering the material causes of the physical manifestations of fear: trembling voice, shivering, loose bowels, flatulence, rapid heartbeat, pallor of face, thirst, silence, contraction of the private parts, urination, and the emission of semen (see chs. 1–3, 6–11). Ch. 3 also discusses spirited men—those who are angry and bold—which has a connection to courage. Courage itself is the topic of chs. 4 and 5.

ΟΣΑ ΠΕΡΙ ΦΟΒΟΝ ΚΑΙ ΑΝΔΡΕΙΑΝ

1. Διὰ τί οἱ φοβούμενοι τρέμουσιν; ἢ διὰ τὴν κατάψυξιν; ἐκλείπει γὰρ τὸ θερμὸν καὶ συστέλλεται· διὸ καὶ αἱ κοιλίαι λύονται τοῖς πολλοῖς. |

947b15 2. Διὰ τί οὖν καὶ διψῶσιν ἔνιοι, καθάπερ οἱ μέλλοντες κολάζεσθαι;οὐ γὰρ ἔδει, καταψυχομένων. ἢ οὐκ ἐν ταὐτῷ τόπῳ ἡ κατάψυξις καὶ ἡ θερμότης, ἀλλ' ἡ μὲν ἐν τῷ ἐπιπολῆς, ἔνθεν ἐκλείπει τὸ θερμόν, ἡ δὲ ἐν τῷ ἐντός, ὥστε ἐκθερμαίνει; σημεῖον δὲ καὶ τὸ λύεσθαι
20 τὰς[1] κοιλίας. ἀναξηραινομένου | δὴ τοῦ κυρίου τόπου, τὸ δίψος. ὅμοιον δὲ ἔοικεν ὥσπερ τοῖς ἠπιαλοῦσιν, οἳ ἅμα τῷ ῥιγοῦν διψῶσιν· οὐδὲ γὰρ ὁ αὐτὸς οὐδ' ἐκεῖ τόπος ψύχεται καὶ θερμαίνεται.

3. Διὰ τί ἐν μὲν τοῖς θυμοῖς εἰς τὸ ἐντὸς ἀθροιζο-

[1] ante τὰς add. καὶ α β a^m Barth.

---

[1] Cf. *Pr.* 27.6–7, 10, 11.31.

[2] Cf. *Pr.* 27.8.

[3] The unusual occurrence of οὖν in the opening question, and the lack of specification for ἔνιοι, make it clear that this is a follow-up question to the previous chapter.

PROBLEMS CONNECTED WITH FEAR AND COURAGE

1.[1] Why do those feeling fear tremble? Is it because of the cooling? For the heat departs and contracts; and this is why the bowels become loose in most of them.

2.[2] Why then are some (*of those feeling fear*) also thirsty,[3] like those who are about to be punished? For they ought not to be, since they are being cooled. Or are the cooling and the heat not in the same area, but the former is on the surface, from which the heat departs, whereas the latter is on the inside, so that it heats (*this area*)? Now the loosening of the bowels is a sign of this as well. But when the authoritative area[4] becomes dry, there is thirst. The same thing seems to happen as it does in those suffering from fever,[5] who at the same time shiver and are thirsty; for in that case as well the same region is not both cooled and heated.

3. Why, in those who are spirited,[6] when the heat col-

[4] Likely the region containing the most important internal organs (cf. *GA* 771b31), though Louis supposes the author is referring to the heart.

[5] Or ague—fever accompanied by chills and shivering.

[6] *ἐν τοῖς θυμοῖς* could equally be translated "in those who are angry," but I want to contrast this formulation with the upcoming *τοῖς ὀργιζομένοις* ("in those feeling anger").

μένου τοῦ θερμοῦ διάθερμοι καὶ θαρραλέοι, ἐν δὲ τοῖς
25 φόβοις ἀνάπαλιν; | ἢ οὐκ εἰς τὸν αὐτὸν τόπον, ἀλλὰ
τοῖς μὲν ὀργιζομένοις περὶ τὴν καρδίαν, διὸ καὶ θαρ-
ρητικοὶ καὶ ἐν ἐρυθήματι καὶ πνεύματος πλήρεις, ἄνω
τῆς φορᾶς οὔσης, τοῖς δὲ φοβουμένοις κάτω, συμφευ-
γόντων τοῦ αἵματος καὶ τοῦ θερμοῦ, διὸ καὶ ἡ λύσις
30 τῶν κοιλιῶν; ἐπεὶ καὶ ἡ τῆς καρδίας πήδησις | οὐχ
ὁμοία, ἀλλὰ τοῖς μὲν ὡς ἂν διὰ τὴν ἔκλειψιν πυκνὴ καὶ
νυγματώδης, τοῖς δὲ ὡς ἂν ἀθροιζομένου πλείονος
θερμοῦ· διὸ καὶ τὸ ἀναζεῖν καὶ τὸ ὀρίνεσθαι τὸν θυμὸν
καὶ ταράττεσθαι, καὶ ὅσα τοιαῦτα λέγουσιν οὐ κακῶς
ἀλλ᾽ οἰκείως. ἆρ᾽ οὖν καὶ διὰ τοῦτο τὸ δίψος, ἐπεὶ τό γε
35 ξηρὸν | πτύειν καὶ ὁ σαυσαρισμὸς[2] καὶ τὰ τοιαῦτα
γίνεται διὰ τὴν ἀναφορὰν τοῦ πνεύματος ἅμα καὶ
θερμοῦ; καὶ τὸ δίψος δὲ δῆλον, ὡς ἐκθερμαινομένου
τοῦ σώματος. πῶς οὖν ὁ αὐτὸς τόπος ἀναξηραίνεται
ἀμφοῖν, ᾧ διψῶμεν, καὶ τῷ φοβουμένῳ καὶ τῷ ὀργι-
948a ζομένῳ; ὁ δὲ φόβος ὅτι διψητικόν, καὶ || οἱ ἐν ταῖς
τροπαῖς δηλοῦσιν· οὐδαμοῦ γὰρ οὕτω διψῶσιν. καὶ οἱ
ἀγωνιῶντες δὲ σφόδρα· διὸ καὶ διακλύζονται καὶ ἐπιρ-
ροφοῦσι, καθάπερ Παρμένων ὁ ὑποκριτής. ἢ τούτοις
μὲν οὐκ ἔστι δίψος, ἀλλὰ ξηρότης πεφευγότος τοῦ

[2] σαυσαρισμὸς (hapax), cf. Hsch. Σ 285 (σαυσαρόν : ψιθυ-ρόν) : *siccitas* Barth. : *linguam haerere* Gaza

---

[7] The term here translated (σαυσαρισμός) is rare and its meaning uncertain.

lects within, they are heated and bold, but in those who are afraid (*the effect*) is the opposite? Or does (*the heat collect*) not in the same area, but in those feeling anger it collects around the heart, and this is why they are bold, red-faced, and full of breath, as the course of the heat is upward, but in those feeling fear the course is downward, as the blood and the heat escape together, and this is why there is a loosening of the bowels? And the beating of the heart is not the same (*in both cases*), since in those feeling fear it is rapid and punctuated, as would happen from the departure (*of heat*), whereas in those feeling anger it is as would happen when a great deal of heat collects; and this is why with respect to spirit people say—not erroneously, but fittingly—"boil up," "stir," "be roused," and other such expressions. Now is it also for this reason that there is thirst, since dry spitting, parched tongue,[7] and such conditions occur owing to the simultaneous upward course of breath and heat? Indeed, it is clear that there is thirst when the body becomes heated. How, then, does the same region—the one in which we feel thirst—become dried up in both cases: in feeling fear and in feeling anger? Now that fear is thirst-producing is shown by men in a rout; for nowhere are people so thirsty. And those feeling great anxiety[8] too are thirsty; and this is why they wash out their mouths and swallow besides, just like Parmenon the actor.[9] Or in these people[10] is this not thirst, but dryness from the blood es-

[8] Or "those engaged in a great struggle," though the example of an actor suggests anxiety (specifically, stagefright).

[9] A comic actor of the mid-fourth century, and thus a contemporary of Aristotle. See *IG* II^2 2325 and Aeschin. *In Tim.* 157.

[10] Those feeling anxiety, in contrast to men in a rout.

5 αἵματος, ὅθεν καὶ | ὠχροί; σημεῖον δὲ τὸ μὴ πίνειν πολύ, ἀλλὰ καὶ βροχθίσαι. οἱ δ' ἐν ταῖς τροπαῖς μετὰ πόνου. διὸ διψῶσι καὶ οἱ μέλλοντες κολάζεσθαι· καὶ οὐθὲν ἄτοπον. ἐν δὲ τοῖς πολεμικοῖς ἔνιοι καὶ τῶν ἀνδρείων, ὅταν διασκευασθῶσι, καὶ τρέμουσιν οὐκ ἐξεστηκότες ἀλλὰ θαρροῦντες· ὧν εἰώθασι μαστιγοῦν |
10 τὸ σῶμα πλατεῖ νάρθηκι, εἰ δὲ μή, ταῖς χερσὶν <ἵν'> ἀναθερμανθῇ.[3] ἔοικε δὴ διὰ τὴν ὀξύτητα καὶ τὴν φορὰν τοῦ θερμοῦ ἀνωμαλία τις εἶναι περὶ τὸ σῶμα ταραχώδης.

4. Διὰ τί οἱ ἀνδρεῖοι ὡς ἐπὶ τὸ πολὺ φίλοινοι; ἢ ὅτι οἱ ἀνδρεῖοι θερμοί, ἡ δὲ θερμότης περὶ τὰ στήθη;
15 ἐνταῦθα γὰρ | καὶ ὁ φόβος φαίνεται, γινόμενος κατάψυξίς τις, ὥστε[4] περὶ τὴν καρδίαν ἧττον μένει,[5] τοῖς δὲ πηδᾷ ψυχομένη. ὅσοι οὖν τὸν πνεύμονα ἔχουσιν ἔναιμον, θερμὸν ἔχουσι τοῦτον ὥσπερ οἰνωμένοι, ὥστε οὐ ψύχει ἡ φαντασία τοῦ δεινοῦ. οἱ δὲ τοιοῦτοι καὶ φιλοπόται. ἥ τε γὰρ τοῦ ποτοῦ ἐπιθυμία διὰ τὴν
20 τούτου | τοῦ μορίου θερμότητά ἐστιν (εἴρηται δὲ περὶ τούτου[6] ἐν ἄλλοις) καὶ τοῦ παυστικοῦ ἡ ἐπιθυμία. ὁ δὲ οἶνος θερμὸς μὲν τὴν φύσιν, παύει δὲ τὴν δίψαν μᾶλλον τοῦ ὕδατος, καὶ μάλιστα τῶν αὐτῶν· δι' ἣν

[3] <ἵν'> ἀναθερμανθῇ Richards : ἀναθερμανθέντες codd. : fort. <ἵν'> ἀναθερμανθῶσι

[4] post ὥστε add. τοῖς μὲν Ruelle

[5] μένει β Barth. : μὲν μένει cett. codd.

[6] τούτου β Barth. : αὐτοῦ cett. codd.

caping, for which reason too they are pale? Now a sign of this is that they don't drink a great deal, but in fact take a gulp. But men in a rout are (*feeling fear and acting*) with exertion. This is why those too who are about to be punished are thirsty;[11] and this is not strange. And in war, even some of the courageous, when they are equipped for battle, also tremble, not because they are distraught, but because they are bold; and they are accustomed to whip their bodies with a flat stick, or if not, with their hands, in order that they may be heated. It is likely that owing to the sharpness and course of the heat there is a disturbing inequality (*of temperature*) with respect to the body.

4.[12] Why are the courageous in most cases wine lovers? Is it because the courageous are hot, and heat is in the region of the chest? For fear manifests itself there as well, arising as a sort of cooling; so that less heat remains in the region of the heart, and in some people the heart beats rapidly as it cools. Therefore, those who have blood in their lungs have hot lungs, like those who have been drinking wine, so that the presentation of terror does not cool them. Now such people are also lovers of drink. For the desire for drink is owing to the heat of this part (this has been discussed in other places)[13] and this desire is for what can stop (*the heat*). Now wine is hot in its nature, and it stops thirst more than water does, and especially in these very people;[14] the reason for which has been discussed in other

[11] An example of those feeling anxiety, not a case similar to men in a rout.

[12] Cf. *Pr.* 3.7.

[13] The work(s) referred to may be lost; but cf. *Pr.* 3.7.

[14] I.e., the courageous.

αἰτίαν, εἴρηται ἐν ἄλλοις. διὸ καὶ οἱ ἐν τῇ περιπνευμονίᾳ καὶ οἱ μαινόμενοι ἀμφότεροι ἐπιθυμοῦσιν |
25 οἴνου· καίτοι τῶν μὲν διὰ τὴν θερμασίαν θερμὸς ὁ πνεύμων, τῶν δὲ διὰ τὴν ταραχήν. ἐπεὶ οὖν οἱ αὐτοὶ ὡς ἐπὶ τὸ πολὺ τῷ γένει διψητικοὶ καὶ ἀνδρεῖοι, οἴνου δὲ οἱ διψητικοὶ ἐπιθυμητικοί, οἱ δὲ τοιοῦτοι φιλοπόται, ἀναγκαῖον ὡς ἐπὶ τὸ πολὺ παρακολουθεῖν ἀλλήλοις
30 τὰς φύσεις. διὸ καὶ οἱ οἰνωμένοι | ἀνδρειότεροι τῶν μή.

5. Διὰ τί μάλιστα τὴν ἀνδρείαν τιμῶσιν αἱ πόλεις, οὐ βελτίστην οὖσαν τῶν ἀρετῶν; ἢ ὅτι διατελοῦσιν ἢ πολεμοῦντες ἢ πολεμούμενοι, αὕτη δὲ ἐν ἀμφοῖν χρησιμωτάτη ἐστίν; τιμῶσι δὲ οὐ τὰ βέλτιστα, ἀλλὰ τὰ αὑτοῖς βέλτιστα. |

35 6. Διὰ τί οἱ φοβούμενοι μάλιστα τρέμουσι τὴν φωνὴν καὶ τὰς χεῖρας καὶ τὸ κάτω χεῖλος; ἢ διότι ἔκλειψίς ἐστι τὸ πάθος θερμοῦ ἐκ τῶν ἄνω τόπων; διὸ καὶ ὠχριῶσιν. διὰ μὲν οὖν τὸ ἐκ τοῦ στήθους ἡ φωνὴ τρέμει, ψυχομένου ᾧ κινεῖται. ὁμοίως δὲ καὶ αἱ χεῖρες·
948b ἐκ τοῦ στήθους γὰρ ἤρτηνται. τὸ δὲ || κάτω χεῖλος, ἀλλ' οὐ τὸ ἄνωθεν,[7] κάτω κρέμαται ᾗ ῥέπει· τὸ δὲ κάτωθεν ἄνω παρὰ φύσιν, ἀλλ' ὑπὸ τοῦ θερμοῦ ἄνω

[7] post ἄνωθεν add. τρέμει, διότι τὸ ἄνωθεν Forster ex Gaza

---

[15] The work(s) referred to may be lost; but see [Arist./Alex.] *Sup.Pr.* 3.14.

[16] I.e., courage and love of wine.

[17] The subject of the main verb is not specified. It likely means people (or citizens of the cities) generally. But if one renders

places.[15] And this is why those suffering from pneumonia and the insane both desire wine; and yet the lungs of the former are hot owing to a process of heating, whereas those of the latter are hot owing to their disorder. Therefore, since the same people are in most cases thirsty and courageous in kind, and those who are thirsty are desirous of wine, and such people are lovers of drink, it necessarily follows that in most cases these natures[16] accompany each other. And this is why those who have been drinking wine are more courageous than those who have not.

5. Why do cities honor courage most of all, though it is not the best of the virtues? Is it because they[17] are continually fighting a war or being fought in a war, and in both cases courage is most useful? So they honor not what is best, but what is best for themselves.

6.[18] Why do those feeling fear tremble most in the voice, the hands, and the lower lip? Is it because this condition is a departure of heat from the upper parts? And this is why they grow pale. Now the voice trembles because of the departure of heat from the chest, when that by which it is set in motion is cooled. And it's the same with the hands as well; for they depend upon the chest. Now the lower lip, but not the upper, hangs downward[19] in the direction it tends (*naturally*); and the lower lip moving in an upward direction is contrary to nature,[20] but it remains up because

διατελοῦσιν "they persevere," then the implied subject could be "courageous men."

[18] Cf. *Pr.* 27.1, 7, 10 and 11.31.

[19] Or, following Forster's emendation (based on Gaza), "the lower lip trembles, but not the upper, because the upper hangs downward," etc.

[20] I.e., contrary to its natural tendency.

ἠρεμεῖ· οὗ ὑφαιρουμένου διὰ τὸ ψύχεσθαι τρέμει. καὶ ἐν τοῖς θυμοῖς δὲ διὰ τὸ αὐτὸ ἀποκρεμάννυται τὸ
5 χεῖλος. δῆλον | δὲ ἐπὶ τῶν παιδίων· συνθεῖ γὰρ εἰς τὴν καρδίαν τὸ θερμόν.

7. Διὰ τί οἱ φοβούμενοι τρέμουσι, καὶ μάλιστα τὴν φωνὴν καὶ τοῦ σώματος τὰς χεῖρας καὶ τὸ κάτω χεῖλος; ἢ διότι ἐκ τούτου τοῦ τόπου ἐκλείπει τὸ θερμὸν ἐν ᾧ ἡ φωνή, τὸ δὲ χεῖλος καὶ τὰς χεῖρας, ὅτι εὐκινη-
10 τότατα καὶ ἥκιστα ἔναιμα; | καὶ προΐενται μὲν τὴν χολήν,[8] συσπῶσι δὲ τὰ αἰδοῖα,[9] προΐενται μὲν διὰ τὸ συντήκειν τὸ καταβαῖνον θερμόν, ἀνασπῶσι δέ, ὅτι ἔξωθεν φόβος· εἰς τοὐναντίον οὖν ἡ φυγή.

8. Διὰ τί οἱ φοβούμενοι καὶ ῥιγῶσι καὶ διψῶσι;[10] ταῦτα δὲ ἐναντία τὰ πάθη. ἢ ῥιγῶσι μὲν ψυχόμενοι,
15 διψῶσι δὲ | θερμαινόμενοι, διότι[11] ἐν τῷ φοβεῖσθαι τὸ θερμὸν ἐκλείπει καὶ τὸ ὑγρὸν ἐκ τῶν ἄνω τόπων; δηλοῖ δὲ τὸ χρῶμα καὶ αἱ κοιλίαι· τὸ μὲν γὰρ πρόσωπον ὠχρόν, αἱ δὲ κοιλίαι ἐνίοτε λύονται. διὰ μὲν οὖν τὸ ἐκλείπειν τὸ θερμὸν ἐκ τῶν ἄνωθεν τὸ ῥῖγος γίνεται, διὰ δὲ τὸ[12] ὑγρὸν ἡ δίψα. |

20 9. Διὰ τί τοῦ τε φόβου λύπης τινὸς ὄντος καὶ τῆς ἀλγηδόνος, οἱ μὲν ἀλγοῦντες ἀναβοῶσιν, οἱ δὲ φοβού-

[8] χολήν : γονήν Sylburg [9] ante τὰ αἰδοῖα add. καὶ β Xa u [10] ῥιγῶσι καὶ διψῶσι codd. (teste Marenghi3), Gaza : διψῶσι καὶ ῥιγῶσι Ya Ca (teste Louis), Barth.
[11] διότι : διὸ β [12] <τὸ> τὸ Richards

[21] Cf. *Pr.* 27.1, 6, 10 and 11.31.

of the heat. So when the heat is withdrawn, owing to the cooling it trembles. And in those who are spirited, the lip hangs down for the same reason. This is clear in the case of children: for the heat goes into the heart.

7.[21] Why do those feeling fear tremble, and especially in the voice and, concerning the body, in the hands and the lower lip? Is it because the heat departs from the part in which the voice resides, and, with respect to the lip and the hands, because these are most easily moved and have the least blood in them? And (*those feeling fear*) emit bile, and their private parts contract: they emit owing to the melting from the descending heat, and they retract because fear comes from outside; so the flight is in the opposite direction.

8.[22] Why do those feeling fear shiver and feel thirsty (these being contrary conditions)? Do they shiver when they are being cooled, and feel thirsty when they are being heated, since in those feeling fear the heat and the moisture depart from the upper parts of the body? Complexion and the bowels make this clear: for the face becomes pale, and the bowels are sometimes loosened. Therefore, shivering occurs owing to the heat departing from the upper parts, whereas thirst occurs owing to the moisture departing.

9.[23] Why, although both fear and pain are a sort of grief,[24] do those feeling pain cry out, whereas those feeling

[22] Cf. *Pr.* 27.2. [23] Cf. *Pr.* 11.32.

[24] Both λύπη and ἀλγηδονῶς can be translated "grief" or "pain." As used here, however, λύπη is meant to be the broader term, and ἀλγηδονῶς refers to physical suffering, thus I translate them "grief" and "pain" respectively.

μενοι σιωπῶσιν; ἢ οἱ μὲν ἀλγοῦντες κατέχουσι τὸ πνεῦμα (διὸ ἀθρόον ἐξιὸν μετὰ βοῆς[13] ἐξέρχεται), τῶν δὲ φοβουμένων κατέψυκται τὸ σῶμα καὶ τὸ θερμὸν
25 κάτω ἐνήνεκται, ὃ ποιεῖ | πνεύματα. ᾗ οὖν ἐνήνεκται μάλιστα, ἐνταῦθα καὶ ποιεῖ αὐτά. διὸ καὶ ἀποψοφοῦσιν οἱ φοβούμενοι. ἡ δὲ φωνή ἐστι φορὰ πνεύματος ἄνω πως καὶ διά τινων γινομένη. τοῦ δὲ τοὺς ἀλγοῦντας κατέχειν τὸ πνεῦμα αἴτιον, ὅτι ταῖς ἐνυπαρχούσαις ἡμῖν βοηθείαις φύσει εὐθὺς πάντες παθόντες
30 ἄνευ | λογισμοῦ χρώμεθα, καθάπερ καὶ τὰ ἄλλα ζῷα· τὰ μὲν γὰρ κέρασι, τὰ δὲ ὀδοῦσι, τὰ δὲ ὄνυξιν ἀμύνεται. πρὸς δὲ τὰ ἀλγήματα πάντα ἢ τὰ πλεῖστα βοηθεῖ ἡ θερμότης. ὃ ποιεῖ ὁ κατέχων τὸ πνεῦμα· θερμαίνει γὰρ καὶ ἐκπέττει τὸ ἄλγημα, συστέλλων ἐντὸς τὸ θερμὸν τῷ πνεύματι. |

35 10. Διὰ τί τοῖς φοβουμένοις αἱ κοιλίαι λύονται καὶ οὐρητιῶσιν; ἢ τὸ θερμὸν τὸ ἐν ἡμῖν ἐστὶν ὥσπερ ζῷον; τοῦτ' οὖν φεύγει ὅ τι ἂν φοβηθῇ. ἔξωθεν οὖν γινομένων τῶν τε ὑπὸ τῆς ἀγωνίας φόβων καὶ τῶν τοιούτων, καὶ ἐκ τῶν ἄνωθεν εἰς τὰ κάτω καὶ ἐκ τῶν
949a ἐπιπολῆς εἰς τὰ ἐντός, ἐκθερμαινόμενοι || δὴ οἱ περὶ τὴν κοιλίαν τόποι καὶ τὴν κύστιν διαλύονται, καὶ ποιοῦσιν αὐτὰς εὐτρεπεῖς. καὶ γὰρ τὰ ἄνηθα καὶ τὰ ἀψίνθια, καὶ ὅσα οὐρητικά, καὶ[14] θερμαντικά. ὁμοίως δὲ καὶ τὰ πρὸς τὴν κοιλίαν φάρμακα, τὰ κάτω θερμαν-

[13] βοῆς α γ δ (praeter u) : φωνῆς β u
[14] καὶ om. γ

fear remain silent? Is it because those feeling pain hold their breath (which is why, exiting in a mass, it exits with a cry),[25] whereas the bodies of those feeling fear cool down and the heat, which creates breath, is carried downward? Now it creates breath most in the place to which it has been carried. And this is why those feeling fear break wind. But the voice is a rush of breath upward in some way and occurring through certain ⟨*passages*⟩. And the reason those feeling pain hold their breath is that all of us, when we suffer, straightaway and without thinking make use of those useful things presented to us by nature, just like the other animals do: for some defend themselves with horns, others with teeth, and others with claws. Now against all or most pains, heat is useful. This is what is done when someone holds his breath; for he heats and concocts the pain, collecting heat within by means of the breath.

10.[26] Why do the bowels[27] loosen in those feeling fear and ⟨*why do those feeling fear*⟩ desire to urinate? Is the heat in us like a living being? Therefore, this flees whatever it fears. Since, then, the fears due to anxiety and such things come from the outside, and from the upper parts to the lower and from the surface to the interior, the regions around the stomach and the bladder, becoming hot, are thoroughly loosened, and so make these organs ready to function. Indeed, anise and wormwood and all the diuretics also produce heat. In the same way, the drugs that affect the stomach also produce heat in the lower parts:

[25] Or, with some mss., "a voice."

[26] Cf. *Pr.* 27.1–2. Gell. (19.4) refers to this chapter and attributes it to Aristotle.

[27] I translate the singular of κοιλία "stomach" and the plural "bowels."

5 τικά· καὶ τὰ μὲν | τῶν εἰσενεχθέντων μόνον[15] λυτικά, τὰ δὲ καὶ ἑτέραν σύντηξιν ποιεῖ, οἷον τὸ σκόροδον εἰς τὸ οὖρον. τὸ αὐτὸ δὲ τοῖς τοιούτοις ἡ ἐκ τῶν ἐπιπολῆς θερμασία εἰς τούτους τοὺς τόπους συνιοῦσα δρᾷ.

11. Διὰ τί οἱ φοβούμενοι συσπῶσι τὰ αἰδοῖα; εἰκὸς 10 γὰρ | ἦν τοὐναντίον, τοῦ θερμοῦ εἰς τοῦτον τὸν τόπον ἀθροιζομένου τῶν φοβουμένων, ἀνίεσθαι αὐτά. ἢ οἱ φοβούμενοι σχεδὸν ἅπαντες ὥσπερ ῥιγοῦντές εἰσιν; ἐκλελοιπότος οὖν ἐκ τῶν ἐπιπολῆς τοῦ θερμοῦ συσπῶσιν. διὸ καὶ βομβυλίζουσιν[16] οἱ δεινῶς δεδιότες. δοκεῖ δὲ συσπᾶν τὸ ἐπιπολῆς καὶ τὸ δέρμα τῶν ῥιγούντων, | 15 ἅτε τοῦ θερμοῦ ἐκκεκριμένου· διὸ καὶ φρίττουσιν. συσπᾶται δὲ καὶ ἡ ὀσχέα τοῦ αἰδοίου ἄνω, καὶ συνεφέλκονται καὶ οἱ ὄρχεις αὐτῇ συστελλομένῃ.[17] θᾶττον δὲ φαίνεται ἐπὶ τῶν ἀφροδισίων· ὁ γὰρ φόβος ἐκκρίνει, καὶ πολλοῖς τῶν ἀγωνιώντων καὶ τῶν περι- 20 φόβων συγκινεῖ ἡ[18] τῆς γονῆς | πρόεσις.

[15] μόνον α γ δ : μόνων β

[16] βομβυλίζουσιν : βομβυλιάζουσιν Xa u : βομβολύζουσιν Am : βομβλύζουσιν R

[17] αὐτῇ συστελλομένῃ Forster ex Gaza : αὐτοῖς συστελλομένων codd.

[18] συγκινεῖ ἡ : συγκινεῖ [ἡ] Richards : συμβαίνει [ἡ] Platt

some drugs when introduced only loosen, whereas others produce further colliquation, as garlic does (*when introduced*) into the urine. Now the heat going from the regions on the surface into these parts accomplishes the same thing as these drugs.

11. Why do those feeling fear contract their private parts? For the opposite would seem likely: since the heat collects in this region in those feeling fear, these parts should be relaxed. Or are those feeling fear almost always as it were shivering? So when the heat has departed from the parts on the surface the private parts contract. And this is why those who are terribly frightened experience rumbling. Now the surface and the skin of those who are shivering seem to contract, because the heat has been excreted; and this is why they shudder. And the scrotum too contracts upward, and the testicles as well are raised up with it as it is drawn together.[28] This is readily apparent in cases of sexual intercourse; for fear causes excretion, and the emission of semen accompanies many of those who are feeling anxiety and in great fear.

[28] Or, following the mss., "the testicles as well are raised up in them (*i.e., those feeling fear*), when they (*i.e., the testicles*) are drawn together."

BOOK XXVIII

INTRODUCTION

In the *Nicomachean Ethics*, Aristotle distinguishes virtue, continence, incontinence, and vice: virtue and vice are the fixed states of character; continence is the state or condition in which one is tempted to do wrong—there is a struggle in one's soul—but in the end one tends to do what is right; incontinence is the state or condition in which one is tempted to do wrong, and after a struggle one does it. Although continence and incontinence arise in the case of every potential virtue, it has a special connection to the virtue of moderation (σωφροσύνη)—the state of character by which one is able rationally to choose the mean in those areas of life involving certain bodily appetites—and its corresponding vice, licentiousness.[1] The topic of *Pr.* 28 is, as its title indicates, moderation, licentiousness, continence, and incontinence

The following works in the *corpus Aristotelicum* deal with these ethical states or conditions: *EN* 3.10–12, *EN* 7 [=*EE* 6] 1–10, *EE* 3.2, and *MM* 1.21. These provide the background or framework for the discussion in *Pr.* 28, but

[1] Of course, moderation is actually a mean between two extremes (two vices): licentiousness (pursuing bodily pleasures too much) and the rare unnamed vice (pursuing bodily pleasures too little). The latter is not mentioned in *Pr.* 28.

in most cases (five of the eight chapters) no sources can be identified.

Pr. 28 is more concerned with issues in Peripatetic ethics than is Book 27, and less with the physiological side of ethical states. Topics discussed are incontinence (chs. 2, 3 and 7), hunger and thirst (5 and 6), licentiousness (1), moderation and continence (4), and laughter (8).

ΟΣΑ ΠΕΡΙ ΣΩΦΡΟΣΥΝΗΝ ΚΑΙ ΑΚΟΛΑΣΙΑΝ, ΚΑΙ ΕΓΚΡΑΤΕΙΑΝ ΚΑΙ ΑΚΡΑΣΙΑΝ

1. Διὰ τί ἔνιοι κάμνουσιν, ὅταν ἐθισθέντες ἀκο-
949a25 λάστως ζῆν | μὴ ἀκολάστως διαιτῶνται· οἷον Διονύ-
σιος ὁ τύραννος, ἐπεὶ ἐν τῇ πολιορκίᾳ ἐπαύσατο πίνων
ὀλίγον τινὰ χρόνον, εὐθὺς ἐφθισίασεν, ἕως πάλιν εἰς
τὴν μέθην μετέβαλεν. ἢ μέγα μέν τι καὶ τὸ ἔθος ἐστὶν
ἑκάστοις; φύσις γὰρ ἤδη γίνεται. καθαπερανεὶ[1] ἰχθὺς
30 ἐν ἀέρι ἢ ἄνθρωπος ἐν ὕδατι διατελῶν | φαύλως ἂν
ἴσχοι, οὕτω καὶ οἱ τὰ ἔθη μεταβάλλοντες χαλεπῶς
ἀπαλλάττουσιν, καὶ τὸ πάλιν εἰς τὰ εἰωθότα ἐλθεῖν
σωτηρία γίνεται αὐτοῖς ὥσπερ εἰς φύσεως κατάστα-
σιν. ἔτι δὲ καὶ συντηκτικοὶ γίνονται, εἰωθότες τροφῇ
χρῆσθαι δαψιλεῖ τῇ ἰδίᾳ· μὴ λαμβάνοντες γὰρ τὴν

[1] καθαπερανεὶ α β x Xᵃ M : καθάπερ ἂν Aᵐ : καθάπερ οὖν εἰ w : καθάπερ οὖν Richards

PROBLEMS CONNECTED WITH MODERATION AND LICENTIOUSNESS, CONTINENCE AND INCONTINENCE

1. Why do some people become ill when, after having been accustomed to live licentiously, they no longer conduct themselves licentiously? For instance Dionysius the tyrant, when during the siege he ceased drinking (*wine*) for a short time, straightaway became consumptive, until he turned back to his drunkenness.[1] Is habit too something big in everyone? For it soon becomes nature. Just as a fish continuing in air or a human in water would do poorly, so too those changing with respect to their character get on with difficulty, and the return to what they were accustomed to becomes their salvation, like a return to their natural condition. Further, they also waste away, if they are accustomed to being supplied with an abundance of spe-

[1] Dionysius I (ca. 430–367) or Dionysius II (ca. 397–343) of Syracuse. Dionysius I is suggested by the fact that Syracuse was besieged by Carthage in 397–396, Dionysius II by the following passage in Ath. 10.435D–F (= Arist. fr. 605,1 Gigon): "Aristotle in his *Constitution of the Syracusians* says that he (*i.e., Dionysus II*) was sometimes drunk for ninety days continuously."

35 εἰωθυῖαν ὥσπερ ὅλως | μὴ λαμβάνοντες διατίθενται. οὐ μὴν ἀλλὰ καὶ τὰ περιττώματα τροφῇ μεμιγμένα πολλῇ ἀφανίζεται, αὐτὰ δὲ ἐπιπολάζει μόνα ὄντα, καὶ φέρεται εἰς ὄμματα ἢ πνεύμονα· προσενεγκαμένοις δὲ 949b τροφὴν κατακεραννύμενα ὑδαρῆ || γίνεται καὶ ἀβλαβῆ. γίνεται δὲ τοῖς ἀκολάστως ζῶσι πλείω τὰ περιττώματα ἄχρι τινὸς λήξασι τοῦ εἰωθότος βίου, διὰ τὸ πολλὴν ἀκαταχώριστον ἐν αὐτοῖς ὕλην ὑπάρχειν ἐκ τοῦ προτέρου βίου, ἧς τηκομένης ὑπὸ τοῦ συμφύτου 5 θερμοῦ, καθάπερ | χιόνος πολλῆς, ῥεύματα ἁδρὰ συμβαίνει γίνεσθαι.

2. Διὰ τί κατὰ δύο μόνας αἰσθήσεις ἀκρατεῖς λέγομεν, οἷον ἁφὴν καὶ γεῦσιν; ἢ διὰ τὰς ἀπὸ τούτων γινομένας ἡδονὰς ἡμῖν καὶ τοῖς ἄλλοις ζῴοις; ἅτε οὖν κοιναὶ οὖσαι ἀτιμόταταί εἰσι, διὸ καὶ μάλιστα ἢ μόναι 10 ἐπονείδιστοί εἰσιν. ὥστε | τὸν ὑπὸ τούτων ἡττώμενον ψέγομεν καὶ ἀκρατῆ καὶ ἀκόλαστον εἶναι φαμέν, διὰ τὸ ὑπὸ τῶν χειρίστων ἡδονῶν ἡττᾶσθαι.

3. Διὰ τί ἀκρατεῖς λέγονται κατὰ[2] τὰς ἐπιθυμίας μόνον, οὔσης τῆς ἀκρασίας καὶ περὶ τὴν ὀργήν; ἢ ὅτι 15 ἀκρατὴς μέν | ἐστιν ὁ παρὰ τὸν λόγον τι πράττων καὶ ἡ[3] ἀκρασία ἡ παρὰ τὸν λόγον ἀγωγή; εἰσὶ δὲ αἱ μὲν ἐπιθυμίαι, ὡς ἐπίπαν εἰπεῖν, παρὰ τὸν λόγον, αἱ δὲ

[2] κατὰ : μετὰ α δ M Ap Barth.
[3] ἡ om. γ

[2] I.e., unmixed. [3] I.e., undigested or not yet excreted.

cial nourishment; for if they do not receive their accustomed nourishment they manage as if they did not receive anything at all. Moreover, residues mixed with a quantity of nourishment disappear, but when they are alone[2] they come to the surface, and travel to the eyes and the lungs; and for those taking nourishment, as it is mixed (*the residues*) become watery and so harmless. Now in those living licentiously the residues become abundant up to a certain point when they abandon their accustomed life, because a quantity of unseparated[3] matter is present in them from their previous life, which when melted by the natural heat, like a quantity of snow, as a result becomes a copious flow.

2.[4] Why do we speak of incontinent people with respect to two senses only, touch and taste? Is it because the pleasures from these senses come to be in us and in the other animals? Being common, therefore, they[5] are the most dishonored, and this is why they are the only ones (or they are most of all) open to reproach. So we blame the one who is defeated by them and declare him to be incontinent and licentious, because he is defeated by the worst pleasures.

3.[6] Why are people called incontinent only with respect to their desires, when incontinence is also connected to anger? Is it because an incontinent person is one who acts in some way contrary to reason, and incontinence is conduct contrary to reason? Now desires are, to speak generally, contrary to reason, but feelings of anger are in accordance

[4] Cf. *Pr.* 28.3 and 7. Sources: *EE* 3.2 and *EN* 3.10 (see also *EN* 7 [= *EE* 6] 4). [5] These two senses or the pleasures from these two senses—likely the latter.

[6] Cf. *Pr.* 28.2 and 7. Sources: *EE* 3.2 and *EN* 3.10 (see also *EN* 7 [= EE 6] 4).

ὀργαὶ μετὰ λόγου, οὐχ ὡς κελεύσαντος τοῦ λόγου, ἀλλ' ὡς δηλώσαντος τὸν προπηλακισμὸν ἢ τὴν αἰτίαν.[4] |

20 4. Διὰ τί τὴν μὲν ἐγκράτειαν καὶ τὴν σωφροσύνην ἐπὶ τῶν νέων καὶ πλουσίων μάλιστα ἐξετάζομεν, τὴν δὲ δικαιοσύνην ἐπὶ τῶν πενήτων; ἢ ὅτι οὗ μάλιστα δεῖταί τις, εἰ τούτου ἀπέχεται, μᾶλλον θαυμάζοιτ' ἂν ἢ τῶν ἐναντίων; ὁ μὲν οὖν πένης εὐπορίας δεῖται, ὁ δὲ

25 νέος καὶ πλούσιος | ἀπολαύσεως.

5. Διὰ τί ἧττον ἀνέχονται διψῶντες ἢ πεινῶντες; πότερον ὅτι λυπηρότερον; σημεῖον δὲ τοῦ λυπηροτέρου, ὅτι ἥδιον τὸ διψῶντα πιεῖν ἢ πεινῶντα φαγεῖν. τὸ δ' ἐναντίον τῷ ἡδεῖ[5] λυπηρότερον. ἢ διότι μᾶλλον

30 δεῖται τοῦ ὑγροῦ ἢ | τοῦ ξηροῦ τὸ θερμόν[6] ᾧ ζῶμεν; ἢ ὅτι δυοῖν ἡ δίψα ἐπιθυμία, ποτοῦ καὶ τροφῆς, ἡ δὲ πεῖνα ἑνὸς μόνου, τροφῆς;

6. Διὰ τί ἧττον καρτεροῦμεν διψῶντες ἢ πεινῶντες; ἢ διότι λυπούμεθα μᾶλλον; σημεῖον δὲ τῆς λύπης ἡ ἡδονὴ σφοδροτέρα.[7] εἶτα ὁ μὲν διψῶν δυοῖν ἐνδεής,

35 τροφῆς τε καὶ | καταψύξεως (ἄμφω γὰρ ἔχει τὸ ποτόν), ὁ δὲ πεινῶν θατέρου μόνον.

7. Διὰ τί οἱ κατὰ τὴν τῆς ἁφῆς ἢ γεύσεως ἡδονήν,

[4] αἰτίαν : αἰκίαν Sylburg [5] τῷ ἡδεῖ : τῷ ἡδίονι Forster (cf. Trap.) : τῷ <μᾶλλον> ἡδεῖ Richards

[6] τοῦ ὑγροῦ ἢ τοῦ ξηροῦ τὸ θερμόν Marenghi[3] (τοῦ ξηροῦ iam Bussemaker ex Gaza; cf. Barth. et Trap.) : τὸ θερμὸν τοῦ ὑγροῦ ἢ τὸ ξηρὸν codd. : τοῦ ὑγροῦ [ἢ τὸ ξηρὸν] τὸ θερμὸν Ross apud Forster [7] σφοδροτέρα : <ἡ> σφοδροτέρα Forster : σφοδροτέρα <οὖσα> Richards

with reason, not in the sense that reason orders them, but that reason indicates the insult or the accusation.

4. Why do we value continence and moderation most in the young and the rich, but justice in the poor? Is it because someone would be admired more if he abstains from what he needs most, than if he abstains from the opposite? Now the poor person needs prosperity, whereas the young and rich need enjoyment.

5.[7] Why do people tolerate being thirsty less than being hungry? Is it because it is more painful? Now a sign of it being more painful is that drinking is more pleasant when one is thirsty than eating is when one is hungry. And the opposite of what is pleasant[8] is more painful. Or is it because the heat by which we live has more need of what is moist than of what is dry? Or is it because thirst is a desire for two things, drink and nourishment, whereas hunger is a desire for only one, nourishment?

6.[9] Why do we endure being thirsty less than being hungry? Is it because we are more pained by it? Now a sign of the pain is that the pleasure is more intense. Next, the one who is thirsty is in need of two things, nourishment and cooling (for drink contains both), whereas the one who is hungry is in need of only one.

7.[10] Why are those who are excessive with respect to the

[7] Cf. *Pr.* 28.6.

[8] Or, with the emendation or Forster or Richards, "what is more pleasant."

[9] Cf. *Pr.* 28.5.

[10] Cf. *Pr.* 28.2 and 3. Sources: *EE* 3.2 and *EN* 3.10 (see also *EN* 7 [= EE 6] 4). Gell. (19.2) quotes from this chapter and attributes it to Aristotle.

οὗ ἂν ὑπερβάλλωσιν, ἀκρατεῖς λέγονται; οἵ τε γὰρ
950a περὶ τὰ || ἀφροδίσια ἀκόλαστοι, οἵ τε περὶ τὰς τῆς
τροφῆς ἀπολαύσεις. τῶν δὲ κατὰ τὴν τροφὴν ἀπ᾽
ἐνίων μὲν ἐν τῇ γλώττῃ τὸ ἡδύ, ἀπ᾽ ἐνίων δ᾽ ἐν τῷ
λάρυγγι, διὸ καὶ Φιλόξενος γεράνου φάρυγγα εὔχετο
5 ἔχειν. οἱ δὲ κατὰ τὴν ὄψιν καὶ τὴν | ἀκοὴν οὐκέτι. ἢ διὰ
τὸ τὰς ἀπὸ τούτων γινομένας ἡδονὰς κοινὰς εἶναι
ἡμῖν καὶ τοῖς ἄλλοις ζῴοις; ἅτε οὖν οὖσαι κοιναὶ
ἀτιμόταταί εἰσι καὶ μάλιστα ἢ μόναι ἐπονείδιστοι.
ὥστε τὸν ὑπὸ τούτων ἡττώμενον ψέγομεν καὶ ἀκρατῆ
καὶ ἀκόλαστον λέγομεν διὰ τὸ ὑπὸ τῶν χειρίστων
10 ἡδονῶν ἡττᾶσθαι. οὐσῶν | δὲ τῶν αἰσθήσεων πέντε,
τά τε ἄλλα[8] ζῷα ἀπὸ δύο μόνων τῶν προειρημένων
ἥδεται, κατὰ δὲ τὰς ἄλλας ἢ ὅλως οὐχ ἥδεται ἢ κατὰ
συμβεβηκὸς τοῦτο πάσχει. ὁρῶν μὲν γὰρ ὁ λέων,[9] ἢ
καὶ ὀσφραινόμενος, χαίρει ὅτι ἀπολαύσει·[10] καὶ ὅταν
πληρωθῇ, οὐδὲ τὰ τοιαῦτα ἡδέα αὐτῷ, ὥσπερ οὐδὲ
15 ἡμῖν ἡ τοῦ | ταρίχου ὀδμή, ὅταν ἄδην ἔχωμεν τοῦ
φαγεῖν. ὅταν δ᾽ ἐνδεεῖς ὦμεν, ἡδέα. ἡ δὲ τοῦ ῥόδου ἀεὶ
ἡδεῖα.

[8] τά τε ἄλλα : τά ἄλλα τε α β
[9] λέων Richards ex *EN* 1118a20 : ὁρῶν codd.
[10] ἀπολαύσει Bonitz : ἀπολαύει

---

[11] See *EE* 1231a15–17: "This is why gluttons do not pray to have a long tongue but the throat of a crane, just as Philoxenus the son of Eryxis did." The author of *Pr.* 28.7 uses two words

pleasures of touch and taste called incontinent? For those who are excessive in sexual intercourse are called licentious, as are those who are excessive in the enjoyments of nourishment. Now of those enjoyments connected with nourishment, in some cases the pleasure is in the tongue, in others in the larynx, and this is why Philoxenus prayed to have the throat of a crane.[11] But those (*who are excessive*) with respect to sight and hearing are never (*called incontinent*). Is it because the pleasures coming from these[12] are common to us and the other animals? Being common, therefore, they are the most dishonored and the only ones (or most of all) open to reproach. So we blame the one who is defeated by them and call him incontinent and licentious, because he is defeated by the worst pleasures. Now although there are five senses, the other animals derive pleasure from only the two already mentioned, and with respect to the other senses either they derive no pleasure at all or experience it incidentally. For the lion[13] rejoices in seeing or even scenting (*his prey*) because he is going to enjoy it; and when he has had his fill, such things are not pleasant to him, just as the scent of preserved meat[14] is not pleasant when we have eaten enough of it. But when we are in need, it is pleasant. The scent of the rose, however, is always pleasant.

for throat (*λάρυγξ* and *φάρυγξ*, which I render "larynx" and "throat"). These are no doubt synonyms here, the latter coming from *EE* 3.2.

[12] I.e., touch and taste.

[13] Or, following the mss., "the one seeing."

[14] Meat (especially fish) smoked, salted, or pickled.

8. Διὰ τί ἧττον κατέχουσι τὸν γέλωτα παρόντων τῶν γνωρίμων; ἢ ὅταν σφόδρα ἐξηρμένον[11] ᾖ τι, εὐκίνητόν ἐστιν; ἡ δ' εὔνοια εἰπεῖν[12] μᾶλλον γελοῖον, ὥστε κινεῖ.[13]

[11] ἐξηρμένον α β δ : ἐξηρτημένον γ
[12] ante εἰπεῖν add. <ποιεῖ> Marenghi[3], <ὡς> Ruelle
[13] ἡ δ' εὔνοια—κινεῖ : ἡ δ' εὔνοια ἐξαίρει ὥστε κινεῖ μᾶλλον τὸ γελοῖον Forster

8. Why do people hold back their laughter less when acquaintances are present? Is it that when anything is very much excited, it is easily set in motion? Now goodwill (*involves people*) saying more of what is laughable, such that it moves us.[15]

[15] Something is likely wrong with the text, though none of the suggested emendations is satisfactory.

BOOK XXIX

INTRODUCTION

The following works in the *corpus Aristotelicum* deal with justice and injustice: *EN* 5 [=*EE* 4] and [Arist.] *MM* 1.33, to which should be added the remarks on justice in the *Rhetoric* and especially the *Politics*. These provide the background or framework for the discussion in *Pr.* 29, the topic of which is, for the most part, specifically *legal* justice, and the actual source for its chapters seems to be the Athenian law code itself.

Most of the chapters discuss why one sort of unjust action is considered more unjust than another—for example, why stealing a deposit is thought to be worse than stealing a loan (see chs. 1,2, 5, 6, 11, 14, 16; cf. ch. 9). Two chapters discuss why poverty exists more among good people and wealth more among base ones (4, 8), and two why the defendant wins in court when the votes are equal (13, 15). Four others deal with assorted topics: two concerning legal issues (3, 12), two broader ethical issues (7, 10). Chs. 13 and 14 are two of the longest and most developed chapters in the entire *Problems*.

ΟΣΑ ΠΕΡΙ ΔΙΚΑΙΟΣΥΝΗΝ ΚΑΙ ΑΔΙΚΙΑΝ

1. Διὰ τί μείζονος ὄντος ἀδικήματος, ἐάν τις βλάπτῃ εἰς τὸ μεῖζον ἀγαθόν, τῆς δὲ τιμῆς οὔσης μείζονος ἀγαθοῦ, ἡ τῶν χρημάτων ἀδικία μᾶλλον δοκεῖ, καὶ οἱ
950a25 ἄδικοι μᾶλλον | εἶναι δοκοῦσι περὶ τὰ χρήματα; ἢ διότι αἱροῦνται τὰ χρήματα μᾶλλον τῆς τιμῆς, καὶ πᾶσίν ἐστι κοινότατον, ἡ δὲ τιμὴ ὀλίγοις, καὶ ὀλιγάκις συμβαίνει ἡ χρῆσις αὐτῆς;

2. Διὰ τί παρακαταθήκην δεινότερον ἀποστερεῖν ἢ δάνειον; ἢ ὅτι αἰσχρὸν[1] ἀδικεῖν φίλον; ὁ μὲν οὖν τὴν
30 παρακαταθήκην | ἀποστερῶν φίλον ἀδικεῖ· οὐδεὶς γὰρ παρακατατίθεται μὴ πιστεύων. οὗ δὲ τὸ χρέος, οὐ φίλος· οὐ γὰρ δανείζει, ἐὰν ᾖ φίλος, ἀλλὰ δίδωσιν. ἢ ὅτι μεῖζον τὸ ἀδίκημα; πρὸς γὰρ τῇ ζημίᾳ καὶ τὴν πίστιν παραβαίνει, δι' ἥν, εἰ καὶ μηδὲν ἕτερον, δεῖ

[1] αἰσχρὸν : αἴσχιον Richards

---

[1] I.e., the greater the good one harms, the greater the injustice.

PROBLEMS CONNECTED WITH JUSTICE AND INJUSTICE

1. Why, although an injustice is greater if one does harm to what is a greater good,[1] and honor is a greater good, injustice with respect to money is thought to be more unjust, and those who are unjust about money are thought be more so?[2] Is it because people prefer money more than honor, and money is most common to all, whereas honor (*is common*) to few, and the use of it seldom occurs?

2.[3] Why is it more terrible to steal a deposit than a loan? Is it because it is shameful[4] to commit an injustice against a friend? Now the one who steals a deposit commits an injustice against a friend; for no one makes a deposit except with one he trusts. But where there is debt, there is no friend; for one does not lend, if it is a friend, but gives. Or is it because the injustice is greater? For in addition to the loss, one has also violated the trust, because of which, if for

[2] Or "injustice with respect to money seems to be more unjust, and those who are unjust about money seem to be more so."

[3] Cf. *Pr.* 29.6, and see [Arist.] *MM* 1195a10 and Arist. *Rh.* 1383b21.

[4] Or, following Richards, "more shameful."

ἀπέχεσθαι τοῦ ἀδικεῖν. ἔτι τὸ μὴ τοῖς ἴσοις ἀμύνεσθαι |
35 φαῦλον· ὁ μὲν οὖν ἔδωκεν ὡς φίλῳ, ὁ δὲ ἀπεστέρησεν ὡς ἐχθρόν· ὁ δὲ δανείζων οὐχ ὡς φίλος ἔδωκεν. ἔτι τῶν μὲν ἡ δόσις φυλακῆς καὶ ἀποδόσεως χάριν, τῶν δὲ καὶ ὠφελείας· ἧττον δὲ ἀγανακτοῦμεν ἀποβάλλοντες, εἰ
950b κέρδος θηρεύομεν, || οἷον οἱ ἁλιεῖς τὰ δελέατα· προφανὴς γὰρ ὁ κίνδυνος. ἔτι παρακατατίθενται μὲν ὡς ἐπὶ τὸ πολὺ οἱ ἐπιβουλευόμενοι καὶ ἀτυχοῦντες, δανείζουσι δὲ οἱ εὐποροῦντες· δεινότερον δέ ἐστι τὸν ἀτυχοῦντα ἢ τὸν εὐτυχοῦντα ἀδικεῖν. |

5 3. Διὰ τί <ἐν>[2] ἐνίοις δικαστηρίοις τοῖς γένεσι μᾶλλον ἢ ταῖς διαθήκαις ψηφιοῦνται;[3] ἢ ὅτι γένους μὲν οὐκ ἔστι καταψεύσασθαι, ἀλλὰ τὸ ὂν ἀποφαίνειν; διαθῆκαι δὲ πολλαὶ ψευδεῖς ἤδη ἐξηλέγχθησαν οὖσαι.

4. Διὰ τί ἡ Πενία παρὰ τοῖς χρηστοῖς τῶν ἀνθρώ-
10 πων | μᾶλλον ἢ παρὰ τοῖς φαύλοις ἐστίν; ἢ διὰ τὸ ὑπὸ πάντων μισεῖσθαι καὶ ἐξελαύνεσθαι πρὸς τοὺς ἐπιεικεῖς καταφεύγει, οἰομένη μάλιστα παρὰ τούτοις σωτηρίας τυχεῖν καὶ διαμεῖναι; εἰ δὲ πρὸς πονηροὺς ἔλθοι, οὐκ ἂν διαμεῖναι ἐν τῇ αὐτῇ δυνάμει αὐτούς,
15 ἀλλ᾿ ἢ κλέπτειν ἢ ληΐζεσθαι, ὧν γινομένων | οὐκ ἂν ἔτι εἶναι αὐτὴν παρ᾿ αὐτοῖς. ἢ ὅτι τοὺς ἐπιεικεῖς οἴεται τῶν ἀνθρώπων ἄριστα ἂν αὐτῇ χρῆσθαι, καὶ ἥκιστα ἂν ὑβρισθῆναι ὑπ᾿ αὐτῶν; καθάπερ οὖν τὰς τῶν χρημάτων παρακαταθήκας πρὸς τοὺς ἐπιεικεῖς τιθέμεθα,

[2] <ἐν> Bekker
[3] ψηφιοῦνται : ψηφίζονται suspic. Bekker

no other reason, one should hold off from doing injustice. Further, it is base not to repay in equal ways: the one (*making a deposit*) gave as to a friend, the other stole as from an enemy; but the one lending did not give as to a friend. Further, in the one case what is given is for the sake of guarding and giving back, but in the other it is also for the sake of profit; and we are less indignant at losing if we are in pursuit of gain, like fishermen losing their bait; for the risk is obvious. Further, in most cases those who are plotted against and unfortunate make deposits, whereas those who are doing well lend; and it is more terrible to commit an injustice against the unfortunate than against the fortunate.

3. Why in some law courts do people vote in accordance with birth rather than in accordance with the terms of the will? Is it because it is not possible to lie concerning matters of birth, rather it is possible to display what is the case? But many wills before now have been proved to be forgeries.

4.[5] Why does Poverty exist among the good people more than among the base? Is it because, being hated and driven away by everyone, she takes refuge with the fair, thinking that among them she is most able to find safety and remain? But if she were to go to the worthless, (*she thinks that*) they would not remain in the same condition, but would steal or plunder, and when this occurred she could no longer exist among them. Or is it because she thinks that the fair people would treat her best, and that she would least of all be treated with hubris by them? Therefore, just as we place deposits of money with the fair,

[5] Cf. *Pr.* 29.8, and see Ar. *Pl.* 87–98.

οὕτω καὶ αὐτὴ ὑπὲρ αὑτῆς[4] διατάττεται. ἢ ὅτι θήλεια
20 οὖσα ἀπορωτέρα ἐστίν, | ὥστε τῶν ἐπιεικῶν δεῖται; ἢ
ὅτι αὐτὴ κακὸν οὖσα πρὸς τὸ κακὸν οὐκ ἂν ἔλθοι; εἰ
γὰρ τὸ κακὸν ἕλοιτο, παντάπασιν ἂν δυσίατον εἴη.

5. Διὰ τί οὐχ ὁμοίως αἱ ἀδικίαι μείζους[5] περὶ τὰ
ῥήματα[6] καὶ τὰ ἄλλα, οἷον ὁ μικρὸν εἰπὼν οὐκ ἂν καὶ
25 τὸ ἀπόρρητον | εἴποι, οὐδ'[7] ὁ ἕνα προδοὺς καὶ πόλιν,
ὥσπερ ὁ ὀβολὸν ἀποστερήσας καὶ τάλαντον;[8] ἢ ὅτι
ἀπὸ[9] μείζονος ἀδικίας ἔνια ἐλάττω ἐστὶ δι' ἀδυναμίαν;

6. Διὰ τί παρακαταθήκην αἴσχιον[10] ἀποστερῆσαι
μικρὰν ἢ πολὺ δανεισάμενον; ἢ ὅτι ὁ τὴν παρακατα-
30 θήκην ἀποστερῶν | τὸν ὑπολαβόντα εἶναι αὐτὸν ἐπιει-
κῆ ἐξαπατᾷ;[11] ἢ ὅτι ὁ τοῦτο κἂν ἐκεῖνο ποιήσειεν;

7. Διὰ τί ἄνθρωπος μάλιστα παιδείας μετέχων
ζῴων ἁπάντων ἀδικώτατόν ἐστιν; ἢ ὅτι πλείστου λογι-
σμοῦ κεκοινώνηκεν; μάλιστα οὖν τὰς ἡδονὰς καὶ τὴν
35 εὐδαιμονίαν ἐξήτακεν· | ταῦτα δ' ἄνευ ἀδικίας οὐκ
ἔστιν.

8. Διὰ τί ὁ Πλοῦτος ὡς ἐπὶ τὸ πολὺ παρὰ τοῖς

[4] ὑπὲρ αὑτῆς : om. Hett [5] ante μείζους add. <αἱ> Richards [6] ῥήματα : χρήματα Y^a^ Y^e^ Barth. Gaza

[7] οὐδ' Forster ex Gaza : ἀλλ' codd. Barth.

[8] καὶ πόλιν . . . καὶ τάλαντον : κἂν πόλιν . . . κἂν τάλαντον Richards [9] ἀπὸ secl. Hett

[10] αἴσχιον Bonitz : αἰσχρὸν codd.

[11] ἐξαπατᾷ Bekker : ἐξαπατᾶται codd.

---

[6] The text from the mss. tradition is not entirely clear, and seems to require emendation.

so too she appoints herself (*to the fair*) for her own sake. Or is it because, being female, she is more helpless, so that she needs the fair? Or is it because, being herself an evil, she won't go to what is evil? For if she (*being an evil*) were to choose what is evil, she would be completely incurable.

5.[6] Why are the injustices concerning speech[7] and the other things not similarly greater? For instance, the one saying something minor would not[8] also say what is forbidden, nor would the one betraying an individual also betray a city, just as the one stealing an obol (*would not steal*) a talent as well. Is it because some things that come from a greater injustice are less owing to a lack of power?

6.[9] Why is it more shameful to steal a small deposit than a large amount that has been loaned? Is it because the one who steals a deposit is deceiving the person who took him to be fair? Or is it because the one who does this would also do the other?

7.[10] Why is man, who of all animals especially partakes of an education, the most unjust? Is it because he has a share of the greatest amount of reasoning? Therefore, he especially has examined pleasures and happiness, and these are not possible without injustice.

8.[11] Why does Wealth in most cases exist more among

[7] Or, with the oldest ms. and Bartholomew, "money." The examples that follow support both readings.

[8] Here and throughout, the sense requires "would not *necessarily or likely or usually*."

[9] Cf. *Pr.* 29.2 and see [Arist.] *MM* 1195a10 and Arist. *Rh.* 1383b21.

[10] Cf. Arist. *Pol.* 1253a31–38, Pl. *R.* 491d–e.

[11] Cf. *Pr.* 29.4, and see Ar. *Pl.* 87–98.

φαύλοις μᾶλλον ἢ τοῖς ἐπιεικέσιν ἐστίν; ἢ διότι, τυφλὸς ὤν, τὴν διάνοιαν οὐ δύναται κρίνειν οὐδὲ αἱρεῖσθαι τὸ βέλτιστον; ||

951a 9. Διὰ τί δικαιότερον εἶναι νενόμισται τοῖς τετελευτηκόσιν ἢ τοῖς ζῶσιν ἐπαμύνειν; ἢ ὅτι οἱ μὲν ζῶντες δύναιντ' ἂν αὑτοῖς ἐπαρκέσαι, ὁ δὲ τετελευτηκὼς οὐκέτι;

10. Διὰ τί ὑγιαίνοντι μὲν ὁ συνὼν οὐδὲν ὑγιέστερος
5 γίνεται, | οὐδὲ ἰσχυρῷ ἢ καλῷ εἰς τὰς ἕξεις ἐπιδίδωσιν οὐθέν, δικαίῳ δὲ καὶ σώφρονι καὶ ἀγαθῷ; ἢ διότι τὰ μὲν ἀμίμητα τὰ δὲ μιμητὰ τῇ ψυχῇ; ἀγαθὸς δὲ τῇ ψυχῇ, ὑγιὴς δὲ τῷ σώματι· ἐθίζεται οὖν χαίρειν ὀρθῶς καὶ λυπεῖσθαι. ὁ δὲ ὑγιεῖ συνὼν οὐκέτι· οὐ γὰρ ἐν τῷ
10 τισὶ χαίρειν ἢ μὴ ὁ ὑγιής· | οὐθὲν γὰρ τούτων ποιεῖ ὑγίειαν.

11. Διὰ τί δεινότερον γυναῖκα ἀποκτεῖναι ἢ ἄνδρα; καίτοι βέλτιον τὸ ἄρρεν τοῦ θήλεος φύσει. ἢ διότι ἀσθενέστερον, ὥστε ἐλάττω[12] ἀδικεῖ; ἢ ὅτι οὐ νεανικὸν τὸ ἰσχυρίζεσθαι πρὸς τὸ πολὺ ἧττον; |

15 12. Διὰ τί ποτε τῷ φεύγοντι ἐν τῷ δικαστηρίῳ τὴν δεξιὰν στάσιν διδόασιν; ἢ διότι ἐπανισοῦν βούλονται; πλεονεκτοῦντος οὖν τοῦ διώκοντος τὴν στάσιν τῷ φεύγοντι διδόασιν. †εἶθ' ὡς ἐπὶ τὸ πολὺ οἱ φεύγοντες

[12] ἐλάττω : μᾶλλον Bonitz : μείζω Ross

---

[12] Cf. *Pr.* 7.4.

[13] I.e., those associating with good people can get used to feel-

the base than among the fair? Is it because, being blind, he is not able to judge intention nor to choose the best?

9. Why is it considered more just to defend those who have died than those who are living? Is it because the living are able to protect themselves, whereas those who have died no longer can?

10.[12] Why does the one associating with a person who is healthy not become healthier, nor (*does associating*) with a strong or beautiful person add anything to one's characteristics, but (*associating*) with the just, the moderate, and the good does? Is it because the former cannot be imitated by the soul, whereas the latter can be imitated? For good is in the soul, but health is in the body; therefore, one can become accustomed to enjoy and to feel pain correctly.[13] But the one associating with the healthy cannot: for health is not found in enjoying or not enjoying certain things; for neither of these produces health.

11. Why is it more terrible to kill a woman than a man? And yet the male is better by nature than the female. Is it because she is weaker, so that she does less injustice?[14] Or is it because it is not befitting a young man to use force against what is much weaker?

12. Why do they give the defendant in a law court the position on the right? Is it because they wish to make things equal? Therefore, as the prosecutor has the advantage they give the defendant this position. †Next, in most

ing joy and pain correctly—in the way good people do—which is an improvement in the soul.

[14] Or, following Bonitz or Ross, "so that he does more injustice" or "commits a greater injustice"—though such an emendation is unnecessary.

παραφυλάττονται· ἐπὶ δεξιὰ δὲ ἡ φυλακὴ γίνεται, ἐὰν ὁ φεύγων ἔχῃ τὴν ἐν δεξιᾷ στάσιν.†[13] |

20 13. Διὰ τί ποτε, ὅταν καὶ[14] τῷ φεύγοντι καὶ τῷ διώκοντι φαίνωνται αἱ ψῆφοι ἴσαι, ὁ φεύγων νικᾷ; ἢ ὅτι ὁ μὲν φεύγων ἐν τῷ ἀγῶνι μόνον ἀκήκοεν αὐτῷ[15] πρὸς ἃ δεῖ αὐτὸν ἀπηγορεῖσθαι[16] καὶ τοὺς μάρτυρας παρασχέσθαι πρὸς τὰ κατηγορημένα ἔχειν,[17] εἴ τι 25 †μέλλουσιν ὠφεληθῆναι†;[18] οὐ ῥᾴδιον | δὲ τὸ μαντεύσασθαί τινα ὧν δεῖ αὐτὸν παρασκευάσασθαι ἢ μάρτυρας ἢ ἄλλο τεκμήριον ὅτι οὐθὲν ἀδικεῖ. τῷ δὲ διώκοντι ἔστιν ὅπως βούλεται, καὶ πρὸ τοῦ τὴν δίκην κλητεύσασθαι, ἐνστήσασθαι τὸ πρᾶγμα, καὶ ἤδη κεκληκότα, πλασάμενον ὅ τι βούλεται πιθανόν, κατηγο- 30 ρεῖν αὐτοῦ. ὁρῶν δὴ | κατὰ πάντα ταῦτα ἐλαττούμενον ὁ νομοθέτης τὸν φεύγοντα, προσέθετο τῷ φεύγοντι ὅ τι ἂν οἱ δικασταὶ ἀμφιδοξήσωσιν. ἀλλὰ μὴν καὶ τοῦτ' ἄν τις ἴδοι· ἐν γὰρ τοῖς φόβοις ὄντες πολλὰ παραλιμπάνουσιν ὧν αὐτοὺς ἔδει εἰπεῖν ἢ πρᾶξαι, οἱ δὲ φεύγοντες ἀεὶ ἐν μείζοσι κινδύνοις ὡς ἐπὶ τὸ πολὺ 35 τυγχάνουσιν | ὄντες, ὥστ' εἰ παραλιμπάνουσιν ὧν δεῖ

[13] *εἶθ' ὡς—δεξιᾷ στάσιν* codd. (obelis inclusi) || *ἡ φυλακὴ γίνεται, ἐὰν ὁ φεύγων* : fort. *ὁ φεύγων γίνεται, ἐὰν ἡ φυλακὴ*
[14] *καὶ* om. Bekker [15] *αὐτῷ* Richards : *αὐτοῦ* codd.
[16] *ἀπηγορεῖσθαι hapax legomenon* [17] *ἔχειν* Richards : *ἔχεσθαι* codd. : [*ἔχεσθαι*] Forster : <*τὸ*> (post *πρὸς*) . . . *ἔχεσθαι* Ruelle [18] *μέλλουσιν ὠφεληθῆναι* plur. codd. (*ὠφεληθήσεσθαι* Y[a], *ὠφεληθήσεται* X[a]) (obelis inclusi) : *μέλλουσιν ὠφελήσειν* Ruelle : *μέλλει ὠφεληθῆναι* vel *μέλλουσιν ὠφελῆσαι* Richards

cases the defendants are guarded; and the guard is on the right, if the defendant has the position on the right.†[15]

13.[16] Why, when the votes for the defendant and for the prosecutor are shown to be equal, does the defendant win? Is it because the defendant has heard, only in the trial itself, the ⟨*charges*⟩ against which he must make a defense and be able to produce the witnesses against the accusations, if †they are to be helped† in some way?[17] Now it is not easy to foresee the things for which he must provide witnesses or other evidence that he did nothing unjust. But the prosecutor can do whatever he wants, both put matters in place before issuing summons to appear in court, and, after the summons has been issued, invent any plausible ⟨*charge*⟩ he wants and accuse him of it. So the lawgiver, seeing that the defendant is disadvantaged in all these respects, sides with the defendant whenever the members of the jury are split in their opinion. Indeed, one should observe this too: those who are in a state of fear omit many of the things they should have said or done, and the defendants in most cases are continually in greater danger, so that if they omit what they should have ⟨*said or done*⟩, when they turn out equal ⟨*with the prosecutors*⟩ in their

[15] I suspect there is something wrong with this line, for as stated it does not provide an explanation for why the defendant is positioned on the right. Perhaps "the guard" and "the defendant" should be switched.

[16] Cf. *Pr.* 29.15, and see also Arist.(?) *Ath.* 69.1 and [Arist.] *Rh.Al.* 1433a4–12.

[17] There is something wrong with the text of this sentence. The obelized part must be emended to read either "if he (*i.e., the defendant*) is to be helped in some way" or "if they (*i.e., the witnesses*) are to be of any help."

αὐτούς, εἴπερ ἐξισοῦνται τοῖς δικαίοις, δῆλον ὅτι εἰ μὴ
παρελίμπανον, ἐκράτουν ἄν. ἔτι δὲ ἕκαστος ἡμῶν
μᾶλλον ἂν προέλοιτο τοῦ ἀδικοῦντος ἀποψηφίσασθαι
951b ὡς οὐκ ἀδικεῖ ἢ τοῦ <μὴ>[19] || ἀδικοῦντος καταψηφί-
σασθαι ὡς ἀδικεῖ, οἷον εἴ τις φεύγει δουλείας ἢ
ἀνδροφονίας. τούτων γὰρ ἑκάστου ὄντων, ἃ κατηγορεῖ
αὐτῶν, μᾶλλον ἂν ἀποψηφίσασθαι ἑλοίμεθα ἢ μὴ
5 ὄντων καταψηφίσασθαι. | ἔστι γάρ, ὅταν τις ἀμφι-
δοξῇ, τὰ ἐλάττω τῶν ἁμαρτημάτων αἱρετέον. δεινὸν
γὰρ καὶ τὸ τοῦ δούλου ὡς ἐλεύθερός ἐστι καταγνῶναι·
πολὺ δὲ δινότερον, ὅταν τις τοῦ ἐλευθέρου ὡς δούλου
καταψηφίσηται. ἔτι δὲ ἐὰν ὁ μὲν τύχῃ ἐγκαλῶν ὁ δὲ
10 ἀμφισβητῶν ὑπὲρ ὁτουοῦν, οὐκ εὐθὺς | οἰόμεθα δεῖν
ἀποδοῦναι τῷ ἐγκαλοῦντι, ἀλλὰ νέμεσθαι τὸν κεκτη-
μένον, ἕως ἂν κριθῇ. τὸν αὐτὸν δὲ τρόπον καὶ ἐπὶ τῶν
πλειόνων, ὅταν ἰσάζῃ τὸ πλῆθος τῶν τε φασκόντων
ἀδικεῖν καὶ τῶν μὴ ὁμολογούντων, ὥσπερ ὅτε ἐξ
ἀρχῆς ὁ μὲν ἐνεκάλει ὁ δὲ ἀπηρνεῖτο, οὐκ οἰόμεθα δεῖν
15 τὸν νομοθέτην προστιθέναι | τῷ ἐγκαλοῦντι, ἀλλὰ τὸν
φεύγοντα κύριον εἶναι, ἕως ἂν ὑπεροχήν τινα ἔχῃ ὁ
διώκων.[20] ὁμοίως δὲ καὶ ἐπὶ τῶν κριτῶν, ἐπειδὴ οὐδε-
μίαν ὑπεροχὴν <ἔχει> ἰσασθεισῶν τῶν ψήφων, κατὰ
χώραν εἴασεν ὁ νομοθέτης [ἔχειν].[21] ἔτι δὲ τῶν μὲν

[19] <μὴ> Sylburg [20] διώκων (vel φεύγων) Bonitz : ἀδικῶν codd. [21] <ἔχει> . . . [ἔχειν] Richards

claims to justice, it is clear that if they had not omitted anything they would have won.

Further, each of us would prefer to vote for an unjust man as one who did not commit an injustice than to vote against a man who is not unjust as one who did commit an injustice, for instance, if one is accused of enslavement or murder. For we should prefer to vote for (*the defendant*), even though the things that accuse either of them[18] are true, rather than to vote against, if the things that accuse him are not true. For when someone is split in his opinion, he should choose the lesser of two offenses. For to decide that a slave is free is serious; but it is much more serious when one votes against a free man as being a slave.

Further, if one person is bringing a charge, while the other is disputing it on behalf of something,[19] we do not think that it should be straightaway given to the one bringing the charge, but that it should be assigned to the possessor until there is a decision. And in the same way, in a case involving many people, when the number of those who claim that an injustice was committed and of those who do not agree is equal (as when one was bringing a charge and the other was denying it from the beginning), we do not think that the lawgiver should hand it over to the one bringing the charge, but that the defendant should be in control, until the prosecutor holds some superiority. And similarly in the case of judges, when the prosecutor holds no superiority because the votes on each side are equal, the lawgiver leaves things as they are.

[18] I assume the person accused of enslavement or the person accused of murder.

[19] This is a case in which two people are disputing ownership of some property.

ἀξιολόγων ἁμαρτημάτων μεγάλαι καὶ αἱ κολάσεις
20 εἰσίν, ὥστε | ἀδίκως μὲν καταψηφισαμένοις καὶ μεταγνοῦσιν[22] οὐκ ἔστιν ἐπανορθοῦσθαι καιρὸν λαβόντας· ἀπολύσασι δὲ παρὰ τὸ προσῆκον, εἰ μὲν οὕτως εὐλαβῶς <ζῴη>[23] ὥστε μηθὲν ἔτι ποτὲ ἁμαρτεῖν, τί ἂν καὶ μέγα ἡμαρτηκότες οἱ κριταὶ εἴησαν, τοιοῦτον ἄνθρωπον ἀπολύσαντες θανάτου; εἰ δέ τι ἐξ ὑστέρου ἁμαρ-
25 τάνοι, | δι' ἀμφότερα ἂν νῦν αὐτὸν[24] κολάζεσθαι ἀξιοῖ. ἢ ἔτι[25] ἀδικωτέρου μέν ἐστιν ἀνδρὸς ταῦτα ἀδικεῖν ἃ ἧττον εἰκός ἐστιν ἀδίκως ἐγκαλεῖσθαι; τὸ μὲν γὰρ ἀδικεῖν καὶ δι' ὀργὴν καὶ διὰ φόβον καὶ δι' ἐπιθυμίαν καὶ δι' ἄλλα πολλὰ γίνεται, καὶ οὐ μόνον ἐκ προνοίας·
30 τὸ δὲ ἀδίκως ἐγκαλεῖν ὡς | τὸ πολὺ ἐκ προνοίας ἐστίν. ὥστε ἐπεὶ ἴσαι αἱ ψῆφοι γεγόνασι, τό τ'[26] ἀδίκως τὸν ἐγκαλοῦντα ἐγκαλεῖν καὶ τὸν φεύγοντα ἀδικεῖν, φαύλου[27] κριθέντος τοῦ ἀδίκως ἐγκαλοῦντος τὸ νικᾶν τῷ φεύγοντι ὁ νομοθέτης ἀπένειμεν. ἔτι δὲ καὶ αὐτοὶ οὕτως ἔχομεν πρὸς τοὺς θεράποντας, ὥστε ὅταν ὑπο-
35 πτεύσωμέν | τι αὐτοὺς ἡμαρτηκέναι καὶ μηθὲν ἀκριβὲς ἔχωμεν, ἀλλ' ὅμως αὐτοὺς ὑπολαμβάνωμεν πεπραχέναι, οὐκ εὐθὺς ἐπὶ τὸ κολάζειν ἐρχόμεθα· καὶ ἐὰν
952a μηθὲν μᾶλλον || δυνώμεθα ἐξετάσαι, ἀφίεμεν ταύτης

[22] μεταγνοῦσιν Richards : μιγνύουσιν Y^a Ap : μὴ γνοῦσιν cett. codd. [23] <ζῴη> Forster : <διάγοι> Richards : <ἔχῃ> Grumach apud Flashar [24] ἂν νῦν αὐτὸν : om. νῦν Bekker : [ἂν] Hett : post αὐτὸν add. <ὁ νομοθέτης> Forster

[25] ἔτι : ὅτι Bekker ex Gaza

[26] τό τ' Bussemaker : τὸ δὲ codd. [27] φαύλου : φαύλως Ap^a : φαυλοτέρου vel <μᾶλλον> φαύλου Richards

Further, the punishments for serious offenses are great, so that if they vote against (*the defendant*) unjustly and change their minds,[20] it is not possible to seize the opportunity to set things right; but if they release (*the defendant*) contrary to what is fitting, if he <lives> so cautiously as never to commit an offense again, what sort of great offense would the judges have committed in releasing such a person from death? Whereas if (*the defendant*) does commit some offense later, they would think him worthy to be punished for both offenses.

Or further, is it characteristic of a very unjust man to commit injustices for which he is less likely to be charged unjustly? For committing an injustice comes about through anger, fear, desire, and many other things, and not only intentionally; but bringing charges unjustly is in most cases intentional. So when the votes turn out to be equal—the one bringing the charge brought the charge unjustly *and* the one who is the defendant committed an injustice—because the one bringing the charge unjustly is judged to be base, the lawgiver awards the victory to the defendant.

Further, this is how we ourselves are with respect to our servants, so that when we suspect that they have committed some offense and have no certainty, but nevertheless we believe that they have done it, we do not straightaway proceed to punish them; and if we are able to prove nothing more,[21] we release them from blame.

[20] Or, with most mss., "and do not know (*that this is what they've done*)."

[21] I.e., nothing more than our suspicions. The Greek could also be rendered "able to examine them no further."

τῆς αἰτίας. ἔτι μείζω μὲν ἀδικεῖ ὁ ἐκ προνοίας ἀδικῶν ἢ ὁ μὴ ἐκ προνοίας. ὁ μὲν δὴ συκοφαντῶν ἀεὶ ἐκ προνοίας ἀδικεῖ, ὁ δὲ ἕτερόν τι ἀδικῶν τὰ μὲν δι'
5 ἀνάγκην τὰ δὲ δι' ἄγνοιαν, τὰ δὲ ὅπως | ἔτυχεν ἀδικεῖν αὐτῷ συμπίπτει. ὅταν δὲ ἴσαι γένωνται αἱ ψῆφοι, ὁ μὲν διώκων κέκριται ὑπὸ τῶν ἡμίσεων ἐκ προνοίας ἀδικεῖν, ὁ δὲ φεύγων ὑπὸ τῶν λοιπῶν αὖ ἀδικεῖν μὲν οὐ μέντοι γε ἐκ προνοίας, ὥστε ἐπεὶ ἀδικεῖν μείζω κέκριται ὁ διώκων τοῦ φεύγοντος, εἰκότως ὁ νομοθέτης
10 νικᾶν ἔκρινε | τὸν τὰ ἐλάττω ἀδικοῦντα. ἔτι δὲ ἀεὶ μὲν ἀδικώτερός ἐστιν ὁ μὴ οἰόμενος λανθάνειν ὃν ἀδικεῖ καὶ ὅμως ἀδικῶν, ἢ ὁ οἰόμενος λανθάνειν. ὁ μὲν γὰρ ἀδίκως τινὶ ἐγκαλῶν οὐκ οἴεται λανθάνειν τοῦτον ὃν συκοφαντεῖ, οἱ δ' ἄλλο τι ἀδικοῦντες ὡς ἐπὶ τὸ πολὺ
15 οἰόμενοι λανθάνειν ὃν ἀδικοῦσιν | ἐπιχειροῦσιν ἀδικεῖν, ὥστε ἀδικώτεροι ἂν κρίνοιντο οἱ διώκοντες ἢ οἱ φεύγοντες.

14. Διὰ τί ποτε, ἐάν μέν τις ἐκ βαλανείου κλέψῃ ἢ ἐκ παλαίστρας ἢ ἐξ ἀγορᾶς ἢ τῶν τοιούτων τινός, θανάτῳ ζημιοῦται, ἐὰν δέ τις ἐξ οἰκίας, διπλοῦν τῆς
20 ἀξίας τοῦ κλέμματος | ἀποτίνει; ἢ ὅτι ἐν μὲν ταῖς οἰκίαις φυλάξαι ὁπωσοῦν ἔστιν; καὶ γὰρ ὁ τοῖχος ἰσχυρὸς καὶ κλεὶς ἐστί, καὶ οἰκέταις τοῖς ἐν τῇ οἰκίᾳ

[22] Cf. Dem. 24.114.
[23] A school or area for sports like wrestling and boxing.

Further, the one committing an injustice intentionally commits a greater injustice than the one who does not do so intentionally. But the one who makes false accusations surely always commits an injustice intentionally, whereas the one committing any other injustice sometimes does so from necessity and sometimes from ignorance, and sometimes it happens to fall to him to commit an injustice. But when the votes are equal, the prosecutor is judged by half ⟨*the jury*⟩ to be committing an injustice intentionally, whereas the defendant is judged by the rest to be committing an injustice, not however intentionally, and so, since the prosecutor is judged to have committed a greater injustice than the defendant, it is reasonable that the lawgiver has decided that the one who has committed the lesser injustice should be victorious.

Further, the person who does not expect to go unnoticed by the one he treats unjustly and nevertheless commits an injustice is always more unjust than the one who expects to go unnoticed. For the person bringing a charge unjustly against someone does not expect to go unnoticed by the one he falsely accuses, whereas those committing any other injustice in most cases expect to go unnoticed by the one they treat unjustly in attempting to commit an injustice, so that the prosecutors ought to be judged more unjust than the defendants.

14.[22] Why, if someone steals from a bathhouse or a palaestra[23] or a market or from any such ⟨*public place*⟩, he is punished by death, whereas if someone steals from a ⟨*private*⟩ house, he pays back double the value of what he has stolen? Is it because in houses it is possible in some manner to keep guard? Indeed, the wall is strong and there is a key, and all the servants in the house are careful to keep

πᾶσιν ἐπιμελές ἐστιν ὅπως σώζηται τὰ ἐνόντα. ἐν δὲ τῷ βαλανείῳ, καὶ ἐν τοῖς οὕτω κοινοῖς οὖσιν ὥσπερ τὸ βαλανεῖον, ῥᾴδιον τῷ βουλομένῳ κακουργεῖν· οὐδὲν | 25 γὰρ ἰσχυρὸν ἔχουσι πρὸς τὴν φυλακὴν οἱ τιθέντες ἀλλ' ἢ τὸ αὑτῶν ὄμμα, ὥστε ἂν μόνον τις παραβλέψῃ, ἐπὶ τῷ κλέπτοντι ἤδη γίνεται. διὸ ὁ νομοθέτης οὐχ ἱκανοὺς ὄντας ἡγησάμενος εἶναι φύλακας, τὸν νόμον αὐτοῖς ἐπέστησεν ἀπειλοῦντα σφοδρῶς ὡς οὐ βιωσο- 30 μένοις ἐάν τι σφετερίζωνται | τῶν ἀλλοτρίων. ἔτι δὲ εἰς μὲν τὴν οἰκίαν ἐπὶ τῷ κεκτημένῳ ἐστὶν ὅν τινα ἂν βούληται εἰσδέχεσθαι, καὶ ᾧ μὴ πιστεύει εἰσφέρεσθαι·[28] τῷ δ' ἐν τῷ βαλανείῳ θεμένῳ τι οὐκ ἔξεστι <κλέπτην> οὐδένα[29] κωλῦσαι οὔτε εἰσιέναι, οὔτε εἰσελθόντα μὴ παρὰ [κλέπτην] τὸ αὑτοῦ <τὸ> ἱμάτιον θέ- 35 σθαι ἀποδύντα [ἄν]·[30] ἀλλ' ὡς οὐ | βούλεται, ἐν τῷ αὐτῷ ἥ τε τοῦ κλέπτου ἐσθὴς καὶ ἡ τοῦ μέλλοντος ἀπολλύναι ἀναμεμιγμέναι κεῖνται. διὸ ὁ νομοθέτης τῷ μὲν ἑκόντι εἰσδεξαμένῳ τὸν κλέπτην καὶ αὐτῷ ἡμαρ- 952b τηκότι || οὐ λίαν μεγάλαις τιμωρίαις βεβοήθηκεν, τοῖς δὲ ἐξ ἀνάγκης κοινωνοῦσι τῆς εἰς τὸ βαλανεῖον εἰσόδου καὶ τῆς ἀναμίξεως μεγάλας τιμωρίας φανερός ἐστι καθιστὰς τοῖς κλέπτουσιν. ἔτι δὲ οἱ μὲν ἐν τοῖς 5 οὕτω κοινοῖς οὖσι τῷ βουλομένῳ | εἰσιέναι κλέπτοντες

[28] εἰσφέρεσθαι : <οὐκ> εἰσφέρεσθαι Sylburg : <μὴ> εἰσφρέσθαι Richards

[29] ἔξεστι <κλέπτην> οὐδένα Richards : ἔξεστιν οὐθένα codd.

safe the things in it. But in the bathhouse, and in places that are as public as the bathhouse, it is easy for anyone who wishes to do evil; for those who place (*their property there*) have no secure safeguard other than their own eye, so that if one merely looks away, it immediately goes to the thief. This is why the lawgiver, holding that the safeguards are not sufficient, has established the law threatening them[24] violently that they shall not live if they appropriate what belongs to others.

Further, in a house it is left to the owner to admit whomever he wants, and so to introduce someone whom he does not trust; but the one placing something in a bathhouse is not able to prevent any thief from entering, nor, when (*the thief*) has entered, can he prevent him from putting his cloak, when he has removed it, next to his own; but contrary to what he wants, the clothes of the thief and of the person about to lose them lie mixed up in the same place.[25] This is why the lawgiver has not assisted with very large penalties the one who voluntarily and by his own mistake admitted the thief, whereas it is evident (*he has assisted*) those who necessarily share the entrance to the bathhouse and the mixing (*of clothes*), setting down heavy penalties for those who steal.

Further, it is obvious that all those who steal in places that are so public that anyone who wants can enter are bad,

[24] I.e., thieves or potential thieves. [25] There are problems with the text here, which seems to require emendation.

---

30 παρὰ [κλέπτην] τὸ αὑτοῦ <τὸ> ἱμάτιον θέσθαι ἀποδύντα [ἄν] Richards : παρὰ κλέπτην (περικλέπτην Xa) τὸ αὑτοῦ ἱμάτιον θέσθαι ἀποδύντα ἄν codd.

καταφανεῖς ἅπασι γίνονται ὅτι πονηροί[31] εἰσιν, ὥστε περιγενόμενοι οὐδὲ καρπισμοῦ ἔτι χάριν ἐπιεικεῖς εἶναι δοκεῖν βούλονται, ὡς μάτην αὐτοῖς ὂν πρὸς τοὺς γνόντας πλάττεσθαι ὅτι ἐπιεικεῖς εἰσίν· καταφανῶς οὖν ἤδη πονηροὶ διατελοῦσιν ὄντες. οἱ δὲ ἑνὶ μόνῳ
10 φανεροὶ γενόμενοι | πρὸς[32] τοὺς ἄλλους ἐπιχειροῦσι πείθειν, ἀποτίσαντές τι, ὅπως μὴ καταφανεῖς αὐτοὺς ποιήσῃ· διὸ οὐ παντελῶς ἂν εἶεν πονηροὶ διὰ τέλους, ἀνθ' ὧν ὁ νομοθέτης ἐλάττω αὐτοῖς τὰ ἐπιζήμια ἐποίησεν. ἔτι δὲ τῶν ἁμαρτιῶν μάλιστα αἰσχύνουσι τὴν πόλιν αἱ ἐν τοῖς κοινοτάτοις συλλόγοις τε καὶ συν-
15 όδοις γινόμεναι, | ὥσπερ καὶ τιμὴν φέρουσι πολὺ μάλιστα αἱ ἐν τῷ κοινῷ εὐταξίαι· καταφανεῖς γὰρ μάλιστα διὰ τῶν τοιούτων καὶ αὐτοῖς καὶ τοῖς ἄλλοις. συμβαίνει οὖν οὐ μόνον ἰδίᾳ τὸν ἀπολέσαντα βλάπτεσθαι ἐκ τῶν τοιούτων τινός, ἀλλὰ καὶ πρὸς τὴν πόλιν
20 λοιδορίας γίνεσθαι. διὸ καὶ τὸν κλέψαντα | ταῖς μείζοσι ζημίαις ἐκόλασε τῶν ἐξ οἰκίας τινὸς ἀφελομένων. ἔτι δὲ καὶ ὁ ἐξ οἰκίας τινὸς ἀπολέσας ἐν τοιούτῳ τόπῳ τυγχάνει ὤν, ὅθεν ῥᾴδιον μήτε παθόντα μήτε χλευασθέντα ὑπό τινων, οἴκοι ὄντα τὸ ἀτύχημα φέρειν. τῷ δ' ἥ τε ἀποχώρησις ἐργώδης γεγυμνωμένῳ, προσέτι
25 δὲ χλευάζεσθαι | ὑπό τινων ὑπάρχει τοῖς πολλοῖς, ὃ πολὺ δυσχερέστερόν ἐστι τῆς ἀπωλείας. διὸ καὶ ὁ νομοθέτης μείζους αὐτοῖς ζημίας ἐνέγραψεν. ἔτι δὲ

[31] πονηροί Richards : φανεροί codd.
[32] om. πρὸς fort.

so that, if they survive, they do not want to be thought to be fair even for the sake of further advantage, as it is folly for them to pretend that they are fair before those who know (*the truth*); therefore, they continue to be obviously bad. But those (*whose crimes*) become known to one person alone attempt to persuade him before the others by paying back what (*they stole*), so that he will not make known their character; this is why they will not likely be completely bad to the end, in return for which the lawgiver has created less severe penalties for them.

Further, those offenses occurring in the most public assemblies and meetings most of all shame the city, just as well-ordered behavior in public brings the city the most honor; for it is by such actions that they become known to themselves and to others. Therefore, the result from such offenses is that not only is the one who lost something harmed in private, but abuse comes to the city as well. And this is why (*the lawgiver*) has punished the one who steals (*from public places*) with greater penalties than those who take something from a house.

Further, the one who loses something from a house happens to be in such a place where it is easy not to suffer and not to be mocked by people, bearing the misfortune while he is at home. But for the one who has been stripped of clothing, his departure (*from the bathhouse*) is irksome, and besides it is a fact that in most cases he will be laughed at by people, which is much harder to take than the loss. And this is why the lawgiver prescribed greater penalties for them.[26]

[26] I.e., for those who steal from public places.

παραπλήσια τούτοις πολλὰ φαίνονται νενομοθετηκότες, οἷον καὶ ἐὰν μέν τις ἄρχοντα κακῶς εἴπῃ,
30 μεγάλα τὰ ἐπιτίμια, ἐὰν δέ τις ἰδιώτην, οὐθέν. | καὶ καλῶς· οἴεται γὰρ τότε οὐ μόνον εἰς τὸν ἄρχοντα ἐξαμαρτάνειν τὸν κακηγοροῦντα, ἀλλὰ καὶ εἰς τὴν πόλιν ὑβρίζειν. τὸν αὐτὸν δὲ τρόπον καὶ τὸν ἐν τῷ λιμένι κλέπτοντα οὐ μόνον τὸν ἰδιώτην βλάπτειν, ἀλλὰ καὶ τὴν πόλιν αἰσχύνειν. ὁμοίως δὲ καὶ ἐν τοῖς
35 ἄλλοις, οὗ κοινῇ που[33] | συνερχόμεθα.

15. Διὰ τί ἐν τοῖς δικαστηρίοις ἐὰν ἴσαι γένωνται ψῆφοι[34] τοῖς ἀντιδίκοις, ὁ φεύγων νικᾷ; ἢ ὅτι ὁ φεύγων
953a ὑπὸ τοῦ || διώκοντος οὐθὲν πέπονθεν, ἀλλ' ἐν τοῖς ἴσοις αὐτῷ[35] ἤδη ἔμελλε νικᾶν;

16. Διὰ τί ἐπὶ μὲν κλοπῇ θάνατος ἡ ζημία, ἐπὶ δὲ ὕβρει, μείζονι οὔσῃ ἀδικίᾳ, τίμησις τί χρὴ παθεῖν ἢ
5 ἀποτῖσαι; ἢ διότι | τὸ μὲν ὑβρίζειν ἀνθρώπινόν ἐστι πάθος, καὶ πάντες πλέον ἢ ἔλαττον αὐτοῦ μετέχουσι, τὸ δὲ κλέπτειν οὐ τῶν ἀναγκαίων; καὶ ὅτι ὁ κλέπτειν ἐπιχειρῶν καὶ ὑβρίζειν ἂν προέλοιτο.

[33] που : fort. ποτε Richards
[34] ante ψῆφοι add. <αἱ> Richards
[35] post αὐτῷ add. <ὢν> Richards

Further, many laws passed resembling these appear, for instance, if one even speaks evilly of an official, the damages are great, whereas if one speaks evilly of a private individual, there are no damages. And rightly so: for (*the lawgiver*) thinks that the one who speaks evil not only wrongs the official, but also treats the city with hubris. Now in the same way too the one who steals in the harbor not only harms the private individual, but also shames the city. And similarly too in other places, wherever we come together in public.

15.[27] Why, in the courts, if the votes for the litigants are equal, does the defendant win? Is it because the defendant has not been affected by the prosecution, but being in an equal position with him beforehand he would have won?

16. Why, in the case of theft, is the penalty death, but in the case of hubris, which is a greater injustice, there is an assessment of what must be suffered or paid? Is it because acting with hubris is a human characteristic, and all share in it more or less, but stealing is not one of the necessary characteristics? Also, it is because the one who attempts to steal would be willing to act with hubris.

[27] Cf. *Pr.* 29.13, and see also Arist.(?) *Ath.* 69.1 and [Arist.] *Rh.Al.* 1433a4–12.

BOOK XXX

INTRODUCTION

Nicomachean Ethics 6 [= *EE* 5] is Aristotle's primary discussion of the intellectual virtues. Although this may serve as the background or framework for some of the discussion in *Pr.* 30, few of its chapters seem to draw on *EN* 6 as their source.

Pr. 30.1, on melancholy, is the longest and most famous chapter in the entire *Problems*. (It is longer than all the other chapters in Book 30 combined.) It was attributed to Aristotle in antiquity. Cicero (*Tusc. Disp.* 1.33) writes: "Aristotle says that all geniuses are melancholic."[1] And Plutarch (*Lys.* 2.5) says: "Aristotle, declaring that the great natures are melancholic, such as Socrates and Plato and Hercules, records that Lysander too—not right away, but when he was older—was afflicted with melancholy." Both authors are clearly referring to passages in *Pr.* 30.1.

It is possible that this chapter was written by Aristotle or largely based on something he wrote; but given the available evidence, there is no way to establish that with certainty. In any case, the author was clearly familiar

[1] See also *Div.* 1.81 and Seneca, *Tranq.* 17.10.

with Aristotle's scattered remarks on melancholy.[2] Another possible source is the *On Melancholy* attributed to Theophrastus by Diogenes Laertius (5.44). No fragments survive, however, so there is no way to make an informed judgment on the relationship between that work and *Pr.* 30.1. Whoever the author, he may (also) have been building on or responding to the discussions of melancholy of Diocles of Carystus (see frs. 108–10 v.d. Eijk) and in the Hippocratic corpus (see *Morb.* 1.30, *Epid.* 3.14, 6.8, 31, *Prorrh.* 1.14 and 18, *Aph.* 3.20, 6.23, 56, 7.40).[3]

Of the other thirteen chapters of Book 30, only one (14, on dreams) mentions melancholy. And along with chs. 1 and 14, only 3 is concerned with the physiological or physical basis of intellectual states. Further, five chapters discuss differences in cognitive abilities—between humans and animals (3, 6, 12) and among humans (5, 13)—and four discuss different sciences or disciplines (2, 8, 9, 10). There are three miscellaneous chapters (4, 7, 11).

[2] See P. van der Eijk, *Medicine and Philosophy in Classical Antiquity: Doctors and Philosophers on Nature, Soul, Health and Disease* (Cambridge, 2005), ch. 5, "Aristotle on Melancholy." This essay is a model of how to approach the *Problems* in light of the authentic works of Aristotle. See p. 161 n. 74 for a complete list of parallels between *Pr.* 30.1 and the authentic works of Aristotle (specifically *Somn., Insomn., Div.Somn., HA, PA, GA, EN, EE, Rh.*).

[3] See also Hp. *Vict.* 1.35. Although it does not discuss melancholy, it contains a lengthy discussion of the physiological basis of φρόνησις.

ΟΣΑ ΠΕΡΙ ΦΡΟΝΗΣΙΝ ΚΑΙ ΝΟΥΝ ΚΑΙ ΣΟΦΙΑΝ

953a10 1. Διὰ τί πάντες ὅσοι περιττοὶ γεγόνασιν ἄνδρες ἢ κατὰ φιλοσοφίαν ἢ πολιτικὴν ἢ ποίησιν ἢ τέχνας φαίνονται μελαγχολικοὶ ὄντες, καὶ οἱ μὲν οὕτως ὥστε καὶ λαμβάνεσθαι τοῖς ἀπὸ μελαίνης χολῆς ἀρρωστήμασιν, οἷον λέγεται τῶν [τε][1] ἡρωϊκῶν τὰ περὶ τὸν
15 Ἡρακλέα; καὶ γὰρ ἐκεῖνος ἔοικε | γενέσθαι ταύτης τῆς φύσεως, διὸ καὶ τὰ ἀρρωστήματα τῶν ἐπιληπτικῶν ἀπ' ἐκείνου προσηγόρευον οἱ ἀρχαῖοι ἱερὰν νόσον. καὶ ἡ περὶ τοὺς παῖδας ἔκστασις καὶ ἡ πρὸ τῆς ἀφανίσεως ἐν Οἴτῃ τῶν ἑλκῶν ἔκφυσις γενομένη τοῦτο δηλοῖ· καὶ γὰρ τοῦτο γίνεται πολλοῖς ἀπὸ μελαίνης
20 χολῆς. συνέβη δὲ καὶ | Λυσάνδρῳ τῷ Λάκωνι πρὸ τῆς τελευτῆς γενέσθαι τὰ ἕλκη ταῦτα. ἔτι δὲ τὰ περὶ

[1] [τε] Flashar

---

[1] There are no perfect English equivalents for the names of these three intellectual virtues (which Aristotle discusses in *EN* 6), though "wisdom" is a good translation of σοφία. Φρόνησις is

PROBLEMS CONNECTED WITH INTELLIGENCE, UNDERSTANDING, AND WISDOM[1]

1.[2] Why is it that all those men who have become extraordinary in philosophy, politics, poetry, or the arts are obviously melancholic,[3] and some to such an extent that they are seized by the illnesses that come from black bile, as is said in connection with the stories about Heracles among heroes? Indeed, he seems to have been of this nature, and this is why the ancients named the illnesses of epilepsy "sacred disease" after him. And his insanity regarding his children and the eruption of sores that occurred before his disappearance on Mount Oeta prove this; for in many cases this occurs as a result of black bile. And these sores also afflicted Lysander the Spartan before he died. Further, there are the stories about Ajax and Bellerophon,

traditionally rendered "practical wisdom" or "prudence"; but in *Pr.* 30, its most common meaning is "intelligence." I translate νοῦς "understanding," which is not its most common rendering, though it makes sense in Book 30.

[2] For the background and possible sources for this chapter, see the introduction to *Pr.* 30. [3] I.e., have an abundance of black bile (μέλας, μελαίνης + χολή).

Αἴαντα καὶ Βελλεροφόντην, ὧν ὁ μὲν ἐκστατικὸς ἐγένετο παντελῶς, ὁ δὲ τὰς ἐρημίας ἐδίωκεν, διὸ οὕτως ἐποίησεν Ὅμηρος

αὐτὰρ ἐπεὶ[2] καὶ κεῖνος ἀπήχθετο πᾶσι θεοῖσιν,
ἤτοι ὁ κὰπ πεδίον[3] τὸ Ἀλήϊον οἶος ἀλᾶτο
25 ὃν | θυμὸν κατέδων, πάτον ἀνθρώπων ἀλεείνων.

καὶ ἄλλοι δὲ πολλοὶ τῶν ἡρώων ὁμοιοπαθεῖς φαίνονται τούτοις. τῶν δὲ ὕστερον Ἐμπεδοκλῆς καὶ Πλάτων καὶ Σωκράτης καὶ ἕτεροι συχνοὶ τῶν γνωρίμων. ἔτι δὲ τῶν περὶ τὴν ποίησιν οἱ πλεῖστοι. πολλοῖς μὲν γὰρ 30 τῶν τοιούτων γίνεται νοσήματα ἀπὸ | τῆς τοιαύτης κράσεως τῷ σώματι, τοῖς δὲ ἡ φύσις δήλη ῥέπουσα πρὸς τὰ πάθη. πάντες δ' οὖν ὡς εἰπεῖν ἁπλῶς εἰσί, καθάπερ ἐλέχθη, τοιοῦτοι τὴν φύσιν. δεῖ δὴ λαβεῖν τὴν αἰτίαν πρῶτον ἐπὶ παραδείγματος προχειρισαμένους.[4] ὁ γὰρ οἶνος ὁ πολὺς μάλιστα φαίνεται παρα-35 σκευάζειν τοιούτους οἵους | λέγομεν τοὺς μελαγχολικοὺς εἶναι, καὶ πλεῖστα ἤθη ποιεῖν πινόμενος, οἷον ὀργίλους, φιλανθρώπους, ἐλεήμονας, ἰταμούς· ἀλλ' οὐχὶ τὸ μέλι οὐδὲ τὸ γάλα οὐδὲ τὸ ὕδωρ οὐδ' ἄλλο τῶν τοιούτων οὐδέν. ἴδοι δ' ἄν τις ὅτι παντοδαποὺς ἀπεργάζεται, θεωρῶν ὡς μεταβάλλει τοὺς πίνοντας ἐκ 953b προσαγωγῆς· παραλαβὼν || γὰρ ἀπεψυγμένους ἐν τῷ νήφειν καὶ σιωπηλοὺς μικρῷ μὲν πλείων ποθεὶς λαλι-

[2] αὐτὰρ ἐπεὶ : ἀλλ' ὅτε δὴ H. *Il.* 6.200
[3] κὰπ πεδίον Forster ex H. *Il.* 6.201 : καππεδίον codd.

of whom the former went completely insane,[4] whereas the latter sought deserted places, which is why Homer wrote (*of Bellerophon*) in this way:

> But when indeed he was hated by all the gods,
> Verily over the Aleian plain he wandered alone,
> Devouring his spirit, avoiding the path of men.[5]

And many other heroes have obviously suffered in the same way as these men. Now in later times, of the well-known people there are Empedocles, Plato, Socrates, and many others. Further, there are most of those connected to poetry. For in many such men diseases have come from this sort of mixture[6] in the body, whereas in others their nature clearly inclines toward these conditions. So they are all, generally speaking, as has been said, such with respect to their nature.

Now the cause should be grasped if we first make use of an example. For more than anything else, a lot of wine appears to produce those qualities that we say are melancholic, and when it has been drunk it produces most of the characteristics, namely, irascibility, benevolence, compassion, and recklessness; but neither honey nor milk nor water nor any other such thing does this. One can see that it brings about all sorts of effects, by observing how it gradually changes the drinkers; for finding them chilled and silent when they are sober, having a bit too much to drink

[4] See Sophocles, *Ajax*.
[5] *Il*. 6.200–202.
[6] Or "temperament."

---

[4] post προχειρισαμένους add. οὐκ ἀτόπου ἐκ τοῦ οἴνου Ruelle ex Gaza

στέρους ποιεῖ, ἔτι δὲ πλείων ῥητορικοὺς καὶ θαρραλέους, προϊόντας δὲ πρὸς τὸ πράττειν ἰταμούς, ἔτι δὲ
5 μᾶλλον πινόμενος ὑβριστάς, ἔπειτα μανικούς, | λίαν δὲ πολὺς ἐκλύει καὶ ποιεῖ μωρούς, ὥσπερ τοὺς ἐκ παίδων ἐπιλήπτους, ἢ καὶ ἐχομένους τοῖς μελαγχολικοῖς ἄγαν. ὥσπερ οὖν ὁ εἷς ἄνθρωπος μεταβάλλει τὸ ἦθος πίνων καὶ χρώμενος τῷ οἴνῳ ποσῷ τινί, οὕτω καθ' ἕκαστον τὸ ἦθος εἰσί τινες ἄνθρωποι. οἷος γὰρ
10 οὗτος μεθύων νῦν ἐστίν, ἄλλος τις | τοιοῦτος φύσει ἐστίν, ὁ μὲν λάλος, ὁ δὲ κεκινημένος, ὁ δὲ ἀρίδακρυς· ποιεῖ γάρ τινας καὶ τοιούτους, διὸ καὶ Ὅμηρος ἐποίησε "καί μέ φησι δάκρυ πλώειν βεβαρημένον οἴνῳ."[5] καὶ γὰρ ἐλεήμονές ποτε γίνονται καὶ ἄγριοι καὶ σιωπηλοί· ἔνιοι γὰρ αὖ ἀποσιωπῶσι, καὶ μάλιστα τῶν
15 μελαγχολικῶν ὅσοι | ἐκστατικοί. ποιεῖ δὲ καὶ φιλητικοὺς ὁ οἶνος· σημεῖον δὲ ὅτι προάγεται ὁ πίνων καὶ τῷ στόματι φιλεῖν, οὓς νήφων οὐδ' ἂν εἷς φιλήσειεν ἢ διὰ τὸ εἶδος ἢ διὰ τὴν ἡλικίαν. ὁ μὲν οὖν οἶνος οὐ πολὺν χρόνον ποιεῖ περιττόν, ἀλλ' ὀλίγον, ἡ δὲ φύσις ἀεί,
20 ἕως τις ἂν ᾖ· οἱ μὲν γὰρ θρασεῖς, οἱ δὲ σιωπηλοί, | οἱ δὲ ἐλεήμονες, οἱ δὲ δειλοὶ γίνονται φύσει. ὥστε δῆλον ὅτι διὰ τὸ αὐτὸ ποιεῖ ὅ τε οἶνος καὶ ἡ φύσις ἑκάστου τὸ ἦθος· πάντα γὰρ κατεργάζεται τῇ θερμότητι ταμιευόμενα. ὅ τε δὴ χυμὸς καὶ ἡ κρᾶσις ἡ τῆς μελαίνης

[5] καί μέ φησι δάκρυ πλώειν βεβαρημένον οἴνῳ : φῇ δὲ δακρυπλώειν βεβαρηότα με φρένας οἴνῳ H. *Od.* 19.122

makes them more talkative, while even more makes them eloquent and bold, and, proceeding to action, they become reckless; still more drinking makes them hubristic, and then insane;[7] and a lot more relaxes[8] them and makes them stupid, like those who are epileptic from childhood, or even very near the melancholic. Therefore, just as an individual changes his character by drinking and using wine in a certain quantity, so there are certain people corresponding to each character. For just as one man is temporarily when he is drunk, so some other is by nature—one is talkative, another agitated, and another prone to tears; for wine produces in some people such qualities, and this is why Homer writes: "And he says that I swim in tears, being heavy with wine."[9] And indeed, they sometimes become compassionate and savage and silent; for some remain silent, especially those melancholic persons who are insane. And wine also makes people affectionate; a sign of this is that the one who is drinking is induced to kiss those whom, because of appearance or age, no one would kiss when sober. Therefore, wine produces extraordinary results, not for a long time, but briefly, whereas nature produces them permanently, for as long as someone exists: for some people are bold, others silent, others compassionate, and others cowardly, by nature. So it is clear that wine and nature produce the character of each person by the same means; for all of these are achieved under the regulation of heat. Now certainly both the juice (*of the grape*) and the

[7] Not permanently, of course. I render ἔκστασις "insane" throughout. [8] Or perhaps "loosens," in the sense of making them less inhibited. [9] *Od.* 19.122.

χολῆς πνευματικά ἐστιν· διὸ καὶ τὰ πνευματώδη πάθη
25 καὶ τὰ | ὑποχόνδρια μελαγχολικὰ οἱ ἰατροί φασιν
εἶναι. καὶ ὁ οἶνος δὲ πνευματώδης τὴν δύναμιν. διὸ δή
ἐστι τὴν φύσιν ὅμοια ὅ τε οἶνος καὶ ἡ κρᾶσις. δηλοῖ
δὲ ὅτι πνευματώδης ὁ οἶνός ἐστιν ὁ ἀφρός· τὸ μὲν γὰρ
ἔλαιον θερμὸν ὂν οὐ ποιεῖ ἀφρόν, ὁ δὲ οἶνος πολύν,
30 καὶ μᾶλλον ὁ μέλας τοῦ λευκοῦ, | ὅτι θερμότερος καὶ
σωματωδέστερος. καὶ διὰ τοῦτο ὅ τε οἶνος ἀφροδισια-
στικοὺς ἀπεργάζεται, καὶ ὀρθῶς Διόνυσος καὶ Ἀφρο-
δίτη λέγονται μετ᾽ ἀλλήλων εἶναι, καὶ οἱ μελαγχολικοὶ οἱ πλεῖστοι λάγνοι εἰσίν. ὅ τε γὰρ ἀφροδισιασμὸς
πνευματώδης. σημεῖον δὲ τὸ αἰδοῖον, ὡς ἐκ μικροῦ
35 ταχεῖαν ποιεῖται | τὴν αὔξησιν διὰ τὸ ἐμφυσᾶσθαι.
καὶ ἔτι πρὶν δύνασθαι προΐεσθαι σπέρμα, γίνεταί τις
ἡδονὴ ἐπὶ παισὶν οὖσιν,[6] ὅταν ἐγγὺς ὄντες τοῦ ἡβᾶν
ξύωνται τὰ αἰδοῖα δι᾽ ἀκολασίαν· γίνεται δὲ δῆλον διὰ
τὸ πνεῦμα διεξιέναι διὰ τῶν πόρων, δι᾽ ὧν ὕστερον τὸ
954a ὑγρὸν φέρεται. ἥ τε ἔκχυσις τοῦ || σπέρματος ἐν ταῖς
ὁμιλίαις καὶ ἡ ῥῖψις ὑπὸ τοῦ πνεύματος ὠθοῦντος

[6] ἐπὶ : ἔτι Bonitz || om. οὖσιν fort.

---

[10] ἡ κρᾶσις ἡ τῆς μελαίνης χολῆς could also be rendered "the melancholy temperament."

[11] The Greek (πνευματώδης) actually means "like wind or breath or air" and so also "windy" or "flatulent." It could also be rendered "full of breath." Throughout, I translate πνεῦμα "breath," though it may simply refer to "air."

[12] Or perhaps simply flatulence.

mixture of black bile[10] contain breath;[11] and this is why the physicians say that pulmonary afflictions[12] and abdominal[13] afflictions are melancholic. And wine, with respect to its power, contains breath. This is why wine and the mixture (*of black bile*) are similar in nature. And the foam shows that the wine contains breath; for oil, though it is hot, does not produce foam, whereas wine produces a lot, and red wine more than white, because it is hotter and has more body. For this reason wine works as an aphrodisiac, and Dionysus and Aphrodite are correctly said to be with each other, and the majority of melancholic people are lustful.[14] For sexual excitement involves the presence of breath. A sign of this is the penis, in that its expansion is produced quickly from a small size, owing to being inflated. Even before seed is able to be emitted, a certain pleasure occurs in the case of children, when they are near puberty, in rubbing their private parts[15] owing to licentiousness; this[16] becomes clear because of the breath passing through the channels through which the moisture later travels. The outflow of the seed in intercourse and its ejection is obviously due to pushing by the breath. So those

13 "Abdominal" is a loose translation of ὑποχόνδριος, literally, "under the cartilage" (of the breastbone); it refers to the internal organs below this cartilage and above the navel.

14 Cf. *Pr.* 4.30.

15 Earlier, I translated the singular (τὸ αἰδοῖον, literally, "the shameful part") "the penis"; here I translate the plural (τὰ αἰδοῖα) "the private parts."

16 The subject of this sentence is left unstated, and has variously been taken to be the inflation of the penis, the emission of seed, or the pleasure (just described) occurring in children.

φανερὸν γίνεσθαι.[7] ὥστε καὶ τῶν ἐδεσμάτων καὶ ποτῶν εὐλόγως ταῦτ' ἐστὶν ἀφροδισιαστικά, ὅσα πνευματώδη τὸν περὶ τὰ αἰδοῖα ποιεῖ τόπον. διὸ καὶ ὁ
5 μέλας | οἶνος οὐδενὸς ἧττον τοιούτους ἀπεργάζεται, οἷοι[8] καὶ οἱ μελαγχολικοὶ, πνευματώδεις.[9] δῆλοι δ' εἰσὶν ἐπ' ἐνίων· σκληφροὶ[10] γὰρ οἱ πλείους τῶν μελαγχολικῶν, καὶ αἱ φλέβες ἐξέχουσιν· τούτου δ' αἴτιον οὐ τὸ τοῦ αἵματος πλῆθος, ἀλλὰ τοῦ πνεύματος. διότι δὲ
10 οὐδὲ πάντες οἱ μελαγχολικοὶ | σκληφροὶ[11] οὐδὲ μέλανες, ἀλλ' οἱ μᾶλλον κακόχυμοι, ἄλλος λόγος. περὶ οὗ δὲ ἐξ ἀρχῆς προειλόμεθα διελθεῖν, ὅτι ἐν τῇ φύσει εὐθὺς ὁ τοιοῦτος χυμὸς ὁ μελαγχολικὸς κεράννυται· θερμοῦ γὰρ καὶ ψυχροῦ κρᾶσίς ἐστιν· ἐκ τούτων γὰρ τῶν δυοῖν ἡ φύσις συνέστηκεν. διὸ καὶ ἡ μέλαινα |
15 χολὴ καὶ θερμότατον καὶ ψυχρότατον γίνεται. τὸ γὰρ αὐτὸ πάσχειν πέφυκε ταῦτ' ἄμφω, οἷον καὶ τὸ ὕδωρ ὂν ψυχρόν, ὅμως ἐὰν ἱκανῶς θερμανθῇ, οἷον τὸ ζέον, τῆς φλογὸς αὐτῆς θερμότερόν ἐστι, καὶ λίθος καὶ σίδηρος διάπυρα γενόμενα μᾶλλον θερμὰ γίνεται ἄνθρακος,
20 ψυχρὰ | ὄντα φύσει. εἴρηται δὲ σαφέστερον περὶ τούτων ἐν τοῖς περὶ πυρός. καὶ ἡ χολὴ δὲ ἡ μέλαινα φύσει ψυχρὰ καὶ οὐκ ἐπιπολαίως οὖσα, ὅταν μὲν οὕτως ἔχῃ ὡς εἴρηται, ἐὰν ὑπερβάλλῃ ἐν τῷ σώματι,

[7] fort. φανερὸν <ὅτι> γίνεται Richards
[8] οἷοι : εἰσὶ <δέ> Richards
[9] πνευματώδεις : om. Forster : fort. πνευματώδης
[10] σκληφροὶ Bussemaker : σκληροὶ codd.
[11] σκληφροὶ Ap Y^e : σκληροὶ cett. codd.

foods and drinks, which produce breath in the region around the private parts, are with good reason aphrodisiacs. And this is why red wine more than anything[17] makes people have such a condition, just like melancholic people, ⟨*namely*⟩ containing abundant breath.[18] Now these are clear in some cases: for the majority of melancholic people are thin,[19] and their veins stand out; and the reason for this is the quantity not of blood, but of breath; but why all melancholic people are neither thin[20] nor dark, but only the evil-humored ones, is another story.

But we prefer to treat what we've been discussing from the beginning, that in nature already such a humor—the melancholic—is mixed: it is a mixture of hot and cold; for its nature consists of these two things. And this is why black bile becomes both very hot and very cold. For the same thing can naturally be affected by both of these, for instance, even water, which is cold: if however it is sufficiently heated, as when it is boiling, it is hotter than the flame itself, and stone and iron made red-hot become hotter than the coal, though they are cold by nature. But these things have been spoken about more clearly in the work *On Fire*.[21] Now black bile, being cold by nature and not on the surface, when it is in the condition mentioned,[22] if it

[17] Literally, "less than nothing" (*οὐδενὸς ἧττον*).

[18] There may be a problem with the text of this line.

[19] Or "hard," following the mss.

[20] Or "hard," following most mss.

[21] This is perhaps a reference to Thph. *Ign*. 35.

[22] I.e., either very hot or very cold (see 954a14–15). In the following list, the first set of characteristics is the result of the black bile being very cold, the second very hot.

ἀποπληξίας ἢ νάρκας ἢ ἀθυμίας ποιεῖ ἢ φόβους, ἐὰν
25 δὲ ὑπερθερμανθῇ, τὰς μετ' | ᾠδῆς εὐθυμίας καὶ ἐκστάσεις καὶ ἐκζέσεις ἑλκῶν καὶ ἄλλα τοιαῦτα. τοῖς μὲν οὖν πολλοῖς ἀπὸ τῆς καθ' ἡμέραν τροφῆς ἐγγινομένη οὐδὲν τὸ ἦθος ποιεῖ διαφόρους, ἀλλὰ μόνον νόσημά τι μελαγχολικὸν ἀπειργάσατο. ὅσοις δὲ ἐν τῇ φύσει συνέστη κρᾶσις τοιαύτη, εὐθὺς οὗτοι τὰ ἤθη
30 γίνονται | παντοδαποί, ἄλλος κατ' ἄλλην κρᾶσιν· οἷον ὅσοις μὲν πολλὴ καὶ ψυχρὰ ἐνυπάρχει, νωθροὶ καὶ μωροί, ὅσοις δὲ λίαν πολλὴ καὶ θερμή, μανικοὶ[12] καὶ εὐφυεῖς καὶ ἐρωτικοὶ καὶ εὐκίνητοι πρὸς τοὺς θυμοὺς καὶ τὰς ἐπιθυμίας, ἔνιοι δὲ καὶ λάλοι μᾶλλον. πολλοὶ
35 δὲ καὶ διὰ τὸ ἐγγὺς εἶναι τοῦ | νοεροῦ τόπου τὴν θερμότητα ταύτην νοσήμασιν ἁλίσκονται μανικοῖς ἢ ἐνθουσιαστικοῖς, ὅθεν Σίβυλλαι καὶ Βάκιδες καὶ οἱ ἔνθεοι γίνονται πάντες, ὅταν μὴ νοσήματι γένωνται ἀλλὰ φυσικῇ κράσει. Μαρακὸς δὲ ὁ Συρακούσιος καὶ ἀμείνων ἦν ποιητής, ὅτ' ἐκσταίη. ὅσοις δ' ἂν ἐπανεθῇ
954b τὴν ἄγαν θερμότητα[13] || πρὸς τὸ μέσον, οὗτοι μελαγχολικοὶ μέν εἰσι, φρονιμώτεροι δέ, καὶ ἧττον μὲν ἔκτοποι, πρὸς πολλὰ δὲ διαφέροντες τῶν ἄλλων, οἱ μὲν πρὸς παιδείαν, οἱ δὲ πρὸς τέχνας, οἱ δὲ πρὸς
5 πολιτείαν. πολλὴν δὲ καὶ εἰς τοὺς κινδύνους | ποιεῖ

12 †μανικοὶ† Grumach apud Flashar

13 ἐπανεθῇ Bussemaker : ἐπανθῇ codd. || ἐπανεθῇ ἡ ἄγαν θερμότης legit Gaza (vid. Bussemaker) : ἐπανθῇ τὴν ἄγαν θερμότητα codd.

abounds in the body, produces apoplexy or torpor or spiritlessness or fear, but if it becomes overheated, it produces high-spiritedness with song, and insanity, and the breaking out of sores and such things. In most people, therefore, arising from their daily nutrition, it produces no differences in character, but only brings about some melancholic disease. But those in whom such a mixture[23] has formed by nature, these straightaway develop all sorts of characters, each difference in accordance with the different mixture; for instance, those in whom (*the black bile*) is considerable and cold become sluggish and stupid, whereas those in whom it is very considerable and hot become mad, clever, erotic, and easily moved to spiritedness and desire,[24] and some become more talkative. But many too, owing to this heat being near the location of the intelligence, are affected by diseases of madness or inspiration, whence come Sibyls and Bakides[25] and all the inspired persons, when (*the condition*) comes not through disease[26] but through natural mixture. Maracus the Syracusan was even a better poet when he was insane. But those in whom the excessive heat is relaxed toward a mean, these people are melancholic, but they are more intelligent, and they are less eccentric, but they are superior to the others in many respects, some in education, others in arts, and others in politics. And in the face of danger, such a state pro-

[23] Or "temperament." [24] Re. "easily moved to spiritedness (or anger, τοὺς θυμοὺς) and desire (τὰς ἐπιθυμίας)": note the continued use of "spirit" (θυμ-) words.

[25] Plural of "Bakis" (also or originally a proper name), an ecstatic or inspired seer. [26] I.e., the "diseases of madness or inspiration" occur not owing to some other disease.

διαφορὰν ἡ τοιαύτη ἕξις τοῦ ἐνίοτε ἀνωμάλους εἶναι ἐν[14] τοῖς φόβοις πολλοὺς τῶν ἀνδρῶν. ὡς γὰρ ἂν τύχωσι τὸ σῶμα ἔχοντες πρὸς τὴν τοιαύτην κρᾶσιν, διαφέρουσιν αὐτοὶ αὑτῶν. ἡ δὲ μελαγχολικὴ κρᾶσις, ὥσπερ καὶ ἐν ταῖς νόσοις ἀνωμάλους ποιεῖ, οὕτω καὶ
10 αὐτὴ ἀνώμαλός ἐστιν· | ὁτὲ μὲν γὰρ ψυχρά ἐστιν ὥσπερ ὕδωρ, ὁτὲ δὲ θερμή. ὥστε φοβερόν τι ὅταν εἰσαγγελθῇ, ἐὰν μὲν ψυχροτέρας οὔσης τῆς κράσεως τύχῃ, δειλὸν ποιεῖ· προωδοπεποίηκε γὰρ τῷ φόβῳ, καὶ ὁ φόβος καταψύχει. δηλοῦσι δὲ οἱ περίφοβοι· τρέμουσι γάρ. ἐὰν δὲ μᾶλλον θερμή, εἰς τὸ μέτριον
15 κατέστησεν | ὁ φόβος, καὶ ἐν αὐτῷ καὶ ἀπαθῆ. ὁμοίως δὲ καὶ πρὸς τὰς καθ' ἡμέραν ἀθυμίας· πολλάκις γὰρ οὕτως ἔχομεν ὥστε λυπεῖσθαι, ἐφ' ὅτῳ δέ, οὐκ ἂν ἔχοιμεν εἰπεῖν· ὁτὲ δὲ εὐθύμως, ἐφ' ᾧ δέ, οὐ δῆλον. τὰ δὴ τοιαῦτα πάθη καὶ τὰ ἐπιπόλαια[15] λεχθέντα κατὰ
20 μέν τι μικρὸν πᾶσι γίνεται· | πᾶσι γὰρ μέμικταί τι τῆς δυνάμεως· ὅσοις δ' εἰς βάθος, οὗτοι δ' ἤδη ποιοί τινές εἰσι τὰ ἤθη. ὥσπερ γὰρ τὸ εἶδος ἕτεροι γίνονται οὐ τῷ πρόσωπον ἔχειν, ἀλλὰ τῷ ποιόν τι τὸ πρόσωπον, οἱ μὲν καλόν, οἱ δὲ αἰσχρόν, οἱ δὲ μηθὲν ἔχοντες περιττόν, οὗτοι δὲ μέσοι τὴν φύσιν, οὕτω καὶ οἱ μὲν μικρὰ |
25 μετέχοντες τῆς τοιαύτης κράσεως μέσοι εἰσίν, οἱ δὲ

[14] ἐν Richards : μὲν codd.

[15] ἐπιπόλαια Forster : παλαιὰ codd. Barth. : πάλαι Sylburg ex Gaza

duces great variation because many of the men are sometimes inconsistent in the presence of fears. For as their body happens to be with respect to such a mixture,[27] so they differ in themselves. Now the melancholic mixture is itself inconsistent, just as it produces inconsistency in those with the (*melancholic*) diseases; for like water, it is sometimes cold and sometimes hot. So when something fearful is announced, if it happens when the mixture is colder, it makes the person cowardly; for it paves the way to fear, and fear cools. Those feeling great fear prove this: for they tremble. But if the mixture is hotter, the fear brings it down to the moderate level, and (*makes the person*) in possession of himself and unaffected.[28] And so it is with respect to daily spiritlessness; for we are often in a condition of feeling grief, though for what reason we are unable to say; and sometimes we are in a cheerful condition, but why is not clear. Such affections and those called superficial come to be in everyone to some small extent, for some of their capacity is mingled in everyone; but those in whom they are deep, these people are already this type with respect to their characters. For just as people come to be different in appearance not by having faces, but by having a certain type of face, some beautiful, some ugly, and some having nothing extraordinary in this respect (those who are naturally average), so too, those having a small share of such a mixture[29] are average, whereas those sharing in

[27] Or "temperament."

[28] I assume "in possession of himself" (ἐν αὐτῷ) should likely be contrasted to "insane" or "out of one's mind" (ἔκστασις), and "unaffected" to "easily moved" (954a33).

[29] Or "temperament"—i.e., the melancholic mixture or temperament.

πλήθους ἤδη ἀνόμοιοι τοῖς πολλοῖς. ἐὰν μὲν γὰρ σφόδρα κατακορὴς ᾖ ἡ ἕξις, μελαγχολικοί εἰσι λίαν, ἐὰν δέ πως κραθῶσι, περιττοί. ῥέπουσι δ', ἂν ἀμελῶσιν, ἐπὶ τὰ μελαγχολικὰ νοσήματα, ἄλλοι περὶ ἄλλο
30 μέρος τοῦ σώματος· | καὶ τοῖς μὲν ἐπιληπτικὰ ἀποσημαίνει, τοῖς δὲ ἀποπληκτικά, ἄλλοις δὲ ἀθυμίαι ἰσχυραὶ ἢ φόβοι, τοῖς δὲ θάρρη λίαν, οἷον καὶ Ἀρχελάῳ συνέβαινε τῷ Μακεδονίας βασιλεῖ. αἴτιον δὲ τῆς τοιαύτης δυνάμεως ἡ κρᾶσις, ὅπως ἂν ἔχῃ ψύξεώς τε
35 καὶ θερμότητος. ψυχροτέρα μὲν γὰρ οὖσα τοῦ | καιροῦ δυσθυμίας ποιεῖ ἀλόγους· διὸ αἵ τ' ἀγχόναι μάλιστα τοῖς νέοις, ἐνίοτε δὲ καὶ πρεσβυτέροις. πολλοὶ δὲ καὶ μετὰ τὰς μέθας διαφθείρουσιν ἑαυτούς. ἔνιοι δὲ τῶν μελαγχολικῶν ἐκ τῶν πότων ἀθύμως διάγουσιν· σβέννυσι γὰρ ἡ τοῦ οἴνου θερμότης τὴν φυσικὴν
955a θερμότητα. τὸ δὲ θερμὸν τὸ περὶ || τὸν τόπον ᾧ φρονοῦμεν καὶ ἐλπίζομεν ποιεῖ εὐθύμους. καὶ διὰ τοῦτο πρὸς τὸ πίνειν εἰς μέθην πάντες ἔχουσι προθύμως, ὅτι πάντας ὁ οἶνος ὁ πολὺς εὐέλπιδας ποιεῖ, καθάπερ ἡ νεότης τοὺς παῖδας· τὸ μὲν γὰρ γῆρας δύσελπί
5 ἐστιν, ἡ δὲ | νεότης ἐλπίδος πλήρης. εἰσὶ δέ τινες ὀλίγοι οὓς πίνοντας δυσθυμίαι λαμβάνουσι, διὰ τὴν αὐτὴν αἰτίαν δι' ἣν καὶ μετὰ τοὺς πότους ἐνίους. ὅσοις μὲν οὖν μαραινομένου[16] τοῦ θερμοῦ αἱ ἀθυμίαι γίνονται, μᾶλλον ἀπάγχονται. διὸ καὶ οἱ νέοι ἢ καὶ οἱ
10 πρεσβῦται μᾶλλον πάγχονται· τὸ μὲν γὰρ | γῆρας

[16] ante μαραινομένου add. <μὴ> Grumach apud Flashar

much of it are unlike the majority. For, if their condition is quite saturated, they are very melancholic, whereas if it is mixed in a certain way, they are extraordinary. But if they are careless,[30] they incline toward melancholic diseases, different people in a different part of the body: indeed, in some the signs are epileptic, in some apoplectic, and in others, there is strong spiritlessness or there are fears, whereas in some there is too much boldness, for instance, as happened to Archelaus, king of Macedonia.[31] The mixture is cause of such power, according to how much cold and heat it contains. For when it is colder than is fitting, it produces irrational despondency; this is why hanging (*oneself*) is most prevalent among the young, though it sometimes occurs among older men as well. Many kill themselves after drunkenness. And some melancholic people continue to be spiritless after drinking; for the heat of the wine extinguishes the natural heat. But heat around the region in which we think and hope makes us cheerful. And for this reason everyone is eager to drink to the point of drunkenness, because a lot of wine makes everyone hopeful, just as youth does children; for old age is hopeless, whereas youth is full of hope. There are some few people who while drinking are seized with despondency, for the same reason some are such after drinking. So those in whom despondency occurs when the heat is put out are more inclined to hang themselves. And this is why the young are more inclined than even the old to hang themselves; for old age puts out the heat, but for the young the

30 I.e., if they neglect their health.

31 Ruled from 413 to 399 BC.

μαραίνει τὸ θερμόν, τῶν δὲ τὸ πάθος φυσικὸν ὂν †καὶ αὐτὸ τὸ μαραινόμενον θερμόν†.[17] ὅσοις δὲ σβεννυμένου[18] ἐξαίφνης, οἱ πλεῖστοι διαχρῶνται ἑαυτούς, ὥστε θαυμάζειν πάντας διὰ τὸ μηθὲν ποιῆσαι σημεῖον πρότερον. ψυχροτέρα μὲν οὖν γινομένη ἡ κρᾶσις ἡ
15 ἀπὸ τῆς μελαίνης χολῆς, ὥσπερ | εἴρηται, ποιεῖ ἀθυμίας παντοδαπάς, θερμοτέρα δὲ οὖσα εὐθυμίας. διὸ καὶ οἱ μὲν παῖδες εὐθυμότεροι, οἱ δὲ γέροντες δυσθυμότεροι. οἱ μὲν γὰρ θερμοί, οἱ δὲ ψυχροί· τὸ γὰρ γῆρας κατάψυξίς τις. συμβαίνει δὲ σβέννυσθαι ἐξαίφνης ὑπό τε τῶν ἐκτὸς αἰτιῶν, ὡς καὶ παρὰ φύσιν τὰ
20 πυρωθέντα, | οἷον ἄνθρακα ὕδατος ἐπιχυθέντος. διὸ καὶ ἐκ μέθης ἔνιοι ἑαυτοὺς διαχρῶνται· ἡ γὰρ ἀπὸ τοῦ οἴνου θερμότης ἐπείσακτός ἐστιν, ἧς σβεννυμένης συμβαίνει τὸ πάθος. καὶ μετὰ τὰ ἀφροδίσια οἱ πλεῖστοι ἀθυμότεροι γίνονται. ὅσοι δὲ περίττωμα πολὺ
25 προΐενται μετὰ τοῦ σπέρματος, οὗτοι | εὐθυμότεροι· κουφίζονται γὰρ περιττώματός τε καὶ πνεύματος καὶ θερμοῦ ὑπερβολῆς. ἐκεῖνοι[19] δὲ ἀθυμότεροι πολλάκις· καταψύχονται γὰρ ἀφροδισιάσαντες διὰ τὸ τῶν ἱκανῶν τι ἀφαιρεθῆναι· δηλοῖ δὲ τοῦτο τὸ μὴ πολλὴν τὴν ἀπορροὴν γεγονέναι. ὡς οὖν ἐν κεφαλαίῳ εἰπεῖν, διὰ
30 μὲν τὸ ἀνώμαλον | εἶναι τὴν δύναμιν τῆς μελαίνης χολῆς ἀνώμαλοί εἰσιν οἱ μελαγχολικοί· καὶ γὰρ

[17] καὶ αὐτὸ τὸ μαραινόμενον θερμόν codd. (obelis inclusi) : secl. Hett : καὶ αὐτὸ [τὸ μαραινόμενον θερμόν] Forster : καὶ αὐτὸ τὸ μαραῖνον θερμόν Richards

condition is natural, †and so the heat is being put out by itself†.[32] And among those people, when (*the heat*) is suddenly extinguished, the majority kill themselves, such that everyone is amazed because they gave no sign of it before. Therefore, when the mixture from the black bile becomes colder, as was said, it produces all kinds of spiritlessness, but when it is hotter, cheerfulness. And this is why children are more cheerful, whereas the old are more despondent. For the former are hot, the latter cold, since old age is a sort of cooling. But it happens that the heat is suddenly extinguished by external causes, just as things heated in fire (*are cooled*) contrary to nature, like coals when doused with water. And this is why some people kill themselves out of drunkeness; for the heat from the wine is foreign, and when it is extinguished this condition[33] results. And after sexual intercourse most people are more spiritless, but those who emit a lot of residue with their seed are more cheerful; for they are relieved of residue and of an excess of breath and heat. But those (*others*) are often more spiritless; for they cool down when they have had sexual intercourse, because they are deprived of something significant; and this is clear from the fact that the outflow (*of seed*) is not great.

So, to sum up, because the power of the black bile is uneven, melancholic people are uneven; for (*the black bile*)

[32] There is likely something wrong with the text of this and the previous line.

[33] That is, being suicidal.

---

18 σβεννυμένου : σβέννυται Forster ex Gaza

19 ἐκεῖνοι : fort. ἕτεροι Forster ex Gaza

ψυχρὰ σφόδρα γίνεται καὶ θερμή. διὰ δὲ τὸ ἠθοποιὸς εἶναι (ἠθοποιὸν γὰρ τὸ θερμὸν καὶ ψυχρὸν μάλιστα τῶν ἐν ἡμῖν ἐστίν) ὥσπερ ὁ οἶνος πλείων καὶ ἐλάττων
35 κεραννύμενος τῷ σώματι ποιεῖ τὸ ἦθος | ποιούς τινας ἡμᾶς. ἄμφω δὲ πνευματικά, καὶ ὁ οἶνος καὶ ἡ μέλαινα χολή. ἐπεὶ δ' ἔστι καὶ εὔκρατον εἶναι τὴν ἀνωμαλίαν καὶ καλῶς πως ἔχειν, καὶ ὅπου δεῖ θερμοτέραν εἶναι τὴν διάθεσιν καὶ πάλιν ψυχράν, ἢ τοὐναντίον διὰ τὸ ὑπερβολὴν ἔχειν, περιττοὶ μέν εἰσι πάντες οἱ μελαγ-
40 χολικοί, | οὐ διὰ νόσον, ἀλλὰ διὰ φύσιν. ||

955b 2. Διὰ τί κατ' ἐνίας μὲν τῶν ἐπιστημῶν ἕξιν ἔχειν λέγομεν, κατ' ἐνίας δὲ οὔ; ἢ καθ' ὅσας εὑρετικοί ἐσμεν, ἕξιν ἔχειν λεγόμεθα; τὸ γὰρ εὑρίσκειν ἀπὸ ἕξεως.

3. Διὰ τί τῶν ζῴων ὁ ἄνθρωπος φρονιμώτατον;
5 πότερον | ὅτι μικροκεφαλώτατον κατὰ λόγον τοῦ σώματος; ἢ ὅτι ἀνωμάλως ἐλάχιστον; διὰ γὰρ τοῦτο καὶ μικροκέφαλον, καὶ αὐτῶν οἱ τοιοῦτοι μᾶλλον τῶν μεγαλοκεφάλων φρονιμώτεροι.

4. Διὰ τί δοκεῖ ἡμῖν πλείων εἶναι ἡ ὁδός, ὅταν μὴ
10 εἰδότες | πόση τίς ἐστι βαδίζωμεν, μᾶλλον ἢ ὅταν εἰδότες, ἐὰν τὰ ἄλλα ὁμοίως τύχωμεν ἔχοντες; ἢ ὅτι τὸ

---

[34] According to Aristotle, a state (ἕξις)—a fixed state of the soul—is the genus of which the intellectual and moral virtues are species (*EN* 2.5–6 and 6.1).

[35] Ἐπιστήμη is best translated "science" (which is how I render it throughout), or "knowledge" (or "branch of knowledge"). It is another of the intellectual virtues discussed by Aristotle (see *EN* 6.6).

becomes both very cold and very hot. And because it is character-forming (for of the things in us, the hot and cold are especially character-forming), just like wine being mixed in the body in greater or less amounts, it produces certain qualities of character in us. Now both wine and black bile are full of breath. But since it is possible that what is uneven is well tempered and in a fine condition, and when it should be the disposition is hotter and then again cold, or the opposite owing to there being an excess, all melancholic people are extraordinary, not owing to disease but owing to nature.

2. Why do we say we have a state (*of the soul*)[34] in some of the sciences,[35] but not in others? Are we said to have a state in those concerned with discovery? For making discoveries comes from a state.

3.[36] Why is the human most intelligent of the animals? Is it because he has the smallest head in proportion to his body? Or is it because it is irregularly smallest?[37] For this is why he also has a small head, and among (*humans*) such people are more intelligent than those with large heads.

4.[38] Why does the road seem to us to be longer, when we walk without knowing how long it is, than when we do know, if we are the same with respect to other factors? Is it

[36] Cf. *GA* 2.6, 744a24–30, *Phgn*. 6, 811b28–12a8.

[37] The meaning of this sentence is unclear. The author is either asking "Is it because (*his head*) is irregularly smallest?" or "Is it because (*the human*) is irregularly smallest (*with respect to certain parts*)?" Neither is completely satisfactory.

[38] Cf. *Pr.* 5.25.

εἰδέναι <πόση>[20] ἐστὶν εἰδέναι τὸν ἀριθμόν; τὸ γὰρ
ἄπειρον καὶ ἀναρίθμητον ταὐτόν, καὶ πλέον ἀεὶ τὸ
ἄπειρον τοῦ ὡρισμένου. ὥσπερ οὖν εἰ ᾔδει ὅτι τοσήδε
15 ἐστί, πεπερασμένην αὐτὴν ἀνάγκη εἶναι, | οὕτως εἰ μὴ
οἶδε πόση τίς ἐστιν, ὡς ἀντιστρέφοντος παραλογίζε-
ται ἡ ψυχή, καὶ φαίνεται αὕτη εἶναι ἄπειρος. ἔτι[21] τὸ
ποσὸν ὡρισμένον ἐστὶ καὶ τὸ ὡρισμένον ποσόν. ὅταν
τοίνυν μὴ φαίνηται ὡρισμένον, ὥσπερ ἄπειρον δόξει
εἶναι, διὰ τὸ τὸ πεφυκὸς ὡρίσθαι, ἂν μὴ ᾖ ὡρισμένον,
20 ἄπειρον εἶναι, | καὶ τὸ φαινόμενον μὴ ὡρίσθαι φαίνε-
σθαι ἀνάγκη πως ἀπέραντον.

5. Διὰ τί πρεσβύτεροι μὲν γινόμενοι μᾶλλον νοῦν
ἔχομεν, νεώτεροι δ᾽ ὄντες θᾶττον μανθάνομεν; ἢ ὅτι ὁ
θεὸς ὄργανα ἐν ἑαυτοῖς ἡμῖν δέδωκε δύο, ἐν οἷς χρη-
25 σόμεθα τοῖς ἐκτὸς | ὀργάνοις, σώματι μὲν χεῖρα, ψυχῇ
δὲ νοῦν; ἔστι γὰρ καὶ ὁ νοῦς τῶν φύσει ἐν ἡμῖν ὥσπερ
ὄργανον ὑπάρχων· αἱ δὲ ἄλλαι ἐπιστῆμαι καὶ τέχναι
τῶν ὑφ᾽ ἡμῶν ποιητῶν εἰσίν, ὁ δὲ νοῦς τῶν φύσει.
καθάπερ οὖν τῇ χειρὶ οὐκ εὐθὺς γενόμενοι χρώμεθα
30 βέλτιστα, ἀλλ᾽ ὅταν ἡ φύσις αὐτὴν ἐπιτελέσῃ | (προϊ-
ούσης γὰρ τῆς ἡλικίας ἡ χεὶρ μάλιστα δύναται ἀπο-
τελεῖν τὸ ἑαυτῆς ἔργον), τὸν αὐτὸν τρόπον καὶ ὁ νοῦς
τῶν φύσει οὐκ εὐθὺς ἀλλ᾽ ἐπὶ γήρως ἡμῖν μάλιστα

[20] <πόση> Sylburg (cf. *Pr.* 5.25, 883b5)
[21] ἔτι Forster (cf. *Pr.* 5.25, 883b9) : ἐπεὶ codd.

---

[39] I.e., to be able to specify its length arithmetically.
[40] The word translated here is a form of the standard term in

because knowing <how long it is>, is to know the number?[39] For the infinite and unnumbered are the same, and the infinite is always greater than the determinate. Therefore, just as if one knows that it is such a length, it must be limited, so too if one does not know how long it is, as though converting (*the proposition*),[40] the soul is led to a false conclusion, and this[41] appears to be infinite. Further, a quantity is determinate and what is determinate is a quantity. So when something does not appear to be determinate, it seems to be as it were infinite, because that which is naturally determinate, if it is not determinate, seems to be infinite, and what appears not to be determinate must appear in a sense infinite.

5.[42] Why do we have more understanding when we get older, whereas we learn more quickly when we are younger? Is it because god has given us two instruments within ourselves, in which we will use external instruments, the hand for the body, understanding for the soul? For the understanding is among the things existing in us by nature as an instrument; and while the other sciences and arts are among the things produced by us, understanding is among the things existing by nature. So, just as we do not use the hand in the best way immediately after we are born, but when nature perfects it (for as our age progresses the hand is most able to complete its function), in the same way too, among the things existing by nature, understanding is present in us most not immediately but in old age, and

Aristotle's logical works for "to convert" (ἀντιστρέφειν), e.g., to convert "every A is B" into "every B is A" (see, e.g., *Pr.An.* 25a6).

[41] This (αὕτη) must refer to the length ("how long," πόση).

[42] Cf. *EN* 6.11, 1143b7–9, *Rh.* 2.13.

παραγίνεται καὶ τότε ἀποτελεῖται μάλιστα, ἂν μὴ ὑπό τινος πηρωθῇ, καθάπερ καὶ τὰ ἄλλα τὰ φύσει ὑπάρ-
35 *χοντα. ὕστερον* | *δὲ τῆς τῶν χειρῶν δυνάμεως ὁ νοῦς παραγίνεται ἡμῖν, ὅτι καὶ τὰ τοῦ νοῦ ὄργανά ἐστι τῶν τῆς χειρός. ἔστι γὰρ νοῦ μὲν ὄργανον ἐπιστήμη (τούτῳ γάρ ἐστι χρήσιμος, καθάπερ αὐλοὶ αὐλητῇ), χειρῶν δὲ πολλὰ τῶν φύσει ὄντων· ἡ δὲ φύσις αὐτή τε*
40 *ἐπιστήμης πρότερον, καὶ τὰ ὑπ' αὐτῆς γινόμενα.* | *ὧν δὲ τὰ ὄργανα πρότερα, καὶ τὰς δυνάμεις πρότερον*
956a *εἰκὸς* || *ἐγγίνεσθαι ἡμῖν· τούτοις γὰρ χρώμενοι ἕξιν λαμβάνομεν. καὶ ἔχει ὁμοίως τὸ ἑκάστου ὄργανον πρὸς αὐτό· καὶ ἀνάπαλιν, ὡς τὰ ὄργανα πρὸς ἄλληλα, οὕτω <ὧν>*[22] *τὰ ὄργανα πρὸς αὐτά. ὁ μὲν οὖν νοῦς διὰ*
5 *ταύτην τὴν αἰτίαν πρεσβυτέροις* | *οὖσιν ἡμῖν μᾶλλον ἐγγίνεται. μανθάνομεν δὲ θᾶττον νεώτεροι ὄντες διὰ τὸ μηδέν πω ἐπίστασθαι. ὅταν δὲ ἐπιστώμεθα, οὐκέτι ὁμοίως δυνάμεθα δέχεσθαι,*[23] *καθάπερ καὶ μνημονεύομεν μᾶλλον οἷς ἂν ἕωθεν πρῶτον ἐντυγχάνωμεν, ἔπειτα προϊούσης τῆς ἡμέρας οὐκέτι ὁμοίως διὰ τὸ* |
10 *πολλοῖς ἐντετυχηκέναι.*

6. *Διὰ τί ἀνθρώπῳ πειστέον*[24] *μᾶλλον ἢ ἄλλῳ ζῴῳ;*

[22] *<ὧν>* Richards

[23] *δυνάμεθα δέχεσθαι* Richards : *δυνάμεθα, δυνάμεθα δὲ ἔχεσθαι* codd.

[24] fort. post *πειστέον* add. *<τὰ ζῷα>* Richards

then it is most of all complete, if it is not incapacitated by something, just like the other things existing in us by nature. But understanding is present in us later than the power of the hands, because the instruments of understanding are (*present later*) than those of the hand. For science is the instrument of understanding (since it is useful to understanding, just as *auloi* are to the *aulos* player), whereas many are the natural instruments of the hands; but nature itself is prior to science, as well as the things that come to be from it. Now with respect to the things to which the instruments are prior, it is reasonable that the powers be prior in us as well; for by using these we acquire a state (*of the soul*).[43] And the instrument of each[44] has a similar relation to it; and conversely, as the instruments are related to each other, so are the things of which they are the instruments related to the same things. For this reason, therefore, understanding comes to be in us more when we are older. But we learn more quickly when we are younger, because we do not yet know anything. Now once we have science, we are no longer in the same way able to acquire it,[45] just as we remember more those whom we first encounter in the morning, then as the day progresses we no longer remember in the same way, because we have encountered many people.

6.[46] Why should the human be obeyed more than an-

[43] See n. 34 above.

[44] The masculine/neuter ἑκάστου ("of each") cannot refer to the preceding feminine δυνάμεις ("powers"). I take it to refer to the instruments provided by god: intelligence and hands.

[45] There is a problem with the text. I have accepted Richards's conjecture.

[46] Cf. *Po*. 4, 1448b4–9.

πότερον ὥσπερ Πλάτων Νεοκλεῖ ἀπεκρίνατο, ὅτι ἀριθμεῖν μόνον ἐπίσταται τῶν ἄλλων ζῴων; ἢ ὅτι θεοὺς νομίζει μόνον; ἢ ὅτι μιμητικώτατον; μανθάνειν γὰρ δύναται διὰ τοῦτο. |

15 7. *Διὰ τί οὐ χαίρομεν μεμνημένοι*[25] *οὐδὲ ἐλπίζοντες ὅτι τὸ τρίγωνον δύο ὀρθαῖς ἴσας ἔχει τὰς ἐντὸς γωνίας, οὐδὲ τῶν ἄλλων τῶν τοιούτων οὐθέν, εἰ μὴ τῇ θεωρίᾳ, αὕτη δὲ ὁμοίως ἐστὶν ἡδεῖα κἂν εἰ τρισὶν ὀρθαῖς ἢ πλείοσιν ἴσας ἔσχεν, ἀλλ' ὅτι Ὀλυμπίᾳ* 20 *ἐνικῶμεν, καὶ περὶ τῆς ναυμαχίας τῆς ἐν* | *Σαλαμῖνι, χαίρομεν καὶ μεμνημένοι καὶ ἐλπίζοντες τοιαῦτα, ἀλλ' οὐ τἀναντία τοῖς τοιούτοις; ἢ ὅτι ἐπὶ μὲν τοῖς τοιούτοις χαίρομεν ὡς γενομένοις ἢ οὖσιν, ἐπὶ δὲ τοῖς κατὰ φύσιν †ὡς κατὰ ἀλήθειαν θεωρίας ἡδονήν, ὡς ἔχει, μόνην ἡμῖν ποιεῖν, τὰς δὲ πράξεις†*[26] *τὴν ἀπὸ τῶν* 25 *συμβαινόντων ἀπ'* | *αὐτῶν; ἀνομοίων οὖν οὐσῶν τῶν*

[25] *μεμνημένοι* conieci (cf. 956a20) : *θεώμενοι* codd.

[26] *ὡς* (*ὅπως* pro *ὡς* Ap Ye) *κατὰ ἀλήθειαν θεωρίας ἡδονήν, ὡς ἔχει, μόνην ἡμῖν ποιεῖν, τὰς δὲ πράξεις* codd. (obelis inclusi) : <*ἢ*> *ὡς κατὰ ἀλήθειαν ἔχει θεωρία ἡδονὴν μόνη ἡμῖν ποιεῖ, αἱ δὲ πράξεις* Ross apud Forster : *ὡς* <*οὖσιν, ὥστε τὴν*> *κατ' ἀληθείας ὡς ἔχει θεωρίαν ἡδονὴν μόνην ἡμῖν ποιεῖν, τὰς δὲ πράξεις* Richards

---

[47] The subject is not stated, and one naturally takes it to refer to humans: Why should one obey humans more than any other kind of animal? Richards argues that it makes more sense to take animals as the subject: Why should *animals* obey a human more than another animal?

other animal?[47] Is it, as Plato replied to Neocles,[48] because he alone of the animals knows how to count? Or because he alone believes in gods? Or because he is the most imitative animal? For he is able to learn because of this.

7. Why do we not enjoy remembering or anticipating the fact that the triangle has interior angles equal to two right angles, nor any other such things, except in the contemplation,[49] and this would be similarly pleasant if they were equal to three or more right angles, but that we were victorious at Olympia, or concerning the sea battle at Salamis, we do enjoy remembering and anticipating such events, but not their opposites?[50] Is it because we feel enjoyment in such things that have occurred or are happening, but in the case of what is according to nature, †the contemplation of the truth produces the only pleasure in us, whereas the actions† produce the pleasures that come from their results?[51] Therefore, since actions are variable,

[48] This reference is unknown; but see the *Epinomis* attributed to Plato, which deals with the issues raised in this chapter.

[49] The mss. reading involves a contradiction: "Why do we not enjoy contemplating (*θεώμενοι*) . . . except in the contemplation" (*εἰ μὴ τῇ θεωρίᾳ*). Most translators attempt to avoid the contradiction by translating *θεώμενοι* "contemplation" and *τῇ θεωρίᾳ* "the speculation," but I find that unsatisfactory. If, however, *θεώμενοι* was a mistake for *μεμνημένοι* ("remembering," cf. l. 20), the contradiction disappears.

[50] I.e., remembering such events in the past, and anticipating such events as they unfold in the present or foreseeable future. A sea battle we lost or were losing is an example of an opposite we would take no pleasure in remembering or anticipating.

[51] The text of this sentence is uncertain; I translate Ross's conjecture.

πράξεων, καὶ τὰ ἀποβαίνοντα ἀπ᾽ αὐτῶν γίνεται τὰ μὲν λυπηρὰ, τὰ δὲ ἡδέα· φεύγομεν δὲ καὶ διώκομεν καθ᾽ ἡδονὴν καὶ λύπην ἅπαντα.

8. Διὰ τί μέχρι ὑγείας πραγματεύονται οἱ ἰατροί; ἰσχναίνει γάρ, εἶτα ἐκ τούτου ξηραίνει, εἶτα ὑγείαν
30 ἐποίησεν, | εἶτα ἐνταῦθα ἔστη. πότερον[27] οὐκ ἔστι δυνατὸν ἐκ τούτου γενέσθαι ἄλλο; ἢ εἰ δυνατόν, ἄλλης ἐπιστήμης, καὶ ἔσται ὅ τις ἐξ ὑγείας ποιήσει ἄλλο τι; εἰ δὴ γίνεται ἐκ τῶν ἐναντίων καὶ τῶν μεταξύ, δῆλον ὅτι ἀρρωστεῖ, ἢ ξηρότερος ἢ ὑγρότερος ἤ τι τοιοῦτον.[28] ποιεῖ δὴ ἐκ ψύχους ἧττον σφόδρα, καὶ |
35 τέλεον[29] ὡδὶ θερμὸν καὶ ὡδὶ ξηρὸν ἢ ὑγρὸν μεταβαῖνον ἐκ τῶν ἐναντίων ἢ μεταξύ, ἕως ἂν ἔλθῃ εἰς τὸ οὕτως ἔχειν, ὃ ἦν τοῦ ὑγιαίνειν· ἔκ τε τούτου οὐ πέφυκεν ἄλλο τι ὂν ἢ τὸ μεταξύ. δύναται μὲν οὖν ποιῆσαι ὁ ἔχων. ὡς γὰρ ἦλθεν, ἀναλῦσαι δύναται καὶ
40 ἀπελθεῖν, οὐ μὴν ἥ γε τέχνη τούτου | ἐστίν. ἀεὶ γὰρ
956b βέλτιον.[30] ὥστε οὔτε ἄλλη οὔτε αὑτὴ[31] ποιήσει || ἐξ ὑγείας ἄλλο τι· οὐθὲν γὰρ ἐγίνετο <ἂν>[32] ἢ τὸ ἐναντίον τούτου, εἴπερ ἡ αὐτὴ ἐπιστήμη. οὕτω καὶ ἐπὶ οἰκίας οὐδὲν ποιήσειεν ἂν τοὐναντίον· οὐκ ἔστιν οὖν ἄλλη[33]

[27] post πότερον add. <ὅτι> Richards
[28] post τοιοῦτον add. <ὤν> Forster
[29] τέλεον : τέλος Forster : fort. τελέως
[30] βέλτιον : βελτίονος Richards
[31] οὔτε ἄλλη οὔτε αὑτὴ Forster : οὐδὲ ἄλλη οὔτε αὐτὴ codd. [32] <ἂν> Richards
[33] οὖν ἄλλη Bussemaker ex Gaza : ἐν ἄλλῃ codd.

with respect to the results coming from them, some are painful, some pleasant; and we avoid and pursue everything according to pleasure and pain.

8. Why do doctors exert themselves only until health is achieved? For the doctor reduces (*the patient*), then after this dries him, then he produces health, then he stops there. Is it not possible for some other condition[52] to come to be from this one? Or if it is possible, does it belong to another science, and will what one produces from health be some other condition? If indeed health is produced from opposite or intermediate conditions, it is clear that one is sick by being too dry or too moist or some such condition. Now from cold, (*the doctor*) produces a less extreme condition, and in the end a certain hot and a certain dry or moist condition moving from the opposite or intermediate conditions, until he reaches the condition, which is that of health; and from this condition no other is possible by nature except the intermediate one.[53] Now the one possessing (*the art of medicine*) is able to produce this. For once he reaches (*the state of health*), he is able to undo it and go back, but his art is not of this character. For always (*his concern is making the patient*) better. So neither any other art nor this one will produce anything else from health; for nothing would come from it or its opposite, if it is the same science. So, too, in the case of a house, nothing could make its opposite. There is no other art, therefore, producing anything out of health, except in the sense of (*producing*

[52] Here and in the rest of the chapter, "condition" does not correspond to any word in the text but is implied.

[53] I.e., intermediate between health and sickness, which of course no doctor would aim at.

τέχνη ἐκ τούτου ποιήσουσα, πλὴν ὡς <ἐκ>[34] μέρους, οἷον ἡ σκυτικὴ ὑπόδημα ἐκ προσχίσματος.[35] ἐξ ἑκατέ-
5 ρου | γὰρ γίνεται διττῶς, ἢ συντιθεμένου ἢ φθειρομένου.

9. Διὰ τί τὸν φιλόσοφον τοῦ ῥήτορος οἴονται διαφέρειν; ἢ ὅτι ὁ μὲν φιλόσοφος περὶ αὐτὰ τὰ εἴδη τῶν πραγμάτων διατρίβει, ὁ δὲ περὶ τὰ μετέχοντα, οἷον ὁ μὲν τί ἐστιν ἀδικία, ὁ δὲ ὡς ἄδικος ὁ δεῖνα, καὶ ὁ μὲν
10 τί ἡ τυραννίς, ὁ δὲ | οἷόν τι ὁ τύραννος;

10. Διὰ τί οἱ Διονυσιακοὶ τεχνῖται ὡς ἐπὶ τὸ πολὺ πονηροί εἰσιν; ἢ ὅτι ἥκιστα λόγου <καὶ> σοφίας[36] κοινωνοῦσι διὰ τὸ περὶ τὰς ἀναγκαίας τέχνας τὸ πολὺ μέρος τοῦ βίου εἶναι, καὶ ὅτι ἐν ἀκρασίαις τὸ πολὺ τοῦ
15 βίου[37] εἰσίν, τὰ δὲ καὶ ἐν ἀπορίαις; | ἀμφότερα δὲ φαυλότητος παρασκευαστικά.

11. Διὰ τί οἱ ἐξ ἀρχῆς τῆς μὲν κατὰ τὸ σῶμα

[34] <ἐκ> Louis ex Gaza

[35] προσχίσματος Ap[a] M X[a] c u Berol.148 Marc.604 : προσχήσματος cett. codd.

[36] λόγου <καὶ> σοφίας Bonitz (cf. Gell. 20.4, λόγου καὶ φιλοσοφίας) : λόγου σοφίας codd.

[37] τὸ πολὺ τοῦ βίου : τὸν πολὺν χρόνον Gell. 20.4

---

[54] By aiming at the health of a leg, say, the doctor is also aiming at the health of the whole patient. In this sense alone, he can be said to produce something (general health) out of health (that of the leg).

[55] For instance, a shoemaker can make a shoe out of new materials (composition) or he can make a shoe out of parts taken

something) out of a part, as the shoemaker's art produces shoes from the front part of a shoe.[54] For one thing can come from another in two ways: from composition or from destruction.[55]

9.[56] Why do people think the philosopher is better than the orator? Is it because the philosopher occupies himself with the forms themselves of things, whereas the orator occupies himself with the things participating in them—for instance, the former says what injustice is, while the latter says that so-and-so is unjust, and the latter says that someone is a tyrant, while the former says that tyranny is such and such?

10.[57] Why are Dionysian artists[58] in most cases bad people? Is it because they least of all partake of reason and wisdom, owing to most of their life being concerned with the necessary arts,[59] and because most of their life is passed in incontinence, and some of it also in difficulties? Both of these prepare the way for baseness.

11.[60] Why did those of old institute a prize for competi-

from an old one (destruction). It's unclear what the analogue is in the case of medicine.

[56] *Pr.* 18.5 is a shorter version of this chapter.

[57] Gellius (20.4) quotes this entire chapter (with some variations), and attributes it to Aristotle's *Προβλήματα ἐγκύκλια*.

[58] I.e., artists connected with the theater, perhaps actors especially (see *Rh.* 1405a23–24).

[59] This is unclear: the arts that are necessary, given their profession, or the arts necessary for providing their daily needs. The point the author is making remains the same.

[60] Cf. Thph. fr. 564 FHSG (= Ath. 13.90, 610A–B), Pl. *Hipp. Min.* 364a.

ἀγωνίας ἆθλόν τι προὔταξαν, σοφίας δὲ οὐθὲν ἔθηκαν; ἢ ὅτι ἐπιεικῶς δεῖ τοὺς κριτάς, ἃ περὶ[38] διάνοιάν ἐστιν, ἢ μηθὲν χείρους τῶν ἀγωνιστῶν εἶναι ἢ κρείτ-
20 τους; εἰ δὲ ἔδει σοφίᾳ τοὺς πρωτεύοντας | ἀγωνίζεσθαι καὶ ἆθλον προὐτέτακτο, κριτῶν ἂν ἠπόρουν αὐτοῖς. ἐπὶ δὲ τῶν γυμνικῶν ἀγώνων ἅπαντός ἐστι κρῖναι, τῇ ὄψει μόνῃ θεασάμενον. ἔτι δὲ ὁ ἐξ ἀρχῆς κατασκευάζων οὐκ ἐβούλετο τοιαύτην ἀγωνίαν προθεῖναι τοῖς Ἕλλησιν, ἐξ ὧν[39] ἔμελλον στάσεις καὶ ἔχθραι μεγά-
25 λαι ἔσεσθαι· οἷον | οἱ ἄνθρωποι, ὅταν τις ἢ ἐκκριθῇ ἢ προσδεχθῇ εἴς τι τῶν κατὰ τὸ σῶμα ἀθλημάτων, οὐ πάντῃ χαλεπῶς φέρουσιν οὐδὲ εἰς ἔχθραν καθίστανται τοῖς κρίνουσιν, ὑπὲρ δὲ τοῦ φρονιμωτέρους ἢ μοχθηροτέρους εἶναι τοῖς κρίνουσι μάλιστα ὀργίζονται καὶ ἀγανακτοῦσιν. στασιῶδες δὲ καὶ μοχθηρὸν τὸ
30 τοιοῦτόν | ἐστιν. ἔτι δὲ δεῖ τῆς ἀγωνίας τὸ ἆθλον κρεῖττον εἶναι. ἐπὶ μὲν γὰρ τῶν γυμνικῶν ἀθλημάτων τὸ ἆθλον αἱρετώτερον καὶ βέλτιον τῆς ἀγωνίας· σοφίας δὲ τί ἂν ἆθλον βέλτιον γένοιτο;

12. Διὰ τί ἄλλο νοεῖ καὶ ποιεῖ ἄνθρωπος μάλιστα; ἢ ὅτι τῶν ἐναντίων ἡ αὐτὴ ἐπιστήμη; ἢ ὅτι ὁ μὲν νοῦς
35 πολλῶν | ἐστίν, ἡ δὲ ὄρεξις ἑνός; ὁ μὲν οὖν ἄνθρωπος τῷ νῷ τὰ πλεῖστα ζῇ, τὰ δὲ θηρία ὀρέξει καὶ θυμῷ καὶ ἐπιθυμίᾳ.

13. Διὰ τί φρόνιμοί τινες κτώμενοι οὐ χρώμενοι

[38] περὶ Bussemaker ex Gaza : παρὰ codd.
[39] ὧν : ἧς Forster

tion involving the body, but establish none for wisdom? Is it because the judges, who are concerned with thought, should in fairness either be no worse than the competitors or superior to them? But if those preeminent in wisdom had to compete and a prize was instituted, they would have a problem finding judges of them. But in the case of gymnastic competitions anyone is able to judge, observing with their eyes alone. Further, the one first creating these did not want to set up such a competition among the Greeks from which great divisions and enmity would arise; for instance, when someone is rejected or accepted in one of the contests involving the body, people do not altogether bear hard feelings or stand in enmity against the judges, but over whether they are more intelligent or more wretched, they most of all are angered and irritated by the judges. And this is divisive and wretched. Further, the prize should be superior to the competition. For in the case of gymnastic contests the prize is more desirable and better than the competition; but what prize could be better than wisdom?

12.[61] Why does man in particular think one thing and do another? Is it because the same science is concerned with opposites? Or is it because understanding is of many things, whereas appetite is of one? Now with respect to most things, man lives by understanding, whereas beasts live by appetite, spirit, and desire.

13.[62] Why do some intelligent people spend their time

[61] See *EN* 7.2.
[62] Cf. *Pol.* 1.9.

διατελοῦσιν; πότερον ὅτι τῷ ἔθει χρῶνται; ἢ διὰ τὸ ἐν ἐλπίδι ἡδύ;

14.[40] . . . ὅτι ἡ αἴσθησις καὶ ἡ διάνοια τῷ ἠρεμεῖν
40 τὴν ψυχὴν | ἐνεργεῖ; ὃ καὶ ἡ ἐπιστήμη δοκεῖ εἶναι, ὅτι
957a τὴν ψυχὴν ἵστησιν· || κινουμένης γὰρ καὶ φερομένης οὔτε αἰσθέσθαι οὔτε διανοηθῆναι δυνατόν. διὸ καὶ τὰ παιδία καὶ οἱ μεθύοντες καὶ οἱ μαινόμενοι ἀνόητοι· διὰ γὰρ τὸ πλῆθος τοῦ θερμοῦ τοῦ ἐνυπάρχοντος πλείστη
5 κίνησις αὐτοῖς καὶ σφοδροτάτη συμβαίνει, | ληγούσης δὲ ταύτης ἐμφρονέστεροι γίνονται· ἀταράχου γὰρ οὔσης τῆς διανοίας μᾶλλον ἐφιστάναι δύνανται αὐτήν. οἵ τ' ἐν τῷ καθεύδειν ἐνυπνιαζόμενοι ἱσταμένης τῆς διανοίας, καὶ καθ' ὅσον ἠρεμεῖ, ὀνειρώττουσιν. μάλιστα γὰρ ἐν τοῖς ὕπνοις ἡ ψυχὴ κινεῖται. περι-
10 ισταμένου γὰρ τοῦ θερμοῦ ἐκ τοῦ ἄλλου | σώματος εἰς τὸν ἐντὸς τόπον, τότε πλείστη καὶ σφοδροτάτη κίνησις ὑπάρχει, οὐχ ὥσπερ οἱ πολλοὶ ὑπολαμβάνουσι τότε ἠρεμεῖν καὶ καθ' αὑτὴν εἶναι, καὶ μάλιστα ὅταν μηδὲν ἴδωσιν ἐνύπνιον. συμβαίνει δὲ τοὐναντίον· διὰ γὰρ τὸ ἐν πλείστῃ κινήσει εἶναι καὶ μηδὲ κατὰ μικρὸν
15 ἠρεμεῖν, οὐδὲ διανοεῖσθαι | δύναται. ἐν πλείστῃ δὲ κινήσει, ὅταν ἥδιστα καθεύδῃ, εἰκότως ἐστίν, ὅτι τότε

[40] ante ὅτι lac. indic. Ruelle : cap. 13 continuatur in codd. || Xa mg et Apmg, λείπει ἡ ἀρχὴ τοιαύτη : διὰ τί οἱ βαθέως καὶ ἥδιστα καθεύδοντες οὐδὲν ἐνύπνιον ὁρῶσιν; ἢ (cf. Barth., *Propter quid qui graviter et suavissime dormiunt nihil somniant*)

acquiring and not using? Is it because they are following habit, or is it due to the pleasure in anticipation?

14.[63] (*Why do those who sleep deeply and pleasantly see no dreams*?)[64] Is it because perception and thought function by the soul being at rest? And this is what science[65] seems to be, because it steadies the soul;[66] for, when the soul is set in motion or traveling, it is able neither to perceive nor to think. And this is why children and those who are drunk and the insane are without understanding; for owing to the quantity of heat present in them, a very great and violent motion results, but when this abates they become more intelligent; for when the thought is undisturbed they can steady it more. Those who dream during sleep when their thought is steadied, and insofar as it is at rest, have dream visions.[67] For the soul is moved most in sleep. For when the heat gathers in the inner region from the rest of the body, the motion is greatest and most violent—not, as most people suppose, at rest and by itself, and especially when they see no dream. But the opposite occurs: because being in the greatest motion and not resting even for a short time, it is unable to think. Now it is naturally in the greatest motion when one sleeps most

[63] Cf. *Pr.* 18.1, *Phys*. 247b1–48a11. [64] Translating the marginal note in Ap and X[a]. [65] Or "knowledge."

[66] A false etymology, deriving ἐπιστήμη from ἵστημι (or ἐφίστημι, see 957a6). Cf. Pl. *Crat*. 437a–b.

[67] This line contains two verbs for dreaming (ἐνυπνιάζω and ὀνειρώσσω). The related nouns (ἐνύπνιον and ὄνειρος) are basically synonyms, though according to Artemidorus (*Onirocriticon* 1.1), ἐνύπνιον refers to simple dreams, whereas ὄνειρος refers to dreams bearing a vision. Such a distinction may be relevant here, and I translate the line accordingly.

μάλιστα καὶ πλεῖστον θερμὸν ἀθροίζεται εἰς τὸν εἴσω τόπον. ὅτι δὲ ἐν τῇ κινήσει οὖσα ἡ ψυχὴ οὐ μόνον ὕπαρ ἀλλ' οὐδ' ἐν τοῖς ὕπνοις δύναται διανοεῖσθαι, κἀκεῖνο σημεῖον· ἐν γὰρ τοῖς μετὰ τὴν πρόσεσιν τῶν
20 σιτίων | ὕπνοις ἥκιστα ἔστιν ἐνύπνια ὁρᾶν, τότε δὲ μάλιστα συμβαίνει κινεῖσθαι αὐτὴν διὰ τὴν ἐπεισενεχθεῖσαν τροφήν. τὸ δὲ[41] ἐνύπνιόν ἐστιν, ὅταν <τοῖς>[42] διανοουμένοις καὶ πρὸ ὀμμάτων τιθεμένοις ὕπνος ἐπέλθῃ. διὸ καὶ ταῦτα μάλιστα ὁρῶμεν ἃ πράττομεν ἢ μέλλομεν ἢ βουλόμεθα· περὶ γὰρ τούτων μάλιστα |
25 πλειστάκις λογισμοὶ καὶ φαντασίαι ἐπιγίνονται. καὶ οἱ βελτίους βελτίω τὰ ἐνύπνια ὁρῶσι διὰ ταῦτα, ὅτι καὶ [οἱ][43] ἐγρηγορότες περὶ βελτιόνων διανοοῦνται, οἱ δὲ χεῖρον ἢ τὴν διάνοιαν ἢ τὸ σῶμα διακείμενοι χείρω. καὶ γὰρ ἡ τοῦ σώματος διάθεσις πρὸς τὴν τῶν
30 ἐνυπνίων φαντασίαν συμβλητικόν· τοῦ | γὰρ νοσοῦντος καὶ αἱ τῆς διανοίας προθέσεις φαῦλαι, καὶ ἔτι διὰ τὴν ἐν τῷ σώματι ταραχὴν ἐνοῦσαν ἡ ψυχὴ οὐ δύναται ἠρεμεῖν. οἱ δὲ μελαγχολικοὶ διὰ τοῦτο ἐξάττουσιν ἐν τοῖς ὕπνοις, ὅτι πλείονος τῆς θερμασίας οὔσης μᾶλλον τοῦ μετρίου ἡ ψυχὴ ἐν κινήσει, σφοδροτέρας
35 δὲ τῆς κινήσεως | οὔσης οὐ δύνανται καθεύδειν.

[41] τὸ δὲ Grumach apud Flashar : τό τε codd.
[42] <τοῖς> addidi
[43] [οἱ] Bekker

pleasantly, because it is then especially that the greatest quantity of heat is collected in the inner region. And a sign that, when it is in motion the soul is not able to think, not only when awake, but even in sleep, is this: seeing dreams is least likely in the sleep that occurs after taking food, but this is when it is most of all moved owing to the introduction of nourishment. Now there is a dream when sleep comes to those who are thinking and have something before their eyes. And this is why we most of all see what we are doing or will do or wish to do; for it is about these things that our reasonings and imaginings most often occur. And better people see better dreams for this reason, because when they are awake they think about better things, but those who are in a worse condition with respect to thinking or the body see worse dreams. For the disposition of the body contributes to the image of our dreams; for the products of the thoughts of the sick man are base, and further, because there is a disturbance in his body, his soul is not able to rest. And for this reason, melancholic people are startled in their sleep, because as the heat is great, the soul is in motion more than the intermediate amount, and as the motion is more violent they are not able to sleep.

BOOK XXXI

INTRODUCTION

The *Problems* ends with eight books focusing on human anatomy (broadly conceived): eyes (31), ears (32), nose (33), mouth (34), touch (35), the face (36), the entire body (37), and skin color (38). Few of the chapters in these books resemble the sophisticated exploration of the functions of the parts of animals found in Aristotle's biological works.

The topics of the thirty[1] chapters of *Pr.* 31 can be broken down as follows: the difference (or lack thereof) between right and left, in the case of the eyes compared to other parts of the body (7, 12, 13, 18, 24, 29); strabismus, the abnormal alignment of the eyes (2, 7, 26, 27, and perhaps 11); seeing with one eye versus with two (2, 4, 10, 20); shortsightedness (8, 15, 16, 25); and seeing double (7, 11, 17a, 17b). Most of the remaining chapters deal with the effects of a wide variety of things or actions on the eyes or vision (3, 6, 9, 14, 19, 21, 28). Four chapters treat miscellaneous topics (1, 5, 22, 23).

Aristotle discusses the eye and vision most fully in *DA* 2.7, *Sens.* 2–3, and *GA* 5.1, and Theophrastus in *De Sensi-*

[1] According to the manuscript tradition there are twenty-nine chapters, but I follow Sylburg in dividing ch. 17 in two.

bus (passim). Although these provide part of the background or framework for the discussion in Book 31 (as do the relevant parts of the Hippocratic corpus, e.g., *On Sight*), none of its chapters seem to draw on them directly.

ΟΣΑ ΠΕΡΙ ΟΦΘΑΛΜΟΥΣ

1. Διὰ τί τρίψαντες τὸν ὀφθαλμὸν παυόμεθα τῶν πταρμῶν; ἢ ὅτι ἀναπνοὴ ταύτῃ γίνεται τῷ ὑγρῷ;
957a40 δακρύει γὰρ | ὁ ὀφθαλμὸς μετὰ τὴν τρῖψιν, ὁ δὲ
957b πταρμὸς διὰ πλῆθος || ὑγροῦ. ἢ ὅτι τὸ ἔλαττον θερμὸν φθείρεται ὑπὸ τοῦ πλείονος, ὁ δ' ὀφθαλμὸς τριφθεὶς πλείω λαμβάνει θερμότητα τῆς ἐν τῇ ῥινί; διὰ τοῦτο δὲ κἂν τις αὐτὴν τὴν ῥῖνα τρίψῃ, παύεται ὁ πταρμός. |

5 2. Διὰ τί τῷ ἑνὶ ὀφθαλμῷ ἀκριβέστερον ὁρῶσιν ἢ τοῖν δυοῖν; ἢ ὅτι πλείους αἱ[1] κινήσεις τοῖν δυοῖν γίνονται, οἷον τοῖς διεστραμμένοις; οὔκουν μία ἡ κίνησις, τοῦ δὲ ἑνὸς ἁπλῆ. ἧττον οὖν ὁρῶσιν ἀκριβέστερον.

3. Διὰ τί ὀργιζόμενοι μὲν τοὺς ὀφθαλμοὺς μάλι-
10 στα[2] ἐπιδιδόασι | πρὸς τὸ ἐρυθριᾶν, αἰσχυνόμενοι δὲ τὰ ὦτα; ἢ διότι οἱ μὲν καταψύχονται ἐν τῇ αἰδοῖ (ἐν

[1] *αἱ* Platt : *οὖσαι* codd. [2] *μάλιστα* codd. (teste Marenghi[3]) || *μᾶλλον* Ap[a] : *μάλιστα* cett. codd. (teste Louis)

---

[1] See *Pr.* 38.8 and [Arist./Alex.] *Sup.Pr.* 2.41.

[2] See *Pr.* 31.4 and 20.

[3] I.e., the abnormal alignment of one or both eyes. The basic

PROBLEMS CONNECTED WITH THE EYES

1.[1] Why, when rubbing the eye, do we stop sneezing? Is it because by this means evaporation occurs in the moisture? For the eye sheds tears after rubbing, and sneezing is due to a quantity of moisture. Or is it because the lesser heat is destroyed by the greater? Now the eye when rubbed receives greater heat than the heat in the nose. And for this reason, even if one rubs the nose itself, the sneezing stops.

2.[2] Why do we see more accurately with one eye than with two? Is it because more movements occur in two eyes, as in those who suffer from strabismus?[3] Therefore, the movement (*of the two eyes*) is not one, but that of the one eye is simple. So they do see less clearly.

3.[4] Why, when becoming angry, do people grow red especially with respect to their eyes, whereas when feeling shame, with respect to their ears? Is it because in shame

meaning of διαστρέφω is "twist or turn about." In discussions of eyes and vision, however, it has usually been translated "squint" (which can mean "be affected by strabismus"). But as the other meaning of "squint" ("to look with the eyes partly closed") is now more dominant, a different translation is preferable.

[4] See *Pr.* 32.1, 8, 12.

ὀφθαλμοῖς γὰρ αἰδώς) <καὶ>[3] ἀντιβλέπειν οὐ δύνανται; καὶ ἡ δειλία κατάψυξίς τίς ἐστιν ἐνταῦθα. μεθίσταται δ' εἰς τοὐναντίον τῷ ἔμπροσθεν τὸ θερμόν.[4] τὰ δὲ ὦτα ἀντίκειται· διὸ καὶ μάλιστα ἐρυθριῶσιν |
15 αἰσχυνόμενοι. ἐν δὲ τῷ κνήθεσθαι ἐπὶ τὸ αἰσθητικώτερον καὶ κινητικώτερον ἡ βοήθεια ὡς ἀδικουμένου· φοβουμένοις γὰρ ἐνταῦθα ἐκλείπει μάλιστα.

4. Διὰ τί θατέρου καταληφθέντος ὀφθαλμοῦ ὁ ἕτερος ἀτενίζει μᾶλλον; ἢ διότι ἐκ ταὐτοῦ ἤρτηνται αἱ
20 ἀρχαὶ τῶν | ὀφθαλμῶν; θατέρου οὖν κινουμένου καὶ ἡ κοινὴ ἀρχὴ κινεῖται, ἐκείνης δὲ κινουμένης καὶ ὁ ἕτερος. ληφθέντος οὖν θατέρου ἡ κίνησις κινήσει αὐτόν, ὥστε δύναται ἀτενίζειν μᾶλλον.

5. Διὰ τί οἱ ἐκ γενετῆς τυφλοὶ οὐ γίνονται φαλακροί; <ἢ>[5] ὅτι πημαίνει τὰ ὄμματα ὑγρότης οὖσα
25 πολλὴ ἐν τῷ περὶ | τὴν κεφαλὴν τόπῳ; διὸ τῶν ῥευματικῶν εἰς τοὺς ὀφθαλμοὺς τάς τε περὶ τοὺς κροτάφους φλέβας κάουσι, πυκνοῦντες τοὺς τῶν ὑγρῶν πόρους, καὶ ξύουσι τὴν κεφαλήν, διατέμνοντες τὸ ἐν αὐτῇ δέρμα. ἐπεὶ οὖν πημαίνει τοὺς ὀφθαλμοὺς τὸ ἐν αὐτῇ περίττωμα γινόμενον, κωλύοι ἂν αὐτοὺς ταὐτὸ τοῦτο
30 ἐξ ἀρχῆς | γίνεσθαι, πλέον συνιστάμενον ἐν αὐτῇ. ἐπεὶ δ' ἐκ περιττωμάτων θρὶξ φύεται, τοῦτο δ' ἐν τῇ

[3] <καὶ> Marenghi[3] : <ὥστ'> Forster
[4] θερμόν Forster ex Gaza : ὄπισθεν codd.
[5] <ἢ> Sylburg

the eyes are cooled (for shame is in the eyes) and they are not able to look straight ahead? Cowardice too involves a sort of cooling there. Now the heat transfers in the direction away from the front (*of the head*), and the ears are in the opposite part; and this is why they redden especially when people feel shame. But in a state of being irritated, help goes to the more sensitive and more movable part, as though it were being treated unjustly; for in those feeling fear it especially departs from there.[5]

4.[6] Why, when one eye is held down, does the other stare more? Is it because the starting points of the eyes are fastened at the same place? So when one is moved, the common starting point is moved as well, and when that is moved, the other eye moves too. Therefore, when one eye is held, the movement (*from that eye*) will move it (*sc. the other eye*), such that it is able to stare more.

5.[7] Why do those who are blind from birth not become bald? Is it because a great deal of moisture present in the region around the head harms the eyes? This is why they burn the veins around the temples of those suffering from a discharge in the eyes, closing off the passages of the moisture, and scrape the head, cutting through the skin on it. Therefore, since the residue forming in the head harms the eyes, this same residue might prevent them from forming at the beginning, by collecting in it in a large quantity. And since hair grows out of residues, and this is abundant

[5] The meaning is unclear. Perhaps the author is saying that when people are irritated, help (i.e., heat) goes to the eyes, whereas in those feeling fear (e.g., cowards) heat leaves the eyes (and travels to the ears). [6] See *Pr.* 31.2 and 20.

[7] See [Arist./Alex.] *Sup.Pr.* 2.61, cf. *GA* 5.3, 783b8–20.

τῶν τυφλῶν κεφαλῇ ἐκ γενετῆς ἐστὶ πολύ, εἰκότως οὐκ εἰσὶ φαλακροί.

6. Διὰ τί οἱ ἐξόφθαλμοι καπνίζονται μᾶλλον; ἢ ὅτι τάχιστα προσπίπτει πρὸς τὰ προέχοντα; |

35 7. Διὰ τί εἰς μὲν τὰ δεξιὰ ἀμφοτέρας τὰς ὄψεις ἅμα διαστρέφειν δυνάμεθα, καὶ εἰς τὰ ἀριστερὰ καὶ πρὸς τὴν ῥῖνα, καὶ εἰς τὸ ἀριστερὸν δὲ ἢ τὸ δεξιὸν τὴν ἑτέραν, ἅμα δὲ εἰς τὸ δεξιὸν καὶ ἀριστερὸν ἀδυνατοῦμεν; ὁμοίως δὲ καὶ εἰς τὸ κάτω καὶ εἰς τὸ ἄνω· ἅμα μὲν
40 γὰρ ἐπὶ ταὐτὸ δυνάμεθα, | χωρὶς δὲ οὔ. ἢ ὅτι αἱ ὄψεις
958a δύο οὖσαι ὁμοίως ἐξ ἑνὸς συνήρτηνται; || ὅσα δὲ τοιαῦτα, ἄκρου θατέρου κινουμένου ἀνάγκη θάτερον ἀκολουθεῖν ἐπὶ ταὐτό. τῷ γὰρ ἑτέρῳ ἄκρῳ ἡ ἀρχὴ θάτερον ἄκρον. εἰ οὖν τὸ ἓν ἀδύνατον ἅμα εἰς τἀναντία κινεῖσθαι, ἀδύνατον καὶ τὰς ὄψεις. τὰ μὲν γὰρ ἄκρα
5 εἰς | τἀναντία ἂν κινοῖτο,[6] εἰ τὸ μὲν ἄνω τὸ δὲ κάτω κινοῖτο, ἡ δ' ἀρχὴ ἀμφοῖν ἂν ἀκολουθοίη· ὅπερ ἀδύνατον. ἡ δὲ διαστροφή ἐστι τῶν ὀμμάτων διὰ τὸ ἀρχὴν ἔχειν τὰς σφαίρας, καὶ μέχρι του[7] στρέφεσθαι εἰς τὰ ἄνω καὶ κάτω καὶ εἰς πλάγιον. ὅταν οὖν ἔχουσαι ὡς ἂν
10 ὁμοίως ἔχοιεν τῇ θέσει ἀλλήλαις, | καὶ ἐν μέσῳ τοῦ

[6] ἂν κινοῖτο Bekker : ἀντικινοίτο codd. (cf. Barth. *contramoverentur*) : <ἂν> ἀντικινοίτο Marenghi[3]
[7] του Bussemaker : τοῦ codd.

---

[8] See *Pr.* 31.21 and 10.51.
[9] See *Pr.* 31.11, 17a, 17b. Much is unclear in this chapter, and there are problems with the text in a number of places.

in the head of blind people from birth, it is reasonable that they are not bald.

6.[8] Why are those with bulging eyes more affected by smoke? Is it because smoke strikes most quickly against the parts that protrude?

7.[9] Why are we able to turn the eyes[10] to the right at the same time, and to the left and toward the nose, and either eye to the left or to the right,[11] but we are unable to turn one to the right and one to the left at the same time? And similarly, (*we are able to turn both eyes at the same time*) in the upward direction and in the downward; for we are able to turn them in the same direction at the same time, but not separately. Is it because the eyes, though they are two, are similarly connected at one point? Now in all such cases, when one extremity is moved the other must follow in the same direction. For the source (*of movement*) for one extremity is the other extremity. Therefore, if it is impossible for one thing to move in opposite directions at the same time, it is also impossible for the eyes to do this. For the extremities would be moving in opposite directions, if the one moved in the upward direction and the other in the downward, and the source of both would follow, which is impossible. Now strabismus is due to the eyeballs having a source, and turning to a certain extent upward and downward and sideways. Therefore, being in such a condition that they are in a similar position to one another, and mid-

[10] Although ὄψις ("sight") can be translated "eye" (i.e., "organ of sight"), its meaning here may be closer to "line of sight" (cf. Forster's "the gaze of both eyes") or "visual ray."

[11] Presumably with a hand over one eye, unless the author is referring to strabismus.

ἐπὶ τὸ ἄνω καὶ κάτω κινεῖσθαι καὶ εἰς πλάγιον, ἐπὶ τοῦ αὐτοῦ σημείου ἑαυτῶν λάβωσι τὴν ὄψιν, αὗται μὲν ἀδιάστροφοί τε καὶ μάλιστα ἀκίνητοι[8] τῇ θέσει· ὅσαι δ' ἐπὶ[9] ταὐτοῦ σημείου λάβωσι τὰς ὄψεις, ἀδιάστροφοι μέν εἰσι, διαφέρουσι δ' ἀλλήλων. καίτοι κρύπτε-
15 ται τοῦ μέλανός | τι καὶ τοῖς ἄνω βάλλουσι τὰ λευκά, οἷον μελλέπταρμοι· ἕτεροι δὲ εἰς τὸ πλάγιον, ὥσπερ οἱ μανικοί, οἱ δὲ εἰς τοὺς μυκτῆρας, ὥσπερ τὰ τραγικὰ πρόσωπα καὶ οἱ στρυφνοί· σύννουν γὰρ τὸ βλέμμα. ὅσοι δὲ μήθ' ὁμοίως κειμένων τῶν σφαιρῶν ἐπὶ ταὐτῷ
20 σημείῳ ἔχουσι τὰς ὄψεις, ἢ ὁμοίως μὲν | κειμένων μὴ ἐπὶ τῷ αὐτῷ δέ, οὗτοι διεστραμμένοι εἰσίν· διὸ ὑποβλέπουσι καὶ συνάγουσι τὰ ὄμματα. πειρῶνται γὰρ ἐπὶ ταὐτὸν καταστῆσαι σχῆμα τὴν σφαῖραν. ὥστε τὸν μὲν ἐῶσι, τὸν δὲ σχηματίζουσι τῶν ὀφθαλμῶν. ἐὰν γὰρ μὴ κατὰ ταὐτὸ[10] σημεῖον τεθῶσιν αἱ ὄψεις,
25 ἀνάγκη διεστράφθαι. ὥσπερ | γὰρ τοῖς ὑποβάλλουσιν[11] ὑπὸ τὸν ὀφθαλμὸν[12] δύο φαίνεται (καὶ γὰρ

8 ἀκίνητοι : ἀκίνηται α β γ : κινητοί Forster ex Gaza

9 ante ἐπὶ add. <ἂν> Ruelle

10 κατὰ ταὐτὸ β Barth. : κατ' αὐτὸ cett. codd.

11 post ὑποβάλλουσιν add. <τὸν δάκτυλον> fort., cf. *Metaph.* 1063a6–10 and *Insomn.* 461b30–462a1

12 post ὀφθαλμὸν add. <τὸ ἓν> Sylburg ex Gaza, cf. *Metaph.* 1063a6–10 and *Insomn.* 461b30–462a1

---

12 This line is unclear. Midway between up and down or to either side suggests the eyes are looking straight ahead. Many edi-

way between moving in an upward and a downward direction and sideways,[12] when they receive the visual ray on the same point of themselves, the eyes are aligned in turning[13] and are especially immobile in their position. Now those eyes that receive visual rays on the same point are aligned in turning, although they differ from each other. And yet, in those who cast up the whites of their eyes, some of the black is hidden, as in those who are about to sneeze; but others turn their eyes sideways, for instance the insane, and others toward the nostrils, just like tragic masks and those who are austere; for the look is thoughtful.[14] But those who hold fast the visual rays on the same point though the eyeballs are not similarly placed, or though they are similarly placed they do not hold them fast on the same point, these people suffer from strabismus; this is why they squint[15] and contract their eyes. For they attempt to set the eyeball in the same position. So they leave one of the eyes alone, whereas they position the other. For if the visual rays[16] are not set on the same point, they necessarily suffer from strabismus. For just as in those putting (*a finger*) under the eye (*what is one*) appears double[17] (for

tors place the comma after κινεῖσθαι, moving εἰς πλάγιον to the next line: "they receive the visual ray from the side," etc.

[13] I.e., they do not suffer from strabismus.

[14] The sideways glance of the insane perhaps describes staring off into space; the latter, thoughtful, look is, I assume, not cross-eyed but downward (i.e., in the same direction as the nostrils, but not toward them). [15] ὑποβλέπω (literally, "look from under") can refer to eyeing with suspicion or anger, blinking, or squinting. [16] αἱ ὄψεις, which here could also be rendered "the eyes" (see n. 10).

[17] See *Metaph.* K 6, 1063a6–10 and *Insomn.* 3, 461b30–62a1.

ἐκείνοις κεκίνηται ἡ ἀρχή), καὶ τούτοις ὁμοίως. ἐὰν μὲν οὖν ἄνω κινηθῇ ὁ ὀφθαλμός, τὸ πέρας κάτω τῆς ὄψεως γίνεται, ἐὰν δὲ κάτω, ἄνω τὸ πέρας. ἐν ἑνὶ δ' ὀφθαλμῷ μεθισταμένῳ κινεῖσθαι μὲν τὸ ὁρώμενον |
30 δοκεῖ διὰ ταὐτὸ[13] ἄνω ἢ κάτω, ὅτι καὶ ἡ ὄψις, δύο δὲ οὐ φαίνεται, ἂν μὴ δύο αἱ ὄψεις ὦσι καὶ διαστραφῶσι[14]. τοιαύτη μὲν τῷ ἑτεροφθάλμῳ γίνεται, ὥστε δύο φαίνεσθαι· κατὰ τὴν θέσιν δὲ γίνεται τῷ μὴ κατὰ μέσον τοῦ ὄμματος κεῖσθαι. |

35 8. Διὰ τί οἱ μύωπες μικρὰ γράμματα γράφουσιν; ἄτοπον γὰρ τὸ μὴ ὀξὺ ὁρῶντας ποιεῖν ἔργον ὀξὺ ὁρώντων. πότερον ὅτι μεγάλα φαίνεται τὰ μικρά, ἐὰν ᾖ ἐγγύς, οἱ δὲ προσάγοντες γράφουσιν; ἢ διὰ τὸ συνάγοντας τὰ βλέφαρα γράφειν; δι' ἀσθένειαν γὰρ
958b τῆς ὄψεως, ἂν μὲν ἀναπεπταμένοις || γράφωσι τοῖς ὄμμασι, διασπωμένη ἡ ὄψις ἀμβλὺ ὁρᾷ, οὕτω δὲ ἀθρόως προσπίπτει· γωνίαν δὲ μικρὰν ποιοῦσα ἐξ ἀνάγκης ποιεῖ μικρὰ γράφειν.

9. Διὰ τί ὀφθαλμιάσαντες ἔνιοι ὀξύτερον ὁρῶσιν; ἢ
5 διὰ | τὸ ἀποκεκαθάρθαι τὰ ὄμματα; πολλάκις γὰρ ἡ ἔξω πυκνότης ἀποστέγει τὴν ὄψιν, ἀποδακρύσαντι δὲ

13 ταὐτὸ : ταῦτα Xa u 14 διαστραφῶσι Marenghi3 (cf. Barth.) : διαστρέφει codd. : διαστροφὴ <γίνεται> Sylburg || ὦσιν. καὶ διαστροφὴ τοιαύτη κτλ. Forster

---

18 Or "for this reason," following some mss. and most editors.

19 ἑτερόφθαλμος can mean "one-eyed" or "having different colored eyes," but neither of those work here. Forster translates it

in these the source has moved), so it is in this case. Therefore, if the eye is moved upward, the limit of the vision goes down, but if it is moved downward, the limit goes up. Now in repositioning one eye, what is seen seems for the same reason[18] to move up or down, because the vision too moves, but it does not appear double, unless the vision of both eyes is double and so they suffer from strabismus. Such happens to a different-eyed person,[19] so that (*what is seen*) appears double; but this is because of the position (*of the visual ray*), in that it does not lie in the middle of the eye.

8.[20] Why do the shortsighted write small letters? For doing the work of those who have acute vision, while not having acute vision, is strange. Is it because small letters appear large if they are near, and the shortsighted bring what they are writing close to them? Or is it because they contract their eyelids to write? For owing to the weakness of their vision, if they write with their eyes wide open, the vision, being dispersed, sees dimly, but in this way[21] (*the object of sight*) strikes them compactly; and producing a small angle, out of necessity it produces writing in small letters.

9.[22] Why do some people suffering from eye disease see more acutely? Is it because the eyes are cleaned off? For often the external thickness keeps out the vision, but this is

"one whose eyes do not correspond," in which case this line may be a summary (and later addition to the text) describing the person whose eyes turn unaligned (as I render it).

[20] See *Pr.* 31.15, 16, 25.

[21] I.e., with the eyelids contracted.

[22] See *Pr.* 20.22.

λύεται. διὸ καὶ τὸ ἀποδάκνεσθαι συμφέρει, οἷον κρόμμυον· θάτερον δὲ πολέμιον, οἷον ὀρίγανον.

10. Διὰ τί τῇ μιᾷ ὄψει ἀπαθέστεροι; ἢ διότι ἔλαττον
10 ἡ | ψυχὴ πάσχει, ὥστε ἔλαττον τὸ πάθος;

11. Διὰ τί τοῖς διισταμένοις[15] δύο φαίνεται; ἢ διότι οὐκ ἀφικνεῖται ἐπὶ τὸ αὐτὸ σημεῖον ἑκατέρου τῶν ὀμμάτων ἡ κίνησις; ὥσπερ οὖν δύο ὁρᾶν τὸ δὶς ὁρᾶν οἴεται ἡ ψυχή. ὅμοιον καὶ ἐπὶ τῶν δακτύλων τῆς
15 ἐπαλλάξεως· δύο γὰρ | τὸ ἓν δοκεῖ, ὡς δὶς ἁπτομένη[16] ἑνί.

12. Διὰ τί οὐ διαφέρουσιν αἱ αἰσθήσεις αἱ ἐν τοῖς δεξιοῖς τῶν ἀριστερῶν, ἐν δὲ τοῖς ἄλλοις πᾶσι κρείττω τὰ δεξιά; πότερον διὰ τὸ ἔθος, ὅτι εὐθὺς ὁμοίως ἀμφοῖν ἐθιζόμεθα αἰσθάνεσθαι; τὰ δὲ δεξιὰ τῷ ἔθει
20 δοκεῖ διαφέρειν, ἐπεὶ ἐθισθεῖσιν | ἀμφιδέξιοι γίνονται. ἢ ὅτι τὸ μὲν αἰσθάνεσθαι πάσχειν τί ἐστι, τὰ δὲ δεξιὰ διαφέρει τῷ ποιητικώτερα εἶναι καὶ ἀπαθέστερα τῶν ἀριστερῶν;

13. Διὰ τί ἐν μὲν τοῖς ἄλλοις κρείττω τὰ δεξιά, ἐν δὲ

[15] διισταμένοις : διεστραμμένοις Forster (cf. *Pr.* 31.2, 957b7) [16] ὡς δὶς ἁπτομένη : ὡς δὶς ἁπτομένῃ Bekker : [ὡς] δὶς ἁπτομένῳ Forster : τῳ δὶς ἁπτομένῳ Hett : [ὡς] δὶς ἁπτομένῃ Louis

---

[23] Presumably, what dries the eyes.

[24] Literally, "more unaffected"—perhaps by problems with vision (for example, of the sort discussed in the following chapter).

[25] See *Pr.* 31.7, 17a, 17b and 35.10.

cleared by tearing. And this is why what causes tearing, such as onion, is beneficial; but the other sort,[23] such as marjoram, is harmful.

10. Why are those who see with one eye less affected?[24] Is it because the soul is affected less, so that the effect is less?

11.[25] Why do things appear double in those whose (*eyes*) diverge?[26] Is it because the movement[27] does not reach the same point in each of the two eyes? The soul, therefore, seeing (*one thing*) twice, thinks it sees two things. And similarly in the case of crossed fingers: one thing seems to be two, as if (*the soul*) was touched twice by one thing.

12.[28] Why are the senses on the right not superior to those on the left, whereas in all other respects the parts on the right are stronger? Is it due to habit, because we straightaway habituate ourselves to perceive similarly on both sides? But the parts on the right seem by habit to be superior, since people become ambidextrous through habituation. Or is it because to perceive is to experience something, whereas the parts on the right are superior by being more active and less affected than the parts on the left?

13.[29] Why are the parts on the right stronger in other

[26] The same word could also be translated "in those whose (*eyes*) are set apart," but that makes less sense. Perhaps the author has in mind seeing cross-eyed. If Forster's conjecture is correct, the author is again discussing strabismus.

[27] Forster's note *ad loc.*: "i.e. of the visual ray from the object seen."

[28] See *Pr.* 31.13, 18, 29.

[29] See *Pr.* 31.12, 18, 29.

ταῖς αἰσθήσεσιν ὅμοια; ἢ διότι ταῦτα μὲν ὁμοίως
25 ἐθιζόμεθα | κατ' ἀμφότερα τῷ ἔθει; ἔτι τὸ μὲν αἰσθάνεσθαι πάσχειν τί ἐστιν, ἡ δὲ τῶν δεξιῶν διαφορὰ τῷ εἰς τὸ ποιεῖν καὶ οὐκ εἰς τὸ πάσχειν.

14. Διὰ τί τὸ γυμνάζεσθαι ἀσύμφορον πρὸς ὀξυωπίαν; ἢ ὅτι ξηρὸν ποιεῖ τὸ ὄμμα ἡ γυμνασία, ὥσπερ
30 καὶ τὸ ἄλλο | σῶμα; ἡ δὲ ξηρότης σκληρύνει τὸ δέρμα πᾶν, ὥστε καὶ τὸ ἐπὶ τῇ κόρῃ. διὸ καὶ οἱ πρεσβῦται οὐκ ὀξὺ ὁρῶσιν· καὶ γὰρ τῶν γερόντων σκληρόδερμα, ἅμα δὲ καὶ ῥυσά, ὥστε ἐπικαλύπτεται ἡ ὄψις.

15. Διὰ τί οἱ μύωπες βλέπουσι μὲν οὐκ ὀξύ, γρά-
35 φουσι δὲ | μικρά; καίτοι τὸ μικρὸν ὀξὺ βλέποντος καθορᾶν ἐστίν. ἢ διότι ἀσθενῆ ἔχοντες τὴν ὄψιν συνάγουσι τὰ βλεφαρὰ εἰς μικρόν; ἀθρόα γὰρ ἐξιοῦσα ἡ ὄψις μᾶλλον ὁρᾷ, ἀναπεπταμένου δὲ τοῦ ὄμματος διασπᾶται. διὰ μὲν οὖν τὴν ἀσθένειαν συνάγουσι ἐις μικρὸν[17] τὸ βλέφαρον,[18] διὰ δὲ τὸ ἐκ μικροῦ ὁρᾶν
959a μικρὸν || μέγεθος ὁρῶσιν. ὅσον δὲ ὁρῶσι μέγεθος, τοσοῦτον καὶ γράφουσιν.

16. Διὰ τί οἱ μύωπες συνάγοντες τὰ βλέφαρα ὁρῶσιν; ἢ δι' ἀσθένειαν τῆς ὄψεως; ὥσπερ καὶ οἱ πρὸς
5 τὰ πόρρω τὴν | χεῖρα προσάγοντες, οὕτω καὶ τὰ βλέφαρα πρὸς τὰ ἐγγὺς προστίθενται †ὥσπερ χεῖρα†.[19] τοῦτο δὲ ποιοῦσιν, ἵνα ἀθροωτέρα ἡ ὄψις ἐξίῃ,

[17] ἐις μικρὸν α β δ : om. γ
[18] τὸ βλέφαρον : fort. τὰ βλέφαρα
[19] ὥσπερ χεῖρα codd. (obelis inclusi) : secl. Hett

respects, but in the senses they are equal (*to those on the left*)? Is it because in both these cases we habituate ourselves similarly by habit? Further, to perceive is to experience something, whereas the superiority of the parts on the right is in acting and not in experiencing.

14. Why is exercising not beneficial with respect to acuteness of vision? Is it because exercise makes the eye dry, as it does the rest of the body? Now dryness hardens all skin, so that it also hardens the skin over the pupil. And this is why old men do not have acute vision; for having hard skin, and also wrinkles, is characteristic of old men, so that their vision is obscured.

15.[30] Why do the shortsighted, though they do not look with acute vision, write small (*letters*)? And yet seeing what is small is characteristic of looking with acute vision. Is it because, having weak vision, they contract the eyelids to a small space? For when the vision goes forth compact it sees better, but when the eye is wide open the vision is dispersed. Therefore, it is due to weakness that they contract the eyelid to a small space, and because they are seeing from a small space they see something large as small. And however much they see something large, in this way too they write.

16.[31] Why do the shortsighted contract their eyelids when they look at something? Is it due to the weakness of their sight? And just like those who put a hand up to look at distant things, so too they position their eyelids—†like a hand†—to look at things nearby. Now they do this in order that the vision may go forth more compact, going forth

[30] See *Pr.* 31.8, 16, 25.
[31] See *Pr.* 31.8, 15, 25.

δι' ἐλάττονος ἐξιοῦσα, καὶ μὴ εὐθὺς ἐξ ἀναπεπταμένου ἐξιοῦσα διασπασθῇ. ὁρᾷ δὲ ἡ πλείων μεῖζον.

17a. Διὰ τί εἰς τὸ πλάγιον κινοῦσι τὸν ὀφθαλμὸν οὐ
10 φαίνεται | δύο τὸ ἕν; ἢ ὅτι ἐπὶ τῆς αὐτῆς γίνεται γραμμῆς ἡ ἀρχή; δύο δὲ φαίνεται ταύτης μεταβαλλούσης ἄνω ἢ κάτω. εἰς δὲ πλάγιον οὐδὲν διαφέρει, ἐὰν μὴ ἅμα καὶ ἄνω <ἢ κάτω>.[20]

17b. <Διὰ> τί δὲ[21] ἐπὶ μὲν τῆς ὄψεως ἔστιν ὥστε φαίνεσθαι τὸ ἓν δύο, ἄν πως τεθῶσιν οἱ ὀφθαλμοὶ
15 πρὸς ἀλλήλους, ἐπὶ δὲ τῶν ἄλλων | αἰσθήσεων οὐκ ἔστιν; ἢ καὶ ἐπὶ τῆς ἁφῆς γίνεται τῇ ἐπαλλάξει τῶν δακτύλων τὸ ἓν δύο; ἐπὶ δὲ τῶν ἄλλων οὐ γίνεται, ὅτι οὔτε ἔξω ἀποτεινομένων αἰσθάνεται, οὔτε[22] δύο. γίνεται δὲ διὰ ταὐτὸ[23] διόπερ καὶ ἐπὶ τῶν δακτύλων· μιμεῖται γὰρ τὴν ὄψιν. |

20 18. Διὰ τί τοῦ μὲν ἄλλου σώματος τὰ ἀριστερὰ ἀσθενέστερα, τῶν δὲ ὀφθαλμῶν οὔ, ἀλλ' ὁμοίως ὀξύ; ἢ ὅτι τὰ μὲν δεξιὰ τῷ ποιητικὰ εἶναι διαφέρουσι, τῷ δὲ παθητικὰ οὐ διαφέρουσιν; αἱ δὲ ὄψεις παθητικαί.

19. Διὰ τί τῇ ὄψει πρὸς μὲν τὰ ἄλλα ἀτενίζοντες
25 χεῖρον | διατιθέμεθα, πρὸς δὲ τὰ χλωρὰ καὶ ποώδη, οἷον λάχανα καὶ τὰ τούτοις ὅμοια, βέλτιον; ἢ ὅτι πρὸς μὲν τὸ λευκὸν καὶ μέλαν ἥκιστα δυνάμεθα ἀτενίζειν

[20] ἅμα καὶ ἄνω : κάτω καὶ ἄνω X^a u Ap^b || <ἢ κάτω> Septalius : post ἅμα add. <κάτω> Marenghi[3]

[21] <Διὰ> τί δὲ (nov. cap.) Sylburg : τί δὴ (cap. continuatur) codd. [22] οὔτε Richards : οὐδὲ codd.

[23] ταὐτὸ Richards : τοῦτο codd.

through a smaller space, and in order that it may not be dispersed by going forth straightaway from a wide open eye. But the larger space sees more.

17a.[32] Why, by moving the eye to the side, does the one thing not appear as two? Is it because the source (*of the vision*) is on the same line? Now two things appear when this line shifts upward or downward, but to the side makes no difference, unless at the same time it also shifts upward ‹or downward›.

17b.[33] But why in the case of sight is it such that one thing appears as two, if the eyes are placed a certain way in relation to each other, but it is not so in the case of the other senses? Or even in the case of touch, does one thing become two by crossing the fingers? But in the case of the other senses this does not occur, because they do not perceive what is extending out from them, nor are they two. But it occurs for the same reason as it does in the case of the fingers; for (*touch*) imitates sight.

18.[34] Why, for the rest of the body, are the parts on the left weaker, whereas for the eyes this is not so, but they are equally acute? Is it because the parts on the right are superior by being active, and not by being passive? But vision is passive.

19. Why are we in a worse position with respect to our vision if we stare at other things, but in a better one if we stare at green and grassy things, such as vegetables and the like? Is it because we are least able to stare at white and

[32] See *Pr.* 31.7, 11, 17b.

[33] See *Pr.* 31.7, 11, 17a and 35.10.

[34] See *Pr.* 31.12, 13, 29.

(ἄμφω γὰρ λυμαίνεται τὴν ὄψιν), τὰ δὲ τοιαῦτα τῶν χρωμάτων μέσον ἔχει τούτων· διὸ μετρίως τῆς ὄψεως
30 διατιθεμένης οὐκ[24] ἐξαδυνατοῦμεν | αὐτῇ, βέλτιον δὲ διατιθέμεθα. τάχα δὲ ἴσως καθάπερ ἐπὶ τῶν σωμάτων σφοδρότερον πονοῦντες χεῖρον ἔχομεν, τὸ μέσον δὲ βέλτιστα διατίθησι, τὸν αὐτὸν τρόπον καὶ τὴν ὄψιν. πρὸς μὲν γὰρ στερεὰ ἀτενίζοντες πονοῦμεν αὐτήν, πρὸς δὲ τὰ ὑγρὰ μηδενὸς ἀντιφράττοντος οὐ διαπο-
35 νοῦμεν. τὰ δὲ χλωρὰ | στερεά τε μετρίως, καὶ ὑγρὸν ἐν αὐτοῖς ἱκανόν. διὸ βλάπτει τε οὐθέν, καὶ διαναγκάζει τὴν ὄψιν πρὸς τούτοις εἶναι, διὰ τὸ τὴν τοῦ χρώματος κρᾶσιν σύμμετρον ἔχειν πρὸς τὴν ὄψιν.

20. Διὰ τί τὰ μὲν ἄλλα ἀμφοτέροις τοῖς ὀφθαλμοῖς μᾶλλον ὁρῶμεν, τὸ δὲ εὐθὺ τὸ[25] ἐπὶ τῶν στίχων τῷ ἑνὶ
40 προσάγοντες | πρὸς τὰ γράμματα μᾶλλον καθορῶμεν;
959b ἢ ἀμφότεραι || μὲν αἱ ὄψεις συμπίπτουσαι, καθάπερ λέγουσιν οἱ περὶ τὰ ὀπτικά, ταραχὴν παρέχουσιν, ἐπειδὰν δὲ τῇ μιᾷ θεωρῶμεν, πρὸς εὐθεῖαν τὴν ὄψιν, ὥσπερ πρὸς κανόνα, μᾶλλον <φαίνεται>[26] τὸ εὐθύ; |

5 21. Διὰ τί ὁ καπνὸς τοὺς ὀφθαλμοὺς μᾶλλον[27] δάκνει; ἢ ὅτι μόνοι ἀσθενέστατοι; ἀεὶ γὰρ τὰ ἔσω τοῦ σώματος ἀσθενέστατα. σημεῖον δὲ ὅτι καὶ τὸ ὄξος καὶ ἕκαστον τῶν δριμέων τὴν μὲν ἔξω σάρκα οὐ δάκνει,

[24] οὐκ β : οὐδὲν Xa u : οὐδὲ cett. codd.
[25] τὸ δὲ εὐθὺ τὸ β Xa u : τὰ δὲ εὐθὺ τὰ a M r t Apa Am : τὰ δὲ εὐθὺ τὸ cett. codd.
[26] <φαίνεται> Sylburg
[27] μᾶλλον : μόνους vel μόνον Richards

black (for both ruin vision), but such colors[35] are intermediate between these? This is why, when our vision is in an intermediate position, we are not incapacitated with respect to it, but are in a better position. But perhaps, as is in the case of our bodies, we soon become worse from extreme strain, whereas the intermediate puts us in the best position, so it is the same way too regarding vision. For when we stare at solid things we strain our vision, but when we look at moist things we do not strain it, as nothing is blocking it. Now green things are moderately solid, and there is sufficient moisture in them. This is why they do no harm, and they urge vision to be directed at them, because the mixture of color is in accord with vision.

20.[36] Why do we tend to see other things better with both eyes, whereas in the case of the straightness of written lines we see better by bringing one eye to the letters? Do both eyes falling together (*on the same point*) cause confusion, as those writing on optics say, but when we look with one eye, the straightness ⟨appears⟩ better to the straight vision,[37] as if along a rod?

21.[38] Why does smoke sting the eyes more (*than other parts*)? Is it because they alone are very weak? For the parts inside the body are always weakest. Now a sign of this is the fact that vinegar and each of the acrid things do not

[35] I.e., green and the color of grassy things, etc.

[36] See *Pr.* 31.2 and 4.

[37] But perhaps ὄψις in the sense of "line of sight" (rather than "vision") better conveys the author's meaning.

[38] See *Pr.* 31.6, 10.51, 20.22; cf. Hp. *Vis.* 9.1.

τὴν δὲ ἐντός, ὅτι ἀραιοτάτη[28] τοῦ σώματος καὶ μάλιστ'
10 ἔχει πόρους· αἱ γὰρ ὄψεις | διά τινων πόρων ἐκπίπτουσιν, ὥστε τὸ ἔσω δηκτικώτατον ἀπὸ τῆς σαρκὸς ἀποπίπτει. ὁμοίως δὲ καὶ τὸ κρόμμυον, καὶ ὅσα ἄλλα δάκνει τοὺς ὀφθαλμούς. τὸ δὲ ἔλαιον μάλιστα τῶν ὑγρῶν, ὅτι λεπτομερέστατον· τοιοῦτον δ' ὄν, εἰσδύνει διὰ τῶν πόρων· τὸ δ' ὄξος ἐν φαρμάκῳ τῇ ἄλλῃ σαρκί. |

15 22. Διὰ τί ὁ ὀφθαλμὸς μόνον τοῦ σώματος, ἀσθενέστατος ὤν, οὐ ῥιγοῖ; ἢ ὅτι πίων ἐστὶν ὁ ὀφθαλμός, σαρκὸς δὲ οὐθέν; τὰ δὲ τοιαῦτα ἄριγά ἐστιν. οὐ γὰρ δὴ ὅτι γε πῦρ ἐστὶν ἡ ὄψις, διὰ τοῦτο οὐ ῥιγοῖ· οὐ γὰρ τοιοῦτόν γέ ἐστι τὸ πῦρ ὥστε θερμαίνειν. |

20 23. Διὰ τί δάκρυα, ἐὰν μὲν κλαίοντες ἀφίωμεν, θερμά ἐστιν, ἐὰν δὲ πονοῦντες τοὺς ὀφθαλμοὺς δακρύωμεν, ψυχρά; ἢ ὅτι τὸ μὲν ἄπεπτον ψυχρόν, τὸ δὲ πεπεμμένον θερμόν; ἡ δὲ μαλακία ὅλως πᾶσά ἐστιν ἐξ ἀπεψίας, καὶ τῶν τοὺς ὀφθαλμοὺς πονούντων ἄπεπτόν
25 ἐστι τὸ δάκρυον· διὸ ψυχρόν. | διὰ τοῦτο καὶ οἱ ἰατροὶ οἴονται σημεῖον εἶναι μεγάλης νόσου τοὺς ψυχροὺς ἱδρῶτας, τοὺς δὲ θερμοὺς τοὐναντίον ἀπαλλακτικούς. ὅταν μὲν γὰρ ᾖ τὸ περίττωμα πολύ, οὐ δύναται τὸ ἐντὸς θερμὸν πέττειν, ὥστε ἀνάγκη ψυχρὸν εἶναι· ὅταν δὲ ὀλίγον, κρατεῖ. γίνονται δὲ ἐκ τῶν περιττωμάτων αἱ |
30 ἀρρωστίαι.

24. Διὰ τί ποτε εὐκινήτων ὄντων τῶν δεξιῶν μερῶν

[28] ἢ ante ὅτι Rmg et Gaza || ἀραιοτάτη γ (praeter r t) : ἀραιότατον cett. codd.

sting the external flesh, but they do sting the internal, because it is the loosest flesh of the body and has the most passages; for the visual rays go out through certain pores, so that what stings the most within goes forth from the flesh. Similarly too with the onion, and all the other things that sting the eyes. And olive oil does this, most of all the liquids, because it has the smallest particles; and being such, it sinks in through the passages. But vinegar is medicine in the rest of the flesh.

22. Why is it that the eye alone of the body, being weakest, does not shiver? Is it because the eye is fat, but none of it is flesh? Such things do not shiver. For it is *not* because the organ of sight is fire, that it does not shiver; for its fire is not such as to heat it.

23. Why are tears hot, if we shed them while weeping, but cold, if we cry from straining the eyes? Is it because what is unconcocted is cold, but what is concocted is hot? Now in general, every weakness is from a lack of concoction, and the tears of those straining their eyes are unconcocted; this is why they are cold. It is for this reason that physicians believe cold sweats are a sign of grave disease, but hot ones on the contrary remove disease. For when the residue is abundant, the internal heat is not able to concoct it, so that it must necessarily be cold; but when there is little residue, the internal heat gains the mastery. And sicknesses arise from residues.

24.[39] Why, though the parts on the right are easily

[39] See *Pr.* 32.7.

ὁ ὀφθαλμὸς ὁ ἀριστερὸς μᾶλλον τοῦ δεξιοῦ συνάγεται; ἢ ὅτι τὰ ἀριστερὰ πάντα ὑγρότερα τῶν δεξιῶν ἐστί, τὰ δὲ ὑγρότερα μᾶλλον συνάγεσθαι πέφυκεν;
35 †εἶτα εἰς τὸ δεξιὸν | [μᾶλλον] ἀποτελεῖν δύναται, τοῦ ἀριστεροῦ δυναμένου καὶ καθ' αὑτό.†[29]

25. Διὰ τί ἀμφότεροι κατὰ ἀσθένειάν τινα τῶν ὀφθαλμῶν διακείμενοι, ὅ τε μύωψ καὶ ὁ πρεσβύτης, ὁ μὲν ἐγγὺς προσάγει, ἄν τι βούληται ἰδεῖν, ὁ δὲ πόρρω
40 ἀπάγει; ἢ ὅτι | οὐχ ὁμοία ἡ ἀσθένεια παρέπεται
960a αὐτοῖς; ὁ μὲν γὰρ πρεσβύτης || αὐτὸ ἰδεῖν ἀδύνατός ἐστιν· οὗ δὴ συμπίπτει ἡ ὄψις αὐτῷ, ἀπάγει τὸ θεώμενον, ἅτε καὶ[30] μάλιστα μέλλων ὄψεσθαι· πόρρω δὲ συμπίπτει. ὁ δ' αὐτὸ μὲν ὁρᾷ, ποῖα δὲ κοῖλα καὶ[31] ποῖα ἐξέχοντα τοῦ ὁρωμένου οὐκέτι δύναται κρίνειν,[32] |
5 ἀλλὰ περὶ ταῦτα ἀπατᾶται. τὰ δὲ κοῖλα καὶ τὰ ἐξέχοντα μάλιστα τῇ αὐγῇ κρίνεται. πόρρωθεν μὲν οὖν οὐ δύναται τὴν αὐγὴν[33] καταμαθεῖν πῶς ἐπιβάλλει ἐπὶ τὸ ὁρατόν· ἐγγύθεν δὲ μᾶλλον καταφανής ἐστιν.

26. Διὰ τί τῶν ζῴων ἄνθρωπος ἢ μόνον ἢ μάλιστα
10 διαστρέφεται; | ἢ ὅτι ἢ μόνον ἢ μάλιστα ἐπίληπτον ἐν τῇ νεότητι[34] γίνεται, ὅτε καὶ διαστρέφεσθαι συμβαίνει πᾶσιν;

27. Διὰ τί οἱ ἄνθρωποι μόνοι τῶν ἄλλων ζῴων τὰ

[29] εἶτα εἰς—καθ' αὑτό codd. (obelis inclusi) || μᾶλλον seclusi : καὶ secl. Louis [30] ἅτε καὶ : ἅτ' ἐκεῖ Richards
[31] καὶ γ : ἢ cett. codd. [32] κρίνειν : διακρίνειν β
[33] τὴν αὐγὴν Bonitz : τῇ αὐγῇ codd.
[34] νεότητι : νηπιότητι *Pr.* 10.50, 896b6–7

moved, does the left eye close more easily than the right? Is it because all the parts on the left are moister than those on the right, and the moister parts naturally close more easily? †Thus, it is possible to accomplish this [more] in the right eye, though it is possible for the left eye also in itself.†[40]

25.[41] Why, though both the shortsighted man and the old man are affected by weakness of the eyes, the former, if he wants to see something, brings it up close, while the latter holds it away? Is it because the kinds of weakness present in them are not similar? For the old man is unable to see it; indeed, he holds what he is looking at away to the point on which his vision[42] falls, as he will then see it best, and it falls far away. The shortsighted man, however, sees it, but is not able to distinguish which parts of the visual object are concave and which are convex, but he is deceived on these points. Now what are concave and what are convex are best distinguished by means of the light. So from a distance he is not able to discern how the light falls on what is seen; but it is more evident when close by.

26.[43] Why does a human alone of the animals or most of all suffer from strabismus? Is it because he alone or most of all is epileptic in his youth, which in every case is when strabismus occurs?

27.[44] Why do humans alone of the animals suffer in the

[40] The text of the last line "appears to be hopelessly corrupt" (Forster, note *ad loc.*). [41] See *Pr.* 31.8, 15, 25; cf. Hp. *Vis.* 9.1. [42] I.e., the line of sight from his two eyes.

[43] This chapter is virtually identical to *Pr.* 10.50. Source: Hp. *Epid.* 2.5.11.

[44] See *Pr.* 31.26. Source: Hp. *Epid.* 2.5.11.

ὄμματα διαστρέφονται; πότερον διὰ τὸ ἐλάχιστον διάστημα εἶναι τῶν ὀμμάτων, καὶ ἐπ' εὐθείας, ὥστε
15 εὔδηλον σφόδρα | γίνεται τὸ μὴ κατωρθωμένον; ἢ διότι τῶν ἄλλων μονόχροα τὰ ὄμματά ἐστι μᾶλλον, εἰ δ' ἦν ἓν χρῶμά τι τοῦ ὄμματος, οὐκ ἦν διαστροφή; ἢ διότι μόνοι ἐν τῷ γένει ἐπίληπτοι γίνονται τῶν ζῴων, ἡ δ' ἐπίληψις διαστροφὴν ποιεῖ, ὅταν γένηται, ὥσπερ
20 καὶ τῶν ἄλλων μορίων; ἀλλ' ἐνίοις ὀψὲ | παντελῶς γίνεται ἡ διαστροφή, ὅσοις τὸ ἀρρώστημα.

28. Διὰ τί πρὸς τὸν λύχνον καὶ πρὸς τὸν ἥλιον προστησάμενοι τὴν χεῖρα πρὸ τοῦ φωτὸς μᾶλλον ὁρῶμεν; ἢ ὅτι τὸ ἀπὸ τοῦ ἡλίου καὶ λύχνου φῶς προσπῖπτον μὲν ἡμῶν πρὸς τὴν ὄψιν ἀσθενεστέραν
25 ποιεῖ δι' ὑπερβολήν; φθείρει γὰρ αὐτὰ | καὶ[35] τὰ συγγενῆ τῇ ὑπερβολῇ. εἰρχθέντα δ' ὑπὸ τῆς χειρὸς, τὴν μὲν ὄψιν οὐ πημαίνει, τὸ δ' ὁρώμενον ὁμοίως ἐστὶν ἐν φωτί. διὸ ἡ μὲν μᾶλλον δρᾷ,[36] τὸ δὲ ὁρώμενον οὐδὲν ἧττον ὁρᾶται.

29. Διὰ τί χεὶρ μὲν καὶ ποὺς διαφορὰν ἔχει πρὸς
30 τὰ[37] δεξιὰ | καὶ[38] τὰ ἀριστερά, ὄμμα[39] δὲ καὶ ἀκοὴ οὔ; ἢ ὅτι τὰ στοιχεῖα τὰ εἰλικρινῆ ἀδιάφορα, ἐν δὲ τοῖς ἐκ τῶν στοιχείων ἡ διαφορά; αὗται δὲ αἱ αἰσθήσεις εἰσὶν ἐξ εἰλικρινῶν, ἡ μὲν ὄψις πυρός, ἡ δ' ἀκοὴ ἀέρος.

[35] αὐτὰ καὶ : καὶ αὐτὰ Richards
[36] δρᾷ : ὁρᾷ Richards
[37] τὰ om. α β A^{m}
[38] καὶ v (teste Marenghi[3]), Ap (teste Louis) : om. cett. codd.
[39] ὄμμα : ὄμματα β v X^{a} u

eyes from strabismus? Is it because there is the smallest distance between the eyes, which are in a straight line, so that when they are not lined up correctly it is very obvious? Or is it because the eyes of the other animals tend to be one color, and if there were only some one eye color, there would be no strabismus? Or is it because humans alone of the kinds of animal become epileptic, and epilepsy, whenever it occurs, produces strabismus, just as ⟨*it produces distortion*⟩[45] in the other parts? But in some—all those in whom there is the sickness—strabismus comes *much* later.

28.[46] Why, if we put a hand out toward the lamp or the sun, in front of the light, we see better? Is it because the light from the sun or the lamp, striking our vision, makes it weaker through its excess? For through excess, it destroys the very things akin to it. But confined by the hand, it does not harm the vision, while the visual object is in the light all the same. This is why the vision does better, whereas the visual object is seen no less.

29.[47] Why do hand and foot differ with respect to the right and the left, but eyesight and hearing do not? Is it because the pure elements are undifferentiated, but there is difference in what consists of ⟨*different*⟩ elements? Now these senses are from pure elements, sight from fire, hearing from air.

[45] διαστροφή should be understood here both narrowly (as strabismus, in the case of eyes) and broadly (as distortion or twisting, in the rest of the body).

[46] See Hp. *Medic.* 2.

[47] See *Pr.* 31.12, 13, 18.

BOOK XXXII

INTRODUCTION

The thirteen chapters in Book 32 discuss various aspects of the ear, including the eardrum, the earlobe, and the outer rim of the ear. A surprisingly large number of chapters are devoted to ear-related problems encountered by divers (see chs. 2, 3, 5, 11, and arguably 10). Three chapters concern the coloring of the ears in those blushing from shame (1, 8, 12); two discuss the connection between poking inside the ear and coughing (6) or yawning (13). No attention is given to the ear as the organ of hearing, though one chapter discusses ringing in the ears (9). Finally, one chapter discusses the bitter taste of earwax (4), and another the claim that a pierced left earlobe closes more quickly than a right one (7). No sources can be discerned for these chapters.

ΟΣΑ ΠΕΡΙ ΩΤΑ

960a35 1. Διὰ τί τὰ ὦτα ὄντα ἀναιμότατα τοῦ προσώπου, ὅταν αἰσχύνωνται, ἐρυθριᾷ μάλιστα; πότερον ὅτι εἰς τὸ κενὸν μάλιστα πορεύεσθαι πέφυκε τὸ ἀλλότριον ὑγρόν, ὥστε ὅταν διαλυθῇ ὑπὸ τῆς θερμότητος, ἣ
40 γίνεται αἰσχυνομένοις, συνέρχεται | εἰς ταῦτα; ἢ διότι
960b ἐπὶ τοῖς κροτάφοις ἐπίκεινται, || εἰς οὓς τὸ ὑγρὸν ἀθροίζεται μάλιστα; αἰσχυνομένων δ' εἰς τὸ πρόσωπον ἔρχεται ἡ ὑγρότης· διὸ καὶ ἐρυθριῶσιν. τοῦ δὲ προσώπου ἥκιστα βάθος ἔχει τὰ ὦτα· καὶ φύσει θερμότατα καὶ εὔχροα, ἐὰν μὴ ἀπηρτημένα πόρρωθεν
5 ᾖ τῷ ψύχει. | διὸ καὶ εὐχρούστατον τῶν ἐν τῷ προσώπῳ μορίων. ὥστε ὅταν σκεδασθῇ ἡ θερμότης, μάλιστα ἐπιπολῆς οὖσα, ἐν τούτοις ποιεῖ ἐρυθρά.[1]

2. Διὰ τί τὰ ὦτα ἐν τῇ θαλάττῃ ῥήγνυται τοῖς κολυμβῶσιν; πότερον διὰ τὸ κατέχειν τὸ πνεῦμα πλη-
10 ρούμενον βιάζεται; | ἢ εἰ τοῦτ' αἴτιον, ἔδει καὶ ἐν τῷ ἀέρι. ἢ ὅτι μὴ ὑπεῖκον διακόπτεται θᾶττον, καὶ ὑπὸ[2] σκληροτέρου ἢ μαλακοῦ; τὸ οὖν πεφυσημένον ἧττον

[1] ἐρυθρά : ἐρυθριᾶν Sylburg [2] ὑπὸ : ἀπὸ Bekker

PROBLEMS CONNECTED WITH THE EARS

1.[1] Why do the ears, though they are the most bloodless parts of the face, grow most red when people feel shame? Is it because the alien moisture naturally moves most readily into the empty space, so that when it is released by the heat, which occurs in those feeling shame, it collects in these parts? Or is it because the ears lie on the temples, into which the moisture most readily gathers? Now when people feel shame, the moisture goes into the face; and this is why they grow red. But of the parts of the face, the ears have the least depth; and they are by nature hottest and well colored, unless they have hung for a long time in the cold. And so they are the most well colored of the parts in the face. Consequently when the heat is dispersed, being mostly on the surface, it produces red in these parts.

2.[2] Why do the ears[3] of divers burst in the sea? Are the ears subject to pressure because holding the breath makes them full? If this is the reason, it ought to happen in the air as well. Or is it because what does not yield is broken more quickly, and more by the hard than by the soft? Now what

[1] See *Pr.* 32.8 and 12, 31.3.

[2] See *Pr.* 32.3, 5, 11.

[3] Particularly the eardrums.

ὑπείκει. τὰ δὲ ὦτα, ὥσπερ εἴρηται, ὑπὸ τοῦ κατέχεσθαι τὸ πνεῦμα ἐμφυσᾶται, ὥστε τὸ ὕδωρ, σκληρότερον ὂν τοῦ ἀέρος, προσπῖπτον διακόπτει. |

15 3. Διὰ τί οἱ κολυμβηταὶ σπόγγους περὶ τὰ ὦτα καταδοῦνται; ἢ ἵνα ἡ θάλαττα βίᾳ ἰοῦσα μὴ ῥηγνύῃ τὰ ὦτα; οὕτω μὲν γὰρ οὐ γίνεται, ὥσπερ ἀφῃρημένων, πλήρη.

4. Διὰ τί ὁ ἐν τοῖς ὠσὶ ῥύπος πικρός ἐστιν; ἢ διότι ἱδρώς ἐστι σαπρός; ἔστιν οὖν ἁλμυρὸν σαπρόν. τὸ δὲ 20 σαπρὸν ἁλμυρὸν | πικρόν.

5. Διὰ τί οἱ σπογγεῖς διατέμνονται τὰ ὦτα καὶ τοὺς μυκτῆρας; ἢ ὅπως εὐπνούστεροι ὦσι; ταύτῃ γὰρ ἐξιέναι δοκεῖ τὸ πνεῦμα. †ἀνατέμνουσι δὲ καὶ τῶν τόπων ταῦτα πρὸς εὔπνοιαν.†[3] πονεῖν γὰρ δή φασι μᾶλλον 25 αὐτοὺς ἐν τῇ δυσπνοίᾳ, | τῷ μὴ δύνασθαι προΐεσθαι θύραζε· ὅταν δὲ ὥσπερ ἐξεράσωσι, κουφίζονται. ἄτοπον οὖν εἰ μὴ δύνανται τυγχάνειν ἀναπνοῆς καταψύξεως χάριν· ἀλλ' ἔοικε τοῦτο ἀναγκαιότερον εἶναι. ἢ εὐλόγως ὁ πόνος πλείων κατέχουσιν, ὀγκουμένων καὶ 30 διατεινομένων; φαίνεται δὲ καὶ αὐτόματός τις | εἶναι φορὰ τοῦ πνεύματος ἔξω· εἰ δὲ καὶ εἴσω, σκεπτέον. ἔοικε δέ· ὁμοίως γὰρ ἀναπνοὴν ποιοῦσι τοῖς κολυμβηταῖς λέβητα καταφέντες. οὐ πίμπλαται γὰρ οὗτος τοῦ ὕδατος, ἀλλὰ τηρεῖ τὸν ἀέρα. μετὰ βίας γὰρ ἡ κάθεσις. ὀρθὸν γὰρ ὁτιοῦν παρεγκλιθὲν εἰσρεῖ. |

[3] ἀνατέμνουσι—εὔπνοιαν om. A^m, non vertit Gaza (obelis inclusi) || τῶν τόπων : τὸν τόπον N^a x X^a u t || ταῦτα a Barth. : om. cett. codd. : καὶ Sylburg

has been inflated is less yielding. But the ears, as has been said, are inflated by holding the breath, so that the water, which is harder than air, strikes against and bursts them.

3.[4] Why do divers bind sponges around their ears? Is it so that the sea, when it moves with violence, does not burst their ears? For in this way the ears do not become filled, as they do when the sponges are removed.

4.[5] Why is earwax[6] bitter? Is it because sweat is putrid? Therefore, it is salty and putrid. And what is putrid and salty is bitter.

5.[7] Why do sponge divers cut through their ears and nostrils? Is it so they may breathe more freely? For in this way the breath seems to go out. †Now they cut into these parts with a view to breathing freely.† For they say that they feel a greater strain from difficult breathing, by not being able to *expel* the breath; but when they as it were vomit forth (*the breath*), they are relieved. It is strange, therefore, if they are not able to achieve breathing for the sake of cooling; but this seems to be more necessary. Or is the strain naturally greater when they hold their breath, since they are swollen and stretched? Now there appears to be in fact an automatic passage of the breath outward; but we must consider whether the movement inward is automatic as well. It seems to be, since they similarly produce breathing in divers by lowering a cauldron. For this does not fill with water, but retains the air. For the letting down is with force. Indeed, for anything (*immersed in water*) upright, when inclined the water flows in.

[4] See *Pr.* 32.2, 5, 11.
[5] See Apollon. *Mir.* 28.
[6] Literally, "the dirt in the ear."
[7] See *Pr.* 32.2, 3, 11.

35 6. Διὰ τί ἔνιοι τὰ ὦτα σκαλεύοντες βήττουσιν; ἢ ὅτι ἐπὶ τοῦ αὐτοῦ πόρου τῷ πνεύμονι καὶ τῇ ἀρτηρίᾳ ἡ ἀκοή; σημεῖον δέ ὅτι, <ἂν> ἀναπληρῶνται, [καὶ][4] γίνονται ἐνεοί. θερμαινομένου οὖν τῇ τρίψει συντήκεται ἐπὶ τὴν ἀρτηρίαν ἀπὸ τοῦ πόρου[5] κάτωθεν ὑγρόν, ὃ ποιεῖ τὴν βῆχα. |

40 7. Διὰ τί τὸ ἀριστερὸν οὖς θᾶττον συμφύεται ὡς 961a ἐπὶ τὸ || πολύ, ὅταν τρυπηθῇ; διὸ καὶ αἱ γυναῖκες τὸ μὲν ἄρρεν τὸ δὲ θῆλυ καλοῦσι τῶν ὤτων. ἢ ὅτι τὰ ἀριστερὰ ὑγρὰ καὶ θερμὰ μᾶλλον, συμφύεται δὲ τὰ τοιαῦτα μάλιστα; διὸ καὶ ἐν φυτοῖς τοῖς χλωροῖς ἡ 5 σύμφυσις· καὶ τὰ τῶν νέων | δὲ ἕλκη <μᾶλλον συμφύεται>[6] ἢ τὰ τῶν πρεσβυτέρων. σημεῖον δὲ ὅτι ὑγρὰ μᾶλλον[7] καὶ ὅλως θηλυκώτερα τὰ ἀριστερά.

8. Διὰ τί τοῖς μὲν αἰσχυνομένοις ἄκρα τὰ ὦτα ἐπιφοινίσσεται, τοῖς δὲ ὀργιζομένοις οἱ ὀφθαλμοί; ἢ 10 ὅτι ἡ μὲν | αἰδὼς ἐν ὀφθαλμοῖς κατάψυξίς τις μετὰ φόβου, ὥστε εἰκότως ἀπολείπει τὸ θερμὸν τοὺς ὀφθαλμούς, χωριζόμενον δὲ εἰς τὸν δεκτικώτατον φέρεται τόπον; τοιοῦτος δὲ ὁ ἐν τοῖς ἄκροις τῶν ὤτων· ὁ γὰρ ἄλλος ὀστώδης. ὀργιζομένοις δ' ἐπανέρχεται τὸ θερ- 15 μόν. μάλιστα δὲ γίνεται φανερὸν ἐν τοῖς | ὀφθαλμοῖς διὰ τὴν χρόαν οὖσαν λευκήν.

[4] <ἂν> ἀναπληρῶνται [καὶ] Ross apud Forster || ἀναπληροῦνται a δ M Ap c t Barth : ἀναπηροῦνται cett. codd.
[5] πόρου : πόνου u t
[6] <μᾶλλον συμφύεται> Sylburg : <μᾶλλον> Marenghi[3]
[7] post μᾶλλον add. <ὅτι μαλακώτερα> Forster ex Gaza

6.[8] Why do some people cough when they poke around in their ears? Is it because hearing is on the same passage to the lung and to the windpipe? Now a sign of this is the fact that, if (*these passages*) fill up, people become deaf.[9] Therefore, when (*the ear*) is heated by rubbing, moisture from the passage below is melted on the windpipe, which produces the cough.

7. Why does the left ear[10] close up more quickly in most cases, when it has been pierced? Indeed, this is why women call the one ear male and the other female. Is it because the left parts are moister and hotter, and such things close up most quickly? And this is why there is closing up in green plants; and the wounds of the young <close up more quickly> than those of older people. And this is a sign that the left parts are moister and generally more feminine.

8.[11] Why do the edges of the ears turn purple in those feeling shame, whereas in those feeling anger the eyes do? Is it because shame is a cooling in the eyes with fear, so that the heat naturally leaves the eyes, and when it departs it travels to the region best able to receive it? And such is the region in the edges of the ears; for the rest of it is bony. But in those feeling anger, the heat rises. It appears most noticeably in the eyes because the color there is light. Now it is especially apparent in the eyes because their color is white.

[8] See *Pr.* 32.13, *HA* 492a13–20.

[9] There seems to be something wrong with the text here.

[10] Particularly the earlobe.

[11] See *Pr.* 32.1 and 12, 31.3.

9. Διὰ τί ὁ ἦχος ὁ ἐν τοῖς ὠσίν, ἐάν τις ψοφήσῃ, παύεται; ἢ διότι[8] ὁ μείζων ψόφος τὸν ἐλάττω ἐκκρούεται;

10. Διὰ τί, ἐὰν εἰς τὸ οὖς ὕδωρ ἐγχυθῇ, ἔλαιον προσεγχέονται, οὐ δυναμένου τοῦ ἐνόντος ὑγροῦ ἐξελ-
20 θεῖν δι' ἄλλου ὑγροῦ; | πότερον διὰ τὸ ἐπιπολῆς γίνεσθαι τὸ ἔλαιον τοῦ ὕδατος, καὶ διὰ γλισχρότητα αὐτοῦ ἔχεσθαι τὸ ὕδωρ ἐξιόντος τοῦ ἐλαίου, ἵνα συνεξίῃ τὸ ὕδωρ; ἢ ἵνα, ὀλισθηροῦ τοῦ ὠτὸς γενομένου, ἐξέλθοι[9] τὸ ὕδωρ; τὸ γὰρ ἔλαιον λεῖον ὂν ποιεῖ ὀλισθαίνειν.

11. Διὰ τί ἧττον τὰ ὦτα ῥήγνυται τοῖς κολυμβῶ-
25 σιν, ἐὰν | προσεγχέωσιν[10] εἰς τὰ ὦτα ἔλαιον;[11] ἢ τοῦ μὲν ῥήγνυσθαι τὰ ὦτα εἴρηται πρότερον ἡ αἰτία, τὸ δ' ἔλαιον ἐγχυθὲν εἰς τὰ ὦτα τὴν ὕστερον θάλατταν ἀπολισθαίνειν ποιεῖ, καθάπερ ἐπὶ τῶν ἔξω τοῦ σώματος συμβαίνει τοῖς ἀληλιμμένοις. ὀλισθαίνουσα δὲ πληγὴν οὐ ποιεῖ εἰς τὸ ἐντὸς τοῦ ὠτός, διόπερ οὐ |
30 ῥήγνυσιν.

12. Διὰ τί τῶν ὤτων ἀναίμων ὄντων μάλιστα οἱ αἰσχυνόμενοι ἐρυθριῶσιν; ἢ ἕκαστον εἰς τὸ κενὸν ἑκάστου μάλιστα φέρεται; δοκεῖ δὲ τοῦ αἰσχυνομένου ἄνω θερμὸν φέρεσθαι τὸ αἷμα. εἰς οὖν τὸ κενώτατον[12]

[8] διότι α δ : ὅτι β γ
[9] ἐξέλθοι : ἐξέλθῃ δ Xᵃ u
[10] προσεγχέωσιν : προεγχέωσιν α γ δ
[11] ἔλαιον γ : τὸ ἔλαιον cett. codd.
[12] post κενώτατον add. <ἰὸν> Bonitz

9. Why does ringing[12] in the ears cease if one makes a noise? Is it because the greater noise knocks out the less?

10.[13] Why, if water has been poured into the ear, do they pour in olive oil, when the liquid inside is not able to go out through the other liquid? Is it because the oil is on the surface of the water, and because of its stickiness the water is held to it when the oil goes out, so that the water goes out with it? Or is it so that, when the ear becomes slippery, the water can go out? For oil, being smooth, makes it slippery.

11.[14] Why do the ears[15] of divers burst less, if they pour olive oil into their ears? The reason why the ears burst has been stated before,[16] but the olive oil poured into the ears makes the subsequent seawater slip off, just as happens in the case of the outer parts of the body to those smeared with oil. And by slipping, the seawater does not produce a blow against the inside of the ear, and so does not burst it.

12.[17] Why, though the ears are the most bloodless parts, do people who feel shame grow red (*there*)? Does each thing travel most readily to the part empty of it? Now when a person feels shame, the hot blood seems to travel upward.[18] It therefore produces red in the emptiest part. This

[12] The Greek (ἦχος) generally means "sound" or "resonating," but it can have the special sense of "ringing (in the ears)" (see Hp. *Prorrh.* 1.18, Thphr. *Sens.* 19).

[13] See *Pr.* 24.1.

[14] See *Pr.* 32.2, 3, 5. Plutarch *QN* 11 (*Mor.* 914F–15A) seems to quote from this chapter and attribute it to Aristotle.

[15] Particularly the eardrums.

[16] See *Pr.* 32.2.

[17] See *Pr.* 32.1 and 8, 31.3.

[18] Or "the blood seems to travel upward hot."

35 ἐρυθριᾶν ποιεῖ. τὸ δ' αὐτὸ τοῦτο | καὶ ἐπὶ τῶν γνάθων. ἔτι δὲ καὶ ὅτι λεπτότατον τὸ δέρμα τὸ περιτεταμένον, μάλιστα δὴ φαίνεται δι' αὐτά.

13. Διὰ τί οὐδεὶς χασμώμενος τὸ οὖς σκαλεύει; ἢ ὅτι ὅτε χασμᾶται, ἐμφυσᾶται καὶ ἡ μῆνιγξ, δι' ἧς ἀκούει; σημεῖον δέ· ἥκιστα γὰρ ἀκούουσι χασμώμε-40 νοι. τὸ γὰρ πνεῦμα, ὥσπερ | καὶ κατὰ τὸ στόμα, καὶ 961b εἰς τὰ ὦτα ἐντὸς πορευόμενον, ἐξωθεῖται || τὸν ὑμένα καὶ κωλύει τὸν ψόφον εἰσιέναι. ἐὰν οὖν οὕτως ἔχοντος ἅψηται τῆς ἀκοῆς ὡς σκαλεύειν, μάλιστ' ἂν[13] βλάψειε· πρὸς ἀντιπῖπτον γὰρ ἡ πληγὴ γίνεται, καὶ οὐ πρὸς ὑπεῖκον τὸ τοῦ πνεύματος. τὸ δὲ δέρμα καὶ τὴν μήνιγ-5 γα | ἀφεστάναι τῶν στερεῶν <δῆλον>.[14] ὥστε πόνον μάλιστα οὕτω ποιεῖ, καὶ τραυματίζοι ἄν.

[13] μάλιστ' ἂν Bekker : μάλιστα codd.

[14] <δῆλον> Sylburg : ante τῶν στερεῶν add. <συμβαίνει> Marenghi[3]

same thing also occurs in the case of the cheeks. And a further reason is the fact that the skin (*of the ears*), being stretched all around, is very thin, so the blood appears especially through it.

13.[19] Why does no one poke around the ear while yawning? Is it because, when one yawns, the eardrum[20] through which one hears is inflated? And there's a sign of this: people hear least well when yawning. For the breath, just as in the mouth, proceeding into the inner ears, pushes out the membrane and prevents the sound from entering. Therefore, if in this condition one touches the organ of hearing so as to poke it, one might do a great deal of harm; for the blow occurs against a resisting, not a yielding, surface of breath. It is clear that the skin and the eardrum are far from being solid things. Consequently, this produces a great deal of pain and could cause a wound.

[19] See *Pr.* 32.6, 7.1.

[20] μῆνιγξ (which I translate "eardrum") and ὑμένα ("membrane," 961b1) seem to be synonyms.

BOOK XXXIII

INTRODUCTION

All but four of the eighteen chapters in Book 33 are devoted to sneezing (1–5, 7–12, 15–17). For the rest, one chapter discusses the treatment of a bloody nose (6), one the way in which deaf people "speak out of their nostrils" (14), and one the supposed connection between curly hair and being snub-nosed (18). Ch. 13, on hiccups, is unconnected to the topic of *Pr.* 33 (but note that 1, 5, and 17 discuss hiccuping in contrast to sneezing). No attention is given in these chapters to the nose as the organ of smell. No sources can be discerned for them.

ΟΣΑ ΠΕΡΙ ΜΥΚΤΗΡΑ[1]

1. Διὰ τί ὁ πταρμὸς λυγμὸν μὲν παύει, ἐρυγμὸν δὲ
961b10 οὐ | παύει; ἢ διότι οὐ τοῦ αὐτοῦ τόπου τὸ πάθος ἑκάτερον, ἀλλ' ὁ μὲν ἐρυγμὸς κοιλίας, ὁ δὲ λυγμὸς τοῦ περὶ τὸν πνεύμονα κατάψυξις καὶ ἀπεψία πνεύματος καὶ ὑγροῦ; κοινωνοῦσι δ' οἱ περὶ τὸν ἐγκέφαλον τόποι τῷ πνεύμονι, οἷον τοῖς ὠσίν.[2] φανερὸν δέ· ἅμα γὰρ
15 ἐνεοὶ καὶ κωφοὶ γίνονται, καὶ αἱ νόσοι | ἀντιπεριίστανται αἱ τοῦ ὠτὸς εἰς τὰ τοῦ πνεύμονος πάθη, ἐνίοις δὲ σκαλεύουσι τὸ οὖς βῆχες ἐγγίνονται. τὸ δὲ περὶ τὸν πταρνύμενον τόπον εἶναι τῆς ῥινὸς κοινωνίαν τῷ πνεύμονι δηλοῖ ἡ ἀναπνοὴ κοινὴ οὖσα, ὥστε πτάρνυται μὲν θερμαινομένου, ταὐτὸ δὲ συμπάσχει[3] ὁ κάτω τό-
20 πος, ἐστὶν[4] ὁ | λυγμός. ἡ δὲ θερμασία πέττει· διὸ ὄξος τε παύει λυγμὸν καὶ ἡ ἀπνευστία, ἐὰν ἠρεμαία ᾖ ἡ λύγξ. ἐκθερμαίνει γὰρ τὸ πνεῦμα κατεχόμενον, ὥστε καὶ ἐν τῷ πταρμῷ ἡ ἀντικατάσχεσις γενομένη τοῦ

[1] μυκτῆρα : μυκτήρων M c : fort. μυκτῆρας vel τὴν μυκτῆρα [2] τοῖς ὠσίν : τὰ ὦτα Forster

[3] ταὐτὸ δὲ συμπάσχει scripsi ex [Arist./Alex.] *Sup.Pr.* 2.45, 8–9 : αὐτοῦ : τῷ δὲ συμπάσχειν codd.

[4] ante ἐστὶν add. <ἐν ᾧ> Sylburg

PROBLEMS CONNECTED WITH THE NOSTRIL

1.[1] Why does sneezing stop hiccuping, but does not stop belching? Is it because each affliction is not of the same region, but belching is of the stomach, whereas hiccuping is a cooling of the region around the lung and a lack of concoction of breath and moisture? Now the regions around the brain are connected to the lung, as they are to the ears.[2] This is obvious: for people become deaf and dumb at the same time, and diseases of the ear transfer into afflictions of the lung, and coughing occurs in those poking around the ear. Respiration being common (*to the nose and the lung*) makes clear that the region of the nose around which sneezing occurs is connected to the lung, so that one sneezes when (*this region of the nose*) is heated, and the lower region[3] experiences the same thing—this is hiccuping. Now heat causes concoction; this is why both vinegar and holding one's breath stop hiccups, if the hiccuping is mild. For it heats the contained breath, such that even in sneezing the counter-containment of the breath

[1] Cf. *Pr.* 33.5 and 17, and [Arist./Alex.] *Sup.Pr.* 2.45. Source: Hp. *Aph.* 6.13.

[2] Or, with Forster's conjecture, "for example, the ears."

[3] I.e., a lung.

πνεύματος τοῦτο ποιεῖ, καὶ οἰκείως ἡ ἔκπνευσις γίνε-
25 ται, καὶ ἐκ τοῦ ἄνω τόπου· ἀδύνατον γὰρ | πτάρειν μὴ ἐκπνέοντα. ἡ οὖν ὁρμὴ ῥήγνυσι τὸ ἐγκατειλημμένον πνεῦμα, ὃ ποιεῖ τὸν λυγμόν.

2. Διὰ τί, ἐάν τις μέλλων πτάρνυσθαι τρίψῃ τὸν ὀφθαλμόν, ἧττον πτάρνυται; ἢ διότι τὸ ποιοῦν τὸν πταρμὸν θερμότης τίς ἐστιν; ἡ δὲ τρῖψις θερμότητα
30 ποιεῖ, ἣ διὰ τὸ πλησίον | εἶναι τῶν ὀφθαλμῶν τὸν τόπον ᾧ πτάρνυται, ἀφανίζει τὴν ἑτέραν, ὥσπερ τὸ ἔλαττον πῦρ ὑπὸ τοῦ πλείονος μαραινόμενον.

3. Διὰ τί δὶς πτάρνυται ὡς ἐπὶ τὸ πολύ, καὶ οὐχ ἅπαξ ἢ πλεονάκις; ἢ διότι δύο εἰσὶ μυκτῆρες; καθ'
35 ἕτερον[5] οὖν διέσχισται | τὸ φλέβιον, δι' οὗ πνεῦμα ῥεῖ.

4. Διὰ τί πρὸς τὸν ἥλιον βλέψαντες πτάρνυνται μᾶλλον; ἢ διότι κινεῖ θερμαίνων; καθάπερ οὖν πτεροῖς θιγγάνοντες. ἀμφότεροι γὰρ τὸ αὐτὸ ποιοῦσιν· τῇ γὰρ κινήσει θερμαίνοντες ἐκ τοῦ ὑγροῦ θᾶττον πνεῦμα
40 ποιοῦσιν. τούτου δ' ἡ ἔξοδος | πταρμός. ||

962a 5. Διὰ τί λύγγα παύει πταρμὸς καὶ πνεύματος ἐπίσχεσις καὶ ὄξος; ἢ[6] ὁ μὲν πταρμός, ὅτι[7] ἀντιπερίστασίς ἐστι τοῦ κάτω πνεύματος, ὥσπερ αἱ ἄνω φαρμακεῖαι πρὸς τὴν κάτω κοιλίαν; ἡ δ' ἀπνευστία τὰς
5 ἀσθενεῖς λύγγας, | ὅτι ἡ μικρὰ ὁρμὴ τοῦ πνεύματος ἡ ἀνιοῦσα, ὥσπερ περὶ τὴν βῆχα,[8] ἐάν τις κατάσχῃ,

[5] καθ' ἕτερον : ἑκάτερον Bussemaker ex Barth. : καθ' ἑκάτερον Forster [6] post ἢ add. ὅτι γ [7] ὅτι : διότι γ
[8] post βῆχα add. <ἤ> Forster

produces this, and exhalation naturally occurs and from the upper region; for it is impossible to sneeze without exhaling. Therefore the onrush (*of the sneeze*) breaks up the enclosed air, which causes hiccuping.

2.[4] Why, if someone who is about to sneeze rubs his eye, does he sneeze less? Is it because what produces the sneezing is a sort of heat, and rubbing produces heat, which, owing to the eyes being near the region in which one sneezes, does away with the other heat, just as the lesser fire is put out by the greater?

3. Why does one sneeze twice in most cases, and neither once nor many times? Is it because there are two nostrils? So the vessel through which breath flows is divided along to each nostril.

4. Why do people, looking at the sun, sneeze more? Is it because the sun, by producing heat, causes movement? So, it is just like tickling with feathers. Both produce the same result: for causing movement by heat they produce breath more quickly from the moisture. And the exit of this is a sneeze.

5.[5] Why do sneezing, delaying the breath, and vinegar stop hiccuping? Does sneezing, because it is the counter-containment of the breath below, just as medicines in the upper parts are for the stomach below? Now not breathing stops weak hiccups, because the small rush of breath rising—just as with the cough, if one holds it down, it is

[4] See *Pr.* 31.1, 33.8, [Arist./Alex.] *Sup.Pr.* 2.41.
[5] Cf. *Pr.* 33.1 and 17.

παύεται, οὕτω καὶ ἐνταῦθα καὶ κατέσπασε καὶ κατέπνιξε καὶ συναπεβιάσατο. τὸ δ' ὄξος παύει, ὅτι τὸ περιεστὸς ὑγρὸν καὶ κωλῦον ἀπερυγεῖν ἐπνευμάτωσε τῇ θερμασίᾳ. ἔστι γὰρ ἐρυγμὸς μέν, ὅταν πνευματωθῇ |
10 τὸ ἐν τῇ ἄνω κοιλίᾳ ὑγρὸν καὶ πεφθῇ, ἡ δὲ λύγξ, ὅταν ὑπὸ ὑγροῦ κατέχηται πνεῦμα περιττὸν περὶ τὸν πνευματικὸν τόπον. τοῦτο γὰρ ὁρμῶν καὶ μὴ δυνάμενον διακόψαι σπασμὸν ποιεῖ, ὁ δὲ σπασμὸς οὗτος καλεῖται λύγξ. καὶ διὰ τοῦτο ῥιγώσαντας λὺγξ λαμ-
15 βάνει, ὅτι τὸ ψῦχος | τὸ ὑγρὸν ποιεῖ συνεστάναι[9] ἐκ τοῦ πνεύματος· ἔτι περιλαμβανόμενον δὲ τὸ ἄλλο πηδᾷ· οὗ ἡ κίνησις λυγμός ἐστιν.

6. Διὰ τί ἐνίοις ὕδωρ ψυχρὸν προσχέομεν [καὶ][10] πρὸς τὸ πρόσωπον, ἡνίκα αἷμα ῥεῖ ἐκ τῶν μυκτήρων; ἢ ἀντιπερίσταται εἴσω τὸ θερμόν; ἂν οὖν ἐπιπολῆς
20 τύχῃ αἷμα, ἐξυγραίνει | μᾶλλον.

7. Διὰ τί τὸν μὲν πταρμὸν θεῖον[11] ἡγούμεθα εἶναι, τὴν δὲ βῆχα ἢ τὴν κόρυζαν οὔ; ἢ διότι ἐκ τοῦ θειοτάτου τῶν περὶ ἡμᾶς τῆς κεφαλῆς, ὅθεν ὁ λογισμός ἐστι, γίνεται; ἢ ὅτι τὰ μὲν ἄλλα ἀπὸ νοσούντων γίνεται, τοῦτο δὲ οὔ; |

25 8. Διὰ τί τρίψαντες τὸν ὀφθαλμὸν παυόμεθα τῶν πταρμῶν; ἢ ὅτι ἀνάπνοια ταύτῃ γίνεται τῷ ὑγρῷ; δακρύει γὰρ ὁ ὀφθαλμὸς μετὰ τρῖψιν, ὁ δὲ πταρμὸς

[9] συνεστάναι Forster : συστὰν codd. : συνιστὰν Y^a mg
[10] [καὶ] Bekker
[11] θεῖον K^a mg (*divinum* Trap., cf. *augurium* Barth.) : θεὸν codd. (cf. *numine* Gaza)

stopped—so too here draws down, stifles, and forces away the hiccups. And vinegar stops hiccuping, because by its heat it vaporizes the surrounding moisture and prevents belching. For there is belching, when the moisture in the upper stomach is vaporized and concocted, whereas there is hiccuping, when excessive breath is held down by moisture in the region around the lung. For this (*breath*) rushing and not being able to break through produces a spasm, and this spasm is called hiccuping. And it is for this reason that hiccuping seizes those who are shivering, because the cold causes the moisture from the breath to set; and the rest (*of the breath*), being still enclosed, leaps, and this movement is a hiccup.

6. Why do we in some cases pour cold water on the face, when blood flows from the nostrils? Does (*cold water*) counter and contain the heat within? Therefore, if the blood happens to be on the surface, (*the heat*) liquefies it more.

7.[6] Why do we consider sneezing to be divine, but not coughing or a runny nose? Is it because it comes out of the most divine part of us, the head, from which there is reasoning? Or is it because the others come from diseases, but this does not?

8.[7] Why, when rubbing the eye, do we stop sneezing? Is it because by this means evaporation occurs in the moisture? For the eye sheds tears after rubbing, and sneezing is

[6] Cf. *Pr.* 33.9 and 11.
[7] See *Pr.* 31.1, 33.2, [Arist./Alex.] *Sup.Pr.* 2.41.

διὰ πλῆθος ὑγρότητος. ἢ ὅτι τὸ ἔλαττον θερμὸν φθείρεται ὑπὸ τοῦ πλείονος, ὁ δ' ὀφθαλμὸς τριφθεὶς πλείω
30 λαμβάνει θερμότητα τῆς ἐν | τῇ ῥινί; διὰ τοῦτο[12] δὲ κἄν τις αὐτὴν τὴν ῥῖνα τρίψῃ, παύεται ὁ πταρμός.

9. Διὰ τί τῶν μὲν ἄλλων πνευμάτων αἱ ἔξοδοι, οἷον φύσης καὶ ἐρυγμοῦ, οὐχ ἱεραί, ἡ δὲ τοῦ πταρμοῦ μόνη;[13] πότερον ὅτι τριῶν τόπων ὄντων, κεφαλῆς καὶ
35 θώρακος καὶ τῆς κάτω | κοιλίας, ἡ κεφαλὴ θειότατον; ἔστι δὲ φῦσα μὲν ἀπὸ τῆς κάτω κοιλίας πνεῦμα, ἐρυγμὸς δὲ τῆς ἄνω, ὁ δὲ πταρμὸς τῆς κεφαλῆς. διὰ τὸ ἱερώτατον οὖν εἶναι τὸν τόπον καὶ τὸ πνεῦμα τὸ ἐντεῦθεν ὡς ἱερὸν προσκυνοῦσιν. ἢ ὅτι ἅπαντα τὰ πνεύματα σημαίνει τοὺς εἰρημένους τόπους βέλτιον
40 ἔχειν ὡς | ἐπὶ τὸ πολύ; μὴ διαχωρούντων γὰρ κουφίζει
962b τὸ πνεῦμα διεξιόν, || ὥστε καὶ ὁ πταρμὸς τὸν περὶ τὴν κεφαλὴν τόπον, ὅτι ὑγιαίνει καὶ δύναται πέττειν. ὅταν γὰρ κρατήσῃ ἡ ἐν τῇ κεφαλῇ θερμότης τὴν ὑγρότητα, τὸ πνεῦμα τότε γίνεται πταρμός. διὸ καὶ τοὺς ἐκθνή-
5 σκοντας κρίνουσι[14] πταρμικῷ, ὡς | ἐὰν μὴ τούτῳ[15] δύνωνται πάσχειν, ἀσώτους ὄντας. ὥσθ' ὡς σημεῖον ὑγείας[16] τοῦ ἀρίστου[17] καὶ ἱερωτάτου τόπου προσκυνοῦσιν ὡς ἱερόν, καὶ φήμην ἀγαθὴν ποιοῦνται.

[12] τοῦτο scripsi ex *Pr.* 31.1, 957b3 : ταῦτα codd.

[13] μόνη scripsi ex [Arist./Alex.] *Sup.Pr.* 2.50, 2 : ἱερά codd.

[14] κρίνουσι Bussemaker ex [Arist./Alex.] *Sup.Pr.* 2.50, 11 : κινοῦσι codd.

[15] τούτῳ : τοῦτο Bussemaker ex [Arist./Alex.] *Sup.Pr.* 2.50, 11

[16] ὑγείας : ὑπὲρ [Arist./Alex.] *Sup.Pr.* 2.50, 12

due to a quantity of moisture. Or is it because the lesser heat is destroyed by the greater, and the eye when rubbed acquires more heat than that in the nose? And for this reason, even if one rubs the nose itself, the sneezing stops.

9.[8] Why are the other escapes of breath, such as the escape of breaking wind or of belching, not sacred, but only the escape of a sneeze is? Is it because of the three regions involved—the head, the chest, and the lower abdomen—the head is the most divine? But breaking wind is breath from the lower abdomen and belching is from the upper, whereas sneezing is from the head. Because this region is most sacred, therefore, they also revere the breath there as sacred. Or is it that all the breaths signify that the regions mentioned are in a better condition generally? For without ⟨*anything else*⟩[9] passing out, the breath in escaping lightens ⟨*the body*⟩, so that even sneezing lightens the region around the head, because it is healthy and able to produce concoction. For when the heat in the head masters the moisture, then the breath becomes a sneeze. And this is why they test those who are dying with what causes sneezing, so that if they are not able to be affected by this, they are past saving. So they revere it as sacred, as a sign of health in the best and most sacred region, and make it a good omen.

[8] Cf. *Pr.* 33.7 and 11, see [Arist./Alex.] *Sup.Pr.* 2.50.

[9] Excrement, for example.

---

17 ἀρίστου Bussemaker ex [Arist./Alex.] *Sup.Pr.* 2.50, 12 : ἀρρώστου codd.

10. Διὰ τί ἄνθρωπος πτάρνυται μάλιστα τῶν ἄλλων ζῴων; πότερον ὅτι τοὺς πόρους εὐρεῖς ἔχει δι᾽ ὧν
10 τὸ πνεῦμα καὶ ἡ | ὀσμὴ[18] εἰσέρχεται; τούτοις γὰρ πληρουμένοις πνεύματος πτάρνυται. ὅτι δ᾽ εὐρεῖς, σημεῖον ὅτι ἥκιστα ὀσφραντικὸν τῶν ζῴων· ἀκριβέστεροι γὰρ[19] οἱ λεπτοὶ πόροι.[20] εἰ οὖν εἰς μὲν τοὺς εὐρεῖς πλεῖον καὶ πλεονάκις εἰσέρχεται τὸ ὑγρόν, οὗ πνευματουμένου ὁ πταρμὸς γίνεται, τοιούτους δὲ μάλιστα
15 τῶν ζῴων | οἱ ἄνθρωποι ἔχουσι, πλειστάκις ἂν πτάρνυντο[21] εἰκότως. ἢ ὅτι[22] ἐλάχιστοι οἱ μυκτῆρες, ὥστε τὸ θερμανθὲν ὑγρὸν ταχὺ ἐξιέναι δύναται πνεῦμα γενόμενον, ἐν δὲ τοῖς ἄλλοις διὰ μῆκος καταψύχεται πρότερον;

11. Διὰ τί οἱ μὲν ἀπὸ μέσων νυκτῶν ἄχρι μέσης
20 ἡμέρας | οὐκ ἀγαθοὶ πταρμοί, οἱ δ᾽ ἀπὸ μέσης ἡμέρας ἄχρι μέσων νυκτῶν; ἢ ὅτι ὁ μὲν πταρμὸς μᾶλλον δοκεῖ ἐπισχεῖν τοὺς ἀρχομένους καὶ ἐν τῇ ἀρχῇ; διὸ ὅταν μέλλουσιν ἄρξεσθαι συμβῇ,[23] μάλιστα ἀποτρεπόμεθα τοῦ πράττειν. ἡ μὲν οὖν ἠὼς καὶ[24] τὸ ἀπὸ
25 μέσων νυκτῶν οἷον ἀρχή τις· διὸ εὐλαβούμεθα | πτά-

[18] ὀσμὴ Bussemaker ex *Pr.* 10.18, 892b23 (cf. [Arist./Alex.] *Sup.Pr.* 2.51, 2) : ῥύμη codd.

[19] γὰρ scripsi ex [Arist./Alex.] *Sup.Pr.* 2.51, 4 : δὲ codd.

[20] λεπτοὶ πόροι : λεπτότεροι Bussemaker ex *Pr.* 10.18, 892b26 (cf. [Arist./Alex.] *Sup.Pr.* 2.51, 4)

[21] πτάρνυντο : πτάρνοιντο Sylburg

[22] ἢ ὅτι Forster ex *Pr.* 10.18, 892b30 (cf. [Arist./Alex.] *Sup.Pr.* 2.51, 7) : ὅσοις codd.

10.[10] Why does the human sneeze most of all animals? Is it because the passages through which the breath and odor enter are wide? For it is when these are full of breath that he sneezes. Now a sign that they are wide is the fact that he is less able to smell than the other animals; for narrow channels are the more accurate. Therefore, if moisture enters these wide passages in greater quantity and more often, and when it is converted into breath a sneeze occurs, and humans most of all the animals have such passages, it is reasonable that he should sneeze most often. Or is it because his nostrils are especially small, so that the heated moisture can exit quickly when it becomes breath, but in the other animals it is cooled beforehand owing to the length of the nostrils?

11.[11] Why is the sneezing that occurs from midnight until midday not good, but the sneezing from midday until midnight is? Is it because sneezing seems rather to check those who are beginning something and are at the beginning? This is why when (*sneezing*) happens when people are about to begin something, we are especially turned back from doing it. Now the dawn and the period after midnight are, as it were, a sort of beginning; this is why we beware sneezing, lest we should prevent what has been

[10] This chapter is virtually identical to *Pr.* 10.18, and very close to [Arist./Alex.] *Sup.Pr.* 2.51. Cf. *Pr.* 10.54.

[11] Cf. *Pr.* 33.7 and 9.

---

23 μέλλουσιν ἄρξεσθαι συμβῇ conieci : μέλλωσιν ἀρχομένοις συμβῆναι codd. : μέλλουσιν ἢ ἀρχομένοις συμβῇ Forster

24 ἠῶς καὶ Xª Ap u: καὶ ἠῶς καὶ cett. codd.

ρειν, μὴ κωλύσωμεν <τὸ>[25] ὡρμημένον. πρὸς δείλης[26] δὲ καὶ ἐπὶ μέσας νύκτας οἷον τελευτή τις καὶ ἐναντίον ἐκείνῳ, ὥστε ἐν τῷ ἐναντίῳ ταὐτὸν αἱρετέον.

12. Διὰ τί οἱ πρεσβῦται χαλεπῶς πτάρνυνται; πότερον <ὅτι> οἱ πόροι συμπεπτώκασι δι᾿ ὧν τὸ πνεῦμα
30 <ἐκκρίνεται>;[27] ἢ ὅτι αἴρειν | αὐτὸ ἄνω οὐκέτι δυνάμενοι ῥᾳδίως,[28] εἶτα βίᾳ ἀφιᾶσι κάτω;

13. Διὰ τί, ἐάν τις ἀπνευστιάζῃ, ἡ λὺγξ παύεται; ἢ διότι ἡ μὲν ὑπὸ καταψύξεως γίνεται (διὸ καὶ οἱ φοβούμενοι καὶ οἱ ῥιγοῦντες λύζουσιν), κατεχόμενον δὲ τὸ πνεῦμα ἐκθερμαίνει τὸν ἐντὸς τόπον; |

35 14. Διὰ τί οἱ κωφοὶ ἐκ τῶν μυκτήρων διαλέγονται ὡς ἐπὶ τὸ πολύ; ἢ ὅτι ὁ πνεύμων ἐστὶ τούτοις πεπονηκώς; τοῦτο γάρ ἐστιν ἡ κωφότης, πλήρωσις τοῦ τόπου τοῦ πνευμονικοῦ. οὔκουν ῥᾳδίως ἡ φωνὴ φέρεται, ἀλλ᾿ ὥσπερ τὸ πνεῦμα τῶν πνευστιώντων ἢ ἀσθμαινόντων
40 δι᾿ ἀδυναμίαν ἀθρόον, οὕτως ἐκείνοις | ἡ φωνή. βιάζε-
963a ται οὖν καὶ διὰ τῶν μυκτήρων. βιαζομένη || δὲ τῇ τρίψει ποιεῖ τὸν ἦχον. ἔστι γὰρ ἡ διὰ τῶν ῥινῶν διάλεκτος γινομένη, ὅταν τὸ ἄνω τῆς ῥινὸς εἰς τὸν οὐρανόν, ᾗ συντέτρηται, κοῖλον γένηται· ὥσπερ κώδων γὰρ ὑπηχεῖ, τοῦ κάτωθεν στενοῦ ὄντος. |

5 15. Διὰ τί μόνον ὁ πταρμὸς ἡμῖν καθεύδουσιν οὐ

[25] <τὸ> Forster [26] πρὸς δείλης : πρὸς δείλην vel πρὸ δείλης Richards [27] <ὅτι> et <ἐκκρίνεται> addidi ex [Arist./Alex.] *Sup.Pr.* 2.52, 1–2

[28] ἢ ὅτι—ῥᾳδίως codd. (αὐτὸ pro τὰ Richards) : ἢ τῷ ἀδυνατεῖν αἴρειν ῥᾳδίως [Arist./Alex.] *Sup.Pr.* 2.52, 2–3

started. But from late afternoon and up to midnight is as it were a sort of ending and opposite to the other period, so that in contrary conditions the same thing (*that was undesirable*) is desirable.

12.[12] Why do old people sneeze with difficulty?[13] Is it because the passages through which the breath <is expelled> have closed? Or is it because they can no longer raise it[14] up easily, so they eject it downward with force?

13.[15] Why, if one holds one's breath, does the hiccuping stop? Is it because hiccuping comes about by cooling (and this is why those who feel fear and those who shiver hiccup), but holding the breath heats the region within?

14.[16] Why do the deaf in most cases speak out of their nostrils? Is it because in them the lung has been affected? For deafness is this, fullness of the region of the lungs. The voice, therefore, does not travel easily, but just as the breath of those who are panting or gasping is accumulated because of weakness, so is the voice in the deaf. Therefore, it is forced through the nostrils. And being forced, it produces an echo through rubbing. For speaking through the nose occurs when the upper part of the nose, which is connected by passage to the palate, becomes hollow; for it echoes like a bell, as the lower part is narrow.

15.[17] Why does sneezing alone not happen to us when

[12] See [Arist./Alex.] *Sup.Pr.* 2.52.

[13] According to Plin. *HN* 28.57, "Theophrastus says that older people have more difficulty in sneezing" (= fr. 348 FHSG).

[14] I.e., the breath.

[15] See [Arist./Alex.] *Sup.Pr.* 2.53. Cf. *Pr.* 33.1, 5, and 17.

[16] Cf. *Pr.* 11.2 and 4.

[17] See [Arist./Alex.] *Sup.Pr.* 2.40.

γίνεται, ἀλλ' ὡς εἰπεῖν ἅπαντα ἐγρηγορόσιν; ἢ ὅτι ὁ μὲν πταρμὸς γίνεται [καὶ][29] ὑπὸ θερμοῦ τινὸς κινήσαντος τὸν τόπον τοῦτον ἀφ' οὗ γίνεται (διὸ καὶ ἀνακύπτομεν πρὸς τὸν ἥλιον, ὅταν βουλώμεθα πτάρειν)· καθευδόντων δ'[30] ἡμῶν ἀντιπεριίσταται τὸ | θερμὸν ἐντός; διὸ καὶ γίνεται τὰ κάτω θερμὰ τῶν καθευδόντων, καὶ τὸ πνεῦμα τὸ πολὺ αἴτιόν ἐστι τοῦ ἐξονειρώττειν ἡμᾶς. εἰκότως οὖν οὐ πταρνύμεθα· ἀπαλλαγέντος γὰρ τοῦ θερμοῦ τοῦ ἐκ[31] τῆς κεφαλῆς, ὃ κινεῖν πέφυκε τὸ ἐνταῦθα ὑγρόν, οὗ ἐξωθουμένου[32] γίνεται ὁ πταρμός, καὶ τὸ συμβαῖνον | πάθος εἰκὸς μὴ γίνεσθαι. ἀποψοφοῦσι δὲ μᾶλλον ἢ πτάρνυνται καὶ ἐρεύγονται καθεύδοντες [ἢ ἐγρηγορότες],[33] ὅτι ἐκθερμαινομένου τοῦ περὶ τὴν κοιλίαν τόπου ἐν τοῖς ὕπνοις μᾶλλον ἐκπνευματοῦσθαι συμβαίνει τὰ περὶ αὐτὴν ὑγρά, πνευματούμενα δὲ εἰς τοὺς ἔγγιστα τόπους φέρεσθαι. ἐνταῦθα γὰρ | καὶ συναπωθεῖται ὑπὸ τοῦ ἐν τῷ ὕπνῳ γινομένου πνεύματος. καθεκτικώτερος γάρ ἐστιν ἢ προετικώτερος ὁ καθεύδων τοῦ πνεύματος, διὸ καὶ συστέλλει τὸ θερμὸν ἐντός. ὁ δὲ κατέχων τὸ πνεῦμα ὠθεῖ κάτω αὐτό· παρὰ φύσιν γάρ ἐστι τῷ πνεύματι ἡ κάτω φορά, διὸ καὶ χαλεπόν ἐστι κατέχειν τὸ | πνεῦμα. τὸ δ' αὐτὸ αἴτιον καὶ τοῦ καθεύδειν ἡμῖν ἐστίν. οὔσης γὰρ τῆς ἐγρηγόρσεως κινήσεως, ταύτης δ' ἐν τοῖς αἰσθητηρίοις ἡμῶν γινομένης μάλιστα ἐν

29 [καὶ] Forster (cf. [Arist./Alex.] *Sup.Pr.* 2.40, 3)

we are asleep, but virtually always when we are awake? Is it because sneezing occurs due to some heat moving that region from which it comes (and this is why we lift up our heads to the sun when we want to sneeze), whereas when we are asleep the heat is compressed within? And this is why the lower parts become hot when we are asleep, and the quantity of breath is the cause of our having nocturnal emissions. It is therefore reasonable that we do not sneeze: for when the heat from the head—which naturally moves the moisture there—is removed (and when this moisture is pushed out, a sneeze naturally occurs), it is reasonable that the resulting experience does not occur. Now people break wind more than they sneeze and belch when sleeping, because as the region around the stomach becomes hot in sleep the moisture around it becomes more vaporized, and as it is vaporized it travels to the nearest regions. For there it is pushed together by the breath that comes in sleep. Indeed, the one who is sleeping is more able to hold his breath than to expel it, and this is why he draws in the internal heat. Now the one holding his breath pushes it downward; for downward motion is contrary to nature for breath, and this is why it is difficult to hold one's breath. And this is the same cause of our sleeping as well. For being awake is movement, and this occurs in our sense organs

---

30 καθευδόντων δὲ Richards (cf. [Arist./Alex.] *Sup.Pr.* 2.40, 5) : ἢ ὅτι καθευδόντων codd.

31 τοῦ ἐκ : ἐκ [Arist./Alex.] *Sup.Pr.* 2.40, 7

32 ἐξωθουμένου scripsi ex [Arist./Alex.] *Sup.Pr.* 2.40, 7 : ἐξαερουμένου R : ἐξαιρουμένου cett. codd.

33 [ἢ ἐγρηγορότες] Forster : ‹μᾶλλον› ἢ ἐγρηγορότες Marenghi[3]

τῷ ἐγρηγορέναι ἡμᾶς, δῆλον ὡς καὶ ἠρεμούντων[34] ἡμῶν καθεύδοιμεν ἄν. ἐπεὶ δὲ τὸ μὲν πῦρ κινητικόν
30 ἐστι τῶν ἐν ἡμῖν μορίων, τοῦτο δ' ἐν τῷ | ὕπνῳ ἐντὸς περιίσταται, λιπὸν τὸν περὶ τὴν κεφαλὴν τόπον, οὗ ἐστὶ τὸ αἰσθητήριον,[35] ἠρεμοίη ἂν μάλιστα ἡμῶν τότε τὰ αἰσθητήρια· ὃ εἴη ἂν αἴτιον τοῦ καθεύδειν.

16. Διὰ τί πτάραντες καὶ οὐρήσαντες φρίττουσιν; ἢ ὅτι κενοῦνται αἱ φλέβες ἀμφοτέροις τούτοις τοῦ πρό-
35 τερον ἐνυπάρχοντος | ἀέρος θερμοῦ; κενωθέντων δ' ἄλλος ἀὴρ ἔξωθεν εἰσέρχεται ψυχρότερος τοῦ προϋπάρχοντος ἐν ταῖς φλεψίν· τοιοῦτος δ' εἰσιὼν ποιεῖ φρίττειν.

17. Διὰ τί τοὺς λυγμοὺς οἱ πταρμοὶ παύουσιν; ἢ ὅτι ὁ λυγμὸς οὐχ ὥσπερ οἱ ἐρυγμοὶ ἀπὸ τῆς τὰ σιτία
40 δεχομένης | κοιλίας ἐστὶν ἀλλ' ἀπὸ τοῦ πνεύμονος,[36]
963b συμβαίνει δὲ μάλιστα || ἀπὸ καταψύξεως ἐκ ῥίγους καὶ λύπης καὶ φαρμακείας τῆς ἄνω μάλιστα γίνεσθαι; θερμὸς γὰρ ὢν φύσει ὁ τόπος, ὅταν καταψυχθῇ, οὐ προίεται[37] τὸ πνεῦμα πᾶν, ἀλλ' ὥσπερ πομφόλυγας
5 ποιεῖ· διὸ καὶ τὸ πνεῦμα κατασχοῦσι παύεται | (ἐκθερμαίνεται γὰρ ὁ τόπος), καὶ τὸ ὄξος, θερμαντικὸν ὄν, προσφερόμενον. τοῦ δὴ θερμοῦ συμβαίνοντος ἀπὸ θερμασίας καὶ τοῦ ἐγκεφάλου, τῶν ἄνω τόπων εἰς τὸν πνεύμονα συντετρημένων, θερμοῦ τοῦ πνεύμονος ὄν-

[34] post ἠρεμούντων add. <τῶν αἰσθητηρίων> Bonitz
[35] τὸ αἰσθητήριον : fort. τὰ αἰσθητήρια

most of all while we are awake, so it is clear that when we are at rest[18] we should sleep. But since fire produces movement in our parts, and this is concentrated within during sleep, leaving the region around the head where the sense organ is, our sense organs would be at rest most of all at that time; and this would be a cause of sleeping.

16.[19] Why do people shiver after they have sneezed or urinated? Is it because in both these cases the veins are emptied of the hot air that was in them before? Now having been emptied, other air—colder than what was in the veins before—enters from the outside; and such air entering produces shivering.

17.[20] Why does sneezing stop hiccuping? Is it because hiccuping (unlike belching, which is from the stomach when it receives food) is from the lung, and results mostly from cooling that arises out of shivering and pain and medicine especially coming to be above? For the region (*of the lungs*) being by nature hot, when it is cooled does not emit all the breath, but as it were produces bubbles; and this is why by holding their breath hiccups stop (for the region is thoroughly heated), and adding vinegar, which produces heat, (*does the same thing*). Since the heat joins together with the heat from the brain as well, the upper regions being connected by passages to the lungs (the lungs being

[18] Or, with Bonitz, "when our <sense organs> are at rest."
[19] This is a longer version of *Pr.* 8.8. Cf. *Pr.* 8.13.
[20] Cf. *Pr.* 33.1 and 5.

---

[36] πνεύμονος β A E Lambeth.1204 R^pc : πνεύματος cett. codd.

[37] προίεται β Barth. : προσίεται cett. codd.

τος, ἥ τε πρὸ τοῦ πταρμοῦ κατοχὴ καὶ ἡ ἄνωθεν κατάκρουσις λύει τὸ πάθος. |

10 18. Διὰ τί οἱ οὐλότριχες, καὶ οἷς ἐπέστραπται τὸ τρίχιον, ὡς ἐπὶ τὸ πολὺ σιμότεροι; ἢ εἴπερ ἡ οὐλότης ἐν παχύτητι, ἡ δὲ παχύτης μετὰ σκληρότητος, σκληρὸν δ' ὂν τὸ αἷμα[38] θερμόν, ἡ δὲ θερμότης οὐ ποιεῖ περίττωσιν, τὸ δὲ ὀστοῦν ἐκ περιττώματος, ὁ δὲ χόν-
15 δρος ὀστοῦν, εὐλόγως ἂν ἔκλειψις | εἴη τοῦ μορίου; σημεῖον δὲ τὸ τὰ παιδία πάντα εἶναι σιμά.

[38] αἷμα : δέρμα Louis ex *GA* 5.3, 783a18

hot), the holding of the breath before the sneeze and the downward pressure from above eliminates the experience.

18. Why are those with woolly hair, and in whom the hair has curled, in most cases very snub-nosed? Is it because woolliness is found in thickness, and thickness comes with hardness, and blood[21] when it is hard is hot, and heat does not produce residue, and bone comes out of residue, and cartilage is bone, so reasonably there would be a lack of that part?[22] Now a sign of this is the fact that all children are snub-nosed.

[21] Or "skin," following the conjecture of Louis.
[22] The implied premise is that a snub nose has less cartilage.

BOOK XXXIV

INTRODUCTION

This brief book shows at least some level of organization (lacking in most books of *Problems*). The subjects covered are teeth (chs. 1–3), the tongue (4–6), and respiration (7–9, 11–12). Ch. 10, however, on the lifeline on the hand, is completely out of place. The author seems aware of, and in some cases raises questions about, Aristotle's biological writings.

ΟΣΑ ΠΕΡΙ ΤΟ ΣΤΟΜΑ ΚΑΙ ΤΑ ΕΝ ΑΥΤΩ

1. Διὰ τί οἱ μανοὺς ἔχοντες τοὺς ὀδόντας οὐ μακρόβιοι; ἢ ὅτι τὰ μακρόβια πλείους ἔχουσιν, οἷον τὰ
963b20 ἄρσενα τῶν θηλειῶν, | ἄνδρες γυναικῶν, πρόβατα προβάτων;[1] οἱ οὖν ἀραιόδοντες[2] ὥσπερ ἂν ἐλάττονας ἔχουσιν ὀδόντας ἐοίκασιν.

2. Διὰ τί οἱ ὀδόντες ἰσχυρότεροι τῶν σαρκῶν ὄντες ὅμως τοῦ ψυχροῦ αἰσθάνονται μᾶλλον; ἢ ὅτι ἐπὶ τοὺς πόρους προσπεφύκασιν, ἐν οἷς ὀλίγον ὂν τὸ θερμὸν
25 ταχὺ ὑπὸ τοῦ ψυχροῦ | κρατούμενον ποιεῖ τὴν ἀλγηδόνα;

3. Διὰ τί τοῦ ψυχροῦ μᾶλλον αἰσθάνονται οἱ ὀδόντες ἢ τοῦ θερμοῦ, ἡ δὲ σὰρξ τοὐναντίον; πότερον ὅτι ἡ μὲν σὰρξ τοῦ μέσου καὶ εὔκρατος, οἱ δὲ ὀδόντες ψυχροί, ὥστε τοῦ ψυχροῦ[3] μᾶλλον αἰσθητικοί; ἢ διότι
30 λεπτῶν πόρων εἰσίν, ἐν οἷς μικρὸν | τὸ θερμόν, ὥστε ταχὺ πάσχουσιν ὑπὸ τοῦ ἐναντίου; ἡ δὲ σὰρξ θερμόν,

[1] προβάτων : τῶν λοιπῶν Ruelle

[2] ἀραιόδοντες Marenghi[3] : ἀραιοὶ ὀδόντες codd. : ἀραιώδοντες Bekker

[3] ψυχροῦ w R^{mg} : ἐναντίου cett. codd.

PROBLEMS CONNECTED WITH THE MOUTH AND THE THINGS IN IT

1.[1] Why are those who have well-spaced[2] teeth not long-lived? Is it because the long-lived have more teeth, for instance males have more than females, men more than women, rams more than ewes? Therefore, those with porous teeth seem to be like those having fewer teeth.

2.[3] Why are teeth, though stronger than flesh, nevertheless more sensitive to cold? Is it because they are attached to passages in which the heat, being slight, is quickly mastered by cold and causes pain?

3.[4] Why are teeth more sensitive to cold than to heat, whereas flesh is the opposite? Is it because flesh shares in the intermediate and temperate, whereas teeth are cold so that they are more sensitive to cold?[5] Or is it because the teeth consist of thin passages in which there is little heat, so that they are quickly affected by the opposite? But flesh is

[1] Cf. *Pr.* 10.48. Source: *HA* 501b22–24; cf. Hp. *Epid.* 2.6.1.

[2] Or "porous," if *μανούς* is a synonym of *ἀραιοί*.

[3] Cf. *Pr.* 34.3.

[4] Cf. *Pr.* 34.2.

[5] Or "to the opposite," with most mss., though that seems to make less sense.

ὥστε οὐδὲν πάσχει ὑπὸ τοῦ ψυχροῦ, τοῦ δὲ θερμοῦ ταχὺ αἰσθάνεται· ὥσπερ γὰρ πῦρ ἐπὶ πυρὶ γίνεται.

4. Διὰ τί ἡ γλῶττα[4] σημαντικὸν πολλῶν; καὶ γὰρ τῶν πυρετῶν ἐν[5] τοῖς ὀξέσι νοσήμασι, καὶ ἐὰν χάλα-
35 ζαι ἐνῶσιν· | †καὶ τῶν ποικίλων προβάτων ποικίλαι†.[6] ἢ ὅτι ὑγρότητος δεκτικόν, καὶ ἐπὶ τῷ πνεύμονι ἐπίκειται, οὗ ἡ ἀρχὴ ἐπὶ τῶν πυρετῶν; πολύχροα δὲ πάντα διὰ τὴν πολύχροιαν τῶν ὑγρῶν· βάπτεται δὲ πρῶτον δι' οὗ πρῶτον ἠθεῖται· ἡ δὲ γλῶττα τοιοῦτον. αἵ τε
40 χάλαζαι διὰ τὸ σομφὴν εἶναι συλλέγονται· | ἔστι γὰρ ἡ χάλαζα οἱονεὶ ἴονθος ἄπεπτος ἐν τοῖς ἐντός. ||

964a 5. Διὰ τί ἡ γλῶττα γλυκεῖα μὲν οὐ γίνεται, πικρὰ δὲ καὶ ἁλμυρὰ καὶ ὀξεῖα; ἢ ὅτι διαφθοραὶ ταῦτ' ἐστί, τῆς δὲ φύσεως οὐκ αἰσθάνεται;

6. Διὰ τί, ὅσας ἂν χρόας ἔχῃ τὸ δέρμα, τοσαύτας
5 ἔχει | καὶ ἡ γλῶττα; πότερον ὅτι ἓν μέρος ἐστὶν ὥσπερ ἄλλο τι τῶν ἔξωθεν, ἀλλ' ἐντὸς περιείληπται; διὰ δὲ τὸ λεπτὸν εἶναι ταύτῃ τὸ δέρμα καὶ ἡ μικρὰ ποικιλία ἐμφαίνεται. ἢ διότι τὸ ὕδωρ ἐστὶν ὃ ποιεῖ μεταβάλλειν τὰς χρόας, ἡ δὲ γλῶττα μάλιστα πάσχει ὑπὸ τοῦ πόματος; |

10 7. Διὰ τί ἐκ τοῦ στόματος καὶ θερμὸν καὶ ψυχρὸν

[4] ἡ γλῶττα : αἱ γλῶτται a δ

[5] ἐν Sylburg : καὶ γὰρ codd.

[6] καὶ τῶν—ποικίλαι codd. (obelis inclusi) : secl. Marenghi[3] : fort. καὶ τῶν πυρετῶν <ἐν τοῖς> προβάτοις ποικίλαι

hot, so that it is not affected by the cold, but is quickly sensitive to heat; for it is like fire added to fire.

4.[6] Why is the tongue a signifier of many things? Indeed, it is a signifier of fevers in acute diseases, especially if there are blisters present, †and those with a variety of colors (*are signifiers*) of sheep with a variety of colors†.[7] Is it because it is capable of receiving moisture, and is situated near the lung, which is the origin of fevers? Now everything multicolored is so through the moisture being multicolored: that through which moisture is first strained is dyed by them, and the tongue has this characteristic. And blisters collect on the tongue through its being spongy; for the blister is as it were a pimple not concocted internally.

5.[8] Why doesn't the tongue become sweet, whereas it does become bitter and salty and acrid? Is it because these are corruptions, but the tongue does not perceive its own nature?

6.[9] Why is it that, however many colors the skin has, the tongue has that many as well? Is it because it is the one part that is like any other of the outside parts, although it is enclosed within? But because the skin on it is thin, even a small variation in color is apparent. Or is it because water is what produces change of color, and the tongue is most affected by drink?

7.[10] Why do people breathe both hot and cold from the

[6] Source: Hp. *Epid.* 6.5.10.

[7] Perhaps this line originally stated that a many-colored tongue was a sign of fever in sheep; but cf. *HA* 6.19, 574a5–8 and *GA* 5.6, 786a23–24.

[8] See Hp. *Epid.* 6.5.10.

[9] Source: *GA* 786a21–29.

[10] Cf. *Pr.* 26.48. Source: Thphr. *Vent.* 20.

πνέουσιν; φυσῶσι μὲν γὰρ ψυχρόν, ἀάζουσι δὲ θερμόν. σημεῖον δὲ ὅτι θερμαίνει, ἐὰν πλησίον προσάγῃ τις τὴν χεῖρα τοῦ στόματος.[7] ἢ ἀμφοτέρως ὁ ἀὴρ κινούμενος θερμός,[8] ὁ δὲ φυσῶν κινεῖ τὸν ἀέρα οὐκ
15 ἀθρόως, ἀλλὰ διὰ στενοῦ τοῦ στόματος; | ὀλίγον οὖν ἐκπνέων, πολὺ κινεῖ τὸν θύραθεν, ἐν ᾧ τὸ θερμὸν ὂν τὸ ἐκ τοῦ στόματος οὐ φαίνεται δι' ὀλιγότητα. ὁ δ' ἀάζων ἀθρόον ἐκπνεῖ· διὸ θερμόν. ἔστι γὰρ φυσασμοῦ τὸ[9] διαφέρειν τῇ συστροφῇ· ὁ δ' ἀασμὸς ἀθρόου ἔκπνευσις.

8. Διὰ τί, ἐὰν σφόδρα καὶ ἀθρόον ἐκπνεύσωσιν,
20 ἀδυνατοῦσι | πάλιν ἐκπνεῦσαι; ὁμοίως δ' ἔχει καὶ ἐπὶ τοῦ ἀναπνεῦσαι· ἀδυνατοῦσι γὰρ δὶς ἐφεξῆς ποιεῖν αὐτό. ἢ ὅτι τὸ μὲν δίωσίς τίς ἐστι, τὸ δὲ συναγωγὴ τόπου, ἃ ἄχρι τινός ἐστι δυνατὰ γίνεσθαι; φανερὸν οὖν ὅτι ἐναλλὰξ ἀνάγκη ἄμφω γίνεσθαι, καὶ ἀδύνατον δὶς ἐφεξῆς. |

25 9. Διὰ τί ἑτέρου τόπου ὄντος ᾗ τὰ σῖτα καὶ τὸ ποτὸν διεξέρχεται καὶ ᾗ ἀναπνέομεν, ἐὰν μείζω ψωμὸν καταπίωμεν, πνιγόμεθα; οὐδὲν δὴ ἄτοπον· οὐ γὰρ μόνον ἐάν τι ἐμπέσῃ εἰς τὸν τόπον τοῦτον, ἀλλὰ κἂν ἔτι

[7] προσάγῃ τις τὴν χεῖρα τοῦ στόματος γ δ : προσαγάγῃ τις τοῦ στόματος τὴν χεῖρα cett. codd.
[8] θερμός w R^{mg} Gaza : ψυχρός cett. codd.
[9] φυσασμοῦ : φυσασμὸς Marenghi[3] ex Barth. : φυσιασμοῦ Sylburg || τὸ Sylburg : τῷ codd.

mouth? For they blow cold, but they "ha"[11] hot. There is a sign that (*breathing*) causes heat: if one brings the hand near the mouth. Or is the air that is moved in both cases hot, but the one who blows out does not move the air all at once but through a narrow mouth? Therefore, although he breathes out little air, he moves more outside, in which case the heat that is from the mouth is not apparent, because there is little of it. But the one who "ha"s breathes out the air all at once, which is why it is hot. For going through in a dense mass is a characteristic of blowing; but the "ha" is a breathing out all at once.

8.[12] Why, if people breathe out violently and all at once,[13] are they unable to breathe out again? And similarly too in the case of breathing in: for people are unable to do it twice in a row. Is it because the one is a sort of dilation, whereas the other is a contraction of the region, both of which can occur up to a certain limit? Therefore, it is evident that both must occur alternately, and neither can occur twice in a row.

9. Why, although it is a different region through which food and drink pass and through which we breathe in, if we swallow a very large morsel, we choke? In fact, this is not strange; for we do so not only if something falls into this region, but if it is further blocked as well, we choke that

[11] The rare ἀάζω is likely an onomatopoetic word (and perhaps a Peripatetic neologism) referring to the gentle release of breath out of a fairly wide-open mouth: "ha." Aside from its two occurrences in this chapter (as well as one occurrence of its cognate ὁ ἀασμός), it appears elsewhere only at Arist. *Mete*. 367b2.

[12] Cf. *Juv*. 27 (= *Resp*. 21).

[13] I.e., breathing out all of the air at once.

φραχθῇ, οὕτω μᾶλλον πνιγόμεθα. ταῦτα δὲ παράλλη-
30 λά ἐστι, καθ' ὅ τε τὰ | σιτία δεχόμεθα καὶ καθ' ὃ
ἀναπνέομεν. ὅταν οὖν ἐμπέσῃ μείζων ψωμός, καὶ ἡ
ἀναπνοὴ συμφράττεται,[10] ὥστε μὴ εἶναι τῷ πνεύματι
ἔξοδον.

10. Διὰ τί, ὅσοι τὴν διὰ χειρὸς τομὴν ἔχουσι δι'
ὅλης, μακροβιώτατοι; ἢ διότι τὰ ἄναρθρα βραχύβια
35 καὶ ἀσθενῆ; | σημεῖον δὲ τῆς μὲν ἀσθενείας τὰ νέα,
τῆς δὲ βραχυβιότητος τὰ ἔνυγρα. δῆλον ἄρα ὅτι τὰ
ἠρθρωμένα τοὐναντίον. τοιαῦτα δέ, ὧν καὶ τὰ φύσει
ἄναρθρα μάλιστα ἤρθρωται. τῆς δὲ χειρὸς τὸ ἔσω
ἀναρθρότατον.

11. Διὰ τί ἐν τῷ μακρὸν ἀναπνεῖν, ἑλκόντων μὲν
964b εἴσω τὸ ‖ πνεῦμα, συμπίπτει ἡ κοιλία, ἐκπνεόντων δὲ
πληροῦται; πιθανὸν δ' ἐστὶ τοὐναντίον συμβαίνειν. ἢ
ὅτι τῶν μὲν ἀναπνεόντων συμπιεζομένη ταῖς πλευ-
ραῖς κάτω, καθάπερ αἱ φῦσαι, προσογκεῖν φαίνεται; |

5 12. Διὰ τί ἀναπνέομεν; ἢ καθάπερ τὸ ὑγρὸν εἰς
πνεῦμα διαλύεται, οὕτω καὶ[11] τὸ πνεῦμα εἰς τὸ πῦρ; τὸ
τῆς φύσεως οὖν θερμὸν ὅταν τὸ πολὺ τοῦ πνεύματος
πῦρ ποιήσῃ, ἀλγηδόνα ἐμποιεῖ, τοῖς δὲ πόροις καὶ
ὄγκον· διόπερ ἐξωθοῦμεν τὸ πῦρ μετὰ τοῦ πνεύματος.
10 ὅταν δ' ἐξέλθῃ τὸ πνεῦμα καὶ | τὸ πῦρ, συμπιπτόντων

[10] συμφράττεται Marenghi³ ex Barth. : συμφράττει codd.
[11] καὶ γ Xᵃ M u : om. cett. codd.

much more. Now these—both the region through which we receive food and the one through which we breathe in—are parallel. Therefore, when a very large morsel falls in, the organ of respiration is also closed, so that there is no exit for the breath.

10.[14] Why are those who have the line[15] across the entire hand long-lived? Is it because the unarticulated animals[16] are short-lived and weak? Now a sign of weakness are the young animals, and of being short-lived the aquatic animals. So it is clear that the articulated animals are the opposite. Such are those animals for whom even the unarticulated parts are mostly articulated. And the inside of the hand is most unarticulated.

11.[17] Why is it that, in breathing in deeply, when drawing in the breath the stomach contracts, but when breathing out it fills up? It is plausible that the opposite happens. Is it because when breathing in the stomach is compressed downward by the ribs, just like bellows, ⟨*and then, when breathing out*,⟩ it appears to swell?

12.[18] Why do we breathe in? Is it that just as moisture dissolves into breath, so too does breath into fire? The heat of nature, therefore, when the greater part of the breath produces fire, causes pain and also pressure in the passages; this is why we push out the fire with the breath. Now when the breath and the fire have gone out, as the passages

[14] Cf. *Pr.* 10.49. Source: *HA* 493b32–94a1.

[15] Literally, "the cut." [16] Smooth animals, with no or few apparent joints or seams. The author likely has in mind animals like the squid (which Aristotle says is short-lived; see *HA* 550b14). [17] Cf. *Juv.* 27 (= *Resp.* 21).

[18] Cf. *Juv.* 27 (= *Resp.* 21) and Hp. *Epid.* 6.5.1.

τῶν πόρων καὶ καταψυχομένων ἀλγηδόνες γίνονται· ἕλκομεν οὖν τὸ πνεῦμα πάλιν. εἶτα ἀνοίξαντες τοῦ πνεύματος[12] τοὺς πόρους καὶ βοηθήσαντες,[13] πάλιν γίνεται τὸ πῦρ, καὶ πάλιν ἀλγοῦντες ἐκπέμπομεν, καὶ διὰ τέλους τοῦτο πράττομεν, καθάπερ καὶ σκαρδαμύσσομεν κατὰ | τὸ καταψύχεσθαι τὸ περὶ τὸν ὀφθαλμὸν σῶμα καὶ ξηραίνεσθαι, καὶ βαδίζομεν οὐ[14] προσέχοντες τῇ βαδίσει τὸν νοῦν, κυβερνωμένης δὲ τῆς διανοίας αὐτῆς.[15] τοῦτον οὖν τὸν τρόπον καὶ τὰ περὶ τὴν ἀναπνοὴν ποιοῦμεν· μηχανώμενοι γὰρ τὸν ἀέρα ἕλκειν ἀναπνέομεν, καὶ πάλιν ἕλκομεν.

15

12 πνεύματος : σώματος γ (praeter Xᵃ aᵐ p)
13 βοηθήσαντες Sylburg (et Vat.1904ᵐᵍ) : βοήσαντες codd.
14 οὐ Bussemaker : οὖν codd.
15 αὐτῆς x t : αὐτοῖς cett. codd. (αὐτοῖς scrip. Marenghi³) || post αὐτοῖς lac. ind. Bekker

contract and are cooled, pains occur; therefore, we draw in the breath again. Then, when we have opened the passages for breath and relieved them,[19] fire comes again, and again feeling pain we expel (*the fire with the breath*), and we continue doing this to the end, just as we also continue blinking in accordance with the cooling and drying of the part of the body around the eye, and we walk without giving thought to the walking, the mind itself steering us. In the same manner, therefore, we do the things involved in breathing; for we breathe in by contriving to draw in the air, and then we draw it in again.

[19] Or with the mss. "and emitted a shout."

BOOK XXXV

INTRODUCTION

Although Aristotle discusses in some detail the sense of touch (e.g. in *DA* 2.11 and 3.13), this is not the topic of *Pr.* 35. Rather, this brief book is concerned with the *results* of certain kinds of touching—especially tickling (chs. 1, 2, 6, 7, 8) and shuddering or shivering (1, 3, 5, 9). The remaining two chapters raise and discuss the following questions: "Why, though summer is hot and winter is cold, are bodies when touched colder in summer than in winter?" (4) and "Why does what is passed along alternatively between fingers appear to be two things?" (10).

Little can be said about the sources for these chapters. *Pr.* 35.3 and 9 are likely responding to Hippocratic texts, and chs. 2, 6, and 8 appear to be drawing on the discussion of tickling and laughing in *PA* 3.10.

ΟΣΑ ΠΕΡΙ ΤΑ ΥΠΟ ΤΗΝ ΑΦΗΝ

1. Διὰ τί μᾶλλον φρίττομεν ἑτέρου θιγόντος πως ἢ αὐτοὶ ἡμῶν; ἢ ὅτι αἰσθητικωτέρα ἡ ἁφὴ τοῦ ἀλλοτρίου ἢ ἡ τοῦ οἰκείου; τὸ γὰρ συμφυὲς ἀναίσθητον.
964b25 καὶ φοβερώτερον τὸ | λάθρᾳ καὶ ἐξαπιναίως γινόμενον, ὁ δὲ φόβος κατάψυξις <τις>·[1] ἡ δὲ ἀλλοτρία ἁφὴ πρὸς τὴν οἰκείαν ἄμφω ταῦτα ἔχει. καὶ ὅλως δὲ παθητικὸν ἕκαστον πέφυκεν ἢ μᾶλλον ἢ μόνον ὑπ' ἄλλου ἢ ὑφ' αὑτοῦ,[2] οἷον καὶ ἐπὶ τοῦ γαργαλίζεσθαι συμβαίνει. |

30 2. Διὰ τί γαργαλίζονται τὰς μασχάλας καὶ τὰ ἐντὸς τῶν ποδῶν; ἢ διὰ τὴν λεπτότητα τοῦ δέρματος; καὶ ὧν ἀσυνήθης ἡ ἁφή, οἷον τούτων καὶ τοῦ ὠτός;

3. Διὰ τί φρίττουσιν οὐκ ἐπὶ τοῖς αὐτοῖς πάντες; ἢ
35 ὅτι οὐκ[3] ἐπὶ | τοῖς αὐτοῖς πάντες ἡδόμεθα, ὥσπερ οὐδὲ λυπούμεθα ἐπὶ τοῖς αὐτοῖς πάντες; ὁμοίως δὴ οὐ

[1] <τις> Marenghi[3] (cf. *Pr.* 35.3, 964b36)

[2] ὑπ' ἄλλου ἢ ὑφ' αὑτοῦ Sylburg : ὑπ' ἄλλου ἐστίν ἢ αὐτοῦ codd.

[3] οὐκ Marenghi[3] : οὐδ' Bekker : οὔτ' codd.

PROBLEMS CONNECTED WITH WHAT DEPENDS ON TOUCH[1]

1. Why do we shudder[2] more when someone else touches us somewhere than when we touch ourselves? Is it because the touch of another is more sensitive than one's own? For what is naturally connected is imperceptible. Also, what occurs secretly and suddenly is more fearful, and fear is <a sort of> cooling. Now another's touch has both these qualities, relative to one's own. And generally, every passive experience is naturally produced either more or solely by another than by oneself, as happens in the case of being tickled.

2.[3] Why are people ticklish in the armpits and on the soles of the feet?[4] Is it owing to the thinness of the skin? And are some parts not used to the sense of touch, like these and the ear?

3.[5] Why do all people not shudder at the same things? Is it because we do not all feel pleasure at the same things, just as we do not all feel pain at the same things? In the

[1] Or perhaps "what falls under (*the heading of*) touch."

[2] The same word (φρίττειν) can also be mean "shiver."

[3] Cf. *Pr.* 35.6, 7, 8.

[4] Literally, "on the inner parts of the feet."

[5] Cf. *Pr.* 7.5. Source: Hp. *Hum.* 9.

φρίττομεν ἐπὶ τοῖς αὐτοῖς· ἔστι γὰρ ἡ αὐτὴ κατάψυξίς τις. διὸ οἱ μὲν τοῦ ἱματίου δακνομένου φρίττουσιν, οἱ δὲ πρίονος ἀκονουμένου ἢ ἑλκομένου, οἱ δὲ κισήρεως τεμνομένης, οἱ δ' ὄνου λίθον ἀλοῦντος.

4. Διὰ τί τοῦ μὲν θέρους ὄντος θερμοῦ, τοῦ δὲ 965a χειμῶνος ψυχροῦ, ‖ τὰ σώματα θιγγανόντων ψυχεινότερά ἐστι τοῦ θέρους ἢ τοῦ χειμῶνος; πότερον ὅτι ὁ ἱδρὼς καὶ ἡ ἴδισις καταψύχει τὰ σώματα, τοῦτο δ' ἐν μὲν τῷ θέρει γίνεται, ἐν δὲ τῷ χειμῶνι οὔ; ἢ ὅτι 5 ἀντιπεριίσταται ἐναντίως τὸ ψυχρὸν καὶ | τὸ θερμὸν τῇ ὥρᾳ, καὶ ἔσω φεύγει ἐν τῷ θέρει, διὸ καὶ ἱδρῶτα ἀνίησιν· ἐν δὲ τῷ χειμῶνι ἀποστέγει τὸ ψῦχος καὶ ἀτμίζει τὸ σῶμα ὥσπερ ἡ γῆ;

5. Διὰ τί φρίττουσιν αἱ τρίχες ἐν τῷ δέρματι; ἢ ὅταν συσπάσωσι[4] τὸ δέρμα, εἰκότως ἐξανέστησαν; 10 συσπῶσι δὲ καὶ | ὑπὸ ῥίγους καὶ ὑπ' ἄλλων παθῶν.

6. Διὰ τί αὐτὸς αὑτὸν οὐθεὶς γαργαλίζει; ἢ ὅτι καὶ ὑπ' ἄλλου ἧττον, ἐὰν προαίσθηται, μᾶλλον δέ, ἂν μὴ ὁρᾷ; ὥσθ' ἥκιστα γαργαλισθήσεται, ὅταν μὴ λανθάνῃ τοῦτο πάσχων. ἔστι δ' ὁ γέλως παρακοπή τις 15 καὶ ἀπάτη. διὸ καὶ | τυπτόμενοι εἰς τὰς φρένας γελῶσιν· οὐ γὰρ ὁ τυχὼν τόπος ἐστὶν ᾧ γελῶσιν. τὸ δὲ

[4] συσπάσωσι Forster ex *Pr.* 8.12, 888a39 : σπάσωσι codd.

---

[6] I.e., in the cases of shuddering, feeling pain, and feeling pleasure.

[7] Or perhaps across some other surface, like metal or stone.

same way, surely, we do not all shudder at the same things; for it is the same sort of cooling.[6] This is why some of us shudder when a cloak is ripped, some when a saw is sharpened or drawn (*across wood*),[7] some when a pumice stone is cut, and some when a millstone is grinding on stone.

4. Why, though summer is hot and winter is cold, are bodies when touched colder in summer than in winter? Is it because sweat and the act of sweating cool bodies, and this occurs in summer but not in winter? Or is it because cold and heat are contained in a manner inverse to the season,[8] and so (*the cold*) flees inward in summer, and this is why (*the body*) releases sweat; whereas in winter, the cold keeps it[9] inside, and the body, like the earth, produces vapor?

5.[10] Why do the hairs bristle[11] on the skin? Is it that when the skin is contracted, it is reasonable that they stand up? And they contract under the influence of chill and other conditions.

6.[12] Why does no one tickle himself? Is it because one also (*feels tickling*) by another less if it is not anticipated, but more if he does not see it? So, one will feel tickling least when one notices this happening. Now laughter is a sort of frenzy and deceit. And this is why people struck in the midriff laugh; for it is not any chance part with which

[8] I.e., in winter, heat is contained by the cold, while in summer, cold is contained by the heat.

[9] Sweat or (more likely) heat.

[10] This chapter is virtually identical to *Pr.* 8.12. Cf. *Pr.* 8.15 and 21.

[11] The same word (φρίττουσιν) translated "shudder" or "shiver" elsewhere.

[12] Cf. *Pr.* 35.2, 7, 8. See *EN* 1150b22–25.

λαθραῖον ἀπατητικόν. διὰ τοῦτο καὶ γίνεται ὁ γέλως καὶ οὐ γίνεται ὑπ' αὐτοῦ.

7. Διὰ τί ποτε τὰ χείλη μάλιστα γαργαλιζόμεθα; ἢ διότι δεῖ τὸ γαργαλιζόμενον μὴ πρόσω τοῦ αἰσθη-
20 τικοῦ εἶναι; | ἔστι δὲ τὰ χείλη περὶ τὸν τόπον τοῦτον μάλιστα. διὰ τοῦτο δὲ γαργαλίζεται τὰ χείλη τῶν περὶ τὴν κεφαλὴν τόπων, ὅτι[5] ἐστιν εὔσαρκα. εὐκινητότατα οὖν μάλιστά ἐστιν.

8. Διὰ τί, ἐάν τις τὸν περὶ τὰς μασχάλας τόπον κνήσῃ, ἐκγελῶσιν, ἐὰν δέ τινα ἄλλον, οὔ; ἢ διὰ τί
25 <πτερῷ τὰς | ῥῖνας κνήσαντες>[6] πτάρνυνται; ἢ τόποι εἰσὶ τῶν φλεβίων, ὧν καταψυχομένων ἢ τοὐναντίον πασχόντων ὑγραίνονται[7] ἢ εἰς πνεῦμα ἐκ τοῦ ὑγροῦ διαλύονται;[8] ὥσπερ ἐὰν τὰς ἐπὶ τοῦ τραχήλου πιέσῃ τις φλέβας, καθεύδουσιν. ἡ μὲν ἡδονὴ θερμασία[9] τίς ἐστιν· τοῦτο δέ, ὅταν πλέον τὸ πνεῦμα ἐγγένηται, |
30 ἀθρόον ἔξω ἀφίεμεν. ὡσαύτως καὶ ἐπὶ τῷ πταρμῷ, πτερῷ[10] διαθερμάναντες καὶ κνήσαντες[11] διελύσαμεν εἰς πνεῦμα· πλέονος δὲ γενομένου ἐξεώσαμεν.

9. Διὰ τί μετὰ τὰ σιτία φρίττομεν πολλάκις; ἢ ὅτι ψυχρὰ εἰσπορευόμενα ἀπὸ πρώτης κρατεῖ μᾶλλον τοῦ
35 φυσικοῦ | θερμοῦ ἢ κρατεῖται;

[5] ὅτι Marenghi[3] : ἅ γ : ὅ cett. codd. [6] <πτερῷ τὰς ῥῖνας κινήσαντες> Sylburg ex Gaza (κνήσαντες pro κινήσαντες Bekker) [7] ὑγραίνονται : ὑγραίνεται α δ

[8] διαλύονται Forster : διαλύεται codd.

[9] καθεύδουσιν. ἡ μὲν ἡδονὴ θερμασία : καθεύδουσιν ἡμῖν, ἡδονὴ θαυμασία Ross apud Forster

we laugh. Now what is unnoticed is deceptive. For this reason too laughter occurs and is not produced by oneself.

7.[13] Why do we feel ticklish especially on the lips? Is it because the part that feels ticklish must not be far from the sense organ? Now the lips especially are near this region. And for this reason the lips—of the regions around the head—are ticklish, because they are fleshy. Therefore, they especially are most easily moved.

8.[14] Why, if someone scratches the region around the armpits, do we laugh out, but not some other region? Or why do people sneeze <when their nose is scratched with a feather>? Are they regions of the veins, and when these are cooled or experience the opposite they become moist or they dissolve from moisture into breath? Just as, if someone puts pressure on the veins on the neck, people sleep. Pleasure is a sort of heat, but when the breath becomes abundant we release it outside all at once.[15] And similarly in the case of sneezing, by heating (*the moisture in the nostril*) and scratching with a feather we dissolve it into breath; and when it becomes abundant we expel it.

9.[16] Why do we often shudder after food? Is it because the cold (*of the food*) introduced from the very first masters the natural heat more than it is mastered?

[13] Cf. *Pr.* 35.2, 6, 8. [14] Cf. *Pr.* 35.2, 6, 7.

[15] The text of these two lines is uncertain. Ross's emendation would yield "... our neck when we are sleeping, there is a wonderful pleasure. But when ..." [16] Source: Hp. *Flat.* 7.

---

[10] τῷ πταρμῷ δ : πταρμῷ cett. codd. || πτερῷ R w : τῷ πτερῷ cett. codd.

[11] κνήσαντες Bonitz : κινήσαντες codd.

10. Διὰ τί τὸ περιαγόμενον ἐναλλὰξ τοῖς δακτύλοις[12] δύο φαίνεται; ἢ διότι δυσὶν αἰσθητηρίοις ἁπτόμεθα; τοῖς γὰρ ἐντὸς[13] τῶν δακτύλων, κατὰ φύσιν ἔχοντες τὴν χεῖρα, ἀμφοτέροις οὐ δυνατὸν θιγεῖν.[14]

[12] ἐναλλὰξ τοῖς δακτύλοις : τοῖς ἐναλλὰξ δακτύλοις Forster ex Gaza

[13] ἐντὸς : ἐκτὸς Forster ex Gaza

[14] θιγεῖν Ross apud Forster : εἰπεῖν codd. : κινεῖν Louis

10.[17] Why does what is passed along alternatively between fingers[18] appear to be two things? Is it because we are touching it with two sensitive parts? For holding our hand naturally, it is not possible to handle (*what is passed along*) with the inside[19] of both fingers.

[17] See *Pr.* 31.7, 11, 17a, 17b.
[18] Or, following Forster, "between crossed fingers."
[19] Or, following Forster, "outside."

BOOK XXXVI

INTRODUCTION

Pr. 36 is the shortest book in the *Problems*. It consists of three unconnected chapters on the face. Ch. 1 asks and briefly answers the question "Why do people create images of the face?" The others deal with sweat (2) and pimples (3). Aristotle discusses the face in *HA* 1.8, which may serve as the background to these chapters.

ΟΣΑ ΠΕΡΙ ΠΡΟΣΩΠΟΝ

965b 1. Διὰ τί τοῦ προσώπου τὰς εἰκόνας ποιοῦνται; πότερον ὅτι τοῦτο δηλοῖ ποῖοί τινες; ἢ ὅτι μάλιστα γινώσκεται;

2. Διὰ τί τὸ πρόσωπον ἰδίουσι μάλιστα, ἀσαρ-
5 κότατον ὄν; | ἢ διότι εὐΐδρωτα μὲν ὅσα ὕφυγρα καὶ ἀραιά, ἡ δὲ κεφαλὴ τοιαύτη; ὑγρότητα γὰρ οἰκείαν ἔχει πλείστην. δηλοῦσι δ' αἱ φλέβες τείνουσαι ἐντεῦθεν, καὶ οἱ κατάρροι γινόμενοι ἐξ αὐτῆς, καὶ ὁ ἐγκέφαλος ὑγρός, καὶ οἱ πόροι πολλοί· σημεῖον δ' αἱ τρίχες,
10 ὅτι πολλοὶ πόροι εἰσὶ περαίνοντες | ἔξω. οὔκουν ἐκ τῶν κάτω ὁ ἱδρώς, ἀλλ' ἐκ τῆς κεφαλῆς γίνεται. διὸ ἰδίουσι καὶ πρῶτον <καὶ>[1] μάλιστα τὸ μέτωπον· ὑπόκειται γὰρ τὸ πρῶτον. τὸ δ' ὑγρὸν κάτω ῥεῖ, ἀλλ' οὐκ ἄνω.

3. Διὰ τί ἐν τῷ προσώπῳ μάλιστα οἱ ἴονθοι; ἢ διότι |
15 μανὸς ὁ τόπος καὶ ὑγρότητα ἔχει; σημεῖον δ' ἥ τε τῶν τριχῶν ἔκφυσις καὶ ἡ τῶν αἰσθήσεων δύναμις· ὁ δ' ἴονθος ὥσπερ ἐξάνθημα ὑγρότητός τινος ἀπέπτου.

[1] <καὶ> Forster ex *Pr.* 2.17, 868a2

PROBLEMS CONNECTED WITH THE FACE

1.[1] Why do people create images of the face? Is it because this shows certain qualities? Or is it because the face especially is recognized?

2.[2] Why do people sweat most on the face, though it is least fleshy? Is it because parts that are moist and porous are inclined to sweat, and the head is like this? For it contains a great deal of natural moisture. Now this is shown by the veins extending from here, and the discharges coming from it, and the brain being moist, and there being many passages; and the hair is a sign that there are many passages extending outward (*from the head*). Therefore, sweat does not come from the lower parts, but from the head. This is why people sweat first and most on the forehead; for it lies in the first place. And moisture flows downward, but not upward.

3. Why do pimples appear most on the face? Is it because this region is porous and contains moisture? Now a sign of this is the outgrowth of hairs and the power of the sensations; and the pimple is as it were an eruption of some unconcocted moisture.

[1] Sources: *HA* 1.8 and *Phgn*. 805a33–b9.

[2] This chapter is virtually identical to *Pr.* 2.17. Source: Thphr. *Sud*. 33. Cf. *Pr.* 2.10.

BOOK XXXVII

INTRODUCTION

This brief book, purportedly on the body as a whole, mainly deals with two subjects: sweating (chs. 1–2) and massage (3, 5, and 6). Its one other chapter (4) attempts to answer the question "Why do we burn and feel pain more by the same heat if we have first been cooled?" Much of Book 37 seems to have been taken from elsewhere in the *Problems*: chs. 1–2 are together virtually identical to 2.22; a large part of ch. 3 (966a13–34) is virtually identical to 1.52 and 5.34; and ch. 4 is virtually identical to *Pr.* 8.19.

There are no clear sources for the chapters of *Pr.* 37, though those on massage may have been responding to medical writings on the subject, e.g., Diocles of Carystus frs. 182–85 (v.d. Eijk) and Hp. *Off.* 17.

ΟΣΑ ΠΕΡΙ ΟΛΟΝ ΤΟ ΣΩΜΑ

965b20 1. Διὰ τί ἀεὶ τοῦ σώματος ῥέοντος καὶ τῆς ἀπορροῆς γινομένης ἐκ τῶν περιττωμάτων, οὐ κουφίζεται τὸ σῶμα, ἐὰν μὴ ἰδίῃ; ἢ διότι ἐλάττων ἡ ἔκκρισις γίνεται; ὅταν γὰρ ἐξ ὑγροῦ μεταβάλλῃ εἰς ἀέρα, πλέον γίνεται ἐξ ἐλάττονος· τὸ γὰρ διακρινόμενον
25 πλέον, ὥστε ἐν πλείονι | χρόνῳ ἡ ἔκκρισις.

2. Διὰ τί δὲ τοῦτο; ἢ διότι δι' ἐλαττόνων πόρων ἡ ἔξοδός ἐστιν; τὸ γὰρ γλίσχρον καὶ τὸ κολλῶδες μετὰ μὲν τοῦ ὑγροῦ ἐκκρίνεται διὰ τὴν κατάμιξιν, μετὰ δὲ τοῦ πνεύματος ἀδυνατεῖ. μάλιστα δὲ τοῦτ' ἐστὶ τὸ
30 λυποῦν. διὸ καὶ | οἱ ἔμετοι τῶν ἱδρώτων κουφίζουσι μᾶλλον, ὅτι συνεξάγουσι τοῦτο ἅτε παχύτεροι καὶ σωματωδέστεροι ὄντες. ἢ καὶ ὅτι τῇ μὲν σαρκὶ πόρρω οὗτος ὁ τόπος, ἐν ᾧ τὸ γλίσχρον καὶ κολλῶδες, ὥστε ἔργον μεταστῆσαι, τῇ δὲ κοιλίᾳ ἐγγύς; ἢ γὰρ ἐν ταύτῃ
35 γίνεται ἢ πλησίον· διὸ καὶ δυσεξάγωγος | ἄλλως.

PROBLEMS CONNECTED WITH THE BODY AS A WHOLE

1.[1] Why, though the body has a continuous flow and there is an efflux of residues, the body does not grow lighter unless it sweats? Is it because the secretion becomes too small? For when there is a change from moisture to air, a great amount of air comes to be from a small amount of moisture. For the amount (*of moisture*) separated out is great, so that the secretion takes a great deal of time.

2. But why does this[2] happen? Is it because the exit is through small pores? For what is sticky and viscous is secreted with the moisture, because it is mixed with it, but it cannot be with the breath. It is particularly this (*sticky and viscous material*) that causes pain. And this is why vomiting has a more lightening effect than sweat, because being denser and more corporeal it takes out this material with it. Or is it also because the region containing what is sticky and viscous is far away from the flesh, so that it is hard work to move it, but near to the stomach? For it is formed in or close to the stomach; and this is why it is difficult to remove it otherwise.

[1] *Pr.* 37.1–2 and 2.22 are virtually identical.
[2] I.e., the volume of moisture.

3. Διὰ τί αἱ τρίψεις σαρκοῦσιν; ἢ ὅτι αὐξητικώτατον τῶν ἐν τῷ σώματι τὸ θερμόν ἐστιν; τοῦ μὲν γὰρ ἐνυπάρχοντος, μείζους οἱ ὄγκοι γίνονται διὰ τὸ ἀεὶ αὐτὸ ἐν κινήσει εἶναι καὶ εἰς τὸ ἄνω φέρεσθαι καὶ

966a πνευματοῦν τὰ ἐν || ἡμῖν ὑγρά, ὃ ἐν τῇ τρίψει γίνεται· ἐκλείποντος δὲ φθίνει καὶ ἐλαττοῦται τὸ σῶμα. ἢ ὅτι ὀγκοτέρα <ἀπὸ> τῆς τροφῆς[1] γίνεται ἡ σὰρξ διὰ τὴν θερμασίαν; ἅπαν γὰρ τὸ θερμὸν ἐπισπαστικὸν τοῦ

5 ὑγροῦ ἐστίν, ἡ δ' εἰς τὴν σάρκα διαδιδομένη | τροφὴ ὑγρά ἐστι, καὶ ἐπιδέχεται τὴν τροφὴν μᾶλλον διὰ τὴν ἀραίωσιν· ἀραιοτέρα γὰρ γινομένη[2] μᾶλλον δύναται δέχεσθαι ὥσπερ σπογγιά. ἡ δὲ τρῖψις εὔπνουν καὶ ἀραιὰν ποιεῖ τὴν σάρκα, καὶ κωλύει συστάσεις γίνεσθαι κατὰ τὸ σῶμα. τούτου δὲ μὴ ὄντος, οὐδὲ συντή-

10 ξεις γίνονται· αἱ | γὰρ ἀτροφίαι καὶ αἱ συντήξεις ἐκ τῶν ἀθροισθέντων εἰσίν. εὐπνούστερα δὲ καὶ ἀραιότερα καὶ ὁμαλέστερα γινόμενα εἰκὸς μᾶλλον ὀγκοῦσθαι. τῆς τε γὰρ τροφῆς δεκτικώτερα καὶ τῶν ἐκκρίσεων προετικώτερα γίνεται, ὅτι οὐ δεῖ πυκνοῦν τὴν σάρκα πρὸς ὑγίειαν, ἀλλ' ἀραιοῦν. ὥσπερ γὰρ πόλις |

15 ὑγιεινή ἐστι καὶ τόπος εὔπνους (διὸ καὶ ἡ θάλαττα ὑγιεινή), οὕτω καὶ σῶμα τὸ εὔπνουν μᾶλλον ὑγιεινόν ἐστι τοῦ ἐναντίως ἔχοντος. δεῖ γὰρ ἢ μὴ ὑπάρχειν μηδέν <περίττωμα>,[3] ἢ τούτου ὡς τάχιστα ἀπαλλάτ-

[1] <ἀπὸ> τῆς τροφῆς Marenghi[3] : τῆς τροφῆς codd. : τῇ τροφῇ Bussemaker

[2] post γινομένη add. <ἡ σὰρξ> Marenghi[3] ex Barth.

[3] <περίττωμα> Forster ex *Pr.* 1.52 (865b21) and 5.34 (884a29)

3.[3] Why do massages produce flesh?[4] Is it because heat most promotes the growth of what is in the body? For the bulk of what is already present in it becomes greater, because it is always in motion and the moisture in us is carried upward and vaporized, which occurs during massage; but when this is abandoned, the body decays and becomes smaller. Or does the flesh become bulkier owing to the heat from nourishment? For everything hot is capable of attracting moisture, and the nourishment distributed into the flesh is moist, and the flesh admits the nourishment more owing to its being porous; for when (*the flesh*) becomes more porous it can admit more (*moisture*), just like a sponge. Now massage makes the flesh have a good flow of air and porous, and prevents accumulations from appearing in the body. But when there is no accumulation, no colliquations come to be; for lack of nourishment and colliquation are from what has been gathered together. And what comes to have a better flow of air and to be more porous and smoother[5] is likely to become bulkier; for they are more able to receive nourishment and more able to eject excretions, because for health one should not thicken the flesh, but make it porous. For just as a city or a region with a good flow of air is healthy (which is why the sea too is healthy), so also a body is more healthy if it has a good flow of air than if it is in the opposite condition. For either there should be no residue, or the body should release it as

[3] Cf. *Pr.* 37.5 and 6. Part of this chapter (966a13–34) is virtually identical to *Pr.* 1.52 and 5.34. See also Diocl. frs. 182, 185, 186 (v.d. Eijk). [4] I.e., make the body fleshier. The word translated "massages" can also be rendered "rubbings."

[5] ὁμαλέστερα might also here mean "more homogenous."

τεσθαι· καὶ δεῖ οὕτως ἔχειν τὸ σῶμα ὥστε λαμβάνον
20 εὐθὺς ἐκκρίνειν τὴν περίττωσιν, καὶ εἶναι ἐν | κινήσει
ἀεὶ καὶ μηδέποτε ἠρεμεῖν. τὸ μὲν γὰρ μένον σήπεται,
ὥσπερ καὶ ὕδωρ τὸ μὴ κινούμενον· σηπόμενον δὲ
νόσον ποιεῖ· τὸ δὲ ἐκκρινόμενον πρὸ τοῦ διαφθαρῆναι
χωρίζεται. τοῦτο οὖν πυκνουμένης μὲν τῆς σαρκὸς οὐ
γίνεται (ὡσπερεὶ γὰρ ἐμφράττονται οἱ πόροι), ἀραιου-
25 μένης δὲ συμβαίνει. | διὸ καὶ οὐ δεῖ ἐν τῷ ἡλίῳ γυμνὸν
βαδίζειν· συνίσταται γὰρ ἡ σὰρξ καὶ κομιδῇ ἀποσαρ-
κοῦται· τὸ μὲν γὰρ ἐντὸς ὑγρὸν διαμένει, τὸ δ' ἐπιπολῆς ἀπαλλάττεται ἐξατμιζόμενον, ὥσπερ καὶ τὰ κρέα
τὰ ὀπτὰ τῶν ἑφθῶν μᾶλλον τὰ ἐντὸς ὑγρά ἐστιν. οὐδὲ
30 τὰ στήθη γυμνὰ ἔχοντα | βαδίζειν ἐν ἡλίῳ· ἀπὸ γὰρ
τῶν ἄριστα ᾠκοδομημένων τοῦ σώματος ὁ ἥλιος φέρει[4] ὃ ἥκιστα δεῖται ἀφαιρέσεως, ἀλλὰ μᾶλλον τὰ
ἐντὸς ξηραντέον. ἐκεῖθεν μὲν οὖν διὰ τὸ πόρρω εἶναι,
ἐὰν μὴ μετὰ πόνου, οὐκ ἔστιν ἱδρῶτα ἄγειν, ἀπὸ
τούτων δὲ διὰ τὸ πρόχειρα εἶναι ῥᾴδιον ἀναλῶσαι τὸ
ὑγρόν. |

35 4. Διὰ τί ψυχθέντες ἀπὸ τῆς αὐτῆς θερμασίας και-
όμεθα μᾶλλον καὶ ἀλγοῦμεν; πότερον διὰ τὴν πυκνότητα στέγει ἡ σὰρξ τὸ προσπῖπτον θερμόν; διὸ μόλι-
βδος ἐρίου θερμότερος. ἢ βίαιος γίνεται τοῦ θερμοῦ ἡ
δίοδος διὰ τὸ πεπηγέναι ὑπὸ ψυχροῦ τὸ σῶμα; ||

966b 5. Διὰ τί αἱ ξηροτριβίαι στερεὰν τὴν σάρκα παρασκευάζουσιν; ἢ ὅτι διὰ τὴν τρῖψιν τῆς θερμασίας

[4] φέρει : fort. ἀφαιρεῖ ex *Pr.* 1.52 (865b34) and 5.34 (884b3)

quickly as possible; and the body should therefore be in such a condition as to excrete the residue as soon as it receives it, and be in motion and never at rest. For what remains still becomes putrid, like water that doesn't move, and what is putrid produces disease; but what is excreted is separated before any decay takes place. So if the flesh is thickened, this[6] does not occur (for the passages are, so to speak, blocked), but it does happen when the flesh is porous. This is why one should not walk naked in the sun; for then the flesh congeals and becomes very fleshy; for what moisture is inside remains, and what is on the surface is released having been vaporized, just as the inner parts are moist in meat that is roasted rather than boiled. Nor should one walk with a chest bare in the sun; for the sun then removes from the best-constructed parts of the body what least requires to be removed, rather than the inside parts, which require drying. Therefore, because they are farther, it is not possible to lead sweat away *(from them)*, except with exertion, but from the outside parts it is easy to use up the moisture, because they are close at hand.

4.[7] Why do we burn and feel pain more by the same heat if we have first been cooled? Does the flesh, owing to its thickness, keep in the heat which it encounters? This is why lead becomes hotter than wool. Or does the penetration of the heat become violent because the body is solidified by the cold?

5.[8] Why do dry massages render the flesh hard? Is it because owing to the heat added by the massage the moisture

[6] I.e., the excretion of residue.

[7] This chapter is virtually identical to *Pr.* 8.19.

[8] Cf. *Pr.* 37.3 and 6.

ἐπιγινομένης τὸ ὑγρὸν καταναλίσκεται; πρὸς δὲ τούτοις ἡ σὰρξ τριβομένη πυκνοῦται· ἅπαντα δὲ ὅσα
5 πλείονος τρίψεως τυγχάνει, | πυκνοῦται καὶ στερεὰ
γίνεται. θεωρῆσαι δὲ τὸ τοιοῦτον ἔστιν ἐπὶ πολλῶν· τὸ
γὰρ σταῖς ἢ πηλὸς ἢ ἄλλο τι τῶν τοιούτων, ἐὰν μὲν
ὕδωρ ἐπιχέας ἕλκῃς, ὑγρὰ καὶ κλυδῶντα διαμένει, ἐὰν
δὲ πλείω τρῖψιν προσάγῃς, πυκνοῦταί τε καὶ στερεοῦ-
ται ταχέως καὶ γλίσχρα γίνεται. |

10 6. Διὰ τί αἱ τρίψεις μᾶλλον σαρκοῦσι τῶν δρόμων;
<ἢ>[5] ὅτι οἱ μὲν δρόμοι περιψύχουσι τὴν σάρκα καὶ οὐ
δεκτικὴν τροφῆς παρασκευάζουσιν, ἀλλὰ τὰ μὲν συσ-
σείεται κάτω, τὰ δ' ἐπιπολῆς[6] τοῦ φυσικοῦ θερμοῦ
ἐπιτελουμένου παντελῶς λεπτυνόμενα εἰς πνεῦμα δια-
15 κρίνεται; ἡ δὲ παλάμη τῇ | τρίψει τὴν σάρκα ἀραιὰν
καὶ δεκτικὴν αὐτῆς παρασκευάζει. καὶ ἡ ἔξωθεν δὴ[7]
ἁφὴ ἐναντιουμένη διὰ τῆς πιλήσεως τῇ φορᾷ αὐτὴν[8]
συνέχει μᾶλλον, καὶ ἀνάκλασιν τῆς σαρκὸς ποιεῖται.

[5] <ἢ> Sylburg

[6] ἐπιπολῆς w R[2] : ἐπὶ πολλοῦ cett. codd. : ἐπιπολῆς πολλοῦ Hett

[7] δὴ a : δὲ cett. codd.

[8] αὐτὴν (sc. τὴν σάρκα) Flashar : αὐτὸν plur. codd. : αὐτὰ w R : αὐτὸ Marenghi[3] : fort. αὐτῆς

is used up? But in addition to these,[9] the flesh when massaged thickens; and anything receiving much massaging thickens and becomes firm. Now this can be seen in many cases: for dough or clay or any other such substance, if you pour water on it and draw it out,[10] it remains moist and watery, whereas if you apply more massage, they quickly thicken and harden, and become sticky.

6.[11] Why do massages produce more flesh than running? Is it because running cools the flesh and renders it unable to receive nourishment, but part (*of the nourishment*) is shaken downward, while the part on the surface, when the natural heat is exhausted, becomes extremely thin[12] and separates in the form of breath? But the palm, through massage, renders the flesh porous and able to receive nourishment. And the external contact, opposing by its pressure the movement, restrains it more[13] and produces a bending back of the flesh.

[9] Presumably, the heat being added and the moisture used up.

[10] The meaning of ἕλκῃς is unclear here: draw the substance out of the water, or spread out the material.

[11] Cf. *Pr.* 37.3 and 5, and (on running) see Hp. *Vict.* 2.63.

[12] Or ". . . is completely exhausted, becomes thin."

[13] This last line is unclear; there is likely something wrong with the text.

BOOK XXXVIII

INTRODUCTION

The final book of the *Problems* contains eleven chapters dealing with complexion, and especially skin color. Nearly half discuss the effects of the sun on complexion (1, 6–8, 11), and three others the influence of various forms of exercise on complexion (3–5). One chapter is on the hair color of those who work on the sea (2), and one on the skin color of those who work with grain (10). There is one chapter on the effects of old age on complexion (9). Four chapters (3, 6–8) are clearly raising questions about passages in the works of Theophrastus.

ΟΣΑ ΠΕΡΙ ΧΡΟΑΝ

966b20 1. *Διὰ τί τὸν μὲν κηρὸν καὶ τοὔλαιον λευκαίνει ὁ ἥλιος, τὴν δὲ σάρκα μελαίνει; ἢ ὅτι τὰ μὲν λευκαίνει ἀπάγων τὸ ὕδωρ (φύσει γὰρ τὸ ὑγρὸν μέλαν διὰ τὴν μῖξιν τοῦ γεώδους*[1]*), τὴν δὲ σάρκα ἐπικαίει;* |

25 2. *Διὰ τί οἱ ἁλιεῖς καὶ πορφυρεῖς καὶ ἁπλῶς οἱ τὴν θάλατταν ἐργαζόμενοι πυρροί εἰσιν; πότερον ὅτι ἡ θάλαττα θερμὴ καὶ αὐχμώδης ἐστὶ διὰ τὴν ἅλμην, τὸ δὲ τοιοῦτον πυρρὰς ποιεῖ τὰς τρίχας, καθάπερ ἥ τε κονία καὶ τὸ ἀρσενικόν; ἢ τὰ μὲν ἐκτὸς γίνονται*
30 *θερμότεροι, τὰ δ' ἐντὸς* | *περιψύχονται διὰ τὸ βρεχομένων αὐτῶν ἀεὶ ξηραίνεσθαι ὑπὸ τοῦ ἡλίου τὰ πέριξ; τούτων δὲ τοῦτο πασχόντων αἱ τρίχες ξηραινόμεναι λεπτύνονται καὶ πυρροῦνται. καὶ πάντες δ' οἱ πρὸς ἄρκτον πυρρότριχες καὶ λεπτότριχές εἰσιν.*

3. *Διὰ τί οἱ μὲν ἐν ἱματίῳ δρόμοι καὶ ἡ τοῦ ἐλαίου*

[1] *γεώδους* α Xa am p : *γεώδους ὕδατος* δ : *ὕδατος* γ

---

[1] Cf. *Pr.* 38.11. [2] Source: [Arist.], *Col.* 794a20–24.

[3] Literally, "purplers" (*πορφυρεῖς*)—divers for the purple murex (see *HA* 5.15), a gastropod the mucus of which was used in making purple dye.

PROBLEMS CONNECTED WITH COMPLEXION

1.[1] Why does the sun whiten wax and olive oil, but darken the flesh? Is it because it whitens the former by removing the water (for moisture is dark by nature, because of its mixture with what is earthy), whereas it burns the flesh?

2.[2] Why do fishermen and murex divers[3] and in general those who work on the sea have reddish hair? Is it because the sea is hot and causes dryness owing to its saltiness, and such things make the hair reddish, just as lye and orpiment[4] do? Or do the outside parts become hotter, whereas the inside parts are cooled, because, although they are getting drenched, the surrounding parts are continually being dried by the sun? Now when they experience this, as the hair dries it becomes thin and turns reddish. And indeed, all those in the north are red-haired and thin-haired.

3.[5] Why does running in a cloak and the smearing of

[4] Orpiment (τὸ ἀρσενικόν) is a yellow (arsenic-sulfide) mineral used as a pigment in painting.

[5] Cf. *Pr.* 2.30, the source of which is Thphr. *Sud.* 39. See also Hp. *Vic.* 2.63 and Diocl. frs. 182 and 184 (v.d. Eijk).

35 εἰς | ἱμάτιον χρῖσις ἄχρους[2] ποιεῖ, οἱ δὲ γυμνοὶ δρόμοι εὔχρους;[3] ἢ ὅτι ἡ μὲν εὔπνοια εὔχροιαν ποιεῖ, ἡ δὲ κατάπνιξις τοὐναντίον; διὰ δὴ τὸ συνθερμαινόμενον τὸ ἐπιπολῆς ὑγρὸν μὴ διαψύχεσθαι ἄχροιαν ποιεῖ. ἄμφω δὲ ταὐτὸν ποιεῖ, ἡ ἐν τῷ ἱματίῳ ἴδισις καὶ ἡ εἰς
967a τὸ ἱμάτιον ἄλειψις· ἐγκατακλείεται || γὰρ ἡ θερμότης. οἱ δὲ γυμνοὶ δρόμοι εὔχρουν[4] ποιοῦσι διὰ τοὐναντίον, ὅτι καταψύχει ὁ ἀὴρ τὰς συνισταμένας ἐκκρίσεις καὶ διαπνεῖ τὸ σῶμα. ἔτι τὸ ἔλαιον ὑγρὸν ὂν καὶ λεπτόν,
5 ὑπαλειφθὲν καὶ τοὺς πόρους ἐμφρᾶττον, | οὔτε τὸ ἐκ τοῦ σώματος ὑγρὸν καὶ πνεῦμα ἔξω ῥεῖν ἐᾷ, οὔτε τὸ ἐκτὸς πνεῦμα ἐντός. διὸ καταπνιγόμενα ἐν τῷ σώματι ὑγρὰ περιττώματα, σηπόμενα ἄχροιαν ποιεῖ.

4. Διὰ τί ἡ εὔπνοια εὔχρους ποιεῖ; ἢ ὅτι ἄχροια ἔοικεν εἶναι οἷον σῆψίς τις χρωτός; ὅταν οὖν τὸ
10 ἐπιπολῆς ὑγρὸν | καὶ θερμὸν ᾖ, τοῦτο συμβαίνει[5] χλωρὸν γίνεσθαι, ἐὰν μὴ ψυχθῇ καὶ ἀποπνεύσῃ τὸ θερμόν.

5. Διὰ τί οἱ μὲν ἱδρώσαντες ἐκ τῶν γυμνασίων εὔχροοί εἰσιν εὐθύς, οἱ δὲ ἀθληταὶ ἄχροοι; ἢ διότι ὑπὸ μὲν τοῦ μετρίου πόνου τὸ θερμὸν ἐκκάεται καὶ ἐπιπο-
15 λάζει, ὑπὸ δὲ | τῶν πολλῶν ἐξηθεῖται μετὰ τοῦ ἱδρῶτος καὶ τοῦ πνεύματος, ἀραιουμένου τοῦ σώματος ἐν τῷ πονεῖν; ὅταν μὲν οὖν ἐπιπολάσῃ τὸ θερμόν, εὔχροοι

[2] ἄχρους : εὔχρους γ [3] οἱ δὲ γυμνοὶ δρόμοι ἄχρους (εὔχρους pro ἄχρους Hett) : om. Yᵃ Ap
[4] εὔχρουν : ἄχρουν Sylburg
[5] συμβαίνει Xᵃ : συμβαίνει καὶ cett. codd.

olive oil inside the cloak produce a pale complexion, whereas running naked produces a good complexion? Is it because a good flow of air produces a good complexion, whereas stifling produces the opposite? Indeed, it produces a pale complexion through the surface moisture being heated and not cooling. And both—sweating in a cloak and anointing beneath the cloak—produce the same result: for the heat is enclosed. But running naked produces a good complexion for the opposite reason, because the air cools the secretions that have formed and ventilates the body. Further, the olive oil—which is moist and light—being smeared under (*the cloak*) and so obstructing the passages, does not allow the body's moisture and breath out, nor does it allow the air[6] from the outside in. This is why the moist residues in the body being stifled causes putrefaction and produces a pale complexion.

4. Why does a good flow of air produce good complexion? Is it because a pale complexion seems to be, as it were, a sort of putrefying of complexion?[7] Therefore, when the surface is moist and hot, it becomes yellow, unless it is cooled and blows off the heat.

5. Why do those who are sweating as a result of exercise immediately have a good complexion, whereas athletes have a pale complexion? Is it because from moderate exertion the heat is burned out and comes to the surface, whereas from a great deal of exertion the heat is filtered through with the sweat and the breath, as the body becomes porous during the exertion? Therefore, when the heat comes to the surface, people acquire a good complex-

[6] *Πνεῦμα* can simply mean "air," as it does here.

[7] Or "of the skin."

γίνονται, καθάπερ οἵ τε θερμαινόμενοι καὶ αἰσχυνόμενοι· ὅταν δ' ἐκλίπῃ, ἄχροοι. οἱ μὲν οὖν ἰδιῶται μέτρια γυμνάζονται, οἱ δ' ἀθληταὶ πολλά. |

20 6. Διὰ τί μᾶλλον καίονται ὑπὸ τοῦ ἡλίου οἱ καθεζόμενοι τῶν γυμναζομένων; ἢ ὅτι οἱ ἐν κινήσει ὄντες ὥσπερ ῥιπίζονται ὑπὸ τοῦ πνεύματος διὰ τὸ κινεῖν τὸν ἀέρα, οἱ δὲ καθήμενοι οὐ πάσχουσι τοῦτο;

7. Διὰ τί ὁ μὲν ἥλιος ἐπικάει, τὸ δὲ πῦρ οὔ; ἢ διότι | 25 λεπτότερός ἐστιν ὁ ἥλιος, καὶ μᾶλλον δύναται διαδύεσθαι εἰς τὴν σάρκα; τὸ δὲ πῦρ, ἐὰν καὶ ἐπικαύσῃ, ἄνω μόνον ποιεῖ τὸ χρῶμα, τὰς φοῖδας[6] καλουμένας· εἴσω δὲ οὐκ εἰσδύεται. ||

967b 8. Διὰ τί τὸ πῦρ οὐ ποιεῖ μέλανας, ὁ δ' ἥλιος ποιεῖ· τὸν δὲ κέραμον ποιεῖ, ὁ δ' ἥλιος οὔ; ἢ οὐχ ὁμοίως ἑκάτερον ποιεῖ, ἀλλ' ὁ μὲν ἐπικάων τὴν χρόαν μελαίνει, τὸ δὲ πῦρ τὸν κέραμον ἀναπιμπλᾷ, ᾗ ἀναφέρει 5 ἀσβόλῳ; τοῦτο | δ' ἐστὶ λεπτῆς μαρίλης, ἀποθραυομένων ἅμα καὶ καομένων τῶν ἀνθράκων. τοὺς δ' ἀνθρώπους ὁ μὲν ἥλιος μελαίνει, τὸ δὲ πῦρ οὔ, ὅτι τοῦ μὲν μαλθακὴ ἡ θερμότης, καὶ διὰ μικρομέρειαν δύναται τὸ δέρμα αὐτὸ κάειν· ὥστε διὰ μὲν τὸ τῆς σαρκὸς 10 μὴ ἅπτεσθαι οὐκ ἀλγεινόν, διὰ δὲ τὸ κάειν | μέλαν ποιεῖ. τὸ δὲ πῦρ ἢ οὐχ ἅπτεται ἢ εἴσω διέρχεται, ἐπεὶ

[6] φοῖδας : φοῖβας δ : φῳδὰς Sylburg : φωΐδας vel φῷδας Marenghi[3]

ion, just as those who are hot or feeling shame; but when the heat departs, they acquire a pale complexion. Now private people exercise moderately, whereas athletes do so much more.

6.[8] Why are those who are sitting more burned by the sun than those who are exercising? Is it because those who are in motion are, as it were, fanned by the wind owing to their moving the air, but those who are sitting do not experience this?

7.[9] Why does the sun burn (*the skin*), whereas fire does not?[10] Is it because the sun is finer,[11] and so is more able to penetrate the flesh? But fire, even if it does burn, produces only on the top of the skin what are called blisters; but it does not penetrate within.

8.[12] Why does fire not make us dark, whereas the sun does, and why does fire make earthenware dark, whereas the sun does not? Or does each of these act in dissimilar ways, the one darkening the skin by burning it, whereas fire saturates earthenware with the soot that it raises up? (Soot is from fine charcoal, when coal simultaneously breaks up and burns.) Now the sun darkens human beings, whereas fire does not, because the heat of the sun is soft, and it is able to burn the skin itself because it consists of small parts; and as it does not touch the flesh, it is not painful, but because it burns it makes it dark. Fire, however, either does not touch the flesh or it enters it, since what is

[8] Source: Thphr. *Ign*. 36. See also *Pr.* 5.36 and 24.12.

[9] Source: Thphr. *Ign*. 38. Cf. *Pr.* 38.8.

[10] I.e., why does the sun cause sunburn, whereas fire does not?

[11] Specifically, the *heat* from the sun (see Thphr. *Ign*. 38).

[12] Source: Thphr. *Ign*. 38–39. Cf. *Pr.* 38.7.

μέλανα καὶ τὰ πυρίκαυτα[7] γίνεται, ἀλλ' οὐ μόνον ἐκεῖνον τὸν τόπον κάει οὗ ἡ χροιά.

9. Διὰ τί οἱ γηράσκοντες μελάντεροι γίνονται; ἢ ὅτι πᾶν σηπόμενον μελάντερον γίνεται, πλὴν εὐρῶτος;
15 ταὐτὸ[8] δ' | ἐστὶ γῆρας καὶ σαπρότης. ἔτι ἐπειδὴ τὸ αἷμα ξηραινόμενον μελάντερον γίνεται, εἰκότως ἂν μελάντεροι εἶεν οἱ πρεσβύτεροι· τοῦτο γάρ ἐστι τὸ χρῷζον ἡμῶν τὰ σώματα φυσικῶς.

10. Διὰ τί ‹οἱ›[9] περὶ τὴν τῶν σιτίων ἐργασίαν, οἱ
20 μὲν περὶ | τὰς κριθὰς ἄχροοι γίνονται καὶ καταρροϊκοί, οἱ δὲ περὶ τοὺς πυροὺς εὐεκτικοί; ἢ διότι εὐπεπτότερος ὁ πυρὸς τῆς κριθῆς, ὥστε καὶ αἱ ἀπόρροιαι;

11. Διὰ τί ὁ μὲν ἥλιος τὸ μὲν ἔλαιον λευκαίνει, τὴν δὲ σάρκα μελαίνει; ἢ ὅτι τοῦ μὲν ἐλαίου ἀπάγει τὸ
25 γεῶδες; | τοῦτο δ' ἦν τὸ μέλαν, ὥσπερ τὸ γεῶδες τοῦ οἴνου. τὴν δὲ σάρκα μελαίνει, ὅτι κάει· τὸ γὰρ γεῶδες καόμενον ἅπαν γίνεται μέλαν.

[7] πυρίκαυτα : πυρίκαυστα γ
[8] ταὐτὸ Forster ex Gaza : τοῦτο codd.
[9] ‹οἱ› addidi ex *Pr.* 21.24, 929b26

burned by fire also becomes dark, but it does not burn only that region where the skin color is.

9. Why do those growing old become darker? Is it because everything that is putrefying becomes darker, except mold? And old age and putridity are the same thing. Further, since blood when it dries becomes darker, it is reasonable that old men would be darker. For blood is what naturally colors our bodies.

10.[13] Why, of those whose work is connected to grain, do those who deal with barley become pale in complexion and subject to discharges, while those who deal with wheat are healthy? Is it because wheat is more easily concocted than barley, and therefore so are the emanations from it?

11.[14] Why does the sun whiten olive oil, but darken the flesh? Is it because it removes what is earthy from the olive oil? This is the dark part of it, like the earthy part of wine. But the sun darkens the flesh, because it burns it; for anything that is earthy, when burned, becomes black.

[13] *Pr.* 38.10 and 21.24 are virtually identical. See also 1.37. Apollonius (*Mir.* 7) paraphrases this material and attributes it to Aristotle's *Problems*.

[14] Cf. *Pr.* 38.1.

INDEX OF NAMES

References are to Bekker numbers.

INDEX OF SUBJECTS

References are to book and chapter number. If an entry represents the subject of an entire book, that book is listed in italics.

RHETORIC TO ALEXANDER

INTRODUCTION

Reference to an expedition to Sicily by Timoleon (8.8) puts the earliest date for this text after 344/343. The discovery of the Hibeh papyrus, which Grenfell and Hunt date to the early part of the third century BC and which contains a lengthy section of the text from 1.13 through 4.3 (with gaps), limits its latest dating to ca. 300 BC. The likelihood that other events, after Timoleon's expedition,[1] would have been mentioned if the text had been composed much later than 344/343 seems to limit the composition of the text to quite a narrow range, perhaps as narrow as 340–338 BC.

Although its broad similarity to Aristotle's *Rhetoric* and its prefatory letter—which purports to be from Aristotle to Alexander but was composed considerably later than the text itself—led the text to be included among those of Aristotle as his entire corpus appeared in western Europe (first in Latin and then in Greek) in the fourteenth and fifteenth centuries, its more common modern attribution to Anaximenes of Lampsacus began already in the sixteenth century with the Florentine humanist Pier Vettori. He relied on Quintilian's citation (*Inst.* 3.4.9) of Anaximenes as the author of a treatise that identified seven species of rheto-

[1] Chaeroneia (338) and Alexander's accession (336) and campaign into Asia (334–) could hardly be omitted.

ric. The seven species coincide with those in this text. The problem has been that Quintilian knew of only two genres in Anaximenes' system, whereas our text mentions three.[2] However, except for two exceptional (and easily discreditable) passages (1.1 1421b7 and 36.1 1441b31), the text largely avoids references to "genres" (γένη), referring instead to seven "species" (εἴδη) of oratory, which are like Aristotle's six species (which are based on three genres) but include a seventh, investigative (ἐξεταστικόν) species. At any rate, a general consensus has now formed around Anaximenes, even if caution prevents embracing the attribution conclusively.

Anaximenes (ca. 380–320) was a historian (*FGrH* 72) as well as a rhetorician. The Suda (*s.v.*) says that he was a student of Diogenes the Cynic (ca. 412/403–ca. 324/321) and Zoilus the Grammarian, the latter a critic of Plato and Isocrates. There is evidence for his having written a *Hellenica*, a *Philippica*, and a work on Alexander the Great. The hypothesis of Isocrates' *Encomium of Helen* identifies him as the author of the work on Helen to which Isocrates says that his own reacts and which he describes more as a defense (*apologia*) than an encomium (cf. Isoc., *Hel.* 14). But no one now takes seriously Jebb's speculation that Anaximenes is the author of the *Encomium of Helen* now ascribed to Gorgias.

Aristotle and Anaximenes were both tutors to Alexan-

[2] Syrianus in the fifth century likewise cites "Aristotle" when discussing the beginning of the text itself. Like Quintilian, however, Syrianus refers to only two genres, so it seems likely that our text was made to conform more closely with the known Aristotelian doctrine of three genres after that time.

der, and the Suda says that Anaximenes followed him on his campaigns. Pausanias (6.18.2–4) reports seeing a statue of him at Lampsacus, the result of his having interceded on behalf of the people of Lampsacus after they had sided with the Persians against Alexander; he won Alexander over through a trick. Pausanias (6.18.5) also mentions that he wrote a polemic against Athens, Sparta, and Thebes in the style and under the name of Theopompus in order to foment hatred against the historian. Diodorus Siculus (15.76) lists him among the memorable men of learning of his time, such as Plato and Aristotle, and Plutarch (*Comp. Cic. Dem.* 2) even suggests that he rivaled Isocrates and Demosthenes as an orator.

There are almost no points of connection between the prefatory letter addressed to Alexander and the treatise itself, and it is generally agreed to be a forgery, which was appended to the text after Quintilian (ca. AD 35–95) and before the time of Athenaeus (fl. ca. AD 200), who quotes from it and attributes the quotation to Aristotle (11.508a). No specific doctrines from the treatise are referred to in the letter, nor are any distinctly Aristotelian ideas used, although there do seem to be some echoes of Isocrates. The letter seems to imagine Alexander as already sovereign (after 336), but there is no reference to his waging war against the Persians and other non-Greeks to the east, which dominated Alexander's life after 334. So the ostensible date for the letter seems in a fairly narrow range, from 336 to 334 BC.

For Aristotle the disciplinary status of rhetoric was of enormous importance. He makes explicit its relationship to other disciplines, such as dialectic, ethics, and politics. But this text lacks any interest in such metarhetorical ques-

tions; it does not even use the word "rhetoric," though it refers once to the activity of the *rhetor* (36.39). Its discussion is thus direct and practical, aimed sometimes at the second person singular, but more often expressed in the first-person plural. The imagined reader appears to be an orator who needs help brainstorming ideas for particular speeches. To what extent it actually reflects oratorical practice and not simply an attempt at a systematic approach to such practice is still an open question. Although particular historical situations are cited, no actual speeches by practicing orators are used explicitly, and there is only one citation, of Euripides' lost *Philoctetes* (18.15).

As a technical handbook concerned with language, this text presents special problems for a translator, and because of its complicated relationship with Aristotle's *Rhetoric*, the terminology that the two treatises share is especially problematic. Both texts put particular emphasis on terms such as *pistis, enthymema, paradeigma, elenchos*, and so on. Yet in some cases they use the terms in very different ways. Where they differ substantially, I have chosen to avoid confusion by anglicizing the Greek word rather than translating it, so ἐνθύμημα appears as "enthymeme," τεκμήριον as "*tekmerion*," and so on. I have despaired over translation of the word δημηγορικόν and so likewise simply anglicized it as "demegoric." In general I have tried to translate what appear to be technical terms, such as the verbs ἀποφαίνειν, δεικνύειν, and δηλοῦν, consistently. In an attempt to modernize the idiom, I have avoided translating the particle γάρ, since its English counterpart, the conjunction "for," now seems archaic, and the logical structure of the ideas comes forth even without it. Some

readers may be struck by my translations for the names of the species of speeches. I prefer "proposition and opposition" rather than "persuasion and dissuasion," and "criticism" rather than "blame," "condemnation," or "vituperation."

The text has three basic parts = chs. 1–5 discuss argumentation specific to the seven species; chs. 6–28 discuss devices for persuasion (*pisteis* chs. 7–17) and style (chs. 18–28); and chs. 29–37 discuss arrangement, again with reference to the seven species. Ch. 38.1–11 makes more general observations; 38.12–25 is thought to be a later addition.

A recurrent pattern in the text is the triad choices (προαιρέσεις), words (λόγοι), and actions (πράξεις).[3] The relationship between this triad and Aristotle's triad of entechnic proofs (character [of the speaker], speech, and emotions [of the audience]) has yet to be fully explored, but their similarities encourage further study. At 7.2 (1428a18), in particular, a distinction is made between proofs that arise from the speeches themselves, from the actions, and from the people, and other proofs that are supplementary (ἐπίθετοι). The latter concur, with one great exception, with Aristotle's atechnic proofs, the witness testimony, oaths, etc. The great exception is in Anaximenes' use of the term "the opinion of the speaker" (ἡ δόξα τοῦ λέγοντος), which appears where Aristotle places "laws." How that came about, what the origins of

[3] The triad (or at least two of its three members) appears in 1.3, 3.1, 5.1, 7.2, 10.2, 13.4, 14.7, 31.2–3, 36.3, 36.32, 36.37, 37.1, 37.5, and 38.2. In 7.2 the triad appears as "speeches, actions, people," in 37.1 as "speech, life, action," and in 37.5 as "acts, speeches, practices (ἔθη)."

the term "opinion of the speaker" are, and in particular what its relationship is to Aristotle's entechnic proofs that are "through (or in) the character of the speaker" (ἐν τῷ ἤθει τοῦ λέγοντος *Rhet*. 1.2 1356a2–3), are questions that have not been settled. Underlying these questions and distinctions, however, there appears to be a very different way of understanding what a "proof" (πίστις) is. In his *Rhetoric* (1.1 1354a21–6) Aristotle complains against those who ignore *pisteis*, but that complaint does not seem properly directed at this text inasmuch as chs. 7–17 are devoted to them.

In the Greek text I have largely followed the Budé edition of Pierre Chiron (2002) while also consulting the excellent Teubner editions of Manfred Fuhrmann (1966, 2000). Students of the Greek text should consult these editions for exhaustive reports and discussion. I will mention two points, however. First, Fuhrmann was inclined to adopt the reading of the Hibeh papyrus wherever possible, which results in a sort of hybrid edition whose parents are separated by hundreds of years, whereas Chiron prints, and translates, wording from both the manuscript tradition and the papyrus. I have not found the divergence between the two to be of such great significance and have generally followed the manuscript tradition, reporting the papyrus readings in the apparatus. Second, in several places I have been perhaps even more convinced than Chiron of the fidelity of the best of the manuscripts, N (*Neapolitanus gr.* 137 [fourteenth century]), and so sought to preserve its readings. In a very few places I have sought to venture my own readings. Divider lines in my text mark (|) the beginning of every fifth line of a Bekker column and (||) the beginning of a new column (a or b); when Bekker's

lineation would otherwise split a word, the divider appears after that word.

I wish to acknowledge the help of the International Society for the History of Rhetoric, as well as my own university, which allowed me to spend several weeks in the rhetorically stimulating atmosphere of the Seminar für allgemeine Rhetorik in Tübingen while I was preparing this text and translation. My thanks are due also to Pierre Chiron and Marie-Pierre Noël, the organizers, as well as the other participants in a very productive colloquium on the *Rhetoric to Alexander* in Paris during my time in Europe.

SIGLA

Earlier Greek Codices

Recension A

F = *Laurentianus* 60, 18 (ca. 1427)
C = *Parisinus gr.* 2039 (15th cent.)
U = *Utinensis gr.* 3 (15th cent.)
H = *Matritensis* 4632 (ca. 1462)
P = *Vaticanus gr.* (15th cent.)
a = *consensus* FCUHP

Recension B

N = *Neapolitanus gr.* 137 (14th cent.)

Later Greek Codices

Recension A

O = Vaticanus Ottobonianus gr. 178 (ca. 1485)

Recension B

A =	*Parisinus gr.* 2038 (15th cent.)
B =	*Urbinas* 47 (15th cent.)
Cant. =	*Cantabrigiensis* 191 (ca. 1441)
D =	*Laurentianus* 86, 19 (15th cent.)
E =	*Laurentianus* 31, 14 (15th cent.)
G =	*Marcianus gr.* 215 (15th cent.)
M =	*Matritensis* 4684 (14th cent.)
V =	*Palatinus Vaticanus gr.* 160 (15th cent.)

Papyrus

Π =	Papyrus Hibeh 26 (ca. 285–250 BC), in B. P. Grenfell-Hunt and A. S. Hunt, eds., *The Hibeh Papyri*, part I, n. 26, pp. 114–38. London, 1906.

Latin Codices

Lat.$^{\alpha}$ =	*Vaticanus lat.* 2995 (14th cent.)
Lat.$^{\beta}$ =	*Urbanensis* 8 (14th cent.)
ρ =	consensus Lat.$^{\alpha\beta}$
Lat.γ =	*Vaticanus lat*. 2083 (c. 1284)

Ancient Commentators

Athenaeus, *Deipnosophistae*
Quintilian, *Institutio oratoriae*
Syrianus, *In Hermogenem Commentaria*

Modern Editions and Commentators (Cited in the Apparatus)

(Ald.) *Rhetores Graeci*, pp. 235r–268v, by Aldus Manutius. Venice, 1508. (*editio princeps*)

Bekker, I. *Aristotelis opera.* Berlin, 1831.

Buhle, T. *Aristotelis opera omnia graece.* Vol. 5, pp. 15–183. Strasbourg, 1791–1800.

Chiron, P. *Ps.-Aristote, Rhétorique à Alexandre.* Paris, 2002.

Didot, A. F. *Aristotelis opera omnia graece et latine.* Vol. 2, pp. 347–73. Lyon, 1848.

Finkh[1], C. E. *Commentatio de auctore rhetoricae, quae dicitur ad Alexandrum.* Heilbronn, 1849.

Finkh[2], C. E. Review of Spengel, *Neue Jahrbücher für Philologie und Pädagogik* 69 (1854) = 630–46.

Forster, E. S. *De Rhetorica ad Alexandrum.* In *The Works of Aristotle Translated into English*, vol. 11, edited by W. D. Ross. Oxford, 1924.

Fuhr, K. "Rezensionen und Anzeigen: The Hibeh Papyri. Part I," *Berliner philologische Woche* 26 (1906) = col. 1416–21.

Fuhrmann, M. *Anaximenis ars rhetorica.* Leipzig, 1966[1], Munich and Leipzig, 2000[2].

Halm, C. "Ad Anaximenis artem rhetoricam," *Philologus* 1 (1846) = 576–81.

Kassel, R. "Textvorschläge zur Rhetorik des Anaximenes," *Philologus* 111 (1967) = 122–26.

Kayser[1], K. L. Review of Spengel[1], *Neue Jahrbücher für Philologie und Pädagogik* 70 (1854) = 271–96.

Kayser[2], K. L. "Beiträge zur Kritik des Antiphon,

Andocides, und Anaximenes," *Rheinisches Museum* 16 (1861) = 62–81.

Patillon, M. "Aristote, Corax, Anaximène et les autres dans la *Rhétorique à Alexandre*," *Revue des Études Grecques* 110 (1997) = 104–25.

Philelphus, F. Latin translation (1491). In C. A. Brandis, *Aristotelis opera*, vol. 3, pp. 727–42. Berlin, 1831.

Rackham, H. Aristotle XVI, *Loeb Classical Library* 317. London, 1937.

Sauppe, H. "Zu Anaximenes' Rhetorik," *Philologus* 15 (1860) = 626–37.

(Sp.[1]) Spengel, L. *Anaximenis Ars Rhetorica quae vulgo fertur Aristotleis ad Alexandrum*. Zurich and Wintertur, 1844.

(Sp.[2]) Spengel, L., and C. Hammer. *Rhetores Graeci*. Vol. 1. Leipzig, 1894.

Stahr, A. *Aristotelia*. Vol. 2, p. 232. Halle, 1832.

Usener, H. *Quaestiones Anaximeneae*. Göttingen, 1856.

Victorius (Pier Vettori). (after 1508) Emendations in the margins of a copy of the Aldine (Ald.) edition located in the Munich library.

Zwierlein, O. "Zum Text der Anaximenes-Rhetorik," *Rheinisches Museum* 112 (1969) = 72–84.

[ΑΡΙΣΤΟΤΕΛΟΥΣ] ΡΗΤΟΡΙΚΗ ΠΡΟΣ ΑΛΕΞΑΝΔΡΟΝ

Ἀριστοτέλης Ἀλεξάνδρῳ εὖ πράττειν

1420a6 Ἐπέστειλάς μοι ὅτι πολλάκις πολλοὺς πέπομφας πρὸς ἡμᾶς τοὺς διαλεξομένους ὑπὲρ τοῦ γραφῆναί σοι τὰς μεθόδους τῶν πολιτικῶν λόγων· ἐγὼ δὲ οὐ διὰ ῥᾳθυμίαν ὑπερεβαλόμην ἐν τούτοις τοῖς χρόνοις, ἀλ-
10 λὰ διὰ τὸ ζητεῖν | οὕτως ὑπὲρ αὐτῶν γραφῆναί σοι διηκριβωμένως ὡς οὐδεὶς ἄλλος γέγραφε τῶν περὶ ταῦτα πραγματευομένων. [2] ταύτην δὲ εἰκότως τὴν διάνοιαν εἶχον· ὥσπερ γὰρ ἐσθῆτα σπουδάζεις τὴν εὐπρεπεστάτην τῶν λοιπῶν ἀνθρώπων ἔχειν, οὕτω δύναμιν λόγων λαβεῖν ἐστί σοι πειρατέον τὴν εὐδοξο-
15 τάτην. | πολὺ γὰρ κάλλιόν ἐστι καὶ βασιλικώτερον τὴν ψυχὴν ἔχειν εὐγνωμονοῦσαν ἢ τὴν ἕξιν τοῦ σώματος ὁρᾶν εὐειματοῦσαν. [3] καὶ γὰρ ἄτοπόν ἐστι τὸν τοῖς ἔργοις πρωτεύοντα φαίνεσθαι τῶν τυχόντων τοῖς λόγοις ὑστερίζοντα, καὶ ταῦτα εἰδότα ὅτι τοῖς μὲν ἐν
20 δημοκρατίᾳ πολιτευομένοις | ἡ ἀναφορὰ περὶ πάντων τῶν πραγμάτων εἰς τὸν νόμον ἐστί, τοῖς δ' ὑπὸ τὴν τῆς βασιλείας ἡγεμονίαν τεταγμένοις πρὸς λόγον. [4] ὥσπερ οὖν τὰς αὐτονόμους τῶν πόλεων διορθοῦν

[ARISTOTLE'S][1] RHETORIC TO ALEXANDER

Aristotle to Alexander: Prosper ![2]

[1] You wrote to me that you have sent many, many envoys to us to discuss my describing for you the methods for writing political speeches. I did not put it off during this time because of laziness but because I sought to write for you in more detail than anyone else has written who has dealt with these matters. [2] This was my reasoning: just as you take it seriously to have the most striking clothing of anyone, so you ought to try to achieve the most highly regarded ability in speech. It is much finer and more royal to have a thoughtful soul than to see one's body well dressed. [3] And it is odd for the man who is foremost in action to take second place to ordinary people in speech even though he knows that although for those participating in democratic politics reference in all matters is to the law, for those governed under royal rule it is to speech. [4] So just as it has been the custom for common law to direct the

[1] It is generally agreed that Aristotle is not the author of the work or the letter. See the Introduction.

[2] This form of address is used also in the *Letters* of Plato.

εἴωθεν ἐπὶ τὸ κάλλιστον ἄγων ὁ κοινὸς νόμος, οὕτω τοὺς ὑπὸ τὴν σὴν βασιλείαν καθεστῶτας ἄγειν δύ-
25 ναιτ' ἂν | ἐπὶ τὸ συμφέρον ὁ σὸς λόγος. καὶ γὰρ ὁ νόμος ἐστὶν ὡς ἁπλῶς εἰπεῖν λόγος ὡρισμένος καθ' ὁμολογίαν κοινὴν πόλεως, μηνύων πῶς δεῖ πράττειν ἕκαστα.

[5] πρὸς δὲ τούτοις οὐκ ἄδηλον ὡς οἶμαί σοι τοῦτό ἐστιν ὅτι τοὺς μὲν λόγῳ χρωμένους καὶ μετὰ τούτου
30 πάντα πράττειν προαιρουμένους ὡς ὄντας | καλούς τε καὶ ἀγαθοὺς ἐπαινοῦμεν, τοὺς δὲ ἄνευ λόγου τι ||
1420b5 ποιοῦντας ὡς ὄντας ὠμοὺς καὶ θηριώδεις μισοῦμεν. [6] διὰ τούτου καὶ ‹τοὺς›[1] κακοὺς τὴν αὐτῶν κακίαν ἐμφανίσαντας ἐκολάσαμεν, καὶ τοὺς ἀγαθοὺς δηλώσαντας αὐτῶν τὴν ἀρετὴν ἐζηλώσαμεν. οὕτω καὶ τῶν μελλόντων κακῶν ἀποτροπὴν εὑρήκαμεν καὶ τῶν
10 ὑπαρχόντων ἀγαθῶν ὄνησιν ἔσχομεν. καὶ διὰ | τούτου καὶ τὰς ἐπιούσας δυσχερείας ἐφύγομεν καὶ τὰς μὴ προσούσας ἡμῖν ὠφελείας ἐπορισάμεθα. ὥσπερ γὰρ βίος ἄλυπος αἱρετός, οὕτω λόγος συνετὸς ἀγαπητός. [7] εἰδέναι δέ σε δεήσει ὅτι παραδείγματά ἐστι τοῖς πλείστοις τῶν ἀνθρώπων τοῖς μὲν ὁ νόμος, τοῖς δὲ ὁ
15 σὸς βίος καὶ λόγος. ὅπως | οὖν διαφέρων ᾖς πάντων Ἑλλήνων καὶ βαρβάρων, πᾶσάν ἐστί σοι σπουδὴν ποιητέον ἵνα τὴν ἐκ τούτων ἀπομίμησιν οἱ περὶ ταῦτα διατρίβοντες τοῖς τῆς ἀρετῆς στοιχείοις καλλιγραφούμενοι μὴ πρὸς τὰ φαῦλα σφᾶς αὐτοὺς ἄγωσιν, ἀλλὰ τῆς αὐτῆς ἀρετῆς μετέχειν ἐπιθυμῶσιν. [8] ἔτι
20 δὲ τὸ | βουλεύεσθαι τῶν περὶ τὸν ἄνθρωπον θειότατόν

independent cities by guiding on the basis of what is noblest, your speech may be able to guide the cities subject to your kingship with a view to advantage. For, simply stated, law is speech defined according to the common agreement of a city, revealing how everything must be done.[3]

[5] In addition, as is not unclear to you I think, we praise those who use speech and choose to do everything by it as being good and noble, but we hate those who do anything without speech as being crude and savage. [6] Through it we stop the wicked from manifesting their wickedness, and we emulate the good who make their virtue clear. In this way we also discovered defense against future evils and enjoyment of present goods. Also through it we avoided oncoming difficulties and we provided benefits that we did not have before.[4] For just as a life without pain is preferable, so speech with intelligence is valuable. [7] It will be necessary for you to know that for most people either the law or your life and speech are models. In order that you may surpass all Greeks and non-Greeks, you must make every effort that those who spend time on these matters, by artfully drawing a copy of them with elements of virtue, do not lead themselves into corruption but desire to share in the same virtue. [8] Moreover, to deliberate is the most divine aspect of humanity, so you must not ex-

[3] The passage is quoted by Athenaeus 11.508a. Cf. 1.8 and 2.13.

[4] Cf. Isocr. 3.7–8 and 15.255.

---

[1] τοὺς add. Stahr cf. Isocr. 15.255

ἐστιν, ὥστε οὐκ εἰς τὰ πάρεργα καὶ μηδενὸς ἄξια τὴν σπουδήν ἐστί σοι καταναλωτέον, ἀλλὰ τὴν μητρόπολιν αὐτὴν τοῦ καλῶς βουλεύεσθαι μαθεῖν βουλητέον. τίς γὰρ δὴ τοῦτ' ἂν ἀμφισβητήσειε τῶν νοῦν
25 ἐχόντων ὅτι τὸ μὲν πράττειν μὴ βουλευσάμενον | σημεῖόν ἐστιν ἀνοίας, τὸ δὲ κατὰ τὴν ὑφήγησιν τοῦ λόγου συντελεῖν τι τῶν ὑπ' ἐκείνου παραγγελθέντων παιδείας; [9] ἰδεῖν δέ ἐστι πάντας τοὺς ἄριστα τῶν Ἑλλήνων πολιτευομένους λόγῳ πρῶτον ἢ τοῖς ἔργοις συγγινομένους, πρὸς δὲ τούτοις καὶ τοὺς μέγιστον
30 ἀξίωμα τῶν βαρβάρων ἔχοντας | τούτῳ πρὸ τῶν πρα-
1421a γμάτων χρωμένους, εἰδότας καλῶς ὡς || ἀκρόπολίς ἐστι σωτηρίας ἡ διὰ τοῦ λόγου γινομένη τοῦ συμφέροντος θεωρία. ταύτην ἀπόρθητον οἰητέον, οὐ τὴν ἐκ τῶν οἰκοδομημάτων ἀσφαλῆ πρὸς σωτηρίαν εἶναι νομιστέον.

[10] ἀλλὰ γὰρ ὀκνῶ ἔτι πλείω γράφειν, μή ποτε
5 καλλωπίζεσθαι | δόξω περὶ τῶν ἀκριβῶς γνωριζομένων ὡς οὐχ ὁμολογουμένων πίστεις ἐπιφέρων. διόπερ ἀφήσω, ἐκεῖνα μόνον εἰπὼν περὶ ὧν ἔνεστι λέγειν εἰς ἅπαντα τὸν βίον, ὅτι τοῦτό ἐστιν, ᾧ διαφέρομεν τῶν λοιπῶν ζῴων· τοῦτο οὖν καὶ ἡμεῖς διαφερόντως τῶν
10 λοιπῶν ἕξομεν ἀνθρώπων οἱ μεγίστης τιμῆς | ὑπὸ τοῦ δαιμονίου τετυχηκότες. [11] ἐπιθυμίᾳ μὲν γὰρ καὶ θυμῷ καὶ τοῖς τοιούτοις χρῆται καὶ τὰ λοιπὰ ζῷα πάντα, λόγῳ δὲ οὐδὲν τῶν λοιπῶν χωρὶς ἀνθρώπων. ἀτοπώτατον οὖν ἂν εἴη πάντων εἰ τούτῳ μόνῳ τῶν λοιπῶν ζῴων εὐδαιμονέστερον βιοῦντες τὸ αἴτιον τοῦ

pend effort on secondary tasks and those of no account, but you must desire to come to know the mother city of noble deliberation itself. Who of those with sense would ever dispute that action without deliberation is a sign of ignorance, but to accomplish something under the guidance of speech is a sign of the education of those who have been instructed by it? [9] One can see that all the Greeks who engage in civic matters interact best through speech first, and then by actions. Moreover, the non-Greeks who have the greatest worth use it first before acting since they well know that observation of advantage through speech is a stronghold of safety. This stronghold must be thought indestructible; the one secured by buildings must not be credited with safety.

[10] I am reluctant to write more, to appear to be showing off by introducing proofs about matters that are understood in detail as if they were not agreed on. Therefore I shall stop, discussing only what I can relate to life in general, that is, how we are different from the rest of the animals; this way we can also be different from the rest of the people, we who have met with the greatest honor from the Divine. [11] All the rest of the animals utilize appetite and passion and so on, but none of the rest except humans utilizes speech. So it would be the oddest thing of all if we lived more happily than the rest of the animals for this reason alone and yet gave up the cause of our living well and

15 καλῶς εἶναι διὰ ῥᾳθυμίαν ἀφεῖμεν | κατολιγωρήσαντες. [12] διακελεύομαι δή σοι πάλαι παρακεκλημένῳ τῆς τῶν λόγων ἀντέχεσθαι φιλοσοφίας. καθάπερ γάρ ἐστι φυλακτικὸν σώματος ὑγίεια, οὕτω ψυχῆς φυλακτικὸν καθέστηκε παιδεία. ταύτης γὰρ προηγουμένης οὐ πταίειν συμβήσεταί σοι περὶ τὰς πράξεις,
20 ἀλλὰ σῴζειν | ἁπάσας ὡς ἔπος εἰπεῖν τὰς ὑπαρχούσας σοι τῶν ἀγαθῶν κτήσεις. [13] χωρὶς δὲ τῶν εἰρημένων, εἰ τὸ τοῖς ὀφθαλμοῖς βλέπειν ἡδύ, τὸ τοῖς τῆς ψυχῆς ὄμμασιν ὀξυδορκεῖν ἐστι θαυμαστόν. ἔτι δὲ ὥσπερ ὁ στρατηγός ἐστι σωτὴρ στρατοπέδου, οὕτω λόγος
25 μετὰ παιδείας ἡγεμών ἐστι βίου. ταυτὶ | μὲν οὖν καὶ τὰ τούτοις ὅμοια παραλιπεῖν νομίζω καλῶς ἡμῖν ἔχειν κατὰ τὸν ὑπάρχοντα καιρόν.

[14] ἔγραψας δέ μοι διακελευόμενος ὅπως μηδεὶς τῶν λοιπῶν ἀνθρώπων λήψεται τὸ βιβλίον τοῦτο, καὶ ταῦτα εἰδώς ὅτι, καθάπερ τοὺς ἐξ αὐτῶν γεννηθέντας
30 οἱ γεννήσαντες τῶν ὑποβαλλομένων | μᾶλλον φιλοῦσιν, οὕτως οἱ εὑρόντες τι τῶν μετεχόντων· ὥσπερ γὰρ ὑπὲρ τέκνων, οὕτω τῶν λόγων ὑπεραποτεθνήκασιν. [15] οἱ μὲν γὰρ Πάριοι λεγόμενοι σοφισταὶ διὰ τὸ μὴ τεκεῖν αὐτοὶ διὰ ῥᾳθυμίαν ἄμουσον οὐ στέργουσιν, ἀλλὰ χρήματα λαβόντες ἀποκηρύττουσι. διὰ τοῦτο
35 οὖν ἐγώ σοι παρακελεύομαι | διαφυλάττειν οὕτω τοὺς λόγους τούτους ὅπως νέοι καθεστῶτες ὑπὸ μηδενὸς χρήμασι διαφθαρήσονται, κοσμίως δὲ μετὰ σοῦ συμβιώσαντες εἰς ἡλικίαν ἐλθόντες δόξης ἀκηράτου τεύξονται.

considered it of little account because of laziness. [12] I truly encourage you—who got the advice long ago—that you persist in the study of speeches.[5] Although health is protective of the body, education has become protective of the soul. When it leads, chances are that you will not stumble in your actions but preserve almost all the goods you have now acquired. [13] Beyond what has been said, if it is pleasing to look with the eyes, it is wondrous to gaze with the eyes of the soul. Moreover, just as the general is the savior of his army, so speech, with education, is a guide in life. These and like matters, however, I think it best for us to leave aside on the present occasion.

[14] You have written directing me that none of the rest of the people should obtain this book, although you know that just as parents love their own children more than adoptive parents do, so also those who have invented something love it more than those who share in it. Just as parents die for children, so do inventors for their words. [15] The Parians, called Sophists, since they did not give birth (to speeches) themselves—because of their uncultured laziness—do not love them but make money by auctioning them off. Because of this I recommend to you to guard these words so that while still young they may not be corrupted by anyone through money, but may by living with you in an ordered way into maturity achieve undefiled glory.

[5] Literally, "philosophy of speeches."

[16] παρειλήφαμεν δέ, καθάπερ ἡμῖν ἐδήλωσε Νικάνωρ, καὶ τῶν λοιπῶν τεχνογράφων εἴ τίς τι γλαφυ-
40 ρὸν ὑπὲρ | τῶν αὐτῶν τούτων γέγραφεν ἐν ταῖς τέχναις.
1421b περιτεύξῃ δὲ || δυσὶ τούτοις βιβλίοις, ὧν τὸ μέν ἐστιν ἐμὸν ἐν ταῖς ὑπ' ἐμοῦ τέχναις Θεοδέκτῃ γραφείσαις, τὸ δὲ ἕτερον Κόρακος. [17] τὰ δὲ λοιπὰ τούτοις ἰδίᾳ πάντα γέγραπται περί τε τῶν πολιτικῶν καὶ τῶν
5 δικανικῶν παραγγελμάτων· ὅθεν πρὸς | ἑκάτερον αὐτῶν εὐπορήσεις ἐκ τῶνδε τῶν ὑπομνημάτων σοι γεγραμμένων. ἔρρωσο.]

1. Τρία[2] γένη τῶν πολιτικῶν εἰσι λόγων, τὸ μὲν δημηγορικόν, τὸ δὲ ἐπιδεικτικόν, τὸ δὲ δικανικόν. εἴδη δὲ τούτων ἑπτά, προτρεπτικόν, ἀποτρεπτικόν, ἐγκωμι-
10 αστικόν, ψεκτικόν, | κατηγορικόν, ἀπολογητικόν, καὶ ἐξεταστικὸν, ἢ αὐτὸ καθ' ἑαυτὸ ἢ πρὸς ἄλλο. [2] τὰ μὲν οὖν εἴδη τῶν λόγων τοσαῦτα ἀριθμῷ ἐστι, χρησόμεθα δὲ αὐτοῖς ἔν τε ταῖς κοιναῖς δημηγορίαις καὶ ταῖς περὶ τὰ συμβόλαια δικαιολογίαις καὶ ταῖς ἰδίαις
15 ὁμιλίαις. οὕτω δ' ἂν ἑτοιμότατον λέγειν περὶ | αὐτῶν δυνηθείημεν, εἰ καὶ καθ' ἓν ἕκαστον εἶδος ἀπολαβόντες ἀπαριθμησαίμεθα τὰς δυνάμεις αὐτῶν καὶ τὰς χρήσεις καὶ τὰς πράξεις.[3] καὶ πρῶτον μὲν τὰς προτροπὰς καὶ ἀποτροπάς, ἐπείπερ ἐν ταῖς ἰδίαις ὁμιλίαις καὶ ταῖς κοιναῖς δημηγορίαις ἐν τοῖς μάλιστα αὐτῶν
20 χρῆσίς ἐστι, | διέλθοιμεν ἄν.

[3] καθόλου μὲν οὖν εἰπεῖν, προτροπὴ μέν ἐστιν ἐπὶ προαιρέσεις ἢ λόγους ἢ πράξεις παράκλησις, ἀποτροπὴ δὲ ἀπὸ προαιρέσεων ἢ λόγων ἢ πράξεων δια-

[16] Just as Nicanor showed us, we have borrowed from the rest of the handbook writers if any has written anything reliable about the same points in their handbooks. You will find two of these books. One of them is mine, in my *Handbooks Written for Theodectes*; the second is Corax's. [17] They have described the rest of the points regarding both political and forensic precepts separately. From them you will be well supplied for both areas from these notes that have been written for you. Farewell.]

1. There are three genres of political speeches: demegoric, epideictic, and forensic. Of these there are seven species: proposition, opposition, praise, criticism, prosecution, defense, and investigation (either itself by itself or with another species). [2] That is how many species of speeches there are, and we use them in public democratic debates, in legal pleading over contracts, and in private discussions. We could speak about these matters most readily if we took them up individually and enumerated their capacities, their uses, and their practices,[6] and if we went through proposition and opposition first, since their use is most common in private discussions and in public democratic debates.

[3] Generally speaking, a proposition speech is an appeal to choices, words, or actions, and an opposition speech is a deterrence of choices, words, or actions.

[6] Spengel suggested "arrangements," the subject of 29–37. "Uses" are discussed in 6–14.

---

[2] Τρία N a : Δύο Syrianus fortasse recte : *iudicialem et contionalem generalis partes esse voluit* Quintilian 3.4.9

[3] *πράξεις* codd. : *τάξεις* Sp.[1] fortasse recte

κώλυσις. [4] οὕτω δὲ τούτων διωρισμένων, τὸν μὲν προτρέποντα χρὴ δεικνύειν ταῦτα ἐφ᾽ ἃ παρακαλεῖ
25 δίκαια ὄντα καὶ νόμιμα καὶ συμφέροντα | καὶ καλὰ καὶ ἡδέα καὶ ῥᾴδια πραχθῆναι· εἰ δὲ μή, δυνατά τε δεικτέον, ὅταν ἐπὶ δυσχερῆ παρακαλῇ, καὶ ὡς ἀναγκαῖα ταῦτα ποιεῖν ἐστι. [5] τὸν δὲ ἀποτρέποντα δεῖ διὰ τῶν ἐναντίων κώλυσιν ἐπιφέρειν, ὡς οὐ δίκαιον οὐδὲ νόμιμόν ἐστιν οὐδὲ συμφέρον οὐδὲ καλὸν οὐδὲ ἡδὺ οὐδὲ
30 δυνατὸν πράττειν | τοῦτο, εἰ δὲ μή, ὡς ἐργῶδες καὶ οὐκ ἀναγκαῖον. ἅπασαι δὲ αἱ πράξεις μετέχουσι τούτων ἀμφοτέρων, ὥστε μηδένα τὴν ἑτέραν[4] τῶν ὑποθέσεων ἔχοντα λόγων ἀπορεῖν.

[6] ὧν μὲν οὖν ὀρέγεσθαι δεῖ τοὺς προτρέποντας καὶ ἀποτρέποντας ταῦτά ἐστιν· ὁρίσασθαι δὲ πειρά-
35 σομαι τούτων ἕκαστον τί ἐστι καὶ | δεῖξαι πόθεν αὐτῶν εἰς τοὺς λόγους εὐπορήσομεν. [7] δίκαιον μὲν οὖν ἐστι τὸ τῶν ἁπάντων ἢ τὸ τῶν πλείστων ἔθος ἄγραφον, διορίζον τὰ καλὰ καὶ τὰ αἰσχρά. τοῦτο δ᾽ ἐστι τὸ γονέας τιμᾶν καὶ φίλους εὖ ποιεῖν καὶ τοῖς εὐεργέταις χάριν ἀποδιδόναι· ταῦτα γὰρ καὶ τὰ τούτοις ὅμοια οὐ |
40 προστάττουσι τοῖς ἀνθρώποις οἱ γεγραμμένοι νόμοι
1422a ποιεῖν, || ἀλλ᾽ ἔθει ἀγράφῳ καὶ κοινῷ νόμῳ νομίζεται. τὰ μὲν οὖν δίκαια ταῦτά ἐστιν. [8] νόμος δ᾽ ἐστιν ὁμολόγημα πόλεως κοινὸν διὰ γραμμάτων προστάττον πῶς χρὴ πράττειν ἕκαστα. [9] συμφέρον δ᾽ ἐστὶ
5 τῶν ὑπαρχόντων ἀγαθῶν φυλακὴ | ἢ τῶν μὴ προσόντων κτῆσις ἢ τῶν ὑπαρχόντων κακῶν ἀποβολὴ ἢ τῶν προσδοκωμένων γενήσεσθαι βλαβερῶν διακώλυσις.

[4] Given these definitions, the proposing speaker must demonstrate that those things for which he is appealing are just, legal, advantageous, noble, pleasant, and easy to do; if not, he must demonstrate that they are possible whenever he is exhorting something difficult, and that they are necessary to do. [5] But the opposing speaker must convey deterrence through the opposite, that to do it is neither just, nor legal, nor advantageous, nor noble, nor pleasant, nor possible; if not, that it requires hard work and is unnecessary. All actions involve both of these, so that no one taking either of these positions will be at a loss for words.

[6] These, then, are the things that proposing and opposing speakers ought to strive for. I shall try to define what each of them is and show where we shall be well supplied with them for the speeches. [7] "Just" is defined as the unwritten custom of all, or of most, which distinguishes the noble from the base. That is, to honor one's parents, to treat friends well, and to return favors to benefactors. The written laws do not direct people to do these and like things, but they are regulated by unwritten custom and common law. These are the things that are just. [8] "Law" is a common agreement of a city directing in writing how everything must be done. [9] The "advantageous" is defined as protection of existing goods, acquisition of nonpresent goods, disposal of existing harms, or the prevention of damages that are expected to occur.

---

[4] *μηδένα τὴν ἑτέραν* Kayser[1] : *μηδετέραν* N a

[10] διαιρήσεις δὲ τοῦτο τοῖς μὲν ἰδιώταις εἰς σῶμα καὶ ψυχὴν καὶ τὰ ἐπίκτητα. σώματι μὲν οὖν ἐστι συμφέρον ῥώμη, κάλλος, ὑγίεια, ψυχῇ δὲ ἀνδρεία,
10 σοφία, | δικαιοσύνη· τὰ δὲ ἐπίκτητα φίλοι, χρήματα, κτήματα· τὰ δ' ἐναντία τούτοις ἀσύμφορα. [11] πόλει δὲ συμφέροντα τὰ τοιαῦτά ἐστιν· ὁμόνοια, δυνάμεις πρὸς πόλεμον, χρήματα καὶ προσόδων εὐπορία, συμμάχων ἀρετὴ καὶ πλῆθος· καὶ συλλήβδην ἅπαντα τὰ
15 τούτοις ὁμοιότροπα συμφέροντα νομίζομεν, | τὰ δὲ τούτοις ἐναντία ἀσύμφορα. [12] καλὰ δ' ἐστὶν ἀφ' ὧν εὐδοξία τις καὶ τιμή τις ἔνδοξος γενήσεται τοῖς πράξασιν. ἡδέα δὲ τὰ χαρὰν ἐργαζόμενα. ῥᾴδια δὲ τὰ μετὰ ἐλαχίστου χρόνου καὶ πόνου καὶ δαπάνης ἐπιτελούμενα. δυνατὰ δὲ πάντα τὰ ἐνδεχόμενα γίνεσθαι.
20 ἀναγκαῖα δὲ | τὰ μὴ ἐφ' ἡμῖν ὄντα πράττειν, ἀλλ' ὡς ἐξ ἀνάγκης θείας ἢ ἀνθρωπίνης οὕτως ὄντα.

[13] τὰ μὲν οὖν δίκαια καὶ τὰ νόμιμα καὶ τὰ συμφέροντα καὶ τὰ καλὰ καὶ τὰ ἡδέα καὶ τὰ ῥᾴδια καὶ τὰ δυνατὰ καὶ τὰ ἀναγκαῖα ταῦτά ἐστιν· εὐπορήσομεν δὲ περὶ τούτων λέγειν ἐξ αὐτῶν τε τῶν προειρημένων |
25 καὶ τῶν ὁμοίων τούτοις καὶ τῶν ἐναντίων αὐτοῖς καὶ τῶν ἤδη κεκριμένων ἢ ὑπὸ θεῶν ἢ ἀνθρώπων ἐνδόξων ἢ ὑπὸ κριτῶν[5] ἢ ὑπὸ τῶν ἀνταγωνιστῶν ἡμῖν.

[14] τὸ μὲν οὖν δίκαιον οἷόν ἂν ᾖ[6] πρότερον ἡμῖν δεδήλωται· τὸ δὲ ὅμοιον τῷ δικαίῳ τοιόνδε ἐστίν·
30 "ὥσπερ γὰρ δίκαιον νομίζομεν τὸ τοῖς | γονεῦσι πείθε-

[10] For individuals you will distinguish it with regard to body, soul, and possessions: for the body, strength, beauty, and health are advantageous; for the soul courage, wisdom, and a sense of justice; possessions include friends, money, and property. The opposite of these are disadvantageous. [11] For a city the following sorts of things are advantageous: harmony, military capacities, money and a good supply of revenues, and a quality and quantity of allies. In sum, we think everything like these advantageous and their contraries disadvantageous. [12] "Noble" are the things from which a good reputation and reputable honor accrues to those who do them. "Pleasant" are those things that produce joy. "Easy" are those things accomplished in the least time and with the least effort and cost. "Possible" are all those things that have the possibility to occur. "Necessary" are things for us to do, not because of ourselves but because of divine or human necessity.

[13] These then are things just, legal, advantageous, noble, pleasant, easy, possible, and necessary. We shall be well supplied to speak about them from what has been said here earlier, from things similar and opposite to them, and from what has been judged already, either by the gods or by reputable[7] people, by judges, or by our adversaries.

[14] What "the just" is we have made clear earlier; what is similar to the just is of this sort: "Just as we think it just to

[7] While the mss. attach "reputable" to "people," the papyrus attaches it to "judges."

---

[5] ἀνθρώπων ἐνδόξων ἢ ὑπὸ κριτῶν codd. : ἀνθρ[ώ]π[ων ἢ] ὑπ᾽ ἐ[νδόξ]ων ἢ [κρι]τῶν Π

[6] ἄν ᾖ N FCUP : ἐστι Sp.[1] cf. 1.17 1422b2 and 1.20 1422b25

σθαι, τὸν αὐτὸν τρόπον προσήκει τοὺς υἱεῖς μιμεῖσθαι τὰς τῶν πατέρων πράξεις·" καὶ "καθάπερ τοὺς εὖ ποιήσαντας ἀντευεργετεῖν δίκαιόν ἐστιν, οὕτω τοὺς μηδὲν ἡμᾶς κακὸν ἐργασαμένους δίκαιόν ἐστι μὴ βλάπτειν." [15] τὸ μὲν οὖν ὅμοιον τῷ δικαίῳ τὸν
35 τρόπον τοῦτον δεῖ λαμβάνειν· ἐκ δὲ | τῶν ἐναντίων <ὧδε[7]> χρὴ καταφανὲς ποιεῖν αὐτὸ [τὸ παράδειγμα]·[8] "καθάπερ γὰρ τοὺς κακόν τι ποιήσαντας δίκαιόν ἐστι τιμωρεῖσθαι, οὕτω καὶ τοὺς εὐεργετήσαντας προσήκει ἀντευεργετεῖν." [16] τὸ δὲ κεκριμένον ὑπό τινων ἐνδόξων δίκαιον οὕτω λήψῃ· "ἀλλ' οὐχ ἡμεῖς μόνοι
40 μισοῦμεν καὶ κακῶς ποιοῦμεν | τοὺς ἐχθρούς, ἀλλὰ καὶ Ἀθηναῖοι καὶ Λακεδαιμόνιοι δίκαιον εἶναι κρίνουσι τοὺς ἐχθροὺς τιμωρεῖσθαι."

1422b [17] τὸ μὲν οὖν δίκαιον || οὕτω μετιὼν πολλαχῶς λήψῃ· τὸ δὲ νόμιμον αὐτὸ μὲν οἷόν ἐστιν ὥρισται ἡμῖν πρότερον, δεῖ δέ, ὅπου ἂν ᾖ χρήσιμον, αὐτόν τε τὸν ἀγορεύοντα καὶ τὸν νόμον[9] λαμβάνειν, εἶτα τὸ ὅμοιον
5 τῷ γεγραμμένῳ νόμῳ. εἴη δ' ἂν τοιόνδε· "ὥσπερ | γὰρ ὁ νομοθέτης μεγίσταις ζημίαις τοὺς κλέπτας ἐκόλασεν, οὕτω δεῖ καὶ τοὺς ἐξαπατῶντας μάλιστα τιμωρεῖσθαι· καὶ γὰρ οὗτοι κλέπτουσι τὴν διάνοιαν·" καὶ "καθάπερ ὁ νομοθέτης κληρονόμους πεποίηκε τοὺς ἐγγυτάτω γένους ὄντας τοῖς ἄπαισιν ἀποθνῄσκουσιν, οὕτω καὶ
10 τῶν τοῦ ἀπελευθέρου χρημάτων | ἐμὲ νῦν προσήκει κύριον γενέσθαι· τῶν γὰρ ἀπελευθερωσάντων αὐτὸν τετελευτηκότων ἐγγυτάτω γένους αὐτὸς ὢν καὶ τῶν ἀπελευθέρων δίκαιος ἂν εἴην ἄρχειν." [18] τὸ μὲν οὖν

obey one's parents, in the same manner it is fitting for sons to imitate their fathers' actions"; and "Just as it is just to reciprocate those who do good, so is it just for us not to harm those doing nothing wrong to us." [15] It is necessary to devise what is similar to the just in this manner. But from the contraries one must make plain (the opposite):[8] "Just as it is just to punish those who have done something wrong, it is also fitting to reciprocate benefactors." [16] You will devise what is judged just by some reputable people in this way: "It is not we alone who hate and do harm to enemies, but the Athenians and Spartans judge it just to punish their enemies."

[17] By proceeding in this way you will get hold of "the just" in many ways. "The legal" itself, what it is, has been defined earlier, but when it is useful, one must take up the speaker himself and the law, and then what is similar to the written law, as follows: "Just as the legislator restrains thieves with the greatest punishments, one must also punish deceivers in particular, for they steal one's thought"; and, "Just as the legislator has made heirs those nearest by kinship to all who die, it is also fitting for me to have authority over the money of the freedman; since I am myself closest to those who freed him and have died, I am just in having control over their freedmen." [18] What is simi-

[8] The editors have deleted the technical term "example" (*paradeigma*).

---

[7] ὧδε add. Kassel cf. 1.22 1422b37–8

[8] τὸ παράδειγμα del. Kayser[1]

[9] ἀγορεύοντα καὶ τὸν νόμον codd. : (*ipsum legislatorem et legem*) Lat.[a] : διαγορεύοντα νόμον Π

ὅμοιον τῷ νομίμῳ τοῦτον τὸν τρόπον λαμβάνεται, τὸ δὲ ἐναντίον ὧδε· "εἰ γὰρ ὁ νόμος ἀπαγορεύει τὰ δημό-
15 σια διανέμεσθαι, | δῆλον ὅτι τοὺς διαιρουμένους αὐτὰ πάντας ἀδικεῖν ὁ νομοθέτης ἔκρινεν·" "εἰ γὰρ τιμᾶσθαι οἱ νόμοι προστάττουσι τοὺς καλῶς καὶ δικαίως τῶν κοινῶν ἐπιστατήσαντας, δῆλον ὡς καὶ τοὺς τὰ δημόσια διαφθείροντας τιμωρίας ἀξίους νομίζουσιν." [19] ἐκ μὲν οὖν τῶν ἐναντίων καταφανὲς οὕτω
20 γίνεται τὸ | νόμιμον, ἐκ δὲ τῶν κεκριμένων ὧδε· "καὶ οὐ μόνον ἐγὼ τὸν νόμον τοῦτον ἕνεκα τούτων φημὶ τὸν νομοθέτην θεῖναι, ἀλλὰ καὶ πρότερον οἱ δικασταὶ διεξιόντος Λυσιθείδου παραπλήσια τοῖς νῦν ὑπ' ἐμοῦ λεγομένοις ἐψηφίσαντο ταὐτὰ περὶ τοῦ νόμου τούτου."

[20] τὸ μὲν οὖν νόμιμον οὕτω μετιόντες πολλαχῶς |
25 δείξομεν· τὸ δὲ συμφέρον αὐτὸ μὲν οἷόν ἐστιν ἐν τοῖς πρότερον ὥρισται, δεῖ δὲ λαμβάνειν εἰς τοὺς λόγους <ὡς ἐκ>[10] τῶν προειρημένων καὶ ἐκ τοῦ συμφέροντος, ἂν ὑπάρχῃ τι, καὶ μετιόντας τὸν αὐτὸν τρόπον ὅνπερ ὑπὲρ τοῦ νομίμου καὶ τοῦ δικαίου διήλθομεν, οὕτω καὶ
30 τὸ συμφέρον πολλαχῶς ἐμφανίζειν. | [21] εἴη δ' ἂν τὸ μὲν ὅμοιον τῷ συμφέροντι τοιόνδε· "ὥσπερ γὰρ ἐν τοῖς πολέμοις συμφέρει τοὺς εὐψυχοτάτους πρώτους τάττειν, οὕτως ἐν ταῖς πολιτείαις λυσιτελεῖ τοὺς φρονιμωτάτους καὶ δικαιοτάτους προεστάναι τοῦ πλήθους·" καὶ "καθάπερ τοῖς ἀνθρώποις ὑγιαίνουσι συμ-
35 φέρει φυλάττεσθαι μὴ νοσήσωσιν, | οὕτω καὶ ταῖς πόλεσιν ὁμονοούσαις συμφέρον ἐστὶ προσκοπεῖν μὴ στασιάσωσι." [22] τὰ μὲν οὖν ὅμοια τῷ συμφέροντι

lar to the legal is achieved in this manner, but the contrary is this way: "If the law forbids sharing out state funds, it is clear that the legislator has judged all those dividing them for themselves to be doing injustice"; "If the laws command that those who care for state funds nobly and justly be honored, it is clear that they think those who abuse state funds worthy of punishment." [19] The legal becomes plain from contraries in this way, and from what has been judged in the following way: "Not only do I claim that the legislator enacted this law for these reasons, but also in the past, when Lysitheides was relating very similar things to what I am saying now, the judges voted for the same interpretation of this law."

[20] By proceeding in this way we shall demonstrate the legal in many ways. "The advantageous" itself, what it is, has been defined in the earlier sections, but we must bring it into our speeches—as with what has been said before so also now with the advantageous—if there is something available, and by proceeding in the same manner in which we went through the legal and the just, in this way also we must elucidate the advantageous in many forms. [21] What is similar to the advantageous is like this: "Just as in wars it is advantageous to place the bravest at the front, so also in government it is beneficial for the most intelligent and just to lead the majority"; and, "Just as it is advantageous for healthy people to guard against becoming ill, so also for harmonious cities it is advantageous to be watchful against falling into civil strife." [22] By proceeding in this manner you will compose many things similar to

---

[10] ὡς ἐκ add. Fuhrmann

τοῦτον τὸν τρόπον μετιὼν πολλὰ ποιήσεις· ἐκ δὲ τῶν ἐναντίων ὧδέ σοι τὸ συμφέρον ἔσται καταφανές· "εἰ γὰρ λυσιτελεῖ τοὺς ἐπιεικεῖς τῶν πολιτῶν τιμᾶν, συμ-
40 φέρον ἂν εἴη καὶ | τοὺς πονηροὺς κολάζειν·" "εἰ γὰρ οἴεσθε οὐ συμφέρον εἶναι τὸ μόνους ἡμᾶς πρὸς Θη-
1423a βαίους πολεμεῖν, συμφέρον ἂν εἴη τὸ || Λακεδαιμονίους συμμάχους ποιησαμένους ἡμᾶς οὕτω Θηβαίοις πολεμεῖν." [23] ἐκ μὲν δὴ τῶν ἐναντίων οὕτω τὸ συμφέρον καταφανὲς ποιήσεις· τὸ δὲ κεκριμένον ὑπ' ἐνδόξων συμφέρον ὧδε χρὴ λαμβάνειν· "Λακεδαιμόνιοί τε γὰρ |
5 Ἀθηναίους καταπολεμήσαντες συμφέρειν αὐτοῖς ᾠήθησαν μὴ τὴν πόλιν αὐτῶν ἀνδραποδίσασθαι, καὶ πάλιν Ἀθηναῖοι [μετὰ] Θηβαίων[11] ἐξὸν αὐτοῖς ἀνοικίσαι τὴν Σπάρτην συμφέρειν σφίσιν ᾠήθησαν περιποιῆσαι Λακεδαιμονίους."

[24] περὶ μὲν οὖν τοῦ δικαίου καὶ τοῦ νομίμου καὶ
10 τοῦ συμφέροντος οὕτω μετιὼν | εὐπορήσεις· τὸ δὲ καλὸν καὶ τὸ ῥᾴδιον καὶ τὸ ἡδὺ καὶ τὸ δυνατὸν καὶ τὸ ἀναγκαῖον ὁμοιοτρόπως τούτοις μέτιθι. καὶ περὶ μὲν τούτων ἐντεῦθεν εὐπορήσομεν.

2. Πάλιν δὲ διορισώμεθα καὶ περὶ πόσων καὶ περὶ ποίων καὶ <ἐκ> τίνων[12] ἔν τε τοῖς βουλευτηρίοις καὶ
15 ταῖς ἐκκλησίαις συμβουλεύομεν. | ἂν γὰρ τούτων ἕκαστα σαφῶς ἐπιστώμεθα, τοὺς μὲν ἰδίους λόγους αὐτὰ τὰ πράγματα καθ' ἑκάστην ἡμῖν συμβουλίαν παραδώσει, τὰς δὲ κοινὰς ἰδέας ἐκ πολλοῦ προειδότες ἐπιφέρειν ἐφ' ἑκάσταις τῶν πράξεων ῥᾳδίως δυνησόμεθα. τούτων οὖν ἕνεκα διαιρετέον ἡμῖν περὶ ὧν κοινῇ |

the advantageous. But the advantageous will be plain to you from contraries in the following way: "If it is beneficial to honor honest citizens, it would also be advantageous to restrain the base"; "If you think it disadvantageous for us to wage war against Thebes by ourselves, it would be advantageous to make an alliance with Sparta and then wage war against Thebes." [23] You will make the advantageous plain from opposites in this way. But it is necessary to devise what has been judged advantageous by reputable men in this way: "After defeating the Athenians the Spartans thought it advantageous for themselves not to enslave their city"; and again, "The Athenians, with the Thebans, although it was possible for them to demolish Sparta, thought it advantageous for themselves to preserve the Spartans."

[24] You will be well equipped concerning the just and the legal and the advantageous by proceeding in this way. Pursue the noble, the easy, the pleasant, the possible, and the necessary in ways similar to these. We shall be well equipped concerning these matters from there.

2. Now let us determine how many things, what sorts, and the means by which we advise about them in both councils and assemblies. If we clearly understand each of these, the subject matter itself will provide the individual speeches at each of our deliberations, and by first knowing the general forms by and large we shall easily be able to apply them to each of our undertakings. For this reason we must analyze the things about which all deliberate in com-

---

11 *μετὰ*] *Θηβαίων* Π : omit. codd.

12 *καὶ* <*ἐκ*> *τίνων* Usener : *καὶ τίνων* N a *ρ* : del. Kayser[1]

20 βουλεύονται πάντες. [2] ἐν κεφαλαίῳ μὲν οὖν εἰπεῖν, εἰσὶν ἑπτὰ τὸν ἀριθμὸν προθέσεις περὶ ὧν δημηγορήσομεν· ἀνάγκη γάρ ἐστι καὶ βουλεύεσθαι καὶ λέγειν ἡμᾶς ἐν βουλῇ καὶ δήμῳ ἢ περὶ ἱερῶν, ἢ περὶ νόμων, ἢ περὶ τῆς πολιτικῆς κατασκευῆς, ἢ περὶ τῶν πρὸς τὰς
25 ἄλλας πόλεις συμμαχιῶν | καὶ συμβολαίων, ἢ περὶ πολέμων ἢ περὶ εἰρήνης, ἢ περὶ πόρου χρημάτων. αἱ μὲν οὖν προθέσεις αὗται τυγχάνουσιν οὖσαι περὶ ὧν βουλευσόμεθα καὶ δημηγορήσομεν· ἑκάστην δὲ πρόθεσιν διελώμεθα καὶ σκοπῶμεν ἐν οἷς τρόποις περὶ τούτων ἐνδέχεται λόγῳ χρήσασθαι.[13]

30 [3] περὶ μὲν οὖν | ἱερῶν τριττῶς ἀναγκαῖον λέγειν· ἢ γὰρ ἐροῦμεν ὡς τὰ καθεστῶτα διαφυλακτέον ἢ ὡς ἐπὶ τὸ μεγαλοπρεπέστερον πως μεταστατέον ἢ ὡς ἐπὶ τὸ ταπεινότερον. ὅταν μὲν οὖν λέγωμεν ὡς δεῖ τὰ καθεστῶτα διαφυλάττειν, εὑρήσομεν ἀφορμὰς ἐκ μὲν τοῦ δικαίου λέγοντες· "τὰ πάτρια ἔθη παρὰ πᾶσι παρα-
35 βαίνειν | ἄδικόν ἐστι," καὶ διότι "τὰ μαντεῖα πάντα τοῖς ἀνθρώποις προστάττει κατὰ τὰ πάτρια ποιεῖσθαι τὰς θυσίας," καὶ ὅτι "τῶν πρώτων οἰκιζόντων τὰς πόλεις καὶ τοῖς θεοῖς ἱδρυσαμένων τὰ ἱερὰ μάλιστα δεῖ διαμένειν τὰς περὶ τοὺς θεοὺς ἐπιμελείας." [4] ἐκ δὲ
1423b τοῦ συμφέροντος, ὅτι "πρὸς χρημάτων || συντέλειαν ἢ τοῖς ἰδιώταις ἢ τῷ κοινῷ τῆς πόλεως συμφέρον ἔσται κατὰ τὰ πάτρια τῶν ἱερῶν θυομένων," καὶ ὅτι πρὸς εὐτολμίαν "λυσιτελεῖ τοῖς πολίταις, ἐπεὶ συμπομπευόντων ὁπλιτῶν ἱππέων ψιλῶν εὐτολμότεροι γένοιντ' ἂν
5 οἱ πολῖται | φιλοτιμούμενοι περὶ ταῦτα." [5] ἐκ δὲ τοῦ

mon. [2] To speak generally, therefore, there are seven subjects concerning which we debate democratically: we must deliberate and speak, in council and assembly, about religious matters, laws, the condition of the city, alliances or treaties with other cities, wars, peace, or fiscal revenues. Since these are the subjects about which we deliberate and debate, let us go through each and examine in what ways it is possible to use speech about them.

[3] About religion one must speak in three ways: we shall say either that we must protect what has been established, or that we must make a change to something somehow more splendid, or to something smaller. Whenever we say that we must protect what is established, we shall find points of departure by talking about justice: "Among all peoples it is unjust to transgress the traditional customs," and therefore, "All prophecies direct people to perform sacrifices according to the traditional ways," and "We really must abide by the religious practices of those who first founded our cities and built the temples to the gods." [4] Then, from the perspective of the advantageous, that "with regard to the contribution of monies, either privately or for the city in common, it will be advantageous if the sacrificial rites are performed according to the traditional ways"; and with regard to bravery, that "it benefits the citizens, since when hoplites, cavalry, and lightly armed soldiers join in the procession, the citizens, by taking pride in these things, would become braver." [5] And from the per-

---

13 λόγῳ χρήσασθαι N F²H² : τοῖς λόγοις χρῆσθαι Π

καλοῦ, εἰ οὕτω λαμπρὰς τὰς ἑορτὰς πρὸς τὸ θεωρεῖσθαι συμβέβηκεν <εἶναι>.[14] ἐκ δὲ τῆς ἡδονῆς, "εἰ καὶ πρὸς τὸ θεωρεῖσθαι ποικιλία τις περὶ τὰς τῶν θεῶν θυσίας." ἐκ δὲ τοῦ δυνατοῦ, "εἰ μήτε ἔνδεια γεγένηται μήτε ὑπερβολὴ περὶ ταύτας."

10 [6] ὅταν μὲν οὖν τοῖς καθεστῶσι | συνηγορῶμεν, οὕτω μετιοῦσι σκεπτέον ἐπὶ τῶν προειρημένων ἢ τῶν τούτοις ὁμοιοτρόπων, καὶ ὧν[15] ἐνδέχεται διδάσκειν περὶ τῶν λεγομένων· ὅταν δὲ ἐπὶ τὸ μεγαλοπρεπέστερον συμβουλεύωμεν μεθιστάναι τὰς ἱεροποιίας, περὶ μὲν τοῦ τὰ πάτρια κινεῖν ἀφορμὰς ἕξομεν εὐπρεπεῖς 15 λέγοντες· [7] "τὸ προστιθέναι | τοῖς ὑπάρχουσιν οὐ καταλύειν ἐστίν, ἀλλ᾽ αὔξειν τὰ καθεστῶτα·" ἔπειθ᾽ ὡς "καὶ τοὺς θεοὺς εἰκὸς εὐνουστέρους εἶναι τοῖς μᾶλλον αὐτοὺς τιμῶσιν·" ἔπειθ᾽ ὡς "οὐδὲ οἱ πατέρες ἀεὶ κατὰ τὰ αὐτὰ τὰς θυσίας ἦγον, ἀλλὰ πρὸς τοὺς καιροὺς καὶ τὰς εὐπραγίας ὁρῶντες καὶ ἰδίᾳ καὶ κοινῇ τὴν πρὸς 20 τοὺς θεοὺς | θεραπείαν ἐνομοθέτουν·" ἔπειθ᾽ ὡς "καὶ ἐπὶ τῶν λοιπῶν ἁπάντων οὕτω καὶ τὰς πόλεις καὶ τοὺς ἰδίους οἴκους διοικοῦμεν." [8] λέγε δὲ καὶ εἰ τούτων κατασκευασθέντων ὠφέλειά τις ἔσται τῇ πόλει ἢ λαμπρότης ἢ ἡδονή, μετιὼν ὥσπερ ἐπὶ τῶν προτέρων εἴρηται.

25 [9] ὅταν δὲ ἐπὶ τὸ ταπεινότερον συστέλλωμεν, | πρῶτον μὲν ἐπὶ τοὺς καιροὺς τὸν λόγον ἀνακτέον· ὅτι "πράττοντες χεῖρον οἱ πολῖται τυγχάνουσι νῦν ἢ πρότερον·" ἔπειθ᾽ ὡς "οὐκ εἰκὸς τοὺς θεοὺς χαίρειν ταῖς δαπάναις τῶν θυομένων, ἀλλὰ ταῖς εὐσεβείαις τῶν

spective of the noble, that "if they happened this way the festivities were splendid to observe"; from pleasure, "if there is some variety in the observance of the sacrifices to the gods"; from the possible, "if there has been neither a deficiency nor an exaggeration in these matters."

[6] Whenever we are advocating for the established ways, we must proceed in this way in our inquiry, on the basis of what has been said before, things similar to these, and what can be taught about what has been said. And whenever we are advising changes to religious practices on the basis of greater magnificence, we shall have ready starting points to talk about changing the traditional ways: [7] "To add to what exists is not to destroy but to enhance the established ways"; then that "surely the gods are more well disposed to those who honor them more"; then that "our ancestors did not always perform sacrifices in the same way; they looked at the circumstances and their affluence, both privately and publicly, and regulated their ministry to the gods"; then that "in everything else we manage both our cities and our private homes in this way." [8] Say also if there will be any benefit for the city if these things are provided, or reward or pleasure, proceeding just as has been said with regard to the earlier points.

[9] Whenever we are cutting back to something smaller, we must first introduce the argument based on circumstances: that "the citizens are actually less well off than they were before"; then, "It is not likely that the gods rejoice in the costs of the sacrifices but in the piety of those

---

[14] εἶναι add. Didot

[15] ὧν Chiron : ὡς N a ρ

θυόντων·" εἶθ' ὡς "πολλὴν ἄνοιαν τούτων καὶ οἱ θεοὶ
30 καὶ οἱ ἄνθρωποι κατακρίνουσιν, ὅσοι παρὰ | δύναμίν τι
ποιοῦσιν·" ἔπειθ' ὅτι "οὐκ ἐπὶ τοῖς ἀνθρώποις μόνοις,
ἀλλὰ καὶ ἐπὶ ταῖς εὐπραγίαις καὶ κακοπραγίαις ἐστὶ
τὰ περὶ τὰς πολιτικὰς δαπάνας."

[10] ἀφορμὰς μὲν οὖν ταύτας καὶ τὰς ὁμοιοτρόπους
ταύταις ὑπὲρ τῶν περὶ τὰς θυσίας προθέσεων ἕξομεν·
35 ἵνα δὲ καὶ τὰ κατὰ τὴν κρατίστην θυσίαν | εἰδῶμεν
εἰσηγεῖσθαι καὶ νομοθετεῖν, ὁριοῦμαι καὶ ταύτην. ἔστι
γὰρ κρατίστη θυσία πασῶν ἥτις ἂν ἔχῃ πρὸς μὲν
τοὺς θεοὺς ὁσίως [καὶ θείως],[16] πρὸς δὲ τὰς δαπάνας
μετρίως, πρὸς δὲ πόλεμον ὠφελίμως, πρὸς δὲ τὰς
θεωρίας λαμπρῶς. [11] ἕξει δὲ πρὸς μὲν τοὺς θεοὺς
1424a ὁσίως, ἂν τὰ πάτρια μὴ καταλύηται· || πρὸς δὲ τὰς
δαπάνας μετρίως, ἂν μὴ πάντα τὰ πεμπόμενα καταναλίσκηται·
πρὸς δὲ τὰς θεωρίας λαμπρῶς, ἐὰν χρυσῷ
καὶ τοῖς τοιούτοις, ἃ μὴ συναναλίσκεται, δαψιλῶς τις
χρήσηται· πρὸς δὲ τοὺς πολέμους ὠφελίμως, ἐὰν
5 ἱππεῖς | καὶ ὁπλῖται διεσκευασμένοι συμπομπεύωσιν.
[12] τὰ μὲν δὴ περὶ τοὺς θεοὺς ἐκ τούτων κάλλιστα
κατασκευάσομεν, ἐκ δὲ τῶν πρότερον εἰρημένων καθ'
οὓς ἐνδέχεται τρόπους δημηγορεῖν περὶ ἑκάστης ἱεροποιίας
εἰσόμεθα.

[13] περὶ δὲ νόμων πάλιν καὶ τῆς πολιτικῆς κατα-
10 σκευῆς ὁμοιοτρόπως διέλθωμεν. εἰσὶ | δὲ νόμοι συλλήβδην
μὲν εἰπεῖν ὁμολογήματα κοινὰ πόλεως, ἃ διὰ
γραμμάτων ὁρίζει καὶ προστάττει πῶς χρὴ πράττειν
ἕκαστα. [14] δεῖ δὲ αὐτῶν τὴν θέσιν ἐν μὲν ταῖς

sacrificing"; then that "both gods and humans condemn the great ignorance of those who do anything beyond their capacity"; then, "Questions of public costs depend not only on people but on prosperity and adversity."

[10] We shall thus have these and similar starting points for proposals regarding sacrifices. In order for us to know how to introduce and legislate matters with regard to the best sacrifice, I shall now define it also. The best sacrifice of all is one that is devout with regard to the gods, moderate with regard to costs, useful with regard to war, and splendid with regard to the observances. [11] It will be devout with regard to the gods if it does not distort the traditional customs, moderate in cost if it does not consume all the offerings, and splendid with respect to the observances if it makes plentiful use of gold and such things, which are not consumed; it will be useful with respect to wars if cavalry and hoplites, fully equipped, join the procession. [12] We shall organize the matters with respect to the gods most nobly in these ways, and from what has been said before about the possible ways to debate democratically we shall know about each religious activity.

[13] Let us go through laws again and political organization in a similar manner. Laws are, in short, common agreements of a city, which define and direct, in written form, how to do everything. [14] In democracies the legis-

---

16 *καὶ θείως* del. Bekker

δημοκρατίαις τὰς μικρὰς ἀρχὰς καὶ τὰς πολλὰς κλη-
ρωτὰς ποιεῖν (ἀστασίαστον γὰρ τοῦτο), τὰς δὲ μεγί-
15 στας χειροτονητὰς | ἀπὸ τοῦ πλήθους. οὕτω γὰρ ὁ μὲν
δῆμος, κύριος ὢν διδόναι τὰς τιμάς οἷς ἂν ἐθέλοι, τοῖς
λαμβάνουσιν αὐτὰς οὐ φθονήσει, οἱ δ' ἐπιφανέστεροι
μᾶλλον τὴν καλοκαγαθίαν ἀσκήσουσιν, εἰδότες ὅτι τὸ
παρὰ τοῖς πολίταις εὐδοκιμεῖν οὐκ ἀλυσιτελὲς αὐτοῖς
20 ἔσται. [15] περὶ μὲν οὖν τὰς ἀρχαιρεσίας ἐν | τῇ δημο-
κρατίᾳ οὕτω δεῖ νομοθετεῖν· περὶ δὲ τὴν ἄλλην διοί-
κησιν καθ' ἓν μὲν ἕκαστον διελθεῖν πολὺ ἂν ἔργον εἴη,
συλλήβδην δὲ δεῖ παραφυλάττειν ὅπως οἱ νόμοι τὸ
μὲν πλῆθος ἀποτρέψωσι τοῖς τὰς οὐσίας ἔχουσιν
ἐπιβουλεύειν, τοῖς δὲ πλουτοῦσιν εἰς τὰς κοινὰς λει-
25 τουργίας ἑκουσίως δαπανᾶν[17] φιλοτιμίαν | ἐμποιήσω-
σιν.

[16] τοῦτο δὲ οὕτως ἄν τις[18] κατασκευάσειεν, εἰ τοῖς
μὲν τὰς οὐσίας ἔχουσιν ἀντὶ τῶν εἰς τὸ κοινὸν δα-
πανωμένων τιμαί τινες ἀπὸ τῶν νόμων ἀφωρισμέναι
τυγχάνοιεν, τῶν δὲ πενομένων τοὺς τὴν χώραν ἐργα-
ζομένους καὶ ναυκληροῦντας τῶν ἀγοραίων μᾶλλον
30 προτιμῷεν, ὅπως οἱ μὲν | πλουτοῦντες ἑκόντες τῇ πόλει
λειτουργήσουσι, τὸ δὲ πλῆθος οὐ συκοφαντίας, ἀλλ'
ἐργασίας ἐπιθυμήσῃ.

[17] δεῖ δὲ πρὸς τούτοις καὶ περὶ τοῦ μήτε χώραν
ποιεῖν ἀνάδαστον μήτε δημεύειν τὰς οὐσίας τῶν <τῇ
πόλει> λειτουργησάντων[19] ἰσχυροὺς κεῖσθαι νόμους
καὶ μεγάλας ἐπικεῖσθαι τιμωρίας τοῖς παραβαίνουσι
35 ταῦτα. χρὴ | δὲ τοῖς ἐν πολέμῳ τελευτῶσιν εἰς ταφήν τι

lation must be done so as to *allot* the minor offices, that is, the majority of them—since this is least likely to cause strife—and to *elect* the most important ones from the common people. In this way the people are sovereign in giving honors to whomever they may wish and will not envy those who receive them, and the more prominent people will exercise more respectability in the knowledge that having a good reputation among the citizens will not lack rewards for them. [15] We must legislate the distribution of offices in this way in a democracy. It would be a lot of work to go through every other aspect of administration in turn, but in short, we must guard that the laws deter the populace from plotting against those who have property and arouse in the wealthy an ambition to take on the costs of public services willingly.

[16] One might organize this in this way if some offices were actually reserved by law for those with wealth in return for their taking on costs for the public and, of the poor, if farmers and shippers were privileged over those who hang about in the marketplace. In this way the wealthy will willingly do services for the city, and the common people will have an appetite for hard work and not malicious litigation.

[17] In addition, there must be strong laws—and great penalties against those transgressing them—that there be no land redistribution and no confiscation of the property of those who have done public services. It is also necessary

---

17 ἑκουσίως δαπανᾶν Patillon cf. Π : ἑκουσίαν ἅπασαν N a

18 τις Π ut vid. : om. N a 19 τῇ πόλει λειτουργησάντων Fuhr : [ca. 15 litt. σ]άντων Π : τελευτῶντων N a

χωρίον δημόσιον ἐν καλῷ πρὸ τῆς πόλεως ἀφωρίσθαι καὶ τοῖς παισὶν αὐτῶν ἕως ἥβης δημοσίαν τροφὴν δίδοσθαι.

[18] τῶν μὲν οὖν ἐν τῇ δημοκρατίᾳ νόμων τὴν θέσιν τοιαύτην δεῖ ποιεῖσθαι. περὶ δὲ τὰς ὀλιγαρχίας, τὰς
40 μὲν ἀρχὰς δεῖ τοὺς νόμους | ἀπονέμειν ἐξ ἴσου πᾶσι
1424b τοῖς τῆς πολιτείας μετέχουσι, τούτων || δὲ εἶναι τὰς μὲν πλείστας κληρωτάς, τὰς δὲ μεγίστας κρυπτῇ ψήφῳ μεθ' ὅρκων καὶ πλείστης ἀκριβείας διαψηφιστάς. [19] δεῖ δὲ τὰς ζημίας ἐν τῇ ὀλιγαρχίᾳ μεγίστας ἐπικεῖσθαι τοῖς ὑβρίζειν τινὰς τῶν πολιτῶν ἐπιχει-
5 ροῦσι· τὸ γὰρ πλῆθος | οὐχ οὕτω τῶν ἀρχῶν ἀγανακτεῖ στερόμενον ὡς ἔχει βαρέως ὑβριζόμενον. χρὴ δὲ καὶ τὰς διαφορὰς τῶν πολιτῶν ὅτι τάχιστα διαλύειν καὶ μὴ χρονίζεσθαι, μηδὲ συνάγειν ἐκ τῆς χώρας ἐπὶ τὴν πόλιν τὸν ὄχλον· ἐκ γὰρ τῶν τοιούτων συνόδων συστρέφεται τὰ πλήθη καὶ καταλύει τὰς ὀλιγαρχίας. |
10 [20] καθόλου δὲ εἰπεῖν δεῖ τοὺς νόμους ἐν μὲν ταῖς δημοκρατίαις κωλύειν τοὺς πολλοὺς ταῖς τῶν πλουσίων οὐσίαις ἐπιβουλεύειν, ἐν δὲ ταῖς ὀλιγαρχίαις ἀποτρέπειν τοὺς τῆς πολιτείας μετέχοντας ὑβρίζειν τοὺς ἀσθενεστέρους καὶ συκοφαντεῖν τοὺς πολίτας.

15 [21] ὧν μὲν οὖν ὀρέγεσθαι δεῖ τοὺς νόμους καὶ | τὴν πολιτικὴν κατασκευήν, ἐκ τούτων οὐκ ἀγνοήσεις. δεῖ δὲ τὸν συναγορεύειν ἐθέλοντα νόμῳ δεικνύειν τοῦτον ἴσον ὄντα τοῖς πολίταις ὁμολογούμενόν τε τοῖς ἄλλοις νόμοις καὶ συμφέροντα τῇ πόλει μάλιστα μὲν πρὸς ὁμόνοιαν, εἰ δὲ μή, πρὸς τὴν τῶν πολιτῶν καλοκαγα-

to assign some ground in a beautiful spot outside the city for the public burial of those who have died in war, and to give their children public support until adulthood.

[18] It is necessary to establish this sort of legislation in democracies. In oligarchies, however, the laws must distribute the offices equally among those who share in government, to allot most of them, and to vote on the most important, with a secret ballot, with oaths and the greatest accuracy. [19] In oligarchies the penalties must be very great for those attempting to abuse any of the citizens. The common people are not as annoyed at being deprived of public offices as they are at being grievously abused. It is necessary to resolve differences among citizens as quickly as possible and not to delay or to have a mob from the countryside collect in the city. The common people gain strength from such meetings and overturn oligarchies. [20] One must say in general that in democracies the laws prevent the many from conspiring against the property of the wealthy, and in oligarchies they discourage those who share in the government from abusing the weaker and persecuting the citizens.

[21] You will know from these things what laws and political organization must strive for. A person wishing to argue for a law must show that it is fair for the citizens, is consistent with the other laws, and benefits the city, especially with regard to unity, or if not that, then with regard to

20 θίαν ἢ πρὸς τὰς κοινὰς | προσόδους ἢ πρὸς εὐδοξίαν τῷ κοινῷ τῆς πόλεως ἢ πρὸς τὴν πολιτικὴν[20] δύναμιν ἢ πρὸς ἄλλο τι τῶν τοιούτων. [22] ἀντιλέγοντα δὲ δεῖ σκοπεῖν πρῶτον μὲν εἰ μὴ κοινὸς ὁ νόμος, ἔπειτα εἰ μὴ τοῖς ἄλλοις ὁμολογῶν, ἀλλ' ὑπεναντίος ἔσται, ἐπὶ τούτοις εἰ μὴ πρὸς μηδὲν τῶν εἰρημένων συμφέρων, |
25 ἀλλὰ τοὐναντίον βλαβερός. περὶ μὲν οὖν νόμων καὶ τῆς κοινῆς κατασκευῆς ἐντεῦθεν καὶ τιθέναι καὶ λέγειν εὐπορήσομεν.

[23] περὶ δὲ συμμαχιῶν καὶ τῶν πρὸς τὰς ἄλλας πόλεις συμβολαίων διελθεῖν ἐπιχειρήσομεν. τὰ μὲν οὖν συμβόλαια καὶ τὰς τάξεις ἀναγκαῖον κατὰ συν-
30 θήκας κοινὰς γίνεσθαι, | συμμάχους δὲ ποιεῖσθαι κατὰ τοὺς καιροὺς τούτους ὅταν τινὲς καθ' ἑαυτοὺς ὦσιν ἀσθενεῖς ἢ πόλεμός ᾖ τις προσδόκιμος, ἢ διὰ τοῦτο ποιήσασθαι συμμαχίαν πρός τινας[21] ὅτι πολέμου ἀποστήσειν τινὰς νομίζουσιν.

[24] αἰτίαι μὲν οὖν αὗται καὶ παραπλήσιαι ταύταις
35 ἄλλαι πλείους τοῦ ποιεῖσθαι | συμμάχους εἰσί. δεῖ δέ, ὅταν συναγορεύειν βούλῃ τῇ γινομένῃ συμμαχίᾳ, τῶν καιρῶν τούτων τοὺς ὑπάρχοντας ἐμφανίζειν καὶ δεικνύναι τοὺς τὴν συμμαχίαν ποιουμένους μάλιστα μὲν δικαίους ὄντας καὶ πρότερόν τι τῇ πόλει ἀγαθὸν πεποιηκότας καὶ δύναμιν μεγάλην ἔχοντας καὶ πλη-
40 σίον τοῖς τόποις | κατοικοῦντας, εἰ δὲ μή, τούτων ἅπερ
1425a ἂν ὑπάρχῃ, ταῦτα || συνάγειν. [25] ὅταν δὲ διακωλύῃς τὴν συμμαχίαν, ἐμφανίζειν ἐνδέχεται πρῶτον μὲν ὡς οὐκ ἀνάγκη ποιεῖσθαι νῦν αὐτήν, ἔπειθ' ὡς οὐ δίκαιοι τυγχάνουσιν ὄντες, εἶθ' ὡς πρότερον ἡμᾶς κακῶς

the respectability of the citizens, the public revenues, the common repute of the city, its power, or something else of this sort. [22] A respondent must examine first whether the law is not in the common interest, then whether it will conflict with other laws and is opposed to them; in addition if it is not advantageous in any way that has been mentioned but is on the contrary harmful. We shall be well supplied both to legislate and to speak about laws and public organization from here.

[23] We shall attempt to go through alliances and transactions with other cities. Transactions and arrangements must be made according to common terms, but allies are made according to the following circumstances: whenever some are themselves weak, or some war is anticipated, or they think that because they make an alliance with some people[9] they may stay out of war with others.

[24] These, and others very like them, are the grounds for making most alliances. When you wish to argue for making an alliance, you must explain and argue that these circumstances are right for making alliances, especially since the allies are just, they have earlier done something good for the city, they have very great power, and they live near the area, or, if not, you must gather whichever of these reasons is the case. [25] Whenever you are trying to deter an alliance, you can explain first that it is not necessary to make it now, then that (the prospective allies) are not in fact just, then that they have treated us badly in the past;

[9] Editors have faulted this text, but the sense seems clear enough.

---

[20] πολιτικὴν N a ρ : πολεμικὴν Kassel fortasse recte cf. 1422a12 [21] διὰ τοῦτο—τινας del. Fuhrmann

πεποιηκότες, < . . . >.[22] εἰ δὲ μή, ὡς μακρὰν τοῖς τόποις
5 ἀπέχοντες | καὶ οὐχ ὑπάρχοντες δύνατοι κατὰ τοὺς προσήκοντας παραγενέσθαι καιρούς. ταῖς μὲν οὖν ἀντιλογίαις καὶ ταῖς συνηγορίαις ταῖς περὶ τῶν συμμάχων ἐκ τούτων καὶ τῶν τούτοις ὁμοιοτρόπων εὐπορήσομεν χρῆσθαι.

[26] περὶ εἰρήνης δὲ πάλιν καὶ πολέμου, τὸν αὐτὸν
10 τρόπον τὰς μεγίστας ἰδέας | ἐκλάβωμεν. προφάσεις μὲν οὖν εἰσι τοῦ πόλεμον ἐκφέρειν πρός τινας αὗται· "δεῖ πρότερον ἀδικηθέντας νῦν καιρῶν παραπεπτωκότων ἀμύνασθαι τοὺς ἀδικήσαντας," ἢ "νῦν ἀδικουμένους ὑπὲρ αὑτῶν πολεμεῖν ἢ ὑπὲρ συγγενῶν ἢ ὑπὲρ εὐεργετῶν," ἢ "συμμάχοις ἀδικουμένοις βοηθεῖν," ἢ
15 "τοῦ τῇ | πόλει συμφέροντος ἕνεκεν ἢ εἰς εὐδοξίαν ἢ εἰς εὐπορίαν ἢ εἰς δύναμιν ἢ εἰς ἄλλο τι τῶν τοιούτων."

[27] ὅταν μὲν οὖν ἐπὶ τὸ πολεμεῖν παρακαλῶμεν, τούτων τε τῶν προφάσεων ὅτι πλείστας συνακτέον καὶ μετὰ ταῦτα δεικτέον ὡς[23] ἐξ ὧν ἔστι περιγενέσθαι τῷ
20 πολέμῳ τούτων ὅτι πλεῖστα τοῖς παρακαλουμένοις | ὑπάρχοντά ἐστιν. [28] περιγίνονται δὲ πάντες πολεμοῦντες ἢ διὰ τὴν τῶν θεῶν εὔνοιαν, ἣν εὐτυχίαν προσαγορεύομεν, ἢ διὰ σωμάτων πλῆθος καὶ ῥώμην ἢ διὰ χρημάτων εὐπορίαν ἢ διὰ στρατηγοῦ φρόνησιν ἢ διὰ συμμάχων ἀρετὴν ἢ διὰ τόπων εὐφυΐαν. τούτων οὖν καὶ τῶν τούτοις ὁμοιοτρόπων τὰ τοῖς πράγμασιν |
25 οἰκειότατα λαμβάνοντες ἐμφανιοῦμεν ὅταν ἐπὶ τὸ πολεμεῖν παρακαλῶμεν, τὰ μὲν τῶν ἐναντίων ταπεινοῦντες, τὰ δ' ἡμέτερα ταῖς αὐξήσεσι μεγάλα καθιστῶντες.

(then, that they are weak.) If not, that they are far away and not actually capable of being present in the required circumstances. We shall be well prepared with responses and advocacy concerning allies with these and similar points.

[26] Let us take up the same method with regard to the most important aspects of war and peace. These are the reasons to wage war on others: "Since we were wronged before, now that the opportunities have come, we must defend ourselves against those who did the wrong," or "Since we are being wronged now we must make war either on behalf of ourselves or our kinsmen or our benefactors, or to help allies who are being wronged, or for the sake of the city's advantage, or its good reputation, resources, or power, or something else of that sort."

[27] When we are recommending going to war we must bring together as many of these reasons as possible and after this show that those to whom we are making the recommendation possess most of the things that give success in war. [28] Everyone succeeds in war either because of the goodwill of the gods, which we call "good fortune," through numbers and strength of personnel, through a good supply of money, through intelligent generalship, through the excellence of allies, or through the natural superiority of their position. By taking up these points and ones similar to these that are most suitable to the situation we shall make things clear when we are recommending going to war by minimizing the points of our opponents and making the most of our own points by amplification.

---

[22] lac. ind. Sp.[2] : εἶθ' ὡς ἀσθενεῖς prop. Chiron
[23] ὡς Π ut videtur : om. N a

[29] ἐὰν δὲ πόλεμον μέλλοντα γίνεσθαι διακωλύειν ἐπιχειρῶμεν, πρῶτον μὲν διὰ προφάσεων δεικτέον ἢ
30 παντελῶς οὐδεμίαν | ὑπάρχουσαν ἢ μικρὰς καὶ ταπεινὰς οὔσας τὰς δυσχερείας, ἔπειθ' ὡς οὐ συμφέρει πολεμεῖν, διεξιόντας τὰ κατὰ τὸν πόλεμον ἀτυχήματα τοῖς ἀνθρώποις· πρὸς δὲ τούτοις τὰ πρὸς νίκας συντείνοντα τοῦ πολέμου τοῖς ἐναντίοις ὑπάρχοντα μᾶλλον δεικτέον· ταῦτα δ' ἐστιν, ἅπερ ἀρτίως κατηρίθμηται. |
35 [30] γίνεσθαι μὲν οὖν πόλεμον μέλλοντα ἐκ τούτων ἀποτρεπτέον· ἤδη δ' ἐνεστῶτα παύειν ἐπιχειροῦντας, ἐὰν μὲν κρατῶσιν οἱ συμβουλευόμενοι, αὐτὸ τοῦτο πρῶτον λεκτέον ὅτι δεῖ τοὺς νοῦν ἔχοντας μὴ περιμένειν ἕως ἂν πταίσωσιν, ἀλλ' ἐν τῷ κρατεῖν ποιεῖσθαι
40 τὴν εἰρήνην· ἔπειτα διότι πέφυκεν ὁ πόλεμος καὶ | τῶν εὐτυχούντων ἐν αὐτῷ πολλοὺς ἀπολλύναι, ἡ δ' εἰρήνη ||
1425b τοὺς μὲν ἡττωμένους σῴζειν, τοὺς δὲ νικῶντας ὧν ἕνεκεν ἐπολέμησαν παρέχειν ἀπολαύειν.[24] διεξιτέον δὲ τὰς μεταβολὰς τὰς ἐν τῷ πολέμῳ ὡς πολλαὶ καὶ παράλογοι γίνονται. [31] τοὺς μὲν οὖν ἐν τῷ πολέμῳ
5 κρατοῦντας ἐκ τῶν τοιούτων ἐπὶ | τὴν εἰρήνην παρακλητέον, τοὺς δὲ ἐπταικότας ἐξ αὐτῶν τε τῶν συμβάντων καὶ ἐκ τοῦ μὴ παροξύνεσθαι τοῖς προαδικήσασι ταῖς συμφοραῖς πειθομένους καὶ ἐκ τῶν κινδύνων τῶν γεγενημένων τῷ μὴ ποιήσασθαι τὴν εἰρήνην καὶ ἐκ τοῦ κρεῖττον εἶναι τοῖς κρείττοσι μέρος τι τῶν ὑπαρ-
10 χόντων | προέσθαι ἢ πολέμῳ κρατηθέντας αὐτοὺς αὐτοῖς κτήμασιν ἀπολέσθαι. [32] συλλήβδην δὲ τοῦθ' ἡμᾶς εἰδέναι δεῖ ὅτι τότε πάντες οἱ ἄνθρωποι τοὺς

[29] If we are attempting to prevent war that is about to happen, we must show first that absolutely none of the reasons for it is present or that the grievances are small and trivial, and then that there is no advantage in making war. In addition, we must show that our opponents have more of what leads to victory in war—these have just been enumerated. [30] From these sources we must avert a war that is about to happen. But if we are trying to stop a war that has started, if those who are seeking your counsel are stronger, it is necessary first to say this: "Those with sense must not wait until they fall but must make peace while they are still stronger"; then, "By nature war also destroys many who are successful in them, but peace both saves the defeated and provides the victors the enjoyment of what they fought over." We must also go through the reverses in war; that they are many and incalculable. [31] We must urge those who are stronger in war, on the basis of such points, to peace. And those who have been defeated we must urge on the basis of the circumstances themselves, of not being embittered—under the influence of their misfortunes—at those who have done injustice on the basis of the dangers that have resulted from not making peace, and on the basis of it being better to forgo part of one's possessions to the stronger than to be defeated in war and to die for one's belongings. [32] In sum, we must understand this, that all people are accustomed to end wars among them-

24 παρέχειν ἀπολαύειν A : ἀπολαύειν N a

πολέμους εἰώθασι διαλύεσθαι πρὸς ἀλλήλους ὅταν
ἤτοι δίκαια ἀξιοῦν τοὺς ἐναντίους ὑπολαμβάνωσιν ἢ
διενεχθῶσι τοῖς συμμάχοις ἢ τῷ πολέμῳ κάμνωσιν |
15 ἢ φοβηθῶσι τοὺς ἐναντίους ἢ στασιάσωσι πρὸς σφᾶς
αὐτούς· ὥστε τούτων τε πάντων καὶ τῶν τούτοις ὁμοιοτρόπων τὰ τοῖς πράγμασιν οἰκειότατα συνάγων οὐκ
ἀπορήσεις ὅθεν χρὴ περὶ πολέμου δημηγορεῖν καὶ
εἰρήνης.

[33] λείπεται δ' ἡμᾶς ἔτι περὶ πόρου χρημάτων
20 διελθεῖν. πρῶτον μὲν οὖν σκεπτέον | εἴ τι τῶν τῆς
πόλεως κτημάτων ἠμελημένον ἐστὶ καὶ μήτε πρόσ-
οδον ποιεῖ μήτε τοῖς θεοῖς ἐξαίρετόν ἐστιν. λέγω δ'
οἷον τόπους τινὰς δημοσίους ἠμελουμένους, ἐξ ὧν
τοῖς ἰδιώταις ἢ πραθέντων ἢ μισθωθέντων πρόσοδος
ἄν τις τῇ πόλει γίνοιτο· κοινότατος γὰρ ὁ τοιοῦτος
25 πόρος ἐστίν. [34] ἂν δὲ μηδὲν | ᾖ τοιοῦτον, ἀπὸ τιμη-
μάτων ἀναγκαῖον ποιήσασθαι τὰς εἰσφοράς, ἢ τοῖς
μὲν πένησι τὰ σώματα παρέχειν εἶναι προστεταγμέ-
νον εἰς τοὺς κινδύνους, τοῖς δὲ πλουτοῦσι τὰ χρήματα,
τοῖς δὲ τεχνίταις ὅπλα. [35] συλλήβδην δὲ <δεῖ>[25]
περὶ πόρων εἰσηγούμενον φάναι αὐτοὺς ἴσους τοῖς
30 πολίταις καὶ πολυχρονίους καὶ | μεγάλους ὄντας, τοὺς
δὲ τῶν ἐναντίων τὰ ἐναντία τούτοις ἔχοντας. τὰς μὲν
οὖν προθέσεις περὶ ὧν δημηγορήσομεν καὶ τὰ μέρη
τούτων ἐξ ὧν τοὺς λόγους συστήσομεν καὶ προτρέ-
ποντες καὶ ἀποτρέποντες, ἐκ τῶν εἰρημένων ἴσμεν.
προθέμενοι δὲ πάλιν ἐφεξῆς τό τε ἐγκωμιαστικὸν
35 εἶδος καὶ τὸ | ψεκτικὸν περιλάβωμεν.

selves when they accept that their opponents have just claims, when they have differences with their allies, when they are tired of war, when they fear their opponents, or when they have strife among themselves. So, by gathering material appropriate to the circumstances from all these and similar points you will not be at a loss if you need to debate peace and war.

[33] It still remains for us to go through revenues. First we must examine whether any of the resources of the city are neglected, neither creating income nor anything dedicated to the gods. I mean, for example, whether there are some neglected public lands from which there may be some income for the city from private individuals either by sale or lease; that is the most common income. [34] If nothing like this exists, it is necessary to create taxes from assessments, for the poor to be assigned to provide personal service in times of danger, for the wealthy to provide money, and for the artisans to provide equipment. [35] In sum, when making a proposal about revenues it is necessary to show that they are fair to the citizens, sustainable over time, and important, but those of the opponent are the contrary. From what has been said we know the subjects about which we debate democratically and their parts, from which we may put together speeches both to propose and to oppose. Now let us set forth and include in turn the species of praise and criticism.

---

25 δεῖ Sp.[2] : om. N a

3. Συλλήβδην μὲν οὖν ἐστιν ἐγκωμιαστικὸν εἶδος προαιρέσεων καὶ πράξεων καὶ λόγων ἐνδόξων αὔξησις καὶ μὴ προσόντων συνοικείωσις,[26] ψεκτικὸν δὲ τὸ ἐναντίον τούτῳ, τῶν μὲν ἐνδόξων ταπείνωσις, τῶν δὲ
40 ἀδόξων αὔξησις. ἐπαινετὰ | μὲν οὖν ἐστι πράγματα τὰ
1426a δίκαια καὶ τὰ νόμιμα καὶ τὰ || συμφέροντα καὶ τὰ καλὰ καὶ τὰ ἡδέα καὶ τὰ ῥᾴδια πραχθῆναι. ταῦτα δὲ αὐτά τε οἷά ἐστι καὶ ὅθεν αὐτὰ πολλὰ ποιήσομεν, ἐν τοῖς πρὸ τούτων εἴρηται. [2] δεῖ δὲ τὸν εὐλογοῦντα δεικνύειν
5 τοῖς λόγοις, ὡς τούτῳ τῷ ἀνθρώπῳ ἢ τοῖς | πράγμασιν ὑπάρχει τι τούτων ὑπ' αὐτοῦ κατεργασθὲν ἢ δι' αὐτοῦ πορισθὲν ἢ ἐκ τούτου ἐπισυμβαῖνον ἢ ἕνεκα τούτου γινόμενον ἢ οὐκ ἄνευ τούτου ἐπιτελούμενον· ὁμοιοτρόπως δὲ καὶ τῷ ψέγοντι τὰ ἐναντία τούτοις δεικτέον προσόντα τῷ ψεγομένῳ. [3] τὸ μὲν[27] ἐκ τούτου· οἷον ἐκ
10 τοῦ φιλογυμναστεῖν τὸ | σῶμα ὑγιαίνειν, καὶ ἐκ τοῦ μὴ φιλοπονεῖν ἐπ' ἀρρωστίαν ἐμπίπτειν, καὶ ἐκ τοῦ φιλοσοφεῖν δεινότερον εἶναι περὶ φρόνησιν, καὶ ἐκ τοῦ ἀμελεῖν ἐνδεᾶ τῶν ἀναγκαίων εἶναι. [4] τὸ δ' ἕνεκα τούτου· οἷον ἕνεκα τοῦ στεφανωθῆναι ὑπὸ τῶν πολιτῶν πολλοὺς πόνους καὶ κινδύνους ὑπομένουσι· καὶ
15 ἕνεκα τοῦ | χαρίσασθαι τοῖς ἐρωμένοις τῶν ἄλλων οὐδὲν φροντίζουσιν. [5] τὸ δὲ μὴ ἄνευ τούτου· οἷον οὐκ ἄνευ τῶν ναυτῶν ναυμαχιῶν νῖκαι, καὶ οὐκ ἄνευ τοῦ πίνειν αἱ παροινίαι. τὰ τοιαῦτα δὲ τοῖς προειρημένοις

[26] μὴ προσόντων συνοικείωσις N a : μὴ ἐνδόξων ταπείνωσις malit Fuhrmann

3. In short, the species of praise is an amplification of reputable choices, acts, and words and an appropriation of those that are not present;[10] criticism is the contrary of this, the diminution of reputable qualities and the amplification of disreputable. Praiseworthy are actions that are just, lawful, advantageous, noble, pleasant, and easy to do. What these are and how we shall formulate them has been stated earlier. [2] The eulogist must show through his words that something of these qualities belongs to the person or to his actions, that it has been accomplished by him, or provided through him, or happened *as a result* of this action, or came about *for the sake* of it, or would *not* have been completed *without* it. In the same way the critic must show that the person being criticized has the contrary qualities. [3] First, results of it: for instance, "Bodily health results from love of exercise"; "Falling into unfitness results from disliking exertion"; "Greater cleverness in practical wisdom results from philosophy"; "Lack of necessities results from indifference." [4] And (second), for its sake: for instance, "They endure many struggles and dangers for the sake of being crowned by the citizens"; "They give no consideration to others for the sake of favoring the ones they love." [5] And (third), not without: for instance, "There are no naval victories without sailors"; "There is no drunkenness without drinking." By pursuing such things

[10] See 35.3–4: people are often praised for their good birth, looks, and so on, which are actually beyond their personal virtue.

---

[27] lac. ind. Kayser[1], sed cf. 1426a6 ἐκ τούτου ἐπισυμβαῖνον

ὁμοιοτρόπως μετιὼν ἐγκωμίων καὶ ψόγων πολλῶν εὐπορήσεις.

20 [6] αὐξήσεις δὲ καὶ ταπεινώσεις [καὶ][28] | συλλήβδην ἅπαντα τὰ τοιαῦτα τόνδε τὸν τρόπον μετιών, πρῶτον μὲν ἀποφαίνων, ὥσπερ ἀρτίως μετῆλθον, ὑπὸ τουτοὺ πολλὰ γεγενῆσθαι ἢ κακὰ ἢ ἀγαθά. [7] εἷς μὲν οὖν τρόπος τῆς αὐξήσεως οὗτος, δεύτερος δὲ κεκριμένον μέγα φέρειν, ἂν μὲν ἐπαινῇς, ἀγαθόν, ἂν δὲ ψέγῃς, 25 κακόν, εἶτα παριστάναι | τὸ ὑπὸ σοῦ λεγόμενον καὶ παραβάλλειν πρὸς ἄλληλα, τοῦ μὲν ὑπὸ σαυτοῦ λεγομένου τὰ μέγιστα διεξιόντα, τοῦ δὲ ἑτέρου τὰ ἐλάχιστα, καὶ οὕτω μέγα φανεῖται. [8] τρίτος δὲ πρὸς τὸ ὑπὸ σαυτοῦ λεγόμενον ἀντιπαραβάλλειν τοὐλάχιστον τῶν ὑπὸ τὴν αὐτὴν ἰδέαν πιπτόντων· φανεῖται γὰρ 30 οὕτω | τὸ ὑπὸ σοῦ λεγόμενον μεῖζον, ὥσπερ οἱ μέτριοι τὰ μεγέθη φαίνονται μείζους ὅταν πρὸς βραχυτέρους παραστῶσιν. [9] ἔσται δὲ ὧδε πάντως αὔξειν· εἰ κέκριται μέγα ἀγαθὸν τοῦτο, τούτῳ τὸ ἐναντίον ἐὰν λέγῃς, μέγα κακὸν φανεῖται. ὡσαύτως δὲ εἰ νομίζεται μέγα 35 κακόν, ἐὰν τούτῳ ‹τὸ›[29] ἐναντίον λέγῃς, | μέγα ἀγαθὸν φανεῖται. [10] ἔστι δὲ καὶ ὧδε μεγάλα ποιεῖν τὰ ἀγαθὰ ἢ τὰ κακά ἐὰν ἀποφαίνῃς αὐτὸν πράξαντα[30] ἐκ διανοίας, συμβιβάζων ὡς ἐκ πολλοῦ προενόησεν, ὡς πολλὰ πράττειν ἐπεβάλλετο, ὡς πολὺν χρόνον ἔπραττεν, ὡς οὐδεὶς ἄλλος πρότερον τούτοις ἐνεχείρησεν, ὡς μετὰ 40 τούτων ἔπραξε | μεθ' ὧν οὐδεὶς ἄλλος, ὡς ἐπὶ τούτοις

[28] καὶ N[1] a : del. N[2] om. A [29] τὸ add. Chiron

in a similar way to what has been said, you will be well supplied with many praises and criticisms.

[6] You will amplify and diminish, in short, by pursuing such things in this way. First, point out, as I just discussed, that many things, either bad or good, have come about through this man here. [7] This is one method of amplification. A second is to bring in something important that has been judged good, if you are praising it, or bad, if you are criticizing, and then to set beside it what you are discussing and compare them with each other, reciting the most important aspects of what you are discussing and the least important of the other, so that what you are discussing will seem important. [8] A third is to contrast the least of the things that fall under the same kind with what you are discussing. In this way what you are discussing will appear more important, just as men of moderate height seem taller when they stand beside shorter men. [9] It will always be possible to amplify in this way. If something has been judged a great good, its contrary, if you speak of it, will appear a great bad. In the same way, if something is thought a great bad, if you speak of its opposite, it will appear a great good. [10] It is possible to magnify good and bad things if you point out that the person did them intentionally, arguing that he planned them long in advance, that he devoted a lot to doing it, that he was doing it over a long time, that no one else attempted these things before, that he did them with those with whom no one else did

---

[30] πράξαντα Π ut videtur : om. N a

1426b ἐφ' οἷς[31] οὐδεὶς ἕτερος, ‖ ὡς ἑκών, ὡς ἐκ προνοίας, ὡς εἰ πάντες τούτῳ ἴσως ποιοῖμεν, εὐδαιμονοῖμεν ἂν ἢ φαύλως πράττοιμεν. [11] χρὴ δὲ καὶ εἰκάζοντα συμβιβάζειν καὶ ἐποικοδομοῦντα τὸ ἕτερον ὡς ἐπὶ τὸ ἕτερον
5 αὔξειν τρόπῳ τοιῷδε· "ὅστις δὲ τῶν φίλων | κήδεται, τοῦτον εἰκὸς καὶ τοὺς αὑτοῦ γονέας τιμᾶν·" "ὅστις δὲ τοὺς γονέας τιμᾷ, οὗτος καὶ τὴν πατρίδα τὴν ἑαυτοῦ εὖ ποιεῖν βουλήσεται." συλλήβδην δέ, ἐὰν πολλῶν αἴτιον ἀποφαίνῃς, ἐάν τε ἀγαθῶν ἐάν τε κακῶν, μεγάλα φανεῖται. [12] δεῖ δὲ καὶ σκοπεῖν[32] τὸ πρᾶγμα
10 ὁποῖον φανεῖται κατὰ μέρη διαιρούμενον | ἢ καθόλου λεγόμενον, ὁποτέρως ἂν μεῖζον ᾖ, τόνδε τὸν τρόπον αὐτὸ λέγειν.

[13] τὰς μὲν οὖν αὐξήσεις οὕτω μετιὼν πλείστας ποιήσεις καὶ μεγίστας. ταπεινώσεις δὲ τοῖς λόγοις καὶ τὰ ἀγαθὰ καὶ τὰ κακὰ τὸν ἐναντίον τρόπον μετιών, ὡς εἰρήκαμεν ἐπὶ τῶν μεγάλων, καὶ μάλιστα μὲν ἂν
15 μηδενὸς | αἴτιον ἐπιδεικνύῃς, εἰ δὲ μή, ὡς ἐλαχίστων καὶ μικροτάτων. [14] ὡς μὲν οὖν ἐγκωμιάζοντες καὶ ψέγοντες αὐξήσομεν καὶ ταπεινώσομεν ἅπερ ἂν ἐθέλωμεν, ἐκ τούτων ἴσμεν. χρήσιμοι δὲ αἱ τῶν αὐξήσεων ἀφορμαὶ εἰσὶν καὶ ἐν τοῖς ἄλλοις εἴδεσιν, ἀλλ' ἡ
20 πλείστη δύναμις αὐτῶν ἐστιν ἐν τοῖς | ἐγκωμίοις καὶ ἐν τοῖς ψόγοις. περὶ μὲν οὖν τούτων ἐντεῦθεν εὐπορήσομεν.

4. Διέλθωμεν[33] δὲ πάλιν ὁμοιοτρόπως τούτοις τό τε

it, that he did it for these reasons that no one else had had, that he did it willingly, with forethought, that if we all did it equally well as he, we would be happy, or miserable. [11] It is necessary to argue by probabilities and to amplify by associating one thing with another in the following way: "Whoever cares for his friends probably honors his parents"; "Whoever honors his parents will want his homeland to prosper." In short, if you point out a cause of many things, whether they are good or bad, they appear important. [12] It is necessary to examine also how the matter appears if divided into parts or discussed altogether. Whichever way it appears more important, discuss in that way.

[13] By proceeding in this way you will create the greatest number and most significant amplifications. You will minimize through speeches by pursuing the good and the bad in the opposite way, as we said with regard to important things, especially if you show that they are the cause of nothing, and if not, then of the least and most insignificant things. [14] We know in these ways how in praising and criticizing we shall amplify and diminish whatever we want. The bases for amplifications are useful in other species of rhetoric, but their greatest potential is in praise and criticism. Concerning these matters, then, we are well equipped.

4. In a way similar to these let us again go through the

---

[31] ἐπὶ τούτοις ἐφ᾽ οἷς Chiron : ἐπὶ τούτοις μεθ᾽ οὓς N FCH2P

[32] δεῖ δὲ καὶ σκοπεῖν Fuhrmann ap. Chiron : σκοπεῖν δὲ καὶ N a : σ[κοπεῖν δὲ 4 litt.]ν Π

[33] Διέλθωμεν Π : Διέλωμεν N a ρ

κατηγορικὸν καὶ τὸ ἀπολογητικὸν εἶδος ὅ περὶ τὴν δικανικήν ἐστι πραγματείαν αὐτά τε ἐξ ὧν συνέστηκε
25 καὶ ὡς δεῖ | αὐτοῖς χρῆσθαι. ἔστι δὲ τὸ μὲν κατηγορικὸν συλλήβδην εἰπεῖν ἀδικημάτων καὶ ἁμαρτημάτων ἐξήγησις,[34] τὸ δ' ἀπολογικὸν ἁμαρτημάτων καὶ ἀδικημάτων κατηγορηθέντων ἢ ὑποπτευθέντων[35] διάλυσις.

[2] ἑκατέρου δὲ τῶν εἰδῶν τὰς δυνάμεις ταύτας
30 ἔχοντος, τὸν κατηγοροῦντα ταῦτα ἀναγκαῖον[36] | λέγειν, ὅταν μὲν εἰς πονηρίαν κατηγορῇ, ὡς αἱ τῶν ἐναντίων πράξεις ἄδικοι καὶ παράνομοι καὶ τῷ πλήθει τῶν πολιτῶν ἀσύμφοροι τυγχάνουσιν οὖσαι, ὅταν δὲ εἰς ἀβελτερίαν, ὡς αὐτῷ τε τῷ πράττοντι ἀσύμφοροι καὶ αἰσχραὶ καὶ ἀηδεῖς καὶ ἀδύνατοι ἐπιτελεσθῆναι. ταῦ-
35 τα | μὲν καὶ τὰ τούτοις ὅμοια κατά τε τῶν πονηρῶν καὶ τῶν ἀβελτέρων ἐπιχειρήματά ἐστιν.

[3] δεῖ δὲ καὶ τοῦτο παρατηρεῖν τοὺς κατηγοροῦντας ἐπὶ ποίοις τῶν ἀδικημάτων οἱ νόμοι τὰς τιμωρίας τάττουσι καὶ περὶ ἃ τῶν ἀδικημάτων οἱ δικασταὶ τὰς ζημίας ὁρίζουσιν. ὅταν μὲν οὖν ὁ νόμος
40 διωρικὼς ᾖ, | τοῦτο δεῖ μόνον σκοπεῖν τὸν κατήγορον
1427a ὅπως ἐπιδείξῃ || τὸ πρᾶγμα γεγενημένον. [4] ὅταν δὲ οἱ δικασταὶ τὸ κατηγορούμενον ἴσασιν,[37] αὐξητέον ἐστὶ τὰ τοῦ ἐναντίου ἀδικήματα.[38] καὶ μάλιστα μὲν δει-

[34] ἐξήγησις Π ρ : ἐξάγγελσις N a [35] ὑποπτευθέντων Π : καθυποπτευθέντων N a [36] τὸν κατηγοροῦντα ταῦτα ἀναγκαῖον ego : κατηγοροῦντα μὲν ἀναγκαῖον N a : τὸν κα[τηγοροῦντα] τ[ο]ῦτ ..[.. ἀνα]γκα[ῖον Π

species of prosecution and defense, which concerns[11] forensic activity, what they consist in and how to use them. The prosecution species is, in short, the exposition of injustices and wrongs, and the species of defense is the refutation of prosecuted or suspected wrongs and injustices.

[2] Since each of the species has these functions, the prosecuting speaker, when his prosecution speech concerns baseness, must say these things: that his opponents' actions are unjust, unlawful, and, in fact, disadvantageous to the majority of citizens. And when his speech concerns negligence,[12] he must say that their actions are disadvantageous for the doer, shameful, unpleasant, and incapable of success. These and like arguments are attacks against base and negligent people.

[3] Those making prosecution speeches must also take care over which wrongs the laws assign punishments to and for which wrongs the judges define the penalties. When the law has defined it, the prosecutor must only look at how to show that the act has occurred. [4] But when the judges know about the prosecuted act, the prosecutor must amplify the wrongs of the opponent. In particular he

[11] Many questions are raised about interpolation of the text and the relationship of species to genres, which may result in the singular (genre?) in the relative clause, which gives way to the plural. See Chiron *ad loc.*

[12] This word is most often translated more strongly, as "foolishness," but it appears to refer to the mistaken acts referred to in 4.5–6.

---

37 *τὸ κατηγορούμενον ἴσασιν* N a : *τιμῶσιν* Π

38 *τὰ τοῦ ἐναντίου ἀδικήματα* Fuhrmann : *τὰ τοῦ ἐναντίου ἀδικήματα καὶ τὰ τῶν ἐναντίων ἀδικήματα* N a

κτέον ὡς ἑκὼν καὶ ἐκ προνοίας οὐ τῆς τυχούσης, ἀλλὰ
5 μετὰ παρασκευῆς | πλείστης ἠδίκησεν. [5] ἐὰν δὲ μὴ
δυνατὸν ᾖ τοῦτο ποιεῖν, ἀλλὰ νομίζῃς δείξειν τὸν
ἐναντίον ὡς ἥμαρτε τρόπον τινά, ἢ ὅτι ταῦτα πρᾶξαι
διανοηθεὶς καλῶς ἠτύχησε, περιαιρετέον τὴν συγγνώ-
μην λέγοντα τοῖς ἀκούουσιν ὡς "οὐ δεῖ πράξαντας
ἡμαρτηκέναι φάσκειν, ἀλλὰ πρὶν πράττειν εὐλαβεῖ-
10 σθαι·" | ἔπειθ' ὡς "εἰ καὶ ἐξήμαρτεν ἢ ἠτύχησεν ἐκεῖνος,
δεῖ διὰ τὰς ἀτυχίας καὶ τὰς ἁμαρτίας ζημιωθῆναι
μᾶλλον αὐτὸν ἢ τὸν μηδέτερον τούτων ποιήσαντα·"
πρὸς δὲ τούτοις, "καὶ ὁ νομοθέτης οὐκ ἀφῆκε τοὺς
ἐξαμαρτάνοντας, ἀλλ' ὑποδίκους ἐποίησεν, ἵνα μὴ
15 πάλιν ἐξαμαρτάνωσι." [6] λέγε δὲ καὶ ὡς | "εἰ τὸν τὰ
τοιαῦτα ἀπολογούμενον ἀποδέξονται, πολλοὺς τοὺς
ἀδικεῖν προαιρουμένους ἕξουσι· κατορθώσαντες μὲν
γὰρ ἅπερ ἂν ἐθέλωσι πράξουσιν, ἀποτυχόντες δὲ
φάσκοντες ἠτυχηκέναι τιμωρίαν οὐχ ὑφέξουσι." τοῖς
μὲν οὖν κατηγοροῦσιν ἐκ τῶν τοιούτων ἡ συγγνώμη
20 περιαιρετέα καί, ὡς πρότερον | εἴρηται, διὰ τῶν αὐξή-
σεων πολλῶν αἴτια κακῶν τὰ τῶν ἐναντίων ἔργα
ἀποδεικτέον.

[7] τὸ μὲν οὖν κατηγορικὸν εἶδος διὰ τῶν μερῶν
ἀποτελεῖται τούτων· τὸ δὲ ἀπολογικὸν διὰ τριῶν μεθ-
όδων συνίσταται [πόθεν ἄν τις ἀπολογήσαιτο].[39] ἢ
γὰρ ἀποδεικτέον τῷ ἀπολογουμένῳ ὡς οὐδὲν τῶν κατ-
25 ηγορουμένων | ἔπραξεν· ἢ ἐὰν ἀναγκάζηται ὁμολογεῖν,

[39] πόθεν ἄν τις ἀπολογήσαιτο del. Sp.[1]

must show that he did wrong willingly, from forethought, and not by chance, but with a great deal of preparation. [5] If it is not possible to do this, but you think that the opponent will argue that he made a mistake in some way, or that although well intended he had bad luck, you must deny him pardon by telling the audience, "They must not act and then claim to have made a mistake; they should take care before acting"; then that "if that man made a mistake or had bad luck, he ought to be penalized for his misfortunes and mistakes rather than the man who has done neither of these." In addition, "The lawmaker did not let the people who make mistakes off; he made them legally responsible so that they would not make mistakes again." [6] Say also that "if they accept someone who makes such defenses, they will have many who choose to do wrong; if they are successful, they will do whatever they wish, and if they are unlucky, by claiming misfortune they will not undergo punishment." Those making prosecution speeches must do away with pardon by such arguments and, as we have said earlier, they must demonstrate through amplifications that the actions of the opponents were the cause of many bad things.

[7] The prosecution species is complete through these parts. The species of defense consists of three methods [how one may speak in defense].[13] The person giving the defense speech must demonstrate either that he did none of the things alleged in the prosecution speech; or, if he is

[13] The bracketed words appear to be a sort of subtitle inserted in medieval times.

πειρατέον δεικνύναι ἔννομον καὶ δίκαιον καὶ καλὸν καὶ συμφέρον τῇ πόλει τὸ πεπραγμένον· ἐὰν δὲ μὴ τοῦτο δύνηται ἀποδεῖξαι, εἰς ἁμάρτημα ἢ εἰς ἀτύχημα ἄγοντα τὰς πράξεις καὶ μικρὰς τὰς βλάβας ἀπ' αὐτῶν
30 γεγενημένας ἀποφαίνοντα, | συγγνώμης τυχεῖν πειρατέον. [8] ἀδικίαν δὲ καὶ ἁμάρτημα καὶ ἀτυχίαν ὧδε ὅρισαι· τὸ μὲν ἐκ προνοίας κακόν τι ποιεῖν ἀδικίαν τίθει, καὶ φάθι δεῖν τιμωρίαν ἐπὶ τοῖς τοιούτοις τὴν μεγίστην λαμβάνειν· τὸ δὲ δι' ἄγνοιαν βλαβερόν τι πράττειν ἁμαρτίαν εἶναι φατέον. [9] τὸ δὲ μὴ δι'
35 ἑαυτόν, | ἀλλὰ δι' ἑτέρους τινὰς ἢ διὰ τύχην μηδὲν ἐπιτελεῖν τῶν βουλευθέντων καλῶς ἀτυχίαν τίθει, καὶ φάθι τὸ μὲν ἀδικεῖν εἶναι τῶν πονηρῶν ἀνθρώπων ἴδιον, τὸ δ' ἐξαμαρτεῖν καὶ περὶ τὰς πράξεις ἀτυχεῖν οὐ μόνου εἶναι ἑαυτοῦ ἴδιον, ἀλλὰ καὶ κοινὸν καὶ τῶν
40 δικαζόντων καὶ τῶν ἄλλων ἀνθρώπων. | ἀξίου δὲ συγγνώμην ἔχειν ἀναγκασθείς τι ὁμολογεῖν τῶν τοιούτων αἰτιῶν, κοινὸν τοῖς ἀκούουσι ποιῶν τὸ ἁμαρτάνειν ||
1427b καὶ τὸ ἀτυχεῖν.

[10] δεῖ δὲ τὸν ἀπολογούμενον πάλιν θεωρεῖν ἐφ' οἷς τῶν ἀδικημάτων οἵ τε νόμοι τὰς τιμωρίας ἔταξαν καὶ οἱ δικασταὶ ζημίας τιμῶσι· καὶ ὅταν ὁ νόμος ὁρίζῃ τὰς τιμωρίας, δεικτέον ὡς οὐκ ἐποίησε ‹ταῦτα›[40] τὸ
5 παράπαν, | ἢ ὡς ἔννομα καὶ δίκαια ἐποίησεν· [11] ὅτε δὲ οἱ δικασταὶ καθεστήκασι τιμηταὶ τῆς ζημίας, ὁμοίως πάλιν οὐ φατέον ὅτι ταῦτα οὐκ ἐποίησεν, ἀλλὰ μικρὰ βεβλαμμένον τὸν ἐναντίον καὶ ἀκούσια ἀποφαίνειν πειρατέον. ἐκ τούτων μὲν οὖν καὶ ἐκ τῶν

compelled to admit them, he must try to show that what was done was lawful, just, noble, and advantageous to the city. If it is not possible to demonstrate this, he must try to gain pardon by ascribing the actions to bad luck and by pointing out that the damage resulting from them was small. [8] Distinguish injustice, mistake, and misfortune in the following way: make "injustice" the doing of something wrong with forethought, and say that the greatest punishment must be applied to such things. One must say that "mistakenness" is the doing of some damage because of ignorance. [9] Make "misfortune" the accomplishment of none of the things that were well planned, not because of oneself, but because of others or some chance, and say that wrongdoing is a trait of base people, but mistakes and misfortune in one's actions are not a personal trait of oneself, but are a common trait both of the judges and of other people. Demand pardon when you have been compelled to admit somehow to such charges by making mistakenness and misfortune a trait in common with the audience.

[10] The defense speaker must observe to which wrongs the laws assign punishments and for which the judges assess penalties. When the law defines the punishment, you must show that he did not do it at all, or that what he did was lawful and just. [11] When the judges become assessors of the penalty, you must similarly not say that he did these things, but try to point out that the opponent suffered little damage and that it was unintentional.

---

[40] ταῦτα add. Chiron

τούτοις ὁμοιοτρόπων ἐν ταῖς κατηγορίαις καὶ ταῖς |
10 ἀπολογίαις εὐπορήσομεν· λείπεται δ' ἡμῖν ἔτι διεξελθεῖν τὸ ἐξεταστικὸν εἶδος.

5. ἐν κεφαλαίῳ μὲν οὖν εἰπεῖν, ἡ ἐξέτασίς ἐστι προαιρέσεων ἢ πράξεων ἢ λόγων πρὸς ἄλληλα ἢ πρὸς τὸν ἄλλον βίον ἐναντιουμένων ἐμφάνισις. δεῖ δὲ
15 τὸν ἐξετάζοντα | ζητεῖν εἴ που ἢ ὁ λόγος ὃν ἐξετάζει ἢ αἱ πράξεις τοῦ ἐξεταζομένου ἢ αἱ προαιρέσεις ἐναντιοῦνται ἀλλήλαις. [2] ἡ δὲ μέθοδος ἥδε· σκοπεῖν ἐν τῷ παροιχομένῳ χρόνῳ, εἴ τῳ πρῶτόν τις φίλος γενόμενος πάλιν ἐχθρὸς ἐγένετο καὶ πάλιν φίλος τῷ αὐτῷ
20 τούτῳ, ἤ τι ἄλλο ἐναντίον ἢ εἰς μοχθηρίαν | φέρον ἔπραξεν ἢ ἔτι πράξει, εἰ καιροὶ παραπέσοιεν αὐτῷ, ἐναντίον τοῖς πρότερον ὑπ' αὐτοῦ πεπραγμένοις. [3] ὡσαύτως δὲ ὅρα καὶ εἴ τι εἰπὼν νῦν λέγει ἐναντίον τοῖς πρότερον αὐτῷ εἰρημένοις, ἢ εἴ τι εἴποι ἂν ἐναντίον τοῖς λεγομένοις ἢ τοῖς πρότερον εἰρημένοις.
25 [4] ὡσαύτως δὲ καὶ εἴ | τι προείλετο ἐναντίον τοῖς πρότερον ὑπ' αὐτοῦ προῃρημένοις, ἢ προέλοιτ' ἂν καιρῶν παραπεσόντων. ὁμοιοτρόπως δὲ τούτοις λαμβάνειν καὶ πρὸς τὰ ἄλλα ἔνδοξα ἐπιτηδεύματα τὰς ἐν τῷ τοῦ ἐξεταζομένου βίῳ ἐναντιώσεις. τὸ μὲν οὖν ἐξεταστικὸν εἶδος οὕτω μετιὼν οὐδένα παραλείψεις τρόπον
30 τῆς | ἐξετάσεως.

[5] ἁπάντων δὲ τῶν εἰδῶν ἤδη διῃρημένων δεῖ καὶ χωρὶς τούτων ἑκάστῳ, ὅταν ἁρμόττῃ, χρῆσθαι καὶ κοινῇ, συμμιγνύντα τὰς δυνάμεις αὐτῶν. ταῦτα γὰρ

In these and similar ways we shall be well supplied in prosecution and defense speeches. It remains for us to discuss the investigative species.

5. To describe it in general terms, investigation is the elucidation of choices or acts or words that contradict each other or the rest of the person's life, and the investigator must examine whether somehow the speech that he is investigating or the actions of the person being investigated or his choices contradict each other. [2] The method is as follows: see whether, at a previous time, after having been at first a friend to someone he became his enemy and again a friend to the same person, or if he has done something else contradictory or leading to baseness, or if he will in future do something contradictory to what he has done in the past, if circumstances present themselves. [3] In the same way, see if after saying something he now says the contrary of what he said before, or if he may say something contrary to what is being said or what has been said earlier. [4] In the same way, see whether he has made some choice contrary to what he is choosing now, or what he would choose if circumstances presented themselves. In ways similar to these, take up contradictions in the life of the person being examined with regard to other behaviors that are held in repute. By proceeding through the investigative species in this way you will not miss any mode of investigation.

[5] All the species have now been differentiated; it is necessary to use each of them separately, when it is fitting, and in common, by combining their capacities together.

ἔχει μὲν διαφορὰς εὐμεγέθεις, < . . . >[41] ἐπικοινωνοῦσι μέντοι κατὰ τὰς χρήσεις ἀλλήλοις, καὶ ταὐτὸ πεπόν-
35 θασι τοῖς τῶν ἀνθρώπων | εἴδεσιν· καὶ γὰρ οὗτοι τῇ μὲν ὅμοιοι, τῇ δὲ ἀνόμοιοι τὰς ὄψεις καὶ τὰς αἰσθήσεις εἰσίν. οὕτω δὲ τῶν εἰδῶν διωρισμένων καὶ ὧν προσδέονται κοινῇ πάλιν ἐξαριθμήσωμεν καὶ διεξέλθωμεν ὡς αὐτοῖς δεῖ χρῆσθαι.

6. Πρῶτον μὲν οὖν καὶ τὸ δίκαιον καὶ τὸ νόμιμον
40 καὶ τὸ συμφέρον καὶ τὸ καλὸν καὶ τὸ ἡδὺ καὶ τὰ τούτοις ἀκόλουθα, καθάπερ ἐν ἀρχῇ διειλόμην, κοινὰ
1428a πᾶσι τοῖς εἴδεσίν || ἐστι, μάλιστα δ᾽ αὐτοῖς τὸ προτρέπειν[42] προσχρῆται. [2] δεύτερον δὲ τὰς αὐξήσεις καὶ ταπεινώσεις χρησίμους ἀναγκαῖον εἶναι παρὰ πάντα τὰ λοιπά, μάλιστα δ᾽ αὐτῶν ἐν τοῖς ἐγκωμίοις
5 καὶ τοῖς ψόγοις αἱ χρήσεις. [3] τρίτον δὲ πίστεις, | αἷς ἀνάγκη μὲν πρὸς πάντα τὰ μέρη τῶν λόγων χρῆσθαι, χρησιμώταται δ᾽ εἰσιν ἐν ταῖς κατηγορίαις καὶ ταῖς ἀπολογίαις· ταῦτα γὰρ πλείστης ἀντιλογίας δέονται. πρὸς δὲ τούτοις προκαταλήψεις καὶ αἰτήματα καὶ παλιλλογίαι καὶ μῆκος λόγου καὶ μετριότης μήκους
10 καὶ βραχυλογία καὶ | ἑρμηνεία· ταῦτα γὰρ καὶ τὰ τούτοις ὅμοια κοινὰς ἔχει πᾶσι τοῖς εἴδεσι τὰς χρήσεις.

7. Περὶ μὲν οὖν τῶν δικαίων καὶ τῶν νομίμων καὶ τῶν τούτοις ὁμοιοτρόπων πρότερον διωρισάμην καὶ τὴν χρῆσιν αὐτῶν διεξῆλθον καὶ περὶ μὲν τῶν αὐξήσεων καὶ ταπεινώσεων εἶπον. |
15 νῦν δὲ περὶ τῶν ἄλλων δηλώσω, πρῶτον ἀπὸ τῶν

The species have considerable differences. ‹ . . . ›[14] Indeed, they share in their uses with each other and they have undergone the same thing as the species of humans: they also are similar in one respect, but dissimilar in their looks and appearances. But since the species have been defined in this way, let us enumerate again what they all, in common, require and discuss how to use them.

6. First, then, the just, the lawful, the advantageous, the noble, the pleasant and what follows from them are common to all the species, just as we distinguished at the beginning, but proposition makes the most use of them. [2] Second, amplification and minimization must be useful in all the rest of the species, but their uses are greatest in praise and criticism. [3] Third, proofs, which must be used in all parts of speeches, are most useful in prosecution and defense speeches; these species require the most debate. In addition to these, there are anticipations, appeals, repetitions, length of speech, moderation of length, brevity of speech, and expression. These and similar things have common uses in all the species.

7. Earlier I gave definitions for the just, the lawful, and what is similar to them, went through their use, and spoke about amplification and minimization.

Now I want to explain the other matters, beginning with

[14] There seems a gap here. It is unclear what "they" in the next sentence refers to.

---

[41] lac. ind. ego

[42] προτρέπειν N : προτρεπτικὸν a ρ

πίστεων ἀρξάμενος. [2] *εἰσὶ δὲ δύο τρόποι τῶν πίστεων· γίνονται γὰρ αἱ μὲν ἐξ αὐτῶν τῶν λόγων καὶ τῶν πράξεων καὶ τῶν ἀνθρώπων, αἱ δ' ἐπίθετοι τοῖς λεγομένοις καὶ τοῖς πραττομένοις. τὰ μὲν γὰρ εἰκότα καὶ*
20 *παραδείγματα καὶ* | *τεκμήρια καὶ ἐνθυμήματα καὶ γνῶμαι καὶ τὰ σημεῖα καὶ οἱ ἔλεγχοι* [*καὶ*] *πίστεις ἐξ αὐτῶν τῶν λόγων καὶ τῶν ἀνθρώπων καὶ τῶν πραγμάτων εἰσίν, ἐπίθετοι δὲ* [*δόξα*],[43] *μάρτυρες, ὅρκοι, βάσανοι.* [3] *δεῖ δὲ τούτων ἑκάστην αὐτήν τε συνιέναι ποία τίς ἐστι, καὶ πόθεν αὐτῶν εἰς τοὺς λόγους*[44]
25 *εὐπορήσομεν, καὶ* | *τί ἀλλήλων διαφέρουσιν.*

[4] *εἰκὸς μὲν οὖν ἐστιν οὗ λεγομένου παραδείγματα ἐν ταῖς διανοίαις ἔχουσιν οἱ ἀκούοντες. λέγω δ' οἷον εἴ τις φαίη τὴν πατρίδα βούλεσθαι μεγάλην εἶναι καὶ τοὺς οἰκείους εὖ πράττειν καὶ τοὺς ἐχθροὺς ἀτυχεῖν καὶ τὰ τούτοις ὅμοια,* <*τοιαῦτα*>[45] *συλλήβδην εἰκότα*
30 *δόξειεν* <*ἂν*>.[46] *ἕκαστος γὰρ* | *τῶν ἀκουόντων σύνοιδεν αὐτὸς αὑτῷ περὶ τούτων καὶ τῶν τούτοις ὁμοιοτρόπων ἔχοντι τοιαύτας ἐπιθυμίας. ὥστε τοῦτο δεῖ παρατηρεῖν ἡμᾶς ἐν τοῖς λόγοις ἀεὶ εἰ τοὺς ἀκούοντας συνειδότας ληψόμεθα περὶ τοῦ πράγματος οὗ λέγομεν· τούτοις γὰρ αὐτοὺς εἰκός ἐστι μάλιστα πιστεύειν.* [5] *τὸ μὲν*
35 *οὖν* | *εἰκὸς τοιαύτην ἔχει φύσιν, διαιροῦμεν δὲ αὐτὸ εἰς τρεῖς ἰδέας. μία μὲν οὖν ἐστι τὸ τὰ πάθη τὰ κατὰ φύσιν ἀκολουθοῦντα τοῖς ἀνθρώποις* <*ἐν*> *τοῖς λόγοις*

[43] *δόξα* H : om. N FCUP *ρ* [44] *αὐτῶν εἰς τοὺς λόγους* Zwierlein et Fuhrmann² : *τῶν εἰς αὐτὴν λόγων* N a

the proofs. [2] There are two kinds of proofs: some arise from the speeches themselves, the actions, and the people; others are supplementary to what is said and done. Plausibilities, examples, *tekmeria,* enthymemes, maxims, signs, and *elenchoi* are proofs from the words, the people, and the acts; supplementary are opinion (of the speaker),[15] witnesses, oaths, and tortures.[16] [3] We must understand each of them, what it is, from what sources of them we shall be equipped for speeches, and how they differ from each other.

[4] There is *plausibility* in what is being said when the audience has examples in their thoughts. I mean, for example, if someone were to say that he wanted his homeland to be great, his friends to do well, his enemies to have misfortune, and similar things, such things would, taken together, appear plausible. Everyone in the audience agrees that he himself has such desires about these and similar things. So we must always take care in speeches that we grasp whether the audience agrees with us about the matter about which we are speaking. It is plausible that they really believe these things. [5] Plausibility has this nature, but we shall divide it into three forms. One is, whether speaking for the prosecution or defense, to take into account in the

[15] Most of the mss. do not have the word "opinion" here, let alone "opinion of the speaker," but see 14.9 1431b18.

[16] What is meant is either statements by someone, usually a slave, who was tortured, or statements that such a person might have made if both parties had agreed to conduct such torture.

---

[45] τοιαῦτα add. Chiron

[46] ἂν add. Sp.[2]

συμπαραλαμβάνειν ἐν τῷ κατηγορεῖν ἢ ἀπολογεῖσθαι, οἷον ἐὰν τύχωσί τινες καταφρονήσαντές τινος ἢ
40 δείσαντες, εἰ[47] καὶ αὐτοὶ[48] τοῦτο τὸ πρᾶγμα | πολλάκις
1428b πεποιηκότες, ἢ πάλιν ἡσθέντες ἢ λυπηθέντες || ἢ ἐπιθυμοῦντες ἢ πεπαυμένοι τῶν ἐπιθυμιῶν ἤ τι τοιοῦτον ἕτερον πεπονθότες πάθος ταῖς ψυχαῖς ἢ τοῖς σώμασιν ἤ τινι τῶν ἄλλων αἰσθήσεων οἷς συμπάσχομεν· ταῦτα
5 γὰρ καὶ τὰ τούτοις ὅμοια κοινὰ τῆς ἀνθρωπείας | φύσεως ὄντα πάθη γνώριμα τοῖς ἀκούουσίν ἐστιν. [6] τὰ μὲν οὖν κατὰ φύσιν τοῖς ἀνθρώποις εἰθισμένα γίνεσθαι τοιαῦτά ἐστιν, ἅ φαμεν δεῖν συμπαραλαμβάνειν ἐν τοῖς λόγοις. ἕτερον δὲ μέρος ἐστὶ τῶν εἰκότων ἔθος, ὃ κατὰ συνήθειαν ἕκαστοι ποιοῦμεν. τρίτον δὲ κέρδος·
10 πολλάκις γὰρ διὰ τοῦτο | τὴν φύσιν βιασάμενοι καὶ τὰ ἤθη προειλόμεθα πράττειν.

[7] οὕτω δὲ τούτων διωρισμένων, ἐν μὲν ταῖς προτροπαῖς καὶ ταῖς ἀποτροπαῖς δεικτέον ὑπὲρ τῶν ζητουμένων ὅτι τοῦτο τὸ πρᾶγμα, ἐφ' ὃ ἡμεῖς παρακαλοῦμεν ἢ ᾧ ἀντιλέγομεν οὕτως ὡς ἡμεῖς φαμεν
15 γίνεται, εἰ δὲ μή, ὅτι τὰ τούτῳ | τῷ πράγματι ὅμοια τοῦτον τὸν τρόπον γίνεται ὃν ἡμεῖς φαμεν ἢ τὰ πλεῖστα ἢ τὰ πάντα. [8] κατὰ μὲν οὖν τῶν πραγμάτων οὕτω τὸ εἰκὸς ληπτέον.

κατὰ δὲ τῶν ἀνθρώπων ἐν μὲν ταῖς κατηγορίαις, ἐὰν ἔχῃς, ἐπιδείκνυε αὐτὸν τοῦτο τὸ πρᾶγμα πολλάκις
20 πεποιηκότα πρότερον, εἰ δὲ μή, | ὅμοια τούτῳ. πειρῶ δὲ ἀποφαίνειν καὶ ὡς λυσιτελὲς ἦν αὐτῷ ταῦτα ποιεῖν· οἱ γὰρ πλεῖστοι τῶν ἀνθρώπων αὐτοὶ τὸ λυσιτελὲς μάλι-

speeches the emotions that naturally follow for humans, for example if certain people happen to despise or fear something, even if they have often done it, or again, if they feel pleasure or pain or desire, or stop desiring, or have experienced some other emotion mentally or physically or in some other sense by which we are affected. These and similar things are well known by the audience to be common emotions in human nature. [6] Such things regularly happen to people by nature, and we say that they ought to be taken into account in speeches. Another part of plausibility is habit, what each of us does by habituation. A third is profit: because of it we often choose to act although doing violence to our nature and characters.

[7] Since these things have been defined in this way, in speeches of proposition and opposition we must show, about the matters in question, that this action, for which we are appealing or against which we are speaking, will turn out as we say it will, and if not, that actions similar to this one will turn out in the way we say, either mostly or always. [8] With regard to actions, we must deal with plausibility in this way.

With regard to people, demonstrate in prosecution speeches, if you can, that he has often done this action before, and if not, then actions similar to this one. Try to point out that doing this was profitable for him; most people themselves really prefer what is profitable and think that

---

47 *εἰ* Chiron : *ἢ* N a
48 *αὐτοὶ* ego : *αὐτὸ* codd.

στα προτιμῶντες καὶ τοὺς ἄλλους νομίζουσιν ἕνεκα τούτου πάντα πράττειν. [9] ἂν μὲν οὖν ἔχῃς ἀπὸ τῶν ἀντιδίκων αὐτῶν τὸ εἰκὸς λαμβάνειν, οὕτως αὐτὸ σύν-
25 αγε, | εἰ δὲ μή, ἀπὸ τῶν ὁμοίων τὰ εἰθισμένα φέρε. λέγω δ' οἷον <εἰ>[49] νέος ἐστὶν οὗ κατηγορεῖς, ἃ οἱ περὶ τὴν ἡλικίαν ταύτην ὄντες πράττουσι, ταῦτα λέγε πεποιηκέναι αὐτόν· πιστευθήσεται γὰρ κατὰ τὴν ὁμοιότητα καὶ τὰ κατὰ τούτου λεγόμενα. τὸν αὐτὸν δὲ
30 τρόπον καὶ ἐὰν | τοὺς ἑταίρους αὐτοῦ δεικνύῃς τοιούτους ὄντας οἷον σὺ τοῦτον φῄς· καὶ γὰρ διὰ τὴν πρὸς ἐκείνους συνήθειαν δόξει τὰ αὐτὰ τοῖς φίλοις ἐπιτηδεύειν. [10] τοὺς μὲν οὖν κατηγοροῦντας οὕτω χρὴ μετιέναι τὸ εἰκός.

τοῖς δὲ ἀπολογουμένοις μάλιστα δεικτέον ὡς οὐδεπώποτε τῶν κατηγορουμένων τι πρότερον οὔτε αὐτοὶ
35 οὔτε | τῶν φίλων οὐδεὶς οὔτε τῶν ὁμοίων αὐτοῖς ἔπραξέ τις, οὐδ' ἐλυσιτέλησεν <ἂν>[50] τοιαῦτα πράττειν. [11] ἂν δὲ φανερὸς ᾖς ταὐτὸ τοῦτο πρότερον πεποιηκώς, αἰτιατέον τὴν ἡλικίαν ἤ τινα πρόφασιν ἄλλην οἰστέον, δι' ἣν εἰκότως ἐξήμαρτες τότε. λέγε δὲ καὶ ὡς οὔτε ταῦτα τότε σοὶ πράξαντι συνήνεγκεν οὔτε νῦν |
40 ἐλυσιτέλησεν ἄν. [12] ἂν δὲ σοὶ μηδὲν ᾖ πεπραγμένον
1429a τοιοῦτον, || τῶν δὲ φίλων σού τινες τυγχάνωσι τοιαῦτα πεποιηκότες, χρὴ λέγειν ὡς οὐ δίκαιόν ἐστι δι' ἐκείνους αὐτὸν διαβάλλεσθαι, καὶ δεικνύναι τῶν αὑτῷ συνήθων ἑτέρους ἐπιεικεῖς ὄντας· οὕτω γὰρ ἀμφί-
5 βολον ποιήσεις τὸ κατηγορούμενον. | ἂν δὲ τῶν ὁμοίων δεικνύωσί τινας τὰ αὐτὰ πεποιηκότας, ἄτοπον εἶναι

others do everything for this reason. [9] If you can take an argument from plausibility from the adversaries themselves, do so, but if not, then bring in what similar people regularly do. I mean, for example, if it is a young man against whom you are giving the prosecution speech, say that he is doing what those who are at that age do. What is said against him will be credible because of his age. In the same way, it will be credible if you argue that his companions are the same as you say that he is. Because of his association with them he will appear to behave in the same way as his friends. [10] Those giving prosecution speeches must pursue plausibility in this way.

Those giving defense speeches must argue that they have never in the past done any of the things the prosecutors are talking about, nor have any of their friends or anyone like them, nor would anyone have profited by doing so. [11] If you have clearly done the same thing earlier, you must blame your age or offer another excuse for why you likely made a mistake then. Say that it was not advantageous for you to do these things then and it would not have profited you now. [12] If you have never done such a thing but some of your friends happen to have done so, you must say that it is not just for you to incur prejudice because of them, and argue that your other acquaintances are honest. In this way you will make what is being accused ambiguous. If they argue that some similar people have done the

---

49 εἰ add. Richards
50 ἂν add. Rackham

φάσκε, [εἰ,][51] διότι ἕτεροί τινες ἐξαμαρτάνοντες φαίνονται, πίστιν εἶναι, ὅτι τῶν ἐγκαλουμένων τι καὶ σὺ πεποίηκας. [13] ἂν μὲν οὖν ἔξαρνος ᾖς μὴ πεποιηκέναι τὴν κατηγορουμένην πρᾶξιν, οὕτως ἐκ τῶν εἰκότων
10 χρή σε ἀπολογεῖσθαι· | ἀπίθανον γὰρ ποιήσεις τὴν κατηγορίαν. ἂν δὲ ὁμολογεῖν ἀναγκάζῃ, τοῖς τῶν πολλῶν ἤθεσιν ἀφομοίου τὰς σαυτοῦ πράξεις ὅτι μάλιστα λέγων ὡς οἱ πλεῖστοι ἢ οἱ πάντες τοῦτο καὶ τὰ τοιαῦτα πράττουσιν οὕτως ὡς σοὶ τυγχάνει πεποιημένον. [14] ἂν δὲ μὴ δυνατὸν ᾖ τοῦτο δεῖξαι, κατα-
15 φευκτέον | ἐπὶ τὰς ἀτυχίας ἢ τὰς ἁμαρτίας καὶ συγγνώμης πειρατέον τυγχάνειν συμπαραλαμβάνοντα τὰ κοινὰ τῶν ἀνθρώπων γινόμενα πάθη δι' ὧν ἐξιστάμεθα τοῦ λογισμοῦ· ταῦτα δ' ἐστὶν ἔρως, ὀργή, μέθη, φιλοτιμία καὶ τὰ τούτοις ὁμοιότροπα. τὸ μὲν οὖν εἰκὸς
20 διὰ ταύτης τῆς μεθόδου | τεχνικώτατα μέτιμεν.

8. Παραδείγματα δ' ἐστὶ πράξεις ὅμοιαι γεγενημέναι καὶ ἐναντίαι ταῖς νῦν ὑφ' ἡμῶν λεγομέναις. τότε δὲ χρηστέον αὐτοῖς ἐστιν ὅταν ἄπιστον ὂν τὸ ὑπὸ σοῦ λεγόμενον [εἶναι][52] φανερὸν ποιῆσαι θέλῃς, ἐὰν διὰ
25 τοῦ εἰκότος μὴ πιστεύηται, | ὅπως πρᾶξιν ὁμοίαν ἑτέραν τῇ ὑπὸ σοῦ λεγομένῃ καταμαθόντες οὕτω πεπραγμένην, ὡς σὺ φῂς πεπρᾶχθαι, μᾶλλον πιστεύσωσι τοῖς ὑπὸ σοῦ λεγομένοις. [2] εἰσὶ δὲ τῶν παραδειγμάτων δύο τρόποι· τὰ μὲν γὰρ τῶν πραγμάτων γίνεται κατὰ λόγον, τὰ δὲ παρὰ λόγον. ποιεῖ δὲ τὰ μὲν κατὰ |
30 λόγον γινόμενα πιστεύεσθαι, τὰ δὲ μὴ κατὰ λόγον ἀπιστεῖσθαι. [3] λέγω δ' οἷον εἴ τις φάσκοι τοὺς

same things, state that it is absurd to believe that you have done any of the things that are alleged because others appear to have done wrongs. [13] If you deny that you have done the alleged action, you must base your defense on plausibilities and so make the prosecution speech unpersuasive. If you are compelled to make an admission, compare your actions to the characteristics of the many by saying as strongly as possible that most or even all do this, and this sort of thing, just as you happen to have done. [14] If it is not possible to make this argument, you must resort to pleas of misfortune or mistakenness and try to win pardon by taking into account the common human emotions through which we lose our reasoning. These are love, anger, drunkenness, pride, and so on. We pursue plausibility most skillfully through this method.

8. *Examples* are actions that have taken place that are similar or contrary to those being discussed by us now. You must use them whenever what you are saying is hard to believe but you want to make clear (if it does not become credible through an argument from plausibility) that once they learn that an action similar to the one being discussed by you has been done as you say it was done, they will believe more in what you are saying. [2] There are two sorts of examples: some events occur according to and others against reasonable expectation. Those that occur according to reasonable expectation create belief; those that occur not according to reasonable expectation create disbelief. [3] I mean, for instance, if someone were to argue that

---

51 εἰ om. ρ
52 εἶναι del. Sp.[2]

πλουσίους δικαιοτέρους εἶναι τῶν πενομένων καὶ φέροι τινὰς πράξεις πλουσίων ἀνδρῶν δικαίας. τὰ μὲν οὖν τοιαῦτα τῶν παραδειγμάτων κατὰ λόγον εἶναι
35 δοκεῖ· τοὺς γὰρ πλείστους <ἔστιν>[53] ἰδεῖν | νομίζοντας τοὺς πλουτοῦντας δικαιοτέρους εἶναι τῶν πενομένων. [4] εἰ δέ τις πάλιν ἀποφαίνοι τινὰς τῶν πλουσίων ἐπὶ χρήμασιν ἀδικήσαντας, τῷ παρὰ τὸ εἰκὸς γενομένῳ παραδείγματι χρώμενος ἀπίστους ἂν ποιοῖ[54] τοὺς πλουτοῦντας. [5] ὡσαύτως δὲ καὶ εἴ τις φέροι παρά-
1429b δειγμα τῶν κατὰ λόγον εἶναι δοκούντων || διότι Λακεδαιμόνιοί ποτε ἢ Ἀθηναῖοι πολλῷ πλήθει χρώμενοι συμμάχων κατεπολέμησαν τοὺς ἐναντίους, καὶ προτρέποι τοὺς ἀκούοντας πολλοὺς συμμάχους ποιεῖσθαι· τὰ μὲν δὴ τοιαῦτα παραδείγματα κατὰ λόγον
5 ἐστίν· ἅπαντες | γὰρ νομίζουσιν ἐν τοῖς πολέμοις τὸ πλῆθος οὐ μετρίαν ῥοπὴν ἔχειν πρὸς τὴν νίκην. [6] εἰ δέ τις ἀποφαίνειν ἐθέλοι μὴ τοῦτ' αἴτιον τοῦ νικᾶν, τοῖς παρὰ τὸ εἰκὸς γενομένοις πράγμασι χρήσαιτ' ἂν παραδείγμασι, λέγων ὡς οἱ μὲν Ἀθήνησι φυγάδες τὸ
10 πρῶτον μετὰ πεντήκοντα ἀνδρῶν Φυλήν | τε καταλαβόντες καὶ πρὸς τοὺς ἐν ἄστει πολλῷ πλείους ὄντας καὶ συμμάχοις Λακεδαιμονίοις χρωμένους πολεμήσαντες κατῆλθον εἰς τὴν ἰδίαν πόλιν· [7] Θηβαῖοι δὲ Λακεδαιμονίων καὶ σχεδὸν ἁπάντων Πελοποννησίων εἰς τὴν Βοιωτίαν ἐμβαλόντων μόνοι περὶ τὰ Λεῦκτρα
15 παραταξάμενοι | τὴν Λακεδαιμονίων δύναμιν ἐνίκησαν· Δίων δὲ ὁ Συρακούσιος μετὰ τρισχιλίων ὁπλιτῶν εἰς Συρακούσας πλεύσας Διονύσιον πολλαπλάσιον ἔχον-

the rich are more just than the poor and cited certain just actions of rich men. This sort of example seems according to reasonable expectation since one can see that most people think that the rich are more just than the poor. [4] But if on the contrary someone pointed out that some rich people have done injustice for money, by using this example, which occurred contrary to plausibility, he would discredit the rich. [5] In the same way, if someone cited an example of things appearing to be according to reason, such as that the Lacedaemonians or the Athenians once used a great number of allies to defeat their opponents in war, he would also be proposing to the audience to make many allies. Such examples are according to reason since everyone believes that in war a great number of allies has a great influence on victory. [6] But if someone wanted to point out that this was not the cause of the victory, he would use as examples events that took place contrary to plausibility such as the exiles at Athens who with fifty men first took Phyle and waged war against the much more numerous men in the city, who were using Spartan allies, and thus entered their own city. [7] And when the Lacedaemonians, together with almost all the Peloponnesians, attacked Boeotia, the Thebans arrayed themselves alone around Leuctra and conquered the Lacedaemonian force. And Dion the Syracusan with three thousand hoplites sailed to Syra-

---

53 ἔστιν add. Cant. Erasm. *est*

54 ποιοῖ Bekker : ποιοῖτο N a

τα δύναμιν κατεπολέμησεν· [8] ὡσαύτως δὲ Κορίνθιοι Συρακουσίοις ἐννέα τριήρεσι βοηθήσαντες Καρχηδο-
20 νίους ἑκατὸν μὲν καὶ πεντήκοντα ναυσὶν ἐπὶ | τοῖς λιμέσι τῶν Συρακουσίων ἐφορμοῦντας, τὴν δὲ πόλιν ἅπασαν πλὴν τῆς ἀκροπόλεως ἔχοντας οὐδὲν ἧττον κατεπολέμησαν. συλλήβδην δὲ ταῦτα καὶ τὰ τούτοις ὅμοια παρὰ λόγον πραχθέντα τὰς κατὰ τὸ εἰκὸς γινομένας συμβουλὰς ἀπίστους ποιεῖν εἴωθεν.

25 [9] τῶν μὲν οὖν παραδειγμάτων | τοιαύτη τις ἡ φύσις ἐστί· χρηστέον δ' αὐτῶν ἑκατέρῳ τρόπῳ, ὅταν μὲν ἡμεῖς λέγωμεν τὰ κατὰ λόγον γινόμενα, δεικνύντας ὡς ἐπὶ τὸ πολὺ τοῦτον τὸν τρόπον ἐπιτελουμένας τὰς πράξεις, ὅταν δὲ τὰ παρὰ λόγον γινόμενα, φέροντας ὅσα παρὰ λόγον δοκοῦντα γενέσθαι τῶν πραγμά-
30 των εὐλόγως | ἀποβέβηκεν. [10] ὅταν δ' οἱ ἐναντίοι λέγωσι τοῦτο, χρὴ δεικνύειν ὡς εὐτυχήματα ταῦτα συνέβη, καὶ λέγειν ὅτι αἱ τοιαῦται πράξεις ἐν τῷ σπανίῳ γεγόνασιν, οἵας δὲ σὺ λέγεις, πολλάκις. τοῖς μὲν οὖν παραδείγμασιν οὕτω χρηστέον.

[11] ὅταν γε μὴν τὰ παρὰ λόγον γινόμενα φέρωμεν, |
35 χρὴ συνάγειν αὐτῶν ὅτι πλεῖστα καὶ λέγειν ὡς οὐδὲν μᾶλλον ἐκεῖνα τούτων εἴωθε γίνεσθαι. [12] δεῖ δὲ χρῆσθαι τοῖς παραδείγμασιν οὐ μόνον ἐκ τούτων, ἀλλὰ καὶ ἐκ τῶν ἐναντίων. λέγω δ' οἷον ἐὰν ἀποφαίνῃς τινὰς πλεονεκτικῶς τοῖς συμμάχοις χρωμένους καὶ
1430a διὰ τοῦτο λυθεῖσαν αὐτῶν τὴν || φιλίαν καὶ λέγῃς· "ἡμεῖς δέ, ἂν ἴσως καὶ κοινῶς πρὸς αὐτοὺς προσφερώμεθα, πολὺν χρόνον τὴν συμμαχίαν φυλάξομεν·"

cuse and defeated Dionysius, who had a much larger force. [8] In the same way, the Corinthians gave the Syracusans the help of (only) nine triremes and nevertheless defeated the Carthaginians, who were blockading the Syracusan harbors with one hundred fifty ships and held the entire city except the acropolis. In short, these and similar things that have been done contrary to reasonable expectation have commonly discredited counsels based on plausibility.

[9] Such is the nature of examples. We must use each sort when we are talking about things that take place according to reasonable expectation, arguing that the actions turn out in this way for the most part, but when we are talking about things that happen against reasonable expectation by bringing in whatever matters seem to have taken place against reasonable expectation and worked out reasonably well. [10] When the opponents say this, we must argue that that was good luck and say that such actions have rarely taken place, but what you are describing takes place often. We must use these examples in this way.

[11] When, however, we are bringing in things that have taken place against reasonable expectation, we must collect as many of them as possible and say that they have taken place no less commonly than those that take place according to reason. [12] We must not only use these examples, but also those based on contraries. I mean, for example, if you point out that some use allies selfishly and that their friendship is destroyed because of it, you may also say, "But if we conduct ourselves fairly in partnership toward them, we shall guard our alliance for a long time."

[13] καὶ πάλιν, ἄν τινας ἑτέρους ἀπαρασκευάστως πολεμήσαντας καὶ διὰ τοῦτο καταπολεμηθέντας ἀπο-
5 φαίνῃς, εἶτα λέγῃς· | "ἂν παρασκευασάμενοι πολεμῶμεν, βελτίους ἂν περὶ τῆς νίκης τὰς ἐλπίδας ἔχοιμεν."
[14] πολλὰ δὲ λήψῃ παραδείγματα διὰ τῶν προγεγενημένων πράξεων καὶ διὰ τῶν νῦν γινομένων· τὰ γὰρ πλεῖστα τῶν ἔργων τῇ μὲν ὅμοια, τῇ δὲ ἀνόμοια
10 ἀλλήλοις ἐστίν, ὥστε διὰ τὴν αἰτίαν ταύτην καὶ | παραδειγμάτων εὐπορήσομεν καὶ τοῖς ὑπὸ τῶν ἄλλων λεγομένοις οὐ χαλεπῶς ἀντεροῦμεν. τῶν μὲν οὖν παραδειγμάτων τούς τε τρόπους ἴσμεν, καὶ ὡς αὐτοῖς χρησόμεθα, καὶ ὅθεν πολλὰ ληψόμεθα.

9. Τεκμήρια δ' ἐστιν ὅσ' ἂν ἐναντίως ᾖ πεπραγμένα |
15 τῷ περὶ οὗ ὁ λόγος καὶ ὅσα ὁ λόγος αὐτὸς ἑαυτῷ ἐναντιοῦται· τῶν γὰρ ἀκουόντων οἱ πλεῖστοι τοῖς συμβαίνουσι περὶ τὸν λόγον ἢ τὴν πρᾶξιν ἐναντιώμασι τεκμαίρονται μηδὲν ὑγιὲς εἶναι μήτε τῶν λεγομένων μήτε τῶν πραττομένων. [2] πολλὰ δὲ λήψῃ τεκμήρια
20 σκοπῶν εἴτε ὁ λόγος τοῦ ἐναντίου | αὐτὸς αὑτῷ [τῷ πράγματι][55] ἐναντιοῦται, εἴτε ἡ πρᾶξις αὐτοῦ ἐναντία τῷ λόγῳ ἐστίν. τὰ μὲν οὖν τεκμήρια τοιαῦτά ἐστι, καὶ οὕτως αὐτὰ πλεῖστα ποιήσεις.

10. Ἐνθυμήματα δ' ἐστὶν οὐ μόνον τὰ τῷ λόγῳ καὶ τῇ πράξει ἐναντιούμενα, ἀλλὰ καὶ τοῖς ἄλλοις ἅπασιν.

[55] τῷ πράγματι om. Lat.[a] Philelphus del. Buhle

[13] And again, you may point out that others have waged war without preparation and been defeated as a result, and then say, "If we wage war after making preparations, we may have better hopes of victory." [14] You will obtain examples through actions that have taken place in the past and through those that are taking place now. Most matters have some similarity or dissimilarity to each other, and for this reason we shall be well supplied with examples and will respond without difficulty to what others say. We now know the kinds of examples, how to use them, and where we shall obtain many of them.

9. *Tekmeria*[17] are whatever has been done in a way contrary to what the speech is about and those things with respect to which the speech is contrary to itself. Most of the audience take as *tekmeria* the contraries that occur in the speech or action and conclude that there is nothing sound in what has been said and done. [2] You will obtain many *tekmeria* by examining whether the speech of the opponent contradicts itself with regard to the act or if the action contradicts the speech. Such are the *tekmeria*, and you will create many of them in this way.

10. *Enthymemes*[18] are contraries not only in word and action, but also in all other ways. You will obtain many of

[17] What Anaximenes means by *tekmeria* (*tekmerion*, sg.) is strikingly different from Aristotle's "sure signs." "Contradictions" may be possible, but it seems better to use the transliterated Greek term.

[18] What Anaximenes means by *enthymeme* (*enthymema*, *enthymemata* pl.) is strikingly different from Aristotle's "rhetorical syllogism." It seems best to use the anglicized term "enthymeme" so long as this difference from Aristotle is understood.

25 λήψῃ | δὲ πολλὰ μετιὼν ὡς ἐν τῷ ἐξεταστικῷ εἴδει εἴρηται, καὶ σκοπῶν, εἴ πῃ ὁ λόγος ἑαυτῷ ἐναντιοῦται ἢ τὰ πεπραγμένα τοῖς δικαίοις ἢ τῷ νόμῳ ἢ τῷ συμφέροντι ἢ τῷ καλῷ ἢ τῷ δυνατῷ ἢ τῷ ῥᾳδίῳ ἢ τῷ εἰκότι ἢ τῷ ἤθει τοῦ λέγοντος ἢ τῷ ἔθει τῶν πραγμά-
30 των. [2] τὰ μὲν οὖν | τοιαῦτα τῶν ἐνθυμημάτων κατὰ τῶν ἐναντίων ἐκληπτέον· τὰ δ' ἐναντία τούτοις ὑπὲρ ἡμῶν αὐτῶν δεῖ λέγειν, ἀποφαίνοντας τὰς πράξεις τὰς ἡμετέρας καὶ τοὺς λόγους ἐναντιουμένους τοῖς ἀδίκοις καὶ τοῖς ἀνόμοις καὶ τοῖς ἀσυμφόροις καὶ τοῖς τῶν
35 ἀνθρώπων τῶν πονηρῶν ἤθεσι, καὶ συλλήβδην | τοῖς μοχθηροῖς νομιζομένοις εἶναι. [3] δεῖ δὲ τούτων ἕκαστα συνάγειν ὡς εἰς βραχύτατα καὶ φράζειν ὅτι μάλιστα ἐν ὀλίγοις τοῖς ὀνόμασιν. τὰ μὲν οὖν ἐνθυμήματα τοῦτον τὸν τρόπον πολλὰ ποιήσομεν, καὶ οὕτως αὐτοῖς ἄριστα χρησόμεθα. |

40 11. Γνώμη δ' ἐστὶ μὲν ὡς ἐν κεφαλαίῳ καθ' ὅλων
1430b τῶν πραγμάτων || δόγματος ἰδίου δήλωσις. δύο δὲ τρόποι τῶν γνωμῶν εἰσιν, ὁ μὲν ἔνδοξος, ὁ δὲ παράδοξος. [2] ὅταν μὲν οὖν ἔνδοξον λέγῃς, οὐδὲν δεῖ τὰς αἰτίας φέρειν· οὔτε γὰρ ἀγνοεῖται τὸ λεγόμενον οὔτ' ἀπιστεῖ-
5 ται· ὅταν δὲ παράδοξον λέγῃς, | χρὴ φράζειν τὰς αἰτίας συντόμως, ἵνα τὴν ἀδολεσχίαν καὶ τὴν ἀπιστίαν διαφύγῃς. δεῖ δ' ἀεὶ τὰς γνώμας οἰκείας φέρειν τῶν πραγμάτων, ἵνα μὴ σκαιὸν καὶ ἀπηρτημένον φαίνηται τὸ λεγόμενον. [3] πολλὰς δὲ ποιήσομεν αὐτὰς ἢ ἐκ τῆς ἰδίας φύσεως ἢ ἐξ ὑπερβολῆς ἢ ἐκ παρομοιώσεως.
10 αἱ | μὲν οὖν ἐκ τῆς ἰδίας φύσεως τοιαίδε τινές εἰσιν·

them by proceeding as has been described regarding the investigative species and examining whether the speech contradicts itself somehow or what has been done contradicts what is just, lawful, advantageous, noble, possible, easy, plausible, the character of the speaker, or the pattern of the facts. [2] We must select such enthymemes against the opponents; but we must say what is contrary to them for ourselves, pointing out that our actions and speeches contradict the unjust, unlawful, disadvantageous, the characters of bad people, and, in short, what is thought to be base. [3] We must collect each of these as briefly as possible and state them in the fewest words. We shall create many enthymemes in this way and so use them best.

11. A *maxim* is basically an explanation of a particular conviction with regard to matters in general, but there are two sorts of maxims, one being conventional, the other paradoxical. [2] Whenever you speak conventionally, there is no need to offer the grounds; what you say is not unknown or disbelieved. But when you speak paradoxically, you must state the grounds concisely so that you may avoid excess subtlety and disbelief. You must always offer the proper maxims for the subject so that what you say does not appear clumsy and incoherent. [3] We shall create many maxims from the individual nature of the situation, from exaggeration, and from drawing similarities. The following are maxims based on the particular nature of the

"οὐκ εἶναί μοι δοκεῖ δεινὸν γενέσθαι στρατηγὸν πραγμάτων ἄπειρον ὄντα." ἑτέρα δ' ἐστὶν ἥδε· "νοῦν ἐχόντων ἀνδρῶν ἐστι τοῖς τῶν προγεγενημένων παραδείγμασι χρωμένους πειρᾶσθαι διαφυγεῖν τὰς ἐκ τῆς
15 ἀβουλίας ἁμαρτίας." [4] ἐκ μὲν οὖν τῆς | ἰδίας φύσεως τοιαύτας ποιήσομεν γνώμας, ἐξ ὑπερβολῆς δὲ τοιάσδε· "δεινότερά μοι δοκοῦσιν οἱ κλέπτοντες τῶν ληϊζομένων ποιεῖν· οἱ μὲν γὰρ λαθραίως, οἱ δὲ φανερῶς τὰ χρήματα περιαιροῦνται." [5] τὰς μὲν οὖν ἐξ ὑπερβολῆς γνώμας τὸν τρόπον τοῦτον πολλὰς ποιήσομεν.
20 αἱ δ' ἐκ παρομοιώσεως | τοιαίδε εἰσίν· "ὁμοιότατόν μοι δοκοῦσιν οἱ τὰ χρήματα ἀποστεροῦντες τοῖς τὰς πόλεις προδιδοῦσι ποιεῖν· πιστευθέντες γὰρ ἀμφότεροι τοὺς πιστεύσαντας ἀδικοῦσιν." [6] ἑτέρα δέ· "παραπλήσιόν μοι δοκοῦσι ποιεῖν οἱ ἀντίδικοι τοῖς τυράννοις· ἐκεῖνοί τε γὰρ ὧν μὲν αὐτοὶ ἀδικοῦσιν, οὐκ
25 ἀξιοῦσι | διδόναι δίκας, ὧν δὲ τοῖς ἄλλοις ἐγκαλοῦσιν, ἀνυπερβλήτως τιμωροῦνται, οὗτοί τε εἰ μέν τι αὐτοὶ τῶν ἐμῶν ἔχουσιν, οὐκ ἀποδιδόασιν, εἰ δέ τι ἐγὼ τούτων ἔλαβον, καὶ αὐτὸ καὶ τοὺς τόκους οἴονται δεῖν κομίσασθαι." γνώμας μὲν οὖν τοῦτον τὸν τρόπον μετιόντες πολλὰς ποιήσομεν. |

30 12. Σημεῖον δ' ἐστὶν ἄλλο ἄλλου, οὐ τὸ τυχὸν τοῦ τυχόντος οὐδ' ἅπαν παντός, ἀλλὰ τό γε εἰθισμένον γίνεσθαι πρὸ τοῦ πράγματος ἢ ἅμα τῷ πράγματι ἢ μετὰ τὸ πρᾶγμα. [2] ἔστι δὲ σημεῖον τό τε γενόμενον οὐ μόνου τοῦ γενομένου, ἀλλὰ καὶ τοῦ μὴ γενομένου,
35 ὡσαύτως δὲ καὶ τὸ μὴ γεγονὸς | οὐ μόνον τοῦ μὴ ὄντος,

situation: "It seems to me impossible to become a general without practical experience." Here is another: "It is characteristic of sensible men to use their experience of past examples to avoid the mistakes of bad planning." [4] We shall make this sort of maxim based on the individual nature of the situation, and the following based on exaggeration: "Thieves seem more dangerous than robbers; thieves steal possessions secretly, but robbers do so openly." [5] We shall create many maxims based on exaggeration in this way. Those based on similarity are like the following: "Those who embezzle money seem to me very like those who betray their cities; although trusted, they both do injustice to those who trust them." [6] And another: "The opponents seem to me to act very like tyrants. Tyrants do injustice and demand not to pay the penalty for it, but they accuse others and claim exaggerated compensation. These people, if they have something of mine, they do not return it, but if I have taken something of theirs, they think it has to be returned with interest." We shall create many maxims if we pursue this method.

12. One thing is a *sign* of another, not a chance event of a chance event, nor everything of everything, but what usually happens before another event, at the same time, or after it. [2] Not only is what happens a sign of what happens, but it is also a sign of what does not happen, and similarly what does not happen is a sign of what is not, and also

ἀλλὰ καὶ τοῦ ὄντος. ποιεῖ δὲ τῶν σημείων τὸ μὲν οἴεσθαι, τὸ δ᾽ εἰδέναι, κάλλιστον δὲ τὸ εἰδέναι ποιοῦν· δεύτερον δὲ τὸ δόξαν πιθανωτάτην ἐργαζόμενον. [3] πολλὰ δὲ ποιήσομεν σημεῖα συλλήβδην εἰπεῖν ἐξ ἑκάστου τῶν πεπραγμένων καὶ λεγομένων καὶ ὁρωμένων, | καθ᾽ ἓν ἕκαστον λαμβάνοντες, ἔκ τε τοῦ μεγέθους καὶ τῆς || μικρότητος τῶν ἀποβαινόντων κακῶν ἢ ἀγαθῶν, ἔτι δὲ καὶ ἐκ τῶν μαρτύρων καὶ ἐκ τῶν μαρτυρουμένων καὶ ἐκ τῶν συμπαρόντων ἡμῖν ἢ τοῖς ἐναντίοις καὶ ἐξ αὐτῶν ἐκείνων καὶ ἐκ τῶν προκλήσεων καὶ ἐκ τῶν χρόνων καὶ ἐξ ἄλλων | πολλῶν. τῶν μὲν οὖν σημείων ἐντεῦθεν εὐπορήσομεν.

40

1431a

5

13. Ἔλεγχος δ᾽ ἐστὶ μέν ὃ μὴ δυνατὸν ἄλλως ἔχειν ἀλλ᾽ οὕτως ὡς ἡμεῖς λέγομεν· λαμβάνεται δὲ ἐκ τῶν φύσει ἀναγκαίων ‹ἢ ἀναγκαίων›[56] ὡς ἡμεῖς λέγομεν [ἢ ὁ ἀντιλέγων][57] καὶ ἐκ τῶν κατὰ φύσιν ἀδυνάτων ἢ ἀδυνάτων ὡς οἱ ἐναντίοι λέγουσιν. | [2] κατὰ φύσιν μὲν οὖν ἀναγκαῖόν ἐστιν οἷον τοὺς ζῶντας σιτίων δεῖσθαι καὶ τὰ τούτοις ὅμοια· ὡς δ᾽ ἡμεῖς λεγομέν ἐστιν ἀναγκαῖον τοὺς μεμαστιγωμένους ὁμολογεῖν ἅπερ οἱ μαστιγοῦντες κελεύουσιν. [3] κατὰ φύσιν δὲ πάλιν ἀδύνατόν ἐστι παιδάριον μικρὸν κλέψαι τοσοῦτον ἀργύριον ὅσον μὴ | δυνατὸν φέρειν, καὶ οἴχεσθαι τοῦτο φέρον· ὡς δ᾽ ἂν ὁ ἐναντίος λέγοι, ἔσται ἀδύνατον ἂν φάσκῃ μὲν ἐν χρόνοις τισὶν Ἀθήνησι ποιήσασθαι τὸ συμβόλαιον, ἡμεῖς δ᾽ ἔχωμεν ἐπιδεῖξαι τοῖς ἀκούουσιν ὡς κατὰ τοὺς τότε καιροὺς ἀπεδημοῦμεν ἐν ἑτέρᾳ πόλει τινί. [4] τοὺς μὲν οὖν ἐλέγχους ἐκ τούτων |

10

15

of what is. One sign creates belief, another knowledge, but the best creates knowledge, and the second best produces very persuasive opinion. [3] We shall create many signs, to state it in sum, from each of the things done, said, and seen, taking them individually, from the size and smallness of the goods and evils that result, and also from witnesses and what is witnessed, from those on our side and on the opponents', from the opponents themselves, and from the challenges,[19] from the times, and from many other things. From them we shall be well supplied with signs.

13. An *elenchos* is what cannot be other than as we say. It is taken from natural necessities or necessities as we claim, and from natural impossibilities or impossibilities as the opponents claim. [2] A natural necessity is for instance that living things require food and similar things. As we claim it, it is a necessity that those who are whipped agree with what those who whip them command. [3] Again, a natural impossibility is that a small child steal an amount of money that it is impossible for him to carry and get away while carrying it. It will be an impossibility as the opponent would claim if he states that we made a contract at a certain time in Athens, but we are able to demonstrate to the audience that on that occasion we were away in some other city. [4] We shall create many *elenchoi* in these and similar

[19] Statements elicited by torture (*basanoi*) and statements sworn by oath normally resulted from litigants' challenges to each other.

---

56 ἢ ἀναγκαίων add. Sp.[1]
57 ἢ ὁ ἀντιλέγων del. Sp.[1]

20 καὶ ἐκ τῶν τούτοις ὁμοιοτρόπων <πολλοὺς>[58] ποιησόμεθα. συλλήβδην δὲ τὰς ἐξ αὐτοῦ τοῦ λόγου καὶ τῶν πράξεων καὶ τῶν ἀνθρώπων πίστεις ἁπάσας διεληλύθαμεν. σκεψώμεθα δὲ καὶ τί ἀλλήλων διαφέρουσιν.

14. Τὸ μὲν τοίνυν εἰκὸς τοῦ παραδείγματος ταύτῃ
25 διαφέρει | διότι τοῦ μὲν εἰκότος ἔχουσιν αὐτοὶ οἱ ἀκούοντες ἔννοιαν, [2] τὰ δὲ παραδείγματα καὶ ἐκ τῶν ἐναντίων καὶ ἐκ τῶν ὁμοίων φέρειν ἔστι. τὰ δὲ τεκμήρια μόνον ἐκ τῶν περὶ τὸν λόγον καὶ τὴν πρᾶξιν ἐναντίων συντίθεται. [3] καὶ μὴν ἐνθύμημα τεκμηρίου
30 ταύτην τὴν διαφορὰν ἔσχηκεν ὅτι τὸ | μὲν τεκμήριον περὶ τὸν λόγον καὶ τὴν πρᾶξιν ἐναντίωσίς ἐστι, τὸ δ᾽ ἐνθύμημα καὶ τὰς περὶ τὰς ἄλλας ἰδέας ἐναντιώσεις ἐξείληφεν· ἢ καὶ διότι τὸ μὲν τεκμήριον οὐκ ἐφ᾽ ἡμῖν ἐστι λαμβάνειν, ἂν μὴ περὶ τὰ πράγματα καὶ τοὺς λόγους ἐναντίωσίς τις ὑπάρχῃ, τὸ δ᾽ ἐνθύμημα πολ-
35 λαχόθεν | οἷόν τε πορίζεσθαι τοῖς λέγουσιν. [4] γνῶμαι δ᾽ ἐνθυμημάτων διαφέρουσιν ᾗ τὰ μὲν ἐνθυμήματα μόνον ἐκ τῶν ἐναντιώσεων σύγκειται, τὰς δὲ γνώμας καὶ μετὰ τῶν ἐναντιώσεων καὶ ἁπλῶς αὐτὰς καθ᾽ αὑτὰς δυνατόν ἐστιν ἐμφανίζειν. [5] τὰ δὲ σημεῖα τῶν
40 γνωμῶν καὶ τῶν προειρημένων ἁπάντων | ταύτῃ διαφέρουσιν ᾗ τὰ μὲν ἄλλα πάντα οἴησιν ἐμποιεῖ τοῖς ἀκούουσι, τῶν δὲ σημείων ἔνια καὶ σαφῶς εἰδέναι ποιήσει τοὺς κρίνοντας· καὶ διότι τῶν μὲν ἑτέρων οὐκ
1431b ἔστιν αὐτοὺς || πορίσασθαι τὰ πλεῖστα, τῶν δὲ σημείων πολλὰ ῥᾳδίως ἔστι ποιήσασθαι. [6] καὶ μὴν ἔλεγχος σημείου ταύτῃ διαφέρει διότι τῶν μὲν σημείων ἔνια

ways. In sum, we have gone through all the proofs from the speech itself, from the actions and from the people. Let us examine how they differ from one another.

14. Plausibility differs from example in this way: the audience has a notion of what is plausible, [2] but it is possible to introduce examples from contraries and from similarities. *Tekmeria* are composed only from contraries with regard to the speech and the action. [3] However, an enthymeme has this difference from a *tekmerion*, that the *tekmerion* is a contrariety with regard to the speech and the action, but the enthymeme admits contrarieties with regard to the other aspects. It is also not possible for us to obtain a *tekmerion* unless some contrariety exists in the acts and words, but speakers can supply the enthymeme from many sources. [4] Maxims differ from enthymemes in that only enthymemes consist of contraries, but it is possible to elucidate maxims both with contrarieties and simply by themselves. [5] Signs differ from maxims and all the aforesaid proofs in this way, that all the others instill belief in the audience, but some signs make judges know clearly. It is also not possible for us to supply most of the other proofs, but it is easy to supply many of the signs. [6] An *elenchos* also differs from a sign because some signs only

[58] πολλοὺς ρ (*multos*) Fuhrmann : om. N a

μόνον οἴεσθαι ποιεῖ τοὺς ἀκούοντας, ἔλεγχος δὲ πᾶς
5 τὴν ἀλήθειαν διδάσκει τοὺς κρίνοντας. [7] | ὥστε τὰς
μὲν τῶν λόγων καὶ τῶν πράξεων πίστεις, οἷαί τέ εἰσι
καὶ ὅθεν αὐτῶν εὐπορήσομεν καὶ τίνι ἀλλήλων διαφέρουσιν, ἐκ τῶν προειρημένων ἴσμεν· τῶν δ' ἐπιθέτων
ἑκάστην πάλιν διέλθωμεν.

[8] ἡ μὲν οὖν δόξα τοῦ λέγοντός ἐστι τὸ τὴν αὑτοῦ
10 διάνοιαν | ἐμφανίζειν κατὰ τῶν πραγμάτων. δεῖ δ' ἔμ-
πειρον ἀποφαίνειν ἑαυτὸν περὶ ὧν ἂν λέγῃς, καὶ ἐπι-
δεικνύναι ὡς συμφέρει σοι τἀληθῆ λέγειν περὶ τούτων, τὸν δ' ἀντιλέγοντα μάλιστα δεικνύναι μηδεμίαν
ἐμπειρίαν ἔχοντα τὸν ἐναντίον περὶ ὧν ἂν λέγῃ ἀπο-
15 φαίνεσθαι τε τήν δόξαν ὁμοίως.[59] [9] ἂν δὲ τοῦτο | μὴ
δυνατὸν ᾖ, δεικτέον ὡς καὶ οἱ ἔμπειροι πολλάκις
ἐξαμαρτάνουσιν, ἂν δὲ τοῦτο μὴ ἐνδέχηται, λέγειν ὡς
ἀσύμφορόν ἐστι τοῖς ἐναντίοις τἀληθῆ περὶ τούτων
εἰπεῖν. ταῖς μὲν οὖν δόξαις τοῦ λέγοντος οὕτω χρησόμεθα καὶ αὐτοὶ ἀποφαινόμενοι καὶ ἑτέροις ἀντιλέ-
γοντες. |

20 15. Μαρτυρία δ' ἐστὶν ὁμολογία συνειδότος ἑκόν-
τος. ἀναγκαῖον δ' εἶναι τὸ μαρτυρούμενον ἢ πιθανὸν ἢ
ἀπίθανον ἢ ἀμφίβολον πρὸς πίστιν, ὡσαύτως δὲ καὶ
τὸν μάρτυρα πιστὸν ἢ ἄπιστον ἢ ἀμφίδοξον. [2] ὅταν
μὲν οὖν τὸ μαρτυρούμενον ᾖ πιθανὸν καὶ ὁ μάρτυς
25 ἀληθινός, οὐδὲν δέονται αἱ μαρτυρίαι | ἐπιλόγων, ἐὰν

[59] ἂν λέγῃ ἀποφαίνεσθαι τε τήν ego : ἀποφαίνεται τήν τε N a ρ (*et opinionem*)

make the audience believe, but every *elenchos* teaches judges the truth. [7] So, from what has been said before, we know we shall be well supplied with proofs—whatever they are, wherever they come from, and how they differ from one another—from the speeches and the actions. Let us again go through each of the supplementary proofs.

[8] The *opinion of the speaker* is the elucidation of his thought concerning the facts. You must point out that you are experienced with what you are saying, and demonstrate that it is to your advantage to speak the truth, and the respondent must argue in particular that his opponent has no experience with what he is talking about and point out that his opinion is similar. [9] If it is not possible to do this, you must show that experienced people often make mistakes, and if this is not possible, say that it is disadvantageous to the opponents to speak the truth about these things. We shall use the opinions of the speaker in this way both in pointing things out ourselves and in responding to the others.

15. *Witness testimony* is a willing corroboration by someone who has knowledge.[20] It is necessary that what is testified be persuasive or unpersuasive or ambiguous as to proof, and likewise that the witness be credible or not credible or doubtful. [2] When what is testified is persuasive and the witness truthful, the testimony needs no com-

[20] The term *suneidon*, "someone who has (eyewitness) knowledge," is a technical term used of witnesses in Athenian forensic oratory as well.

μὴ βούλῃ γνώμην ἢ ἐνθύμημα συντόμως εἰπεῖν τοῦ ἀστείου ἕνεκεν· ὅταν δὲ ὑποπτεύηται ὁ μάρτυς, ἀποδεικνύειν δεῖ ὡς οὔτε χάριτος ἕνεκεν οὔτε τιμωρίας οὔτε κέρδους ὁ τοιοῦτος ἂν τὰ ψευδῆ μαρτυρήσειε. [3] δεῖ δὲ καὶ διδάσκειν ὅτι οὐ συμφέρει τὸ ψεῦδος
30 μαρτυρεῖν· αἱ μὲν γὰρ | ὠφέλειαι μικραί, τὸ δ' ἐξελεγχθῆναι χαλεπόν, γνωσθέντα δ' οὐ μόνον εἰς ἀργύριον οἱ νόμοι ζημιοῦσιν, ἀλλὰ καὶ εἰς δόξαν καὶ εἰς ἀπιστίαν. [4] τοὺς μὲν οὖν μάρτυρας οὕτω πιστοὺς ποιήσομεν· ἀντιλέγοντας δὲ μαρτυρίᾳ δεῖ τὸν τρόπον τοῦ μάρτυρος διαβάλλειν, ἂν ᾖ πονηρός, ἢ τὸ μαρτυρού-
35 μενον | ἐξετάζειν, ἂν ἀπίθανον <ὂν>[60] τυγχάνῃ, ἢ καὶ συναμφοτέροις τούτοις ἀντιλέγειν, συνάγοντας τὰ φαυλότατα τῶν ἐναντίων εἰς ταὐτό. [5] σκεπτέον δὲ καὶ εἰ φίλος ἐστὶν ὁ μάρτυς ᾧ μαρτυρεῖ, ἢ εἰ μέτεστιν ποθεν αὐτῷ τοῦ πράγματος, ἢ ἐχθρός ἐστιν οὗ κατα-
40 μαρτυρεῖ, ἢ πένης· τούτων γὰρ οἱ μὲν διὰ χάριν, οἱ | δὲ διὰ τιμωρίαν, οἱ δὲ διὰ κέρδος ὑποπτεύονται τὰ ψευδῆ μαρτυρεῖν. [6] καὶ τὸν τῶν ψευδομαρτυριῶν νόμον ἐπὶ τούτοις τεθεικέναι φήσομεν τὸν νομοθέτην· ἄτοπον
1432a οὖν εἶναι τοῦ νομοθέτου || τοῖς μάρτυσι μὴ πιστεύσαντος τοὺς κρίνοντας πιστεύειν αὐτοῖς, κατὰ τοὺς νόμους κρινεῖν ὀμωμοκότας. τοὺς μὲν οὖν μάρτυρας οὕτως ἀπιθάνους ποιήσομεν.

[7] ἔστι δὲ καὶ κλέπτειν τὴν μαρτυρίαν τρόπῳ
5 τοιῷδε· "μαρτύρησόν μοι, ὦ Λυσικλῆς·" | "μὰ τοὺς θεοὺς οὔκουν ἔγωγε· κωλύοντος γὰρ ἐμοῦ ταῦτα ἔπραξεν οὗτος." καὶ διὰ τούτου ἐν ἀποφάσει ψευδομαρτυρήσας

ment, unless you wish briefly to say a maxim or enthymeme for the sake of urbanity. When the witness is suspect you must show that such a man would not testify falsely out of favor or revenge or profit. [3] You must teach that false witnessing is not advantageous: the benefits are small and being refuted is a hard thing; the laws punish someone convicted not only with a fine but also with regard to his reputation and credibility. [4] We shall make witnesses credible in this way. But when speaking in response to witness testimony you must provoke prejudice against the behavior of the witness if he is base, or investigate what is being testified, whether it may in fact be unpersuasive, or respond in both ways, collecting the most base aspects of the opponents against it. [5] You must examine whether the witness is a friend of the person for whom he is testifying, or if he has some interest in the case somehow, or if he is an enemy of the person against whom he is testifying, or if he is poor. For some people are suspected of giving false testimony because of favor, others for revenge, and others because of profit. [6] We shall say that the legislator established the law against false testimony for these reasons. It would be odd if the legislator did not trust the witnesses but the judges did inasmuch as they have sworn to judge according to the laws. We shall attack the credibility of the witnesses in this way.

[7] It is also possible to sneak in witness testimony in this way: "Lysicles, testify for me." "By the gods I will not. This man did it even though I forbade it." In this way, although he has testified falsely in his refusal, he will not in-

60 ἂν add. Sp.[1]

ψευδομαρτυρίου δίκην οὐχ ὑφέξει. [8] τοιγαροῦν ὅταν μὲν ἡμῖν συμφέρῃ κλέπτειν τὴν μαρτυρίαν, οὕτως αὐτῇ χρησόμεθα· ἐὰν δὲ οἱ ἐναντίοι τοιοῦτόν τι ποιή-
10 σωσιν, ἐμφανιοῦμεν τὴν κακοποιίαν | αὐτῶν καὶ συγγραψαμένους μαρτυρεῖν κελεύσομεν. μάρτυσι μὲν οὖν καὶ μαρτυρίαις ἐκ τούτων ἴσμεν ὡς δεῖ χρήσασθαι.

16. Βάσανος δ' ἐστὶ μὲν ὁμολογία παρὰ συνειδότος, ἄκοντος δέ. ὅταν μὲν οὖν συμφέρῃ ἡμῖν αὐτὴν ποιεῖν ἰσχυράν, λεκτέον ὡς οἵ τε ἰδιῶται περὶ τῶν
15 σπουδαιοτάτων καὶ αἱ | πόλεις περὶ τῶν μεγίστων ἐκ βασάνων τὰς πίστεις λαμβάνουσι, καὶ διότι πιστότερόν ἐστι βάσανος μαρτύρων· τοῖς μὲν γὰρ μάρτυσι συμφέρει πολλάκις ψεύσασθαι, τοῖς δὲ βασανιζομένοις λυσιτελεῖ τἀληθῆ λέγειν· οὕτω γὰρ παύσονται τάχιστα τῆς κακοπαθείας. [2] ὅταν δὲ βούλῃ τὰς
20 βασάνους | ἀπίστους ποιεῖν, πρῶτον μὲν λεκτέον ὡς οἱ βασανιζόμενοι τοῖς ἐκδιδοῦσι πολέμιοι γίνονται καὶ διὰ τοῦτο πολλὰ τῶν δεσποτῶν καταψεύδονται· ἔπειθ' ὅτι πολλάκις τοῖς βασανίζουσιν ὁμολογοῦσιν οὐ τὰς ἀληθείας, ἵν' ὡς τάχιστα τῶν κακῶν παύσωνται.
25 [3] δεικτέον δ' ὅτι καὶ τῶν ἐλευθέρων πολλοὶ | ἤδη βασανιζόμενοι καθ' ἑαυτῶν ἐψεύσαντο βουλόμενοι τὴν παραυτίκα κακοπάθειαν ἐκφυγεῖν, ὥστε πολὺ μᾶλλον εὔλογον τοὺς δούλους ψευσαμένους κατὰ τῶν δεσποτῶν βούλεσθαι τὴν αὑτῶν τιμωρίαν ἐκφυγεῖν ἢ πολλὰς κακοπαθείας τοῖς σώμασι καὶ ταῖς ψυχαῖς
30 ὑπομείναντας, ἵν' ἕτεροι | μηδὲν πάθωσιν, αὐτοὺς βούλεσθαι μὴ ψεῦδος εἰπεῖν. τὰς μὲν οὖν βασάνους ἐκ

cur a suit for false testimony. [8] Therefore, when it is advantageous for us to sneak in the witness testimony, we shall do it in this way. But if the opponents do some such thing, we shall expose their misdeed and call on them to commit the witness testimony to writing. In this way then we know how we must employ witnesses and witness testimony.

16. A statement derived from *torture*[21] is a corroboration from one who has knowledge but is unwilling. When it is to our advantage to make it strong, we must say that both private individuals about the most serious matters and cities about the most important matters obtain their proofs from torture and that torture is more credible than witnesses. It is often advantageous for witnesses to lie, but it profits those who are being tortured to tell the truth. In this way they will stop their suffering most quickly. [2] When you want to discredit torture, first you must say that those who are being tortured become enemies to those who surrender them and for this reason they say many false things against their masters; then, that they often agree with their torturers and not the truth in order to end their troubles as quickly as possible. [3] You must argue that many free people, once tortured, have lied about themselves in the desire to escape suffering immediately, so it is much more reasonable that slaves lie against their masters in the wish to escape their punishment than that they would endure a lot of suffering in body and soul and say nothing false in order that others not suffer. We shall

[21] The Greek word *basanos* can refer to torture itself, a statement derived from torture, or even a challenge to have torture performed.

τῶν τοιούτων καὶ τῶν τούτοις ὁμοιοτρόπων πιθανὰς καὶ ἀπιθάνους καταστήσομεν.

17. Ὅρκος δ' ἐστὶ μετὰ θείας παραλήψεως φάσις ἀναπόδεικτος. δεῖ δ' αὐτὸν ὅταν μὲν αὔξειν θέλωμεν,
35 λέγειν | οὕτως· "οὐδεὶς ἂν ἐπιορκεῖν βούλοιτο φοβούμενος τήν τε παρὰ τῶν θεῶν τιμωρίαν καὶ τὴν παρὰ τοῖς ἀνθρώποις αἰσχύνην," καὶ διεξιέναι ὅτι τοὺς μὲν ἀνθρώπους λαθεῖν ἔστι, τοὺς δὲ θεοὺς οὐκ ἔστιν. [2] ὅταν δὲ οἱ ἐναντίοι καταφύγωσιν εἰς ὅρκον καὶ βουλώμεθα ταπεινοῦν αὐτόν, δεικτέον ὡς τῶν αὐτῶν |
40 ἐστιν ἀνθρώπων τὰ πονηρὰ πράττειν καὶ μὴ φρον-
1432b τίζειν || ἐπιορκοῦντας· ὅστις γὰρ κακουργῶν οἴεται λανθάνειν τοὺς θεούς, οὗτος οὐδὲ ἐπιορκῶν τιμωρίας οἴεται τεύξεσθαι. καὶ περὶ μὲν τῶν ὅρκων ὁμοιοτρόπως τοῖς προειρημένοις μετιόντες λέγειν εὐπορήσομεν [ὑπὲρ αὐτῶν].[61]

5 [3] Συλλήβδην δὲ τὰς πάσας πίστεις | ἤδη, καθάπερ ὑπεθέμεθα, διεξεληλύθαμεν καὶ δεδηλώκαμεν οὐ μόνον ἣν ἑκάστη αὐτῶν δύναμιν ἔσχηκεν, ἀλλὰ καὶ τί ἀλλήλων διαφέρουσι καὶ πῶς αὐταῖς χρηστέον. νῦν δ' ὑπὲρ τῶν ὑπολοίπων, ἃ τῶν ἑπτὰ εἰδῶν ἐστι καὶ περὶ πάντας τοὺς λόγους χρήσιμα γίνεται, διδάσκειν
10 ἐπιχειρήσομεν. |

18. Προκατάληψις μὲν οὖν ἐστι δι' ἧς τά τε τῶν ἀκουόντων ἐπιτιμήματα καὶ τοὺς τῶν ἀντιλέγειν μελλόντων λόγους προκαταλαμβάνοντες ὑπεξαιρήσομεν τὰς ἐπιφερομένας δυσχερείας. [2] καὶ τὰς μὲν τῶν
15 ἀκουόντων ἐπιτιμήσεις ὧδε χρὴ | προκαταλαμβάνειν·

make torture persuasive and unpersuasive in these and similar ways.

17. *Oath* is an undemonstrated statement with an appeal to the gods. When we wish to amplify it, we must speak in this way: "No one would want to commit perjury so long as he fears the gods' punishment and disgrace among people," and to continue that "it is possible to escape human notice, but it is not possible to escape the gods'." [2] When the opponents take refuge in an oath and we wish to denigrate it, we must argue that it is characteristic of the same people to do base things and to be unconcerned about perjury. Whoever commits evil and thinks he escapes the gods' notice also thinks he will not meet punishment for perjury. By proceeding in a way similar to what was said before, we shall be well supplied to speak about oaths.

[3] In sum, we have now gone through all the proofs, just as we set out to, and we have explained not only what capacity each of them has but also how they differ from each other and how to use them. Now we shall attempt to teach the rest of the things that belong to the seven species and that are useful for all speeches.

18. *Anticipation* is that through which we shall anticipate both the reproaches of the audience and the speeches of those who will respond and remove the difficulties that they impose. [2] We must anticipate the reproaches of the

---

61 *ὑπὲρ αὐτῶν* del. Fuhrmann

"ἴσως δέ τινες ὑμῶν θαυμάζουσιν ὅτι νέος ὢν οὕτω περὶ μεγάλων πραγμάτων ἐπεχείρησα δημηγορεῖν·" καὶ πάλιν· "μηδεὶς ἀπαντήσῃ μοι δύσκολος ὅτι μέλλω συμβουλεύειν ὑμῖν περὶ ὧν ὀκνοῦσί τινες ἄλλοι παρρησιάζεσθαι πρὸς ὑμᾶς." [3] περὶ μὲν οὖν τῶν μελλόν-
20 των δυσχεραίνεσθαι | τοῖς ἀκούουσιν, οὕτω δεῖ προκαταλαμβάνοντα φέρειν αἰτίας παρ' ἃς ὀρθῶς ποιεῖν δόξεις συμβουλεύων, δεικνύντα τὴν ἐρημίαν τῶν λεγόντων <ἢ>[62] τὸ μέγεθος τῶν κινδύνων ἢ τὸ τῷ κοινῷ συμφέρον ἢ ἄλλην τοιαύτην αἰτίαν δι' ἧς λύσεις τὴν
25 ἐπιφερομένην δυσχέρειαν. [4] ἂν δὲ μηδὲν | ἧττον θορυβῶσιν οἱ ἀκούοντες, χρὴ λέγειν συντόμως ἢ ὡς ἐν γνώμης ἢ ὡς <ἐν>[63] ἐνθυμήματος σχήματι, διότι "πάντων ἀτοπώτατόν ἐστιν ἥκειν μὲν ὡς περὶ τῶν πραγμάτων βουλευσομένους τὰ κράτιστα, νῦν δὲ μὴ βουλομένους ἀκούειν τῶν λεγόντων οἴεσθαι καλῶς ἂν
30 βουλεύσασθαι·" καὶ πάλιν, ὅτι | "καλόν ἐστιν ἢ αὐτοὺς ἀνισταμένους συμβουλεύειν ἢ τῶν συμβουλευόντων ἀκούσαντας, ἅπερ ἂν αὐτοῖς δοκῇ χειροτονεῖν." [5] ἐν μὲν οὖν ταῖς δημηγορίαις οὕτω καὶ ταῖς προκαταλήψεσι χρηστέον καὶ τοῖς θορύβοις ἀπαντητέον.

ἐν δὲ ταῖς δικαιολογίαις προκαταληψόμεθα μὲν
35 ὁμοιοτρόπως τοῖς προειρημένοις, | ἀπαντήσομεν δὲ τοῖς θορύβοις, ἐὰν μὲν ἐν ἀρχαῖς γίνωνται τῶν λόγων, ὧδε· [6] "πῶς οὐκ ἄλογον [οὖν][64] ἐστι τὸν μὲν νομοθέτην προστάξαι δύο λόγους ἑκάστῳ τῶν ἀντιδίκων

[62] ἢ add. Rackham [63] add. Finkh[1]

audience in this way: "Perhaps some of you are surprised that although young I have attempted to debate important matters." And again, "Do not let any grumbler interrupt me because I am going to give counsel to you about matters that some others have hesitated to discuss frankly with you." [3] On matters that are going to create difficulties for the audience, you must anticipate by offering reasons why you think you are right to be giving counsel, mentioning the lack of speakers, the size of the dangers, the common advantage, or any other reason by which to remove the difficulty that has been imposed. [4] If the audience creates no less a disturbance, you must say, concisely or in the form of a maxim or enthymeme, that "it is most odd that those who came to deliberate over the most important matters now think that they will deliberate well even though they are unwilling to listen to the speakers." And again, that "it is right either to stand up oneself and give counsel or to listen to those who are giving counsel and vote for what seems best." [5] In public speeches we must use anticipations in this way and counter disturbances.

In legal pleading we shall anticipate in a way similar to what has been said and we shall counter disturbances if they occur at the beginning of speeches, in this way: [6] "How is it not unreasonable that the lawgiver prescribed two speeches, for each of the litigants to give one,[22]

[22] It is possible that the Greek means that each litigant gives two speeches.

---

64 οὖν del. Hammer

ἀποδοῦναι, τοὺς δὲ δικάζοντας ὑμᾶς ὀμωμοκέναι κατὰ τὸν νόμον κρινεῖν, εἶτα μηδὲ τὸν ἕνα λόγον ἀκοῦσαι
40 βούλεσθαι; | καὶ ἐκεῖνον μὲν ὑμῶν τοσαύτην πρόνοιαν
1433a ἔχειν, ὅπως ἀκούσαντες ‖ πάντων τῶν λεγομένων εὐόρκως θῆσθε τὴν ψῆφον, ὑμᾶς δὲ περὶ τούτων οὕτως ὀλιγώρως ἔχειν ὥστε μηδὲ τὰς ἀρχὰς αὐτὰς ὑπομείναντας τῶν λόγων ἤδη νομίζειν ἀκριβῶς ἅπαντα γι-
5 νώσκειν;" [7] καὶ ἄλλως· "πῶς οὐκ ἄλογόν ἐστι | τὸν μὲν νομοθέτην τάξαι τῶν ψήφων ἴσων γινομένων τὸν φεύγοντα νικᾶν, ὑμᾶς δὲ οὕτως ἐναντίως γινώσκειν περὶ τούτων ὡς μηδὲ ἀπολογουμένων τῶν διαβεβλημένων ἀκούειν; κἀκεῖνον μὲν διὰ τὸ μᾶλλον κινδυνεύειν τοὺς φεύγοντας ἀπονεῖμαι ταύτην τὴν πλεονεξίαν
10 αὐτοῖς ἐν ταῖς ψήφοις, | ὑμᾶς δὲ τοῖς μὲν ἀκινδύνως κατηγοροῦσι μὴ φιλονεικεῖν, τοὺς δὲ μετὰ φόβων καὶ κινδύνων περὶ τῶν κατηγορουμένων ἀπολογουμένους θορυβοῦντας ἐκπλήττειν;"

[8] ἐὰν μὲν οὖν ἐν ἀρχαῖς οἱ θόρυβοι γίνωνται, τοῦτον τὸν τρόπον αὐτοῖς ἀπαντητέον· ἐὰν δὲ προελη-
15 λυθότος τοῦ λόγου θορυβῶσιν, ἐὰν μὲν | ὀλίγοι τινὲς τοῦτο ποιῶσιν, ἐπιτιμητέον τοῖς θορυβοῦσι καὶ πρὸς αὐτοὺς λεκτέον ὅτι δίκαιον νῦν μὲν αὐτοὺς ἀκούειν ἐστίν, ἵνα μὴ κωλύωσι τοὺς ἄλλους ὀρθῶς δικάζειν, ἐπὰν δὲ ἀκούσωσι, τότε ποιεῖν ὅ τι ἂν ἐθέλωσιν· [9] ἐὰν δὲ τὸ πλῆθος θορυβῇ, μὴ τοῖς κρίνουσιν, ἀλλὰ
20 ἑαυτῷ ἐπίπληξον· τὸ μὲν γὰρ | ἐκείνοις ἐπιτιμᾶν ὀργὴν ἐργάζεται, τὸ δ' ἑαυτῷ ἐπιπλῆξαι καὶ λέγειν ἐν τῷ λέγειν ἡμαρτηκέναι συγγνώμης ποιήσει τυχεῖν. δεῖ δὲ

and that you judges have sworn to judge according to the law, but are unwilling to listen to one of the speeches. He had such great forethought for you, that you hear everything that is said and cast your vote according to your oath, but do you make such light about these matters that you do not even wait for the beginnings of the speeches because you think you already know everything precisely?" [7] And in another way: "How is it not unreasonable that the lawgiver dictated that the defendant win when the votes are equal, but you have decided so differently that you do not listen to defendants who have incurred prejudice? Because defendants run the greater risk, he allocated them this advantage in the votes, but you do not quarrel with those giving the prosecution speech without danger, but terrify with your disturbances those who are in fear and danger defending themselves against the allegations?"

[8] If there are disturbances at the beginning, meet them in this way. But if they create a disturbance when the speech is advanced, if only a few are doing it, you must reproach the disturbers and say to them that it is just for them to listen, so that they do not prevent others from judging correctly, and once they listen, then they may do whatever they want. [9] If the majority is creating a disturbance, admonish not the judges, but yourself. Criticizing them generates anger, but admonishing yourself and saying that you made a mistake in your speech will win you

καὶ δεῖσθαι τῶν κρινόντων εὐμενῶς αὐτοὺς ἀκοῦσαι τοῦ λόγου, καὶ <μὴ>[65] περὶ ὧν μέλλουσι κρύβδην τὴν ψῆφον φέρειν, ἤδη τὴν διάνοιαν φανερὰν τίθεσθαι.
25 [10] συλλήβδην δὲ τοῖς | θορύβοις ἀπαντήσομεν κεφαλαιωδῶς ἢ γνώμαις ἢ ἐνθυμήμασι, δεικνύντες τοὺς θορυβοῦντας ἢ τοῖς δικαίοις ἢ τοῖς νόμοις ἢ τῷ συμφέροντι τῆς πόλεως ἢ τῷ καλῷ ἐναντιουμένους· ἐκ γὰρ τῶν τοιούτων ἔστιν ὅτι μάλιστα παῦσαι τοὺς ἀκούοντας θορυβοῦντας.

30 [11] ταῖς μὲν οὖν πρὸς τοὺς ἀκροατὰς | προκαταλήψεσιν ὡς δεῖ χρῆσθαι καὶ ὅπως τοῖς θορύβοις ἀπαντητέον, ἐκ τῶν προειρημένων ἴσμεν· τὰ δὲ ὑπὸ τῶν ἀνταγωνιστῶν ἐπίδοξα λέγεσθαι πάλιν ὡς δεῖ προκαταλαμβάνειν ὑποδείξω· "ἴσως οὖν ὀδυρεῖται αὑτοῦ πενίαν, ἧς οὐκ ἐγώ, ἀλλ' ὁ τούτου τρόπος ὑπαίτιός
35 ἐστι·" καὶ πάλιν· | "πυνθάνομαι αὐτὸν τὸ καὶ τὸ μέλλειν λέγειν." [12] ἐν μὲν οὖν τοῖς προτέροις λόγοις, οὕτω δεῖ τὰ ἐπίδοξα λέγεσθαι ὑπὸ τῶν ἐναντίων προκαταλαμβάνοντα διαλύειν καὶ ἀσθενῆ ποιεῖν· καὶ γὰρ κἂν πάνυ ἰσχυρὰ ᾖ τὰ προδιαβεβλημένα, οὐχ ὁμοίως
40 φαίνεται μεγάλα τοῖς ἤδη προακηκοόσιν. | [13] ἐὰν δὲ
1433b τοὺς ὑστέρους λόγους ἔχωμεν καὶ οἱ ἐναντίοι || προκατειληφότες ὦσιν ἃ μέλλομεν λέγειν, ἀντιπροκαταληπτέον ἐστὶν αὐτὰ λύοντας τόνδε τὸν τρόπον· [14] "οὗτος δ' οὐ μόνον μου κατέψευσται πολλὰ πρὸς ὑμᾶς, ἀλλὰ καὶ σαφῶς εἰδὼς ὅτι ἐξελέγξω αὐτόν,
5 προκατέλαβέ μου τὸν λόγον | καὶ προδιέβαλεν, ἵν' ὑμεῖς μὴ ὁμοίως αὐτῷ προσέχητε ἢ ἐγὼ μὴ εἴπω πρὸς

pardon. You must ask the judges to listen to the speech in a friendly way, and about matters about which they are going to cast a vote secretly not to make clear their intention already. [10] In sum, we shall counter disturbances chiefly with maxims and enthymemes, arguing that those who disturb are opposed to justice, the laws, the advantage of the city, and what is noble. In these ways it is most possible to stop the audience's disturbances.

[11] We know from what has been said how to use anticipations in response to the audience and how to counter disturbances. I shall now illustrate how to anticipate what you expect the adversaries to say: "Perhaps he will lament his poverty, for which not I but his behavior is to blame." And again: "I perceive that he is going to say thus and so." [12] In first speeches, we must, by anticipating what the opponents are expected to say, unravel and weaken it. Even if they are very strong, arguments that have had prejudice raised against them do not appear as great to those who have heard about them before. [13] If we have the second speech and the opponents have anticipated what we are going to say, we must perform an anti-anticipation by refuting them in this way: [14] "This man has not only told you many lies about me, but since he knew very well that I am going to refute him he anticipated my speech and created prejudice so that you would not give it the same at-

[65] μὴ add. Victorius

ὑμᾶς αὐτὸν διὰ τὸ διασεσύρθαι πρότερον ὑπὸ τούτου· ἐγὼ δ' οἶμαι δεῖν τοὺς ἐμοὺς λόγους παρ' ἐμοῦ πυνθάνεσθαι ὑμᾶς, ἀλλὰ μὴ παρὰ τούτου, εἰ δὲ καὶ ταῦθ' οὗτος προδιέσυρε λέγων ἅ φημι, οὐ μικρὰ σημεῖα |
10 εἶναι τοῦ μηδὲν ὑγιὲς τοῦτον λέγειν." [15] κέχρηται δὲ καὶ Εὐριπίδης ἐν Φιλοκτήτῃ τεχνικῶς τούτῳ τῷ εἴδει διὰ τοῦδε·

> λέξω δ' ἐγώ, κἄν μου διαφθείρας δοκῇ
> λόγους ὑποφθάς,[66] αὐτὸς ἠδικηκέναι·
> ἀλλ' ἐξ ἐμοῦ γὰρ τ' ἀμὰ †μαθήσῃ[67] κλύων,
> ὁ δ' αὐτὸς αὐτὸν †ἐμφανιεῖ σοι[68] λέγων.

15 ταῖς μὲν οὖν προκαταλήψεσιν | ὡς δεῖ χρῆσθαι καὶ πρὸς τοὺς κριτὰς καὶ πρὸς τοὺς ἐναντίους, ἴσμεν διὰ τούτων.

19. Αἰτήματα δ' ἐστὶν ἐν τοῖς λόγοις, ἃ παρὰ τῶν ἀκουόντων οἱ λέγοντες αἰτοῦνται. τούτων δ' ἐστὶ τὰ μὲν ἄδικα, τὰ δὲ δίκαια. δίκαιον μὲν οὖν ἐστι τό τε
20 προσέχειν τοῖς λεγομένοις | αἰτεῖσθαι καὶ μετ' εὐνοίας ἀκούειν, δίκαιον δὲ καὶ τὸ κατὰ τοὺς νόμους αὐτῷ βοηθῆσαι καὶ τὸ μηδὲν παρὰ τοὺς νόμους ψηφίσασθαι καὶ τὸ τοῖς ἀτυχήμασι συγγνώμην ἔχειν. †ἐὰν δὲ ᾖ παρὰ τοὺς νόμους, ἄδικον, ἐὰν δὲ μή, δίκαιον†.[69] [2] τὰ μὲν οὖν αἰτήματα ταῦτά ἐστι, διειλόμεθα δ' |
25 αὐτῶν τὰς διαφοράς, ἵν' εἰδότες τό τε δίκαιον καὶ τὸ

[66] ὑποφθάς Weil ap. Nauck²-Kannicht *TrGF* 5 p. 841 cf. *preveniens* Lat.ᵃ : ὑποστάς N a

[67] τἀμὰ μαθήσῃ nullo metro codd. (*addisces* Lat.ᵃ)

tention or I would not speak it to you because he had torn it to pieces. But I think you need to learn my arguments from me and not from him, and if he has already torn to pieces what I am saying, it is no small sign that there is nothing sound in what he says." [15] In *Philoctetes* Euripides has skillfully used this form in this way:

> I shall speak for myself, even if he gives the appearance, by having destroyed
> My words by anticipation himself, of having (already) done (me) wrong.
> No, from me you will learn my views, when you listen,
> And he will explain himself, when he speaks to you.[23]

We know in this way how we must use anticipations, with regard both to the judges and the opponents.

19. *Appeals*, in speeches, are what the speakers appeal for from the audience. Some of them are unjust, others just. It is just to appeal for attention to what is being said and for a friendly hearing, and it is just that they help the speaker according to the laws, vote nothing contrary to the laws, and pardon misfortunes. If it is contrary to the laws it is unjust, if not, it is just. [2] These then are appeals, and we have distinguished their differences so that by knowing the just and the unjust we may use them at the correct time

[23] Euripides, *Philoctetes* fr. 797 Nauck[2] (= *LCL* 506 pp. 400–401 Collard and Cropp).

---

[68] ἐμφανιεῖ σοι nullo metro codd. (*demonstrabit* Lat.[a])
[69] ἐὰν—δίκαιον cruces posuit Kayser[1]

ἄδικον χρώμεθα κατὰ τὸν καιρὸν καὶ μὴ λανθάνωσιν ἡμᾶς οἱ ἐναντίοι ἄδικόν τι αἰτοῦντες τοὺς δικάζοντας. καὶ περὶ μὲν τούτων ἐκ τῶν εἰρημένων οὐκ ἀγνοήσομεν.

20. Παλιλλογία δ' ἐστὶ μὲν σύντομος ἀνάμνησις,
30 δεῖ δ' | αὐτῇ χρῆσθαι καὶ περὶ τῶν μερῶν καὶ περὶ τῶν ὅλων λόγων τὰς τελευτάς. παλιλλογήσομεν δ' ἐν κεφαλαίοις ἢ διαλογιζόμενοι ἢ ἀπολογιζόμενοι ἢ ἐκ προαιρέσεως[70] ἢ προσερωτῶντες. [2] δείξω δ' αὐτῶν οἷον ἕκαστόν ἐστιν. τὸ μὲν οὖν διαλογίζεσθαι τοιόνδε
35 τί ἐστιν· "ἀπορῶ δ' ἔγωγε τί ἂν | ἐποίησαν οὗτοι, εἰ μὴ φανεροὶ μὲν ἦσαν ἡμᾶς πρότερον ἐγκαταλελοιπότες, ἐξηλέγχοντο δὲ ἐπὶ τὴν πόλιν ἡμῶν στρατεύσαντες, οὐδὲν δὲ πώποτε ὧν ὡμολογήκασι ποιήσαντες." [3] τὸ μὲν οὖν διαλογίζεσθαι τοιοῦτόν ἐστι, τὸ δὲ ἀπολογίζεσθαι τοιόνδε· "ἀπέδειξα δ' αὐτοὺς διαλύσαντας προ-
40 τέρους | τὴν συμμαχίαν καὶ πρῶτον ἐπιθεμένους ἡμῖν,
1434a ὅτε πρὸς || Λακεδαιμονίους ἐπολεμοῦμεν, καὶ μάλιστα σπουδάσαντας ἐξανδραποδίσασθαι τὴν πόλιν ἡμῶν." [4] τὸ μὲν οὖν ἀπολογίζεσθαι τοιοῦτόν ἐστι, τὸ δ' ἐκ προαιρέσεως ἀναμιμνήσκειν τοιόνδε· "ἐνθυμεῖσθαι δὲ
5 δεῖ ὅτι συμβέβηκεν ἡμῖν, ἐξ ὅτου | τὴν φιλίαν πρὸς τούτους ἐποιησάμεθα, μηδέποτε κακὸν ὑπὸ τῶν πολεμίων παθεῖν· βοηθήσαντες γὰρ ἡμῖν πολλάκις ἐκώλυσαν Λακεδαιμονίους τὴν χώραν ἡμῶν διαφθεῖραι, χρήματα δὲ πολλὰ καὶ νῦν φέροντες διατελοῦσιν." [5] ἐκ προαιρέσεως μὲν οὕτως ἀναμνήσομεν, ἐξ ἐπε-
10 ρωτήσεως δὲ | τόνδε τὸν τρόπον· "ἡδέως δ' ἂν αὐτῶν

and take notice of our opponents when they appeal to the judges for something unjustly. From what has been said, we shall not be ignorant concerning these matters.

20. *Repetition* is a concise reminder, and we must use it at the ends both of parts and of entire speeches. We shall repeat under the headings contemplation, calculation, choosing, or questioning. [2] I shall demonstrate instances of each of them. Contemplation is of this sort: "I have no idea what they would have done if it were not clear that they had deserted us earlier, that they had been exposed as having fought against our city, and that they had never done anything that they had agreed to."[24] [3] This then is an instance of contemplation, but calculation is as follows: "I have demonstrated that they were the first to break the alliance. They attacked us first when we were at war with the Lacedaemonians, and they were especially eager to enslave our city."[25] [4] This is an instance of calculation; the following is an instance of recalling choice: "We must consider what has happened to us since we established friendship with them: we have suffered nothing bad at the hands of our enemies. They have often helped us prevent the Lacedaemonians from destroying our territory and they continue to contribute a lot of money to us even now."[26] [5] In this way we recall choice, and in the following way we recall through interrogation: "I would be

[24] Cf. Is. 7.45 and Isocr. 6.90.
[25] Cf. Dem. 24.108.
[26] Cf. Aesch. 2.35.

---

70 ἐκ προαιρέσεως N² M F²H² : om. N¹

πυθοίμην διὰ τί τὰς συντάξεις ἡμῖν οὐκ ἀποδιδόασιν· οὐ γὰρ ὡς ἀποροῦσιν εἰπεῖν ἂν τολμήσαιεν, οἳ τοσαῦτα χρήματα καθ' ἕκαστον ἐνιαυτὸν ἐκ τῆς χώρας ἐπιδεικνύονται λαμβάνοντες, οὐδ' αὖ φήσουσιν εἰς τὴν τῆς πόλεως διοίκησιν πολλὰ δαπανᾶν· παντελῶς |
15 γὰρ ἐλάχιστα τῶν νησιωτῶν ἀναλίσκοντες φαίνονται." ἐκ μὲν οὖν ἐπερωτήσεως οὕτω παλιλλογήσομεν.

21. Εἰρωνεία δ' ἐστὶ λέγειν τι μὴ λέγειν προσποιούμενον ἢ [ἐν] τοῖς ἐναντίοις ὀνόμασι τὰ πράγματα προσαγορεύειν. εἴη δ' ἂν αὐτῆς τὸ σχῆμα
20 τοιοῦτον ἐν τῷ περὶ τῶν εἰρημένων | συντόμως ἀναμιμνῄσκειν· "οὐδὲν δ' οἶμαι δεῖν λέγειν ὅτι οὗτοι μὲν οἱ φάσκοντες πολλὰ ἀγαθὰ πεποιηκέναι πλεῖστα φαίνονται τὴν πόλιν κεκακουργηκότες, ἡμεῖς δ' οὓς οὗτοί φασιν ἀχαρίστους εἶναι, τούτοις τε πολλάκις βοηθήσαντες καὶ τοὺς ἄλλους οὐδὲν ἀδικοῦντες." [2] τὸ μὲν
25 οὖν ἐν προσποιήσει | παραλείψεως λέγοντα συντόμως ἀναμιμνῄσκειν τοιοῦτόν ἐστι, τὸ δὲ τοῖς ἐναντίοις ὀνόμασι προσαγορεύειν τὰ πράγματα πάλιν τοιόνδε· "οὗτοι μὲν οἱ χρηστοὶ πολλὰ φαίνονται τοὺς συμμάχους κακὰ πεποιηκότες, ἡμεῖς δ' οἱ φαῦλοι πολλῶν ἀγαθῶν αὐτοῖς αἴτιοι καταστάντες." διὰ τούτων μὲν |
30 οὖν συντόμως ἀναμιμνῄσκοντες ταῖς παλιλλογίαις χρησόμεθα καὶ περὶ τῶν μερῶν καὶ περὶ τῶν ὅλων λόγων τὰς τελευτάς.

22. Ὅθεν δ' ἐστὶν ἀστεῖα λέγειν καὶ τὰ μήκη τῶν λόγων ποιεῖν ὅπως ἄν τις θέλῃ, τοῦτο διέξιμεν πάλιν.
35 ἀστεῖα μὲν | οὖν λέγειν ἐκ τούτου τοῦ τρόπου[71] ἔστιν

pleased to learn from them why they have not paid us the assessments. They would not dare to say that they lack funds since they are shown to receive so much money each year from their land. Nor will they say that they spend a lot on the administration of their city; their costs appear to be the least of all the islanders'." In this way we shall repeat by questioning.

21. *Irony* is to say something while pretending not to say it or to address matters with the opposite words. In recalling concisely what has been said it takes the following form: "I do not think I need to say that these people who claim to have done much good appear to have worked much evil against the city, but we, who, they say, are disrespectful, have often helped them and done no wrong to others." [2] The following is an instance of concise repetition with the pretense of leaving something out of the speech: "These good men appear to have done the allies much harm, but we base men turned out to be the cause of many benefits to them." By concisely recalling in these ways, we shall use repetitions at the ends both of parts and of whole speeches.

22. We shall now go through *how to speak urbanely* and how to make the lengths of speeches however one wishes. Urbane speech in this way is, for instance, to speak enthy-

---

[71] τρόπου UHP : τόπου NFC ρ

οἷον τὰ ἐνθυμήματα λέγοντας ὅλα ἢ ἡμίση, ὥστε τὸ ἥμισυ αὐτοὺς ὑπολαμβάνειν τοὺς ἀκούοντας. [2] δεῖ δὲ καὶ γνώμας συμπαραλαμβάνειν. χρὴ δὲ τούτων <τινὰ>[72] κατὰ πάντα τὰ μέρη συγκαταλέγειν, διαλλάττοντα τοὺς λόγους καὶ μηδέποτε ὅμοια εἰς τὸ αὐτὸ |
40 πολλὰ τιθέντα, καὶ οὕτως ὁ λόγος ἀστεῖος φανεῖται.
1434b [3] μηκύνειν || δὲ τοὺς λόγους βουλόμενον δεῖ μερίζειν τὸ πρᾶγμα καὶ ἐν ἑκάστῳ μέρει τὰ ἐνόντα οἷά τέ ἐστι τὴν φύσιν διδάσκειν, καὶ τὴν χρῆσιν καὶ ἰδίᾳ καὶ κοινῇ καὶ τὰς προφάσεις αὐτῶν ἐκδιηγεῖσθαι. ἂν δὲ
5 καὶ ἔτι μακρότερον θελήσωμεν | τὸν λόγον ποιεῖν, δεῖ πολλοῖς ὀνόμασι περὶ ἑκάστου χρῆσθαι. [4] χρὴ δὲ καὶ παρὰ μέρος ἕκαστον τοῦ λόγου παλιλλογεῖν καὶ τὴν παλιλλογίαν σύντομον ποιεῖσθαι, ἐν δὲ τῇ τελευτῇ τοῦ λόγου ταῦτα περὶ ὧν καθ' ἓν ἕκαστον εἴρηκας, ἀθρόα συντιθέναι καὶ περὶ ὅλων τῶν πρα-
10 γμάτων λέγειν. | τοῦτον μὲν οὖν τὸν τρόπον μῆκος ἕξουσιν οἱ λόγοι.

[5] βραχυλογεῖν δὲ βουλόμενον <δεῖ>[73] ὅλον τὸ πρᾶγμα ἑνὶ ὀνόματι περιλαμβάνειν, καὶ τούτῳ ὃ ἂν ὑπάρχῃ βραχύτατον τῷ πράγματι. χρὴ δὲ καὶ συνδέσμους ὀλίγους ποιεῖν, τὰ πλεῖστα δὲ ζευγνύναι.
15 ὀνομάζειν μὲν οὕτω, τῇ δὲ λέξει εἰς δύο | χρῆσθαι, καὶ παλιλλογίαν τὴν σύντομον ἐκ τῶν μερῶν ἀφαιρεῖν, ἐν δὲ ταῖς τελευταῖς μόνον παλιλλογεῖν. καὶ τοῦτον μὲν τὸν τρόπον βραχεῖς τοὺς λόγους ποιήσομεν.

[6] ἐὰν δὲ βούλῃ μέσως λέγειν, <δεῖ>[74] τὰ μέγιστα τῶν μερῶν ἐκλέγοντα περὶ τούτων ποιεῖσθαι τοὺς

memes in wholes or in halves, so that the audience itself assumes the other half. [2] It is also necessary to include maxims. They must be cited in every part, varying their words and never being cast with many of the same expressions for the same thing. In this way the speech appears urbane.

[3] If you wish to lengthen speeches you must divide the subject into parts and in each part teach the nature of its contents and relate their use, both specifically and generally, and their rationale. If we wish to make the speech still longer we must use many words for each thing. [4] We must also do a repetition for each part of the speech and make the repetition concise. At the end of the speech you must put together those things about which you have spoken individually and speak about the entire matter. In this way the speeches will have length.

[5] If you wish to make a short speech, you must incorporate the entire matter with a single expression and it must be the shortest there is for that matter. You must use only a few conjunctions to connect the most things. Use wording in this way, but make the expression do double service: remove the concise repetition from the parts, and repeat only at the end. In this way we shall make the speeches short.

[6] If you wish to speak at moderate length, you must pick out the most important parts and make the speech

---

[72] τινὰ add. Chiron

[73] δεῖ add. Fuhrmann

[74] δεῖ add. Fuhrmann

20 λόγους. χρὴ δὲ καὶ τοῖς ὀνόμασι | τοῖς μέσοις χρῆσθαι καὶ μήτε τοῖς μακροτάτοις μήτε τοῖς βραχυτάτοις μήτε πολλοῖς περί γε ἑνός, ἀλλὰ μετρίοις. [7] χρὴ δὲ καὶ τοὺς ἐπιλόγους ἐκ τῶν ἀνὰ μέσον μερῶν μήτε παντελῶς ἐξαιρεῖν μήτε πᾶσι τοῖς μέρεσιν ἐπιφέρειν, ἀλλ' ἅπερ ἂν μάλιστα βούλῃ κατανοῆσαι τοὺς ἀκού-
25 οντας, ἐπὶ τούτων | μάλιστα παλιλλογεῖν ἐπὶ τῇ τελευτῇ.

[8] τὰ μὲν οὖν μήκη τῶν λόγων ἐκ τούτων ποιήσομεν ἡνίκα ἂν θέλωμεν· ἂν δὲ ἀστεῖον γράφειν θέλῃς λόγον, παραφύλαττε ὡς μάλιστα ὅπως τὰ ἤθη τῶν λόγων ὁμοιοῦν τοῖς ἀνθρώποις δυνήσῃ. τοῦτο δὲ
30 ποιήσεις, ἂν ἐπιθεωρῇς τὰ μεγάλα τῶν ἠθῶν καὶ | τὰ ἀκριβῆ καὶ τὰ μέτρια. περὶ μὲν οὖν τούτων ἐντεῦθεν οὐκ ἀγνοήσεις, περὶ δὲ ὀνομάτων συνθέσεως δηλώσομεν· καὶ γὰρ τοῦτο τῶν ἀναγκαίων ἐστί.

23. Πρῶτον μὲν οὖν τρόποι ὀνομάτων εἰσὶ τρεῖς, ἁπλοῦς ἢ σύνθετος ἢ μεταφέρων. ὡσαύτως δὲ καὶ
35 θέσεις τρεῖς· μία | μὲν εἰς φωνῆεν τελευτᾶν ‹ἐν›[75] ταῖς συμβολαῖς καὶ ἀπὸ φωνήεντος ἄρχεσθαι, δευτέρα δὲ ἀπὸ ἀφώνου ἀρξάμενον εἰς ἄφωνον τελευτᾶν, τρίτη δὲ τὰ ἄφωνα πρὸς τὰ φωνήεντα συνδεῖν. [2] τάξεις δὲ τέτταρες· μία μὲν τὰ ὅμοια τῶν ὀνομάτων ἢ παράλ-
40 ληλα τιθέναι ἢ διασπείρειν, ἄλλη δὲ τοῖς | αὐτοῖς
1435a ὀνόμασι χρῆσθαι ἢ μεταβάλλειν εἰς ἕτερα, τρίτη || δὲ ἑνὶ ἢ πολλοῖς ὀνόμασι τὸ πρᾶγμα προσαγορεύειν, τετάρτη δὲ ἑξῆς τὰ πραχθέντα ὀνομάζειν ἢ ὑπερβιβάζειν. ὅπως δὲ καλλίστην ποιήσεις τὴν ἑρμηνείαν, νῦν δηλώσομεν.

about them. You must use words of moderate length, neither the longest nor the shortest, nor many about just one thing, but a moderate number. [7] You must not remove the conclusions from the parts in the middle nor attach them to every part, but whatever points you wish the audience to understand thoroughly, repeat them, especially at the end.

[8] In this way we shall make the lengths of speeches as long as we want. If you want to write an urbane speech, take care especially, as much as you are able, to liken the characters of the speeches to the people. You will do this if you observe the large aspects of the characters, the precise aspects, and the middle aspects. In this way you will know about these things, but we shall explain the composition of words. That is a necessity.

23. First, there are three sorts of words, simple, combined, or metaphorical. There are likewise three positions: one ends in a sounded syllable in the transitions (between words) and begins from a sounded, a second begins from an unsounded syllable and ends in an unsounded, and a third connects unsounded syllables to sounded. [2] There are also four arrangements: one either sets similar words beside each other or spreads them out, another uses the same words or changes to others, a third refers to a matter with one or many words, and a fourth names what has been done in order or transposes it. Now we shall explain how you will make your expression as attractive as possible.

---

[75] ἐν add. Fuhrmann

24. Πρῶτον μὲν οὖν εἰς δύο ἑρμηνεύειν, εἶτα σαφῶς
5 δεῖ | λέγειν. σχήματα δ' ἐστὶ τοῦ εἰς δύο λέγειν τάδε· ἓν
μὲν ὅτι αὐτὸς δύναται καὶ τοῦτο καὶ ἕτερον, δεύτερον
δὲ ὅτι οὗτος μὲν οὐ δύναται, ἕτερος δὲ δύναται, τρίτον
δὲ ὅτι οὗτος καὶ τοῦτο καὶ ἕτερον δύναται, τέταρτον δὲ
ὅτι οὔτ' αὐτὸς οὔθ' ἕτερος δύναται, πέμπτον δὲ ὅτι
10 ἐκεῖνος μὲν δύναται, αὐτὸς | δὲ οὐ δύναται, ἕκτον δὲ ὅτι
αὐτὸς μὲν ἕτερον δύναται, ἐκεῖνος δὲ οὐ δύναται ἕτερον. [2] ἕκαστον δὲ τούτων ἐπὶ τῶνδε θεωρήσεις. ὅτι
μὲν γὰρ αὐτὸς δύναται καὶ τοῦτο καὶ ἕτερον, τοιόνδε
ἐστίν· "ἐγὼ δὲ οὐ μόνον τούτων αἴτιος ὑμῖν ἐγενόμην,
ἀλλὰ καὶ Τιμόθεον μέλλοντα στρατεύειν ἐφ' ὑμᾶς |
15 διεκώλυσα." [3] ὅτι δὲ οὗτος μὲν οὐ δύναται, ἕτερος
δὲ δύναται, τοιόνδε· "αὐτὸς μὲν οὖν ἀδυνάτως ἔχει
πρεσβεύειν ὑπὲρ ἡμῶν, οὗτος δὲ φίλος ἐστὶ τῇ πόλει
τῶν Σπαρτιατῶν καὶ μάλιστ' ἂν δυνηθείη πρᾶξαι ἃ
βούλεσθε." [4] τὸ δὲ ὅτι οὗτος καὶ τοῦτο καὶ ἕτερον
20 δύναται, τοιόνδε· "οὐ μόνον δὲ ἐν τοῖς πολέμοις | εὔ-
ρωστον αὑτὸν παρέσχεν, ἀλλὰ καὶ βουλεύσασθαι τῶν
πολιτῶν οὐχ ἥκιστα δύναται." [5] τὸ δὲ ὅτι οὔτ' αὐτὸς
οὔθ' ἕτερος δύναται, τοιόνδε· "οὔτ' ἂν αὐτὸς δυνηθείην
ὀλίγην δύναμιν ἔχων καταπολεμῆσαι τοὺς ἐναντίους
οὔτ' ἄλλος οὐδεὶς τῶν πολιτῶν." [6] τὸ δὲ ὅτι ἐκεῖνος
25 μὲν δύναται, αὐτὸς δὲ οὐ | δύναται, τοιόνδε· "οὗτος μὲν
γὰρ ἔρρωται τῷ σώματι, ἐγὼ δ' ἀρρωστῶν τυγχάνω."
[7] τὸ δὲ ὅτι αὐτὸς μὲν ἕτερον δύναται, ἐκεῖνος δὲ οὐ
δύναται ἕτερον, τοιόνδε· "ἐγὼ μὲν γὰρ κυβερνῆσαι
δυνατός εἰμι, οὗτος δὲ οὐδὲ κωπηλατῆσαι δύναται."

24. First, you must express double statements, and then you must speak clearly. The following are forms of double statements: one is, "He himself can do this thing and the other thing"; a second is, "This man cannot do it, but the other can"; a third is, "This man can do this thing and the other thing"; a fourth is, "Neither this man nor the other can do it"; a fifth is, "That man can do it, but he himself cannot"; a sixth is, "He can do the other thing, but that man cannot do the other thing." [2] You will observe each of these in the following. That he himself can do this and the other thing is as follows: "I was not only responsible for these things for you, but I also prevented Timotheus from coming to fight against you." [3] That this man cannot do it but the other can: "He himself is incapable of going on a embassy for us, but this man is a friend to the Spartans' city and is very capable of doing what you wish." [4] That he can do this and the other thing: "He not only offers himself fit for war but he is also not the least capable citizen at deliberation." [5] That neither he himself nor the other can do it: "Because I had little power, I was unable to prosecute the war against the enemy, nor could any other citizen." [6] That that man can do it, but he cannot: "This man is physically robust, but I am actually weak." [7] That he can do the other thing, but that man cannot do the other thing: "I can steer, but this man cannot even row." You will create

σχήματα μὲν οὖν τοῦ εἰς δύο ἑρμηνεύειν ὧδε ποιήσεις, |
30 ἐπὶ τῶν πραγμάτων ἁπάντων τὸν αὐτὸν τρόπον μετιών. σαφῶς δὲ ὅθεν δηλώσεις, τοῦτο πάλιν σκεπτέον.

25. Πρῶτον μὲν οὖν ὀνόμαζε τοῖς οἰκείοις ὀνόμασιν ὅ τι ἂν λέγῃς, διαφεύγων τὸ ἀμφίβολον. εὐλαβοῦ δὲ περὶ τὰ φωνήεντα τῶν γραμμάτων ὅπως μὴ ἑξῆς
35 τεθήσονται. πρόσεχε | δὲ καὶ τοῖς καλουμένοις ἄρθροις ὅπως ἐν τῷ δέοντι προστιθῆται. σκόπει δὲ καὶ τὴν σύνθεσιν τῶν ὀνομάτων ὅπως μήτε συγκεχυμένη μήθ' ὑπερβατὴ ἔσται· τὰ γὰρ οὕτω λεγόμενα δύσγνωστα συμβαίνει. μετὰ δὲ συνδέσμους, οὓς ἂν προείπῃς, ἀποδίδου τοὺς ἀκολουθοῦντας. [2] τὸ μὲν οὖν συνδέ-
40 σμους | ἀποδιδόναι τοὺς ἀκολουθοῦντας τοιόνδε ἐστίν·
1435b "ἐγὼ μὲν || παρεγενόμην οὗ ἔφην, σὺ δὲ φάσκων ἥξειν οὐκ ἦλθες·" πάλιν ὅταν ὁ αὐτὸς σύνδεσμος ἀκόλουθος ᾖ, οἷον· "σὺ γὰρ κἀκείνων αἴτιος ἐγένου, καὶ τούτων αἴτιος σύ." [3] περὶ μὲν οὖν τῶν συνδέσμων εἴρηται,
5 καὶ ἀπὸ τούτων τεκμαίρεσθαι δεῖ καὶ περὶ | τῶν ἄλλων. δεῖ δὲ καὶ τὴν σύνθεσιν τῶν ὀνομάτων μήτε συγκεχυμένην μήτε ὑπερβατὴν ποιεῖν. τὸ μὲν γὰρ συγκεχυμένον τοιόνδε ἐστίν ὡς ὅταν εἴπῃς· "δεινόν ἐστι τοῦτον τύπτειν τοῦτον·" ἄδηλον γάρ [ἦν][76] ὁπότερος ἂν ἦν ὁ τύπτων. ἐὰν δὲ εἴπῃς οὕτως, δῆλον ποιήσεις· "δεινόν
10 ἐστι τοῦτον ὑπὸ | τούτου τύπτεσθαι." [4] τὸ μὲν οὖν συγχεῖν τὴν σύνθεσιν τῶν ὀνομάτων τοιοῦτόν ἐστι. τὸ

[76] ἦν del. Sp.[1]

forms to express two things in this way, pursuing the same method in all matters. How you will explain clearly must now be examined.

25. First, name everything by its proper name whatever you say, avoiding ambiguity. Take care about vowels that they are not placed in order. Give attention to the so-called articles, that they are placed in the required position. Examine also the connection of words so that there will be no confusion or transposition. What is said that way turns out hard to understand. After connectives that you speak first, supply those that follow. [2] Here is an instance of supplying connectives that follow: "I *on the one hand* was present where I claimed; you *on the other hand*,[27] although claiming that you would arrive, did not come." Again, an instance of when the same particle follows: "You were the cause *both* of those things, *and*[28] of these you were the cause." [3] I have discussed the connectives; from them inferences must be drawn about others. The connection of words must create neither confusion nor transposition. There is an instance of confusion when you say, "It is terrible that *this* man *this* man strikes." It is unclear who the striker is. You will make it clear when you speak as follows: "It is terrible that *this man* is struck by *this man*."[29] [4] That is an instance of the confusing connection of words. See

[27] The Greek particle *men* ("on the one hand") anticipates the following *de* ("on the other hand"); they are a very common way of indicating coordinating structures, such as antithesis, within sentences. [28] Greek repeats that particle *kai* ("and") to create the expression "both . . . and." [29] In the first example, "this (man)" has the same form both times; in the second, its grammatical function, and so form, changes.

δὲ προσέχειν τοῖς ἄρθροις ὅπως ἐν τῷ δέοντι προστιθῆται, ἐπὶ τῶνδε ὅρα· "οὗτος ὁ ἄνθρωπος τοῦτον τὸν ἄνθρωπον ἀδικεῖ." νῦν μὲν οὖν ἐγγενόμενα τὰ ἄρθρα σαφῆ ποιεῖ τὴν λέξιν, ἐξαιρεθέντα δὲ ἀσαφῆ ποιήσει. | 15 ἔσθ' ὅτε δὲ συμβαίνει καὶ τὸ ἀνάπαλιν. [5] τὰ μὲν οὖν ἐν τοῖς ἄρθροις τοιαῦτά ἐστιν.

τὰ δὲ φωνήεντα μὴ τίθει παράλληλα, ἂν μή ποτε ἄλλως ἀδύνατον ᾖ δηλῶσαι, ἢ ἀνάπτυξις ᾖ τις ἢ ἄλλη διαίρεσις. [6] τὸ δὲ τὰ ἀμφίβολα διαφεύγειν τοιόνδε 20 ἐστίν· ἔνια τῶν ὀνομάτων ταὐτὰ ἐπὶ | πλείοσι πράγμασι κεῖται, οἷον ὀδὸς τῶν θυρῶν καὶ ὁδὸς ἣν βαδίζουσιν. δεῖ δ' ἐπὶ τοῖς τοιούτοις τὸ ἴδιον ἀεὶ συμπαραλαμβάνειν. καὶ σαφῶς μὲν ἐν τοῖς ὀνόμασιν, ἂν ταῦτα ποιῶμεν, διαλεξόμεθα, εἰς δύο δ' ἑρμηνεύσομεν διὰ τῆς προτέρας μεθόδου. |

25 26. Περὶ δὲ ἀντιθέτων καὶ παρισώσεων καὶ ὁμοιοτήτων λέγωμεν ἤδη· δεησόμεθα γὰρ καὶ τούτων. ἀντίθετον μὲν οὖν ἐστι τὸ ἐναντίαν τὴν ὀνομασίαν ἅμα καὶ τὴν δύναμιν <ἐν>[77] τοῖς ἀντικειμένοις ἔχον, ἢ τὸ ἕτερον τούτων. [2] τοῖς μὲν οὖν ὀνόμασιν εἴη ἂν 30 ἐναντίον ἅμα καὶ τῇ δυνάμει τόδε· "οὐ | γὰρ δίκαιον τοῦτον μὲν τὰ ἐμὰ ἔχοντα πλουτεῖν, ἐμὲ δὲ τὰ ὄντα προϊέμενον οὕτω πτωχεύειν." [3] τοῖς δ' ὀνόμασι μόνοις· "διδότω γὰρ ὁ πλούσιος καὶ εὐδαίμων τῷ πένητι καὶ ἐνδεεῖ." τῇ δὲ δυνάμει· "ἐγὼ μὲν τοῦτον νοσοῦντα ἐθεράπευσα, οὗτος δ' ἐμοὶ μεγίστων κακῶν αἴτιος 35 γέγονεν." ἐνταῦθα μὲν | γὰρ τὰ ὀνόματα οὐκ ἐναντία, αἱ δὲ πράξεις ἐναντίαι. κάλλιστον μὲν οὖν εἴη ἂν τὸ κατ'

from the following how attention must be given to how articles are placed: "This person wrongs this person." The presence of the articles now makes the expression clear; their removal will make it unclear. But the reverse happens sometimes. [5] Those are instances of articles.[30]

Do not place vowels side by side, unless it is impossible to achieve clarity otherwise or there is some opening or another separation. [6] The following is an instance of avoiding ambiguities: some words have the same form in many contexts, such as "doorway" and "pathway."[31] In such instances you must always include the particular context. Our wording will be clear if we do these things, and we shall express two things through the earlier method.[32]

26. Let us now discuss antithesis, parisosis, and similarity. We need them also. It is an antithesis to have simultaneously contrary wording or meaning, or both, in antithetical clauses. [2] The following is an instance of contrariety in both simultaneous wording and meaning: "It is not just that this man by having my things is wealthy, but I by giving up my property am impoverished." [3] Of wording alone: "Let the rich and prosperous person give to the poor and needy." In meaning: "I nursed this person when he was ill, but he has been the cause of my greatest troubles." Here the words are not contrary, but the actions are. Antithesis

[30] Editors have placed a lacuna here because the suggested discussion of transposition does not occur.

[31] The Greek words *odos* ("sill") and *(h)odos* ("road") differ only in the breathing mark, which creates the *h* sound.

[32] Cf. 24.1.

---

77 ἐν add. Kassel

ἀμφότερα ἀντίθετον, καὶ κατὰ τὴν δύναμιν καὶ κατὰ τὴν ὀνομασίαν. ἔστι δὲ καὶ τὰ λοιπὰ δύο ἀντίθετα.

27. Παρίσωσις δ' ἐστὶ μέν ὅταν δύο ἴσα λέγηται
40 κῶλα· | εἴη δ' ἂν ἴσα καὶ πολλὰ μικρὰ ὀλίγοις μεγά-
1436a λοις, καὶ || ἴσα τὸ μέγεθος καὶ[78] ἴσα τὸν ἀριθμόν. ἔχει δὲ τοιόνδε τὸ σχῆμα ἡ παρίσωσις· "ἢ διὰ χρημάτων ἀπορίαν ἢ διὰ πολέμου μέγεθος." ταῦτα γὰρ οὔτε ὅμοια οὔτε ἐναντία, ἀλλ' ἴσα μόνον ἀλλήλοις. |

5 28. Παρομοίωσις δ' ἐστὶν ἡ μείζων τῆς παρισώσεως· οὐ γὰρ μόνον ἴσα τὰ κῶλα ποιεῖ, ἀλλὰ καὶ ὅμοια ἐξ ὁμοίων ὀνομάτων, οἷον· "†δεῖ σε†[79] λόγου μίμημα, φέρε πόθου τέχνασμα." μάλιστα δὲ <δεῖ>[80] ποιεῖν ὅμοια τὰ τελευταῖα τῶν ὀνομάτων· ταῦτα γὰρ
10 μάλιστα ποιεῖ τὴν ὁμοίωσιν. ὅμοια δ' | ἐστὶν ὀνόματα τὰ ἐξ ὁμοίων συλλαβῶν, ἐν αἷς πλεῖστα γράμματα τὰ αὐτά ἐστιν, οἷον· "πλήθει μὲν ἐνδεῶς, δυνάμει δὲ ἐντελῶς." [2] ὅσα δὲ ἔξω τέχνης κεῖται, τὸ αὐτόματον αὐτὸ δείξει.[81]

Περὶ μὲν οὖν τούτων ἀπόχρη· καὶ γὰρ τὸ δίκαιον
15 καὶ τὸ νόμιμον[82] καὶ | τὸ καλὸν καὶ τὸ συμφέρον καὶ τὰ λοιπὰ αὐτά τε ἴσμεν οἷά ἐστι καὶ ὅθεν αὐτὰ πολλὰ ποιήσομεν. ὡσαύτως δὲ καὶ τὰς αὐξήσεις καὶ τὰς ταπεινώσεις < . . . >[83] γινώσκομεν αἵ τινές τ' εἰσι καὶ

[78] καὶ (*et*) Lat.$^{\beta}$ Rackham : om. N a [79] loc. desp. apud Fuhrmann [80] δεῖ (*oportet*) Lat.$^{\beta}$: om. N a
[81] ὅσα—δείξει del. Fuhrmann
[82] καὶ τὸ νόμιμον (*et legitimum*) Lat.$^{\beta}$: om. N a
[83] lac. ind. Chiron

in both ways would be finest, both in meaning and in wording. There are two antitheses remaining.

27. There is *parisosis* when two equal colons are spoken. Many short elements may be equal to a few long ones, and both the size and number may be equal. Parisosis has the following form: "either because of a lack of money or because of the size of a war." These are neither similar nor contrary but only equal to each other.

28. *Paromoiosis* is a greater form of *parisosis*. Not only does it make the colons equal, but they are similar as a result of similar wording, for instance: "You must speak a verbal imitation; offer an emotional fabrication." You must make the endings of the wording similar; it creates the similarity. Words constructed from similar syllables, in which most of the letters are the same, are similar, such as "in number defective, but in power effective." [2] But whatever is outside the art[33] shows itself spontaneously.

Enough about these things. We know about the just, the lawful, the noble, the advantageous, etc., what they are and how to create many arguments about them. In the same way we also understand amplification and minimization and < . . . >,[34] what they are and how to be well sup-

[33] Some editors have doubted the authenticity of this sentence, especially with its unique reference to the "art" (*techne*) of rhetoric.

[34] Chiron sees a gap here, where reference to the proofs would have been expected.

ὅθεν αὐτῶν εἰς τοὺς λόγους εὐπορήσομεν. [3] ὁμοιοτρόπως δὲ τούτοις τάς τε προκαταλήψεις καὶ τὰ παρὰ
20 τῶν | ἀκουόντων αἰτήματα καὶ τὰς παλιλλογίας καὶ τὰς ἀστειολογίας καὶ τὰ μήκη τῶν λόγων καὶ τῆς ἑρμηνείας τὴν σύνθεσιν ἅπασαν ἴσμεν. [4] ὥστε τὰς κοινὰς δυνάμεις ἁπάντων τῶν εἰδῶν καὶ τὰς διαφορὰς καὶ τὰς χρήσεις αὐτῶν ἐκ τῶν προειρημένων εἰδότες, ἂν
25 ἐθίσωμεν ἡμᾶς αὐτοὺς καὶ | γυμνάσωμεν ἀναλαμβάνειν αὐτὰς κατὰ τὰ προγυμνάσματα, πολλὴν εὐπορίαν καὶ γράφοντες καὶ λέγοντες ἐξ αὐτῶν ἕξομεν. [5] κατὰ μέρη μὲν οὖν οὕτως ἀκριβέστατα ἂν διέλοις τὰς τῶν λόγων μεθόδους.

ὡς δ' ἐπὶ τοῖς εἴδεσι χρὴ τάττειν τοὺς λόγους
30 σωματοειδῶς, τίσι τε πρώτοις τῶν μερῶν | χρῆσθαι καὶ πῶς τούτοις αὐτοῖς, ταῦτα πάλιν δηλώσω. προοίμιον μὲν οὖν προτάττω· κοινὸν γάρ ἐστι τῶν ἑπτὰ εἰδῶν καὶ ἐπὶ πᾶσι τοῖς πράγμασιν ἁρμόσει λεγόμενον.

29. Ἔστι δὲ προοίμιον καθόλου μὲν εἰπεῖν ἀκροατῶν παρασκευὴ καὶ τοῦ πράγματος ἐν κεφαλαίῳ μὴ
35 εἰδόσι δήλωσις, | ἵνα γινώσκωσι περὶ ὧν ὁ λόγος παρακολουθῶσί τε τῇ ὑποθέσει, καὶ ἔτι προσέχειν παρακαλέσαι καὶ καθ' ὅσον τῷ λόγῳ δυνατὸν εὔνους ἡμῖν αὐτοὺς ποιῆσαι. τούτων μὲν οὖν εἶναι δεῖ τὸ προοίμιον παρασκευαστικόν. ὡς δὲ αὐτῷ χρησόμεθα, πρῶτον μὲν ἐπὶ τῶν δημηγορικῶν καὶ προτρεπτικῶν, |
40 τοῦτο δείξω.

1436b [2] τὸ μὲν οὖν προεκτιθέναι τὸ πρᾶγμα || τοῖς ἀκούουσι καὶ φανερὸν ποιεῖν τοιόνδε ἐστίν· "ἀνέστην συμ-

plied with them for speeches. [3] We similarly know about anticipations, appeals to the audience, repetitions, urbanities, lengths of speeches, and the entire composition of expression. Since we know the common powers of all the species and their differences and uses from what has been said before, if we accustom ourselves and practice taking them up according to preliminary exercises, we shall have a large supply of them for writing and speaking. [5] In this way, then, you would divide most precisely the methods of speeches by their parts.

But since we must *arrange* speeches coherently with regard to the species, I shall clarify these matters again, which parts to use first and how to use them. An introduction, therefore, I arrange first. It is common to all seven species and fits all matters when spoken.

29. An introduction is, in general, a preparation of the audience and a description of the headings of the matter for those who do not know it (so that they may know the subject of the speech and may follow its premise), and in particular, it calls for attention and, as much as is possible for a speech, makes the audience friendly toward us. The introduction must be preparative of these things. I shall first show how we shall use it with regard to demegoric and proposition speeches.

[2] Present the matter to the audience and make it clear in this way: "I have come forward to advise that we must

βουλεύσων ὡς χρὴ πολεμεῖν ἡμᾶς ὑπὲρ Συρακουσίων·" "ἀνέστην ἀποφανούμενος ὡς οὐ χρὴ βοηθεῖν ἡμᾶς Συρακουσίοις." [3] τὸ μὲν οὖν φράζειν ἐν κεφαλαίῳ τὸ πρᾶγμα τοιοῦτόν ἐστιν. |

5 προσέχειν δὲ παρακαλεῖν ἐκ τούτων ἂν εἰδείημεν, εἰ κατανοήσαιμεν αὐτοί ποίοις μάλιστα καὶ λόγοις καὶ πράγμασι βουλευόμενοι προσέχομεν. [4] ἆρ' οὖν οὐ τούτοις ὅταν ἢ ὑπὲρ μεγάλων ἢ φοβερῶν ἢ τῶν ἡμῖν οἰκείων βουλευώμεθα; ἢ φάσκωσιν [ἐπιδείξειν][84] οἱ
10 λέγοντες ὡς δίκαια καὶ καλὰ καὶ | συμφέροντα καὶ ῥᾴδια καὶ ἡδέα ἐπιδείξουσιν ἡμῖν ἐφ' ἃ πράττειν παρακαλοῦσιν; ἢ δεηθῶσιν ἡμῶν ἀκοῦσαι αὐτῶν προσέχοντας τὸν νοῦν; [5] ὥσπερ οὖν αὐτοὶ τοῖς ἄλλοις, οὕτω καὶ ἡμεῖς τὰ οἰκειότατα τῶν προειρημένων τοῖς ὑφ' ἡμῶν πράγμασι λεγομένοις λαμ-
15 βάνοντες καὶ τοῖς ἀκούουσιν ἐνδεικνύμενοι | προσέχειν αὐτοὺς ποιήσομεν. [6] ἐπὶ μὲν οὖν τὸ προσέχειν διὰ τούτων παρακαλοῦμεν.

τὴν εὔνοιαν δὲ παρασκευασόμεθα διασκεψάμενοι πρῶτον πῶς πρὸς ἡμᾶς αὐτοὺς τυγχάνουσιν ἔχοντες, εὐνοϊκῶς ἢ δυσμενῶς ἢ μήτε εὖ μήτε κακῶς. [7] ἐὰν μὲν οὖν εὖνοι τυγχάνωσιν ὄντες, περίεργον λέγειν |
20 περὶ εὐνοίας· ἂν δὲ πάντως βουλώμεθα, χρὴ συντόμως μετ' εἰρωνείας εἰπεῖν τοῦτον τὸν τρόπον· "ὅτι μὲν οὖν "εὔνους εἰμὶ τῇ πόλει καὶ πολλάκις μοι πεισθέντες συμφερόντως ἐπράξατε, καὶ διότι πρὸς τὰ κοινὰ δίκαιον ἐμαυτὸν παρέχω καὶ μᾶλλόν τι τῶν ἰδίων προϊέμε-
25 νον ἢ ἀπὸ | τῶν δημοσίων ὠφελούμενον, περίεργον

wage war on behalf of the Syracusans"; "I have come forward to point out that we must not help the Syracusans." [3] Say what the headings of the matter are in this way.

We may know how to appeal for attention if we recognize just what kinds of arguments and facts we ourselves pay attention to when deliberating. [4] Is it not when we are deliberating about important or alarming matters or matters that closely concern ourselves? Or is it when those who are speaking claim that they will show that they are appealing to us to do something just, noble, advantageous, easy, and pleasant? Or is it when they ask us to pay attention when listening to them? [5] Therefore, just as we pay attention to others, we shall make them attentive by taking up from what has been previously discussed what is most relevant to the facts being discussed by us and demonstrating them to the audience. [6] In this way we shall make appeals to be attentive.

Friendliness we shall create by first examining how they happen to be disposed toward us, with friendliness, ill will, or neither well nor poorly. [7] If they happen to be friendly, it is superfluous to talk about goodwill. But if we really want to do so we have to speak briefly, with irony, as follows: "Because I have goodwill toward the city and you have often acted advantageously when advised by me, and because I offer myself justly for public service, forgoing my private interests rather than benefiting from public interests, I think it is unnecessary to say to you what you

---

[84] ἐπιδείξειν del. Bekker

εἶναι νομίζω πρὸς ὑμᾶς τοῦτό γε σαφῶς εἰδότας λέγειν· ὡς δὲ εἰ καὶ νῦν μοι πεισθεῖτε, καλῶς βουλεύσεσθε, τοῦτο πειράσομαι διδάσκειν." [8] τοῦτον μὲν οὖν τὸν τρόπον τοῖς εὖ διακειμένοις ἐν ταῖς δημηγορίαις τῆς εὐμενείας ὑπομνηστέον.

30 τοῖς δὲ μήτε | διαβεβλημένοις μήτε εὖ διακειμένοις ῥητέον ὡς δίκαιόν ἐστι καὶ συμφέρον τοῖς πεῖραν μὴ δεδωκόσι τῶν πολιτῶν εὔνους ἀκροατὰς γενέσθαι. [9] ἔπειτα τοὺς ἀκούοντας ἐπαίνῳ θεραπευτέον, δικαίως καὶ νουνεχῶς τοὺς λόγους, "ὡς εἰώθασι," δοκιμάζειν. ἔτι δὲ τὰς ἐλαττώσεις οἰστέον λέγοντας ὡς "οὐ
35 δεινότητι | πιστεύων ἀνέστην, ἀλλὰ νομίζων τῷ κοινῷ τὸ συμφέρον εἰσηγήσεσθαι." [10] καὶ τοῖς μὲν μήτε εὖ μήτε κακῶς διακειμένοις ἐκ τῶν τοιούτων τὴν εὔνοιαν ποριστέον.

τοὺς δὲ διαβεβλημένους ἀναγκαῖον τὰς διαβολὰς ἢ αὐτοὺς ἔχειν, ἢ τὰ πράγματα ὑπὲρ ὧν λέγουσιν, ἢ
40 τὸν λόγον. αὗται δὲ αἱ | διαβολαὶ γίνονται ἢ ἐκ τοῦ
1437a παρόντος ἢ ἐκ τοῦ παροιχομένου ‖ χρόνου. [11] ἐκ μὲν οὖν τοῦ παροιχομένου χρόνου ἐάν τις ὑποπτεύηται εἰς πονηρίαν τινά, πρῶτον μὲν τῇ πρὸς τοὺς ἀκροατὰς προκαταλήψει χρῆσθαι καὶ λέγειν ὡς "οὐδ' αὐτὸς ἀγνοῶ διαβεβλημένος, ἀλλ' ἐπιδείξω ψευδεῖς οὔσας
5 τὰς | διαβολάς." [12] ἔπειτα κεφαλαιωδῶς ἐν τοῖς προοιμίοις ἀπολογητέον, ἂν ἔχῃς τι λέγειν ὑπὲρ ἑαυτοῦ, καὶ τὰς κρίσεις ψεκτέον. ἀναγκαῖον γάρ, ἄν τε πρὸς τὸ δημόσιον ᾖ τις διαβεβλημένος, ἄν τε πρὸς τοὺς ἰδιώτας, ἢ γεγενῆσθαι κρίσιν ἢ μέλλειν γενήσεσθαι ἢ

clearly know already. But I shall try to teach that if you follow my advice now, you will deliberate well." [8] This is the way in public speeches to remind those who are well disposed of their goodwill.

To those without prejudice or bias in our favor we must say that it is just and advantageous to listen with goodwill to citizens who have not proven themselves. [9] Then we must apply some praise to our audience, that they scrutinize speeches justly and sensibly, "as they usually do." Then we must acknowledge our weaknesses, saying, "I have not come forward out of confidence in my cleverness but in the belief that my proposal is advantageous to the common good." [10] We must create goodwill in those who are neither well nor ill disposed (to us) in this way.

Those who have incurred prejudice must suffer the prejudice with regard to themselves, with regard to the matters about which they are speaking, or with regard to their speech. Prejudice arises either from present circumstances or from a previous time. [11] If someone is suspected of some corruption in the past, he must first employ anticipation toward the audience and say, "I am also not unaware that there is prejudice against me, but I shall show that the prejudice is false." [12] Then you must make a summary defense in your introduction if you have something to say in your favor, and you must criticize the judgments. If someone has incurred prejudice in public or in private, a judgment must either have occurred or be going to occur, or else those who are making the accusation do

10 μὴ βούλεσθαι τοὺς τὴν αἰτίαν | ἐπενεγκόντας λαβεῖν κρίσιν. [13] καὶ ῥητέον ὡς ἀδίκως ἡ κρίσις ἐγένετο, καὶ ὡς ὑπὸ τῶν ἐχθρῶν κατεστασιάσθημεν· ἢ ἐὰν τοῦτο μὴ ἐνδέχηται, λέγειν ὡς ἱκανὸν ἡμῖν ἀτυχήσασι τότε, καὶ ὡς δίκαιόν ἐστιν τῶν πραγμάτων ἤδη κεκριμένων μὴ περὶ τῶν αὐτῶν ἔτι διαβολὴν ἔχειν. [14] ἂν
15 δ' ἐπίδοξος ἡ | κρίσις ᾖ γενέσθαι, λεκτέον ὡς ἕτοιμος εἶ περὶ τῶν διαβολῶν ἐν τοῖς καθημένοις ἤδη κρίνεσθαι, κἂν ἐλεγχθῇς τι τὴν πόλιν ἀδικῶν, ἀποθνῄσκειν ὑποτιμᾷ. [15] ἐὰν δὲ οἱ ἐγκαλέσαντες μὴ ἐπεξίωσιν, αὐτὸ τοῦτο χρὴ σημεῖον ποιεῖσθαι διότι τὴν διαβολὴν
20 ψευδῶς ἡμῶν κατήνεγκαν· οὐ γὰρ εἰκὸς | εἶναι δόξει τοὺς ἀληθῶς ἐγκαλοῦντας μὴ βούλεσθαι κρίσιν λαβεῖν.

[16] ἀεὶ δὲ κατηγορεῖν χρὴ διαβολῆς καὶ λέγειν ὡς δεινὸν καὶ κοινὸν καὶ πολλῶν κακῶν αἴτιον. ἐμφανιστέον δ' ὅτι καὶ πολλοὶ ἤδη διεφθάρησαν ἀδίκως διαβληθέντες. χρὴ δὲ καὶ διδάσκειν ὡς εὔηθές ἐστιν
25 ὑπὲρ τῶν κοινῶν βουλευομένους | μὴ παρὰ πάντων τοὺς λόγους ἀκούοντας τὸ συμφέρον σκοπεῖν, ἀλλὰ ταῖς ἐνίων διαβολαῖς δυσχεραίνειν. δεῖ δὲ καὶ ἐπαγγέλλεσθαι καὶ ὑποσχνεῖσθαι δίκαια καὶ συμφέροντα καὶ καλὰ ἐπιδείξειν ἃ ὑπέσχου συμβουλεύειν. [17] τοὺς μὲν οὖν ἐκ τοῦ παροιχομένου χρόνου διαβεβλημένους |
30 τοῦτον τὸν τρόπον ἐν ταῖς δημηγορίαις τὰς διαβολὰς λυτέον· ἐκ δὲ τοῦ παρόντος χρόνου διαβάλλει τοὺς λέγοντας πρῶτον μὲν ἡλικία. ἐάν τε γὰρ νέος παντελῶς ἐάν τε πρεσβύτης δημηγορῇ, δυσχεραίνεται· τῷ

not want a judgment to be made. [13] We must also say that the judgment occurred unjustly and that our enemies' faction overcame us. Or, if that is not possible, say that we suffered sufficient misfortune on that occasion and that it is just, when matters have already been judged, not to continue incurring prejudice over the same things. [14] If a trial is anticipated, you must say that with regard to the prejudices you are ready to be judged before those already seated, and if you are convicted of harming the city in any way, you propose the death penalty. [15] If the accusers do not prosecute, that must be taken as a sign that they caused this prejudice falsely; it will seem implausible that those making true accusations would not wish to go to trial.

[16] It is always necessary to condemn prejudice and to say that it is a terrible thing, a concern to all, and a cause of much harm. Explain that many people have been ruined by unjust prejudice. Teach that it is foolish when deliberating matters of common concern to examine what is advantageous without hearing arguments from everyone but to be annoyed by the prejudices of some. You must also declare and promise that you will show that what you have undertaken to advise will be just, advantageous, and honorable. [17] Those who have incurred prejudice from a former time must in this way refute the prejudices in public speeches. From the present time, age is the first thing that evokes prejudice against the speakers. When a very young man or an old man speaks publicly, there is annoyance:

μὲν γὰρ οὔπω ἦρχθαι, τῷ δὲ ἤδη πεπαῦσθαι προσ-
35 ήκειν οἴονται. [18] ἔπειτα ἐὰν | συνεχῶς εἰώθῃ λέγειν· πολυπράγμων γὰρ εἶναι δοκεῖ οὗτος. καὶ ἐὰν μηδέποτε πρότερον εἰρήκῃ· καὶ γὰρ οὗτος κέρδους[85] ἕνεκά τινος ἰδίου δοκεῖ παρὰ τὸ ἔθος δημηγορεῖν. [19] ἐκ μὲν οὖν τοῦ παρόντος χρόνου διαβολαὶ περὶ τὸν δημηγοροῦντα τοιαῦται γενήσονται.

προφασίζεσθαι δὲ ὑπὲρ αὑτῶν δεῖ τὸν μὲν νεώτερον |
40 ἐκ τῆς ἐρημίας τῶν συμβουλευόντων καὶ ἐκ τοῦ προσ-
1437b ήκοντος || αὐτῷ, λέγω δ' οἷον ὑπὲρ λαμπαδαρχίας ἢ ὑπὲρ γυμνασίας ἢ ὑπὲρ ὅπλων ἢ ἵππων ἢ περὶ πολέμου· τούτων γὰρ οὐκ ἐλάχιστον μέρος τῷ νέῳ μέτεστιν. [20] ῥητέον δὲ καὶ ὡς εἰ μήπω καθ' ἡλικίαν τὸ
5 φρονεῖν, ἀλλὰ κατὰ φύσιν | καὶ ἐπιμέλειαν. ἐμφανιστέον δὲ καὶ ὡς ἁμαρτόντι μὲν ἴδιον τὸ ἀτύχημα, κατορθώσαντι δὲ κοινὴ ἡ ὠφέλεια.

[21] τῷ μὲν οὖν νέῳ ἐκ τῶν τοιούτων προφασιστέον, <τῷ δὲ> γέροντι[86] ἔκ τε τῆς ἐρημίας τῶν συμβουλευόντων καὶ ἐκ τῆς ἐμπειρίας αὐτοῦ, πρὸς δὲ
10 τούτοις καὶ ἐκ τοῦ μεγέθους | καὶ ἐκ τῆς καινότητος τῶν κινδύνων καὶ ἐκ τῶν ἄλλων τῶν τοιούτων· [22] τῷ δὲ λίαν εἰθισμένῳ ἐκ τῆς ἐμπειρίας καὶ ἐκ τοῦ αἰσχρὸν εἶναι πρότερον ἀεὶ λέγοντα νῦν μὴ[87] ἀποφαίνεσθαι γνώμας· τῷ δὲ μὴ εἰθισμένῳ ἔκ τε τοῦ μεγέθους τῶν
15 κινδύνων καὶ ἐκ τοῦ ἀναγκαῖον εἶναι πάντα τινά | ᾧ τῆς πόλεως μέτεστιν ὑπὲρ τῶν νῦν προκειμένων ἀποφαίνεσθαι γνώμην. [23] τὰς μὲν οὖν περὶ αὐτὸν τὸν

they think it proper for the one not to be speaking yet and for the other to have stopped. [18] Next is when someone is accustomed to speak frequently; he seems to be a busybody. Another is when someone has never spoken before; this man seems to make a public speech, contrary to his habit, for the sake of some private profit. [19] These are the sorts of prejudice that will arise from the present time regarding someone engaged in public speech.

The young man must make the excuse that it is because of a lack of advisers and because it is pertinent to him, I mean for example, the supervision of a torch race or of the gymnasium, or weapons or horses or war. The young have not a small part in these matters. [20] He must also say that even if he does not yet have intelligence through his age, he does have it through his nature and training. Explain that the misfortune of someone who fails is his private affair, but the benefits of a successful man are shared.

[21] The young man must excuse his age in this way, but the old man must say it is because of a lack of advisers and his experience, and in addition because of the importance and the novelty of the dangers and other such things. [22] The man who is accustomed to speak excessively must say that it is because of his experience and because it would be shameful not to express his views now when earlier he spoke regularly. The man who is not accustomed to speak must say it is because of the magnitude of the dangers and because everyone who has a share in the city must express his view concerning the matters at hand. [23] In public

---

85 κέρδους (*utilitatem*) Lat.^{a} : om. N a Lat.$^{\beta}$

86 τῷ δὲ γέροντι H^{2} Fuhrmann : λέγοντι N FCUH^{1}P

87 μὴ H^{2} (*silere*) Lat.$^{\beta}$ A edd. : om. N FCUH^{1}P

ἄνθρωπον διαβολὰς ἐν ταῖς δημηγορίαις ἐκ τῶν τοιούτων λύειν ἐπιχειρήσομεν.

αἱ δὲ περὶ τὸ πρᾶγμα γίνονται μὲν ὅταν τις ἡσυχίαν πρὸς τοὺς μηδὲν ἀδικοῦντας ἢ πρὸς τοὺς κρείτ-
20 τονας | συμβουλεύῃ <λύειν>[88] ἢ εἰρήνην ποιεῖσθαι αἰσχράν, ἢ παραινῇ περὶ τὰς θυσίας μικρὰ συντελεῖν, ἤ τι τοιοῦτον εἰσηγῆται. [24] δεῖ δὲ περὶ τῶν τοιούτων πρότερον μὲν πρὸς τοὺς ἀκροατὰς προκαταλήψει χρῆσθαι, ἔπειτα τὴν αἰτίαν εἰς τὴν ἀνάγκην καὶ τὴν τύχην καὶ τοὺς καιροὺς καὶ τὸ συμφέρον ἀναφέρειν καὶ |
25 λέγειν ὡς οὐχ οἱ συμβουλεύοντες τῶν τοιούτων, ἀλλὰ τὰ πράγματά ἐστιν αἴτια. [25] καὶ τὰς μὲν περὶ τὸ πρᾶγμα διαβολὰς ἐκ τῶν τοιούτων ἀπὸ τῶν συμβουλευόντων ἀπάξομεν.

ὁ δὲ λόγος ἐν ταῖς δημηγορίαις διαβάλλεται ὅταν ἢ μακρὸς ἢ ἀρχαῖος ἢ ἄπιστος λέγηται. [26] ἐὰν μὲν
30 οὖν μακρὸς ᾖ, | τὸ πλῆθος αἰτιατέον τῶν πραγμάτων, ἐὰν δὲ ἀρχαῖος, διδακτέον ὅτι νῦν καιρὸς αὐτοῦ, ἐὰν δὲ ἀπίθανος, ὑπισχνεῖσθαι δεῖ ὡς ἀληθῆ ἐπιδείξεις ἐπὶ τοῦ λόγου.

[27] τὰς μὲν οὖν δημηγορίας ἐκ τούτων καταστησόμεθα. τάξομεν δὲ πῶς; ἐὰν μὲν μηδεμίαν διαβολὴν
35 ἔχωμεν μήτε αὐτοὶ μήτε ὁ λόγος | μήτε τὸ πρᾶγμα, τὴν πρόθεσιν ἐν ἀρχῇ εὐθέως ἐκθήσομεν, ἐπὶ δὲ τὸ προσέχειν καὶ τοῦ λόγου εὐμενῶς ἀκούειν ὕστερον παρακαλέσομεν. [28] ἐὰν δὲ διαβολή τις ᾖ τῶν προειρημένων περὶ ἡμᾶς, προκαταλαβόντες τοὺς ἀκροατὰς καὶ περὶ τῶν διαβολῶν τὰς ἀπολογίας καὶ τὰς προφάσεις συν-

speeches we shall attempt to refute prejudices against the person himself in these ways.

Prejudices arise concerning the subject matter when one advises disrupting peace against those who are doing no injustice or against the stronger or making a disgraceful peace, or recommends making small contributions to a sacrifice, or introduces some such thing. [24] Concerning such matters one must first employ anticipation with regard to the audience, and then attribute the cause to necessity, luck, the circumstances, and advantage and say that it is not the advisers who are responsible but the facts. [25] Through such arguments we shall draw away prejudice with regard to the subject from the advisers.

In public speeches, the speech encounters prejudice whenever it is long or old-fashioned, or not credible. [26] If it is long, you must blame the large quantity of facts; if it is old-fashioned, you must teach that it is now timely; if it is unpersuasive, you must promise to demonstrate its truth in the course of the speech.

[27] We shall construct public speeches from this material. But how shall we arrange them? If we encounter no prejudice, either toward ourselves, the speech, or the subject, we shall lay out the proposal straightaway at the beginning, and call for attention and a favorable hearing for the speech later. [28] If there is some prejudice arising from what has been said about us, after anticipating the audience and introducing concise defenses and excuses

---

88 λύειν add. Rhys Roberts apud Forster

40 τόμως | ἐνεγκόντες, οὕτω προθήσομεν καὶ τοὺς ἀκρο-
1438a ατὰς ἐπὶ || τὸ προσέχειν παρακαλέσομεν. τοῦτον μὲν οὖν τὸν τρόπον τὰς καταστάσεις τῶν δημηγοριῶν ποιητέον.

30. Μετὰ δὲ τοῦτο ἀναγκαῖον ἡμᾶς ἐστιν ἢ τὰς προγεγενημένας πράξεις ἀπαγγέλλειν ἢ ἀναμιμνή-
5 σκειν, ἢ τὰς νῦν | οὔσας μερίζοντας δηλοῦν, ἢ τὰς μελλούσας γενήσεσθαι προλέγειν.

[2] ὅταν μὲν οὖν πρεσβείαν ἀπαγγέλλωμεν, πάντα δεῖ τὰ ῥηθέντα καθαρῶς διεξελθεῖν, ἵνα πρῶτον μὲν μέγεθος ὁ λόγος ἔχῃ (ἀπαγγελία γὰρ μόνον ἔσται ἡ τοιαύτη καὶ οὐδὲν ἄλλο λόγου σχῆμα παρεμπεσεῖται),
10 [3] ἔπειθ' ὅπως, ἂν | μὲν ἀποτετυχηκότες ὦμεν, μὴ διὰ τὴν ἡμετέραν ῥᾳθυμίαν οἱ ἀκούοντες οἴωνται διαμαρτάνειν τῆς πράξεως, ἀλλὰ δι' ἄλλην τινὰ αἰτίαν· ἂν δὲ ἐπιτύχωμεν, μὴ διὰ τύχην ὑπολάβωσι τοῦτο γεγενῆσθαι, ἀλλὰ διὰ τὴν ἡμετέραν προθυμίαν. ταῦτα δὲ πιστεύσουσιν, ἐπειδὴ τοῖς πράγμασιν οὐ παρεγένοντο |
15 πραττομένοις, ἐὰν ἐπὶ τοῦ λόγου τὴν προθυμίαν ἡμῶν θεωρῶσι μηδὲν παραλειπόντων ἀλλ' ἀκριβῶς ἕκαστα ἀπαγγελλόντων. [4] ὅταν μὲν οὖν πρεσβείαν ἀπαγγέλλωμεν, διὰ τὰς αἰτίας ταύτας ἕκαστα ὃν τρόπον ἐγένετο ἀπαγγελτέον.

ὅταν δὲ αὐτοὶ δημηγοροῦντες τῶν παρεληλυθότων |
20 τι διεξίωμεν ἢ [καὶ][89] τὰ παρόντα δηλῶμεν ἢ τὰ μέλλοντα προλέγωμεν, δεῖ τούτων ἕκαστον ποιεῖν βραχέως καὶ σαφῶς καὶ μὴ ἀπίστως· [5] σαφῶς μέν, ὅπως καταμάθωσι τὰ λεγόμενα πράγματα, συντόμως

against the prejudices, we shall make the proposal and call for attention. This is the way we must compose the bases for public speeches.

30. After this we must either report or recall previous events, or divide into parts and explain those that are current, or discuss in advance those that are going to occur.

[2] When we are reporting an embassy, we must go through everything that was said cleanly, first so that the speech may have importance (such a speech will only be a report and no other form of speech intrudes); [3] then, if we have been unsuccessful, in order that the audience does not believe that the failure of the endeavor was due to our inattention but to some other cause. If we have been successful, they should suppose that it was not due to luck but to our diligence. Since they were not present at the events that transpired, they will believe this if they observe our diligence in the speech as we leave nothing out and report each thing precisely. [4] For these reasons, when we are reporting an embassy, we must report each thing as it happened.

When we ourselves are recounting in debate something from the past, or are explaining present circumstances, or discussing in advance what is to come, we must do each of these things briefly, clearly, and credibly: [5] it must be clear so that they will understand the facts described; it

[89] καὶ om. Lat.$^{\beta}$ Ald. del. Sp.[1]

δέ, ἵνα μνημονεύσωσι τὰ ῥηθέντα, πιστῶς δέ, ὅπως
25 μὴ πρὸ τοῦ ταῖς πίστεσι καὶ ταῖς | δικαιολογίαις βε-
βαιῶσαι τὸν λόγον ἡμᾶς τὰς ἐξηγήσεις ἡμῶν οἱ
ἀκούοντες ἀποδοκιμάσωσιν. [6] σαφῶς μὲν οὖν δηλώσομεν ἀπὸ τῶν ὀνομάτων ἢ ἀπὸ τῶν πραγμάτων. ἀπὸ
μὲν οὖν τῶν πραγμάτων[90] ἐὰν μὴ ὑπερβατῶς αὐτὰ
δηλῶμεν, ἀλλὰ τὰ πρῶτα πραχθέντα ἢ πραττόμενα ἢ
30 πραχθησόμενα | πρῶτα λέγωμεν, τὰ δὲ λοιπὰ ἐφεξῆς
τάττωμεν, καὶ ἐὰν μὴ προαπολιπόντες τὴν πρᾶξιν
περὶ ἧς ἂν ἐγχειρήσωμεν λέγειν, πάλιν ἑτέραν ἐξαγ-
γείλωμεν. [7] ἀπὸ μὲν οὖν τῶν πραγμάτων σαφῶς
οὕτως ἐροῦμεν· ἀπὸ δὲ τῶν ὀνομάτων, ἐὰν ὅτι μάλιστα
35 τοῖς οἰκείοις τῶν πραγμάτων ὀνόμασι τὰς | πράξεις
προσαγορεύωμεν καὶ τοῖς κοινοῖς, καὶ ἐὰν[91] μὴ ὑπερβατῶς αὐτὰ τιθῶμεν, ἀλλ' ἀεὶ τὰ ἐχόμενα ἑξῆς τάττωμεν. [8] σαφῶς μὲν οὖν δηλώσομεν ταῦτα διαφυλάτ-
τοντες, συντόμως δέ, ἐὰν ἀπὸ τῶν πραγμάτων καὶ τῶν
ὀνομάτων περιαιρῶμεν τὰ μὴ ἀναγκαῖα ῥηθῆναι, ταῦ-
40 τα | μόνα καταλείποντες ὧν ἀφαιρεθέντων ἀσαφὴς
1438b ἔσται ὁ λόγος. || [9] καὶ συντόμως μὲν τοῦτον τὸν
τρόπον δηλώσομεν, οὐκ ἀπίστως δέ, ἂν περὶ τὰς
ἀπιθάνους πράξεις αἰτίας φέρωμεν παρ' ἃς εἰκότως τὰ
λεγόμενα δόξει πραχθῆναι. ὅσα δ' ἂν λίαν ἄπιστα
5 συμβαίνῃ, δεῖ παραλείπειν. [10] ἐὰν δὲ ἀναγκαῖον | ᾖ
λέγειν, εἰδότα δεῖ φαίνεσθαι καὶ ἐπιπλέξαντα αὐτὰ τῷ

[90] ἀπὸ μὲν οὖν τῶν πραγμάτων A² edd. : om. N a ρ

must be concise so that they remember what has been said; and it must be credible so that the audience does not refuse to accept our accounts before we can support the speech with proofs and legal argumentation.[35] [6] We shall explain things clearly by means of the words we use and the facts, by means of the facts, however, if we do not explain them in reverse order but tell the first things that happened, are happening, or will happen first, and if we arrange the rest in order, and if we do not, by leaving out the activity about which we are attempting to speak, report again on something else. [7] We shall speak clearly by means of the facts in this way, and by means of the words we use if we describe the activities with the very most appropriate terms for the actions and those in common use, and if we do not place them in a reversed order but always arrange them in succession. [8] By taking these precautions, we shall make a clear explanation. It will be concise if we strip away from the facts and words those that do not have to be said, leaving only those whose removal would make the speech unclear. [9] We shall explain things concisely in this way. We shall explain things credibly with regard to unpersuasive matters if we offer reasons according to which what is being said will seem likely to have happened. Whatever occurs too incredibly must be left out. [10] If it must be discussed, you must appear to know (that it is incredible) and weave it in with the device of omission

[35] Cf. 36.19–25.

91 καὶ τοῖς κοινοῖς, καὶ ἐὰν ego : καὶ ἐὰν τοῖς κοινοῖς, καὶ N a

τῆς παραλείψεως σχήματι ὑπερβάλλεσθαι καὶ προϊόντος τοῦ λόγου ἐπιδείξειν ἀληθῆ ὑπισχνεῖσθαι, προφασισάμενον ὅτι τὰ προειρημένα πρῶτον βούλει ἀποδεῖξαι ἀληθῆ ὄντα ἢ δίκαια ἤ τι τῶν τοιούτων.
10 *[11] καὶ τοῦτον μὲν τὸν | τρόπον τὰς ἀπιστίας ἰασόμεθα. συλλήβδην δὲ τὰς ἀπαγγελίας καὶ τὰς δηλώσεις καὶ τὰς προρρήσεις ἐξ ἁπάντων τῶν εἰρημένων σαφεῖς καὶ βραχείας καὶ οὐκ ἀπίστους ποιήσομεν.*

31. *Τάξομεν δὲ αὐτὰς διὰ τριῶν τρόπων. ὅταν μὲν*
15 *γὰρ | ὦσιν ὀλίγα τὰ πράγματα περὶ ὧν λέγομεν καὶ γνώριμα τοῖς ἀκούουσι, τῷ προοιμίῳ συνάψομεν, ἵνα μὴ βραχὺ τοῦτο τὸ μέρος καθ' ἑαυτὸ τεθὲν γένηται. [2] ὅταν δὲ λίαν ὦσιν αἱ πράξεις πολλαὶ καὶ μὴ γνώριμοι, παρ' ἕκαστον συναπτὰς ποιήσομεν καὶ δι-*
20 *καίας καὶ συμφερούσας καὶ καλὰς ἀποφανοῦμεν, | ἵνα μὴ μόνον πραγματολογοῦντες ἁπλοῦν τὸν λόγον καὶ μὴ ποικίλον ποιῶμεν, ἀλλὰ καὶ τῶν ἀκουόντων τὰς διανοίας ἀναλαμβάνωμεν. [3] ἂν δ' ὦσιν αἱ πράξεις μέτριαι καὶ ἀγνοούμεναι, τὴν ἀπαγγελίαν ἢ τὴν δήλωσιν ἢ τὴν πρόρρησιν ἐπὶ τῷ φροιμίῳ δεῖ σωματοειδῆ*
25 *τάττειν. | τοῦτο δὲ ποιήσομεν, ἐὰν ἀπὸ τῆς ἀρχῆς τῶν πραγμάτων ἐπὶ τὸ τέλος διέλθωμεν, μηδὲν ἄλλο συμπαραλαμβάνοντες, ἀλλὰ τὰς πράξεις αὐτὰς ψιλὰς φράζοντες. καὶ τὰς μὲν διηγήσεις ἐπὶ τοῖς προοιμίοις ὡς δεῖ τάττειν, οὕτως εἰσόμεθα.*

32. *Μετὰ δὲ ταύτας ἐστὶ βεβαίωσις δι' ἧς τὰς προ-*
30 *ειρημένας | πράξεις ἐκ τῶν πίστεων καὶ τῶν δικαίων καὶ τῶν συμφερόντων, οἵας ὑπεθέμεθα δείξειν βεβαι-*

and the promise to demonstrate its truth in the course of the speech and the plea that you wish to show first that what you have said is true or just or something of this sort. [11] In this way we shall cure a lack of credibility. In sum, we shall make our reports, explanations, and advance discussions clear, brief, and credible from what has been said.

31. We shall arrange them[36] in three ways. When the matters about which we are speaking are few in number and well known to the audience, we shall attach them to the introduction so that this part, set by itself, does not become too brief. [2] When the facts are very many and unfamiliar, we shall make them connected to each other and point out that they are just, advantageous, and honorable, so that we do not just discuss the facts in plain and unadorned speech but engage the thoughts of the audience. [3] If there is a moderate number of facts and they are unknown, we must arrange the report, explanation, or advance discussion coherently with the introduction. We shall do this if we go through the facts from beginning to end, including nothing else but describing the bare facts themselves. In this way we shall know how to arrange the narrations in relation to the introductions.

32. After them there is confirmation, through which we shall confirm, through proofs and claims of justice and advantage, that the previously stated facts are as we promised

[36] The reports, explanations, advance discussions, and so on.

ώσομεν. ὅταν μὲν οὖν < . . . >[92] συναπτὰς δεῖ ποιεῖν.
οἰκειόταται <δὲ>[93] ταῖς δημηγορίαις εἰσὶ πίστεις τά τε
τῶν πραγμάτων ἔθη καὶ τὰ παραδείγματα καὶ τὰ
35 ἐνθυμήματα καὶ ἡ δόξα τοῦ λέγοντος. χρηστέον | δὲ
καὶ ἄν τις τῶν ἄλλων πίστεων παρεμπέσῃ.

[2] τάττειν δὲ αὐτὰς ὧδε δεῖ· πρῶτον μὲν τὴν τοῦ
λέγοντος δόξαν, εἰ δὲ μή, τὰ τῶν πραγμάτων ἔθη,
δεικνύντας ὅτι ταῦθ' ἃ λέγομεν ἢ τὰ τούτοις ὅμοια
οὕτως εἴθισται γίνεσθαι. [3] ἐπὶ δὲ τούτοις παρα-
40 δείγματα οἰστέον, καὶ εἰ ὁμοιότης τίς ἐστι πρὸς | τὰ ὑφ'
ἡμῶν λεγόμενα προσακτέον. λαμβάνειν δὲ δεῖ τὰ ||
1439a παραδείγματα <τὰ>[94] οἰκεῖα τῷ πράγματι καὶ τὰ ἐγ-
γύτατα τοῖς ἀκούουσι χρόνῳ ἢ τόπῳ, ἐὰν δὲ μὴ
ὑπάρχῃ τοιαῦτα, τῶν ἄλλων τὰ μέγιστα καὶ γνωρι-
μώτατα· μετὰ δὲ ταῦτα γνωμολογητέον. δεῖ δὲ καὶ
5 περὶ τὰ μέρη τῶν εἰκότων καὶ τῶν | παραδειγμάτων ἐπὶ
τελευτῆς ἐνθυμηματώδεις καὶ γνωμολογικὰς τὰς τε-
λευτὰς ποιεῖσθαι.

[4] καὶ τὰς μὲν πίστεις οὕτως ἐπὶ ταῖς πράξεσι
προσακτέον· ἐὰν δὲ πιστεύηται τὰ πράγματα εὐθέως
ῥηθέντα, τὰς μὲν πίστεις παραλειπτέον, τῷ δὲ δικαίῳ
10 καὶ τῷ νομίμῳ καὶ τῷ συμφέροντι καὶ τῷ | καλῷ καὶ τῷ
ἡδεῖ καὶ τῷ ῥᾳδίῳ καὶ τῷ δυνατῷ καὶ τῷ ἀναγκαίῳ τὰς
προειρημένας πράξεις βεβαιωτέον. [5] καὶ εἰ μὲν ὑπ-
άρχει, πρῶτον τὸ δίκαιον τακτέον, διεξιόντας δι' αὐτοῦ
τε τοῦ δικαίου καὶ τοῦ ὁμοίου τῷ δικαίῳ καὶ τοῦ
ἐναντίου καὶ τοῦ κεκριμένου δικαίου. δεῖ δὲ καὶ τὰ
15 παραδείγματα <τὰ>[95] τοῖς | ὑπὸ σοῦ λεγομένοις δι-

to show. Whenever < . . . >, you must make them connected.[37] The most appropriate proofs in public speeches are the patterns of the facts, examples, enthymemes, and the opinion of the speaker. But if any of the other proofs presents itself, you must also use it.

[2] Arrange them in this way: first, the opinion of the speaker, and if not, the patterns of the facts, showing that they follow in this way the patterns we say or those that are similar to them. [3] After this bring in examples and mention whether there is some similarity to what you are saying. Take the examples that are appropriate to the subject and closest to the audience in time or place. But if there are none of these, use others that are very important and well known; and after them use maxims. With regard to the parts on plausibilities and examples, make the conclusions, at the end, in the form of enthymemes and maxims.

[4] Add proofs to discussions of the facts in this way: if the facts being discussed have immediate credibility, pass over the proofs and confirm the previous discussions of fact with reference to justice, law, advantage, honor, pleasure, ease, possibility, and necessity. [5] If possible, arrange justice first, going through justice itself, what is like justice, the opposite of justice, and judicial precedent. Bring in examples that are like the claims of justice you are

[37] The presence of the gap in the text, which was indicated by Fuhrmann, seems clear. The reference to making things "connected" seems related to that in 31.2, in which the facts are "very many and unfamiliar."

---

92 lac. ind. Fuhrmann　　93 δὲ add. Fuhrmann
94 τὰ add. Halm　　95 τὰ add. Finckh2

καίοις ὅμοια φέρειν. πολλὰ δὲ ἕξεις λέγειν ἔκ τε τῶν ἰδίᾳ παρ' ἑκάστοις δικαίων ὑπολαμβανομένων καὶ ἐκ τῶν ἐν αὐτῇ τῇ πόλει ἐν ᾗ λέγεις, καὶ ἐκ τῶν ἐν ταῖς ἄλλαις πόλεσιν. [6] ὅταν δὲ ἅπαντα τοῦτον τὸν τρόπον
20 μετιόντες διέλθωμεν, ἐπὶ τελευτῆς αὐτοῦ γνώμας | καὶ ἐνθυμήματα μέτρια καὶ ἀλλήλοις ἀνόμοια ἐνεγκόντες, ἂν μὲν μακρὸν ᾖ τὸ μέρος καὶ βουλώμεθα μνημονεύεσθαι, συντόμως παλιλλογήσομεν· ἐὰν δὲ μέτριον ᾖ καὶ μνημονεύηται, αὐτὸ τὸ μέρος ὁρισάμενοι πάλιν ἕτερον προθησόμεθα. ἔστι δὲ ὃ λέγω τοιόνδε· "ὡς μὲν
25 δίκαιόν ἐστιν ἡμᾶς | βοηθεῖν Συρακουσίοις, ἐκ τῶν εἰρημένων ἱκανῶς ἐπιδεδεῖχθαι νομίζω· ὡς δὲ καὶ συμφέρει ταῦτα πράττειν, ἐπιχειρήσω διδάσκειν." [7] πάλιν δὲ περὶ τοῦ συμφέροντος ὁμοιοτρόπως τοῖς προειρημένοις ἐπὶ τοῦ δικαίου μετιὼν καὶ ἐπὶ τῇ τελευτῇ <τούτου>[96] τοῦ μέρους ἢ παλιλλογίαν ἢ ὁρισμὸν
30 ἐπιθείς, | πάλιν ἕτερον ὅ τι ἂν ὑπάρχῃ σοι προτίθει. τοῦτον δὲ <δεῖ>[97] τὸν τρόπον ἄλλο ἄλλῳ συνάπτειν μέρει καὶ συνυφαίνειν τὸν λόγον. [8] ὅταν δὲ πάντα διέλθῃς ἐξ ὧν ἐνδέχεταί σοι βεβαιῶσαι τὴν προτροπήν, ἐπὶ τούτοις ἅπασι κεφαλαιωδῶς μετὰ ἐνθυμη-
35 μάτων καὶ γνωμῶν ἢ σχημάτων δείκνυε ὡς | ἄδικον καὶ ἀσύμφορον καὶ αἰσχρὸν καὶ ἀηδὲς μὴ ποιεῖν ταῦτα, καὶ ἀντιτίθει κεφαλαιωδῶς ὡς δίκαιον καὶ συμφέρον καὶ καλὸν καὶ ἡδὺ πράττειν ἐφ' ἃ παρακαλεῖς. [9] ὅταν δὲ ἱκανῶς ἤδη ᾖς ἐγνωμολογηκώς, τὴν προτροπὴν πέρατι ὅρισαι. καὶ τοῦτον μὲν τὸν τρόπον βεβαι-
1439b ώσομεν τὰ || προτεθέντα, μετὰ δὲ τοῦτο τὸ μέρος λέξομεν τὴν προκατάληψιν.

discussing. You will have many to discuss from the conceptions of justice held by each individual, from those in the city in which you are speaking, and from those in other cities. [6] When we have gone through everything in this way, at the end of it bring in maxims and medium-length and diverse enthymemes: if one part is long and we wish to do a reminder, we shall repeat concisely; but if it is medium-length and easily recalled, we shall limit this part and again set forth another part. This is the sort of thing I mean: "That it is just for us to help the Syracusans I think has been sufficiently demonstrated from what has been said; I shall attempt to teach that doing these things is also advantageous." [7] Again, concerning what is advantageous, after proceeding in a way similar to what was said before about justice and placing a repetition or a limit at the end of this part, add whatever else is available to you. In this way you must connect one part to another and weave the speech together. [8] When you have gone through everything that is available to confirm your proposition, in addition to all these things show succinctly, with enthymemes and maxims, or figures, that not to do this would be unjust, disadvantageous, shameful, and unpleasant, and make the counterproposal that what you are calling to do is just, advantageous, honorable, and pleasant. [9] When you have employed maxims sufficiently, put a limit to the proposition. In this way we shall confirm the proposals, and after this part we shall discuss anticipation.

---

96 *τούτου* add. Sp.[1]
97 δεῖ (*oportet*) Lat.[β]

33. Αὕτη δ' ἐστὶ δι' ἧς τὰς ἐνδεχομένας ἀντιλογίας
ῥηθῆναι τοῖς ὑπὸ σοῦ εἰρημένοις προκαταλαμβάνων
5 διασύρεις. | δεῖ δὲ τὰ μὲν ἐκείνων μικρὰ ποιεῖν, τὰ δὲ
σαυτοῦ αὔξειν, ὡς ἐν ταῖς αὐξήσεσι προακήκοας.
[2] χρὴ δὲ παρατιθέναι καὶ ἓν πρὸς ἕν, ὅταν τὸ σὸν
μεῖζον ᾖ, καὶ πρὸς πλείω πλείω καὶ ἓν πρὸς πολλὰ καὶ
πολλὰ πρὸς ἕν, διαλλάττοντα κατὰ πάντας τοὺς τρό-
10 πους καὶ τὰ μὲν σαυτοῦ αὔξοντα, τὰ δὲ | τῶν ἐναντίων
ἀσθενῆ καὶ μικρὰ ποιοῦντα. [3] καὶ τοῦτον μὲν τὸν
τρόπον ταῖς προκαταλήψεσι χρησόμεθα.

ταῦτα δὲ διελθόντες ἐπὶ τελευτῇ παλιλλογήσομεν
τὰ προειρημένα, σχήματα διαλογισμοῦ λαβόντες ἢ
ἀπολογισμοῦ ἢ προαιρέσεως ἢ [ἐξ][98] ἐπερωτήσεως ἢ
εἰρωνείας. |

15 34. Ἐὰν δὲ ἐπὶ τὸ βοηθεῖν τισι προτρέπωμεν ἢ
ἰδιώταις ἢ πόλεσιν, ἁρμόσει συντόμως εἰπεῖν καὶ εἴ
τις προϋπάρχει τούτοις πρὸς τοὺς ἐκκλησιάζοντας
φιλία ἢ χάρις ἢ ἔλεος· μάλιστα γὰρ τοῖς οὕτω διακειμένοις ἐθέλουσιν ἐπαμύνειν. [2] φιλοῦσι μὲν οὖν πάν-
τες <τούτους>[99] ὑφ' ὧν οἴονται κατὰ τὸ προσῆκον εὖ |
20 πεπονθέναι ἢ πάσχειν ἢ πείσεσθαι ἢ ὑπ' αὐτῶν ἢ τῶν
φίλων, ἢ αὐτοὶ ἢ ὧν κηδόμενοι τυγχάνουσι. [3] χάριν
δ' ἔχουσι τούτοις ὑφ' ὧν οἴονται παρὰ τὸ προσῆκον
ἀγαθόν τι πεπονθέναι ἢ πάσχειν ἢ πείσεσθαι, ἢ ὑπ'
αὐτῶν ἢ τῶν φίλων, ἢ αὐτοὶ ἢ ὧν κηδόμενοι τυγχάνου-
25 σιν. [4] τούτων μὲν οὖν ἄν τι | ἐνῇ, χρὴ συντόμως
διδάσκειν, καὶ ἐπὶ τὸν ἔλεον ἄγειν. εὐπορήσομεν δὲ
ἐλεεινὰ ποιεῖν ἅπερ ἂν ἐθέλωμεν, ἐὰν συνειδῶμεν ὅτι

33. This is the way you tear up the possible objections to what you have said. You must minimize their arguments and amplify your own as you have heard earlier, in the discussion of amplifications.[38] [2] You must set the arguments side by side, whenever yours is stronger, or multiple arguments against multiple, or one against many, or many against one, comparing them in every way and amplifying your own but making your opponents' weak and small. [3] We shall use anticipation in this way.

After going through these things we shall repeat at the end what has been said before, taking up the forms of reflection or calculation or choice or interrogation or irony.[39]

34. If we are proposing to give aid to someone, either private citizens or cities, it will be fitting to state concisely whether there is some preexisting friendship, favor, or compassion with the members of the assembly; they are especially willing to give assistance to those in these circumstances. [2] Everyone feels friendship toward those from whom they think that they themselves, or those for whom they really care, have benefited, do benefit, and will benefit in a fitting way, from them themselves or from their friends. [3] They are thankful to those from whom, either themselves or their friends, they think that they themselves or those they care for have received, are receiving, or will receive some benefit *beyond* what is due. [4] If any of these are the case, teach them concisely and urge compassion. We shall be well equipped to make whichever arguments we want on the basis of compassion if we realize

[38] Cf. 3.6–14. [39] Cf. 20.

[98] ἐξ del. Fuhrmann [99] τούτους add. Sp.[1]

πάντες ἐλεοῦσι τούτους οὓς οἰκείως ἔχειν αὑτοῖς ὑπειλήφασιν καὶ οἴονται ἀναξίους εἶναι δυστυχεῖν. [5] δεῖ δὲ ταῦτα ἀποφαίνειν ἔχοντας οὓς ἐθέλεις ἐλεεινοὺς
30 ποιεῖν, καὶ | ἐπιδεικνύειν αὐτοὺς ἢ κακῶς πεπονθότας ἢ πάσχοντας ἢ πεισομένους, ἐὰν μὴ οἱ ἀκούοντες αὐτοῖς βοηθῶσιν. [6] ἐὰν δὲ ταῦτα μὴ ἐνῇ, δεικτέον ὑπὲρ ὧν λέγεις ἀγαθῶν ἐστερημένους ὧν τοῖς ἄλλοις ἅπασιν ἢ τοῖς πλείστοις μέτεστιν, ἢ ἀγαθοῦ μηδέποτε τετυχη-
35 κότας ἢ μὴ τυγχάνοντας ἢ μὴ | τευξομένους, ἐὰν μὴ νῦν οἱ ἀκούοντες οἰκτείρωσιν. ἐκ τούτων μὲν οὖν ἐπὶ τὸν ἔλεον ἄξομεν.

[7] τὰς δὲ ἀποτροπὰς ἐκ τῶν ἐναντίων ποιήσομεν, τὸν αὐτὸν τρόπον φροιμιαζόμενοι καὶ τὰ πράγματα διεξιόντες, ταῖς τε πίστεσι χρώμενοι καὶ τοῖς ἀκούουσι δεικνύντες ὡς ἔστιν ἃ πράττειν ἐπιχειροῦσιν ||
1440a ἄνομα καὶ ἄδικα καὶ ἀσύμφορα καὶ αἰσχρὰ καὶ ἀηδῆ καὶ ἀδύνατα καὶ ἐργώδη καὶ οὐκ ἀναγκαῖα. ἡ δὲ τάξις ὁμοιότροπος ἔσται οἵα καὶ τῷ προτρέποντι. [8] τοῖς μὲν οὖν καθ' αὑτοὺς ἀποτρέπουσιν οὕτω τὰς τάξεις ποιητέον.

5 τοὺς δὲ | πρὸς τὰς ὑφ' ἑτέρων εἰρημένας προτροπὰς ἀντιλέγοντας πρῶτον μὲν ἐν τῷ προοιμίῳ δεῖ οἷς μέλλουσιν ἀντιλέγειν προθέσθαι, τὰ δ' ἄλλα καθ' αὑτὰ προοιμιάζεσθαι, [9] μετὰ δὲ τὰ προοίμια μάλιστα μὲν ἕκαστα τῶν προειρημένων καθ' ἓν ἕκαστον προτιθέμενον ἐπιδεικνύειν ὡς οὐκ ἔστι δίκαια οὐδὲ |
10 νόμιμα οὐδὲ συμφέροντα οὐδὲ τούτοις ἀκόλουθα ἐφ' ἃ παρακαλεῖ ὁ ἐναντίος. τοῦτο δὲ ποιήσεις ἀποφαίνων ἢ

that all have compassion for those whom they assume to be closely associated with themselves and think do not deserve to suffer misfortune. [5] You must point out that this is the experience of those for whom you wish to create compassion and demonstrate that they either have suffered badly, are suffering badly, or will suffer badly unless the audience helps them. [6] If this is not possible, show that those for whom you are speaking have been deprived of goods that all or most others share, or that they have not had, are not having, or will not have good luck unless the audience now takes pity. In these ways we shall urge compassion.

[7] We shall compose opposition speeches from the opposite points, making introductions in the same way and going through the facts, and using proofs and showing the audience that what they are attempting to do is illegal, unjust, disadvantageous, shameful, unpleasant, impossible, laborious, and unnecessary. The arrangement will be similar as that for the proponent. [8] Those speaking in opposition on their own account must do arrangement in this way.

Those speaking against proposals discussed by others must first, in the introduction, put forward what they are going to speak against, [9] and after the introduction demonstrate that each and every one of the things said in each and every proposal is neither just, nor legal, nor advantageous, nor consistent with what the opponent is advocating. You will do this by pointing out that what he is

ἄδικα ὄντα ἃ λέγει, ἢ ἀσύμφορα ἢ τούτοις ὅμοια ἢ ἐναντία τοῖς δικαίοις καὶ τοῖς συμφέρουσι καὶ τοῖς κεκριμένοις εἶναι τοιούτοις. ὁμοιοτρόπως δὲ καὶ τῶν
15 ἄλλων τὰ ὑπάρχοντα μέτιθι. | [10] κράτιστος μὲν οὖν ὁ τρόπος τῆς ἀποτροπῆς οὗτός ἐστιν· ἐὰν δὲ μὴ ἐνδέχηται τοῦτο ποιεῖν, ἐκ τοῦ παραλελειμμένου τόπου ἀπότρεπε λέγων οἷον ἐὰν ὁ ἐναντίος δίκαιον ἀποφήνῃ, σὺ ἐπιχείρει δεικνύναι ὡς ἔστιν αἰσχρὸν ἢ ἀσύμφορον ἢ ἐργῶδες ἢ ἀδύνατον ἢ ὅ τι ἂν ἔχῃς τοιοῦτον. ἐὰν δὲ
20 ἐκεῖνος | ἔχῃ τὸ συμφέρον, σὺ ἐπιδείκνυε ὡς ἄδικον κἄν τι ἄλλο ἔχῃς πρὸς τούτῳ. [11] δεῖ δὲ καὶ τὰ μὲν αὐτοῦ αὔξειν, τὰ δὲ τοῦ ἐναντίου ταπεινοῦν, ποιοῦντα ὡς ἐν τῷ προτρεπτικῷ εἴρηται. χρὴ δὲ καὶ γνώμας φέρειν καὶ ἐνθυμήματα καθάπερ ἐκεῖσε, καὶ τὰς προκατα-
25 λήψεις λύειν καὶ ἐπὶ τελευτῇ | παλιλλογεῖν.

[12] πρὸς δὲ τούτοις ἐν μὲν ταῖς προτροπαῖς ἀποφαίνειν ἢ φιλίαν ὑπάρχειν οἷς βοηθεῖν προτρέπομεν πρὸς τοὺς προτρεπομένους ἢ χάριν τοὺς προτρεπομένους ὀφείλοντας ἔχειν τοῖς δεομένοις, οἷς δ'οὐκ ἐῶμεν βοηθεῖν ἢ ὀργῆς ἢ φθόνου ἢ ἔχθρας ἀξίους ὑπάρχοντας. [13] ἔχθραν μὲν οὖν ἐμποιήσομεν ὑπ'
30 ἐκείνων οὐ | προσηκόντως τοὺς ἀποτρεπομένους ἀποφαίνοντες κακῶς πεπονθότας <ἢ ὑπ' αὐτῶν>[100] ἢ τῶν φίλων, ἢ αὐτοὺς ἢ ὧν κηδόμενοι τυγχάνουσιν· [14] ὀργὴν δέ, ἐὰν ἐπιδεικνύωμεν παρὰ τὸ προσῆκον ὠλιγω-

[100] ἢ ὑπ' αὐτῶν add. Sp.[1]

saying is unjust, or disadvantageous, or similar to them, or that it is opposed to what is just and advantageous and what has been judged to be so. Pursue the other possible points in a similar way. [10] This is the strongest way to oppose. But if it is not possible to do this, make your opposition speech on the basis of some topic that has been left out. For instance, if the opponent points out that something is just, you attempt to argue that it is shameful, disadvantageous, laborious, impossible, or whatever you can. If he holds that it is advantageous, you demonstrate that it is unjust, or whatever you can in response. [11] You must also amplify your own position, and minimize the opponent's, doing as was said in the section on the proposition species.[40] You must also introduce maxims and enthymemes as you did there, refute anticipations, and repeat at the end.

[12] In addition to this, in proposition speeches you must point out either that friendship exists between those for whom we are proposing help and those to whom we are making the proposal or that those to whom the proposal is made owe a favor to those who are requesting it; but those for whom we do not permit help are worthy of anger, envy, or hostility. [13] We shall create hostility by pointing out that those before whom we are speaking in opposition have not been appropriately treated by those people, having suffered badly either at their hands, or their friends' hands, either themselves or those for whom they care. [14] We shall create anger if we demonstrate that either we

[40] Cf. 33.1–2.

ρημένους ἢ ἠδικημένους ὑπ᾽ ἐκείνων ἢ τῶν φίλων,[101] ἢ αὐτοὺς ἢ ὧν κηδόμενοι τυγχάνουσιν αὐτοί. [15] φθό-
35 νον δὲ παρασκευάσομεν | συλλήβδην πρὸς τούτους οὓς ἀποφαίνομεν ἀναξίως εὖ πεπραχότας ἢ πράττοντας ἢ πράξοντας, ἢ ἀγαθοῦ μηδέποτε ἐστερημένους ἢ μὴ στερομένους ἢ μὴ στερησομένους, ἢ κακοῦ μηδέποτε τετυχηκότας ἢ μὴ τυγχάνοντας ἢ μὴ τευξομένους. [16] φθόνον μὲν οὖν καὶ ἔχθραν καὶ ὀργὴν τοῦτον τὸν |
40 τρόπον ἐμποιήσομεν, φιλίαν δὲ καὶ χάριν καὶ ἔλεον
1440b ἐκ || τῶν ἐν ταῖς προτροπαῖς· συνθήσομεν δὲ καὶ τάξομεν ἐξ ἁπάντων τῶν προειρημένων αὐτὰς τόνδε τὸν τρόπον. τὸ μὲν οὖν προτρεπτικὸν εἶδος αὐτό τε ἴσμεν, οἷόν ἐστι καὶ ἐξ ὧν συνέστηκε καὶ ὡς αὐτῷ χρηστέον. |

5 35. Τὸ δὲ ἐγκωμιαστικὸν καὶ τὸ κακολογικὸν πάλιν προθέμενοι σκοπῶμεν. φροιμιαστέον οὖν καὶ περὶ τούτων πρῶτον προθέμενοι τὰς προθέσεις· καὶ τὰς διαβολὰς ἀπολύομεν ὁμοίως ὥσπερ ἐν τοῖς προτρεπτικοῖς. [2] ἐπὶ τὸ προσέχειν δὲ παρακαλοῦμεν ἔκ τε
10 τῶν ἄλλων τῶν ἐν ταῖς δημηγορίαις | εἰρημένων καὶ ἐκ τοῦ θαυμαστὰ καὶ περιφανῆ φάσκειν καὶ αὐτὸν ἴσα καὶ τοὺς ἐγκωμιαζομένους καὶ τοὺς ψεγομένους ἀποφανεῖν πεπραγότας· ὡς γὰρ ἐπὶ τὸ πολὺ τῶν τοιούτων εἰδῶν οὐκ ἀγῶνος, ἀλλ᾽ ἐπιδείξεως ἕνεκα λέγομεν.

[3] τάξομεν δὲ πρῶτον τὰ προοίμια τὸν αὐτὸν
15 τρόπον ὅνπερ ἐπὶ τῶν | προτροπῶν καὶ ἀποτροπῶν. μετὰ δὲ τὸ προοίμιον δεῖ διελόμενον τὰ ἔξω τῆς ἀρετῆς ἀγαθὰ καὶ τὰ ἐν αὐτῇ τῇ ἀρετῇ ὄντα ποιεῖν οὕτως· τὰ μὲν οὖν ἔξω τῆς ἀρετῆς εἰς εὐσθένειαν[102] καὶ

or people for whom we happen ourselves to have concern have been inappropriately diminished or wronged by them or their friends. [15] We shall generate envy, in short, against those whom we show to have been, to be, or to be about to be, unworthily prosperous, or never to have been, to be, or to be about to be deprived of some good, or never to have had, to have, or in future to have bad fortune. [16] We shall create envy, hostility, and anger in this way, and friendship, favor, and compassion from the methods used in proposition speeches. We shall construct and arrange them in this way from everything that was said before. Therefore we know the proposition species, what it is, from what it is composed, and how to use it.

35. Let us set forth again the species of praise and criticism for examination. In the introduction we must first set forth the proposals also about these matters. We refute prejudices much as in proposition speeches. [2] We call for attention by the same means as we discussed for other speeches, particularly demegoric ones, by claiming that the acts are both remarkable and well known, and by pointing out that he has done acts equal to those by people who are praised and criticized for having done them. In most speeches of these species we are not contesting a trial but giving a display.

[3] We shall first arrange the introductions in the same way as in proposition and opposition speeches. After the introduction, we must divide the goods external to virtue and those that are inherent in virtue itself, as follows: those external to virtue, then, are fitness, strength, beauty, and

101 ὑπ' ἐκείνων ἢ τῶν φίλων (*ab illis aut/vel amicis eorum*) Lat.[αβ] Hammer 102 εὐσθένειαν N a : εὐγένειαν A[2] edd.

ῥώμην καὶ κάλλος καὶ πλοῦτον, τὴν δ' ἀρετὴν εἰς σοφίαν καὶ δικαιοσύνην καὶ ἀνδρείαν καὶ ἐπιτηδεύ-
20 ματα ἔνδοξα. | [4] τούτων δὲ τὰ μὲν τῆς ἀρετῆς δικαίως ἐγκωμιάζεται, τὰ δ' ἔξω κλέπτεται· τοὺς γὰρ ἰσχυροὺς καὶ τοὺς καλοὺς καὶ τοὺς εὐγενεῖς καὶ τοὺς πλουσίους οὐκ ἐπαινεῖν, ἀλλὰ μακαρίζειν προσήκει.

[5] ταῦτα δὴ διαλογισάμενοι μετὰ τὰ προοίμια πρώτην τὴν γενεαλογίαν τάξομεν· πρῶτον γὰρ τοῖς
25 ἀνθρώποις | καὶ τοῖς ἄλλοις ζῴοις τοῦθ' ὑπάρχει ἔνδοξον ἢ ἄδοξον. τοιγαροῦν <ὅταν>[103] μὲν ἄνθρωπον ἤ τι ἄλλο τοιοῦτον ζῷον <ἐγκωμιάζωμεν>[104] εὐλόγως γενεαλογήσομεν. ὅταν δὲ πάθος ἢ πρᾶγμα ἢ λόγον ἢ κτῆμα, ἀπ' αὐτῶν εὐθὺς τῶν προσόντων ἐνδόξων ἐπαινέσομεν. [6] γενεαλογεῖν δὲ δεῖ ὧδε· ἐὰν μὲν ὦσιν οἱ
30 πρόγονοι | σπουδαῖοι, πάντας ἐξ ἀρχῆς ἀναλαβόντα μέχρι πρὸς τὸν ἐγκωμιαζόμενον ἐφ' ἑκάστῳ τῶν προγόνων κεφαλαιωδῶς ἔνδοξόν τι περιτιθέναι· [7] ἐὰν δὲ οἱ πρῶτοι μὲν ὦσι σπουδαῖοι, τοὺς δὲ λοιποὺς συμβεβήκῃ μηδὲν ἀξιόλογον πρᾶξαι, τοὺς μὲν πρώτους
35 τὸν αὐτὸν τρόπον διελθεῖν, τοὺς δὲ φαύλους | παραλιπεῖν, προφασισάμενον ὅτι διὰ πλῆθος τῶν προγόνων οὐ θέλεις λέγων αὐτοὺς μακρολογεῖν, ἔτι δὲ οὐκ ἄδηλον εἶναι πᾶσιν ὅτι τοὺς ἐξ ἀγαθῶν γενομένους εἰκός ἐστι τοῖς προγόνοις ὁμοιοῦσθαι. [8] ἐὰν δὲ οἱ παλαιοὶ πρόγονοι φαῦλοι τυγχάνωσιν ὄντες, οἱ δὲ
40 πρὸς αὐτὸν ἔνδοξοι, τούτοις δεῖ γενεαλογεῖν | καὶ λέ-
1441a γειν ὅτι περὶ μὲν ἐκείνων περίεργον ἂν εἴη || μακρολογεῖν, τοὺς δὲ πλησίον γεγονότας τῶν ἐπαινουμένων

wealth, and virtue consists of wisdom, a sense of justice, bravery, and reputable behavior. [4] Those internal to virtue are justly praised; the external are deceptive. It is not fitting to extol the strong, the beautiful, the wellborn, and the wealthy, but to congratulate them.

[5] After having made these distinctions in the introduction we shall arrange the genealogy first. Both for humans and for other animals, this is the first basis of good and bad repute. Whenever we praise a human or another comparable animal, we shall reasonably discuss genealogy, but when it is an emotion, action, speech, or possession, we shall praise on the basis of the directly inherent reputable qualities themselves. [6] Genealogy must be done in the following way: if the ancestors were important, they must all be taken up from the beginning until the person being eulogized, and something reputable must be attributed in summary form to each of the ancestors; [7] if the first ancestors were important but the rest happen to have done nothing worth mentioning, run through the first ones in the same way but leave out the inferior ones, giving the excuse that because of the multiplicity of ancestors you do not wish to make too long a speech but that it is clear to all that those born from good people are likely to resemble their ancestors. [8] If the oldest ancestors were in fact inferior but those closer were reputable, you must base your genealogy on them and say it would be superfluous to talk at length about the others but show that those who lived

---

103 ὅταν add. Kassel

104 ἐγκωμιάζωμεν add. Kassel

τούτους ὄντας ἀγαθοὺς ἐπιδείξειν· καὶ δῆλον ὡς οἵ γε
τούτων πρόγονοι σπουδαῖοί τινες ἦσαν· οὐ γὰρ εἰκὸς
φανῆναι τοὺς τοιούτους καλοὺς ἢ ἀγαθοὺς εἶναι ἐκ
5 μοχθηρῶν προγόνων γεγονότας. | [9] ἐὰν δὲ μηδὲν ἀπὸ
τῶν προγόνων ἔνδοξον ὑπάρχῃ, λέγε ὡς αὐτός ἐστι
γενναῖος, συμβιβάζων ὡς εὖ γεγόνασι πάντες οἱ πρὸς
τὴν ἀρετὴν εὖ πεφυκότες. ἐπιτίμα δὲ καὶ τοῖς ἄλλοις
ὅσοι τοὺς προγόνους ἐπαινοῦσι, λέγων ὅτι πολλοὶ
προγόνων ἐνδόξων τυχόντες ἀνάξιοι γεγόνασι. λέγε |
10 δὲ καὶ ὅτι τοῦτον, οὐ τοὺς προγόνους πρόκειται νῦν
ἐγκωμιάζειν. [10] ὁμοιοτρόπως δὲ καὶ κακολογοῦντα
ἐπὶ τῶν μοχθηρῶν προγόνων ποιητέον τὴν γενεαλογίαν. καὶ τοῦτον μὲν τὸν τρόπον ἐν τοῖς ἐπαίνοις καὶ
ταῖς κακολογίαις τὰς γενεαλογίας τακτέον, [11] εἴ τι
15 δὲ ἔνδοξον αὐτῷ διὰ τὴν τύχην | ὑπῆρξε, τοῦτο μόνον
διαφυλάττοντα πῶς τὰ πρέποντα ταῖς ἡλικίαις ἐρεῖς
καὶ μὴ μακρά. τοὺς γὰρ παῖδας οὐχ οὕτω δι᾿αὑτοὺς ὡς
διὰ τοὺς ἐφεστῶτας οἴονται κοσμίους εἶναι καὶ σώ-
φρονας· διὸ βραχυλογητέον περὶ αὐτῶν.

[12] ὅταν δὲ τοῦτον τὸν τρόπον διέλθῃς, ἐπὶ τῇ
20 τελευτῇ τοῦ μέρους ἐνθύμημα καὶ | γνώμην εἰπὼν ὅρι-
σαι τοῦτο τὸ μέρος. καὶ ἐπὶ τῇ τοῦ νεανίσκου ἡλικίᾳ
τὴν πρόθεσιν ποιήσας καὶ προτιθέμενος ἢ τὰ ἔργα
τοῦ ἐπαινουμένου ἢ τὸν τρόπον ἢ τὰ ἐπιτηδεύματα
αὖξε, καθάπερ εἴπομεν πρότερον ἐν ἀρχαῖς ἐπὶ τοῦ
ἐγκωμιαστικοῦ εἴδους, διεξιὼν ὅτι ὑπὸ τούτου τοῦ
25 ἐπαινουμένου ἐν ταύτῃ | τῇ ἡλικίᾳ ὄντος τὸ καὶ τὸ
γέγονεν ἔνδοξον ἢ ὅτι διὰ τούτου ἢ ὅτι διὰ τοῦ

closer in time to those being praised were good men; and it is clear that their ancestors at least were some important people; it is unlikely that such honorable and good men were born from disreputable ancestors. [9] If there is nothing reputable about the ancestors, say that the man himself is noble, reasoning that all who are well endowed with virtue are wellborn. Criticize others who praise ancestors, saying that in fact many worthless men have been born from reputable ancestors. Say also that it is not the ancestors but the man himself who is now to be praised. [10] You must do the genealogy of base ancestors in a similar way when doing criticism. You must arrange genealogies in speeches of praise and criticism in this way, [11] and if he possesses something (else) of repute because of luck, take care only how to say what fits with his age, and not at length. They think that children are orderly and temperate not because of themselves but because of those who raise them; therefore you must speak briefly about these things.

[12] When you have proceeded in this way, at the end of the part conclude it by saying an enthymeme and a maxim. With regard to the age of a youth make your point by setting forth either his exploits or his character or his behavior and amplify it—just as we said earlier at the beginning of the species of praise—by recounting that this or that reputable thing was done by the person being praised when he was at this age, either through himself or through his en-

ἐπιτηδεύματος ἢ ἐκ τούτου ἢ ἕνεκα τούτου. [13] δεῖ δὲ καὶ ἑτέρων νέων ἐνδόξους πράξεις παριστάναι καὶ ὑπερβάλλειν ταύτας ἐκείνων, τοῦ μὲν ἑτέρου τἀλάχιστα τῶν ὑπαρχόντων λέγοντα, τοῦ δ᾽ ὑπὸ σοῦ ἐπαι-
30 νουμένου | τὰ μέγιστα. χρὴ δὲ καὶ παρ᾽ ἄλλα σμικρὰ ἔνδοξα πράγματα παριστάναι ‹τὰ›[105] ὑπὸ σοῦ λεγόμενα, ‹καὶ› οὕτω μεγάλα φανεῖται.[106] [14] δεῖ δὲ καὶ εἰκάζοντα τὰς πράξεις αὔξειν ὧδε· "καίτοι ὅστις νέος οὕτω φιλόσοφος ἐγένετο, οὗτος πρεσβύτερος γενό-
35 μενος μεγάλην ἂν ἐπίδοσιν | ἔσχεν·" "καίτοι ὅστις ἐρρωμένως τοὺς ἐν τοῖς γυμνασίοις ὑπομένει πόνους, σφόδρα τὴν ἐν τῇ φιλοσοφίᾳ φιλοπονίαν ἀγαπήσει." τοῦτον μὲν οὖν τὸν τρόπον εἰκάζοντες αὐξήσομεν.

[15] ὅταν δὲ καὶ περὶ τῆς ἡλικίας τοῦ νεανίσκου διέλθωμεν, καὶ ἐπὶ τῇ τελευτῇ τούτου τοῦ μέρους
1441b γνώμας καὶ ἐνθυμήματα || τάξομεν· καὶ παλιλλογήσαντες συντόμως τὰ προειρημένα ἢ πέρατι τὸ μέρος τελευταῖον ὁρισάμενοι, πάλιν ‹διέξιμεν›[107] ἃ διεπράξατο ὁ ὑφ᾽ ἡμῶν ἐγκωμιαζόμενος ἀνήρ· [16] ‹καὶ›[108] προθέμενοι τὴν δικαιοσύνην πρῶτον καὶ ὁμοιοτρόπως
5 τοῖς προειρημένοις | αὐξήσαντες ἥξομεν ἐπὶ τὴν σοφίαν, ἐὰν ὑπάρχῃ· καὶ ταύτην τὸν αὐτὸν τρόπον διελθόντες, προθέμενοι τὴν ἀνδρείαν, ἐὰν ᾖ, καὶ τὴν αὔξησιν ταύτης πάλιν διαδραμόντες, ὅταν ἐπὶ τῇ τελευτῇ τοῦ μέρους γενώμεθα καὶ πάντα τὰ εἴδη διεξεληλυ-
10 θότες ὦμεν, παλιλλογήσαντες ἐν | κεφαλαίῳ τὰ προειρημένα ἐπὶ τελευτῇ ἤτοι γνώμην ἢ ἐνθύμημα παντὶ τῷ λόγῳ ἐπιθήσομεν. ἁρμόσει δὲ ἐν τοῖς ἐπαίνοις καὶ

deavor or as a result of him or for his sake. [13] You must also compare the reputable actions of other youth, saying that these actions surpass those (discussing the least of those done by them and the greatest done by the youth being praised by you). You must also compare the actions you are discussing with other small, reputable actions, and in this way they will seem great. [14] You must also amplify the actions by plausibility, as follows: "Whoever becomes such a philosopher when young will be capable of great progress when he has grown old"; "Whoever withstands the labors of the gymnasium with strength will certainly love the exertion of philosophy." We shall amplify by speculating in this way.

[15] When we have gone through his youth, at the end of this part we shall arrange maxims and enthymemes. After concisely recapitulating what was said or ending this part with a close, we shall again go through what the man being praised by us has accomplished. [16] And we shall set forth his sense of justice first and, after amplifying it in a way similar to what has been said before, we shall go on to his wisdom, if possible. Going through it in the same way, we shall point out his courage, if he has some, and having again run through its amplification, when we come to the end of this part and have gone through all the species (of virtue), having repeated what has been said in a summary at the end, we shall add either a maxim or an enthymeme to the entirety of the speech. It will be fitting in speeches of

---

105 παριστάναι τὰ Sp.[1] : παριστάμενα N a

106 καὶ οὕτω μεγάλα φανεῖται Fuhrmann cf. 1426a27 : οὕτω μεγάλα φαίνεσθαι N a   107 διέξιμεν add. Sauppe

108 καὶ add. Sauppe

πολλοῖς ὀνόμασι περὶ ἕκαστον χρησάμενον μεγαλοπρεπῆ τὴν λέξιν ποιῆσαι.

[17] τὸν δ' αὐτὸν τρόπον ἐπὶ τῶν μοχθηρῶν πρα-
15 γματολογοῦντες τὰς κατηγορίας | συστήσομεν. δεῖ δὲ μὴ σκώπτειν ὃν ἂν κακολογῶμεν, ἀλλὰ διεξιέναι τὸν βίον αὐτοῦ· μᾶλλον γὰρ οἱ λόγοι τῶν σκωμμάτων καὶ τοὺς ἀκούοντας πείθουσι καὶ τοὺς κακολογουμένους λυποῦσιν. τὰ μὲν γὰρ σκώμματα στοχάζεται τῆς ἰδέας ἢ τῆς οὐσίας· οἱ δὲ λόγοι τῶν ἠθῶν καὶ τῶν
20 τρόπων εἰσὶν οἷον | εἰκόνες. [18] φυλάττου δὲ καὶ τὰς αἰσχρὰς πράξεις μὴ αἰσχροῖς ὀνόμασι λέγειν, ἵνα μὴ διαβάλῃς τὸ ἦθος, ἀλλὰ τὰ τοιαῦτα αἰνιγματωδῶς ἑρμηνεύειν καὶ ἑτέρων πραγμάτων ὀνόμασι χρώμενος δηλοῦν τὸ πρᾶγμα. [19] χρὴ δὲ καὶ ἐν ταῖς κακολο-
25 γίαις εἰρωνεύεσθαι καὶ καταγελᾶν τοῦ ἐναντίου ἐφ' | οἷς σεμνύνεται καὶ ἰδίᾳ μὲν καὶ ὀλίγων παρόντων ἀτιμάζειν αὐτόν, ἐν δὲ τοῖς ὄχλοις κοινὰς μάλιστα κατηγορίας λοιδορεῖν· αὔξειν δὲ καὶ ταπεινοῦν τὸν αὐτὸν τρόπον τὰς κακολογίας ὅνπερ καὶ τὰ ἐγκώμια. περὶ μὲν οὖν τούτων τῶν εἰδῶν ἐντεῦθεν εἰδήσομεν τὴν χρῆσιν. |

30 36. Λοιπὸν δ' ἐστὶν ἡμῖν εἶδος τό τε κατηγορικὸν καὶ τὸ ἐξεταστικόν. ταῦτα πάλιν ὡς ἐν τῷ δικανικῷ γένει συνθήσομεν καὶ τάξομεν διέλθωμεν. [2] πρῶτον μὲν οὖν ἐν τοῖς προοιμίοις προθήσομεν τὸ πρᾶγμα περὶ οὗ κατηγορήσομεν ἢ ἀπολογησόμεθα, ὥσπερ ἐπὶ
35 τῶν ἄλλων εἰδῶν. προσέχειν | δὲ παρακαλέσομεν ἐκ τῶν αὐτῶν ὧν ἐν τῷ προτρεπτικῷ καὶ ἐν τῷ ἀποτρεπτικῷ.

praise to use many words for each thing to make the style impressive.

[17] We shall compose prosecution speeches in the same way, by discussing the actions of base people. We must not ridicule the person we are criticizing, but go through his life. Reports persuade an audience better than ridicule and give greater pain to those being criticized. Ridicule takes aim at appearance or at wealth; reports are in a way reflections of the character and personality. [18] Take care not to refer to shameful acts with shameful language so that you do not create prejudice against (your own) character. Instead, express such things allusively and make the matter clear by using language for other matters. [19] You must also use irony in criticism and laugh at your opponent on matters that he takes seriously, and dishonor him privately, when few people are present, but in crowds deride him with the most general verbal attacks. Amplify and diminish your criticism in the same way as eulogies. From here we shall understand the usage of these forms of speech.

36. There remains the prosecution species and the investigative. Let us go through them again, how we shall compose and arrange them in the forensic genre. [2] First, in the introduction, we set out the matter about which we are giving the prosecution speech or the defense as in the other species. We shall call for attention in the same way as in the proposition and opposition species.[41]

[41] Cf. 29.1–7.

[3] ἔτι δὲ καὶ περὶ τῆς εὐμενείας τῷ μὲν εὖ διακειμένῳ ἐκ τοῦ παροιχομένου χρόνου ἢ τοῦ παρόντος καὶ μήτε διαβεβλημένῳ τῷ πρὸς αὐτὸν ἢ πρὸς τὸ πρᾶγμα
1442a ἢ πρὸς τὸν λόγον τοὺς ἀκούοντας δυσχεραίνειν || τὸν αὐτὸν τρόπον, ὡς περὶ ἐκείνων εἴρηται, τὴν εὐμένειανποριστέον· [4] τῷ δὲ μήτε εὖ μήτε κακῶς διακειμένῳ ἢ ἐκ τοῦ παροιχομένου χρόνου ἢ ἐκ τοῦ παρόντος ἢ δι'
5 ἑαυτὸν ἢ τὸ πρᾶγμα ἢ τὸν λόγον | διαβεβλημένῳ, ἔνια μὲν μεμιγμένως, ἔνια δ' ἰδίως, [5] οὗτος μὲν οὖν ὁ τρόπος ἔσται δι' οὗ τὴν εὐμένειαν ποριστέον· τοὺς μὲν γὰρ μήτε εὖ μήτε κακῶς διακειμένους αὐτοὺς μὲν συντόμως ἐπαινετέον καὶ τοὺς ἐναντίους κακολογη-
10 τέον. δεῖ δὲ αὐτοὺς ἐκ τούτων ἐπαινεῖν | ὧν μάλιστα μέτεστι τοῖς ἀκούουσι, λέγω δὲ φιλόπολιν, φιλέταιρον, εὐχάριστον, ἐλεήμονα καὶ τὰ τοιαῦτα, τὸν δ' ἐναντίον κακολογεῖν ἐκ τούτων ἐφ' οἷς οἱ ἀκούοντες ὀργιοῦνται, ταῦτα δ' ἐστὶ μισόπολιν, μισόφιλον, ἀχάριστον, ἀνελεήμονα καὶ τὰ τοιαῦτα. [6] χρὴ δὲ καὶ
15 τοὺς δικαστὰς ἐπαίνῳ θεραπεῦσαι ὡς | δικασταὶ δίκαιοι καὶ δεινοί εἰσιν. συμπαραληπτέον δὲ καὶ τὰς ἐλαττώσεις, εἴ που τῶν ἀντιδίκων καταδεεστέρως ἔχει πρὸς τὸ λέγειν ἢ πράττειν ἢ ἄλλο τι τῶν περὶ τὸν ἀγῶνα. πρὸς δὲ τούτοις ἐμβλητέον τό τε δίκαιον καὶ τὸ νόμιμον καὶ τὸ συμφέρον καὶ τὰ τούτοις ἀκόλουθα.
20 [7] τῷ μὲν οὖν | μήτε εὖ μήτε κακῶς διακειμένῳ ἐκ τούτων ἐν τοῖς δικασταῖς τὴν εὔνοιαν ποριστέον.

τῷ δὲ διαβεβλημένῳ, ἐὰν μὲν ἐκ τοῦ παροιχομένου

[3] With regard to friendliness, for the person who is in a good position as a result of the past or the present and has not incurred prejudice by annoying the audience, either with regard to himself or to the matter at hand or to his speech, you must create friendliness in the same way as has been said about those matters.[42] [4] For the person who is neither in a good nor a bad position as a result of the past or the present or who has incurred prejudice either because of himself or the matter at hand or the speech, [5] this will be the way in which to furnish friendliness, some of it in mixed ways and some separately:[43] when we are in neither a good nor a bad position we must briefly praise ourselves and criticize the opponents. We must praise ourselves especially on the basis of those things that interest the audience (i.e., patriotism, loyalty, gratitude, compassion, and so on), and criticize the opponent for those things that anger the audience (i.e., treachery, disloyalty, ingratitude, a lack of compassion, and so on). [6] We must also pamper the judges by praising them as just and skillful. We must also include our weaknesses if he is at any disadvantage to the adversaries in speech, action, or any other aspect of the trial. In addition, add in justice, law, advantage, and things that follow from them. [7] For the person who is in neither a good position nor a bad position, create benevolence among the judges in this way.

For the person against whom there is prejudice, if the

[42] Cf. 29.25–26.

[43] The interpretation of 36.3–4 has been vexed. The last phrase I have brought into 5, since it appears to me that what is being mixed and separated is praise of the speaker's side and criticism of the opponent's.

χρόνου αἱ διαβολαὶ ὦσιν περὶ τὸν λόγον, ἴσμεν ὡς δεῖ τὰ τοιαῦτα λύειν ἐκ τῶν προτέρων, ἐὰν δὲ ἐκ τοῦ παρόντος χρόνου περὶ αὐτὸν τὸν ἄνθρωπον, ἀναγ-
25 καῖον | διαβεβλῆσθαι ἐὰν ἀπρεπὴς ᾖ τῷ παρόντι ἀγῶνι ἢ ὑπεναντίος τοῖς ἐγκλήμασιν ἢ ὁμολογούμενος τῇ κατηγορίᾳ. [8] ἀπρεπὴς μὲν οὖν γένοιτ' ἄν, ἐὰν ἀγωνίζηται νεώτερος ἢ πρεσβύτερος ὑπὲρ ἄλλου, ὑπεναντίος δέ, ἐάν τις ἰσχυρὸς ὢν ἀσθενεῖ δικάζηται αἰκίας,
30 ἢ ἐάν τις ὑβριστὴς ὢν ὕβριν | ἐγκαλῇ σώφρονι, ἢ ἐάν τις πάνυ πλουσίῳ δικάζηται πάνυ πένης χρημάτων [ἐγκαλῶν]. [9] οἱ μὲν οὖν τοιοῦτοι ὑπεναντίοι εἰσὶ τοῖς ἐγκλήμασιν· ὁμολογούμενος δ' ἔσται, ἐάν τις ἰσχυρὸς ὢν ὑπὸ ἀσθενοῦς αἰκίας διώκηται, ἢ ἐάν τις κλέπτης
35 δοκῶν εἶναι κλοπῆς δίκην φεύγῃ. ὅλως δὲ οἱ τὰς | περὶ αὑτῶν δόξας ὁμοιοτρόπους αὐτοῖς ἔχοντες ὁμολογούμενοι τοῖς ἐγκλήμασι δόξουσιν εἶναι. [10] περὶ μὲν οὖν αὐτὸν τὸν ἄνθρωπον ἐκ τοῦ παρόντος χρόνου τοιαῦται γενήσονται διαβολαί. αἱ δὲ περὶ τὸ πρᾶγμα συμβαίνουσιν,[109] ἐάν τις πραγματεύηται πρὸς οἰκεί-
1442b ους, φίλους ἢ ξένους ἢ ἰδίους, ἢ περὶ || μικρῶν ἢ αἰσχρῶν· ταῦτα γὰρ ἀδοξίαν τοῖς δικαζομένοις ποιεῖ.

[11] πῶς οὖν τὰς διαβολὰς τὰς προειρημένας ἀπολύσομεν, τοῦτο δηλώσω. δύο μὲν δὴ στοιχεῖα λέγω κοινὰ κατὰ πάντων· τὸ μέν, οἷς ἂν νομίζῃς τοὺς κριτὰς
5 ἐπιπλήξειν, | προκαταλάμβανε αὐτοὺς καὶ ἐπίπληττε, τὸ δὲ ἕτερον, εἰ τὰς πράξεις μάλιστα μὲν εἰς τοὺς ἀντιδίκους ἀποτρέψεις, εἰ δὲ μή, εἰς ἄλλους τινάς,

prejudice against the speech arose in the past, we know how to refute such things from what was said earlier.[44] But if it arises from the present time against the person himself, the prejudice is unavoidable if a man is unsuited to the present trial, at odds with his charges, or if he matches the prosecution speech. [8] A younger or older person would be unsuitable if he disputed on another's behalf. A strong man would be at odds if he brought suit against a weak man for assault, or if some brutal person accused a temperate man of brutality, or if a very poor man sued a very wealthy one for defaulting on a loan. [9] Such people are at odds with the charges. But if a strong man is prosecuted by a weak one for assault, he will match what is said in the prosecution speech, or if someone with a reputation as a thief is on trial for theft. In general, those having reputations that are like their actual personalities will appear to match the charges. [10] Such are the prejudices that will arise from the present time against the person himself. Prejudices occur with regard to the action if someone is dealing with intimates, friends, guests, or family members, about either small or shameful matters. These things create disrepute among judges.

[11] I shall now explain how we shall refute the aforementioned prejudices. I claim that there are two elements common to all of them. First, whatever you think may have an impact on the judges, anticipate your opponents and make the impact. Second, ascribe the actions to your adversaries, and if not, to someone else, using the excuse that

[44] Cf. 29.25–26.

---

109 *συμβαίνουσιν* (*contingunt*) Lat.^{a} : *συμβαίνουσαι* N a om. Lat.$^{\beta}$

προφάσει χρώμενος ὅτι οὐχ ἑκών, ἀλλ' ὑπὸ τῶν ἀνταγωνιστῶν ἀναγκαζόμενος εἰς τὸν ἀγῶνα κατέστης. [12] καθ' ἑκάστην δὲ τὴν διαβολὴν τάδε χρὴ προ-
10 φασίζεσθαι· | τὸν μὲν νεώτερον πρεσβυτέρων φίλων ἀπορίαν τῶν ἀγωνιουμένων ὑπὲρ αὑτοῦ ἢ μέγεθος ἀδικημάτων ἢ πλῆθος ἢ προθεσμίαν χρόνου ἢ ἄλλο τι τοιοῦτον. [13] ἐὰν δὲ ὑπὲρ ἄλλου λέγῃς, ῥητέον ὡς διὰ φιλίαν συνηγορεῖς ἢ δι' ἔχθραν τοῦ ἀντιδίκου ἢ διὰ τὸ
15 τοῖς πράγμασι παραγενέσθαι | ἢ διὰ τὸ τῷ κοινῷ συμφέρον ἢ διὰ τὸ ἔρημον εἶναι καὶ ἀδικεῖσθαι ᾧ συνηγορεῖς. [14] ἐὰν δὲ ὁμολογούμενος τῷ ἐγκλήματι ἢ ὑπεναντίος τῇ κατηγορίᾳ γένηται, τῇ τε προκαταλήψει χρῆσθαι καὶ λέγειν ὡς οὐ δίκαιον καὶ νόμιμον οὐδὲ συμφέρον ἐκ τῆς ὑπολήψεως ἢ τῆς ὑποψίας προ-
20 κατακρίνειν | πρὶν τοῦ πράγματος ἀκοῦσαι. [15] τὰς μὲν οὖν περὶ τὸν ἄνθρωπον αὐτὸν διαβολὰς οὕτω λύσομεν· τὰς δὲ περὶ τὸ πρᾶγμα οὕτως ἀπωσόμεθα, τὴν αἰτίαν εἰς τοὺς ἐναντίους τρέποντες ἢ λοιδορίαν ἐγκαλοῦντες αὐτοῖς ἢ ἀδικίαν ἢ πλεονεξίαν ἢ φιλο-
25 νεικίαν ἢ ὀργήν, προφασιζόμενοι ὅτι τοῦ δικαίου | δι' ἄλλου τρόπου τυχεῖν ἀδύνατον. τὰς μὲν οὖν ἰδίας διαβολὰς ἐπὶ τῶν δικαστηρίων οὕτω λύσομεν, τὰς δὲ κοινὰς πᾶσι τοῖς εἴδεσιν ὡς ἐπὶ τῶν προτέρων εἰδῶν εἴρηται. [16] τάξομεν δὲ τὰ δικανικὰ προοίμια τὸν αὐτὸν τρόπον ὅνπερ καὶ τὰ δημηγορικά. κατὰ τὸν
30 αὐτὸν δὲ λόγον καὶ τὰς | ἀπαγγελίας συνάψομεν τῷ προοιμίῳ [καὶ][110] ἢ παρὰ τὰ μέρη πιστὰς καὶ δικαίας ἀποφανοῦμεν ἢ αὐτὰς ἐφ' ἑαυτῶν σωματοειδεῖς ποιήσομεθα.

you have come to trial unwillingly, but forced to do so by your adversaries. [12] To each prejudice, these are the excuses that must be pleaded: a younger man's lack of older friends to plead on his behalf, the gravity or number of the wrongs, or the time limit, or another such thing. [13] If you are speaking on behalf of another, say that you are co-pleading because of friendship, or because of dislike of his adversary, or because you were at the events, or because of the common good, or because the person for whom you are co-pleading is alone and injured. [14] If he matches the charge or is at odds with his prosecution speech, use anticipation and say that it is unjust, illegal, and disadvantageous to convict on the basis of assumption and suspicion before hearing the matter. [15] We shall refute prejudices against a person himself in this way. We shall rebut those concerning his action in the following way, by turning the accusation against the opponents, accusing them of slander, injustice, greed, contentiousness, or anger, and making the excuse that it is impossible to gain justice in another way. We shall refute private prejudices before the courts in this way and public ones with all the forms of argument that have been discussed with regard to the earlier species. [16] We shall arrange forensic introductions in the same way as demegoric introductions. By the same reasoning we shall attach reports of facts to the introduction or demonstrate throughout the parts that the reports are credible and just or make them coherent by themselves.

---

110 καὶ del. Finkh[1]

[17] τὰ δὲ μετὰ ταῦτα ἔσται βεβαίωσις, ἂν μὲν ἀντιλέγηται τὰ πράγματα ὑπὸ τῶν ἀντιδίκων, ἐκ τῶν
35 πίστεων, ἂν δὲ ὁμολογῆται, ἐκ τῶν δικαίων | καὶ ἐκ τῶν συμφερόντων καὶ ἐκ τῶν τούτοις ἀκολούθων. [18] τάττειν δὲ δεῖ τῶν μὲν πίστεων πρώτας τὰς μαρτυρίας καὶ τὰ ἐκ τῶν βασάνων ἡμῖν ὁμολογηθέντα, ἂν ὑπάρχῃ· ἔπειτα βεβαιοῦν, ἂν μὲν πιθανὰ ᾖ, γνώμαις καὶ ἐνθυμήμασιν, ἐὰν δὲ μὴ παντελῶς πιθανὰ ᾖ, τῷ εἰκότι,
1443a ἔπειτα τοῖς παραδείγμασι || καὶ τοῖς τεκμηρίοις καὶ τοῖς σημείοις καὶ τοῖς ἐλέγχοις, τελευταῖον δὲ τοῖς ἐνθυμήμασι καὶ ταῖς γνωμολογίαις. ἐὰν δὲ ὁμολογῆται τὰ πράγματα, τὰς μὲν πίστεις ἐατέον, τῇ δὲ δικαιολογίᾳ
5 ὥσπερ ἐν τοῖς ἔμπροσθεν | χρηστέον. καὶ τοῦτον μὲν τὸν τρόπον βεβαιώσομεν.

[19] μετὰ δὲ τὴν βεβαίωσιν τὰ πρὸς τοὺς ἀντιδίκους τάττοντες προκαταληψόμεθα αὐτῶν τὰ ἐπίδοξα λέγεσθαι. ἐὰν μὲν οὖν ἐξαρνῶνται τὸ πρᾶγμα, τὰς μὲν ὑφ' ἡμῶν πίστεις εἰρημένας αὐξητέον, τὰς δ' ὑπ'
10 ἐκείνων μελλούσας λέγεσθαι διασυρτέον | καὶ ταπεινωτέον. [20] ἐὰν δὲ ὁμολογοῦντες ἀξίωσιν[111] ἔννομα καὶ δίκαια, ἀποφαίνειν χρὴ[112] τοὺς γεγραμμένους νόμους οὓς ἡμεῖς παρεχόμεθα καὶ τοὺς ὁμοίους τούτοις δικαίους καὶ καλοὺς καὶ συμφέροντας τῷ κοινῷ τῆς πόλεως <καὶ> κεκριμένους ὑπὸ πολλῶν τοιούτους εἶναι
15 πειρατέον ἐπιδεικνύειν, | τοὺς δὲ τῶν ἀντιδίκων τὰ ἐναντία. [21] ἐὰν δὲ μὴ ἐνδέχηται ταῦτα λέγειν, ὑπομίμνῃσκε τοὺς δικαστάς ὅτι οὐχ ὑπὲρ τοῦ νόμου ἀλλὰ τοῦ πράγματος δικάζουσιν, ὀμόσαντες κατὰ τοὺς νό-

[17] The part after this will be confirmation. If the opponents contest the facts, the confirmation will be based on proofs. But if they admit them, it will be based on arguments about justice, advantage, and what follows from them. [18] Of the proofs, we must arrange witness testimony first and what has been corroborated for us through torture, if anything has been. Then base the confirmation on maxims and enthymemes, if they are persuasive. But if they are not entirely persuasive, base it on plausibility, then on examples and *tekmeria* and signs and *elenchoi*, and finally on enthymemes and formulations of maxims. If the facts are admitted, you may leave out the proofs and use argumentation about justice, just as before. We shall do confirmation in this way.

[19] After the confirmation we shall anticipate what we expect the opponents to say and arrange arguments in response to them. If they deny the facts, we must amplify the proofs we have stated and tear apart and minimize those we expect them to use. [20] If while admitting the facts they claim that they are lawful and just, we must point out the written laws that we are supplying and try to show that those like them are adjudged by many to be just, noble, and advantageous to the common good of the city, but those of our adversary are the opposite. [21] If it is not possible to say this, remind the judges that they are not judging the law but the facts, having sworn to cast their votes

---

[111] *ἀξίωσιν* ego cf. 1443a41; *ὦσιν* N a
[112] *χρὴ* ego cf. 1443b1; *κατὰ* N a

μους τοὺς κειμένους τὴν ψῆφον οἴσειν, καὶ δίδασκε ὅτι
οὐ νῦν νομοθετεῖν προσήκει, ἀλλ' ἐν ταῖς περὶ τούτων
20 κυρίαις | ἡμέραις. [22] ἂν δ' ἡμῖν συμβαίνῃ τὸ παρὰ
μοχθηροῖς δοκοῦσιν εἶναι νόμοις τὸ πρᾶγμα πε-
πρᾶχθαι, ῥητέον ὡς οὐ νόμος, ἀλλ' ἀνομία τὸ τοιοῦτόν
ἐστιν· ὁ μὲν γὰρ νόμος ἐπὶ τῷ ὠφελεῖν τίθεται, οὗτος
δὲ βλάπτει τὴν πόλιν. [23] ῥητέον δὲ καὶ ὡς οὐ
παρανομήσουσιν, ἂν τούτῳ τῷ νόμῳ ἐναντίαν ψῆφον |
25 θῶνται, ἀλλὰ νομοθετήσουσιν, ὥστε μὴ χρῆσθαι
δόγμασι πονηροῖς καὶ παρανόμοις. δεῖ δὲ καὶ τοῦτο
συμβιβάζειν ὡς οὐδεὶς νόμος κωλύει τὸ κοινὸν εὖ
ποιεῖν, τοὺς δὲ φαύλους νόμους ἀκύρους ποιεῖν εὐερ-
γετεῖν τὴν πόλιν ἐστίν.

[24] περὶ μὲν οὖν τῶν σαφῶς εἰρημένων νόμων
30 ὁποίους ἂν αὐτῶν | ἔχωμεν, ἐκ τῶν τοιούτων προκατα-
λαμβάνοντες ἀντιλέγειν εὐπορήσομεν· περὶ δὲ τῶν
ἀμφιβόλων ἐὰν οὕτως ὑπολαμβάνωσιν ὡς σοὶ συμφέρει, δεῖ ταῦτα ὑποδεικνύειν, ἂν δ' ὡς ὁ ἐναντίος
λέγει, χρὴ διδάσκειν ὡς ὁ νομοθέτης οὐ τοῦτο διενο-
εῖτο <ἀλλ'>[113] ὃ σὺ λέγεις, καὶ ὅτι συμφέρει αὐτοῖς
35 οὕτω λέγειν | τὸν νόμον. [25] ἐὰν δὲ μὴ δυνατὸς ᾖς ἐπὶ
τὸ ἐναντίον μεθιστάναι, δείκνυε ὡς οὐδὲν ἄλλο λέγειν
ὁ ἐναντίος δύναται νόμος ἢ ὃ σύ. καὶ περὶ μὲν νόμων
ὡς δεῖ χρῆσθαι, τοῦτον τὸν τρόπον μετιὼν εὐπορήσεις. καθόλου δὲ ἂν ὁμολογήσαντες ἐκ τῶν δικαίων
40 καὶ τῶν νομίμων τὴν ἀπολογίαν ποιεῖσθαι | μέλλωσιν,
ἐκ τούτων τὰ ἐπίδοξα ῥηθήσεσθαι προκαταληπτέον.

[26] ἐὰν δὲ ὁμολογήσαντες συγγνώμης ἀξιῶσι

according to the existing laws, and explain that it is not fitting to be legislators at the present time but on the days authorized for these matters. [22] If it happens to us that the action that was committed seems contrary to laws that appear flawed, you must say that such a thing is not law but illegality. Law is legislated to help the city, but this one harms it. [23] You must say that they will not be breaking the law if they cast their vote against this law, but they will be legislating in order to avoid using notions that are base and illegal. You must also reason that no law forbids acting for the common welfare, and to invalidate poor laws is to benefit the city.

[24] Concerning clearly stated laws, whichever we have, we shall be well equipped to speak against them in anticipation with such arguments. Concerning ambiguous laws, if the judges take them in a way that benefits you, you must illustrate this. But if they take them as your opponent says, you must teach that the legislator did not intend this but what you say, and that it will benefit them if the law means this. [25] If you are unable to turn around the law to its opposite, show that the opposing law cannot mean anything other than what you say. Concerning law and how to use it you will be well equipped by proceeding in this way. In general, if they are going to admit the facts and base their defense on considerations of justice and the law, you must anticipate what they are expected to say through these points.

[26] If they admit the facts but make a claim to gain par-

---

113 ἀλλ' add. Sp.[1]

1443b τυχεῖν, || ὧδε χρὴ περιαιρεῖσθαι τὰ τοιαῦτα τῶν ἀντιδίκων. πρῶτον μὲν λεκτέον ὡς κακοηθέστερον ἦν καὶ ὡς τὰ τοιαῦτα ἐξαμαρτάνειν φασίν ὅταν γνωσθῶσιν, ὥστε "εἰ τούτῳ συγγνώμην ἔχετε, καὶ τοὺς ἄλλους 5 πάντας τῶν τιμωριῶν ἀφήσετε." [27] ἔτι | δὲ λέγε ὡς· "εἰ τῶν ὁμολογούντων ἐξαμαρτάνειν ἀποψηφιεῖσθε, πῶς τῶν μὴ ὁμολογούντων καταψηφιεῖσθε;" λεκτέον δὲ ὅτι· "εἰ καὶ ἐξήμαρτεν, οὐκ ἐμὲ δεῖ διὰ τὴν τούτου ἁμαρτίαν ζημιοῦσθαι." πρὸς δὲ τούτοις ῥητέον ὡς "οὐδὲ ὁ νομοθέτης τοῖς ἁμαρτάνουσι συγγνώμην ἔχει· 10 οὐκοῦν δίκαιον οὐδὲ τοὺς | δικαστὰς κατὰ τοὺς νόμους κρίνοντας." [28] ἐκ μὲν οὖν τῶν τοιούτων τὰς συγγνώμας περιαιρησόμεθα, καθάπερ ἐν ἀρχαῖς δεδηλώκαμεν. συλλήβδην δὲ τὰ ὑπὸ τῶν ἀντιδίκων μέλλοντα λέγεσθαι καὶ πρὸς πίστιν καὶ δικαιολογίαν καὶ συγγνώμην ἐκ τῶν προειρημένων προκαταληψόμεθα.

15 [29] μετὰ δὲ | ταύτην τὴν αἰτίαν, ἀναλογιστέον ἐν κεφαλαίῳ τὸν λόγον ὅλον, καὶ συντόμως, ἐὰν ἐνδέχηται, πρὸς μὲν τοὺς ἐναντίους ἔχθραν ἢ ὀργὴν ἢ φθόνον τοῖς δικασταῖς ἐμποιητέον, πρὸς δὲ ἡμᾶς φιλίαν ἢ χάριν ἢ ἔλεον. ὅθεν δὲ ταῦτα γίνεται, ἐν τῷ δημηγο- 20 ρικῷ καὶ ἐπὶ τῶν προτροπῶν καὶ ἀποτροπῶν | εἰρήκαμεν καὶ ἐν τῷ ἀπολογικῷ εἴδει πάλιν ἐπὶ τελευτῆς διέξιμεν. [30] τὸν μὲν οὖν πρῶτον λόγον, ἐὰν κατηγορῶμεν, ἐν τοῖς δικανικοῖς οὕτω συνθήσομεν καὶ τάξομεν.

ἐὰν δὲ ἀπολογώμεθα, τὸ μὲν προοίμιον ὁμοιοτρόπως τῷ κατηγοροῦντι συστήσομεν. [31] τῶν δὲ κατ-

don, you must deprive your opponents of such claims in the following way: first, say that it is more wicked that they are saying that they make such mistakes only after being convicted, so that "if you give pardon to this man, you will release everyone else from punishment." [27] Say also, "If you vote to acquit those who admit mistakes, how will you vote against those who do not make an admission." You must also say, "If he has made a mistake, you must not punish me for his mistake." In addition, say, "The lawgiver has no pardon for those who make mistakes, so it not just for the judges to do so who judge according to the laws." [28] We shall remove pleas for pardon through such arguments just as we made clear at the beginning. In sum, we shall anticipate what is going to be said by our opponents with regard to proof and argumentation concerning justice and pardon from what has been said before.[45]

[29] After this accusation, we must sum up the entire speech, in point form and concisely, if possible, and excite hostility, anger, and envy in the judges against the opponents, and friendship, gratitude, and compassion toward ourselves. Where these arise from we have discussed in the section on demegoric and with regard to proposition and opposition speeches and we shall go through it again at the end of the section on defense speeches.[46] [30] We shall compose and arrange the first speech in this way if we are giving the prosecution speech in forensic matters.

If we are giving the defense speech, we shall compose the introduction in the same way as the person giving the prosecution speech. [31] We shall pass over what the pros-

[45] Cf. 4.7–9.
[46] Cf. 36.47–51.

25 ηγορουμένων | ἃ μὲν εἰδέναι τοὺς ἀκούοντας ἐποίησε παραλείψομεν, ἃ δὲ δοξάζειν ταῦτα προθέμενοι μετὰ τὸ προοίμιον διαλύσομεν, τούς τε μάρτυρας καὶ τὰς βασάνους καὶ τοὺς ὅρκους ἀπίστους ποιήσομεν, ὡς προακήκοας· εἰ μὲν τὰ πράγματα πιστὰ εἴη, τὴν ὑπὲρ
30 αὐτῶν ἀπολογίαν | ἐπὶ τὸν ἐκ τοῦ παραλειπομένου τόπον μεταβιβάζωμεν, εἰ δ' εἶεν οἱ μάρτυρες ‹ἢ›[114] οἱ βασανισθέντες πιστοί, ἐπὶ τὸν λόγον ἢ τὴν πρᾶξιν ἢ ὅ τι ἂν ἄλλο ἔχῃς ἐπὶ τῶν ἐναντίων πιστότατον. [32] ἂν δὲ τὸ λυσιτελὲς ἢ τὸ ἔθος ἐπιφέρων σοῦ κατηγορήσῃ, ἀπολογοῦ μάλιστα μέν ὡς ‹οὐ›[115] λυσιτελές ἐστι τὸ
35 κατηγορούμενον, | εἰ δὲ μή, ὅτι οὐκ εἴθισαι τὰ τοιαῦτα πράττειν οὔτε σὺ οὔτε οἱ σοὶ ὅμοιοι, ἢ ὅτι οὐ τοῦτον τὸν τρόπον. [33] τὸ μὲν οὖν εἰκὸς οὕτω λύσεις.

τὸ δὲ παράδειγμα πρῶτον μέν, ἂν δύνῃ, δείκνυε ὡς οὐχ ὅμοιόν ἐστι τῷ ἐγκαλουμένῳ, εἰ δὲ μή, ἕτερον
40 φέρε αὐτὸς παράδειγμα ἐκ τῶν ἐναντίων παρὰ | τὸ εἰκὸς γενόμενον. τὸ δὲ τεκμήριον λύε φράζων παρ' ἃς αἰτίας ἐναντιωθῆναι συνέβη. [34] τὰς δὲ γνώμας καὶ τὰ
1444a ἐνθυμήματα || ἢ παράδοξα ἀπόφαινε ἢ ἀμφίβολα. τὰ δὲ σημεῖα πλειόνων ὄντα ἀπόφαινε σημεῖα καὶ μὴ μόνου τοῦ σοὶ ἐγκαλουμένου. καὶ τὰ μὲν τῶν ἐναντίων ἐπὶ τὸ ἐναντίον ἄγοντες ἢ ἐπὶ τὸ ἀμφίβολον ἀπίθανα τοῦτον
5 τὸν τρόπον | καταστήσομεν.

[35] ἂν δὲ ὁμολογῶμεν τὰ ἐγκαλούμενα πεποιηκέναι, ἐκ τῶν δικαίων καὶ νομίμων μετιόντες ἐννομώτερα

[114] ἢ add. Sp.[1]   [115] οὐ add. Fuhrmann

ecuting speakers let the audience know, but we shall set forth and refute what they made them believe. We shall also discredit their witnesses and arguments based on torture and oaths, as you have heard before.[47] If the facts are credible, we pass from a defense about them to the topic of omission; if the witnesses or torture victims are credible, let us pass to the speech or action or anything else you have that is most credible against the opponents. [32] If the prosecution speech makes reference to profit or habit, reply in defense above all that what is being said in the prosecution speech is not profitable, and if not that, then that it is neither your habit nor that of people like you to do such things, or not to do them in this way. [33] You will refute argumentation based on plausibility in this way.

With regard to an example, show first, if you can, that it is not comparable to what is being accused, and if not that, then bring in yourself another example that has occurred contrary to plausibility. Refute a *tekmerion* by claiming that it actually occurred contrary to the accusations. [34] Point out that the maxims and enthymemes are either paradoxical or ambiguous, and point out that the signs are signs of many things and not only of what you have been accused. We shall make the arguments of the opponents unpersuasive in this way by drawing them in the opposite direction or toward ambiguity.

[35] If we admit that we did what is accused, by pursuing arguments from justice and legality we shall try to show

[47] Cf. 15.4, 16.2, 17.2.

καὶ δικαιότερα τὰ ἡμέτερα ἀποδεικνύναι πειρασόμεθα· ἐὰν δὲ μὴ τοῦτο ἐνδέχηται, εἰς ἁμάρτημα ἢ ἀτύχημα καταφεύγοντας καὶ σμικρὰς τὰς βλάβας ἀποφαίνον-
10 τας συγγνώμης | τυγχάνειν πειρατέον, τὸ μὲν ἁμαρτάνειν κοινὸν πάντων ἀνθρώπων ἐπιδεικνύοντας, τὸ δ' ἀδικεῖν ἴδιον τῶν πονηρῶν. [36] λέγε δέ καὶ ὅτι ἐπιεικὲς καὶ δίκαιον καὶ συμφέρον ἐστὶ συγγνώμην ἔχειν ταῖς ἁμαρτίαις· οὐδεὶς γὰρ οἶδεν ἀνθρώπων εἴ τι
15 τοιοῦτον αὐτῷ συνεμπέσοι. ἀπόφαινε | καὶ τὸν ἐναντίον, εἴ τι ἐξήμαρτε, συγγνώμης τυχεῖν ἀξιώσαντα.

[37] μετὰ δὲ ταῦτα αἱ προκαταλήψεις αἱ ὑπὸ τῶν ἐναντίων εἰρημέναι. τὰς μὲν οὖν ἄλλας ἐξ αὐτῶν τῶν πραγμάτων εὐπορήσομεν λύειν· ἐὰν δὲ διαβάλλωσιν ἡμᾶς ὡς γεγραμμένους λόγους λέγομεν ἢ λέγειν μελε-
20 τῶμεν ἢ ὡς | ἐπὶ μισθῷ τινι συνηγοροῦμεν, χρὴ πρὸς τὰ τοιαῦτα ὁμόσε βαδίζοντας εἰρωνεύεσθαι, καὶ περὶ μὲν τῆς γραφῆς, λέγειν μὴ κωλύειν τὸν νόμον ἢ αὐτὸν γεγραμμένα λέγειν ἢ ἐκεῖνον ἄγραφα· τὸν γὰρ νόμον οὐκ ἐᾶν τοιαῦτα πράττειν, λέγειν δὲ ὅπως ἄν τις
25 βούληται συγχωρεῖν. [38] ῥητέον δὲ καὶ | ὅτι· "οὕτως ὁ ἐναντίος οἴεται μεγάλα ἠδικηκέναι ὥστ' οὐ νομίζει με κατ' ἀξίαν <ἂν>[116] κατηγορῆσαι, εἰ μὴ γράφοιμι καὶ πολὺν χρόνον σκεψαίμην." περὶ μὲν οὖν τὰς τῶν γεγραμμένων λόγων διαβολὰς οὕτως ἀπαντητέον· [39] ἂν δὲ φάσκωσιν ἡμᾶς λέγειν μανθάνειν καὶ
30 μελετᾶν, ὁμολογήσαντες | ἐροῦμεν· "ἡμεῖς μὲν οἱ μανθάνοντες, ὡς φῄς, οὐ φιλόδικοί ἐσμεν, σὺ δὲ ὁ λέγειν μὴ ἐπιστάμενος, καὶ νῦν ἡμᾶς καὶ πρότερον ἑάλως

that our actions were more legal and more just. If this is not possible, we must try to win pardon by appealing to a mistake or misfortune and by pointing out that the damages were small, and by arguing that to err is common to all humans but doing injustice is characteristic of the wicked. [36] Say also that it is fair, just, and advantageous to grant pardon for mistakes: no human knows whether some such thing may happen to him. Point out also that the opponent, if he had made a mistake, would also be demanding to receive pardon.

[37] After this come the anticipations that have been expressed by the opponents. The facts themselves will equip us well to refute other anticipations, but if they create prejudice against us because we read prepared speeches or practice speaking or because we co-plead for some payment, we must proceed against such things directly with irony. About writing, say that the law does not forbid either you speaking written remarks or him unwritten remarks. The law does not allow certain acts, but you can speak however you wish. [38] Say also that "my opponent thinks that he has done such a serious wrong that he does not think I could do a prosecution speech worthily unless I wrote it out and examined it for a long time." Respond to prejudices against written speeches in this way. [39] If they claim that we study and practice speaking, we shall admit it and say, "We who study speaking, as you say, are not litigious, but you, the one who does not know how to speak, have been caught maliciously prosecuting us,

116 ἂν add. Halm

συκοφαντῶν·" ὥστε λυσιτελὲς φανεῖται τοῖς πολίταις κἀκεῖνον μανθάνειν ῥητορεύειν· οὐ γὰρ οὕτω πονηρὸν οὐδὲ συκοφάντην αὐτὸν εἶναι. [40] τὸν αὐτὸν δὲ τρό-
35 πον κἂν | ἡμᾶς ἐπὶ μισθῷ συνηγορεῖν λέγῃ τις, ὁμολογήσαντες εἰρωνευσόμεθα καὶ τὸν αἰτιώμενον ἡμᾶς ἐπιδείξομεν τοῦτο ποιοῦντα καὶ τοὺς ἄλλους ἅπαντας. [41] τῶν δὲ μισθῶν διαιροῦ τὰ εἴδη, καὶ λέγε ὡς οἱ μὲν ἐπὶ χρήμασιν, οἱ δὲ ἐπὶ χάρισιν, οἱ δὲ ἐπὶ τιμωρίαις,
40 οἱ δὲ ἐπὶ τιμαῖς συνηγοροῦσιν· | αὐτὸν μὲν οὖν ἀπό-
1444b φαινε διὰ χάριν συνηγοροῦντα, τὸν δ' || ἐναντίον λέγε οὐδ' ἐπὶ μικρῷ μισθῷ συνηγορεῖν· ὅπως γὰρ λάβῃ ἀργύριον ἀδίκως, οὐχ ὅπως μὴ ἐκτίσῃ, δικάζεται. [42] τῷ αὐτῷ δὲ τρόπῳ καὶ ἐάν τις ἡμᾶς δικάζεσθαί τινας λέγῃ διδάσκειν ἢ λόγους δικανικοὺς συγγρά-
5 φειν· ἀπόφαινε | γὰρ καὶ τοὺς ἄλλους ἅπαντας, καθ' ὅσον δύνανται, τοὺς φίλους ὠφελεῖν καὶ διδάσκοντας καὶ συμβουλεύοντας. καὶ οὕτως ἐντέχνως περὶ τῶν τοιούτων ἀπαντήσεις.

[43] χρὴ δὲ καὶ περὶ τὰς ἐρωτήσεις καὶ τὰς ἀποκρίσεις ὁπόσαι πίπτουσιν εἰς τὰ τοιαῦτα εἴδη μὴ
10 ῥᾳθύμως ἔχειν, ἀλλὰ διακρίνειν | τὰς ὁμολογίας καὶ τὰς ἀρνήσεις ἐν ταῖς ἀποκρίσεσιν. ὁμολογίαι μὲν οὖν εἰσιν αἱ τοιαίδε· "ἀπέκτεινάς μου τὸν υἱόν·—ἀπέκτεινα πρότερον ἐπ' ἐμὲ σίδηρον αἰρόμενον." "συνέκοψάς μου τὸν υἱόν·—ἔγωγε ἀδίκων χειρῶν ἄρχοντα." "κατέαξάς μου τὴν κεφαλήν·—ἐγὼ βιαζομένου σου νύκτωρ εἰς
15 τὴν ἐμὴν | οἰκίαν εἰσιέναι." [44] αἱ μὲν οὖν τοιαῦται ὁμολογίαι τῷ νόμῳ πιστεύουσαι ὁμολογοῦνται. αἱ δὲ

now and before." In this way it will appear profitable to the citizens for him also to study to be an orator; it is not because of this that he is such a wicked litigant. [40] In the same way, if someone says that we are co-pleading for pay, we shall admit it, ironically, and show that our accuser does this, as does everyone else. [41] Distinguish the kinds of payments, and say that some co-plead for money, others as a favor, others for revenge, and others for honor. Point out that you are co-pleading as a favor, but say that the opponent co-pleads for a large payment. He goes to court to earn money unjustly, not to avoid paying it. [42] In the same way, if someone says that we teach certain people how to go to court or how to compose forensic speeches, point out that everyone else, as much as he is able, helps friends by teaching and advising. In this way you will respond skillfully concerning such matters.

[43] With regard to interrogations and answers, as many as occur in such species (of speech), you must not be careless; you must distinguish admissions and denials in your answers. Admissions take the following form: "Did you kill my son?" "I killed him when he first raised a sword at me." "Did you beat my son?" "I beat him when he started a fight." "Did you fracture my head?" "I did, as you were violently entering my home at night." [44] Such admissions rely on what is legal. The following denials re-

τοιαίδε ἀρνήσεις παρακλίνουσι τὸν νόμον· "ἀπέκτεινάς μου τὸν υἱόν—οὐκ ἔγωγε, ἀλλ' ὁ νόμος." τὰ δὲ τοιαῦτα πάντα οὕτω δεῖ ἀποκρίνεσθαι, ὅταν τῶν νό-
20 μων ὁ μὲν κελεύῃ τοῦτο ποιεῖν, ὁ δὲ κωλύῃ. τὰ μὲν | οὖν πρὸς τοὺς ἀντιδίκους ἐκ τούτων ἁπάντων συνάξεις.

[45] μετὰ δὲ ταῦτα παλιλλογία τῶν εἰρημένων ἤδη σύντομος ἀνάμνησις. χρήσιμος δ' ἐστὶ παρὰ πάντας τοὺς καιρούς, ὥστε καὶ παρὰ μέρος καὶ παρὰ εἶδος τῇ παλιλλογίᾳ χρηστέον, μάλιστα δ' ἁρμόττει πρὸς τὰς
25 κατηγορίας καὶ τὰς ἀπολογίας, | ἔτι δὲ πρὸς τὰς προτροπὰς καὶ ἀποτροπάς· οὐ γὰρ μόνον ἀναμνῆσαι δεῖν φαμεν περὶ τῶν εἰρημένων ἐνταῦθα, καθάπερ καὶ ἐπὶ τῶν ἐγκωμίων καὶ τῶν κακολογιῶν, ἀλλὰ καὶ πρὸς ἡμᾶς τοὺς κριτὰς εὖ διαθεῖναι καὶ πρὸς τοὺς ἐναντίους
30 κακῶς. [46] τελευταῖον δὲ τοῦτο τῶν ἐν | τῷ λόγῳ μερῶν τάττομεν. ἔστι δὲ μνημονικὸν ποιεῖν ἐν κεφαλαίῳ ἀπολογιζόμενον περὶ τῶν εἰρημένων ἢ διαλογιζόμενον ἢ προσερωτῶντα τῶν μὲν σαυτοῦ τὰ βέλτιστα, τῶν δ' ἐναντίων τὰ φαυλότατα, εἰ δὲ βούλει, ἐπερωτήσεως σχῆμα ποιησάμενον. οἷον δὲ τούτων ἕκαστόν ἐστιν,
35 ἐκ τῶν προτέρων | ἴσμεν.

[47] εὖ δὲ διαθήσομεν ἡμᾶς καὶ τοὺς ἐναντίους κακῶς ὥσπερ ἐπὶ τῶν προτροπῶν καὶ ἀποτροπῶν, ὑποφαίνοντες κεφαλαιωδῶς ἐφ' οἷς εὖ πεποιήκαμεν τοὺς ἀδικοῦντας ἢ ποιοῦμεν ἢ ποιήσομεν, ἢ αὐτοὶ ἢ ἡμέτεροι φίλοι, ἢ αὐτοὺς ἢ ὧν κηδόμενοι τυγχάνου-
40 σιν, ἢ πάλιν τοὺς κρίνοντας αὐτοὺς | ἢ ὧν κηδόμενοι
1445a τυγχάνουσι, καὶ διεξιόντες αὐτοῖς ὡς νῦν ‖ καιρὸς χάρι-

flect the law: "Did you kill my son?" "It was not me, but the law." You must answer in all of these ways whenever one law calls on you to do the thing and another forbids it. You will collect responses to your adversaries from all of these things.

[45] After this there is repetition, a concise reminder of what has already been said. It is useful on all occasions, so you must use repetition for a part and for a species (of speech), and it especially suits prosecution and defense speeches, as well as proposition and opposition speeches. We say that we must not only recall what has been already said, just as in speeches of praise and criticism, but also make the judges well disposed to us and badly disposed to the opponents. [46] We arrange this part of the speech last. It improves memory to summarize the points that have been said by calculation, by contemplation, or by posing additional questions of the best of your points and the worst of your opponents', and if you like, making use of the form of interrogation. We know what each of these is from what has been said before.[48]

[47] We shall put ourselves in a good light and our opponents in a bad light if, just as in proposition and opposition speeches, we suggest succinctly on what bases we have benefited the wrongdoers, are benefiting them, or will benefit them, either ourselves or our friends, either themselves or those for whom they care, and indicate to them that now they have an opportunity to render thanks

[48] Cf. 20.

τας ἡμῖν τῶν ὑπηργμένων ἀποδοῦναι, καὶ πρὸς τούτοις ἐλεεινοὺς ἡμᾶς αὐτοὺς καθιστάντες, ἐὰν ἐνδέχηται. [48] τοῦτο δὲ ποιήσομεν ἐπιδεικνύντες ὡς πρὸς
τοὺς ἀκούοντας οἰκείως ἔχομεν καὶ ἀναξίως δυστυ-
χοῦμεν κακῶς πρότερον | πεπονθότες ἢ νῦν πάσχοντες,
ἢ πεισόμενοι ἐὰν μὴ βοηθῶσιν ἡμῖν οὗτοι· ἐὰν δὲ μὴ
τοιαῦτα ὑπάρχῃ, διεξιόντες τίνων ἀγαθῶν ἐστερήμεθα
ἢ στερισκόμεθα, ἢ στερησόμεθα ὀλιγωρηθέντες ὑπὸ
τῶν κρινόντων, ἢ ὡς ἀγαθοῦ μηδέποτε ἐπετύχομεν[117] ἢ
μὴ ἐπιτυγχάνομεν ἢ μὴ ἐπιτευξόμεθα μὴ | τούτων ἡμῖν
συμβοηθησάντων. ἐκ γὰρ τούτων ἐλεεινοὺς καταστήσομεν ἡμᾶς αὐτοὺς καὶ πρὸς τοὺς ἀκούοντας εὖ διαθήσομεν.

[49] διαβαλοῦμεν δὲ τοὺς ἀντιδίκους καὶ φθονεῖ-
σθαι ποιήσομεν ἐκ τῶν ἐναντίων τούτοις, ἀποφαίνον-
τες ὑπὸ τούτων ἢ τῶν τούτοις φίλων τοὺς ἀκούοντας ἢ
ὧν αὐτοὶ κήδονται, | κακῶς πεπονθότας ἢ πάσχοντας ἢ
πεισομένους παρὰ τὸ προσῆκον. ἐκ γὰρ τῶν τοιούτων
καὶ μῖσος καὶ ὀργὴν πρὸς αὐτοὺς ἕξουσιν. ἂν δὲ μὴ
ταῦτα ἐνδέχηται, συνάξομεν ἐξ ὧν φθόνον τοῖς ἀκούουσι κατὰ τῶν ἐναντίων ἐργασόμεθα· τὸ γὰρ φθονεῖν
πλησίον τοῦ μισεῖν ἐστιν. [50] φθονήσονται δὲ συλ-
λήβδην, | ἐὰν ἀναξίως αὐτοὺς εὖ πράττοντας ἀποφαί-
νωμεν καὶ πρὸς τοὺς ἀκούοντας ἀλλοτρίως ἔχοντας,
διεξιόντες ὡς ἀγαθὰ πολλὰ πεπόνθασιν ἀδίκως ἢ
πάσχουσιν ἢ μέλλουσι πείσεσθαι, ἢ ἀγαθοῦ οὐδέποτε
πρότερον ἐστερήθησαν ἢ νῦν οὐ στερίσκονται ἢ οὐ
στερήσονται, ἢ κακοῦ οὐδέποτε τετυχηκότες ἢ | νῦν οὐ

to us for our services and, in addition, if possible, to make ourselves pitiable. [48] We shall do this by showing that we have close relations with the audience and that we are unduly unfortunate in having suffered before, suffering now, or being about to suffer, if they do not help us. If this is not possible, recite which goods we have been, are being, or will be deprived of if we are disregarded by those judging the case, or that we have not attained, do not attain, and will never attain good luck without their help. In these ways we shall make ourselves pitiable and put ourselves in a good light with the audience.

[49] We shall create prejudice and envy against the adversaries in the opposite ways by pointing out that the audience or those they care about have been treated, are being treated, or will be treated badly by them or their friends, improperly. In this way they will incur hatred and anger. If this is not possible, we shall collect points from which we shall fashion envy in the audience against the opponents. Envy is close to hatred. [50] They will be envied, in sum, if we point out that they are unduly prosperous and that their interests are different from the audience's, indicating that they enjoyed, enjoy, and will enjoy many benefits, or that they have never before been deprived, are not now being deprived, or will not be deprived of a benefit, or that they have never had, do not now have, and will not

---

117 ἐπετύχομεν Finkh[1] : ἐτύχομεν N a

τυγχάνοντες, ἢ οὐ τευξόμενοι ἐὰν μὴ νῦν αὐτοὺς οἱ κριταὶ κολάσωσιν. [51] ἐκ τούτων μὲν οὖν ἐν τοῖς ἐπιλόγοις εὐμενῶς μὲν αὑτούς, κακῶς δὲ τοὺς ἐναντίους διαθήσομεν· ἐκ δὲ τῶν προειρημένων ἁπάντων ἐντέχνως καὶ τὰς κατηγορίας καὶ τὰς ἀπολογίας τάξομεν. |

30 37. Τὸ δ' ἐξεταστικὸν εἶδος αὐτὸ μὲν καθ' ἑαυτὸ οὐ πολλάκις συνίσταται, τοῖς δὲ ἄλλοις εἴδεσι μίγνυται καὶ μάλιστα πρὸς τὰς ἀντιλογίας χρήσιμόν ἐστιν. οὐ μὴν ἀλλ' ὅπως μηδὲ τούτου τὴν τάξιν ἀγνοῶμεν, ἄν ποθ' ἡμῖν λόγον ἢ βίον ἢ πρᾶξιν ἀνθρώπων ἢ διοίκη-
35 σιν πόλεως ἐξετάζειν | συμβῇ, διέξειμι καὶ περὶ τούτου κεφαλαιωδῶς. [2] φροιμιαστέον μὲν οὖν σχεδὸν ὁμοιοτρόπως τοῖς διαβεβλημένοις καὶ τοῖς ἐξετάζουσι ταῦτα, ὥστε προφάσεις ἐν ἀρχαῖς εὐλόγους ἐνεγκόντες δι' ἃς δόξομεν εἰκότως τοῦτο ποιεῖν, οὕτως ἐπὶ τὴν ἐξέτασιν ἥξομεν. [3] αἱ τοιαίδε δὲ ἁρμόσουσιν· ἐν
40 μὲν τοῖς | πολιτικοῖς συλλόγοις, ὡς "οὐ φιλονεικίᾳ τὸ
1445b τοιοῦτον ποιοῦμεν, || ἀλλ' ὅπως μὴ λάθῃ τοὺς ἀκούοντας," εἶτα ὅτι "ἡμᾶς οὗτοι πρότερον ἠνώχλησαν·" ἐν δὲ τοῖς ἰδίοις ἢ ἔχθραν ἢ τὰ ἤθη τῶν ἐξεταζομένων φαῦλα ὄντα ἢ φιλία πρὸς τοὺς ἐξεταζομένους, ἢ ὅπως
5 συνέντες ἃ πράττουσι, μηκέτι ταῦτα ποιήσωσιν· | ἐν δὲ τοῖς δημοσίοις, τὸ νόμιμον <καὶ>[118] τὸ δίκαιον καὶ τὸ τῷ κοινῷ συμφέρον. [4] φροιμιασάμενοι δ' ἐκ τούτων καὶ τῶν τούτοις ὁμοιοτρόπων ἐφεξῆς ἕκαστον προτιθέμενοι τῶν ῥηθέντων ἢ πραχθέντων ἢ διανοηθέντων ἐξετάσομεν, ἐνδεικνύντες αὐτὰ καὶ τοῖς δικαίοις καὶ

have bad luck unless the judges punish them now. [51] In these ways we shall, in the conclusions, put ourselves in a friendly light and the opponents in a bad light. From everything that was said before, we shall arrange both prosecution and defense speeches skillfully.

37. The investigative species does not occur often by itself but is mixed with other species and is particularly useful for debates. Nevertheless, in order that we not be ignorant of its arrangement if it ever falls upon us to investigate a speech or life or action of people or the administration of a city I shall also go through it summarily. [2] For those who have incurred prejudice and for those doing an investigation the introduction should be very similar, so that, by bringing in reasonable pretexts, as a result of which we seem to be acting reasonably, we come to the investigation on this basis. [3] The following sorts of pretexts are appropriate: in political meetings, that "we are doing this not out of contentiousness but so that it does not escape our audience's attention"; then, that "these people injured us first"; in private meetings (the pretext will be) either dislike or that the characters of those being investigated are bad, or friendship toward those being investigated, or so that if they know what they are doing they may no longer do it. In public matters, the pretext will be what is legal, just, and in the common interest. [4] After doing an introduction in this way, or in ways like it, by setting forth each of the things said or done or thought in turn, we shall do the investigation, pointing out that they contradict what is just,

118 καὶ add. Rackham

10 τοῖς νομίμοις καὶ τοῖς ἰδίᾳ | καὶ κοινῇ συμφέρουσιν ἐναντιούμενα, καὶ πάντα σκοποῦντες εἴ που αὐτὰ αὑτοῖς ἐστιν ἐναντία ἢ τοῖς ἤθεσι τῶν χρηστῶν ἀνθρώπων ἢ τοῖς εἰκόσιν. [5] ἵνα δὲ μὴ μηκύνωμεν καθ᾽ ἓν ἕκαστον λέγοντες, ὅσῳ ἂν πλείοσι τῶν ἐνδόξων ἐπιτηδευμάτων ἢ πραγμάτων ἢ λόγων ἢ ἐθῶν ἐναντιούμενα
15 τὰ | τῶν ἐξεταζομένων ἀποφαίνωμεν τοῖς ἀκούουσι, τοσούτῳ μᾶλλον οἱ ἐξεταζόμενοι ἀδοξήσουσι. [6] δεῖ δὲ πικρῷ τῷ ἤθει μὴ ἐξετάζειν, ἀλλὰ πρᾳεῖ· τοῦτον γὰρ τὸν τρόπον οἱ λόγοι γινόμενοι πιθανώτεροι φανήσονται τοῖς ἀκούουσιν, οἱ δὲ λέγοντες αὑτοὺς ἥκιστα
20 διαβαλοῦσιν. [7] ὅταν δὲ πάντα ἀκριβῶς | ἐξητακὼς αὐξήσῃς αὐτά, παλιλλογίαν ἐπὶ τῇ τελευτῇ σύντομον ποίησαι καὶ τοὺς ἀκροατὰς περὶ τῶν εἰρημένων ἀνάμνησον.

τὰ μὲν οὖν εἴδη πάντα τοῦτον τὸν τρόπον τάττοντες ἐντέχνως αὐτοῖς χρησόμεθα.

38. Δεῖ δὲ καὶ λέγοντας καὶ γράφοντας ὅτι μάλι-
25 στα | πειρᾶσθαι κατὰ τὰ προειρημένα τοὺς λόγους ἀποδιδόναι καὶ συνεθίζειν αὑτοὺς τούτοις ἅπασιν ἐξ ἑτοίμου χρῆσθαι. καὶ περὶ μὲν τοῦ λέγειν ἐντέχνως καὶ ἐν τοῖς ἰδίοις καὶ ἐν τοῖς κοινοῖς ἀγῶσι κἐν ταῖς πρὸς τοὺς ἄλλους ὁμιλίαις ἐντεῦθεν πλείστας καὶ
30 τεχνικωτάτας ἀφορμὰς ἕξομεν· [2] χρὴ | δὲ καὶ τὴν ἐπιμέλειαν ποιεῖσθαι μὴ μόνον περὶ τοὺς λόγους, ἀλλὰ καὶ περὶ τὸν βίον τὸν αὑτοῦ, διακοσμοῦντα ταῖς ἰδέαις ταῖς εἰρημέναις· συμβάλλεται γὰρ ἡ περὶ τὸν βίον παρασκευὴ καὶ πρὸς τὸ πείθειν καὶ πρὸς τὸ δόξης ἐπιεικοῦς τυγχάνειν.

legal, and in the private and common interest, and investigating all of them, whether they contradict with themselves or with the behavior of good people or with plausibility. [5] In order to avoid speaking at length on each point, (suffice it to say that) as much as we point out to the audience that the pursuits or actions or words or practices of the people being investigated contradict most reputable pursuits, actions, words and practices, the more the people being investigated will fall into disrepute. [6] The investigation must be done not in a bitter spirit but in a mild one. In this way the arguments will appear to become more trustworthy to the audience and the speakers will cause themselves the least prejudice. [7] When you have investigated everything in detail and amplified it, do a concise repetition at the end and remind the audience what has been said.

By arranging all the species in this way, we shall use them skillfully.

38. Both in speaking and in writing we must attempt as much as possible to deliver speeches according to what has been said here and to accustom ourselves to use it all readily. We shall have the greatest number and the most technically sound bases for skillful speaking both in private and in public contests, as well as in discussions with others. [2] We must be disciplined not only in speeches but also in life by ordering ourselves according to the norms that have been stated. Life preparation contributes both to persuasion and to gaining an honest reputation.

[3] πρῶτον μὲν οὖν διελέσθαι χρὴ τὰ πράγματα |
35 κατὰ τὴν ὅλην τοῦ παιδεύματος διαίρεσιν, ὅ τι πρῶτον ἢ δεύτερον ἢ τρίτον ἢ τέταρτον μεταχειριστέον, εἶτα σαυτοῦ ποιεῖσθαι παρασκευήν, ὥσπερ ἐν τοῖς προοιμίοις διήλθομεν τὰ περὶ τῶν ἀκροατῶν. [4] εὐμενῆ μὲν οὖν τὰ περὶ σεαυτὸν ποιήσεις, ἐὰν οἷς ὁμολογεῖς
40 ἐμμένης καὶ διαφυλάττης | φίλους τοὺς αὐτοὺς διὰ
1446a παντὸς τοῦ βίου καὶ περὶ τῶν ἄλλων || ἐπιτηδευμάτων φαίνῃ μὴ μεθιστάμενος, ἀλλ' ἀεὶ τοῖς αὐτοῖς χρώμενος. προσέξουσι δέ σοι, ἐὰν μεγάλας καὶ καλὰς μεταχειρίζῃ τὰς πράξεις καὶ τοῖς πολλοῖς συμφερούσας.

[5] εὐμενεῖς δὲ γενόμενοι, ὅταν ἐπὶ τῶν πράξεων
5 γένῃ, ὅσαι | τῶν κακῶν ἀποτροπὴν ἔχουσι τῶν δ' ἀγαθῶν παρουσίαν, ταύτας μὲν ὡς συμφερούσας αὑτοῖς ἀποδέξονται, ὅσαι δὲ τἀναντία παρασκευάζουσιν αὑτοῖς, ταύτας ἀποδοκιμάσουσιν. [6] ἀντὶ δὲ τοῦ ταχεῖαν καὶ σαφῆ καὶ μὴ ἄπιστον τὴν διήγησιν λέγεσθαι
10 τὰς πράξεις δεῖ τοιαύτας ποιεῖσθαι. ταχέως | μὲν οὖν ἐπιτελέσεις, ἂν μὴ πάντα πράττειν ἅμα βούλῃ, ἀλλὰ πρότερον τὸ πρῶτον, ἔπειτα τὸ ἑξῆς· [7] καθαρῶς δέ, ἂν μὴ ταχὺ τῆς πράξεως παυόμενος ἄλλα πράγματα μεταχειρίζῃ πρὶν ταύτην ἐπιτελέσαι· μὴ ἀπίστως δέ, ἂν μὴ παρὰ τὸ ἦθος τὸ σαυτοῦ πράττῃς, πρὸς δὲ
15 τούτοις, ἂν | μὴ προσποιῇ τοὺς αὐτοὺς ἐχθροὺς καὶ φίλους εἶναί σοι.

[8] ἐκ δὲ τῶν πίστεων ληψόμεθα, περὶ ὧν μὲν ἐπιστήμην ἔχομεν, κατὰ τὴν ταύτης ἐξήγησιν τὰς

[3] You must first divide the matters according to the entire system of instruction, whatever you must attempt first, second, third, or fourth, then do the preparation of yourself, just as in the introductions we discuss matters regarding the audience. [4] You will put these aspects of yourself in a friendly light if you abide by what you agree to, keep the same friends throughout your whole life, and appear not to change the rest of your behavior, but always keep it the same. They will give you attention if you pursue great and noble actions that benefit the many.

[5] Once they have become friendly, when you get to the actions that avoid troubles and create goods they will accept them as advantageous to themselves, and those that bring about the contrary for them they will reject. [6] Rather than making your narration rapid, clear, and credible, you must describe the actions as advantageous or disadvantageous. However, you will achieve rapidity if you do not try to do everything at once, but the first thing first and then the rest in order. [7] You will speak cleanly if you do not suddenly interrupt a subject and start on other matters before finishing it. You will speak credibly if what you are doing is not contrary your character, and in addition, if you do not make the same people your enemies and friends.

[8] Regarding proofs, about matters about which we have knowledge, we shall undertake its guidance in deal-

πράξεις ἐπιτελεῖν, περὶ ὧν δὲ τυγχάνομεν ἀγνοοῦντες, κατὰ τὸ ὡς ἐπὶ τὸ πολὺ συμβαῖνον· ἀσφαλέστατον
20 γὰρ πράττειν περὶ τῶν οὕτως ἐχόντων | πρὸς τὸ εἰωθὸς ἀποβλέποντας. [9] εἰς δὲ τὸν πρὸς τοὺς ἀντιδίκους ἀγῶνα ἐν μὲν τοῖς λόγοις ἐκ τῶν λελεγμένων ποιήσομεν βεβαιότητα παρ' ἡμῶν· ἐν δὲ τοῖς συμβολαίοις τοῦτο ποιήσομεν, ἐὰν κατὰ τοὺς νόμους αὐτὰ μεταχειριζώμεθα τοὺς ἀγράφους καὶ τοὺς γεγραμμένους μετὰ
25 μαρτύρων | ὡς βελτίστων ὁριζόμενοι χρόνους.

[10] ἐκ δὲ τοῦ ἐπιλόγου περὶ μὲν τῶν λελεγμένων μνημονικοὺς ποιήσομεν ἐκ τοῦ πάλιν λέγειν κεφαλαιωδῶς· περὶ <δὲ>[119] τῶν πεπραγμένων ἐξ ὧν [δὲ][120] πράττομεν ἀναμνήσομεν οὕτως, ἐπειδὰν τὰς αὐτὰς πράξεις ἢ τὰς ὁμοίας μεταχειριζώμεθα ταῖς προ-
30 τέραις. [11] φιλικῶς δὲ διακείσονται | πρὸς ἡμᾶς, ἐὰν πράττωμεν ἐξ ὧν εὖ πεπονθέναι δόξουσιν ἢ πάσχειν ἢ πείσεσθαι. μεγάλα δὲ πράξομεν, ἐὰν πολλῶν αἰτίας καλῶν τὰς πράξεις μεταχειριζώμεθα.

καὶ τοῦτον μὲν τὸν τρόπον χρὴ τὰ κατὰ τὸν βίον παρασκευάζειν, ἐκ δὲ τῆς προτέρας συντάξεως περὶ
35 τοὺς | λόγους γυμνάζεσθαι.

[12] [Τὰς δὲ θυσίας δεῖ ποιεῖν, ὡς προείρηται, πρὸς μὲν <τοὺς> θεοὺς ὁσίως, πρὸς δὲ τὰς δαπάνας μετρίως, πρὸς δὲ τὰς θεωρίας λαμπρῶς, πρὸς δὲ τοὺς πολέμους[121] ὠφελίμως. καὶ πρὸς μὲν τοὺς θεοὺς ὁσίως

119 δὲ add. Finkh¹ 120 δὲ del. Finkh¹
121 πολέμους Kassel : πολίτας codd.

ing with the subjects. But about matters about which we are ignorant, we shall follow what happens for the most part. It is safest in such situations to act with a view to what is usual. [9] For a trial against adversaries, with regard to the speeches, we shall compose our confirmation from what has been said by us, but with regard to contracts,[49] we shall do this if we handle them according to the laws, both the unwritten and the written, with the best witnesses possible in a limited time.

[10] Regarding the conclusion, we shall remind the audience what has been said by again discussing the headings. We shall recall what was done when we are putting our hand to the same actions or actions similar to those earlier. [11] They will be friendly to us if we act in such a way that they will think that they have been treated, are being treated, or will be treated well. We shall do important things if we put our hands to actions that cause many good things.

We must bring about this behavior with regard to our life; by means of the earlier part of the treatise we must practice doing speeches.

[12] [Sacrifices must be performed, as has been said, with piety toward the gods, with moderation toward the costs, with splendor with regard to the observances, and with benefit toward wars. They will be pious toward the

49 The distinction "speeches" (λόγοις)—"contracts" (συμβολαίοις) seems a sloppy way of making the distinction between deliberative and forensic oratory.

1446b ἕξουσιν, ἐὰν κατὰ τὰ πάτρια θύωμεν· πρὸς ‖ δὲ τὰς δαπάνας μετρίως, ἐὰν μὴ τὰ πεμπόμενα πάντα τοῖς δαπανωμένοις συναναλίσκηται· πρὸς δὲ τὰς θεωρίας λαμπρῶς, ἐὰν μεγαλοπρεπῶς ὦσι κατεσκευασμένα· πρὸς δὲ τοὺς πολέμους ὠφελίμως, ἐὰν ἱππεῖς καὶ
5 ὁπλῖται διεσκευασμένοι | συμπομπεύωσιν. [13] τὰ μὲν δὴ πρὸς τοὺς θεοὺς οὕτω [ἂν][122] γινόμενα ὁσίως ἂν ἔχοι.

φιλίαν δὲ συστησόμεθα πρὸς τοὺς ὁμοιοτρόπους ἡμῖν καὶ οἷς ταὐτὰ συμφέρει καὶ οἷς περὶ τὰ μέγιστα ἀναγκαῖόν ἐστιν ἡμῖν κοινωνεῖν· ἡ γὰρ τοιαύτη μάλιστα συμμένει φιλία. [14] συμμάχους δὲ δεῖ ποιεῖσθαι
10 τοὺς | δικαιοτάτους καὶ τοὺς δύναμιν πολλὴν ἔχοντας καὶ τοὺς πλησίον κατοικοῦντας, ἐχθροὺς δὲ τοὺς ἐναντίους τούτοις. [15] πόλεμον δὲ δεῖ αἱρεῖσθαι πρὸς τοὺς ἀδικεῖν ἐπιχειροῦντας τὴν πόλιν ἢ τοὺς φίλους ἢ τοὺς συμμάχους αὐτῆς. [16] τὰς δὲ φυλακὰς ἀναγκαῖον ἔχειν ἢ δι' ἑαυτῶν ἢ διὰ τῶν συμμάχων ἢ διὰ ξένων, |
15 καὶ κράτιστον μὲν δι' ἑαυτῶν, δεύτερον δὲ διὰ τῶν συμμάχων, τρίτον δὲ διὰ ξένων. [17] περὶ πόρου δὲ χρημάτων κράτιστον μὲν ἀπὸ τῶν ἰδίων προσόδων ἢ κτημάτων, δεύτερον δὲ ἀπὸ τῶν τιμημάτων, τρίτον δὲ τῶν πενήτων τὰ σώματα παρεχόντων λειτουργεῖν, τῶν
20 δὲ τεχνιτῶν ὅπλα, | τῶν δὲ πλουσίων χρήματα.

[18] περὶ πολιτείας δὲ δημοκρατία μὲν ἀρίστη ἐν ᾗ οἱ νόμοι τοῖς ἀρίστοις τὰς τιμὰς ἀπονέμουσι, τὸ δὲ πλῆθος μήτε χειροτονίας μήτε ψηφοφορίας ἐστέρηται, κακίστη δέ, ἐν ᾗ τῷ πλήθει παραδιδόασιν οἱ

gods if we sacrifice according to the ancestral customs; they will be moderate with regard to the costs if the entire procession's budget is not spent on costly items; they will be splendid with regard to the observance if the preparations are magnificent; they will be beneficial for wars if cavalry and foot soldiers are equipped for the procession. [13] Our duty to the gods would be piously fulfilled in this way.

We shall create friendship with those who are similar to us, with those for whom the same things are advantageous, and with those with whom we must share the most important matters. That is how friendship most often endures. [14] We must make allies out of the most just, the most powerful, and the closest neighbors, and enemies out of their opposites. [15] We must choose war against those attempting to do injustice to the city, its friends, or its allies. [16] We must have protection, either through ourselves, through allies, or through foreigners, and it is best when it is through ourselves, second best through allies, and third through foreigners. [17] With regard to revenue, it is best through private income and property, second best from assessments, and third from the performance of liturgy, the poor offering their bodies, artisans weapons, and the rich money.

[18] With regard to politics, a democracy is best in which the laws distribute honors to the best, and the majority is not deprived of its vote in the assembly or the courts. It is worst when the laws hand over to the majority

---

122 οὕτω MA2 edd. : οὕτως ἂν N a

νόμοι τοὺς πλουτοῦντας ὑβρίζειν. ὀλιγαρχιῶν δ' εἰσὶ
25 δύο τρόποι· | ἢ γὰρ ἐξ ἑταιρείας ἢ ἀπὸ τιμημάτων.

[19] ποιεῖσθαι δὲ συμμάχους ἀναγκαῖόν ἐστιν, ὅταν οἱ πολῖται μὴ τυγχάνωσι δι' ἑαυτῶν δυνατοὶ τὴν χώραν καὶ τὰ φρούρια φυλάττειν ἢ τοὺς πολεμίους ἀμύνεσθαι· παρίεσθαι δὲ δεῖ συμμαχίαν, ὅταν μὴ
30 ἀνάγκη τις ᾖ ποιεῖσθαι αὐτὴν ἢ μακρὰν | τοῖς τόποις ἀπέχωσι καὶ ἀδύνατοι ὦσι κατὰ τοὺς προσήκοντας παραγίνεσθαι καιρούς.

[20] πολίτης δὲ ἀγαθός ἐστιν ὅστις φίλους μὲν χρησιμωτάτους τῇ πόλει παρασκευάζει, ἐχθροὺς δὲ ἐλαχίστους καὶ ἀσθενεστάτους, καὶ ὅστις πλείστας προσόδους παρασκευάζει τῶν ἰδιωτῶν μηδένα δημεύ-
35 ων, καὶ | ὅστις ἑαυτὸν δίκαιον παρέχων τοὺς ἀδικοῦντάς τι τῶν κοινῶν ἐξετάζει. [21] δωροῦνται δὲ πάντες ἐλπίζοντες ὠφεληθήσεσθαι ἢ τῶν προτέρων εὐεργεσιῶν χάριν ἀποδιδόντες. ὑπηρετοῦσι δὲ πάντες κέρδους ἕνεκεν ἢ τιμῆς ἢ ἡδονῆς ἢ φόβου. συναλλάττουσι δὲ πάντες ἢ κατὰ προαίρεσιν ἢ ἀκουσίως· αἱ ||
1447a γὰρ πράξεις ἐπιτελοῦνται πᾶσαι ἢ διὰ βίας ἢ διὰ πειθοῦς ἢ δι' ἀπάτης ἢ διὰ προφάσεως.

[22] ἐν δὲ πολέμῳ περιγίνονται πολεμοῦντες ἢ διὰ τύχην ἢ διὰ σωμάτων πλῆθος ἢ ῥώμην ἢ διὰ χρη-
5 μάτων εὐπορίαν ἢ διὰ τόπων εὐφυΐαν | ἢ δι' ἀρετὴν συμμάχων ἢ διὰ στρατηγοῦ γνώμην. [23] ἐγκαταλιπεῖν δὲ τοὺς συμμάχους ὑπολαμβάνουσι δεῖν ἢ διὰ τὸ μᾶλλον συμφέρειν τοῦτο ἢ διὰ τὸ καταλύσασθαι τὸν
1447b πόλεμον. || [24] δίκαια δὲ πράττειν ἐστὶ τὸ τοῖς κοινοῖς

the ability to abuse the wealthy. There are two kinds of oligarchy, based on cronyism or assessments.

[19] We must make allies when the citizens are not actually capable of guarding the land and its fortifications or of fighting off the enemy. But we should forgo alliance whenever there is no necessity to make one or when they are greatly separated by territories and unable to come at the right moments.

[20] A good citizen is one that generates the most useful friends for the city, the fewest and weakest enemies, and who generates a lot of income while expropriating no private money, and who while being himself just investigates those who do any injustice to the common good. [21] Everyone gives gifts in the expectation of gaining a benefit or to return the favor of previous good works. Everyone does service for the sake of profit, honor, pleasure, or fear. Everyone interacts by choice or unwillingly; all (unwilling) actions are performed through force, persuasion, deceit, or pretense.

[22] In war those gain the upper hand who wage war by luck, greater numbers, strength, a good supply of money, a naturally strong position, the courage of allies, or the understanding of the general. [23] They suppose that they must abandon their allies either because of greater advantage or the ending of the war. [24] Doing justice means fol-

τῆς πόλεως ἔθεσιν ἕπεσθαι, τοῖς νόμοις πείθεσθαι καὶ ταῖς ἰδίαις ὁμολογίαις ἐμμένειν. [25] συμφέρει δὲ σώματι μὲν εὐεξία καὶ κάλλος καὶ ῥώμη καὶ ὑγίεια,
5 ψυχῇ δὲ σοφία, φρόνησις, ἀνδρεία, | σωφροσύνη, δικαιοσύνη, συναμφοτέροις δὲ τούτοις χρήματα φίλοι· ἀσύμφορα δὲ τἀναντία τούτων. πόλει δὲ συμφέρον πλῆθος πολιτῶν ἀγαθῶν.]

lowing the common customs of the city, obeying the laws, and abiding by one's agreements. [25] For the body fitness, beauty, strength, and health are advantageous; for the soul, wisdom, intelligence, courage, moderation, a sense of justice; for both, money and friends. The opposites of these are disadvantageous. For a city, a great number of good citizens is advantageous.]

INDEX OF TERMS